THE JAZZ BOOK

FROM RAGTIME TO FUSION AND BEYOND

JOACHIM E. BERENDT

REVISED BY GÜNTHER HUESMANN

Translated by
**H. and B. Bredigkeit
with Dan Morgenstern
and Tim Nevill**

LAWRENCE HILL BOOKS

Library of Congress Cataloging-in-Publication Data

Berendt, Joachim Ernst.
    [Grosse Jazzbuch. English]
    The jazz book : from ragtime to fusion and beyond / Joachim E. Berendt ;
revised by Günther Huesmann ; translated by H. and B. Bredigkeit with Dan
Morgenstern ; new sections translated by Tim Nevill.
      p. cm.
    Translation of: Das grosse Jazzbuch.
    Discography: p.
    Includes index.
    ISBN 1-55652-099-9 (cloth) : $29.00. — ISBN 1-55652-098-0 (pbk.) : $16.95
    1. Jazz—History and criticism.   I. Huesmann, Günther, 1957–   II. Title.
ML3506.B4513   1991
781.65'09—dc20   92-17412
                                                 CIP
                                               MN

© Fischer Taschenbuch Verlag GmbH., Frankfurt am Main
1953, 1959, 1968, 1973, 1981, 1989.

English language translation and discography © 1975, 1982, 1992
Lawrence Hill Books, Brooklyn, New York
All rights reserved

New sections for the 1992 edition were translated from the German
by Tim Nevill

Printed in the United States of America
Sixth edition
First printing
Published by Lawrence Hill Books, Brooklyn, New York
An imprint of Chicago Review Press, Inc.
814 North Franklin Street
Chicago, Illinois 60610

You've got to love to be able to play.
Louis Armstrong

The most important contribution you
can make to the tradition is to create
your own music, create a new music.
Anthony Davis

There is something in music which is
more than melody and more than
harmony: music.
Giuseppe Verdi

Contents

CONTENTS

Preface

Ever since its first appearance in 1953, this book has accompanied three generations of jazz musicians and fans, and has grown from a slender volume to more than 450 pages. By now I've almost lost track of the many revisions and new editions: six in Germany alone, four in North America, three in Japan, two in both Latin America and France, as well as translations into Italian, Polish, Yugoslav, Dutch, Czech, and Indonesian. My German publisher reports that one and a half million copies of the book are in print, but this figure doesn't include the samizdat edition in the Soviet Union. Because the Russian edition appeared "illegally," it is impossible to determine how many copies are in circulation in that vast country.

When the need for a new edition covering jazz from the eighties to the nineties became apparent, it was clear to me that I could no longer undertake this task. For more than thirty-five years, I worked on the various revisions of *The Jazz Book* in intimate contact with the musicians of the times. When, for example, cool jazz, hard bop, and free jazz thrust themselves onto the scene, I wrote under the direct impact of these new styles and ways of playing. Jazz criticism is only alive if a critic lives with the music, and so it seemed important that I should find a collaborator who experienced the musicians and styles of the eighties, as I did the fifties, sixties, and seventies. Writing about jazz suffers from the fact that many critics develop a feeling only for a single style, living off that forever after without becoming aware of the need to constantly reassess and revise their sensibilities and knowledge. Also, my more recent work—on the need for a new appreciation of listening in our one-sided "visual culture"—prevents me from devoting as much time to jazz as I did in the years when earlier editions of this book were produced.

It wasn't difficult to find someone who could take on this revision and expansion of *The Jazz Book*. In 1980, Günther Huesmann (who was born in 1957) was a trainee in my jazz department at Southwest German Radio, attracting attention for his musical sensitivity and empathy. He studied music, theater, cinema, and television at Cologne University and Berlin's Technical University; was for seven years a jazz critic for a Cologne newspaper during the period when the city became the capital of Federal German jazz; and has made a name for himself with his many contributions to music magazines and radio programs in Germany and elsewhere.

The aim of this book continues to be the presentation of *the whole range* of jazz from ragtime and New Orleans to the present day. Because jazz expanded so greatly in the eighties, the decade could have been the subject of a book in its own right. Therefore, in order to do justice to the abundance of new musicians, the principle of completeness had to be sacrificed in the sections on the instruments. Musicians who today no longer seem crucial have been dropped from this edition. However, we believe that all the musicians who have shaped styles and ways of playing are represented here. Anyone who nevertheless craves comprehensiveness should consult previous editions of the book.

There is also a linguistic problem in writing about the music of the eighties. In jazz's earlier styles almost every musician could be clearly distinguished from his or her colleagues. Just think, the entire Chicago style, the dominant style in the twenties, is represented by fewer musicians than there are ways of playing a single instrument in the nineties. Language simply isn't capable of differentiating between the plethora of musicians and their styles. Music—and this is the problem in writing about it—is more differentiated than the words at our disposal.

Although many musicians belong to more than one group, we had no choice but to introduce most of them in the context of a single group if the abundance of names and facts were to remain manageable. We found this particularly unfortunate in the sections on the tenor saxophone, the piano, the guitar, and the drums, which include innumerable musicians. We don't, however, see any solution to the problem. Criticism and narrative are not possible without generalization. Egon Friedell, the eminent cultural historian, once said: "All the classifications man has ever devised are arbitrary, artificial, and false, but simple reflection also shows that such classifications are useful, indispensable, and above all unavoidable since they accord with an innate aspect of our thinking."

Any musician mentioned in this book is portrayed at a specific point in the development of jazz. In reality, however, a human life doesn't occupy a point in time; it is linear, a sequence of numerous points. Yet in the sections on individual instruments the emphasis can only be on a single "point"—one way of playing, resulting in one category to which the musician is assigned. We have endeavored to assign each musician to the category in which the majority of critics place him or her and ideally where the musicians see themselves.

As in previous revisions, each page of the existing text has been critically scrutinized, and, accordingly, shortened or expanded, revised or rewritten. Completely new are the sections entitled "Wynton Marsalis and David Murray," "From the Eighties to the Nineties," and "Saxophone Ensembles," and the section on keyboards is virtually so. The sections on Ornette Coleman and Miles Davis have been much expanded, taking into account their development in the eighties. Important additions and changes have also been incorporated into the sections on ragtime, the seventies, Louis Armstrong, Duke Ellington, and the elements of jazz. About a third of the sections on the various instruments, male and female vocalists, big bands, and combos is new. And of course the book follows the times in presenting the European jazz scene in greater detail.

We want to give the reader an overview of the totality and unity of the development of jazz. So we've tried to avoid the one-sidedness, exaggeration, and fanaticism characteristic of adherents to and specialists in single styles. Anyone who writes, as one critic has, that "eclecticism is irreconcilable with taste" has forgotten that jazz is essentially an eclectic form of music. Jazz was a "bastard" right from the start, and always will be. In jazz, as in other art forms, the distinction between purity and eclecticism simply involves the fact that what may seem pure to us today came into existence so long ago that we have forgotten how eclectic, how impure it used to be.

Critics have asked why a book on jazz comes from Germany. To be quite honest, I don't know. In the United States at least, this question probably relates to Europe rather than just Germany. So why does this book come from our old continent? Here I can give an answer: Jazz came into existence in the United States, but jazz criticism developed in Europe. The first serious evaluation of jazz came from Swiss conductor Ernest Ansermet in 1919. The first book on jazz was written by a Belgian, Robert Goffin, in 1929. The first jazz magazine was edited by a Frenchman, Hugues Panassié, starting in the late 1920s. The first jazz discography was also compiled by a Frenchman, Charles Delaunay, at the end of the 1930s. By that time jazz was accepted by European artists and intellectuals as an art form that should be taken seriously. Great European artists—from Hindemith to Stravinsky, from Picasso to Matisse—devoted attention to jazz, paying tribute to it in their works. But in the United States where jazz came into being, it was long viewed as a superior form of circus music. Even as late as 1976, at an international conference in Washington, D.C. called "The United States in the World" commemorating the American bicentennial, it was scholars, artists, and writers from Poland, Hungary, France, Germany, Italy, Thailand, and Japan who supported my thesis that jazz is America's most autonomous and important contribution to world culture. Whereas American intellectuals thought other fields, which all originally developed in Europe, more significant. "Why do Americans take all new ideas seriously if they come from painting or literature, but not if they come from a saxophone?" Ornette Coleman said that in 1982, and his observation still holds true today.

In 1965, John Coltrane won for the first time *Down Beat* magazine's critics poll (the leading annual survey of the most important musicians). Of the critics who voted for Coltrane, 64 percent were European and only 32 percent American. The Europeans had in fact voted for him for years, but had previously failed to generate enough votes. At the end of the sixties, it was again the European critics who first drew attention to the decisive steps being taken by musicians in Chicago's AACM (Association for the Advancement of Creative Musicians) to advance the development of free jazz. But only at the end of the seventies—ten years later!—did a respectable number of AACM musicians gain U.S. recognition in the *Down Beat* poll.

Albert Ayler, Cecil Taylor, Eric Dolphy, Ornette Coleman, Chick Corea, Lester Bowie, Joseph Jarman, Roscoe Mitchell, Anthony Braxton, Pat Metheny, and Shannon Jackson were stars in Europe long before they became famous in the United States. The world's greatest jazz journal is not, as one might expect, American but Japanese (*Swing Journal* published in Tokyo), followed by the International Jazz Federation's *Jazz Forum*, brought out in Warsaw. Three of America's leading jazz critics—Leonard Feather, Dan Morgenstern, and Stanley Dance—were born in Europe.

All the editions of this book have been produced in close, often lifelong contact with hundreds of jazz musicians. The teachers among musicians make use of the book in college and university classrooms, from Marion Brown in Atlanta to Richard Davis at the University of Wisconsin, and from Anthony Davis at Yale University to John Handy in San Francisco. Musicians are inclined to be skeptical about critics and scholars. I have always felt their acceptance to be a special privilege, and am grateful for it.

Creative artists in all spheres are of the opinion that the critic's main task doesn't involve criticizing but rather describing, that is, mediating understanding. I have always felt this to be my main goal. To be sure, this book is filled with criticism, but the idea of critically assessing every single musician would amount to overestimating the role of the critic, resulting in the know-it-all pedantry of which musicians (and other artists) have accused critics ever since (jazz) criticism came into being.

Jazz, as Eric Dolphy put it, is "human music." Many musicians share his opinion. Duke Ellington loved talking about "humanity." Jazz, according to pianist JoAnne Brackeen, means "making people spiritual." I would be happy if something of this philosophy is apparent in the pages of this book.

The knowledgeable reader should bear in mind that this book also serves as an introduction to jazz, and that, particularly in this respect, its style and structure have stood the test of the past three decades. Our aim has been to adhere to current internationally accepted views within jazz criticism and scholarship, ignoring the many "secondary theories" that have sprung up everywhere.

This book can be read selectively. You can decide for yourself in what order you want to read the various chapters. You could, for instance, start with "The Elements of Jazz" or with the sections on big bands and combos. If you are fond of jazz singing, you could begin with the chapter on jazz vocalists; and if you play an instrument, you could read the relevant section. There's nothing to be said against reading the chapter on jazz styles or the great formative musicians only after first reading many other sections.

It was easy to select the most important musicians of jazz's earlier epochs. Since the seventies, however, there hasn't been any single musician who represents a decade's developments. Henry Threadgill, James Newton, John Zorn, or Bill Frisell could have been chosen for the eighties, but the decade's "conservative" trend is nowhere more fascinatingly apparent than in the music of David Murray, on the one hand, and Wynton Marsalis, on the other—and in the area of tension between them.

Inevitably a book of this kind also owes much to the works that preceded it. We must particularly acknowledge Leonard Feather's *Encyclopedia of Jazz*; André Hodeir's *Jazz—Its Evolution and Essence*; Nat Shapiro and Nat Hentoff's *Hear Me Talkin' To Ya* and *The Jazz Makers*; Charles Keil's *Urban Blues*; John Storm Roberts' *The Latin Tinge*; Ian Carr, Digby Fairweather, and Brian Priestley's *Jazz—the Essential Companion*; Ekkehard Jost's *Jazz in Europa*; and Bert Noglik's *Jazz–Werkstatt International*. The last two works were especially helpful with regard to the presentation of musicians from the European scene.

Some of the information that doesn't derive from such books, or whose source isn't specified in the text, comes from contributions to the well-known jazz magazines: *Down Beat, JazzTimes,* and *Cadence* in the United States; *Coda* in Canada; *Wire* in England; *Jazz Hot* and *Jazz Magazine* in France; *Jazz Podium* and *Jazzthetik* in Germany; and *Jazz Forum* in Poland.

Both Günther Huesmann and I would like to thank all those whose suggestions and criticism have helped us. I owe a particular debt of gratitude to Shoichi Yui and Dan Morgenstern, who have translated, edited, and generally taken care of various editions of this book in Japan and the United States.

We would like to thank Kevin Whitehead for taking on the difficult task of assembling the American discography for this edition of *The Jazz Book*. The problem in creating such a discography is, of course, not so much what to choose, but what to omit. We know that Kevin solved this problem with knowledge and sensitivity.

First and foremost, however, we want to thank the musicians, naturally for their help and advice, but even more for their friendship, and above all for their music. It may be self-evident that their music constitutes the basis of jazz criticism, but this has to be enunciated because critics of all persuasions tend to overvalue their own activities.

The reader will have sensed that this preface is also written on behalf of Günther Huesmann. This particularly applies to the following lines which appear in a similar form in all of my books: We can't claim to have avoided all errors, or expect anyone to adopt our views. No critic has ever attained "papal" infallibility, and anyone who holds this belief only reveals that he or she hasn't understood the nature of the critic's task. But the many previous editions of this book have served so many jazz fans—and potential fans—that we felt obliged to carry on the work. We will be grateful to any reader who draws our attention to errors or something worthy of criticism that we have overlooked so that we may incorporate corrections in future editions.

Joachim-Ernst Berendt
Baden-Baden
April 1991

THE STYLES OF JAZZ

The Styles of Jazz

Jazz has always been the concern of a minority—always. Even in the age of Swing, the thirties, the jazz of creative black musicians was—except for very few recordings—recognized by only a few. Still, taking an active interest in jazz means working for a majority, because the popular music of our times feeds on jazz: All the music we hear in TV series and on Top 40 radio, in hotel lobbies and on elevators, in movies, and through Walkmen; all the music to which we dance, from Charleston to rock, funk and hip-hop; all those sounds that daily engulf us—all that music comes from jazz (because beat came to Western music through jazz).

Taking an active interest in jazz means improving the quality of the "sounds around us"—the level of musical quality, which implies, if there is any justification in talking about musical quality, the spiritual, intellectual, human quality—the level of our consciousness. In these times, when musical sounds accompany the takeoff of a plane as well as a detergent sales pitch, the "sounds around us" directly influence our way of life, the quality of our lives. That is why we can say that taking an active interest in jazz means carrying some of the power, warmth, and intensity of jazz into our lives.

Because of this, there is a direct and concretely demonstrable connection between the different kinds, forms, and styles of jazz on the one hand and the periods and spaces of time of their creation on the other hand.

The most impressive thing about jazz, aside from its musical value, in our opinion is its stylistic development. The evolution of jazz shows the continuity, logic, unity, and inner necessity that characterize all true art. This development constitutes a whole, and those who single out one phase

3

and view it as either uniquely valid or as an aberration destroy this
wholeness of conception. They distort that unity of large-scale evolution
without which one can speak of fashions, but not of styles. It is our
conviction that the styles of jazz are genuine and reflect their own particular
times in the same sense that classicism, baroque, romanticism, and
impressionism reflect their respective periods in European concert music.

Let's suggest one way of getting an impression of the wealth and scope of
the different jazz styles. After reading about the early styles, ragtime and
New Orleans, skip a few chapters and jump into the one on free jazz,
listening to some of the characteristic records as well (which can easily be
found with the help of the discography at the end of the book). What other
art form has developed such contrasting, yet clearly interrelated, styles
within a span of only fifty years?

It is important to be aware of the flowing, streamlike character of jazz
history. It certainly is no coincidence that the word *stream* has been used
again and again by jazz critics and musicians in connection with different
jazz styles—interestingly enough, as "mainstream" first for Swing jazz, later
for the main tendency of today's jazz, or as in "third stream." There is one
mighty stream that flows from New Orleans right up to our contemporary
music. Even breaks or revolutions in this history, such as the emergence of
bebop or, later, free jazz, appear in retrospect as organic or even inevitable
developments. The stream may flow over cataracts or form eddies or rapids
from time to time, but it continues to flow on as ever the same stream. No
one style "replaces" another. Each incorporates what went before—
everything that went before.

Many great jazz musicians have felt the connection between their playing
styles and the times in which they live. The untroubled joy of Dixieland
corresponds to the days just prior to World War I. The restlessness of the
Roaring Twenties comes to life in Chicago style. Swing embodies the
massive standardization of life before World War II; perhaps, to quote
Marshall Stearns, Swing "was the answer to the American—and very
human—love of bigness." Bebop captures the nervous restlessness of the
forties. Cool jazz seems to reflect the resignation of men who live well yet
know that H-bombs are being stockpiled. Hard bop is full of protest, soon
turned into conformity by the fashion for funk and soul music. This protest
gains uncompromising, often angry urgency in free jazz, which characterized the period of the civil rights movement and the student revolt. In the
seventies there was a renewed phase of consolidation. Some aspects of
jazz-rock went along with the age's faith in technology. The jazz of the
eighties, on the other hand, expresses much of the skepticism of people who
live amid affluence but also know where ongoing unquestioned progress has
brought them. What has been said in such a generalized and simplified way

here is even more applicable to the many different styles of individual musicians and bands.

Many jazz musicians have viewed attempts at reconstructing past jazz styles with skepticism. They know that historicism runs counter to the nature of jazz. Jazz stands and falls on being alive, and whatever lives, changes. When Count Basie's music became a worldwide success in the fifties, Lester Young, who had been one of the leading soloists of the old Basie band, was asked to participate in a recording with his old teammates for the purpose of reconstructing the Basie style of the thirties. "I can't do it," Lester said. "I don't play that way any more. I play different; I live different. This is later. That was then. We change, move on." Obviously, this is also true about contemporary reconstructions of historical jazz styles.

Around 1890: Ragtime

Jazz originated in New Orleans: a truism, with all that is true and false about such statements. It is true that New Orleans was the most important city in the genesis of jazz. It is false that it was the only one. Jazz—the music of a continent, a century, a civilization—was too much in the air to be reducible to the patented product of a single city. Similar ways of playing evolved in Memphis and St. Louis, in Dallas and Kansas City, in other cities of the South and Midwest. And this, too, is the hallmark of a style: different people in different places making the same (or similar) artistic discoveries independently of each other.

It has become customary to speak of New Orleans style as the first style in jazz. But before New Orleans style developed, there was ragtime. Its capital was not New Orleans but Sedalia, Missouri, where Scott Joplin had settled. Joplin, born in Texas in 1868, was the leading ragtime composer and pianist—and thus we have made the decisive point about ragtime: It was largely composed, primarily pianistic music. Since it was composed, it lacks one essential characteristic of jazz: improvisation. Yet ragtime swings, at least in a rudimentary sense, and so it is considered part of jazz. And the practice of not only interpreting rags but also using them as themes for jazz improvisations began quite early.

What today seems the epitome of ragtime—the piano rags of Scott Joplin and others—is in fact a late peak in a long development involving an abundance of ragtime forms: vocal ragtime songs, Texan banjo rags (which musicologists assume served as the basis for piano ragtime), ragtimes for brass bands and rags for strings, and ragtime waltzes written by composers who were often more popular than Joplin, even though today they are only known to specialists.

Posterity only remembers the "classic" piano ragtime. Justly so, since it crystallized not only the most artistically valuable aspects of ragtime but also the elements that were to influence jazz most (whereas ragtime songs became important for the tradition of the popular song).

"Classic" ragtime seems to be composed in the style of nineteenth-century piano music. Sometimes it appears to adhere to the trio form of the classical minuet; at others it consists of several successive formal units, as in the waltzes of Johann Strauss. It is, however, important to realize—and this characterizes the complexity of the development of African-American music—that the forms of ragtime also have African origins. Additive forms are even more important in African than in European music. When black ragtime musicians "borrowed" from the additive forms of European music, they actually were drawing on their own history.

Pianistically too, ragtime reflects much of nineteenth-century music. Everything of importance at that time can be found there, from Chopin and above all Liszt to marches and polkas, all recast in the black rhythmic conception and dynamic way of playing. And that was also how it was perceived: Ragtime is, as the name suggests, "ragged time." Unlike in European music, rhythm dictates the melody.

Ragtime was particularly popular in the camps of workers building the great railroads across the American continent. Ragtime was heard everywhere—in Sedalia and Kansas City, in St. Louis and Texas, Joplin's home state. The composers of rags hammered their pieces into player-piano rolls, which were distributed by the thousands.

That was way before the time of the phonograph, and, for a long period little was known about all this. Only in the fifties were substantial numbers of the old piano rolls rediscovered, sometimes quite accidentally in places like antique stores and junk shops, and transferred to records.

Aside from Joplin, there were many other ragtime pianists: Tom Turpin, a St. Louis bar owner (particularly melodically inventive); Joseph Lamb, a textile merchant (celebrated for the complex motivic interweavings in his rags); Louis Chauvin; May Aufderheide; and, above all, Eubie Blake. At the age of ninety, Blake made a spectacular comeback at the great 1973 Newport–New York Jazz Festival and even had his own Broadway show in the late seventies. Blake made thousands of young people who no longer knew what ragtime was, "rag conscious" once again. He died in 1983, just a few days after his hundredth birthday.

There were several whites among the great rag pianists around the turn of the century, and it is significant that even experts were not able to detect differences in playing style between blacks and whites. Ragtime, as Orrin Keepnews once put it, is "on the cool side."

Scott Joplin was a master of melodic invention. He was amazingly productive, and among his even thirty rags are such melodies as "Maple Leaf Rag" and "The Entertainer" (which became immensely popular in 1973,

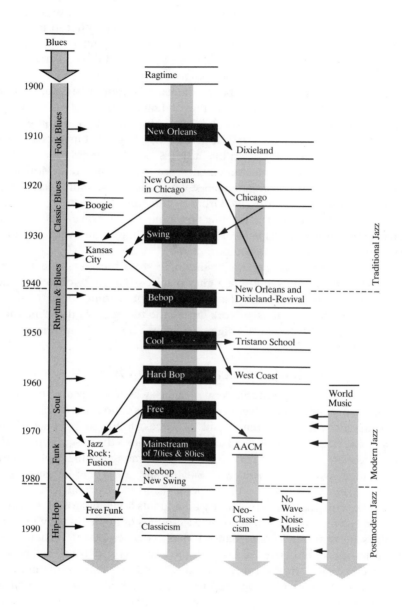

The Evolution of Jazz

almost sixty years after Joplin's death, through the motion picture *The Sting*). In Joplin, as in ragtime per se, the old European tradition merged with the black rhythmic feeling. Ragtime, more than any other form of jazz, may be described as "white music, played black." How much Joplin was at home in the European tradition is apparent not only in the construction of his rags, but also in the fact that he composed two operas.

Among the first musicians to liberate themselves from the strictures of the composer-imposed interpretation of rags and take a freer and more jazzlike approach to melodic material was Jelly Roll Morton, one of the important musicians with whom the New Orleans tradition begins. "I invented jazz in 1902," he once claimed, and on his business card he described himself as "creator of ragtime." Both statements are hyperbole, but Morton is important as the first known jazz pianist who improvised on themes, mostly his own, that were rags or derived from ragtime music.

In Morton we recognize for the first time the decisive fact that the personality of the performing musician is more important in jazz than the material contributed by the composer.

Jelly Roll carried the ragtime tradition to the Chicago of the Roaring Twenties, and even to California. Other pianists—James P. Johnson, Willie "The Lion" Smith, and young Fats Waller—kept ragtime, or at least the ragtime tradition, alive in New York during the twenties. At that time there was scarcely a pianist whose origins could not be traced, in one way or another, to ragtime.

Turn of the Century: New Orleans

At the turn of the century, New Orleans was a witches' cauldron of peoples and races. The city had been under Spanish and French rule prior to the Louisiana Purchase. French and Spaniards, followed by English and Italians, and lastly joined by Germans and Slavs, faced the descendants of the countless Africans brought here as slaves. And among the black population as well there were differences in nationality and culture no less significant than those, say, between the whites from England and the whites from Spain.

All these voluntary and involuntary immigrants loved first of all their own music: what they wanted to keep alive as sounds of home. In New Orleans, people sang British folk songs, danced Spanish dances, played French dance and ballet music, and marched to the strains of brass bands based on Prussian or French models. In the many churches could be heard the hymns and chorales of Puritans and Catholics, Baptists and Methodists; mingled with all these sounds were the "shouts" of the black street vendors, and the black dances and rhythms. Deep into the 1880s, blacks congregated periodically in Congo Square to perform voodoo rites, thus preserving a cult with origins in ancient, half-forgotten African traditions. Recent converts to Christianity, they celebrated the new god in song and dance much as they had honored the deities of their native land. Old New Orleans must have been an incredibly musical city. We know of some thirty orchestras from the first decade of this century. To appreciate what that means, you have to know that the Delta City had little more than 200,000 inhabitants then. And in a city of that size, there were thirty orchestras, playing a vital, new kind of music.

All this created an atmosphere that made the New Orleans of those days a symbol of strange, exotic romanticism for travelers from all parts of the earth. It is certainly a myth that this city in the Mississippi delta was the sole birthplace of jazz, but New Orleans was indeed the point where many important aspects of the music first crystallized. New Orleans was a watershed—for the music of the countryside, such as the work songs of the black plantation laborers; for the spirituals that were sung during the religious services for which they gathered under open skies; and for the old "primitive" blues-folk songs. All these things merged in the earliest forms of jazz.

W. C. Handy, the composer of blues, related that the music played in Memphis around 1905 was not very different from that of New Orleans. "But we didn't discover until 1917 that New Orleans had such music too," Handy said. "Every circus band played this way." The entire Mississippi delta was full of the new sounds—all rising independent of each other. "The river and the city were equally important to jazz."

New Orleans, in spite of this, held a special place. Well into the thirties more than half of the important jazz musicians came from there. Four reasons may have been decisive:

- First, the old French-Spanish urban culture of the Delta City favoring interchanges, unlike other American cities where Puritanism and Victorian values predominated.
- Second, the tensions and challenges arising from the fact that, as we shall see, two decidedly different black populations confronted each other here.
- Third, the intense musical life of the city, in terms of European "serious" and popular music, with which the blacks constantly came in touch.
- And finally, the fact that all these varied elements came together in Storyville, the city's red-light district, relatively free of prejudice or class consciousness.

The two black populations of New Orleans were the Creoles and the "American Negroes." However, obviously, the Creoles, in the geographical sense, were just as "American" as other blacks—perhaps even more so. The Creoles of Louisiana emerged from the old French colonial culture. They were not, like other blacks, descendants of slaves who gained freedom at the end of the Civil War. Their ancestors had been free much longer. Many of them had been freed by rich French planters or merchants for reasons of distinguished service. The term *Free Negro* was an important one in old New Orleans.

The Creole blacks had made French culture their own. Many were wealthy businessmen. Their main language was not English but Creole, a French patois with admixtures of Spanish and African words. Their names were French: Alphonse Picou, Sidney Bechet, Barney Bigard, Albert Nicholas, Buddy Petit, Freddie Keppard, Papa and Louis deLisle Nelson, Kid Ory, etc. It was an honor to be a Creole. Jelly Roll Morton took great pains to make clear that he was a Creole and that his real name was Ferdinand Joseph La Menthe.

Compared to the Creoles, the American blacks were more African. Their masters were of Anglo-Saxon origin, and thus they were not exposed to the more liberal social attitudes of the French-Spanish orbit. The American blacks constituted the black proletariat of New Orleans. The Creoles looked down on them with a particular class- and color-consciousness that "at that time was even more prejudiced to other blacks than the attitude of white people to the colored generally was," as guitarist Johnny St. Cyr put it.

Consequently, there were two very different groups of New Orleans musicians, and the difference found expression in the music. The Creole group was more cultured and educated (skilled in reading notes); the American more vital and spontaneous (handing down its music orally). The main instrument of the French group was the clarinet, which has a great tradition in France. This old French woodwind tradition remained alive well into the thirties in the playing of the leading Swing clarinetists. In fact, Eric Dolphy, in the late fifties, was the first to drop it totally.

In New Orleans itself, the French influence can hardly be overestimated. Many of the things that gave the city the fascinating atmosphere without which its jazz life would have been inconceivable stem from France. Thus, there is the famous Mardi Gras, which has become the expression of the city's lust for life. Even the funerals, during which a band escorts the deceased to the cemetery with sad music and then leads the procession back home with joyful sounds, derive from a French custom; it prevails to this day in rural districts of southern France.

In the mingling of the many ethnic and musical strains in New Orleans, which occurred almost automatically in the laissez-faire climate of Storyville, New Orleans style was born. It is characterized by a "free counterpoint" played by the three melody instruments: cornet (or trumpet), trombone, and clarinet. The lead is taken by the brilliant sound of the cornet, effectively contrasted by the heavy, weighty trombone. The clarinet entwines the two brasses in an intricate pattern of melodic lines. This front line is supported by the rhythm section: string or brass bass, drums, banjo or guitar, and occasionally piano.

The early New Orleans rhythm is still very close to European march rhythm. The peculiar "floating" effect of jazz rhythm, stemming from the fact that 1 and 3 remain the strong beats but 2 and 4 are accented, is as yet absent. The stress is still on 1 and 3, just as in a march.

The early New Orleans jazz bands resembled the marching and circus bands of the day in other respects too, such as instrumentation and social function.

New Orleans style is the first example of "hot' playing. *Hot* connotes the emotional warmth and intensity of the music and has come to stand for the peculiar sound, phrasing, "attack," and vibrato that characterize this style. From that point on, all this becomes individualized. The instrument is not so much played as made to "talk"—to express the individual feelings of the musician.

The Teens: Dixieland

In New Orleans, playing jazz was not exclusively a privilege of the black man. There seem to have been white bands almost from the start. "Papa" Jack Laine led bands in New Orleans from 1891 on. He is known as the "father" of white jazz. Bands traveled through the city on carts, known as band wagons, or marched along the streets. When two bands met, a contest or "battle" ensued. It sometimes happened that black and white bands became engaged in such contests, and when the white band was led by Papa Laine, it often "blew out" its opponent.

From the earliest time, there was a white style of playing jazz: less expressive, but sometimes better versed technically. The melodies were smoother, the harmony "purer," the sonorities not so unorthodox. There were fewer sliding notes, less expressive vibrato, fewer portamenti and glissandi. Whenever these effects were used, there was an element of self-consciousness involved, of knowing that one *could* also play "legitimately"; often the music approached the eccentric, even the downright comic. In contrast, the music of the black bands, whether joyful or blue, always contained the aspect of *having* to be that way.

All the successful early white bands stem from Papa Laine. And there is no doubt that the first successful groups in jazz were white: first and foremost the Original Dixieland Jazz Band, and then the New Orleans Rhythm Kings. The ODJB, as it has come to be known, with its punchy, collective style (there were almost no solos), made famous many early jazz standards. Among them were "Tiger Rag" and "Original Dixieland One-Step" (recorded in 1917) and "At the Jazz Band Ball" (recorded in 1919). The New

Orleans Rhythm Kings, with their two outstanding soloists, Leon Rappolo, clarinet, and Georg Brunis, trombone, devoted more room to solo improvisation. They first recorded in 1922 and became famous in the early twenties.

In 1917, the ODJB played at Reisenweber's Restaurant on Columbus Circle in New York and made a tremendous hit. From that time on, the word *jazz*—at first usually spelled "jass"—became known to the general public. Bandleader Tom Brown claims to have used the word publicly for the first time in Chicago in 1915. But it appears as early as 1913 in a San Francisco newspaper. Prior to that, "jass" (and the earlier "jasm" and "gism") were in use as slang expressions for speed and energy in athletic pursuits, and in sexual contexts as well.

It has become customary to label all New Orleans white jazz "Dixieland," thus separating it from essential New Orleans style, but the borderlines remain fluid. Especially in later years, with black musicians playing in white bands or vice versa, it no longer made any sense to argue about which style was being played.

With ragtime, New Orleans and Dixieland, the history of jazz begins. What was earlier belongs to what Marshall Stearns has called "jazz prehistory." Jazz does not belong to Africa, where it was unknown at its time of origin and where until this day it is less understood than in most other parts of the world, albeit appreciated. The most often cited statement in this context is Barry Ulanov's: "There is more of the sound of jazz in mid-European Gypsy fiddling than in a whole corps of African drummers." To which Leonard Feather adds, "In melodic and harmonic construction, the early jazz bears considerably more resemblance to such tunes of the 1850s as 'Arkansas Traveler' and 'Turkey in the Straw' than to any known African music." When drummer Art Blakey returned from a trip to Africa, where he studied black music, he said, "You can't mix what comes out of the African culture with what came out of our culture." (We will return to this problem repeatedly in the course of this book.)

Jazz was born in the encounter between black and white. That is why it originated where this meeting took place in the most intensive fashion: the southern part of the United States. Until this day, jazz is conceivable only in terms of this interaction. It loses its fundamental rationale when one or the other element is overemphasized, or even given a status of exclusiveness, as has been done.

The contact between the races, which has been so important in the evolution and development of jazz, symbolizes that spirit of "togetherness" per se that characterizes jazz in musical, national, international, social, sociological, political, expressive, aesthetic, ethical, and ethnological terms.

The Twenties: Chicago

We have chosen to divide the evolution of jazz into decades for the purpose of overall perspective. To be sure, ragtime and New Orleans were alive at the beginning of our century, but both styles were still being played later, up to our time. On the other hand, what is decisive is not how long a style was cultivated, but when it originated and when it unfolded its greatest vitality and musical power. From this point of view, it is a fact that a new style has come into being roughly every ten years, often at the beginning of a decade.

There are three essential things about jazz in the twenties: the great period of New Orleans music in Chicago, classic blues, and Chicago style.

The development of New Orleans jazz in Chicago is generally connected with the entry of the United States into World War I. This connection appears somewhat dubious but may, along with other factors, have played a certain role. New Orleans became a war port. The secretary of the navy viewed the goings on in Storyville as a danger to the morale of his troops. Storyville was closed by official decree.

This decree deprived not only the ladies of Storyville but also many musicians of their daily bread—particularly the pianists mainly employed in Storyville, at that time known as "Professors." Even before that, hundreds of other musicians for whom Storyville wasn't as important had already experienced economic hardship. Many left town, most of them to Chicago. The "Windy City" on Lake Michigan had previously been a source of fascination for many New Orleans musicians. Now came the great exodus of New Orleans musicians to Chicago, and it is clear that this was only a part of the general migration of blacks from south to north. It developed that the first jazz style, though called New Orleans, actually had its really great period in the Chicago of the twenties. It was in Chicago that the most famous New Orleans jazz recordings were made, as the phonograph became increasingly popular after World War I.

King Oliver was the leader of the most important New Orleans band in Chicago. It was here that Louis Armstrong formed his Hot Five and Hot Seven, Jelly Roll Morton his Red Hot Peppers, Johnny Dodds his New Orleans Wanderers, etc. What is known as New Orleans style today is not the archaic and barely recorded jazz that existed in New Orleans in the first two decades of this century, but the music made by New Orleans musicians in Chicago during the third decade.

The blues also had its great period in the Chicago of the twenties. Certainly blues songs existed long before there was jazz, at least from the middle of the nineteenth century. In those days, they were heard in the rural districts of the South, mostly without a steady jazz beat and often lacking the standard twelve-bar pattern that characterizes the blues today. Itinerant blues singers traveled—as they still do today—from town to town, from plantation to plantation, with a banjo (or guitar) and a bundle containing all their worldly possessions, singing those songs with the drawn-out "blue" notes known today as country or "archaic" blues.

When the first marching bands began to play in New Orleans, there was a difference between their budding "jazz" and the blues. But soon the rural blues began to flow into the mainstream of jazz, and from then on jazz and blues became so interwoven that, as Ernest Borneman has written, all of jazz is "nothing but the application of the blues to European music, or vice versa." Even the most modern and "freest" jazz musician of today is indebted to the blues; in fact, blues consciousness is higher in today's jazz than in many previous styles.

The twenties are considered the period of "classic" blues. Bessie Smith was its greatest singer. In later chapters, Bessie Smith herself and the harmony, melody, and form of the blues will be discussed. It is with good reason that the blues are treated in a special section as an "element of jazz." It was not only a certain style of jazz in the early times, but it has left its mark on all forms of jazz and on the whole history of the music. The intention here is to give a summary of the development of jazz in its entirety for easier orientation in the following chapters.

Around the great jazz instrumentalists from New Orleans and the famous blues singers there developed in Chicago a jazz life hardly less active than that of New Orleans in the Golden Age. Centered on the South Side, Chicago's black district, it lacked the happy exuberance of the old New Orleans days but reflected the hectic pace of the metropolis and, increasingly, the problems of racial discrimination.

Stimulated by the jazz life of the South Side, young white high school and college students, amateur and professional musicians began to develop what has been called "Chicago style." They had become so inspired by the greats of New Orleans jazz that they wanted to emulate their style. As imitation their music was unsuccessful; instead they came up with something new: Chicago style. In it, the profusion of melodic lines, so typical of New Orleans style, is more or less absent. The voicings, if there is more than one line, are in most cases parallel. The individual has become the ruler. From this point on, the solo becomes increasingly important in jazz. Many Chicago-style recordings consist of hardly more than a sequence of solos or, in jazz terminology, "choruses."

Only now the saxophone, which to many laymen represents jazz incarnate, begins to gain importance. Chicago may be considered the second "cool" style of jazz (the first being piano ragtime). Bix Beiderbecke is the foremost representative of this style, which will be discussed at greater length in the section about him.

The Thirties: Swing

The older styles of jazz are grouped together under the heading "two-beat jazz." Toward the end of the twenties the two-beat styles seemed all but exhausted. In Harlem, and even more in Kansas City, a new way of playing developed around 1928–29. With the second great exodus in jazz history—the journey from Chicago to New York—Swing begins. Swing may be characterized as "four-beat jazz," because it puts stress on all four beats of the bar. This is true in general, but as is so often the case in jazz, there are confusing exceptions. Louis Armstrong (and some Chicago-style players) were already conversant with four-beat style in the twenties. On the other hand, Jimmie Lunceford's big band at the height of the Swing era employed a beat that was simultaneously 2/4 and 4/4.

The word *swing* is a key term in jazz, and it is used in two different senses. This may lead to a certain amount of confusion. First, swing connotes a rhythmic element from which jazz derives the tension classical music gets from its formal structure. This swing is present in all styles, phases, and periods of jazz. It is so essential that it has been said that if music does not swing, it is not jazz.

The other use of the term refers to the dominant jazz style of the thirties—the style through which jazz won its greatest commercial success before the emergence of fusion music. In the Swing era Benny Goodman became the "King of Swing."

There is a difference between saying that a jazz piece swings and that it *is* Swing. Any jazz tune that is Swing also swings—if it is any good. But, conversely, not all jazz that swings is necessarily Swing. In order to avoid confusion, it was suggested in an earlier edition of this book that the *style* Swing should be capitalized, while lower-case swing should connote the rhythmic element. Many jazz scholars all over the world have adopted this practice. In the chapter on "Rhythm" the nature of swing (lower case) will be described further.

One feature of the Swing era was the development of big bands. In Kansas City (e.g., in the bands of Bennie Moten and later Count Basie), the "riff" style developed. This was an application of the old, important call-and-response pattern (originating from Africa) to the sections of a large jazz band. These sections are trumpets, trombones, and saxes. Another contribution to big-band jazz was made by the white Chicago style: a more "European" approach to the music. In Benny Goodman's band, the different styles flowed together: some New Orleans tradition, through Fletcher Henderson, who arranged for the band; the riff technique of Kansas city; and that white precision and training through which this brand of jazz somehow lost so much of its expressivity. On the other hand, the easy melodic quality and clean intonation of Goodman's band made it possible to sell jazz to a mass audience.

It only seems to be a contradiction that the individual soloist gained in importance alongside the development of big bands. Jazz has always been simultaneously collective and individualistic. That jazz, more than any other music, can be both at the same time clarifies much about its nature. This is jazz's particular characteristic (we'll talk about it later), mirroring the social situation of the modern era.

Thus, the thirties also became the era of great soloists: the tenor saxists Coleman Hawkins and Chu Berry; the clarinetist Benny Goodman; the drummers Gene Krupa, Cozy Cole, and Sid Catlett; the pianists Fats Waller and Teddy Wilson; the alto saxists Benny Carter and Johnny Hodges; the trumpeters Roy Eldridge, Bunny Berigan, and Rex Stewart; and many more.

Often these two tendencies—the orchestral and the soloistic—merged. Benny Goodman's clarinet seemed all the more glamorous against the backdrop of his big band. Louis Armstrong's trumpet stood out in bold relief when accompanied by a big band. And the voluminous tone of Coleman Hawkins' or Chu Berry's tenor sax seemed to gain from the contrast to the "hard" sound of Fletcher Henderson's big band.

The Forties: Bebop

Toward the end of the thirties, Swing had become a gigantic business enterprise. It has been called the "greatest music business of all time" (which was true then, but the record sales of the thirties and forties were modest compared to the dimensions of today's music business). The word *Swing* became a marketing device for all sorts of goods, from cigarettes to articles of female clothing, while the music, conforming to general commercial demands, often became a matter of endlessly repeated clichés.

As is so often the case in jazz when a style or way of playing becomes too commercialized, the evolution turned in the opposite direction. A group of musicians who had something new to say found each other in a healthy, although not in all cases deliberate, reaction against the general Swing fashion.

This new music developed—at first in spurts—originally in Kansas City and then, most of all, in the musicians' hangouts in Harlem (particularly in a place called Minton's Playhouse) and once again at the beginning of a decade. Contrary to what has been claimed, this new music did *not* develop when a group of musicians banded together to create something new, at whatever cost, because the old was no longer a draw. The old style drew very well—it was still the "greatest music business of all time." Nor is it true that the new jazz style was shaped as a conscious effort by an interrelated group of musicians. The new style was formed in the minds and instruments of different musicians in different places, independent of each other. But Minton's became a focal point, as New Orleans had been forty years earlier. And just as Jelly Roll Morton's claim to have invented jazz was absurd, so would be the claim of any musician in the forties to have "invented" modern jazz.

The new style was eventually named bebop, a word that seemed to mirror the vocalization of the then best-loved interval of the music: the flatted fifth. The term *bebop* came into being spontaneously when someone attempted to "sing" these melodic leaps. This is the explanation that trumpeter Dizzy Gillespie, one of the main exponents of the new style, gave for the origin of the term *bebop*. There are as many theories about the origin of this word as there are about most jazz expressions.

The flatted fifth became the most important interval of bebop, or, as it was soon called, bop. Until then, this device would have been felt to be erroneous, or at least "wrong" sounding, although it might have been used in passing chords or for the special harmonic effects that Duke Ellington and pianist Willie "The Lion" Smith liked to use as early as in the twenties. But now it characterized an entire style, as the narrow harmonic base of earlier jazz forms was constantly broadened. Within ten or twelve years (as we shall see) the flatted fifth was to become a "blue note," as common as the undetermined thirds and sevenths familiar in traditional blues.

The most important musicians who gathered at Minton's were Thelonious Monk, piano; Kenny Clarke, drums: Charlie Christian, guitar; trumpeter Dizzy Gillespie; and alto saxist Charlie Parker. The latter was to become the real genius of modern jazz as Louis Armstrong was the genius of traditional jazz.

One of these musicians—Christian—not only belongs among the founders of modern jazz but also among those who fashioned from Swing the foundations for its development. There is a whole group of such pioneers, at once the "last" generation of Swing and the pathbreakers for bop. And almost every instrument had its own bebop pioneer; among trumpeters, it is Roy Eldridge; among pianists, Clyde Hart; among tenors, Lester Young; among bassists, Jimmy Blanton; among drummers, Jo Jones and Dave Tough; among guitarists, Charlie Christian.

To the listener of that time, the sounds characteristic of bebop seemed to be racing, nervous phrases that occasionally appeared as melodic fragments. Every unnecessary note was excluded. Everything was highly concentrated. As a bop musician once said, "Everything that is obvious is excluded." It is a kind of musical shorthand, and you have to listen to it in the same way you would read a stenographic transcript, establishing ordered relationships from a few hasty signs.

The improvisations are framed by the theme presented in unison at the beginning and the end of each piece, generally played by two horns, in most cases a trumpet and saxophone (Dizzy Gillespie and Charlie Parker are the archetypes). This unison alone—even before the musicians began to improvise—introduced a new sound and a new attitude. Music psychology knows that unisons, wherever they appear—from Beethoven's "Ode to Joy" and even earlier in the main motif of the Ninth Symphony's first movement to North African Bedouin music and to the choirs of the Arabic world—signal, Listen, this is *our* statement. It is *we* who are talking. And you to whom we speak, you are different from us and probably our opponents.

Under the influence of the then avant-garde bop sound, many friends of jazz didn't know what to make of this new turn in the evolution of the music. With great determination, they oriented themselves backward, toward the basic forms of jazz. "Simple" music was demanded. There was a New Orleans renaissance—or, as it was called, "revival"—that spread all over the world.

This development began as a sound reconsideration of the roots of jazz—the tradition that to this day nourishes jazz in all its forms and phases. But soon the revival led to a simplified and cliché-ridden "traditional" jazz from which black musicians turned away. (With the exception of the surviving New Orleans jazz musicians, for whom traditional jazz was the logical form of expression, no important black musicians participated in the Dixieland revival—strange as this may sound to some.) Amateurs often worked against the commercialization of Dixieland, but they regularly fell victims to it themselves as they attained professional status.

After World War II, the "jazz boîtes" in Saint-German-des-Prés in Paris became the headquarters of the traditional movement, fortified with existentialist philosophy. But soon the young existentialists discovered that their philosophy was better suited to a music that did not reflect the happy, carefree attitudes of the early years of the century, but rather the unrest of their own times. They gravitated toward more contemporary jazz forms, and the center of the movement shifted to England. In that county, Dixieland concerts were organized with the same commercial effort and success as presentations of rock 'n' roll singers.

In this section, bebop and the New Orleans revival have been contrasted in the same way that they appeared to be in contrast to each other to jazz fans at that time: as extremes of antagonistic opposition. Today—and actually since the genesis of free jazz in the sixties—these poles have approached each other, for today's young listener can no longer appreciate this contrast. To him, Charlie Parker is just as much a part of the jazz tradition as Louis Armstrong.

In describing bebop, we have used terms like *racing, nervous, melodic fragments, cypher, hasty.* But in the face of what is racing, nervous, fragmented, and hasty in today's scene, most of the jazz of the forties seems of almost classic completeness to the young listener today. One can only hope that listeners and critics of today's jazz learn from this development and use greater caution in the application of extreme words and concepts. The critics who foresaw the "end of jazz" or even the "end of music" in reaction to the "nervousness" of bop seem a bit ridiculous today, but there were a lot of them once. They are here today, too, in reaction to what seems nervous and loud.

Today, over forty years later, we should pause and consider what has become of the great musicians who created bebop. Only one of them, Max Roach, is still creatively active in the vein of today's scene: with his contemporary percussion group, for instance; or with his duo concerts with musicians like Cecil Taylor, Anthony Braxton, Dollar Brand, and Archie Shepp; or playing together with string quartets. Another of the bop fathers, Dizzy Gillespie, is still creative in the bebop style. The others have either become artistically rigid or have died—most of them after psychological or physical illness, after heroin or alcohol addiction. And even though they died young (Charlie Parker, e.g., was thirty-four), they were past the peak of their creativity at the time of their deaths, at an age when other artists often only begin to gain real stature.

Compare the bebop musicians with creative personalities of European art—figures like Stravinsky or Schönberg, Picasso, Kandinsky, or Chagall. They lived to a ripe old age and remained creative, and the whole world respects and admires them. For the creative musicians of bebop, however, early death was often the rule, and nobody is writing papers and essays about it. That seems to be the toll jazz artists in America have to pay to society, which accepts it without batting an eyelash.

But that is also the backdrop that makes this music so powerful and impressive and that makes the work of these soon rigidified or perished artists seem that much more admirable. And it is no accident that at the end of the seventies we witnessed a bebop revival that hardly anyone would have forecast some years ago. Bebop has become the embodiment of classical modernity in jazz. An entire generation of young people plays this music, and today at the start of the nineties more than ever before. They won't suffer breakdowns or die from heroin like their forerunners. This revival is occurring over thirty years after Charlie Parker's death, forty years since Bud Powell's first breakdown, and thirty-five years after bop trumpeter Fats Navarro died, right after his twenty-sixth birthday.

The Fifties: Cool, Hard Bop

Toward the end of the forties, the "unrest and excitement of bop" were more and more replaced by a tendency toward calm and smoothness. This trend first became apparent in the playing of trumpeter Miles Davis. As an eighteen-year-old, he had played in Charlie Parker's Quintet of 1945 in the "nervous" style of Dizzy Gillespie; not much later, however, he began to blow in a relaxed and "cool" manner. The trend also showed up in the piano improvisations of John Lewis, an anthropology student from New Mexico who traveled with Dizzy Gillespie's big band to Paris in 1948 and only then decided to remain in music; and in the arrangements Tadd Dameron wrote in the second half of the forties for the same Gillespie big band and for various small combinations. Miles Davis' trumpet solos of 1947 with Charlie Parker, such as "Chasin' the Bird," or John Lewis' piano solo in Dizzy Gillespie's " 'Round Midnight," recorded at a 1948 concert in Paris—these are the first cool solos in jazz history, excepting Lester Young's tenor sax solos with Count Basie from the late thirties, in which he paved the way for the cool conception even before the bebop era had begun.

With these three musicians—Miles Davis, John Lewis, and Tadd Dameron—the style known as "cool jazz" begins.

The cool conception dominates all the jazz of the first half of the fifties, but it is notable that it found its most valid and representative expression at a moment almost coincidental with its origin: in the famed recordings of the Miles Davis Orchestra, which was formed for a brief engagement at New York's Royal Roost in 1948 and was recorded by the Capitol label in 1949 and 1950. In the chapter dealing with Davis, this group—of decisive importance to the ensemble sound and musical conception of the decade—will be discussed in detail.

Lennie Tristano (1919–1978), a blind pianist from Chicago who came to New York in 1946 and founded his New School of Music there in 1951, gave a theoretical foundation to cool jazz through his music and thinking. The musicians of the Tristano school (notably altoist Lee Konitz, tenorman Warne Marsh, and guitarist Billy Bauer) were to a large extent responsible for the layman's idea of cool jazz as cold, intellectual, and emotionless music. However, there can be no doubt that Tristano and his musicians improvised with remarkable freedom, and that linear improvisation stood at the center of their interests. Thus Tristano let himself be advertised as Lennie Tristano and His Intuitive Music; he wanted to emphasize the intuitive character of his conception and ward off the lay opinion that his was an intellectually calculated music. Still, Tristano's music held for many listeners a coolness often bordering on a chill. The evolution of modern jazz soon found less abstract, more sensuous and vital forms. The problem was, as Stearns has said, "to play cool without being cold."

The influence of the Tristano school has remained traceable throughout all of modern jazz, however far removed from the "Tristano-ite" mode of coolness. This is true harmonically, but most of all in a distinct preference for long, linear melodic lines.

After Tristano, the center moved initially to the West Coast. Here evolved, directly connected to the Miles Davis Capital Orchestra, a "West Coast jazz," often played by musicians who made their living in the Hollywood studio orchestras. Trumpeter Shorty Rogers, drummer Shelly Manne, and clarinet-ist-saxophonist Jimmy Giuffre became the style-setting musicians of the West Coast. Their music contained elements of the academic European musical tradition; direct and vital jazz content was often pushed into the background. The experts frequently pointed out that New York remained the true capital of jazz. This was where real and vital jazz was made: modern, yet rooted in jazz tradition. West Coast jazz was confronted with "East Coast jazz."

Since then, it has become apparent that both "coasts" were not so much stylistic entities as advertising slogans promoted by record companies. The real tension in the evolution of the jazz of the fifties was not between two coasts but between a classicist direction and a group of young musicians, mostly black, who played a modern version of bebop, so-called hard bop.

The new fifties jazz classicism—as French critic André Hodeir has called it—found its "classics" in the music Lester Young and Count Basie had played in the thirties, first in Kansas City and later in New York. Many musicians from either coast, white or black, were oriented toward this music: Al Cohn, Joe Newman, Ernie Wilkins, Manny Albam, Johnny Mandel, Chico Hamilton, Buddy Collette, Gerry Mulligan, Bob Brookmeyer, Shorty Rogers, Quincy Jones, Jimmy Giuffre. In the fifties, a massive number of "Count Basie tributes" were recorded. Basie's name stands for clarity, melodiousness, swing, and certainly that "noble simplicity" of which Winckelmann, a German scholar of the eighteenth century, spoke in his famous definition of classicism. (It is amazing how often it is possible to employ, almost literally, the words of the German classicists of the Goethe period when speaking of jazz classicism. One needs only to substitute for the names and concepts from Greek art and mythology Count Basie and Lester Young, swing, beat, and blues.)

Confronting this classicism stood a generation of young musicians whose foremost representatives lived in New York, though few of them were born there. Most were from Detroit or Philadelphia. Their music was the purest bop, enriched by a greater knowledge of harmonic fundamentals and a greater degree of instrumental-technical perfection. This hard bop was the most dynamic jazz played in the second half of the fifties—by groups under the leadership of, among others, drummers Max Roach and Art Blakey and pianist Horace Silver; by musicians like trumpeters Clifford Brown, Lee

Morgan, and Donald Byrd, and tenor men Sonny Rollins, Hank Mobley, and others, including initially John Coltrane.

In hard bop, something new was created without sacrificing vitality. All too often, the new in jazz can only be attained at the expense of vitality. Drummer Shelly Manne, for example, had to pay for the amazing musical refinement of his playing with some reduction in directness and vitality. His colleague Elvin Jones, on the other hand, managed to discover rhythms that simultaneously possess a complexity of structure *and* a vitality the likes of which, in such a relationship, were previously unheard-of in jazz. Horace Silver rediscovered new ways of combining the thirty-two-bar song structure, which is the foundation for most jazz improvising, with other forms—combining them into "groups" of forms (as had been done in similar fashion by the ragtime pianists, Jelly Roll Morton, and other musicians of the early jazz period under the influence of both European and African additive styles). Tenor saxophonist Sonny Rollins created through his improvisations grandiose structures, which at that time were considered "polymetric," while striding across the given harmonic materials with a freedom and ease that not even the Tristano school could match.

Marshall Stearns said:

Indeed, modern jazz as played in New York by Art Blakey and his Messengers, Jay and Kai, Max Roach and Clifford Brown, Art Farmer and Gigi Gryce, Gillespie, Davis, and others . . . has never lost its fire. The harmonies of cool jazz—and bop—were taken over, the posture of resignation disappeared, the light sound remained, but the music always has a biting sharpness. In a word: It has changed, but fundamentally it remained "hot" and "swinging". . . . The word "cool" has lost its meaning—unless it is taken in a general sense of "sensitive" and "flexible."

The last sentence applies to both directions of the jazz of the fifties: Basie-Young classicism and new bop.

It is also true of both movements that they had found a new relationship to the blues. Pianist-composer Horace Silver—and with him a few others—broke through with a manner of playing known as "funky": slow or medium blues, played hard on the beat, with all the feeling and expression characteristic of the old blues. And not only the blues, but also the gospel songs of black churches began to play a new, powerful role in jazz: in a playing style called "soul," connected again with Horace Silver, but also with singer and pianist Ray Charles and vibraharpist Milt Jackson. Jazz musicians of all persuasions on both coasts threw themselves into funk and soul with notable enthusiasm. They did so in a manner that, since musical reasons are not readily apparent, leads one to conclude that extramusical influences were present. In a letter to the editor of *Down Beat* magazine (spring 1958), a reader suggested that "the cool musician, in his use of the funky-blues framework, may be thinking about the content which is hidden behind this framework. . . . This content expresses a 'warm'—as opposed to 'cool'—relationship to life. . . . Though the content of the real blues may be sad, it is not a hopeless sadness." The letter continues with talk of a "spiritual transformation" of the cool jazz musician.

The tendency toward funk and soul expresses the wish to belong and the desire for something offering a semblance of security in a world of cool realism. Soul with its roots in the music of the gospel churches, experienced a large-scale success in popular music during the late sixties; funk, which comes from blues, did the same in the seventies. The important thing is to remember that both were born from jazz or, more generally, from black tradition and feeling.

This tendency toward a feeling of security and belonging became even clearer a decade later, in free jazz. Albert Ayler, for example, transplanted circus, country, and marching music—clearly motifs from the safe and sane "good old days"—into his free, atonal, ecstatic improvisations. Other free-jazz musicians overemphasized their hate for the white world and found a substitute realm of group acceptance and security in communion with those who shared this hate—a psychological reaction familiar to anyone conversant with psychoanalysis.

During the cool-jazz period, the contrapuntal and linear music of Johann Sebastian Bach fulfilled this need to belong in the Modern Jazz Quartet of pianist John Lewis. A whole tide of jazz fugues rose in the first half of the fifties; it subsided as power and vitality returned to the scene with hard bop.

The Sixties: Free Jazz

These are the innovations of the jazz of the sixties—free jazz:

1. A breakthrough into the open space of "free tonality."
2. A new rhythmic conception, characterized by the disintegration of meter, beat, and symmetry.
3. The flow of "world music" into jazz, which was suddenly open to all the great musical cultures—from India to Africa, from Japan to Arabia.
4. An emphasis on intensity unknown to earlier styles of jazz. Jazz had always been superior in intensity to other musical forms of the Western world, but never before had the accent been on intensity in such an ecstatic, orgiastic—sometimes even religious—sense as in free jazz. Many free-jazz musicians actually made a "cult" of intensity.
5. An extension of musical sound into the realm of noise.

Around the early sixties, jazz music broke through into the realm of free tonality, or even atonality, as concert music had done forty or fifty years earlier. Jazz specialists had expected this development for some fifteen years; it was anticipated in Lennie Tristano's "Intuition" and "Digression" of 1949; some important musicians of the fifties, particularly George Russell and Charles Mingus, paved the way for it. A "new music," a "new jazz," was born like many innovations in the arts, initially relying on shock value. The power and hardness of the new jazz, along with a revolutionary, partially extramusical pathos, affected the jazz scene of the sixties vehemently. This vehemence was even stronger because so many things had been bottled up in the fifties, when the breakthrough was imminent but was avoided with almost pathological anxiety. All these bottled-up things came down like an avalanche on a contented jazz public, which had accommodated itself to Oscar Peterson and the Modern Jazz Quartet.

For the younger generation of free-jazz musicians, the music preceding them had been depleted in terms of playing and procedural possibilities, harmonic structure, and metric symmetry. It had become rigid in its clichés and predictable formulas, similar to the situation twenty years earlier when bebop was created. Everything seemed to run according to the same, unchangeable pattern in the same, unchanging way. All possibilities of traditional forms and conventional tonality seemed exhausted. That is why the young musicians searched for new ways of playing; in the process, jazz again became what it had been in the twenties when the white public discovered it: a great, crazy, exciting, precarious adventure. At last, there was collective improvisation again, with lines rubbing against and crossing each other wildly and freely. That, too, is reminiscent of New Orleans—with modifications to be discussed later.

Don Heckmann, the critic and musician, once said, "I think there's been a natural tendency toward this freeing of the improvisatory mind from harmonic restrictions throughout the history of jazz."

In jazz, free tonality, however, is understood in a basically different way from that of European concert music. The free jazz of the New York avant-garde around 1965 featured—much more so than, say, the "serial" European avant-garde music—so-called "tonal centers" (see the section dealing with harmony). This means that the music loosely partakes in the general gravitation from the dominant to the tonic but has a wide range of "freedom" in all other aspects.

This development was so spontaneous and nonacademic that the European term *atonality* cannot be used in an exclusively academic sense. Small wonder that many free-jazz musicians have expressed their explicit contempt for academic music and its vocabulary (Archie Shepp: "Where my own dreams sufficed, I disregarded the Western musical tradition altogether"). In the new jazz, "atonality"—or better, "free tonality"—has a wide range of meaning: It includes all steps, from the intimated "tonal centers" to complete harmonic freedom. However, in the face of radical atonality, the tendency to realize that the harmonic system cannot simply be replaced by "nothing"—by no system at all—has become stronger.

In spite of the brevity of its history, jazz has a much longer atonal tradition than European music. The shouts and field hollers, the archaic blues of the southern plantations, indeed, nearly all musical forerunners of jazz—which also survived as elements of jazz—were "free tonal," often enough simply because the singers didn't know anything about European tonality. In the old days of New Orleans, too, there were musicians unconcerned with harmonic laws. Certain Louis Armstrong records from the twenties (*Two Deuces* with Earl Hines, e.g.) are among his most beautiful, though they contain notes that are "wrong" in terms of European academic tonality.

Marshall Stearns, who pointed out all these things when they first surfaced during the hard-bop era, claimed, "The knack for harmonic liberties, which jazz musicians well knew how to take within the system of perfect intonation of European music, moves steadily toward a predictable goal: the freedom of the street cry and the field holler."

In other words, there is a tradition of atonality—or of harmonic freedom—in the whole history of jazz, while atonality in European music was first introduced by an avant-garde—the "classical" avant-garde beginning with Schönberg, Webern, and Berg. Thus, jazz atonality has become the meeting ground for tradition and avant-garde—a truly advantageous point of departure rarely encountered in an art in flux!

There is no doubt that musicians like Ornette Coleman, Archie Shepp, Pharoah Sanders, and Albert Ayler are closer to the "concrete," folk-music-like harmonic freedom of the field cry and of the archaic folk blues than to "abstract," intellectual European atonality. Ornette Coleman, for instance, didn't realize that there was also free tonality in European music until he met John Lewis and Gunther Schuller in 1959–60. At that time he had already developed his own musical concept. Free jazz is a part of jazz tradition, not a break with it.

For a number of years we were at a point where the freedom of free jazz was often understood as freedom from any musical system formed in Europe, with the emphasis on "formed in Europe." The formal and harmonic emancipation from the music of the "white continent" was a part of a greater racial, social, cultural, and political emancipation. "Black music," as it was interpreted by many of these musicians and by LeRoi Jones (Amiri Baraka), one of their most eloquent spokesmen, became "blacker" than ever before in this process of breaking its strongest link with the European tradition, the harmonic laws. (See the quotes by Jones and one of his associates in the section on Ornette Coleman and John Coltrane.)

There is a parallel between jazz and modern European concert music, but only insofar as both displayed a growing disgust with the mechanistic, machinelike character of the traditional system of functional harmonics. This system had become a roadblock in the development of the musics by increasingly substituting for individual decisions its own functional mechanics, and its abolition is a legitimate development familiar from many other arts, cultures, and traditions. When a structuring principle has been worn out and the creative artists become convinced that within its limits everything possible has been said, the principle must be abandoned. And after seventy years of modern concert music, nobody would seriously argue that this traditional principle is the *only* correct one.

The claim of exclusive validity for European harmonics is contradicted not only by artistic and physical considerations, but also by the many different principles and systems that have proven their value in other musical cultures of the world. Especially in view of today's political and cultural developments, the contention has become untenable that one system could have all the answers. On the other hand, it remains to be seen to what extent the free harmonic conception is the answer. It is not correct, however, to simply invalidate this conception as "incomprehensible," since it is a fact that it was immediately understood without prior discussion by a minority of listeners and a majority of young jazz musicians all over the world.

Jazz should be seen as a spiritual and cultural phenomenon within the spiritual and cultural movements of this century. Parallels of a more than accidental nature can be found between the liberation of jazz from functional harmonics and similar developments in other contemporary arts. We have discussed concert music. The parallel with modern literature is just as obvious. The antigrammatical and antisyntactic tendencies of so many modern writers—Raymond Queneau, Arno Schmidt, Helmut Heissenbüttel, Butor, William Burroughs, and, first and foremost, Mallarmé and James Joyce plus many others in all important languages—in many respects correspond to the antiharmonic tendencies of the free-jazz musicians. Increasingly, the gravitation of syntax and grammar draws language into the same functional and causal tunnel into which music moved under the influence of functional harmonics. Each step derived directly and necessarily from the preceding one, so that the creative artist finally could do little more than choose from a catalog determined by syntax, grammar, and harmonics.

Modern philosophy, which moves further and further away from closed systems, is another example of the same phenomenon. Once a philosophical system was established, any further philosophizing within that system showed the same characteristics of mechanically answering grammatical or harmonic rules.

All new jazz styles have created new rhythmic concepts. Free jazz is no exception. Two basic facts determine the different rhythmic concepts in the history of jazz from New Orleans to hard bop: A fixed meter, generally 2/4 or 4/4 (until the emergence of the waltz and other uneven meters in the fifties), is carried out constantly. Second, the jazz beat produces accents that do not necessarily correspond to those a classically trained musician would place within that same meter. Free jazz demolished the two pillars of conventional jazz rhythm—meter and beat. The beat was replaced by the pulse, and the meter, which was passed over by some free-jazz drummers as if it did not exist, was replaced by wide arches of rhythmic tension, built up with an incredible intensity. (More about this in the sections on rhythm and the drums.) Sunny Murray, one of the leading free-jazz drummers, called traditional drum rhythm "cliché beats" that are "like slavery or poverty. Freedom drumming is an aspiration toward a better condition."

Just as important to jazz as harmonic and rhythmic innovation was gaining access to world music. Jazz developed within a dialectic—the meeting of black and white. In the first sixty years of jazz history, the counterpart of jazz was European music. Interaction with the European musical tradition was by no means a marginal activity. Nearly all styles of jazz came into being in and through this dialectical interaction.

In the process, the realm of what was meant by "European music" grew continually larger. To the ragtime pianists of the turn of the century it meant the piano compositions of the nineteenth century. To the New Orleans musicians it meant French opera, Spanish circus music, and European marches. Bix Beiderbecke and his Chicago colleagues of the twenties discovered Debussy. The Swing arrangers learned orchestration skills from the late romantic symphonic period. Finally, when the development had gone beyond cool jazz, jazz musicians had incorporated almost all elements of European music they could possibly use, from baroque to Stockhausen.

Thus, the role of European music as the stimulating counterpart of jazz—at least as its only counterpart—had run out. Aside from this musical reason, there were extramusical ones—racial, social, and political—as we have already mentioned. This is why jazz musicians discovered new partners with growing fervor: the great non-European musical cultures.

The Arabic and Indian cultures and musics have held a special fascination. There have been Islamic tendencies among African-Americans since the mid-forties, since the time, in other words, when modern jazz originated. Dozens of jazz musicians converted to Islam and occasionally took Arabic names. For a couple of years, drummer Art Blakey was known to his Muslim friends as Abdullah Ibn Buhaina; in the forties, saxophonist Ed Gregory had already become Sahib Shihab.

In this turning away from "the white religion," the emancipation from the white man is given particularly effective expression. James Baldwin, the black writer, said, "Whoever wishes to become a truly moral human being must first divorce himself from all the prohibitions, crimes, and hypocrisies of the Christian church. The idea of God is only valid and useful if it can make us greater, freer and more capable of loving." Millions of black Americans believe—"after two hundred years of vain attempts"—that the Christian God cannot do that. For that reason, says Baldwin, "it is time we got rid of Him."

It was only a small step from religious conversion to Islam to a growing interest in Islamic music. Musicians like Yusef Lateef, Ornette Coleman, John Coltrane, Randy Weston, Herbie Mann, Art Blakey, Roland Kirk, Sahib Shihab, and Don Cherry in the United States, and, among others, George Gruntz and Jean-Luc Ponty in Europe—many of them not Muslims by faith—have expressed their fascination with Arabic music in compositions and improvisations.

Even stronger than Arabic music was the interest in Indian music with its great classical tradition. What fascinates jazz musicians most about Indian music is, above all, its rhythmic wealth. The great classical music of India is based on talas and ragas.

Talas are rhythmic series and cycles of immense variety, from three to 108 beats. You have to be aware that Indian musicians and sophisticated listeners are able to appreciate even the longest tala—108 beats—as a series and as a predetermined musical structure and to recall it as such.

Talas usually have a great wealth of rhythmical structuring possibilities. A tala consisting of ten beats, for example, can be conceived as a series of 2-3-2-3 or 3-3-4 or 3-4-3 beats. Within the series, there is ample room for free improvisation; the improvising musicians can wander far away from each other. But the tension characteristic of Indian music is to a large extent founded on the fact that the individual lines of improvisation finally must meet again on the first beat, "one"—the so-called *sam.* After the widely diverging melodic movements, this meeting very often is felt like an almost orgiastic relief.

It is this rhythmic wealth of Indian music that particularly attracts modern jazz musicians. They want to liberate themselves from the 4/4 uniformity of the metrically conventional, constant jazz beat, while at the same time searching for rhythmic and metric structures that create a jazzlike intensity.

In contrast to the rhythmically well-defined tala, the *raga* is a melodic row in which many elements categorized in numerous ways in European music come together: theme, key, mood, phrase, and the form determined by the melodic flow. A particular raga may require, for example, that a certain note can be used only after all other notes of the raga have been played. There are ragas that can be played only in the morning, at night, at full moon, or only with religious thoughts in mind. And, above all, ragas are "modes," which makes them correspond ideally to the tendency toward modality in modern jazz (cf. the section on harmony).

A large number of jazz musicians have studied with the great masters of Indian classical music. The word *classical*, by the way, should be read with emphasis, because this is not folklore music. It is as "classical" as the corresponding music in European culture. The openness with which dozens of jazz musicians of the fifties and sixties have approached the great exotic musical cultures goes far beyond comparable developments in modern European concert music. Overwhelming intensity and complexity are generated when Don Ellis derives big-band compositions, such as "3-3-2-2-2-1-2-2-2" and "New Nine," from Indian talas; when Miles Davis and Gil Evans transform Joaquin Rodrigo's "Concierto de Aranjuez" into Flamenco jazz; when Yusef Lateef converts Japanese, Chinese, and Egyptian elements into blues on his record *A flat, G flat and C*; and when Sahib Shihab, Jean-Luc Ponty, and George Gruntz play with Arab Bedouins on the album *Noon in Tunisia*. Compared to that, Debussy's, Messiaen's and Roussell's use of Indian and Balinese sounds and the influence of Chinese rhythms on the modern German composer Boris Blacher seem timid and marginal.

The new jazz musicians transform world music into swinging sounds. They do this with the liberating joy of the adventurer and discoverer, and with a fervor whose messianic, all-embracing gesture of love is manifest in many of their album titles: in Albert Ayler's *Spiritual Unity* and *Holy Ghost*; Don Cherry's *Complete Communion*; Carla Bley's *Communication*; Schlippenbach's *Globe Unity*; Yusef Lateef's *Try Love*; Ornette Coleman's *Peace*; John Coltrane's "Love," *Love Supreme*, "Elation," and *Ascension*; or in tunes such as "Sun Song," "Sun Myth," and "Nebulae" from *Heliocentric Worlds* by Sun Ra and his Solar Arkestra. The message of these titles can be felt when they are seen in a single context: "spiritual unity to complete communion and communication with the globe as a unity—and, through that, love and peace for everybody and salvation in pan-religious ecstasy . . . cosmic ascension and elation to mythological suns and nebulae and heliocentric worlds."

It is important to note that the jazz musicians merely emphasize artistically and musically what the more aware members of the black community have been realizing extramusically. In March 1967, for instance, teachers and students of a predominantly black New York high school boycotted all concerts of classical European music, not because they were not interested in European concert music (quite the contrary—musical activity at this school was above average) but because they felt it was wrong to be offered only concerts of European music, not jazz or Indian, Arabian, African, etc., music: "This selection is arbitrary, based on European history, not ours."

The opening of musical sounds into the realm of noise has to do with both world music and even more so with increased intensity. For centuries, there have been sounds in different exotic musical cultures, which may not necessarily seem "musical" to a classically trained ear. Their explosive intensity has literally burst open the conventional sound barriers of the instruments of many free-jazz musicians. Saxophones sound like the intensified "white noise" of electronic music, trombones like the noises of conveyor belts, trumpets like steel vessels bursting from atmospheric pressure, pianos like crackling wires, vibraphones like winds haunting metal branches; collectively improvising groups roar like mythical, howling primeval creatures.

Indeed, the border between musical sound and noise, which seems so clear and natural to the average listener, is not physically definable; it is founded on traditional, tacit conventions. Fundamentally, music can use anything audible. In fact, this is its goal: the artistic utilization of what is audible. This goal cannot be reached when only some sounds are deemed suitable for music while all others are branded inappropriate.

Stockhausen said:

> Sounds previously classified as noise are now being incorporated into the vocabulary of our music. . . . All sounds are music . . . music using all sounds is the music of today, not tomorrow, in our space age where the movement, direction, and speed of sounds are calculated elements of a composition. The object is to refresh and renew our known world of sounds with the available means of our time, just as every period of history has done.

To be sure, Stockhausen said this essentially as a result of his experiences with electronic music. But it is true about every acoustic process generated by man. Pianos can be played not only on the keys but also inside, on the strings; violins can be beaten; trumpets can be used (without mouthpiece) as blowpipes. People ridiculing these ways of playing instruments simply prove that to them, music is nothing but fulfilling conventional rules. An instrument exists to produce sounds. There are no laws governing the procedure of this production. On the contrary, it is the job of the musician to continually find new sounds. In doing so, he or she can use conventional instruments in new ways, or invent new instruments, or further develop conventional instruments. This job has become a major challenge for many musicians. For an edition of the avant-garde magazine *Microphone*, many modern British percussionists wrote detailed, page-long statements, but jazz drummer Tony Oxley simply wrote one sentence: "The most important activity for me is the enlargement of my vocabulary." This opinion is characteristic of many contemporary musicians.

We are living in an age that has created new sounds of unimaginable variety: jet planes and atomic explosions, the noises of oscillation and the ghostly crackling in the assembly buildings of precision industry. Big-city dwellers are subject to a barrage of decibels that people of former times not only would have been unable to withstand physically, but that would have cast them into paroxyms of psychological confusion. Scientists have amplified the sounds of plant growth by millions of decibels so that they become a deafening roar. We now know that fish, deemed to be the quietest of all creatures by the romantics of the last century, exist in an environment of continual sounds. Every human being alive today is affected by this expansion of the realm of the audible. Are musicians, whose subject is sound, supposed to be the only ones unaffected?

Within a few years, free jazz became a richly varied means of expression, mastering the gamut of human emotions. We should free ourselves from the misconception that this music only voices anger, hate, and protest. This highly one-sided impression was created mainly by a small group of New York critics and musicians far from representative of all of free jazz. Besides the protest, there are the hymnlike religious fervor of John Coltrane, the joyous air of the folk musician in Albert Ayler, the intellectual yet humorous coolness of Paul Bley or Ran Blake, the cosmic amplitude of Sun Ra, the sensibility of Carla Bley.

During the sixties, increasingly, young musicians and jazz fans all over the world were finding their way to the new sounds. While critics and unappreciative fans were still crying "chaos," the new jazz was finding its audience—not only in the United States but also in Europe, where an autonomous type of free music, European free jazz, evolved. Free jazz finally gave European jazz an unmistakable identity. With free jazz the emancipation of European jazz gets under way—not coincidentally somewhat later than American developments in the mid-sixties. Only with liberation from functional harmony and ongoing rhythm did European musicians really liberate themselves from imitation of American jazz. Of course, there had already been Django Reinhardt and Stan Hasselgard—the great exceptions—who exerted a stylistic influence on American jazz. But up to that point European musicians had been spellbound by American models.

It's interesting that initially, with the emergence of free jazz, nothing changed in this imitative relationship. Just as they had previously copied and imitated Swing and bebop, cool jazz and hard bop, European musicians now copied and imitated the free jazz of Ornette Coleman, Cecil Taylor, and Albert Ayler. But in doing so they also absorbed free jazz's explosive inner message, which says that no musical rule is self-evident. It may sound paradoxical, but European musicians found themselves because they copied black free jazz. By taking over this model of openness and freedom from rules, they were thrown back on themselves. A vacuum developed that European adherents of free jazz had to fill, and they filled it in a highly individual, diverse, and colorful way. There can be no doubt that free jazz produced more internationally recognized European musicians than any other style before or since.

Various languages of free jazz, often intermingling during international encounters, immediately developed in Europe, establishing diverse national and regional characteristics. Interest in the sound's inner life predominated on the English scene among such musicians as guitarist Derek Bailey, saxophonist Evan Parker, and drummer Tony Oxley.

Nowhere else in Europe were experiments and sound collages taken so far as in England. This trip into sound's nuclear center automatically resulted in British free-jazz musicians becoming more involved in electronic music. In the Netherlands there dominated a free jazz characterized by biting wit and mocking humor and propelled by an inclination toward burlesque and parody. Musicians like Han Bennink and Willem Breuker developed theatrical elements out of their playing. A predilection for weight and power was apparent in West German free jazz, whether in Peter Brötzmann's frenetic overblown performances or in Manfred Schoof's and Gunter Hampel's emphasis on clarity. At the end of the sixties, free jazz also got under way in the German Democratic Republic, with such an emphasis on accuracy and order (despite multiple incursions of irony) that people talked about a "Prussian" variant of free jazz.

One claim keeps appearing in the countless critiques that this new style of music has spawned: the new freedom will ultimately end in chaos. However, after understandable initial elation over the new freedom, the musicians began to emphasize that freedom was not the only point. Sunny Murray, the free-jazz drummer already mentioned, said, "Complete freedom you could get from anyone who walks down the street. Give them $20, and they'll probably do something pretty free." Similar statements have been made with increasing frequency since the end of the sixties. One reason for this is certainly that musicians became more aware that free jazz was developing its own clichés. And soon these free-jazz clichés—lacking a tradition—appeared even emptier than the clichés of conventional jazz that had just been so eagerly destroyed. In this way the majority of free-jazz musicians developed a new, dynamic interest in the jazz tradition. But there are other reasons why "chaos" is an inappropriate concept. Let's take a look at the history of European music.

Three times in that history, a "new music" appeared. First, there was *Ars Nova,* appearing around 1350; its most important composer was Guillaume de Machaut. Two and a half centuries later, around 1600, *Le Nuove Musiche* came into existence with the monodical music of the *Stilo Rappresentativo,* centering on composers like Orazio Vecchi and Monteverdi. Both times, secular and religious musical authorities agreed that the new music meant the beginning of chaos in music. From this point on, that fear never vanished: Johann A. Hiller spoke "with disgust" of Bach's "crudities." Copies of the first edition of Mozart's quartets were returned to him because the engraving was "quite imperfect." "Many chords and dissonances were thought to be engraving faults" (Franz Roh).

The reactions of critics contemporaneous with Beethoven are applicable to today: "All neutral music specialists were in full accord that something as shrill, incoherent, and revolting to the ear was utterly without parallel in the history of music." (This about the overture to "Fidelio"!) Brahms, Bruckner, and Wagner at one time or another were all in the "guild of chaotics." Then came the third "new music"—with all the well-documented scandals, misinterpretations, and misunderstandings. One need only recall the turbulence at the premiere of Stravinsky's "Sacre du printemps" in Paris in 1913; the various Schönberg scandals; or the premiere of Debussy's "Pelléas et Mélisande" in 1902 (it was labeled "brain music" and an example of "nihilistic tendencies"). Today, all this music is considered "classical." Hollywood composers are using harmonies and sounds borrowed from it.

It was similar in jazz. At first, the "new music" from New Orleans sounded chaotic to the "legitimate" ear: a wild, free departure to a confusing new land. However, by the turn of the fifties, New Orleans jazz had become party music for the young bourgeois.

When bebop appeared in 1943, the nearly universal opinion was that chaos had finally taken over, that jazz was nearing the end. Today, Dizzy Gillespie's trumpet and vocals sound as gay and familiar to us as "When the Saints Go Marching In."

The conclusion to be drawn from all this is that the word *chaos* is merely a refrain that rhymes with *history of music*, as simply as *fun* and *sun*. *Free jazz* also rhymes with it very well.

A bourgeois world that agrees on nothing as readily as on its need for security first of all needs to be aware of the chaos surrounding it, if it wants to avoid totally despairing of consciously living. By bringing order to chaos, by giving it artistic expression, free jazz is one avenue for this consciousness. Ordering chaos, of course, is possible only by getting closer to it. This is where the sound of chaos enters—first in classical European music, then, since the sixties, in jazz.

Free jazz wants to force us to cease understanding music as a means to self-affirmation. Human beings, who build computers and send satellites to Venus, have better means of self-affirmation. And the person whose racial problems and power politics are still in the style of the nineteenth century does not deserve self-affirmation anyway.

By self-affirmation in music we mean the way all of us have been listening to music: always anticipating a few bars ahead, and when it comes out exactly (or at least nearly) as expected we feel confirmed and note with pride how right we have been. Music has had no other function than to cause such self-esteem. Everything has worked out perfectly. The few places where things deviated have simply increased the fascination.

Free jazz must be listened to without this need for self-affirmation. The music does not follow the listener anymore; the listener must follow the music—unconditionally—wherever it may lead. The members of a German avant-garde group, the Manfred Schoof Quintet, have spoken of the absolute "emptiness," the tabula rasa indispensable to that kind of musical experience. It was observed in the United States that children could be enraptured by free jazz. They simply listen to what is happening—and a lot is! Wherever the sounds go, children follow. There is no place in their minds or sensory systems that, in the middle of each musical phrase, demands, this is the way it must continue; that is where it has to go; if it does anything else, it is "wrong." They demand nothing, and so get everything. The adults, however, for whom a piece of music—or a poem or picture—has almost no other function but to fulfill their demands, should not fool themselves. Except for guaranteed self-affirmation, they get nothing.

The Seventies

> "The fusion has to happen inside you. Otherwise, it's not going to happen at all."—John McLaughlin

Up to this point, we have been able to match each decade with a particular style—certainly at the cost of some fine distinctions, but with greater clarity as a result. With the beginning of the seventies, we have to drop this principle. This decade showed at least seven distinct tendencies:

1. Fusion or jazz-rock: the combination of jazz improvisation with rock rhythms and electronics.

2. A trend toward European romanticist chamber music, an "aestheticization" of jazz, so to speak. Suddenly, large numbers of unaccompanied solos and duos appear on the scene, often without any rhythm section—no drums, no bass. Much that had been considered essential to jazz is dispensed with: explosive power, hardness, tremendous expressiveness, intensity, ecstasy, and no fear of "ugliness." As an American critic put it, jazz was being "beautified"—or as we just put it, "aestheticized."

3. The music of the new free-jazz generation. When fusion music took over the scene in the early seventies and immediately became a commercial success, many critics wrote that free jazz is dead. But that was a rash

judgment. Free music had gone underground (and "underground" back then also meant to Europe). The years 1973–74 marked the comeback of free playing, centered on the Chicago-based AACM, an association of musicians founded by pianist-composer Muhal Richard Abrams. In the course of the seventies, free-jazz musicians, spearheaded by the AACM players, became increasingly prominent, stressing clear structures and a "new simplicity." And it only seems contradictory that free jazz of the seventies is more self-conscious on the one hand, while on the other (at least for the black players) it relates strongly and deliberately to the African roots of black music. The AACM musicians no longer call their music "jazz" but, proudly, "Great Black Music." (More about the AACM appears in the section on jazz combos.)

4. An astonishing comeback for Swing. Suddenly there is an entire generation of young musicians who appear to be playing rock or fusion but in fact are making music reminiscent of the great masters of the Swing age—tenor saxophonists like Ben Webster and Coleman Hawkins, and trumpeters like Harry Edison and Buck Clayton. The most successful of these young musicians are tenor sax player Scott Hamilton, trumpeter Warren Vaché, and guitarist Cal Collins. Reissues of classic Swing recordings have attracted astonishing interest.

5. An even more amazing and widespread comeback for bebop, sparked off by Dexter Gordon, the great tenor saxophonist. For many years he had led a withdrawn existence in Europe (mainly Copenhagen), but then, in late 1976, he went to New York to appear at the Village Vanguard club. What was supposed to be a short engagement led to a triumphant comeback for both Gordon (who remained in the States until his death in 1990) and bebop itself.

This is the third bebop wave in jazz history, following the original bebop in the forties and hard bop in the second half of the fifties. Just as hard bop incorporated the experience of cool jazz (particularly the extended melodic phrases), the new bebop at the end of the seventies similarly took into account all that had happened in the interim. The work of two musicians who were no longer alive, Charles Mingus and John Coltrane, seems to be omnipresent in this new bebop. But there are also musicians whose way of playing bebop responds to experiences of free jazz, thereby creating a kind of "free bop." They include drummer Barry Altschul and saxophonists Arthur Blythe, Oliver Lake, Dewey Redman, and Julius Hemphill.

6. European jazz finds itself. This development opened up with the free jazz of the sixties. New, however, is the fact that European music now goes beyond the more confined sphere of free jazz and also includes tonal ways of playing. Just as the black musicians of the AACM remembered their African roots, European players often started reflecting their own origins.

All the same, the European jazz musician's *roots* lack the unity and coherence of the tradition of black music. These roots are split—not so much because they are culturally diverse in accordance with national and regional differences, but because they separate into at least two basic strands:

- Some European musicians seek their identity by relating to the tradition of European concert music—in the tonal sphere particularly to romantic and impressionist music, and in the realm of free jazz to modern concert music from Webern by way of Berg to Stockhausen, Boulez, and above all Eisler and Weill.
- Others find roots and stimuli in European folklore, the ethnic music of their cultures and others again in world folklore and the great non-European musical cultures.

These spheres of influence often exist in a conflict-ridden state of tension. Since European jazz musicians generally have a more contradictory and disrupted relationship to their musical traditions than African-Americans, European jazz frequently leans toward parody, irony, and elements of distancing and fragmentation. American jazz's confident "This is how things must be" sometimes becomes an ambiguous "both/and" in European music making.

7. The gradual development of a new kind of musician who transcends and integrates jazz, rock, and various musical cultures.

Among all these trends, there are countless overlaps and interconnections. All of these playing styles developed through the interaction of free jazz with conventional tonality and musical structure, traditional jazz elements, modern European concert music, and elements of exotic musical cultures (India, above all), with European romanticism, blues, and rock. "There's no longer just a free style of playing; it's all together," said clarinetist Perry Robinson. Of course, the fundamentally new aspect is that the categorical nature of all these elements is dissolving. The elements no longer exist as distinct entities, as in earlier amalgams; they lose their singular nature and become pure music.

The jazz of the seventies is mainly cool, even where it seems hot. There is a similar kind of "classicist" relation between the styles of the seventies and the sixties as there was between the cool jazz of the fifties and the bebop of the forties.

The freedom of free jazz did not simply mean caprice and chaos. Many free-jazz musicians knew and emphasized this from the beginning, but from the early seventies on, even outsiders have recognized it. The question of what goals the freedom of the sixties had set for itself found its answer in the music of the seventies. The musicians understood why freedom had been necessary: not so that everyone could do as they pleased, but rather to enable jazz musicians to freely make use of all the elements whose authoritarian and automatic characteristics they had overcome.

Harmonically, for example, jazz musicians did not abandon all harmony by learning to play with "free tonality." They merely liberated themselves from the automatic, machinelike functioning of conventional school harmony that, once a certain harmonic structure had been established, determined all harmonic progressions. The free-jazz musicians have broken through this authoritarian, machinelike circularity of the harmonic process. By doing so, they are now that much better equipped to play aesthetically "beautiful" harmonies.

Another example may be found in rhythm. Today we see that the regular meter of conventional jazz was not dissolved in order to destroy it, as it appeared to some fanatics in the initial phase of free jazz. Rather, it was dissolved because the automatic, mechanistic nature of the constant beat was in question. Indeed, an even, constant meter had become so taken for granted during the first sixty years of jazz history that personal artistic decisions in this realm were more or less impossible. Since the first half of the sixties, nothing in rhythm is taken for granted any longer. Now, all kinds of rhythms and meters, constant or not, can be used, with that much more freedom and independence.

Free jazz was a process of liberation. Only now can the jazz musician be really free—free also to play all the things that were strictly taboo for many creative musicians of the free-jazz period: thirds and triads, functional harmonic progressions, waltzes, songs and four-beat meters, discernible forms and structures, and romantic sounds.

The jazz of the seventies melodicizes and structuralizes the freedom of the jazz of the sixties. To the nonspecialist, the seventies are primarily the decade of fusion music or, as it is often called in Europe, jazz-rock. But, as already mentioned, there were a lot of elements besides jazz and rock that were fusioned into this music.

The first signs of fusion could be seen in the late sixties in groups like the Gary Burton Quartet, flutist Jeremy Steig's Jeremy and the Satyrs, the John Handy Quintet, pianist Mike Nock's Fourth Way, the Charles Lloyd Quartet, the Free Spirits of guitarist Larry Coryell, Tony Williams' first Lifetime group, in the group Dreams with saxophonist Michael Brecker and trumpeter Randy Brecker, and in various so-called compact big bands modeled after Blood, Sweat & Tears.

Interestingly enough, the fusion development was initially much stronger in Great Britain (beginning in 1963), but it also came to an end much faster there (around 1969) than in the United States. With a bit of exaggeration one could say that in Great Britain the sixties were already the decade of fusion music, in groups like the Graham Bond Organisation of organist Graham Bond; Colosseum and Cream; Soft Machine; and in musicians like guitarist John McLaughlin, bassist Jack Bruce, drummers Ginger Baker and Jon Hiseman, and saxophonist Dick Heckstall-Smith.

And yet, it was no doubt Miles Davis who made the breakthrough for fusion jazz with his album *Bitches Brew,* released in 1970. Miles was the first to reach a balanced and musically satisfactory integration of jazz and rock. He was the catalyst of jazz-rock—not only with his own records, but also because many of the decade's important players emerged from his groups.

The point in time when all this occurred is noteworthy. As we mentioned, *Bitches Brew* was released in 1970, the time of the *Götterdämmerung* of the rock age: Jimi Hendrix, Janis Joplin, Brian Jones, Jim Morrison, and Duane Allman died; the Beatles broke up. The worst disaster of the rock age occurred in Altamont, California, at a Rolling Stones concert: Four persons died, hundreds were wounded; all the wonderful good will of Woodstock was destroyed; and Woodstock—the miracle of the "Woodstock Nation," of a new, young society full of love, tolerance, and solidarity—showed its true business face. In New York and San Francisco, Fillmore East and Fillmore West, centers of rock music, closed their doors for the last time. Suddenly the rock age had lost its drive; the age had lost its rock. No new groups or individual artists were appearing on the scene to tower above it. Toward the end of this period, Don McLean sang the sad, resigned refrain about the "day the music died," in his hit song "American Pie," the closing hymn of the rock age. It was interpreted that way by the whole world.

All that has been enumerated here happened between 1969 and 1972. The new jazz developed in exact parallel to these events, integrating rock and jazz. The year 1969 marked the release of Miles Davis' *In a Silent Way,* the album that paved the way for *Bitches Brew.* In 1971, Weather Report and the Mahavishnu Orchestra were formed. From 1972 on, the new jazz is here, full-fledged, with all the groups to be introduced in the combo chapter. Anybody who "integrates," who does not always focus on the one, rock *or* jazz, cannot help but conclude that this chronological parallel is not totally accidental. The rock age (or at least the best elements of it) flowed into the new jazz. The new jazz sensitized the rock music of the sixties, as the latter had similarly sensitized the rock 'n' roll of the fifties.

This point becomes clearer when one notes that there is a rock influence on jazz in four essential aspects: the electronization of instruments, rhythm, a new attitude toward the solo, and—connected with that—a stronger emphasis on composition and arrangement as well as on collective improvisation. In each of these aspects, the new jazz makes more sophisticated a characteristic of rock that rock musicians were unable to develop further.

In the area of electronics, several instruments and accessories were added to the store of jazz instrumentation, usually divided into two groups. The first group comprises electroacoustic instruments where the sound is mechanically generated and then electronically amplified and treated: electric pianos, clavinets, guitars, saxophones, trumpets, and even drums. They are often used in connection with wah-wah and fuzz pedals, echolettes, phase shifters, ring modulators, and feedback units; varitones, multividers, harmonizers, etc., for octave duplication and automatic harmonization of melodic lines; and double-neck guitars, combining the possibilities of both six-string and twelve-string guitar or of guitar and bass. The second group includes instruments where sounds are generated completely electronically: organs and other keyboards, and above all a great variety of synthesizers, monophonic at the start of the decade, polyphonic later.

Recording technology achieved similar importance. The modern recording studio has become so important that it has assumed the stature of an "instrument" of equal value to those played by the musicians. A good recording engineer must have the same background knowledge and the same sensitivity as a musician—plus all the required technological expertise—because he or she "plays" the controls and devices. The musicians, on the other hand, have acquired a level of technological know-how scarcely lower than that of many an engineer. Manipulating sound has become an art; with the aid of such devices as phasers, flangers, or chorus machines sound is made to change, scintillate, "migrate." Some of these techniques are also used when recording conventional jazz, but of course much more discretely than with jazz-rock or fusion.

At a superficial first glance, the tempting impression is that the jazz musicians simply took over all this equipment from rock and pop music; but on closer inspection, one discovers that the electric guitar, for example, was first featured by Charlie Christian in 1939 in Benny Goodman's sextet. And the electric organ first became popular in black rhythm and blues music, played by such musicians as Wild Bill Davis; it found its way into mass consciousness through the great success of jazz organist Jimmy Smith after 1956. The music world first became aware of the sparkling sound of the electric piano through Ray Charles' hit "What'd I Say" in 1959. White rock music did not incorporate the instrument until Miles Davis recorded "Filles de Kilimanjaro" with Herbie Hancock and Chick Corea on electric piano in 1968. The first experimentation with electronically amplified horns, varitones, and multividers was done by jazz musicians Sonny Stitt (1966) and Lee Konitz (1968). The synthesizer comes from concert music, where it had been developed and tested since 1957 by R. A. Moog in cooperation with Walter Carlos. Ring modulators, phase shifters, and feedback techniques were also first developed in the electronic studios of concert music.

The impression that all these sounds are sounds of rock is essentially the result of the gigantic publicity machine of the rock media and the record industry. Thus these sounds reached general mass consciousness. It must be seen, however, that the production of "purely" electronic sounds first came from avant-garde concert music. The pioneer work in electrically amplifying and electronically manipulating conventional instruments was done by black musicians, as acknowledged by Charles Keil and Marshall McLuhan.

In this connection, it might be interesting to remember that it was a black singer in the thirties, Billie Holiday, who was the first to realize the potential of the microphone for a completely new use of the human singing voice. It has been said the Billie Holiday's style, which at the time was felt to be new and revolutionary, consisted mainly in "microphonizing" the voice, in a way of singing unthinkable without the microphone. This "microphonic" style has become so commonplace for all kinds of popular music that hardly anyone can imagine how revolutionary it was when Billie Holiday created it.

In summary, we have shown that black musicians set the stage for using instruments electronically and that "purely" electronic sounds were first developed in the studios of electronic concert music. The rock scene merely popularized these sounds. Jazz, rhythm and blues, electronic concert music, rock, and pop all worked together. Such widespread cooperation, covering so many different areas of music, allows the conclusion that the introduction of electronics to music was a demand of the times. Not only the instruments but also the auditory needs of modern man are "electronicized"—of modern man from all social strata and classes, from the slums and ghettos to the music festivals of the intellectual world. Electronics, according to American composer Steve Reich, have become "ethnic"; electronics "transport" the music that "the people" want to hear, as animal hide and wood once transported the music in Africa. The music of an era is always transported by that element that is the general determinant of life. Today that function is carried by electronics.

The question of loudness also belongs in this context. This point causes the outsider as many problems as did the constant beat of the basic meter thirty years ago. So many things have been said about loud volume. We have heard them all: that it is physiologically wrong, incommensurate with the potential of the human ear; that it therefore endangers the auditory faculties or eventually destroys them. There is always an otologist who can confirm this "from daily experience," and the press loves to print things like that. However, increased volume can also create new sensibilities. In the sixties, nobody would have been able to discover as many subtleties as could be heard a decade later in the gale-force range of sound waves generated by the Mahavishnu Orchestra or the group Weather Report, to name two. The new volume is a new challenge: Those who meet that challenge will be capable of working with acoustic maxima that just yesterday seemed impossible for the ear to differentiate. In other words, loud volume widens human capacity and thus human consciousness—and therein lies its challenge. At a time when the sounds of our daily lives have reached decibels of unimagined dimensions, music cannot and must not remain fixed to the volume of yesterday or the day before. That would mean relinquishing the artistic breakthrough into the auditory ranges in which we live, in the sense sketched in the section on the jazz of the sixties regarding the question of "noise."

So much for electronics. Now let's consider rhythm. The inadequacies of the jazz-rock combinations of the sixties were due mainly to the fact that the conventional rock rhythms of the popular groups were much too undifferentiated to be of interest to such a highly sensitized music as the jazz of today. Already in the early sixties, drummers like Elvin Jones, Tony Williams, and Sunny Murray were beating out rhythms without equal in Western music in their highly stratfied complexity and intensity. In the face of this, the work of even the best rock drummers seems regressive. Interestingly, only jazz drummers have generally been successful in dealing with the extroverted, aggressive attitude of rock rhythms in such a way that structures corresponding to the high standards of jazz were produced. In the early seventies, the leading drummers in this field were Billy Cobham (of the first Mahavishnu Orchestra) and Alphonse Mouzon (of the first Weather Report). Both formed their own groups later.

The third aspect of the rock influence on jazz is the new approach to the solo. In all its periods, jazz always had its true culmination in the solo improvisations of outstanding individual artists. However, in the sixties— first in the United States, then even more in Europe—an increasing number of free-jazz collectives came into being who began to doubt the validity of the conventional solo principle. Many of these jazz musicians, consciously or subconsciously, felt that the practice of individual improvisation, in which only the top individual performance counts, reflects all too faithfully the performance principle of the capitalist system. Parallel to the growing social and political criticism of this principle (in fact, even a few years before its rise), a questioning of the value of the principle of individual improvisation had begun. The tendency to improvise collectively became stronger and stronger. The way for this was paved by bassist Charles Mingus, in whose groups there was a lot of free collective improvising as early as the late fifties. At the time it could not be forseen that just a few years later such "collectives" would be the hallmark of an entire musical development—in Europe even more so than in the United States. Bands of the caliber of the Mahavishnu Orchestra showed such a high degree of complex interplay when improvising that one could barely tell which of the five musicians was leading at any given moment, not to speak of soloing in the traditional sense. Pianist Joe Zawinul said about his band, Weather Report, "In this group, either nobody plays solo, or we all solo at the same time."

From the start, record companies and producers played a bigger role in jazz-rock and fusion music than in any of the preceding jazz styles. They had a larger say about what was going to be recorded than the musicians themselves. And they made these decisions more with business than music in mind. Within a span of about five years, the musical impetus of fusion jazz got bogged down by this—in much the same way that, half a decade before, it got bogged down in Great Britain within five years' time.

As early as 1975, critic Robert Palmer wrote, "Electric jazz/rock fusion music is a mutation that's beginning to show signs of adaptive strain. . . . Fusion bands have found that it's a good idea to . . . stick with fairly simple chord voicings. Otherwise, the sound becomes muddy and overloaded. This means that the subtleties of jazz phrasing, the multilayered textures of jazz drumming and the music's rich harmonic language are being abandoned."

The seventies produced an overwhelming inundation of jazz-rock records. Which have endured? At the highest quality level, certainly not much more than the two initial Miles Davis albums, all the records of the first Mahavishnu Orchestra (none by the other Mahavishnu formations!), a couple (and this is where the reservations start) by Chick Corea and Herbie Hancock and Weather Report, and four or five other albums. Not much, really, if you consider that during the peak of bebop—or during the Swing age before that—important, timeless recordings came out month after month; today, over forty years later, these are reissued because they have brilliantly stood the test of time. You can't help but wonder what will remain of jazz-rock and fusion music after so many years.

Many of the best jazz-rock musicians have felt a deficit in their music. Especially during the second half of the seventies, they increasingly returned to acoustic music in studio work or in concerts. ("Acoustic music" is the name for all nonelectronic sounds of conventional instruments—not a particularly fitting term, since of course all music is "acoustic.") When two of the most successful jazz-rock artists, Herbie Hancock and Chick Corea, went on their great duo tours, they dispensed with all the electronics they normally used and played only on the good old concert grand piano. And the group V.S.O.P. brought musicians together on acoustic instruments who had been particularly successful in electronic jazz-rock, among them Herbie Hancock, Tony Williams, Freddie Hubbard, and Wayne Shorter. It is striking how all these musicians really blossom out when they finally can play "just music" again on "normal" instruments without all the complicated electronics.

One of the main reasons why rock elements could be integrated so smoothly into jazz is that, conversely, rock has drawn nearly all its elements from jazz—especially from blues, spirituals, gospel songs and the popular music of the black ghetto, rhythm and blues. Here the regular, steady rock beat, the gospel and soul phrases, the blues form and sound, the dominating sound of the electric guitar, etc., had all been in existence long before the appearance of rock. Drummer Shelly Manne once said, "If jazz borrows from rock, it only borrows from itself." A key figure in this development is blues guitarist B. B. King, who originated almost every element in the music of today's young rock and Top 40 guitarists. Among these, one of the most successful is Eric Clapton, who was honest enough to admit: "Some people talk about me like a revolutionary. That's nonsense—all I did was copy B. B. King." This is what vibraharpist Gary Burton meant when he said, "There is no rock influence on us. We only have the same roots."

We have talked about the way in which improvisation has become increasingly collective. You can hear this trend in the most diverse modern jazz styles, from free jazz to contemporary mainstream and on to fusion jazz. But as is almost always the case in jazz, it also has its countertrend, toward the solo unaccompanied by a conventional rhythm section, a trend initiated by vibraharpist Gary Burton. There have been many such unaccompanied solo or duo performances since the late sixties, from pianists McCoy Tyner, Chick Corea, Keith Jarrett, Cecil Taylor, Oscar Peterson; saxophonists Archie Shepp, Anthony Braxton, Steve Lacy, and Roland Kirk; vibraharpist Karl Berger; trumpeter Leo Smith; trombonist George Lewis; guitarists John McLaughlin, Larry Coryell, Attila Zoller, John Abercrombie, Ralph Towner, and many others; and in Europe by Gunter Hampel, Martial Solal, Derek Bailey, Terje Rypdal, Albert Mangelsdorff, Alexander von Schlippenbach, and John Surman; and in Japan by Masahiko Satoh and others.

Certainly, there had been earlier unaccompanied jazz solos. Coleman Hawkins recorded the first *a cappella* horn solo in 1947, "Picasso." Above all, unaccompanied playing was favored by the great pianists, from the ragtime masters around the turn of the century to James P. Johnson and Fats Waller and on to Art Tatum and beyond. As in almost all areas of jazz, Louis Armstrong was a forerunner in the field of the unaccompanied solo, too: in his duet with Earl Hinnes in 1928, "Weather Bird," and in dozens of solo cadenzas and solo breaks.

However, these musicians merely paved the way for what has been, since the first half of the seventies, a clear tendency reflecting the social alienation and the isolation of the jazz musician—and, in general, of modern man—the opposite of the collective spirit described earlier.

The trend toward the unaccompanied solo performance in the seventies

was a romantic tendency—away from the loudness of electronic amplification and toward an intimate, extremely personalized, and sensitized form of
expression, a symptom of a growing trend toward a new, objective, clear
romanticism. It is only fitting that in the history of this solo and duo
movement (and also in the parallel movement toward an "aestheticization"
of jazz) Europe has played a special role. The first concerts in jazz history in
which all the artists played without accompaniment took place at the jazz
festival on the occasion of the Munich Olympic Games and at the Berlin Jazz
Days in 1972 (both produced by Joachim-Ernest Berendt). Among the
artists appearing were Gary Burton, Chick Corea, Albert Mangelsdorff,
Jean-Luc Ponty, John McLaughlin, Pierre Favre, Gunter Hampel, and ragtime
pianist Eubie Blake. The Munich record company ECM has developed a
concept and sound that have become exemplary for this tendency toward
the accent on aesthetics.

The gradual emergence of a new type of musician (which had already
begun in free jazz, but is now becoming more of a worldwide tendency) was
of greater importance in the seventies than most of the trends already
described. On the one hand, this new type of musician remains in touch with
the jazz scene; on the other hand, he or she uses jazz only as a starting point,
or even as merely one component among many others. These artists have
integrated elements from a large number of musical cultures into their
music—above all from India and Brazil, but also from Arabia, Bali, Japan,
China, the various African cultures, and many others, and occasionally also
from European concert music. They feel what McCoy Tyner put into these
words: "I see connections between all these different kinds of music. The
music of the whole world is interrelated. . . . What I see in music is
something total." And free-jazz trombonist Roswell Rudd, who was professor
of music ethnology at the University of Maine, said, "We're slowly starting to
understand that there really is such a thing and that you can play it: world
music. . . . Today, we can listen to the musics of the whole world, from the
Amazon jungles to the Malaysian highlands and to the recently discovered
native people of the Philippines. All that music is now at our disposal. . . .
What's really important now is a new kind of hearing and seeing, right
through these cultures."

The prototype of this new breed of musician is Don Cherry, the former
partner of Ornette Coleman. In the early sixties, we could still call him a
free-jazz trumpeter. But what do we call him today? Cherry has become
more deeply involved in the musics of the world than just about any other
musician. And he has also learned to play instruments from different
cultures, from Tibet, China, India, or Bali. His own answer to the question is,
"I'm a world musician." And he calls his music "primal music."

The development toward this new type of musician was initiated by John Coltrane, even though he himself was not yet of that type. Clarinetist Tony Scott, who spent years in Asia and was one of the first to incorporate elements of many Asian music cultures, and flutist Paul Horn, who recorded a number of moving solos at the Taj Mahal in India, fit this description as early as the sixties. During the seventies, more and more of these "world musicians" emerged, and this trend continues (see the section From the Eighties to the Nineties). Among the second generation of world musicians are such artists as American sitar and tabla player Collin Walcott, Brazilian guitarist and composer Egberto Gismonti, the members of guitarist Ralph Towner's group Oregon, and Stephan Micus. In the seventies, there in fact existed a music center whose program included world music: the Creative Music Studio of German vibraharpist Karl Berger in Woodstock, New York. Said Berger, "When we started here in the early seventies, we may have called ourselves a 'jazz school.' But what actually interests us today, what we do and play and teach here, that's world music."

From the Eighties to the Nineties

No single style can illustrate eighties jazz. On the one hand, the jazz of the eighties unceasingly fragmented and transcended stylistic limits. Just because it did that, and because it exploded categories and ignored delimitations in an incessant process of blending and intermingling, eighties jazz was syncretistic and eclectic. Never before—not even in the seventies when this development was already emerging—had there been such an astonishingly colorful juxtaposition, so joyously undertaken, of so many different trends and styles. The exciting and fascinating thing about eighties jazz was its enormous diversity.

On the other hand, transcending stylistic boundaries became such a formative component in the jazz of the eighties that this freedom from any circumscribed style became the decade's "style." Aware of its abundance and diversity, and conscious that this *style* entails an open-minded attitude toward playing rather than an actual style, jazz became postmodern. It's a trend that continues in jazz today.

Up until the sixties the development of jazz followed a clear-cut, binding line of progress. The currently topical and most recently developed style was viewed as being not only the most up-to-date but also the most musically apposite compared to what preceded it. The jazz world of the eighties abandoned this perspective. Postmodern jazz says that no style explains the world on its own, that every style is musically acceptable—not only contemporary and modern jazz, but also traditional forms of playing, from hard bop back to bebop, swing, New Orleans jazz, and even earlier elements. And the musicians quickly applied what we have said about style in general to all forms of music. All musical means, not just those belonging to jazz, are usable and may be mixed and amalgamated with one another.

Belief in the equal value of all musical genres and styles is thus the foundation of postmodern jazz. Three aspects have therefore determined jazz since 1980:

1. All of a sudden, everything dating back to before the onset of the New Jazz—all the riches of jazz—became available to the contemporary jazz musician. The eighties' improvised music involved an intensive dialogue with jazz tradition.
2. Postmodern jazz creates unity amid the multiplicity of differing and disparate stylistic elements. It plays with contradictions and rapid paradoxes by integrating contrasting elements into a whole. "The harmony of the disharmonious" is a principle often found in postmodern jazz.
3. The art of quotation became a decisive force in the jazz of the eighties. Postmodern jazz is, as drummer David Moss has shown, a "music of hyphens" where musical fragments are quoted, paraphrased, compared, and combined.

In the early forms of jazz, a musician spent a lifetime mastering a single style. Today's young musicians master several styles and ways of playing simultaneously, often with such sovereign virtuosity that it's scarcely possible to assign them to a single category. Collin Walcott, the tabla virtuoso and sitar player who died in 1984, time and again said that he felt like a wandering eccentric—neither an Indian musician, jazz stylist, salsa player, nor African percussionist, but rather someone who roams around in the no-man's-land between these spheres. "More and more musicians have this background, knowing a little bit about many things and usually not the least about something specific," he said. "It's like walking a tightrope. When I feel bad, I think I'm a dilettante, but when things are going well I feel I know a lot." Alto saxophonist and composer John Zorn said, "Musicians of my generation reject the idea that music is a hierarchy: the so-called more complex forms (the classics) above jazz, which is in turn more complex and thus more elevated than the blues, which is itself put above pop music. . . . Everything is on the same level! And everything should be respected in the same way!" Postmodern jazz musicians are primarily multistylists because they believe that stylistic purism is a fraud.

Postmodern jazz doesn't say either-or. It advocates both-and. The freedom of eighties jazz was freedom of choice—the possibility, as pianist Anthony Davis put it, "of feeling no restraints in taking something over from any conceivable source of influence." Real freedom, felt by an increasing number of musicians at the start of the eighties, is only possible for someone who can both apply over and decide between everything offered: between free meter and playing with beat, open form and the thirty-two-bar standard form, free tonality and major-minor triads, free jazz and world music, bebop, minimal music, rock, New Orleans jazz, trash rock, tango, hip-hop. . . . The message of eighties jazz was, Anything goes.

People have attacked postmodern jazz and its colorful amalgams for being flashy and arbitrary products of fashion. But in an age when modern communications produce a deluge of information and reduce the distance between countries and cultures, musicians are constantly exposed to the greatest possible diversity of sounds, melodies, and stimuli. They're absolutely bombarded with musical information. "The influences are inescapable," said drummer David Moss. "They are just there. We can't get away from them. We hear them all the time."

The development of postmodern jazz thus also has its cultural, social, and political catalysts. The exuberant eclecticism and colorful games played with disparate stylistic elements, wittily penetrating and recombining them, constitute a simultaneously despairing and joyous attempt at establishing meaning and relationship in a world of fragmentation and dissolution. At a time when digital and computerized communication technologies have brought us a gigantic overabundance of news, a musician's world appears as a huge heap of resounding shards out of which he or she has to construct a personal, individual view of reality. Truth is no longer achievable as a whole in postmodern jazz, or in the other arts. Only fragments, partial truths exist.

It goes without saying that yearning for the whole is particularly (and ironically) present in this process of assembling stylistic fragments—a yearning for security, which the invocation of jazz tradition has time and again rekindled. The jazz of the eighties was predominantly conservative. It isn't just a coincidence that this traditionalist, historicist phase of development was paralleled by a resurgence of political conservatism in the Western world.

"There are hundreds of styles today," according to electricbassist and producer Bill Laswell. Nevertheless, a number of eighties ways of playing jazz were more dominant and important than other equally interesting developments. They're listed sequentially here for clarity's sake, but it's important to see that they didn't exist in isolation. Delimitations are fluid and all conceivable permutations exist. The important eighties jazz styles are the following:

• *Neoclassicism* translates jazz's great traditional legacy into contemporary consciousness, using the means of free jazz. Elements of free jazz are mixed and combined with traditional forms of playing. American jazz critic Gary Giddins was the first person to apply the term *neoclassicism* to jazz.

* *Classicism* developed as a countermovement to neoclassicism. Excluding free jazz, it carries on from where the seventies bebop revival left off, further developing the achievements of classical modern jazz in conservative form. Classicism brings a reevaluation of craftsmanship in jazz.
* With jazz-rock as a model, *free funk* has come into being—a combination of free horn improvisations with the rhythms and sounds of funk, new wave, and even punk.
* The development of *world music* continues. More and more musicians integrate elements of Asian, African, Indian, Middle Eastern, and many other musical cultures into their playing.
* The friction between free jazz on the one hand and rock and punk on the other gives rise to *no wave* (also known as noise music or art rock)—a lurid mixture of free jazz improvisation and the wild, unruly sounds and rhythms of punk, heavy metal, trash rock, minimal music, ethnic music, and numerous other influences.

By the start of the eighties the achievements of free jazz, principally through the AACM from Chicago and the Black Artists Group from St. Louis, had become so defined in terms of melody and structure that one could no longer speak of free jazz as strictly defined. The current of the former avant-garde flowed into the mainstream of eighties jazz. Looking backward toward jazz history it became neoclassicism. When the avant-garde trio Air released its *Air Lore* album in 1979, which links free jazz with Scott Joplin's ragtime melodies and Jelly Roll Morton's New Orleans sounds, that was a sensation. At that time, when the avant-garde world was preoccupied with innovation, it still took courage to turn again to the old masters of jazz. But it wasn't long before free-jazz players' return to the imposing achievements of jazz heritage became something that was taken for granted.

It was alto saxophonist Arthur Blythe whose 1980 album *In the Tradition* provided neoclassicism with a slogan. All the important musicians within neoclassicism, coming from free jazz and entering into a dialogue with jazz's legacy, really do play in the tradition: pianist and composer Muhal Richard Abrams; saxophonist, flutist, and composer Henry Threadgill and his sextet; tenor saxophonist David Murray and his octet and big band; trumpeters Lester Bowie and Olu Dara; bassist Dave Holland; flutist James Newton; and many others.

The style a seventies neobop musician reconstructed could still be defined with a degree of precision: updated bebop adapted to contemporary tastes. But what style does a neoclassicist, say, David Murray, reconstruct today? You hear everything in his music: from the collective improvisations of New Orleans jazz to the Duke Ellington Orchestra's jungle sounds, from the agitated motivic vortex of bebop by way of the tempo displacements of a Charles Mingus to the emphatically overblown sounds of free jazz and the shuffle meters of rhythm and blues. That is astonishingly different from earlier retrospective currents in jazz—the New Orleans revival or neobop. The neoclassicist doesn't reconstruct a single style but rather views jazz tradition as a whole.

To be sure, neoclassicism is conservative and nostalgic, but some critics failed to see it isn't only that. Its adherents modernize and update jazz tradition, making it of contemporary interest. They have served to integrate (in the best sense of the word) the music—not just returning contemporary jazz to its roots but also moving in the other direction, filling traditional forms with present-day awareness—and highly infectiously and vitally, too. That's what was involved when trumpeter Lester Bowie said, "We are trying to take what has gone before, mill it around in our minds, add some of *us* to it and then: This is *our* vision of what has happened."

As so often in jazz, the new relationship to what went before became most apparent in rhythm. More and more neoclassicist musicians, formerly associated with the pulse structures of free jazz, found their way back in the course of the eighties to playing with a regular beat. What was frowned upon by many representatives of free jazz and thought a cliché even in melodized seventies free jazz—the time-playing, the playing with an ongoing fundamental rhythm—was rehabilitated within neoclassicism. Its musicians discovered, going beyond the self-restrictions of free jazz, that playing with a specific meter involves certain irreplaceable qualities. Interestingly, they didn't simply take over the classic time-playing but rather permeated that with the unconfined, flowing rhythms of free jazz, refracting the conventional rhythms of bebop, swing, New Orleans jazz, etc., and enriching them with contemporary awareness. What such free jazz musicians as Albert Ayler, Archie Shepp, or Pharoah Sanders cautiously felt is celebrated and lived by neoclassicists with enormous vitality and openness. They affirm that free tonality begins not with free jazz but with country blues and archaic New Orleans jazz; and that the liberation of meter wasn't an invention of sixties jazz but is basically present in everything that goes back (by way of bebop, swing, and the march rhythms of New Orleans parades) to African music's enormously flexible way of treating meters.

Free jazz developed new clichés even though it deliberately broke with old ones. Neoclassicism—this is the difference—breaks with clichés by consciously retaining and playing with them while maintaining (alongside all the quotation, humor, and parody) a profound respect for the great legacy of jazz tradition. "Nothing is contemporary" said guitarist John McLaughlin, "unless you feel the tradition behind it."

The first neoclassicist (although unknowingly) was Duke Ellington. More than anyone else in the abundantly rich history of jazz, Ellington linked innovation with tradition, creating something modern by referring back to the great old forms of African-American music. It's not just accidental that eighties jazz was so shaped by numerous tributes to Ellington. James Newton, the World Saxophone Quartet, Chico Freeman, and many others dedicated entire albums to Duke. Many musicians intuitively sensed the parallels linking Duke Ellington and the jazz of the eighties. Both move in realms beyond categories, dissolving such restrictions in their playing.

Classicism developed as a countermovement to neoclassicism. To be sure, it too updated jazz tradition, but, distancing itself from free jazz, it pursued the course prepared by seventies neobop, further developing and disseminating the legacy of bebop. At the start of the eighties more and more young musicians built on the great tradition of Charlie Parker, Dizzy Gillespie, Fats Navarro, Clifford Brown, Bud Powell, and others, but since then so many nonbop elements—modality (see the section on harmony), tempo displacements, formal freedoms—have been flowing into this revival that neobop can no longer be narrowly defined. The stream of neobop thus enters into classicism.

All the important classicist musicians (including trumpeter Wynton Marsalis, saxophonists Donald Harrison and Bobby Watson, trumpeter Terence Blanchard, pianist Mulgrew Miller, drummer Jeff "Tain" Watts, and bassist Charnett Moffett) are united by the certainty that bebop is *the* foundation of modern jazz. Nevertheless, classicism doesn't update and modernize only bebop but also everything that led up to the beginnings of free jazz: John Coltrane's modality, Wayne Shorter's abstract hard bop, the harmonic and rhythmic daredevilry of the legendary second Miles Davis Quintet, the melodic complexity of the early Eric Dolphy, etc. All that is no longer merely a refreshing contribution to the bebop style, as in neobop, but stands alongside it as something of equal value.

It is strikingly apparent that classicism developed alongside a boom in jazz pedagogy. Since the seventies, influenced by the great model provided by Boston's Berklee College of Music, thousands of clinics, master classes, courses, workshops, and conservatories have come into being. Today's young musician is besieged by hundreds of books containing transcriptions, exercises in improvisation, studies in scales, theories of harmony, analyses of chords, examples of patterns, etc.

The situation was strikingly different in earlier decades. What bebop innovators used to learn largely orally and intuitively, spending night after night at clubs and listening to records over and over, many of today's young musicians acquire rationally—and that's how it sounds: docile and diligent, very accurate and technically brilliant, but with little feeling and expression. Nowhere in eighties jazz have critics so frequently complained of a lack of individual creativity as in the realm of classicism. Making jazz an academic pursuit seems to promote the very thing people originally wanted to avoid: an institutionalization of facelessness. Drummer Marvin "Smitty" Smith said, "They formulate everything. Like, you play lick number 37 combined with licks number 152, 338, and 1,012, and you have a perfect phrase for the first four bars of 'All the Things You Are.' . . . Unfortunately, that's not how the music evolves . . . Discovering myself—that's something nobody can share. It's a big revelation, and it's exciting because it's you *alone* that did all the research."

Jazz schools, conservatories, and courses are important. They further knowledge of jazz and help young musicians build up a vocabulary. But up to now there has never existed any school, any book, or any introduction to improvisation providing a satisfactory explanation of how musical individuality comes into being and how it can be achieved. "Jazz," said trumpeter Woody Shaw, "is a lifestyle. You must live jazz."

Some critics have charged classicist musicians with copying the masters of bebop—and very badly at that, "with mistakes in syntax and grammar." But there's no doubt that it is just these supposed mistakes—errors of harmonic, melodic, and rhythmic character—that constitute the charm of classicism. Classicism's splendid young drummers—Jeff "Tain" Watts, Marvin "Smitty" Smith, Carl Allen, and others—build on the rich bebop tradition: from Max Roach and Art Blakey by way of Roy Haynes to rhythmic advances through Tony Williams and Elvin Jones. Nevertheless, their playing sounds contemporary and different; it's more powerful, aggressive, and hard. They play the rhythms of modern jazz aware of fusion and jazz-rock having existed. They carry something of the energy and weight of rock-oriented styles into the new bebop. Of course, that does involve "mistakes in syntax and grammar," but obviously every innovation in jazz, every attempt at autonomy and individuality—whether of a stylistic or a personal nature—begins with such deviations from existing rules and structures, with "mistakes."

Also astonishing about jazz classicism is that it shows what great possibilities of differentiation can exist within similarity; "sounding like" and "reminiscent of" still contain niches for "sounding like myself." Both in the course of a concert and often within a piece or even a phrase, tenor saxophonist Ricky Ford is reminiscent of Dexter Gordon, and then again of Ben Webster and Don Byas, of John Coltrane and Sonny Rollins. Yet no one would charge Ford with imitation. He always sounds like himself. It may seem paradoxical, but the more he quotes, the more individual he becomes.

Some eighties jazz (not just classicism) succumbed to the danger entailed in such a process. The quotation used as a cue remains a fragment and an empty phrase. Musicians have time and again pointed out that any quotation must really be felt and lived if it is to be more than a background effect. That's why the neotraditionalist plays with and on the legacy of jazz tradition as if on an instrument. He knows he must become one with this instrument if he wants to shape everything he quotes and paraphrases with his own musical signature and personality.

Tensions between neoclassicism and classicism were fundamental within eighties jazz. The following overview sums up what has been said about these two ways of playing, but it goes without saying that transitions between the two realms are possible.

Neoclassicism	*Classicism*
A view of tradition on this side of free jazz. Evaluates jazz history in the spirit of the former avant-garde. Neoclassicism underlines the totality of jazz history, extending, as drummer Beaver Harris said, "from ragtime to no time."	A view of tradition on that side of free jazz. Classicism stresses the legacy of classic modern jazz from bebop to the beginnings of free jazz.
Combination of elements from free jazz with traditional ways of playing. Shows that jazz possesses a tradition of renewal.	Extensive adherence to tonality and beat. Emphasizes that jazz has a tradition of conservation.
Individuality as a medium for tradition.	Tradition as a medium for individuality.
Duke Ellington as inspiration.	Miles Davis as main point of reference (especially the second Miles Davis Quintet from 1964–1968).
Rediscovery of sound as an expressive element: growl and "dirty timbre."	Stress on clarity of line. Phrasing more important than sound.
Quoting through combination of jazz styles.	Quoting through combination of personal styles.
David Murray as spokesperson.	Wynton Marsalis as leading figure.

Development of free funk in the eighties was largely unaffected by classicism and neoclassicism. Free funk catches up with what seventies jazz-rock either neglected or simply forgot. It utilizes the means accessible to free jazz for liberating and opening up the rhythms and melodies of jazz-rock. And, conversely, free funk with its danceable funk and rock rhythms transmits symmetry, motor energy, and tangible physicality to free jazz. At the start of the eighties the interpenetration of jazz and rock at long last again became an exceptionally exciting, infectious adventure.

It is striking that this process of liberation began at a time when signs of stagnation were unmistakable in fusion and jazz-rock, in 1977 with Ornette Coleman's *Dancing in Your Head* album. Ornette's Prime Time band's seething "free" funk rhythms and electrifying untempered collective improvisation didn't only indicate a way out of the dead-end reached by a jazz-rock that had run out of ideas. *Dancing in Your Head,* and later *Body Meta,* were also years ahead of the whole of free funk.

To be sure, there had been previous experiments aimed at melding free jazz and funk. In his 1968 album *New Grass,* Albert Ayler mixed elements of rhythm and blues and soul with free jazz. At the beginning of the seventies Rashid Ali, once the drummer in John Coltrane's last band, headed a group that played free funk. In 1974, the Human Arts Ensemble, grouped around drummer Charles Bobo Shaw in St. Louis, recorded free-jazz improvisation linking rock, rhythm and blues, and funk. Yet there is no doubt that Ornette Coleman achieved the first artistically satisfying integration of free-jazz and funk rhythms on *Dancing in Your Head.*

Ornette Coleman guided and influenced free funk in the same sovereign fashion as Miles Davis shaped and advanced jazz-rock in the seventies. From Coleman comes everyone of significance in the eighties border area between free jazz on the one side and the rhythms of funk, rock, and pop on the other: drummer Ronald Shannon Jackson and his various Decoding Societies, guitarist James "Blood" Ulmer, and electric bassist Jamaaladeen Tacuma (who all played in Ornette's Prime Time band). But also musicians and groups without any close personal contact with Coleman have been lastingly influenced by his music: the Slickaphonics around trombonist Ray Anderson, the Five Elements with alto saxophonist Steve Coleman, Greg Osby, the Noodband in Europe, saxophonist Kazutoki Umezu in Japan, and others.

Even though the rhythmic patterns produced by seventies jazz-rock drummers went considerably beyond rock rhythms, they were a step backward compared with the complex and multilayered rhythms of modern jazz. Their symmetry and two-beat regularity seemed rigid and schematic. Free funk at long last opened up jazz-rock rhythms. All of a sudden funk rhythms *breathe.* They are extended and compressed. The meter is suddenly reinterpreted and played with in a multitude of ways.

All the same, it gradually became apparent during the eighties that the rhythmic patterns in funk could only be liberated to a certain extent, or else they lost the very feature that characterized this music: its motorpower and dance-oriented rhythmic impetus. Funk's riff techniques and its ostinato interlocking figures are diametrically opposed to the open form and liberated conception of free jazz.

Free and funk thus clash. Since that is the case, free funk always fluctuates between two tendencies: either transposing the pulsating funk rhythms into metrically free playing, thereby losing funk qualities, or stressing funk's rigid beat, thereby restricting free jazz's melodic and harmonic independence.

It is part of the diversity and complexity of postmodern jazz that many musicians don't regard this inner contradiction within free funk as something disturbing. On the contrary, it inspires them to creativity. Drummer Shannon Jackson masterfully incorporated this conflict within the rhythmic concept underlying his group Decoding Society. There the freely flowing slow rubato horn themes constitute an intensively provocative contrast to Jackson's strongly pulsating, funk-inspired rhythmic figures.

On the other hand, it is clear that conflicts of such intensity cannot be maintained over the long term, so it wasn't surprising that free funk—in amazingly similar fashion to jazz-rock—began to show clear-cut signs of fatigue after a brief and vehement flourishing at the start of the eighties.

Free funk's dilemma very much involves the fact that its rhythms rarely contain the interactive, group-forming qualities present in all great jazz rhythms. The relative compactness of such ostinato patterns creates problems for what is indispensable in living, vital jazz as created by all the great drummers from New Orleans to free jazz: musical conversation and open dialogue.

That's why free funk—again astonishingly like jazz-rock—has only given rise to a few records satisfying the highest artistic demands: above all Ornette Coleman's *Dancing in Your Head,* some early recordings by Ronald Shannon Jackson's Decoding Society (*Street Priest* and *Nasty*), and some work by James "Blood" Ulmer (*Odyssey*). Ornette Coleman with his Prime Time band is still the leading figure in free funk, even more than ten years after *Dancing in Your Head,* because he mediates, unifies, and integrates in an environment that obstructs mediation, unification, and integration.

Parallel to free funk flows a stream (with many branches leading in other stylistic directions) that first bore fruit in the seventies: the further development of world music.

World music got under way in the sixties as an additive process. Jazz musicians added what interested them—Indian, Balinese, Japanese, African, and Brazilian elements—to what they already played. Only in the seventies did this world music achieve initial high-quality artistic results, blending and integrating the various influences.

Since 1980 this process of amalgamation has proceeded further, even more intensively, within groups such as Codona and Oregon and with musicians like drummer Mark Nauseef, bassist David Friesen, the Europe-based oud player Rabih Abou-Khalil, saxophonist Charlie Mariano, Swedish percussionist Bengt Berger, trumpeter Jon Hassell, percussionist Nana Vasconcelos, and many others. World music goes beyond categories as it already had in the seventies, so it is *the* catalyst for syncretic, eclectic, and style-dissolving forms. More than any other stream in jazz, even free jazz, world music has called into question distinctions between styles, forms, and categories taken to be binding. The world musician is the prototype of the postmodern musician because he or she seeks unity in diversity. Trombonist Roswell Rudd said, "We discovered Pygmy music and realized that it's our own music." And Karl Berger, for years director of the Creative Music Studio in Woodstock, New York, concurred: "When you listen to all the different musics, you suddenly become aware that they all have something in common. They all share the same roots."

Many musicians believe that their musical travels to other cultures are in reality trips within themselves. During his world music courses at Woodstock, Berger time and again stressed, "Listen into yourself. Find everything in yourself."

Consider drummer Ed Thigpen, a man of the older conservative jazz generation, completely different from youthful world musicians. When T. A. S. Mani, the South Indian percussionist, explained in 1984 a difficult 11/8 rhythm frequently found in Indian music but nowhere in jazz, Ed responded (once he'd "understood" the rhythm and played with a group of Indian musicians for a couple of minutes), "It's funny but somehow I knew all that. As if it had always been in me. Who knows?"

That sense of recognition was already felt by the man who sparked off today's world music: John Coltrane, who died in 1967. When he first became acquainted with Indian and Arabic music, he thought he was really hearing a music hidden within himself—"a trip into your inner self." So there also exists psychological motivation for the world music movement—the discovery of musical archetypes.

After the failed utopias of free jazz, world music is the last (to date) and only utopia that has remained to jazz in these sobered and skeptical times. Belief in common roots for all music and the universal energy of music are the motor for world music. Such a belief has time and again inspired jazz musicians to seek musical archetypes, to ignore barriers and divisions between musical cultures, and to set about creative bridge building. Percussionist and sitar player Collin Walcott loved saying that world music is a model of how people on our overpopulated planet can live together more humanely and thoughtfully.

On the other hand, the eighties showed clearly that someone who views African, Tibetan, Balinese, Brazilian, etc., material as something interchangeable doesn't achieve any geniune integration. Some elements of world music have produced terribly superficial results. Many musicians have constantly stressed that you must be aware of the significance and meaning of what you want to amalgamate if the individual elements are to be melded into a whole.

The music of other cultures can't be learned in crash courses. If musicians in a non-Western culture require half a lifetime (wiser musicians would say an entire lifetime) to penetrate and incorporate the symbolical, mythical, religious, and functional aspects of their music, then it would be presumptuous to assume that a jazz musician could internalize the riches of such music within a short period or even after years of hard study. The problem is even more acute because the world musician is usually involved in several different musical cultures rather than a single one.

World music thus tends toward superficiality—inherently rather than because of lack of interest. Stature and musical quality are required if that danger is to be avoided. Astonishingly, many musicians have been successful there. The "colonialist plundering of the self-service shops of global musical cultures," which has also been a part of this movement, pales into insignificance alongside the high artistic achievements of world music.

To be sure, the jazz musician encounters the great non-Western musical cultures as a dilettante. Collin Walcott, together with Don Cherry (*the* world musician in terms of the universal awareness present in his music), repeatedly said that he felt himself to be a self-taught layman during his trips into the music of other cultures. But jazz has always shown—and Collin Walcott's excellent music making confirms this—that dilettantism doesn't inevitably have to be negative. Dilettantes are after all children, at least where love, empathy, and sympathy are concerned. Well-performed world music is open, childlike, and playful. And it is that very intuitive and light-hearted way of encountering the unfamiliar that has enabled the world musicians of jazz to discover and make accessible more of what musical cultures have in common, outstripping modern European concert music's intellectually and theoretically overloaded attempts in that direction.

Toward the end of the eighties it became increasingly apparent that fewer and fewer musicians are playing the kind of world music involving nothing but a conscious encounter between improvised music and the great non-Western musical cultures. Instead, world music, transcending itself, is increasingly flowing into other styles, fertilizing and enlivening all of the eighties eclecticism from free funk by way of neoclassicism to noise music, no wave, etc. So toward the end of the eighties we already had a third phase of world music. After the additive beginnings in the sixties and the initial integrative achievements in the seventies, world music extended beyond itself, influencing other musical styles since 1980. Hardly a single eighties musician was not influenced by the idea of world music, incorporating elements of ethnic music into his or her performances.

No Wave or noise music developed alongside world music, much influenced by it. People have gotten used to viewing no wave as incorporating all the multitudinous tendencies, ways of playing, and fashions resulting from the friction between free jazz on the one hand and, on the other, punk, experimental rock, minimal music, ethnic elements, and various other influences. The proliferation of labels is as rampant as the musical outcome is diverse: art rock, punk jazz, out music, fake jazz, etc. Despite all their differences, these styles are unified by the fact that their bizarre, eccentric playing around with mosaiclike stylistic elements evade any clear-cut categorization—hence no wave, a music directed against all waves and fashions even though some of it shows unmistakable signs of modishness.

Among the outstanding no wave musicians are alto saxophonist and composer John Zorn; guitarists Arto Lindsay, Fred Frith, and Elliott Sharp; drummer David Moss; scratcher Christian Marclay; keyboardist Wayne Horvitz; bassist Bill Laswell; and others.

No Wave or noise music employs the means developed by punk, trash rock, minimal music, and numerous other influences in pursuing what free jazz started—the emancipation of noise. It breaks even more shockingly, aggressively, and wildly with what previously seemed musically valid and binding, transposing all the everyday sounds that surround us into free music.

In the process, no wave musicians went beyond the restrictions free jazz imposed on itself with the same élan and radicality once directed by free jazz against functional harmony, beat, and tonality. Noise music calls into question what is self-evident for free jazz in at least four areas:

1. No Wave separates itself from free jazz's ideas about development. Instead of extended arches of ecstatic tension, often long prepared in collective improvisation, it stresses short, isolated sound events. Noise music and no wave musicians disintegrate and atomize the prolonged formal processes of free jazz, turning them into rapidly changing sound events.

   Free jazz integrates sounds; no wave isolates them. The musical fracture is noise music's most important method, and its favorite medium is the collage—the linking of apparently unrelated musical

processes and sounds. It goes without saying that musical relationships and order develop on a superordinate level but are disrupted and
teased ambivalently.

2. Free jazz's ideas about tempo are intensified and accelerated. No Wave
   concentrates the pulse of free jazz to establish highly charged tempos
   where time is foreshortened. Pieces and forms become ever more
   compressed and shorter at these frantically breakneck speeds. Percussionist and singer David Moss: "If a piece lasts for a minute, that's
   sometimes too long for us."

3. Free jazz rejected much that went before but persisted unwaveringly
   with the idea of craftsmanship and virtuosity. No Wave breaks with
   even that ideal. Out of protest it incorporates the dilettantish, kitschy,
   and banal, all the acoustic junk that surrounds us day in and day out,
   ironically fragmenting, distancing, and parodying.

4. No wave musicians play without free jazz's utopias. The ominous
   fragmented sound of noise music and no wave have completely
   abandoned any belief that music can directly bring abut political and
   social change. The vision of a better, more humane world has been
   replaced by the noise musicians' sober, cynical "that's how it is"
   attitude, criticizing the inhospitability of cities and the madness of an
   ecologically butchered and militarily overarmed world by reflecting
   and dismantling reality in all of its brutality and aggressiveness. In no
   wave you hear the sounds of urban chaos, the roar of exploding nuclear
   power stations, the screechings of totally computerized factory halls
   with their industrial robots, the squeaking and squawking of demented
   video games, the edgy crackling of omnicabled media networks, and
   the like.

Of course, some of those features, attributed here to noise music and no
wave, could also be found in isolated examples of free jazz. The difference
between the two ways of playing consists, however, in the fact that noise
music overstates and exceeds, more cheekily and ambivalently, what was
merely suggested in some aspects of free jazz.

There has been much talk of noise music and no wave being destructive.
But it's not the no wave musicians who are aggressive, brutal, and violent; it
is the conditions of existence influencing their penetration of the acoustic
environment. Ever since art has existed, the charge has always been the
same. Artists are made responsible for something to which they, as sensitive,
alert human beings, are usually the first to draw attention. "Just ride a bike
down Broadway about one in the afternoon, and you'll experience
everything that's in our music," said saxophonist and composer John Zorn.

Noise music has conspicuously remained a style for white musicians. In no other jazz style, except perhaps for the West Coast jazz of the fifties, have white musicians been so isolated. In fact, no wave's noisy, angular rhythms and its somber punk-inspired sounds are particularly remote from the mainstream of jazz and its principal current, the blues. Noise music is "square" in the eyes of African-American musicians because it merely describes what life is like. It doesn't creatively transpose (as a hipster would) everyday circumstances into new reality, thereby mastering those circumstances, which is what matters. In the mid-eighties, many no wave musicians realized that one-sided insistence on sound improvisations had exhausted itself. More and more noise musicians started structuring and melodizing their music. More "ordered" rhythmic patterns, harmonies, and formal categories attracted interest again. This return to structure and form becomes apparent in compositions and "game pieces" by John Zorn, in the music of keyboardist Wayne Horvitz, and in the playing of guitarists Arto Lindsay and Elliott Sharp, drummer David Moss, and many others.

In conclusion, we would like to stress once again that classicism, neoclassicism, free funk, world music, and no wave are not ways of playing isolated from one another. Indeed, they often appear in colorfully confusing admixtures. The situation is complicated even further by the fact that many musicians openly jump around between these ways of playing and trends. It's increasingly impossible to assign a musician's way of playing to a single category. That is astonishingly different from previous decades when a single style usually predominated, with at most two others making themselves felt.

THE MUSICIANS OF JAZZ

The Musicians of Jazz

"I play what I live," said Sidney Bechet, one of the great men of old New Orleans. And Charlie Parker stated, "Music is your own experience, your thoughts, your wisdom. If you don't live it, it won't come out on your horn."

We shall see how the unmistakable sounds of the great jazz soloists, right down to technical elements, depend on their personalities. The jazz musician's life is constantly transformed into music—without regard for "beauty," "form," and the many other concepts that mediate between music and life in the European tradition. That is why it is important to speak of the lives of the jazz musicians and why the jazz enthusiast's desire to know the details of their lives is legitimate. And it is also legitimate that such details make up a great part of the literature of jazz. They help us understand the music itself and thus are quite a different story from the details fan magazines report about the lives of Hollywood stars.

"A person has to have lived to play great jazz, or else he'll be a copy," said Milt Hinton, the bassist. Only a few musicians who exemplify this dictum could be selected for this book. But they are musicians in whom the history of a style is involved, with each one representing a specific period. Louis Armstrong stands for the great New Orleans period; Bessie Smith for the blues and jazz singing; Bix Beiderbecke for Chicago style; Duke Ellington for orchestral Swing; Coleman Hawkins and Lester Young for combo Swing; Charlie Parker and Dizzy Gillespie for bebop and modern jazz itself; Miles Davis for the whole development from cool jazz to the music of the seventies; Ornette Coleman and John Coltrane for the jazz revolution of the sixties; John McLaughlin for the fusion music of the seventies; and David Murray and Wynton Marsalis for the jazz classicism of the eighties.

Louis Armstrong

Until the rise of Dizzy Gillespie in the forties, there was no jazz trumpeter who did not stem from Louis Armstrong—or "Satchmo," as he was called—and even after that, every player has been at least indirectly indebted to him.

The immense size of this debt became clear when impresario George Wein made the 1970 Newport Jazz Festival into one big birthday celebration for seventy-year-old Armstrong. (Satchmo claimed to have been born on July 4, 1900, but Gary Giddins has established that his baptismal certificate states August 4, 1901.) World-famous jazz trumpeters competed for the most appropriate homage to Louis. Bobby Hackett called himself "Louis Armstrong's number one admirer." Joe Newman took exception: he himself should be called Louis's "A-number one fan." Jimmy Owens said that if he could not claim to be Armstrong's number one fan or even A-one fan, he was at least his "youngest fan." Dizzy Gillespie said, "Louis Armstrong's station in the history of jazz . . . all I can say is UNIMPEACHABLE. If it weren't for him, there wouldn't be any of us. So I would like to take this moment to thank Louis Armstrong for my livelihood."

Musicians other than trumpeters have also expressed their great debt to Armstrong. Frank Sinatra has pointed out that Armstrong made an art of singing popular music.

When Louis Armstrong died on July 6, 1971, Duke Ellington said, "If anyone was Mr. Jazz, it was Louis Armstrong. He was the epitome of jazz and always will be. Every trumpet player who decided he wanted to lean towards the American idiom was influenced by him. . . . He is what I call an American standard, an American original. . . . I love him. God bless him."

Louis Armstrong spent his youth in the turmoil of the great port on the Mississippi—in New Orleans' old Creole quarter. His parents—his father was a factory worker, his mother a domestic—were separated when Louis was still an infant. Nobody paid much attention to him. Once or twice the authorities considered putting him in a reformatory, but nothing was done until, one New Year's Eve, Louis fired a pistol loaded with blanks in the streets. Then they put him in the reformatory. He became a member of the school choir that performed at funerals and festivities. Louis received his first musical instruction on a battered old cornet from the leader of the reform school band.

One of the first bands in which Louis played was that of New Orleans' leading trombonist, Kid Ory. Little Louis happened to be passing by with his cornet as Ory's band was playing in the street. Somebody asked for whom he was carrying the instrument. "Nobody. It's mine," said Louis. Nobody would believe him. So Louis started to blow. . . .

When during World War I the red-light district of Storyville was closed down by the secretary of the navy and the great exodus of musicians had long been underway, Louis was among those who remained. He did not go to Chicago until 1922, when King Oliver sent for him to join his band, then playing at the Lincoln Gardens. King Oliver was the second "King of Jazz" following the legendary New Orleans trumpeter Buddy Bolden (who never made any recordings). Louis Armstrong was to become the third king.

Oliver's band—with the King himself and Louis on cornet, Honoré Dutrey on trombone, Johnny Dodds on clarinet, his brother Baby Dodds on drums, Bill Johnson on banjo, and Lil Hardin on piano—was then the most important jazz band. When Armstrong left it in 1924, it began to decline. To be sure, Oliver made several good recordings in later years (such as the 1926–27 series with his Savannah Syncopators), but by then other bands had become more important (Jelly Roll Morton's Red Hot Peppers, Fletcher Henderson, young Duke Ellington). The end of Oliver's career presents the tragic spectacle of an impoverished man, without teeth, unable to play and earn money to live, hiding from his friends because he is ashamed and yet was once king of jazz. Here is an example of the tragedy of artistic existence, and there are many such tragedies in the annals of jazz. Louis Armstrong escaped this fate in an almost supernatural way. The ups and downs that characterize the lives of so many jazz musicians hardly ever affected him. For him there was only one direction: up.

It is a mark of Louis Armstrong's superiority that throughout his long career he had only two ensembles worthy of him—actually only one, because the first of these was a group organized for recording purposes only: Louis Armstrong's Hot Five (and later, Hot Seven) from 1925 to 1928. The other was the Louis Armstrong All Stars of the late forties, with trombonist Jack Teagarden, clarinetist Barney Bigard, and drummer Sid Catlett. With these All Stars—and they really were—Armstrong won tremendous acclaim all over the world. With them he gave one of the most famous concerts of his career in Boston in 1947; it was later released on record.

The musicians who surrounded Satchmo in his Hot Five and Hot Seven are among the great personalities in traditional jazz. Johnny Dodds, the clarinetist, was there, as was trombonist Kid Ory, who many years earlier had given Louis a job in New Orleans. Later, pianist Earl Hines was added. He created a style of piano playing based on Armstrong's trumpet that became (and still is) a model for many pianists throughout the world.

There are few artists whose work and personality are as closely joined as Armstrong's. It is almost as if they had become interchangeable, and thus even the musically flawed Armstrong was made effective through his personality. In the liner notes to a record taken from Edward R. Murrow's film, *Satchmo the Great,* Armstrong said:

When I pick up that horn . . . the world's behind me, and I don't concentrate on nothing but that horn. . . . I mean, I don't feel no different about the horn now than I did when I was playing in New Orleans. No, that's my living and my life. I love them notes. That's why I try to make them right. . . . That's why I married four times. The chicks didn't live with that horn. . . . I mean, if I have an argument with my wife, that couldn't stop me from enjoying the show that I'm playing. I realize I could blow a horn after they pull away. . . . I've expressed myself in the horn. I fell in love with it and it fell in love with me. . . . What we play is life and a natural thing. . . . If it's for laughs, for showmanship; it would be the same as if we were in a backyard practicing or something. Everything that happens there is real. . . . Yeah, I'm happy. Doing the right thing, playing for the highest people to the lowest. . . . They come in Germany with them lorgnettes, and looking at you and everything, and by the time they get on the music, they done dropped the lorgnettes, and they're swinging, man! . . . When we played in Milano, after I finished my concert . . . I had to rush over to the La Scala and stand by those big cats like Verdi and Wagner . . . and take pictures, cause they figure our music's the same. We play them both from the heart.

In such passages more is revealed about Armstrong's nature and music than from all the words a critic can say about them. The musical findings are, anyhow, as simple and immediate as the music itself: Louis Armstrong made jazz "right." He brought together emotional expression and musical technique. After Armstrong, it is no longer possible to make excuses for wrong notes with claims of vitality or authenticity. Since Armstrong, jazz has to be just as right as other music.

A brilliant article written on the occasion of Armstrong's death by critic Ralph Gleason has this to say:

He took the tools of European musical organization—chords, notation, bars and the rest—and added to them the rhythms of the church and of New Orleans and (by definition) Africa, brought into the music the blue notes, the tricks of bending and twisting notes, and played it all with his unexcelled technique. He went as far with it as he could by using the blues and popular songs of the time as skeletons for his structural improvisations.

Many of the young people who love to use the term *revolution* have forgotten that Armstrong was the greatest of all jazz revolutionaries. They may be thinking about Charlie Parker or Cecil Taylor and John Coltrane when they talk of musical revolutions. But the difference between the music before Armstrong and what he made of it is greater than the difference between the music before Parker or Taylor or Coltrane and what they made of it. So, the jazz revolution started by Armstrong is certainly the greater one.

A young fusion drummer, Bob Melton, was right when after Armstrong's death he wrote in a letter to the editor of *Down Beat* magazine:

We've lost some great ones in the last five years. . . . Today we lost the most daring innovator of all. . . . I'm young, a "long-hair," a "jazz-rock" drummer. . . . I've just played over and over about 20 times a 1947 Town Hall concert track of "Ain't Misbehavin" with Pops. . . . I've played it over that many times because in the last three years I've been filling my head with "free" tenor men and rock guitarists, and I've forgotten how audacious . . . is that the word? . . . I've forgotten how *outrageous* it *really was*. . . . I mourn especially that so many of my generation . . . never heard Pops' message, and might not have listened if they had. You know that line of bull about not trusting anybody over thirty? Pops is one of the few people in this century I trusted!

Louis Armstrong made the rhythmic quality of Swing an essential element in jazz. In early New Orleans jazz many musicians still phrased in ways long established in march music and the ragtime tradition: rhythmically angular, stiff, and by today's standards prudish. Of course, musicians were beginning to produce rhythmically rounded, springy, swinging phrasing, but in those days swing was a secondary business, almost as expendable and interchangeable as dynamics and tremolos. It could be used, but it didn't have to be. Since Louis Armstrong, jazz without swing has been unthinkable. With Satchmo flexible triplet jazz phrasing gets under way, and it immediately starts with a high point. Much of what Louis Armstrong sang and played—his nuances of phrasing and his highly exciting rhythmic stretchings and curtailings—was so boldly in advance of its time that it pointed the way toward aspects of modern jazz phrasing. Satchmo made Swing the sine qua non of jazz.

The abandonment of two-beat jazz and transition to playing over four beats began with Louis Armstrong too. He also introduced solo playing into jazz long before it became customary in the Chicago style. His explosive inventiveness literally blew apart the brief and constrained variations of New Orleans jazz, giving rise to expansive and enormously compelling solos.

Between the Armstrong of the Hot Five and Hot Seven and the Armstrong of the All Stars of the forties and fifties stands the Armstrong of the big bands. This period began when Armstrong became a member of Fletcher Henderson's orchestra for a year, starting in 1924 immediately following his departure from King Oliver. Armstrong brought so much stimulation to the rather commercial and mediocre Henderson aggregation of the time that one could say the year 1924 marks the real beginning of big-band jazz. There is a lot of significance and logic in the fact that Armstrong, the most important personality of the New Orleans jazz tradition, was cofounder of the jazz phase that years later replaced the great era of New Orleans: the Swing era of the thirties, with its big bands. Even with the recordings of his Hot Five and Hot Seven, however, Armstrong soon placed himself beyond the New Orleans form, with its three-voiced interweaving of trumpet, trombone, and clarinet. Armstrong is the man who, precisely with the most significant records of the Hot Five and Seven, dissolved this fabric—an achievement characteristic of many stylistic developments in jazz. Again and again, the important personalities within a style have paved the way for the next style when at the zenith of their own. Only the fans demanded a standstill in one particular style. The musicians have always wanted to go on.

Armstrong's playing in Fletcher Henderson's band at the Roseland Ballroom in New York was a sensation among musicians. Armstrong himself found much inspiration in the (for that time) compact section sounds of the big band. Later he became convinced that his trumpet could unfold better against the backdrop of a big band than with a small ensemble—a feeling not shared by many jazz fans.

This feeling may be related to the fact that from the start Armstrong wanted to reach a larger audience—a wish that perhaps was the prime mover of his musical career. It might also account for the records through which the Armstrong of later years so often entered the realm of popular music. In fact, what is lost in simply saying that essentially all of Armstrong's music was meant to be "popular" music, no matter how this might clash with the more or less naive ideas of many a jazz fan?

"There is a definite implication that Louis had a primary interest in pleasing his audiences," George Avakian stated. Many jazz fans ignored Armstrong's success in the hit charts with "Hello Dolly" with a determination that could imply that they were somewhat discomforted by this success. For Armstrong, however—and maybe even more so for his wife, Lucille—the real climax of his career came in 1964, when he took the top spot on the record charts away from the reigning Beatles and held it for weeks with "Hello Dolly."

Louis Armstrong transposed more pop music into jazz than any other musician. Conversely, he translated jazz so convincingly and artistically into pop music that even when he sang the schmaltzy hits of the day, something of jazz's power, warmth, and vitality still shone through. If twentieth-century popular music viewed as a whole constitutes a single, unceasingly flowing river, which arises in the blues and jazz and then branches into an ever-broader delta of rock and pop, funk and disco, rap and hip-hop, then Louis Armstrong symbolizes the oneness holding this river together. No one else made more vividly apparent all the streaming currents linking jazz and popular music.

To Armstrong, singing was at least as important as trumpet playing—not just during his final years when, sometimes hardly able to blow his horn because of failing health, he remained a brilliant singer. During all phases of his career, he knew he could reach a larger audience as a singer than as an instrumentalist. His singing—husky, hoarse, squeezed, rough—shocked listeners in the twenties. Here was someone who dared, in a world still shaped by Victorianism and bourgeois hypocrisy, to transform what he felt into music, directly and honestly. The carefree naturalness and sincerity with which Louis Armstrong made music was an important sign of the times for the contemporary public. His voice, his trumpet, said, Show your feelings. That became a message for the century. The entire world understood it. By now there are hundreds of singers who express their own feelings, not just jazz singers. Any rock singer does so, and almost every pop singer. The fact that no one today is shocked any longer about a singer expressing what he or she feels indicates, more than anything else, Louis Armstrong's status. Armstrong was once alone there; now there are thousands.

Rex Stewart, himself a trumpeter (in fact, one of the best) had to admit:

Louis has bestowed so many gifts upon the world that it is almost impossible to assess in which area his definitive impact has been most felt. My vote would be for his tremendous talent of communication. As profoundly creative as his trumpet ability is, I would place this in a secondary position. He was revered mostly by other professionals, whereas his gravel-voiced singing has carried his message far and wide, to regions and places where not only was the music little known, the language foreign, but where there also was the further barrier of a political system having labeled jazz as decadent. But when Satchmo sang, the entire picture changed. People saw the truth.

In a television program produced on the occasion of the 1970 Newport Jazz Festival, Louis said:

Well, people love me and my music and, you know, I love them and I have no problems at all with people. The minute I walk on the bandstand they know they're going to get something good and no jive and they know what they're there for and that's why they come . . . . I'm the audience myself. I'm my own audience and I don't like to hear myself play bad or something, so I know it ain't no good for you . . . . Some of the critics say I'm a clown, but a clown, that's something great. It's happiness to make people happy. Most of those critics don't know one note from the other . . . . When I play, I just think of all my happy days . . . and the notes come by themselves. You've got to love to be able to play.

During all of Armstrong's life, again and again, there was talk of the impending "end of jazz music" or "death of jazz" in papers and magazines, from the twenties right on up to the seventies. The communicative genius in Armstrong never believed such talk: "I'd get me a record company and record nothing but what people said was finished—and we'd make a million dollars. You get those boys blowing out there—waitin' for that one gig, that one recording session, and we'd get together and set up, you know—we wouldn't go wrong. Everybody's looking for that top banana, but they're asleep on the good music that started all this," he told Dan Morgenstern.

Louis Armstrong's success is, in a very important sense, the success of his personality. Anybody who knew him or worked with him can tell of an experience that illuminates the warmth and sincerity of Armstrong's personality. In 1962, Joachim Berendt produced a television show in New York with the Armstrong All Stars. Only a short time before, Satchmo had been on camera sending regards to his German fans, asking them to have his *sauerkraut* and *wurst* ready for his upcoming tour. Then he and the crew were done; in a few minutes the studio had become dark and empty. Berendt was next door, discussing the editing of the film. Satchmo, surrounded by a throng of fans, had left. About forty-five minutes later, the elevator door opens and out comes Louis Armstrong, to tell Berendt that he had already been sitting in a taxi when he realized he had not said good-bye. Somewhat in doubt, Berendt suspected he had forgotten something. No, said Satchmo, he had just come back up to say good-bye. Which he did—and then he left. Jack Bradley, the jazz photographer, commented, "Yes, that's the way he is."

In the sixties, it became fashionable to call Armstrong an "Uncle Tom" who had not shown any involvement in the black liberation struggle. However, in 1957 Satchmo said to a reporter of the Grand Forks (North Dakota) *Herald,* "The way they are treating my people in the South—the Government can go to hell!" And then he canceled a tour of the Soviet Union organized by the State Department, refusing to go abroad for a government led by such a president. "The people over there ask me what's wrong with my country. What am I supposed to say? I have had a beautiful life in music, but I feel the situation the same as any other Negro." His words resounded around the globe.

On a Scandinavian tour in 1965, as he was watching television coverage of the black protest in Selma, Alabama, he told a reporter, "They would beat Jesus if he was black and marched."

Louis Armstrong had human solidarity and human compassion, but he was not a political man. "He loves people so much, he would even find good in a criminal. He is not capable of hate," a British critic once wrote.

"Of how many American artists can it be said that they formed our century?" asked Martin Williams, who then answered, "I am not sure about our writers, painters, our concert composers. But I am certain Louis Armstrong has formed it."

In a television program on the occasion of Louis Armstrong's death, Joachim Berendt said:

There is no sound today on radio, television, or record which could not somehow be traced back to Armstrong. He must be compared with the other great innovators in the arts of this century—Stravinsky, Picasso, Schöenberg, James Joyce. . . . He was the only native American among them. Without Armstrong, there would be no jazz—without jazz, there would be no modern popular music and no rock. All the sounds that surround us daily would be different without Satchmo; they would not exist without him. If it had not been for Armstrong, jazz would have remained the local folk music of New Orleans—as obscure as dozens of other bodies of folk music.

"Folk music?" Louis once asked. "Why, daddy, I don't know no other kind of music *but* folk music. I ain't never heard a horse sing a song."

Soviet poet Yevgeny Yevtushenko wrote this poem in the days when the news of Louis Armstrong's death was going around the world:

> Do as you did in the past
> And play.
> Cheer up the state of the angels,
> And so the sinners won't get too
>   unhappy in Hell
> Make their lives a bit more hopeful
> Give to Armstrong a trumpet
> Angel Gabriel.

Bessie Smith

> Papa, Papa, you're in a good man's way
> Papa, Papa, you're in a good man's way
> I can find one better than you any time of day.
>
> You ain't no good, so you'd better haul your freight
> You ain't no good, so you'd better haul your freight
> Mama wants a live wire, Papa, you can take the gate.
>
> I'm a red hot woman, just full of flamin' youth
> I'm a red hot woman, just full of flamin' youth
> You can't cool me, daddy, you're no good, that's the truth.

"There was no pretense. It was the real thing: a woman cutting her heart open with a knife until it was exposed for all to see," Carl Van Vechten wrote.

Bessie Smith is the greatest of the many singers from the classical period of the blues, the twenties. She made 160 records, was featured in a movie short, and was so successful at the peak of her career during the early and mid-twenties that her record sales saved the old Columbia Record Company from bankruptcy. Nearly ten million Bessie Smith records were sold. Bessie was the "Empress of the Blues."

Her personality had an awesome effect. She often elicited responses from her listeners similar to religious experiences. They would shout "amen" when she finished a blues number, as they did after spirituals or gospel songs in churches. At this time, nowhere else could one see as clearly the relationship between spirituals and the blues.

Mahalia Jackson, the great singer of the modern spirituals, the gospel songs, said, "Anybody that sings the blues is in a deep pit yelling for help." The blues tells of many things that have been lost: lost love and lost happiness, lost freedom and lost human dignity. Often the blues tells its story through a veil of irony. The coexistence of sorrow and humor is characteristic of the blues. It is as if what one is singing about becomes more bearable because it is not taken quite seriously; even the most desperate situation may reveal something amusing. At times, the comic element arises because one's misfortune is so limitless that it cannot be presented in adequate words. And always there is hope in the blues. As in "Trouble in Mind": "I won't be blue always 'cause the sun will shine in my back door some day."

Bessie Smith sang like someone who hopes that the sun one day will shine in her back door. And the sun did shine. Bessie earned a great deal of money, but she lost it all. She spent it on drink and on whatever else she wanted; she gave it away to relatives and people who seemed needy, or lost it to the men she was in love with.

Bessie Smith was born on April 15, 1894, in Chattanooga, Tennessee. Nobody took care of her, but she started to sing early. One day, blues singer Ma Rainey—the "Mother of the Blues"—came to town. She heard Bessie and took her in tow as a member of her troupe.

Bessie sang in the circus and tent shows in the cities and towns of the South. Frank Walker heard her and signed her to a contract. In 1923 she made her first record: "Downhearted Blues." It was a sensation. It sold 800,000 copies—almost all bought by blacks. However, only one of her records was a real success among the white audience of those years, and that one for the wrong reason: her "Empty Bed Blues," recorded in 1928 with trombonist Charlie Green, which was banned in Boston as obscene. "But," said George Hoefer, "it's hard to believe that the Boston censor understood the words, not to speak of the music. The word 'bed' alone did it."

Aside from Bessie, there were many divas of the classic blues: Ma Rainey; Mamie Smith, who in 1920 made the first recording of a blues; Trixie Smith and Clara Smith, like Mamie, not related to Bessie; Ida Cox, who made "Hard Times Blues" and was rediscovered and recorded in 1961 when she was past seventy; and Bertha "Chippie" Hill, who recorded "Trouble in Mind" with Louis Armstrong in 1926 and again with Lovie Austin's Blues Serenaders in 1946. But Bessie towers above them all.

It is hard to describe the magic of her voice. Maybe it is that its hardness and roughness seem to be edged with deep sorrow, even in the most frisky and humorous songs. Bessie sang as a representative of a people that had lived through centuries of slavery and, after emancipation, often had to live through human situations that seemed worse than the darkest days of slavery. The fact that her sorrow found expression, without a trace of sentimentality, precisely in the rough hardness of her voice may be her secret.

On her recordings Bessie Smith often had first-rate accompanists—musicians like Louis Armstrong or James P. Johnson, Jack Teagarden, Chu Berry, Benny Goodman, Tommy Ladnier, Eddie Lang, Frankie Newton, Clarence Williams, and more of the best jazz musicians of the day. Fletcher Henderson—director of the then leading jazz orchestra—was responsible for her supporting combos for several years and placed his best men at her service.

No female singer in jazz is not influenced to some degree, directly or indirectly, by Bessie Smith. Louis Armstrong said of her, "She used to thrill me at all times, the way she would phrase a note with a certain something in her voice no other blues singer could get. She had music in her soul and felt everything she did. Her sincerity with her music was an inspiration."

Her decline began in the later twenties. By 1930, Bessie Smith, who five years earlier had been the most successful artist of her race (and one of the most successful in America), was in such dire straits that she had to accept bookings no longer in the great theaters of the North but back where she had started from: rural traveling shows in the Deep South.

On September 26, 1937, Bessie Smith died after a highway collision near Clarksdale, Mississippi. In an earlier edition of this book, a story of Bessie Smith's death was retold that reflected a belief still widespread in jazz circles: The singer died because the white hospital to which she was taken after the accident refused to treat a black patient; she bled to death "on the steps" of this hospital.

While it must be granted that this story reflects the situation of the American Deep South at that time, it seems to have been proven that the jazz world was misinformed in the case of Bessie Smith (B. J. Skelton of the Clarksdale *Press Register* in the magazine *The Second Line,* vol. 9, nos. 9 & 10, 1959). She died in an ambulance en route to a black hospital in Clarksdale. Nevertheless, the details surrounding her death still remain uncertain. *Down Beat* reported in 1981 that two ambulances may have previously passed by, the drivers refusing to take the singer because of the color of her skin.

But the story of Bessie Smith's life and work does not end here. In 1971, Columbia Records rereleased the complete life work of Bessie Smith on five double albums. The Empress of the Blues thus received an honor unprecedented in popular music: Thirty-four years after her death, she gained worldwide fame for the second time. Marketing analyses have shown that mainly young people bought the results of this "most important and biggest single reissue project in history." This shows that the words of Bessie Smith's great fan and rediscoverer, John Hammond, were understood: "What Bessie sang in the twenties and thirties *is* the blues of today."

This renaissance of the music and name of Bessie Smith was also the cause for the fact that her grave (a hardly identifiable hill in range 12, lot 20, section 10 of the Mount Lawn Cemetery in Sharon Hill, Pennsylvania) finally received a headstone. Black Philadelphia citizens and Janis Joplin, the white singer from Texas who had learned so much from Bessie, contributed toward the $500 bill for the tombstone. The inscription reads, "The Greatest Blues Singer in the World Will Never Stop Singing—Bessie Smith—1895–1937."

Bix Beiderbecke

Bix Beiderbecke is among those musicians so well hidden by the myth that has evolved about them that it is difficult to discover the reality of the man. He was an inhibited person who never seemed satisfied with his achievements and always set unattainable goals for himself. "I think one of the reasons he drank so much was that he was a perfectionist and wanted to do more with music than any man possibly could. The frustration that resulted was a big factor," said trumpeter Jimmy McPartland, who came particularly close to him musically.

Paul Whiteman related, "Bix Beiderbecke, bless his soul, was crazy about the modern composers—Schöenberg, Stravinsky and Ravel. . . . One evening I took him to the opera. It happened to be *Siegfried.* When he heard the bird calls in the third act, with those intervals that are modern today, when he began to realize that the leitmotifs of the opera were dressed, undressed, disguised, broken down, and built up again in every conceivable fashion, he decided that old man Wagner wasn't so corny after all and that Swing musicians didn't know such a helluva lot."

Why Bix played in the dance orchestras of Whiteman and Jean Goldkette has often been misunderstood. The fans usually say he had to because he could not make a living from jazz. But Bix was one of the most successful musicians during the second half of the twenties. He was in a position to play where he wanted and always earn enough money. George Avakian said, "No one put a pistol in his back to make him join these bands." Actually Bix joined Whiteman—the epitome of commercial music of the day—because he was fascinated by the fancy arrangements written for the band. Here he could at least hang on to a reflection of the colorful orchestral palettes of Ravel, Delius, Stravinsky, and Debussy.

And thus it was—later in the thirties and forties—that record collectors all over the world bought the old records of Paul Whiteman to listen over and over again to eight or sixteen bars of solo blown by Bix. These recordings have repeatedly been reissued up to this day. (Indeed, no other musical form from the first half of the century has remained so alive on records as jazz. In opera, reissues of Caruso and a few other great stars are still an exception, for example. In jazz, on the other hand, the rerelease of the most important records of the outstanding musicians from the first fifty years of jazz has become the rule.)

When Beiderbecke's work in Whiteman's orchestra is viewed from a contemporary perspective, the difference between it and the jazz records made by Bix with his friends is really not too great. Few of the musicians with Bix on his own recording dates could shine his shoes. Not much lasts on them aside from Bix's cornet: the ensemble passages he leads and the solos he improvises.

Bix Beiderbecke is, more than any other musician, the essence of Chicago style. The following musicians—although some only stem from it and gained real importance in other styles—were part of Chicago style: saxophonist Frankie Trumbauer; trumpeters Muggsy Spanier and Jimmy McPartland; drummers Gene Krupa, George Wettling, and Dave Tough; the Dorsey Brothers (Jimmy on alto and clarinet, Tommy on trombone); tenor man Bud Freeman; violinist Joe Venuti, one of the few jazz violinists of those times; guitarists Eddie Lang and Eddie Condon; trombonists Glenn Miller and Jack Teagarden; clarinetists Pee Wee Russell, Frank Teschemacher, Benny Goodman, and Mezz Mezzrow; pianist Joe Sullivan; and a dozen or so others.

Their history is tragic in more ways than one. Rarely was so much enthusiasm for jazz concentrated in any single place as among them. Even so, most of their records from the period are unsatisfactory. The chief reason may be that there was no single band that, on a higher level, represented Chicago style per se. There is no ensemble like Louis Armstrong's Hot Seven or Jelly Roll Morton's Red Hot Peppers, which immediately come to mind when New Orleans style is mentioned; or like the bands of Count Basie or Benny Goodman and the Teddy Wilson combos in Swing; or the Charlie Parker Quintet in bop. From an ensemble point of view (in the sense explicated in the combo chapter of this book), Chicago style failed to produce a single satisfying recording. Almost always, only solo passages are remarkable: the unmistakable clarinet sound of Frank Teschemacher, the tenor improvisations of Bud Freeman, the "cool" alto lines of Frankie Trumbauer, and most of all Bix Beiderbecke's cornet.

It has been argued that Chicago style is not really a "style." Its best recordings, indeed, come so close to Dixieland or New Orleans that what is most typical of Chicago style seems to be only the unfinished quality of its few fine records. And yet, there are a few musical signposts—mainly the rather novel emphasis on solo contributions—which differentiate Chicago from New Orleans and Dixieland. Most of all, the *human* unity and rapport among the Chicagoans was so strong and was reflected in their music with such immediacy that one hesitates—even now—to tear them apart on theoretical and academic grounds.

Bix Beiderbecke was born in Davenport, Iowa, in 1903, the son of a family of German immigrants. His ancestors had been clergymen and organists in Pomerania and Mecklenburg for generations. One of this father's given names was Bismarck, and this name—shortened to Bix—was inherited by the son. As a boy, Bix sang in the chorus of the Lutheran church in Davenport. His grandfather led a German male glee club.

Bix was a musical prodigy. It is said that he first became acquainted with jazz through the riverboats that docked on the Mississippi; some of them had bands from New Orleans, and the music carried across the water.

Soon Bix became so absorbed in music that people began to think him a bit strange. He was expelled from school because he was interested only in music. The image of young Beiderbecke wandering the streets like a dreamer, his beat-up cornet wrapped in newspaper, became proverbial to all who knew him.

With Beiderbecke German romanticism—and the whole spectrum of feelings that belongs to it—entered jazz. Perhaps it was this romantic heritage, fraught with yearning and melancholia, that created in Bix a state of mind similar to that which had come to black people through their American experience. What to the great New Orleans musician was the musical heritage of Africa, if preserved only subconsciously, was to Beiderbecke the "Blue Flower" of German romanticism. He was a Novalis (a lyric poet of German romanticism [1772–1801]) of jazz, transported into the jazz age of the roaring twenties with all the life-hungry characters of F. Scott Fitzgerald.

Beiderbecke was, aside from the old ragtime pianists, the first great "cool" soloist of jazz history. From his cool conception a line leads straight to Miles Davis.

At eighteen, he began to play in public. In 1923, he was with the first real Chicago-style band, the Wolverines. In 1924, he met saxophonist Frank Trumbauer, with whom he made many of his finest records. There followed jobs with a variety of groups—with Jean Goldkette, Hoagy Carmichael, and other bands—until, by the late twenties, Bix was among the select musicians who gave the music of Paul Whiteman its jazz spice.

Around 1927 a lung complaint became noticeable. Bix paid no attention. He played and played, and when he wasn't playing, he drank or went to symphony concerts. He experimented in the harmonic world of Debussy, primarily at the piano. He wrote a few pieces that captured, in astonishingly simple, naive fashion, Impressionism. The titles are revealing: "In a Mist," "In the Dark," "Flashes."

As a trumpeter he was mainly a jazz musician; at the piano he was rather more indebted to the European tradition.

Finally, Whiteman sent him to Davenport for a rest. (He kept him on salary.) But it was too late. Bix could not stay home long. A woman—one of the few in his life—persuaded him to move to Queens and got him an apartment.

Bix spent the last weeks of his life in the apartment of bassist George Kraslow. Here something occurred that is characteristic of the love Bix inspired in everyone. He was in the habit of getting up around three or four in the morning to play his cornet. It is hard to imagine a jazz musician doing such a thing without bringing down upon himself the wrath of all the neighbors. Nothing of the sort happened. The neighbors told Kraslow, "Please don't mention we said anything. We would hate for him to stop."

In August 1931, Beiderbecke died of pneumonia in Kraslow's apartment. In Germany, on the "Lüneburger Heide" south of Hamburg, there are still Beiderbeckes. We asked them about Bix once. They had never heard of him.

Duke Ellington

Duke Ellington's Orchestra is a complex configuration of many spiritual and musical elements. To be sure, it was Duke Ellington's music that was created here, but it was just as much the music of each individual member of the band. Many Ellington pieces were genuine collective achievements, but it was Ellington who headed the collective. Attempts have been made to describe how Ellington recordings came into being, but the process is so subtle that verbalization appears crude. Duke, or his alter ego, the late arranger and jazz composer, Billy Strayhorn, or one of the members of the band would come to the studio with a theme. Ellington would play it on the piano. The rhythm section would fall in. One or another of the horn men would pick it up. Baritone saxophonist Harry Carney might improvise a solo on it. The brass would make up a suitable background for him. And Ellington would sit at the piano and listen, gently accenting the harmonies—and suddenly he'd know: This is how the piece should sound and no other way. Later, when it was transcribed, the note paper only happened to retain what was, in the real meaning of the word, improvised into being.

The dynamic willpower with which Ellington stamped his ideas on his musicians, yet giving them the impression that he was only helping them to unfold and develop their hidden powers, was one of his many great gifts. Owing to this relationship between Duke and his musicians, which can barely be put into words, everything he had written seemed to be created for him and his orchestra—to such a degree that hardly anyone can copy it. Once, it is said, Paul Whiteman and Ferde Grofé, his arranger, went night after night to the club where Ellington was playing, because they wanted to assimilate some of Ellington's typical sounds. Finally they gave up: "You can't steal from him."

Duke Ellington has written countless popular melodies—melodies in the genre of Jerome Kern, Richard Rodgers, Cole Porter, or Irving Berlin. But even the most popular among them— "Sophisticated Lady," "Mood Indigo," "Creole Love Call," "Solitude,"—have seldom become big hits. No matter how memorable and melodic, they seem to lose too much of their essence when not played by Ellington himself.

When Ellington was eighteen, he wanted to become a painter. By becoming a musician he only seemed to have abandoned painting. He painted not in colors but in sounds. His compositions, with their many colors of timbre and harmony, are musical paintings. Sometimes this is revealed by the titles: "The Flaming Sword," "Beautiful Indians," "Portrait of Bert Williams," "Sepia Panorama," "Country Girl," "Dusk in the Desert," "Mood Indigo," and so forth. Even as a conductor, Ellington remained the painter: in the grand manner in which he confronted the orchestra and, with a few sure movements of the hand, placed spots of color on a canvas made of sounds.

It may be due to this that he perceived his music as "the transformation of memories into sounds." The memories are pictures. Ellington said, "The memory of things gone is important to a jazz musician. I remember I once wrote a sixty-four-bar piece about a memory of when I was a little boy in bed and heard a man whistling on the street outside, his footsteps echoing away."

Again and again Ellington has expressed his pride in the color of his skin. Many of his larger works took their themes from black history: "Black, Brown, and Beige," the tone painting of the American Negro who was "black" when he came to the New World, became "brown" in the days of slavery, and today is "beige"—not only in his color, but in his being as well; "Liberian Suite," a work in six movements commissioned by the small republic on the west coast of Africa for its centennial; "Harlem," the work in which the atmosphere of New York's black city has been captured; "Deep South Suite," which reminds us of the locale of the origins of jazz, or "New World A-comin'," the work about a better world without racial discrimination.

"I want to create the music of the American Negro," Ellington once said, placing the accent on "American." He was conscious of the fact that the American Negro had more in common with the world of the white man than with that of black Africa. To a man who once wrote him that he should take his jungle music and go back to Africa as soon as possible, he replied with extreme courtesy that this unfortunately was impossible, inasmuch as the blood of the American Negro in the course of generations had become so mixed with that of the letter writer that he would hardly be accepted there. But if it were all right with the writer, he would go to Europe. "There we are accepted."

Many critics have said that Ellington often comes too close to European music. They point to his concern with larger forms. But in this very concern is revealed an insufficiency in the molding of these forms which is certainly not European: an astonishing, amiable naiveté. This naiveté was also present in those medleys—long series of his many successful tunes—with which Duke again and again upset many of his more sophisticated fans at his concerts. Ellington simply failed to see why the idea of the hit medley should be alien to an artistic music.

In 1923 he joined a five-piece combo, which already included three of his later-to-be famous instrumentalists: Otto Hardwick, alto sax; Sonny Greer, drums; Arthur Whetsol, trumpet. The combo took the name the Washingtonians from the capital, where Ellington was born in 1899 and where he spent a sheltered, carefree youth.

The Washingtonians went to New York where, as Duke told it, they sometimes had to split a hot dog five ways to keep from starving. After six months they gave up.

Three years later, Ellington tried again. This time it worked. Soon he was playing in Harlem's most expensive nightspot, the Cotton Club, located in Harlem but nevertheless catering to white tourists—to give them the feeling that they had "really been to Harlem." Ellington's first famous records were made: "East St. Louis Toodle-oo," "Jubilee Stomp," "Birmingham Breakdown," and "Black and Tan Fantasy."

The germ cell of his Cotton Club orchestra was preserved by Ellington well into the fifties. No other band leader has known so well how to keep an orchestra together. While other successful bands had personnel changes every few months, Ellington in twenty years only had six or seven significant alterations. Among the important soloists with Ellington at the Cotton Club were trumpeter Bubber Miley, trombonist Joe "Tricky Sam" Nanton, and baritone saxophonist Harry Carney. Ellington created his "jungle style" with Miley and Nanton. The expressive growl sounds of trumpet and trombone were reminiscent of voices moaning in a jungle night.

The jungle style is one of the four styles identified with Duke Ellington. The other three are (in a somewhat simplistic but synoptically clear grouping) "mood style," "concerto style," and "standard style," which came rather directly from Fletcher Henderson, the most important band leader of the twenties, and initially did not contribute much that was new. What it did have to offer, though, was clothed in typically Ellingtonian colors and sounds. In addition, of course, there is every imaginable mixture of these styles.

The mood style partakes of blues feeling, even in pieces that are not really blues. Ellington's most ambitious compositions in terms of tonal color are linked to this mood style. "Solitude," which says more in three minutes about the feeling its title describes than many a bulky book, is the most famous example.

As far as the concerto style is concerned, there are really two: real small concertos for different soloists in the Ellington orchestra (such as the famous "Concerto for Cootie" for trumpeter Cootie Williams) and the aforementioned attempts to write jazz in larger forms.

The history of Duke Ellington is the history of the orchestra in jazz. No significant big band—and this includes commercial dance bands—has not been directly or indirectly influenced by Duke. This list of innovations and techniques introduced by Ellington and subsequently picked up by other orchestras or players is unrivaled.

In 1927, he was the first to use the human voice as an instrument. The voice was Adelaide Hall's; the tune, "Creole Love Call." Later, he was to create similar effects with Kay Davis' coloratura soprano. Today, the expression "voice as instrument" has become a household phrase.

With his 1937 recording "Caravan," a tune written with his Puerto Rican trombonist Juan Tizol, he paved the way for what has been called "Cuban jazz" since the forties—what is today called "Latin jazz": the combination of Latin American rhythms with the melodies and harmonies of North American jazz.

Duke Ellington was first to use so-called echo chambers in recording. Today, echo chambers are taken for granted. In 1938, Johnny Hodges' solo on "Empty Ballroom Blues" was the first solo ever to be recorded with echo chamber.

Toward the end of the twenties there is evidence of the flatted fifth, the interval so characteristic of bop, in more than one Ellington piece.

With his baritone saxophonist, Harry Carney, Ellington created a place for the baritone in jazz.

For years, the history of the jazz bass was so closely tied to the Ellington orchestra that it might be as appropriate to discuss it here as in the later section about the bass. There is a straight-line development from the first recording with amplified bass—"Hot and Bothered" with bassist Wellman Braud in 1928—to the playing of Oscar Pettiford and especially of Jimmy Blanton, who as a member of the Ellington band around 1940 made the bass the instrument it is in jazz today.

With Duke Ellington we discover for the first time in jazz how sound becomes independent. The discovery that sound itself, that tonal color, can be a uniquely determining element (just as important as rhythm, melody, and harmony) was first made by Duke Ellington, long before it became a standard feature of sixties jazz. Everything involved in ensemble sound and jazz instrumentation derives almost exclusively from Ellington.

Most important of all, Ellington was decades ahead of his time in solving the paradox of integrating composed music into predominantly improvised music. Duke didn't compose for instruments. He wrote for individuals. Ever since Duke Ellington, jazz composition, if it strives for quality, must entail dialogue between the composer and the performers. Out of composing (an individual's inner monologue) he made an act comprising an exchange of musical ideas between creator and interpreter. Without such empathy and understanding of the character of the particular musicians involved, jazz composition is no longer conceivable. On the level where jazz compositions are written today, Ellington was almost alone between 1925 and 1945. Only then came all the others: John Lewis, Ralph Burns, Jimmy Giuffre, Bill Russo, George Russell, Gerry Mulligan, Charles Mingus, Carla Bley, Gil Evans, Oliver Nelson, Toshiko Akiyoshi, Muhal Richard Abrams, Henry Threadgill, David Murray, Edward Wilkerson, and so forth.

Incomparable, too, is the way in which Ellington dealt with the problem of the piano in jazz (about which we will hear later). The piano became an extension of his conducting hands. He played only what was most necessary, indicated harmonies, bridged gaps, and left everything else to his musicians. His piano breaks were like a drummer's. Duke often executed them without using the piano stool, but they are filled with admirable tension, and when he played one of his rare solos, one feels to this day his roots in the old, genuine ragtime.

Ellington's two most famous orchestras were that of the late twenties, with Bubber Miley and "Tricky Sam" Nanton, and that of the early forties, with bassist Jimmy Blanton and tenor man Ben Webster. Modern big-band jazz begins with the latter; "Ko Ko" is its best-known piece. After that, there was occasional talk about the decline of Ellington. Some people advised him to disband his orchestra, or to keep it together for only a few months of the year and spend the rest of his time composing. But Duke needed his musicians: "I want to have them around me," Leonard Feather quoted him, "to play my music. I'm not worried about creating music for posterity; I just want it to sound good right now!"

Besides, Duke Ellington himself put an end to the "decline" of which hasty critics had spoken. This occurred at the Newport Festival in 1956. Ellington was billed as just another of the many attractions. Nobody expected anything out of the ordinary, but his appearance proved to be the climax of the whole festival. Duke played his old (1937) "Diminuendo and Crescendo in Blue," one of his first extended compositions; Paul Gonsalves blew twenty-seven choruses of stimulating tenor sax on it, and the band generated a vitality and drive the likes of which had not been heard from Ellington in a long time.

It was one of the great jazz nights of the fifties. And what had been forgotten for a few years again became apparent: Duke Ellington was still the "grand old man" of big-band jazz. A string of new masterpieces came into being, first and foremost the Shakespeare suite "Such Sweet Thunder," dedicated to the Shakespeare Festival at Stratford, Ontario. With its spirited glosses, persiflages, and caricatures of great Shakespearean characters, it is one of the most beautiful of the larger Ellington works.

In 1967, Billy Strayhorn died; in 1970, altoist Johnny Hodges. Since the death in 1932 of trumpeter Bubber Miley, who together with Ellington had formed the jungle style with his "growl play" between 1925 and 1929 (and who was replaced by another outstanding soloist, Cootie Williams), Ellington had not taken any personal loss so hard as the death of these two great musicians. The rich, sensuous solos of Johnny Hodges had reflected almost uninterruptedly since 1928 (for forty-two years!) the romantic, sensuous, impressionistic side of Ellington's character. Composer and arranger Billy Strayhorn had contributed many important pieces to the band's repertoire, such as "Lush Life," "Chelsea Bridge," and "Take the A Train," the theme song of the Ellington orchestra. As an orchestrator, he tuned in to Duke so perfectly that even specialists often were hard put to differentiate between what was written by Ellington and what by Billy "Sweet Pea" Strayhorn.

But Strayhorn's death unearthed once again a host of new creative powers in Ellington. During the sixties, he had increasingly left the main composing and arranging work to Strayhorn. Now he began—alone again—to take the initiative himself. A large number of important new great works were created: the *Sacred Concert* and, following that, *Second Sacred Concert;* Duke Ellington's *70th Birthday Concert* (chosen in 1969 as "Jazz Record of the Year" all over the world); the "Far East Suite" (in which Ellington reflects on a tour of Asia, sponsored by the State Department, in a highly personal manner); and, above all, the *New Orleans Suite,* which became the 1970 "Record of the Year." In the latter recording, Ellington salutes the New Orleans heritage of the jazz tradition and transforms it into Ellingtonian music.

Jazz specialists have said that the years after Strayhorn's death comprise one of the richest and most fruitful periods in Ellington's fifty-year life work—in terms of composition as well as the number of concerts and tours by the Ellington orchestra.

In 1970, the Ellington band went on one of the longest tours ever made by a jazz orchestra: the Soviet Union, Europe, Latin America—all without a break, for three months. And again and again, one had the impression that seventy-year-old Ellington was the youngest, most active, most dynamic man in this orchestra of his juniors. Often, when the other band members seemed to drift into sweet slumber behind their music stands, Ellington would fascinate his audience with his humor, spirit, and charm. And when his musicians would be exhausted toward the end of a concert, he would gather a small group of four or five soloists and create with them rare apexes of youthful vitality.

In 1969, we turned the Berlin Jazz Days into a grand birthday celebration for the seventy-year-old Ellington, and dozens of famous musicians—not only the older generation, but also personalities like Miles Davis and Cecil Taylor—paid tribute to Duke. And a critic wrote that Ellington had been "the youngest musician at the whole festival."

Five years later, on May 25, 1974, Duke Ellington—the "Great Orchestrator of Jazz"—died of pneumonia in a New York hospital. Just a couple of weeks before, *Down Beat,* on the occasion of his seventy-fifth birthday, had dedicated to him a whole issue full of congratulations. From Leonard Bernstein to Miles Davis, the music world paid homage to him. Drummer Louis Bellson, possibly, found the most moving words: "You, the MAESTRO, have given me a beautiful education musically and have guided me to be a good human being. Your valued knowledge and friendship will be with me forever. You are the model citizen of the world. Your music is Peace, Love and Happiness."

Duke Ellington's music will remain with us—not only in the Duke Ellington Orchestra, which was taken over by his son Mercer after his death and which continues to play the compositions of the Grand Old Man. It is with an occasional tinge of disappointment that you hear this band now, but finally with the respect that is due the son of the great Duke Ellington.

First and foremost, though, Duke Ellington's music continues to live in the hundreds of musicians who learned from him and who, in turn, pass on their experiences and developments to their students and successors: a stream of "Ellingtonia" that will continue to flow as long as there is jazz.

Coleman Hawkins and Lester Young

Until the late sixties, when the guitar and electronic instruments came into the foreground, the sound of modern jazz was—to use a favorite term of arranger Bill Russo—"tenorized." The man who tenorized it was Lester Young.

More important musicians play tenor saxophone than any other instrument. The sound of Miles Davis' Capitol Orchestra has been described as the orchestration of Lester Young's tenor sound. The other important jazz sound of the fifties—the "Four Brothers" sound of the Woody Herman band—is tenorized, too. The tenor men who played it, almost all other important tenorists, and even trumpeters, trombonists, pianists, alto and baritone saxists of the cool jazz of the fifties—all were influenced by Lester Young.

With Lester "Pres" (from President) Young, cool jazz, the jazz of the fifties, began long before there was bebop, the jazz of the forties. It began with the solos played by Lester in the old Count Basie band: "Song of the Islands" and "Clap Hands, Here Comes Charlie," recorded in 1939; "Lady Be Good," recorded by a Count Basie combo in 1936; or even earlier, when Lester became a member of Fletcher Henderson's band in 1934. "The whole band was buzzing on me," Lester reminisced, "because I had taken Hawk's place. I didn't have the same kind of sound he had. I was rooming at the Henderson's house, and Leora Henderson would wake me early in the morning and play Hawkins' records for me so I could play like he did. I wanted to play my own way, but I just listened. I didn't want to hurt her feelings."

Coleman Hawkins and Lester Young—these two names designate two great eras of jazz. Since "Bean" and Pres both played tenor, and since each of them holds approximately the same position in the phase of jazz he represents, no two other personalities could show more clearly how wide the scale of being and meaning in jazz really is. At one end stands Coleman Hawkins—the extroverted rhapsodist with the voluminous tone. Hard and gripping on fast pieces, erotically expressive on slow numbers, always vitally communicative, never shying away from quantity in utterances or notes, he is a Rubens of jazz. And opposite him stands Lester Young—the introverted lyricist with the supple, soft tone, friendly and obliging on fast pieces, full of tender abandon on slow numbers, reserved in utterance, never stating a nuance more than is absolutely necessary. He is a Cézanne of jazz, as Marshall Stearns has called him, which not only indicates his artistic but also his historical position: As Cézanne paved the way for modern painting, so Young paved the way for modern jazz.

It would be an oversimplification, however, to assign one man to the jazz tradition and the other to modern jazz. Both stem from the tradition; both were "modern." Coleman Hawkins emerged from the Jazz Hounds, the group accompanying blues singer Mamie Smith. Lester Young was born near New Orleans and in his youth received the same impressions that affected the old New Orleans musicians: street parades, Mardi Gras, and New Orleans funerals. When the modern jazz of the forties sprang up, Coleman Hawkins was the first noted "traditional" jazz musician to play with the young bebop revolutionaries. And in the second half of the fifties, the period just preceding the death of Young (who after years of almost constant indulgence in alcohol and marijiuana was only a shadow of his former self), the man who preceded him—Coleman Hawkins—retained his old, indestructible vitality and power.

Hawkins is the "father of the tenor saxophone." To be sure, there were some tenor players before him, but the instrument was not an acknowledged jazz horn. At that time it fell into the category of strange noise makers, like the euphonium, the sousaphone, or the bass sax.

Coleman Hawkins was twenty-one when he came to New York with Mamie Smith in 1923. He was playing blues and jazz in the style of that time, similar possibly to King Oliver and Louis Armstrong, and he was one of the few black musicians who played with the young Chicago-style jazzmen. That same year, he joined the first important big band—Fletcher Henderson's—and remained until 1934. He was the first real tenor saxophone soloist, in the sense of the great virtuosos of the Swing period. He was one of the first to make records with the young European musicians who were just then beginning to hear the jazz message: in 1934 with Jack Hylton in England, in 1935 with the Ramblers in Holland and with Django Reinhardt in Paris. And as modern jazz began—as we have mentioned—he was again one of the first to participate. Hawkins could always be found where original jazz was being created.

His first famous solo on record was the 1926 rendition of "Stampede" with Fletcher Henderson. In 1929 came "One Hour" with the Mound City Blue Blowers, who included some of the Chicago-style practitioners. Then in 1934, again with Henderson, "Talk of the Town"—probably the first great solo ballad interpretation in jazz history, the foundation for everything now meant by ballad playing in modern jazz. (Miles Davis said, "When I heard Hawk, I learned to play ballads.") Then came the European recordings, such as "I Wanna Go Back to Harlem" with the Dutch Ramblers and "Stardust" with Django Reinhardt. When Hawkins returned to the United States in 1939, he almost immediately scored the greatest success of his career: "Body and Soul," a jazz record that became a worldwide hit. Hawkins could not understand it: "I've been playing like that all my life. . . . it wasn't anything special." In 1943, he blew a breathtaking solo on "The Man I Love" with Oscar Pettiford's bass and Shelly Manne's drums, and then, in 1947, came "Picasso"—a long improvisation for unaccompanied tenor saxophone, based on the harmonies of the piece identified with Hawkins, "Body and Soul." It is reminiscent in structure and delineation of Johann Sebastian Bach's Chaconne from the D-minor Partita for solo violin, and full of the same baroque vitality and linearity.

On all these records, and in almost everything he has ever played, Hawkins is the master of the chorus of improvising on a given chord scheme. A Hawkins solo, it has been said, is the classic example of how to develop a solo statement from a phrase. And almost every phrase Hawkins has blown could itself be used again as the theme for a jazz improvisation. There is only one musician who can be compared to him in this respect, the one who in almost every other respect is his opposite: Lester Young.

While everything about Hawkins, the human being, is simple and comprehensible, everything about Lester is strange and incomprehensible. A booking agent, Nat Hentoff related, gave up working with Lester because he couldn't talk to him. "I'd talk to him," the agent said, "and all he'd say was 'Bells!' or 'Ding dong!' I finally decided I'd go to Bellevue if I wanted to talk to crazy people."

He left the Count Basie band, from which he emerged and with which he was connected as Hawkins had been with Fletcher Henderson's band, because Basie had set a recording date for a Friday the thirteenth—and Lester refused to play on that day.

His jargon was almost a language in itself, which made it hard for people to understand him in conversation. No one has coined as many jazz expressions as he—right down to the word *cool*—so that not only the style but also the expression stems from him. He called his colleagues "lady" and addressed club owners as "Pres"; he asked pianist Bobby Scott about his "left people" when he wanted to tease Scott about the habit (shared by many modern pianists) of running hornlike lines with his right hand while the left hardly came into play. Norman Granz said that Lester for a time pretended to be speaking a foreign language: "It was gibberish, but he did it with a straight face and with conviction."

Lester had the sensibility of a Baudelaire or James Joyce. "He lives in his own world," an agent said about him. What was outside of this world was, according to Lester's convictions, not in the world at all. But this world of his was a wonderful world, a world that was mild and friendly and lovely. "Anything that hurts a human being hurts him," said drummer Jo Jones.

Jones said:

> Everyone playing an instrument in jazz expresses what's on his mind. Lester would play a lot of musical phrases that were actually words. He would literally talk on his horn. That's his conversation. I can tell what he's talking about in 85 percent of what he'll play in a night. I could write his thoughts down on paper from what I hear from his horn. Benny Goodman even made a tune out of a phrase Lester would play on his horn—"I want some money."

Because Lester talked on his horn, he loved to listen to singers: "Most of the time I spend in listening to records is listening to singers and getting the lyrics to different songs."

When improvising on a melody, Lester Young attempted to convey the lyrics of this melody to the listener directly and without the aid of words. Thus, he recorded some of his most beautiful solos as accompanist to singer Billie Holiday, the greatest female singer since Bessie Smith—perhaps simply the greatest, in any case the personification of Swing singing, as Bessie Smith was the personification of the classic blues. The way in which Pres backed "Lady Day"—the name he gave her—set the standard for accompaniments to singing in jazz, with such pieces as "Time on My Hands," "Without Your Love," or "Me, Myself and I."

What Lester tells us when he improvises freely on his tenor sax might sound something like this: "I was born near New Orleans, August 27, 1909. I stayed in New Orleans until I was ten. During the carnival season we all traveled with the minstrel show, through Kansas, Nebraska, South Dakota, all through there.

"I played drums from the time I was ten to about thirteen. Quit them because I got tired of packing them up. I'd take a look at the girls after the show, and before I'd get the drums packed, they'd be gone.

"For a good five or six years after that I played the alto, and then the baritone when I joined Art Bronson's band. Ran away from my father when I was about eighteen. . . . I joined Art Bronson and his Bostonians. Played with him for three or four years . . . anyway, I was playing the baritone and it was weighing me down. I'm real lazy, you know. So when the tenor man left, I took over his instrument.

"Used to hear the Basie band all the time on the radio and figured they needed a tenor player. They were at the Reno Club in Kansas City. It was crazy, the whole band was gone, but just this tenor player. I figured it was about time, so I sent Basie a telegram.

"But Basie was like school. I used to fall asleep in school, because I had my lesson, and there was nothing else to do. The teacher would be teaching those who hadn't studied at home, but I had, so I'd go to sleep . . . you had to sit there and play it over and over again. Just sit in that chair.

"I joined Fletcher Henderson in Detroit in 1934. Basie was in Little Rock then, and Henderson offered me more money. Basie said I could go . . . was with Henderson only about six months. The band wasn't working very much . . . then back to Basie until 1944 and the army."

The army broke Lester Young, according to Nat Hentoff. He was harassed, and his individuality and sensitivity were deadened, in the way armies all over the world deaden individuality and sensitivity. Through the army, hate came into his life—hate particularly for whites, or so Hentoff supposed. For a musician whose message was lyricism, tenderness, and amiability there was not much left.

The other thing that oppressed him, subconsciously and sometimes consciously, was the fact that almost every tenor player was playing à la Pres, until during the last years of his life Sonny Rollins and the musicians of his school came up. The worst thing was that there was a man who often played a "better" Lester Young than Lester himself: Paul Quinichette, Lester called him "Lady Q." Lester's manager tells of the time when both were playing at Birdland—the famous, now defunct jazz club in New York—and Lester came off the stand saying, "I don't know whether to play like me or like Lady Q, because he's playing so much like me."

It was a peculiar brand of irony: On the one hand, nothing underlined Lester's enormous artistic success more than that an entire generation of tenor men should play like him; on the other hand, as an uncompromising individualist he found it intolerable that they all should play like him, and he like them.

Most of the records Lester made in the fifties—such as the ones for Norman Granz's Verve label—were only a pale reflection of the great President. But often there were sparks, and one could still feel something of the genius of this great musician—for instance, on the record "Jazz Giants of 1956" with Teddy Wilson, Roy Eldridge, Vic Dickenson, and other great Swing musicians.

For years Lester traveled with Norman Granz's concert unit, Jazz at the Philharmonic, all over the world. Night after night, he witnessed how Flip Phillips brought audiences to their feet with the exhibitionism of his tenor solos. He disliked this ecstatic way of playing tenor, but it reached the point where he himself often utilized it—and from this, too, he must have suffered. For years, Lester Young lived almost uninterruptedly in a state of intoxication, until, in March 1959, he died after a tragic engagement at the Blue Note, a Paris jazz club. Ben Benjamin, the club owner, reported, "Lester was very sick when he worked for me. He was almost apathetic. He wanted to go home because, as he said, he couldn't talk to the French doctors. He had ulcers, and I think he drank a little too much."

Lester came back to New York in time to die. On the early morning of his arrival, he died in the Hotel Alvin, on the "musician's crossroad" at 52nd Street and Broadway where he had lived during the last years of his life.

The only thing Lester retained throughout the crisis periods of his life, and down to his last days, was his sound—as Coleman Hawkins retained his. "The only thing nobody can steal from you is your sound. Sound alone is important," Hawkins once said.

Lester's sonority stems from Frankie Trumbauer and Bud Freeman, the Chicago-style musicians. "Trumbauer was my idol. . . . I imagine I can still play all those solos off the records. He played the C-melody saxophone. I tried to get the sound of a C melody on a tenor. That's why I don't sound like other people. . . . I did like Bud Freeman very much. Nobody played like him." The line that leads from Chicago style via Lester Young to cool jazz is direct.

The name of Lester Young even stands at the beginning of bebop. Kenny Clarke told about it:

They began to talk about Bird [Charlie Parker] because he was playing like Pres on alto. People became concerned about what he was doing. We thought that was something phenomenal because Lester Young was the pace setter, the style setter at that time. . . . We went to listen to Bird at Monroe's [a Harlem club] for no other reason except that he sounded like Pres . . . until we found out that he had something of his own to offer . . . something new.

And Parker himself said: "I was crazy about Lester. He played so clean and beautifully, but I wasn't influenced by Lester. Our ideas ran on differently."

Indeed, these were two different directions. It would be possible to show that modern jazz as a whole, even up to free jazz, has developed in the counterplay of the ideas of Lester Young and Charlie Parker. Lester came first; then, when Parker arrived, *his* influence became dominant. But then, in the fifties, Pres' hour struck again, with a host of musicians playing "cool" *à la* Lester Young, until finally, with the coming of hard bop, Bird's influence again assumed overwhelming importance. And with this Bird influence, with the sonority of Sonny Rollins' tenor sax, we return (and so the circle of this chapter closes) to Coleman Hawkins. His hard, dramatic style now was in the right place, after Lester Young's desire to make the world "nice and cozy" had proven vain, although it had been shared by all jazz musicians for so many years. Hawkins, whose career preceded Young's by almost ten years, also survived Lester by ten years. His health was as robust as his playing (with the exception of the last years of his life), and only weeks before his death—in June 1969—he appeared in concerts and on television. The tenor saxophonists of free jazz who meanwhile had so radically changed jazz—Archie Shepp, Pharoah Sanders, Albert Ayler, and others—all agreed on who had given the first impulses to those expanding inflections of tenor sound that were their main focus: Coleman Hawkins. Archie Shepp said it clearly: "I play Hawk today."

For Coleman Hawkins, this whole rich era he had lived through—from Mamie Smith in 1922 to the post-Coltrane period in 1969—was not as varied as it seems to us today. It was *one* style and *one* era. The style was jazz; from the beginning until today and beyond, it was the era of jazz. Progress was a foreign word to Hawkins. He once said to critic Stanley Dance, "What Charlie Parker and Dizzy were doing was 'far out' to a lot of people, but it was just music to me." And he made recordings with the young bebop people only because "they needed help." When Dance talked to him about Mamie Smith and Fletcher Henderson and the good old days, Hawkins said, "I don't think I ever was a child."

Charlie Parker and Dizzy Gillespie

"Just a week before his death," Leonard Feather said, "Parker ran into Gillespie at Basin Street. He was desperate, pitiful, pleading. 'Let's get together again,' he urged Dizzy. 'I want to play with you again before it is too late.' "

"Dizzy can't get over Bird saying that to him," recalled Loraine, Dizzy's wife. "His eyes get full of water even now when he thinks about it."

Charlie Parker and Dizzy Gillespie are the Dioscuri of bebop.

Charlie Parker came from Kansas City. He was born on August 29, 1920. When he died in 1955, the doctors who performed the autopsy said that he might as well have been fifty-five.

Dizzy Gillespie comes from South Carolina. He was born on October 21, 1917. In all phases of his life he has appeared to be five to eight years younger than he is.

Both grew up in the world of racial discrimination and from early youth experienced the humiliations that are a part of it.

Nobody cared much about young Charlie. Throughout his youth, he lacked love and the warmth of the nest.

None of the few family members close to Charlie Parker were musical. At thirteen, he was playing baritone horn. A year later, alto sax was added.

Dizzy had a sheltered youth and grew up in a well-ordered family environment.

Dizzy Gillespie's father was an amateur musician. He taught his kids to play several instruments. At fourteen, Dizzy's chief horn was the trombone. A year later, trumpet was added.

It has always been a mystery why Charlie Parker became a musician. The alto saxophonist Gigi Gryce— one of his best friends—said: "Parker was a natural genius. If he had become a plumber, I believe he would have been a great one."

It seemed decided from the start that Dizzy would become a musician. He studied theory and harmony.

At fifteen, Charlie Parker was forced to earn his own keep. "We had to play," he said, "from nine in the evening to five in the morning without a break. We usually got $1 or $1.25 a night."

At fifteen, Dizzy completed the studies paid for by his father.

In 1937, at seventeen, Charlie became a member of Jay McShann's

In the same year—1937—Dizzy took over Roy Eldridge's chair in band, a typical Kansas City riff and blues orchestra. Parker said he was "crazy about Lester Young," but it is questionable whether he had a real model. It is probable that his colleagues at first considered his style terrible because he played "different" from anybody else.

Parker's real schooling and tradition was the blues. He heard it constantly in Kansas City and played it night after night with Jay McShann.

Teddy Hill's band. Roy was Dizzy's great model. The Hill band had grown out of the Luis Russell orchestra, and Russell himself had taken over the King Oliver band in 1929. Thus, the jazz genealogy from Dizzy back to King Oliver and Louis Armstrong is surprisingly short.

Gillespie, too, has roots in the jazz tradition, but it is rather the happy tradition of New Orleans and Dixieland music.

The titles of the first records made by both men are symbolic:

Charlie Parker recorded "Confessin' the Blues" on April 30, 1941, in Dallas, Texas, with Jay McShann's band (however, there are earlier recordings, e.g., a 1940 radio session with the Jay McShann Band. The oldest surviving documentation of Charlie Parker is an unaccompanied saxophone solo based on "Honeysuckle Rose" and "Body and Soul," probably recorded by another musician in 1937).

Dizzy Gillespie recorded, in mid-1937, just after becoming a member of Teddy Hill's band, Jelly Roll Morton's "King Porter Stomp."

Charlie Parker at first did not get far from Kansas City. He lived a dreary, joyless life and became acquainted with narcotics almost simultaneously with music. It is believed that Parker had become a victim of "the habit" by the time he was fifteen.

Dizzy went to Europe with Teddy Hill's band in the summer of 1937. Teddy Hill wrote, "Some of the guys threatened not to go if the frantic one went too. But it developed that youthful Dizzy, with all his eccentricities and practical jokes, was the most stable man of the group. He was able to save so much money that he encouraged the others to borrow from him so that he'd have an income in case things got rough back in the States."

The inhibitions and complexes of his life began the moment he became a musician. Charlie Parker played with Jay McShann until 1941. Once he landed in jail for twenty-two days when he refused to pay his cab fare and wounded the driver with a knife. Then he fled to Chicago. He arrived there dirty and tattered as if he had "just got off a freight car." But he was playing "like you never heard."

For three months he was a dishwasher in a Harlem restaurant. Sometimes he didn't even have a horn to play on. "I was always in a panic," is one of his best-known quotes. He slept in garages. "Worst of all was that nobody understood my music."

When Parker once played in a jam session in Kansas City with members of the Basie band and nobody liked what he was blowing, drummer Jo Jones "as an expression of his feelings took his cymbal off and threw it almost the entire distance of the room. Bird just packed up his horn and went out."

Parker said, "I'd been getting bored with the stereotyped changes that were being used all the time at the

Dizzy Gillespie was successful from the moment he began to play. In Paris it was first noticed that his playing was different. A French drummer wrote at the time, "There is in the band of Teddy Hill a very young trumpeter who promises much. It is a pity that he has no opportunity to make recordings here. He is—along with trombonist Dickie Wells—by far the most gifted musician in the band. His name is Dizzy Gillespie."

Upon his return from Europe, Dizzy Gillespie became a successful musician, playing in different bands. In 1939, he became a member of Cab Calloway's orchestra.

Cab Calloway didn't like the way Dizzy played, nor did he care for Dizzy's penchant for practical jokes and, occasionally, for quarreling also. During an engagement in Hartford, someone (not Dizzy) threw a spitball out on the stage, hitting the bandleader. After the curtain, Cab blamed Diz, "and an argument ensued," bassist Milt Hinton related. "Cab made a pass at Dizzy, and Dizzy came at him with a knife. I grabbed Diz's hand . . . but Cab was nicked in the scuffle. Cab hadn't realized he'd been cut until he was back in the dressing room."

Dizzy said, "When I was growing up, all I wanted to play was Swing. Eldridge was my boy. All I ever did

time, and I kept thinking there's bound to be something else. I could hear it sometimes, but I couldn't play it."

"Well, that night I was working over 'Cherokee,' and, as I did, I found that by using the higher intervals of a chord as a melody line and backing them with appropriately related changes, I could play the thing I'd been hearing. I came alive."

When he was not playing with Jay McShann, Charlie Parker pulled through with menial jobs. He participated in every jam session he could find.

In 1941 he came to New York with the McShann band. They played at the Savoy Ballroom in Harlem.

was try to play like him, but I never quite made it. I'd get all messed up because I couldn't get it. So I tried something else. That has developed into what became known as bop."

One of the first records Dizzy made with Cab Calloway's band had the odd title, "Chop, Chop, Charlie Chan" on March 8, 1940. A dozen years later, Parker appeared on the last record made by Dizzy and Bird together under the pseudonym "Charlie Chan." (Chan was his wife's first name.)

Starting in 1939 Dizzy had begun to arrange. Successful bands like Woody Herman's, Jimmy Dorsey's, and Ina Ray Hutton's bought his arrangements.

Dizzy Gillespie came by to sit in.

Bird and Dizzy had met in Kansas City in 1939, but it was most likely on this night that they really played together for the first time.

Soon, the McShann band left New York. Parker went along to Detroit. Then he no longer could stand the routine arrangements and left the band, without saying anything. He never cared much for big bands.

Dizzy Gillespie evolved more and more into a big-band musician. After the row with Calloway he worked in the big bands of Benny Carter, Charlie Barnet, Lucky Millinder, Earl Hines (1943), Duke Ellington, and Billy Eckstine (1944).

After he left the McShann band, Charlie Parker went almost daily to Minton's in Harlem. A band consisting of pianist Thelonious Monk, guitarist Charlie Christian, trumpeter Joe Guy, bassist Nick Fenton, and drummer Kenny Clarke was playing there. "Nobody," Monk was to say later, "was sitting there trying to make up something new on purpose. The job at Minton's was a job we were playing, that's all." Yet Minton's became the point of crystallization for bop. There Charlie Parker and Dizzy Gillespie met again.

Monk relates that Charlie Parker's ability and authority were immediately accepted when he began to show up at Minton's. All could feel his creative productive genius.

Billy Eckstine related, "Now Diz is like a fox, you know. He's one of the smartest guys around. Musically, he knows what he is doing backwards and forwards. So what he hears—that you think maybe is going through—goes in and stays. Later, he'll go home and figure it all out just what it is."

Charlie Parker and Dizzy Gillespie became inseparable. In 1943, they played together in Earl Hines's band; in 1944 they were both with Billy Eckstine. In the same year they co-led a combo on 52nd Street, which became the "Street of Bop." They also made their first joint recording in 1944.

Tony Scott said, "And Bird came in one night and sat in with Don Byas. He blew 'Cherokee' and everybody just flipped. . . . When Bird and Diz hit the Street regularly a couple of years later, everybody was astounded and nobody could get near their way of playing music. Finally, Bird and Dizzy made records, and then guys could imitate and go from there. Everybody was experimenting around 1942, but nobody had set a style yet. Bird provided the push."

In Leonard Feather's words, "Dizzy's followers were aping his goatee, beret and glasses, even his gait." Dizzy created then what was to go around the world as "bebop fashion." Fan magazines advertised "bebop ties."

Charlie Parker had found, in the quintet format of bebop, the instrumentation most congenial to him: sax, trumpet, and three rhythm. The Charlie Parker Quintet became as significant to modern jazz as Louis Armstrong's Hot Five had been to traditional.

Deep inside, Dizzy is a big band man. In 1945 he founded his first own big band. From 1946 to 1950 he had large bands almost steadily. In 1948, he took one to Europe. His Paris concert had long-lasting effects on European jazz.

It becomes clearer: Dizzy Gillespie in those days was the most frequently mentioned bebop musician. If he did not bring to this music the creative impulses that radiated from Charlie Parker, he gave it the glamor and power without which it could not have conquered the world.

Billy Eckstine said, "Bird was responsible for the actual playing of [bebop], more than anyone else. But for putting it down, Dizzy was responsible."

With his Charlie Parker Quintet, Bird made the most important combo recordings of bebop: "Koko," based on the changes to "Cherokee"; "Now Is the Time," a blues; "Chasin' the Bird," with the fugato entry of trumpeter Miles Davis, commencing the fashion of fugues and fugatos in modern jazz; "Embraceable You," the first modern jazz recording based on themeless improvisation (even though, as André Hodeir shows, that was hinted at in "Koko"); and countless others. Accompanied by Erroll Garner he recorded "Cool Blues," relating coolness and the blues in the title itself.

"Things to Come" became the most important record of the Gillespie big band, an apocalyptic vision of the things that were to come: a broiling, twitching mass of lava out of which for a few seconds arise ghostly figurations, to disappear again at once. But above it all the clear and triumphant sound of Dizzy's trumpet. "Music of chaos," as some people said then, but also music about man's victory over chaos!

Charlie Parker's alto sax became the most expressive voice of modern jazz —each note arising from the blues tradition, often imperfect, but always from the depths of a tortured soul.

Bird became the basic improviser, the chorus man par excellence, interested more than anything in the flow of the lines he played. Parker made the nineteen-year-old trumpeter Miles Davis a member of his quintet—the man who was to become the dominant improviser of the next phase in modern jazz. Parker encouraged Davis, who had begun à la Gillespie and Parker, to find a style of his own.

Dizzy Gillespie's trumpet became the clearest, most clarionlike, and yet most flexible trumpet voice in the history of jazz. Almost every phrase he played was perfect.

Dizzy Gillespie became more and more interested in the percussive aspects of the new jazz. In the words of Billy Eckstine, "If you ever listen to Diz humming something, he hums the drum and bass part and everything because it all fits in with what he's doing. Like 'Oop-Bop-Sh'Bam.' That's a drum thing. And 'Salt Peanuts' was another. It was a drum lick."

Years later, when Parker was under contract to Norman Granz, he recorded with Machito's orchestra. But the results were hardly representative Bird. Parker's formula remained the quintet: the smallest instrumentation in which it was possible to create "form" through the unison statement of theme at beginning and end, while retaining complete improvisatory freedom for the remainder.

In Charlie Parker's words: "I'd be happy if what I played would simply be called 'music.' "

On another occasion, Charlie Parker said, "Life used to be so cruel to musicians, just the way it is today. They say that when Beethoven was on his deathbed he shook his fist at the world because they just didn't understand. Nobody in his own time ever really dug anything he wrote. But that's music."

In 1946 Charlie Parker had the first major breakdown of his life. It came during the recording of "Lover Man" at the Dial studios. When Charlie came home after the session, he started a fire in his hotel room and ran, naked and screaming, into the hall.

According to Orrin Keepnews, "There can be little doubt that he was a tortured man, and there are several who emphasize his loneliness." Often he would stay up all night, riding aimlessly around on the subway. As a

Dizzy was interested in Afro-Cuban rhythms. He played with musicians from the Cuban orchestra of Machito. In 1947 he added the Cuban drummer Chano Pozo to his band and thus brought a wealth of ancient West African rhythms and drum patterns into modern jazz.

To the question how the future of jazz would develop Gillespie answered, "Probably it will go back to where it all started from: a man beating a drum."

According to Leonard Feather, Dizzy Gillespie never took himself, or the music he created, as seriously as did the countless music lovers and musicians who have spent so much time investigating, discussing, and imitating everything.

Leonard Feather: "The other musicians who took part in the incubating process that evolved into bop today are dead, or struggling intermittently with the drug habit. Gillespie apparently has never suffered any major frustration or neurosis."

The more it became apparent that Dizzy could not keep his big band together permanently, the more consciously he became the comedian of his music. As the "clown of bebop" he attempted to sell that which other-

musician, on stage, he never developed the ability to "sell" himself and his music. He just stood there and played.

wise had proven itself unsaleable. He was not only the best trumpeter of bop but also one of its foremost vocalists. Always, he retained controlled superiority.

In the years 1948 to 1950, both Dizzy and Bird made recordings with large string ensembles—Bird in New York, Dizzy in California. This was to become the only major financial success of Parker's career. The fanatics among the fans beat their breasts: Bird and Dizzy had gone commercial. It was revealing how differently the two reacted:

Parker, for whom recording with strings was the fulfillment of a life long wish, and for whom the strings represented that aura of the symphony which he had always admired, suffered from the prejudiced judgment of the fans.

Gillespie, for whom the string recordings actually had meant not much more than another record date, made fun of the ignorance of those who talked about commercialism.

Charlie Parker was never satisfied with himself. He never knew how to answer the question of what recordings he thought to be his best. In answer to the question about his favorite musicians, a jazz man only came in third place: Duke Ellington. Before him came Brahms and Schöenberg; after him, Hindemith and Stravinsky. But more than any musician he loved Omar Khayyám, the Persian poet.

In 1954, at a birthday party for his wife, somebody fell over Dizzy's trumpet and bent the horn so that the bell pointed upward. "After his anger had subsided," Feather reported, "Dizzy tried to play the horn and found that the sound seemed to reach his ears better. . . . The next day he went to a trumpet manufacturer to ask whether he could put the idea into mass production." Dizzy wanted to take out a patent. But it was discovered that a similar instrument had been patented 150 years earlier.

Leonard Feather: "Charlie drank more and more in a desperate attempt to stay away from narcotics while still avoiding the terrors of sober reality."

At a time when there was hardly a musician playing anywhere in the world who was not in some degree or fashion under Bird's influence—

Dizzy Gillespie became the first "world statesman" of the international jazz tours organized by the U.S. State Department. With the help

when this influence had even penetrated into the world of dance and
pop music—Parker was only playing
occasionally. According to Orrin
Keepnews, "He had given up the
fight towards the end. In 1954 he
sent [his former wife] Doris a poem.
. . . in part it sets forth a credo that
might easily have been his own:
'Hear the Words! Not the doctrine.
Hear the speech! Not the meaning.
. . . Death is an imminent thing. . . .
My fire is unquenchable.' "

On March 12, 1955, he died. He had
been watching television, laughing
at a joke on "The Tommy Dorsey
Show."

The Parker myth began almost immediately. Among those who paid
him tribute was disc jockey Al
"Jazzbo" Collins: "I don't believe
that in the whole history of jazz
there was a musician more recognized and less understood than he."

"Bird Lives!" This is still true to-
day—and especially today again. In
the seventies, all the important al-
toists were shaped directly by Park-
er: Ornette Coleman, Phil Woods,
Lee Konitz, Charlie Mariano, Sonny
Stitt, Gary Bartz, Jackie McLean,
Frank Strozier, Cannonball Adderley,
Charles McPherson, Anthony
Braxton, Oliver Lake, Richie Cole,
Arthur Blythe, Paquito D'Rivera,
Christopher Hollyday, Greg Osby;
Steve Coleman.

of funds from Washington, he managed to put together a big band
again. He went on worldwide
tours—first to Asia and southeastern
Europe, later to Latin America. In
Athens he gave the most triumphant
concert of his career at the height of
the Cyprian crisis of 1956. The
Greeks were furious at the Americans. The headlines in the newspa-
pers asked why the Americans were
sending a bunch of jazz musicians
instead of guns to chase the British
out of Cyprus. Dizzy's concert began
in a very tense atmosphere. But
when the four white and nine black
musicians swung into Dizzy's "Tour
de Force," written shortly before the
tour, the audience broke into wild
applause. All Athens was filled with
enthusiasm over the Gillespie band,
and the political climate changed so
markedly that a newspaper stated,
"Dizzy Gillespie is a better diplomat
than all the diplomats the U.S.A. ever
had in this part of the world."

More than anyone else, Dizzy has
carried the bop idiom through all
subsequent styles and ways of playing: cool and hard bop, free, and
rock-influenced—and yet, he remained unmistakably Dizzy Gillespie.

For the young audience of the seventies and eighties, he stands right next
to Louis Armstrong. This audience
does not realize any more—and justifiably—that John Birks Gillespie
once had begun as Satchmo's antipode.

The new bebop had become a major style at the end of the seventies and enjoyed even greater influence by way of eighties classicism. Young musicians are now playing Charlie Parker's compositions more frequently than in the twenty-five years since his death. And the bebop renaissance in the form of innumerable reissues of Parker's recordings was reinspired at the end of the eighties by Clint Eastwood's movie *Bird,* which vividly and sensitively presents the musician's life.

Miles Davis

"Don't we have to admit" asked André Hodeir as early as 1956, "that the only complete aesthetic achievements since the great period of Parker and Gillespie belong to Miles Davis?" And the British critic Michael James stated, "It is no exaggeration to say that never before in jazz had the phenomenon of loneliness been examined in so intransigent a manner [as by Miles Davis]."

Our first quotation establishes the historical situation of Davis' music, the second its aesthetic situation. Both are contained, at least up to the beginning of the seventies, in the sound with which he blows. His tone—one of great purity, full of softness, almost without vibrato or attack—represents an image of the world; in each sound of Miles this image is contained.

The sound of Miles Davis is the sound of sadness and resignation. Sadness and resignation, paired with an unconditional, less musical than personal protest, exist independently of whatever else Miles has to say. No doubt he says many amusing, pleasant, and friendly things, but he says it all in this tone of sadness and resignation.

Arranger Gil Evans said, "Miles couldn't play like Louis [Armstrong] because the sound would interfere with his thoughts. Miles had to start with almost no sound and then develop one as he went along, a sound suitable for the ideas he wanted to express. He couldn't afford to trust those thoughts to an old means of expression. If you remember, his sound now is much more highly developed than it was at first."

Gil Evans is the man who translated the Miles Davis sound into orchestral terms. Evans arranged for the Claude Thornhill band during the forties, when Lee Konitz was in the band. He said, "At first, the sound of the band was almost a reduction to an inactivity of music, a stillness . . . everything was moving at a minimum speed . . . and was lowered to create a sound. The sound hung like a cloud."

When improviser Miles Davis and arranger Gil Evans met, it was one of the great moments in the history of jazz. The result was the Miles Davis Cool Band, (later referred to as the Capitol Orchestra) formed for a two-week engagement in September 1948 at the Royal Roost and actually in existence only for those two weeks. "The instrumentation," Evans recalled, "was caused by the fact that this was the smallest number of instruments that could get the sound and still express all the harmonies the Thornhill band used. Miles wanted to play his idiom with that kind of sound." This band consisted of Miles on trumpet, a trombone (J. Johnson or Kai Winding), two saxophones (Lee Konitz, alto; Gerry Mulligan, baritone), and, as sound factors, two instruments rarely used in jazz: French horn and tuba. In addition, there was a rhythm section of Al Haig or John Lewis on piano, Joe Shulman or Nelson Boyd on bass, and Max Roach or Kenny Clarke on drums.

Mulligan and Lewis also arranged for this group, but its sound was created by Evans in collaboration with Davis. Evans also arranged its two most significant pieces, "Boplicity" and "Moon Dreams." With these pieces, the texture of sound that became a model for the entire evolution of cool jazz was created. It was, of course, more than just the Thornhill sound with fewer instruments. It was a jazz sound; and if at all comparable to a cloud, the clouds were frequently pierced by rays of improvised sunshine, which struck the listener through the gentle veil of a fog.

The most "modern" piece recorded by this group was "Israel" by John Carisi, a trumpeter and student of the modern symphonic composer, German-born Stefan Wolpe, with whom many first-rate jazz musicians have studied. "Israel" is a minor blues, and characteristically this piece, whose harsh, brittle sounds opened new tonal horizons, remains indebted to the core of the jazz tradition: the blues.

This Davis Orchestra, recorded by Capitol in 1949 and 1950, was of a size between combo and big band. In 1957 Miles Davis went a step further. He recorded with a large orchestra, and naturally he asked Gil Evans—of whom little had been heard in the interim—to do the arrangements. "Gil," says Gerry Mulligan, "is the one arranger I've ever played with who can really notate a thing the way the soloist would blow it." And Miles himself said: "I haven't heard anyone that knocks me out as consistently as he does since Charlie Parker."

Gil put together a unique big band. There was no saxophone section, but in its place—alongside the conventional trumpets and trombones—there was a strange, unreal-sounding combination of French horns, tuba, alto saxophone, clarinet, bass clarinet, and flute. In some of the pieces—like "Miles Ahead," a theme by Miles Davis—Gil realizes a "continuation" of the Capitol Orchestra's sound; here it becomes apparent which big-band sound the old Capitol Orchestra aimed at: not the sound of Claude Thornhill in the late forties, but rather the sound of this Gil Evans-Miles Davis big band of 1957. It has consciously been stripped of every trace of heated attack. It is calm, lyrical, static—each climax planned way in advance. Broad lines are always preferred, in terms of melody as well as dynamics. But it moves above the old, swinging, pulsating rhythm, laid down by Paul Chambers, bass, and Art Taylor, drums.

Further climaxes in the Evans-Davis collaboration were reached with the album of Gershwin's music from *Porgy and Bess* (1958) and, above all, with the great *Sketches of Spain* (1959), incorporating Spanish, flamenco-conscious compositions. Here, too, Miles made a decisive contribution to a jazz tendency that since has steadily gained in importance: the opening up of jazz to world music.

There can be no doubt: Miles is an improviser. But he improvises out of a great feeling for arrangement and composition. Probably eighteen-year-old Miles, when he asked Dizzy Gillespie and Charlie Parker how to play right, took Dizzy's advice literally: "Learn to play the piano, man, and then you can figure out crazy solos of your own." Marshall Stearns, who tells of this, concluded, "It was the turning point in the playing of Miles Davis." This fits in with Evans' story of the Royal Roost engagement: "There was a sign outside: 'Arrangements by Gerry Mulligan, Gil Evans, and John Lewis.' Miles had it put in front; no one before had ever done that, given credit in that way to arrangers."

Until the mid-fifties, Miles had made his most beautiful recordings in quartets, accompanied only by a rhythm section, often with John Lewis or Horace Silver on the piano. Up to that time, he had never had lasting success with audiences. Then, at the 1955 Newport Festival, the turning point came.

All of a sudden, the name of Miles Davis—until then known only to informed fans and critics—could be heard everywhere. Since then success has never left. For the first time in jazz history, the best-paid and most successful musician of an era was not white, but black—Miles Davis. It is self-evident why Miles became the image-setter for a whole generation of black musicians, not only musically, but in terms of personality as well. Proud black parents—even in Africa—began to name their sons "Miles" or even "Miles Davis."

The quintets Miles Davis has led since then are of crucial importance. Two have been particularly praised. The first—with John Coltrane (tenor), Paul Chambers (bass), Red Garland (piano), and Philly Joe Jones (drums)—set standards for those that followed, indeed for all quintets in modern jazz between 1956 and 1970. After this quintet, which attained peaks of combo integration within hard bop between 1955 and 1957, even greater achievement seemed scarcely possible. But Miles Davis is an exception, so just a few years later he got together another quintet that was artistically the equal of the first and perhaps even more intensively integrated. This quintet stayed together from 1964 to 1968—longer than any other of Miles' groups—with young musicians at that time inspired by free jazz: Herbie Hancock (piano), Wayne Shorter (tenor saxophone), Ron Carter (bass), and Tony Williams (drums). People have rightly become used to calling this the "second" Miles Davis Quintet even though it came very much later in the chronology of Davis quintets. Both musically and in terms of the influence exerted and standards set, this group followed on from where the first quintet had stopped. The second Miles Davis Quintet was an important model for "acoustic" quintets in the seventies mainstream, and it was by far the chief source of inspiration for the groups involved in eighties classicism.

Another greatly influential Davis band was the *Kind of Blue* group (1959) with pianist Bill Evans. Here the new freedom just recently discovered by musicians like Mingus, Coltrane, Evans, and Miles himself for the first time became a group-integrating force, leading to a lyricism and sensitivity unknown in this kind of music until then. The history of over thirty years of jazz combos has been shaped by Miles Davis groups, indicating the extent to which Miles has influenced the development of modern jazz beyond the realm of the trumpet.

An important factor in Miles' great popularity also is his way of playing the muted trumpet—almost as if he were "breathing" into the microphone. The solo he recorded in this manner on Thelonious Monk's " 'Round Midnight" was particularly successful; the muted solo on "All of You" has been praised, especially by musicians, as one of the most beautiful jazz solos of the fifties. Even more than his open-horn playing, Miles' muted work makes it apparent that there is no definitive attack. No longer does the sound begin in one definite, clearly stated moment, as it does in traditional jazz and particularly with most other trumpeters. His sound begins in a moment that cannot be grasped; it seems to come out of nowhere, and it ends equally undefined. Without the listener quite knowing when, it fades into nothingness. And yet, as arranger Gil Evans has indicated, this sound, apparently so withdrawn and timid, contains an incisive intensity, a strength and presence in expression never attained by anyone else on the harmon mute (a stemless mute made from aluminum). Since Miles first used such a harmon mute for his "Oleo" in 1954, its employment has become so customary in jazz, rock, pop music, and even modern concert music that it must be stressed: Miles first made this sound popular.

Miles' muted trumpet playing close to the microphone showed early traces of two important aspects of his later work: first, his then developing feeling (in the mid-fifties!) that electronics are "the continuation of music by· other means"; and second, the unconditional striving for success he shares with Louis Armstrong, his true antipode. Miles' ambitions have often caused him to listen with special care to and absorb the music of successful players—in the mid-fifties (as Gunther Schuller has shown) to someone like pianist Ahmad Jamal, in the late sixties to Jimi Hendrix and Sly Stone, and in the eighties to Prince, Michael Jackson, and Cyndi Lauper.

But let's return to the fifties: Miles Davis is the most significant creative musician of a movement in jazz best defined as having applied the findings of bop to Lester Young. The basic difference between Young's music and that of Davis and his followers is that Miles plays with the knowledge that between himself and Lester there was bop. André Hodeir's remark, "Miles Davis is the only trumpeter who could give to Parker's music that intimate quality in which lies a considerable part of its charm," may be interpreted in this sense. The "intimate quality" is Lester Young.

This intimate quality is also found in the simplicity of Miles' playing. No other musician in jazz has developed simplicity with such refinement and sophistication. The basic contradiction between complexity and simplicity ceases to exist in Miles' playing. In his desire to play simply, Miles (since the second half of the fifties) tends to free his improvisations from the underlying structure of chord changes. He bases his solo work on "scales." About his big-band version of Gershwin's *Porgy and Bess,* Miles said, "When Gil wrote the arrangement of 'I Love You, Porgy,' he only wrote a scale for me to play. No chords. This gives you a lot more freedom and space to hear things." One of Miles' most influential compositions, "So What," is based in its first sixteen measures on a single scale; relieved in the bridge by another scale, it returns to the first scale for the final eight bars.

Miles, and with him John Coltrane, who then was in Davis' Quintet, made this method of improvisation based on scales standard practice for the whole jazz world, thus creating the last step required for the total freedom of free jazz. This is also referred to as "modal" improvisation. (See the section dealing with harmony.)

The simple phrases, often consisting of only a few notes, that Miles makes up on such "scales," have not only an aesthetic but also a practical basis. From an instrumental point of view the possibilities of Miles Davis, the trumpeter, are limited, especially when he is compared to his chief competitor among modern trumpeters, Dizzy Gillespie, a masterful musician who seems able to execute anything conceivable on his horn. If Miles wanted to maintain himself alongside Dizzy, to top him in popularity, he had to make a virtue of his instrumental limitations. Hence the cult of simplicity. Significantly, recording directors agree that Miles always selects for issue those takes from a record date that are instrumentally most perfect, though he may have played with more ideas and inspiration on others. Miles does not seem to want his record audience to know that there are frequent "clams" in his playing.

This "sophistication of simplicity" may be related to the fact that Miles—no matter how many avenues for new possibilities in jazz he may have opened—very often chose tradition when faced with a choice between it and avant-garde. He once complained that pianist Thelonious Monk was playing "wrong chords," though no doubt Monk's chords were not "wrong," but merely more abstract and modern than was suitable to Miles' conception at the time. Miles complained bitterly to the recording director who had hired Monk for a record date. The results, however—whether Miles likes it or not—were some of the most important and artistically successful recorded works of the fifties (Miles, Monk, and Milt Jackson on Prestige).

A further example of Miles Davis' traditionalism is the sharp words with which for years he assessed one of the most important members of the jazz avant-garde, the late Eric Dolphy—some of them insults that Davis had to retract in later years.

When an ultramodern fanatic once called Art Blakey "old-fashioned," Miles said, "If Art Blakey is old-fashioned, then I'm white." About the avant-garde of the sixties, he said, "What's so avant-garde? Lennie Tristano and Lee Konitz were creating ideas fifteen years ago that were stranger than any of these new things. But when they did it, it made sense."

Once, when tenor saxophonist Stan Getz was making some snide remarks about Coleman Hawkins being basically "old-fashioned," Davis rebuked him by pointing out that, if it weren't for Hawk, Getz probably would not be able to play as he did.

Often Miles makes harsh judgments—not only about outsiders (which would be understandable), but also about his colleagues. In a "Blindfold Test" with critic Leonard Feather, Davis voiced such gross insults in connection with many well-known jazz musicians that *Down Beat* magazine hesitated to spell out all his four-letter words. Reputable musicians like Clark Terry, Ellington, Dolphy, Jaki Byard, Cecil Taylor, and others were insulted by Davis at that time.

On the other hand, it must be seen that no other musician—with the exception of Charles Mingus, George Russell, and Dolphy—led the "tonal" jazz of the fifties closer and closer to the "free tonal" jazz of the sixties with such increasing consistency as Miles Davis. Justifiably, Dan Morgenstern calls Miles one of the "spiritual fathers" of the new jazz. In the mid-sixties, the members of the previously mentioned second quintet played "free" or almost free on their own records (mostly on the Blue Note label): Tony Williams (drums), Herbie Hancock (piano), Ron Carter (bass), and Wayne Shorter (tenor)—musicians discussed in the instrument sections. Only Miles himself avoided the final step across the border at that time. But the relevant fact remains that the free tonal musicians also admired him greatly and looked up to him as an example.

Davis' goal in this area of tension between traditionalism and avant-garde is not license, but rather controlled freedom. "Look, you don't need to think to play weird. That ain't no freedom. You need controlled freedom."

With this "controlled freedom," Miles Davis was diametrically opposed to many extreme avant-garde musicians of the sixties. But in the context of the new jazz of the seventies, and to an even greater extent, postmodern jazz since 1980, "controlled freedom" was the actual cue term—no longer just for Miles' music, but for a whole generation of young musicians continuing where Davis' electric jazz only seemingly leaves off.

In 1972, Japanese critic Shoichi Yui went so far as to speak of Davis as the "absolute apex of the development up to this point." He held that Davis is superior even to Louis Armstrong and Charlie Parker, each of whom dominated the jazz scene for only a few years, while Davis "has been the dominating personality from the end of the forties until today—longer than anybody else." Armstrong's influence, for instance, essentially originates in his playing during the period between his first Fletcher Henderson engagement in 1924, and his first visit to Europe in 1932. The period during which Charlie Parker made his most important recordings is even shorter: from the Dizzy Gillespie session with "Groovin' High" and Parker's first own session in 1945—when, among others, "Now's the Time" was created—to Norman Granz's session of 1951 with Miles Davis, when "K.C. Blues" was recorded—six years!

It is hard to say which is more admirable: the power with which a musician like Parker made a host of creative, new recordings within such a short timespan in a concentrated, explosive eruption, or the permanence with which Miles Davis, for a quarter of a century, has continued to set new signposts relevant to the majority of jazz musicians.

In order to be able to gain a perspective on this period of a quarter century, one should remember that Davis has basically gone through five different stylistic phases, including all the overlaps and interconnections that, of course, have existed between these phases:

1. Bebop: from playing with Charlie Parker in 1945 to 1948
2. Cool jazz: from the launching of the Miles Davis Capitol Orchestra in 1948 to the big-band recordings with Gil Evans in 1957–58
3. Hard bop: from the success of the first Davis quintet with John Coltrane in 1955 , via the many subsequent Davis quintets and the sextet with Bill Evans, to 1963 (during this period, an increasingly clear tendency toward modal improvisation)
4. Controlled freedom: The second Miles Davis quintet (1964–68) abstracted modal playing so that it almost became free jazz without Miles ever completely crossing the dividing line.
5. Electric: from *In a Silent Way* (1969) and *Bitches Brew* (1970) by way of the pared-down funk of *We Want Miles* (1982) to the pop Miles of *You're under Arrest* (1985), *Amandla* (1989), until today.

The term *electric jazz* aptly characterizes the music Davis has been making since *Bitches Brew,* incorporating electronic sounds. Records like

Jack Johnson and *Live Evil* also belong to this movement, with such musicians as saxophonist Wayne Shorter and British guitarist John McLaughlin, and, above all, with the collective sound of different pianists playing electric instruments. Among the latter are such players as Chick Corea, Larry Young, Herbie Hancock, Keith Jarrett, the Brazilian Hermeto Pascoal, and the transplanted Viennese Joe Zawinul, who has played a special role in this phase of Davis' work. Miles began to electrify his music after he had heard Joe Zawinul playing the electric piano in Cannonball Adderley's hit "Mercy, Mercy, Mercy."

Even more important, however, were the impulses given by rock musicians Jimi Hendrix and Sly Stone. Filled with self-assurance, Miles declared that he could form a better rock group than even Jimi Hendrix.

Miles' change-over from "acoustic" to electric jazz didn't occur all of a sudden; it was the outcome of a prolonged, cautious process of feeling his way and experimenting, leading to innumerable studio sessions between 1967 and 1970. Canadian jazz critic Jack Chambers makes clear that most of these recordings have remained unissued up to the present day.

Davis' circumspect and highly cautious approach to this transition suffices to refute the critical charge that with his 1970 *Bitches Brew* he had simply jumped onto a fashionable bandwagon. Miles is not an unconditional innovator. The fact that he puts off and holds back from stylistic changes until they finally become unavoidable accords with his basically conservative nature. "Do you know why I don't play ballads any more?" Miles asked pianist Keith Jarrett at the start of the seventies. "It's because I love to play them so much."

What is interesting is the fact that Miles Davis' music (which after *In a Silent Way* corresponded to its title) became more and more percussive, particularly after he hired the percussion player Mtume, a man inspired by African music. Davis paid tribute to the opening of jazz to world music by using Indian instruments like the sitar and tabla drums.

Miles now played trumpet with a wah-wah pedal and through an amplifier. In most cases, the pure, clear, "lonely," always somewhat sad sound of the earlier Miles is hardly recognizable. But Miles was reaching a youthful mass audience—something no black jazz musician since Louis Armstrong had accomplished. He explored the wah-wah pedal to the limits of its technical and musical possibilities. No one who plays an electrically amplified trumpet today can do so without referring to Miles' results.

Davis, the electric trumpeter, has sometimes been accused of breaching jazz tradition. In fact his use of the wah-wah pedal brings the jazz trumpet full circle. This electronic equipment was originally devised to allow electric guitar players to achieve effects corresponding to the wah-wah sounds—the rough growl and muted effects—of brass. Miles' use of the wah-wah pedal was nothing but a return to the jungle sounds of Ellington trumpeters Bubber Miley and Cootie Williams, of course modified and transformed into the electronic age's awareness of sound.

The electrifying success of the "electronic Miles" led to a point when the world of rock and popular music wanted to seize upon Miles Davis. In the summer of 1970, when he was supposed to play with rock musicians like Eric Clapton and Jack Bruce at the Randall's Island Festival in New York, Miles had music people all over the world holding their breath for several weeks, but then he said no; he wouldn't play except with his own group. "I don't want to be a white man. Rock is a white man's word."

Miles Davis had the same kind of leadership position in the jazz scene of the early seventies as Louis Armstrong or Charlie Parker had during earlier jazz periods. But he does not play his role with Satchmo's natural ease. Miles, exactly like Armstrong, wants to "make it" with a large audience. But he reflects the pride, self-assurance, and determination to protest that is characteristic of today's black generation. He plays "black music," but he must also acknowledge the fact that his audience—the buyers of his records and the listeners at his concerts—is mainly white. In a revealing interview with Michael Watts of the London publication *Melody Maker,* Miles said, "I don't care who buys the records as long as they get to the black people so I will be remembered when I die. I'm not playing for any white people, man. I wanna hear a black guy say, 'Yeah, I dig Miles Davis.' "

The cover of Miles' album *On the Corner,* for instance, consciously aims—according to the trumpeter's express wishes—at the black market: a comic-strip-style display of a group of dancing, "hip" street blacks, with slogans like "Vote Miles" and "Free Me" on their shirts and hats.

Again and again, he has said to dozens of critics and reporters, "I just do what I feel like doing." If a man says something like that too often, he obviously has a reason for saying it—he does *not* simply do what he feels like. Miles asked the above-mentioned reporter Michael Watts how long he had waited before deciding to ring his doorbell. And then, Miles was noticeably eager for Watts to take a grand tour of his "rococo house" and enjoyed that his visitor was astonished and impressed by the luxury with which Davis surrounds himself.

Miles Davis mirrors himself in his surroundings and his audience, and he needs this mirror. This is his dilemma: The whites mirror him, but he wants to be heard by the blacks. He may curse at the whites, but he can depend on their applause more than on that of the blacks.

The fact that Miles frequently played with his back to the audience certainly also has to do with that. Miles said, "What should I do? Smile at 'em?" And then comes the sentence that reappears so often: "I just do what I feel like doing."

Any man with so many complexes, so split within himself, must truly have charisma to be successful. Davis' charisma often takes astounding forms. Miles has been involved in violent public encounters twice. Once, gangsters shot at him when he was sitting with a woman in his parked car in Brooklyn. Miles set a reward of $10,000 for the capture of the two assailants. Nobody collected the reward, but a few weeks later the two gangsters were mysteriously shot.

Several years earlier, Miles was standing in front of the Birdland club on Broadway, when a white policeman asked him to move on, then hit him over the head with a club. "The cop was killed, too. In a subway," Miles claimed.

Miles Davis is a devoted sports car fan. In 1972, he broke both ankles in an accident. Since then, and especially after hip surgery some time later, he rarely appeared in public. This retreat into seclusion certainly involves musical and psychological as well as medical reasons. Miles wants to be "the greatest," not just because he's become used to that but because this aspiration is the mainspring of his musical and personal development. In the mid-seventies Miles' music had become so ornate and disoriented that he could no longer be sure of his preeminence.

After 1972, Miles' music became ever denser, more African and percussive: a cooking, seething cosmos of exploding rhythms and sounds in which every player sounded like a huge electronically amplified percussion instrument. Amid such extreme density hardly any space remained for the unique Miles Davis radiance, and he played his trumpet less and less. Everything in Miles' music from 1972 pointed toward a withdrawal, and yet the shock impact was considerable when in 1975 he quit the scene for six years. It wasn't just coincidental that this period of silence was also the time when fusion and jazz-rock stagnated most strikingly.

"Let's all just *forget* about Miles Davis, huh?" wrote an irritated *Down Beat* reader in 1980 when there were innumerable rumors about the possibility of the trumpeter's comeback. "I'm so sick and tired of readers bitching and moaning about his lack of new recordings and his apparent disdain for his audience. . . . Miles is not a god." Yet Miles was treated like a god when, after six years of expectation and speculation, he finally made his comeback at the 1981 New York Jazz Festival. He played great music, driving his group of predominantly young musicians to a climax of glowing, incandescent beauty. He blew more and better trumpet, without distancing electronic equipment, than in the years before his withdrawal. At last it was there again: the warm, dark Davis glow—simultaneously triumphant and resigned.

Stylistically there was nothing new. Miles Davis still played jazz-rock and fusion, stimulated, it's true, by eighties funk rhythms and pop sounds, but time and again interwoven with flashbacks: from the early fusion Miles back by way of the *Sketches of Spain* phase at the end of the fifties to the blues

Miles of cool jazz and hard bop. It was obvious that Miles had lived in such isolation that he was unaware of how much had in the meantime changed through such manifestations as noise music, free funk, and world music.

The jazz world expected something superhuman from Miles. He has changed the course of jazz three times, and it isn't fair to demand that he should do so once again. Miles has done enough.

Jazz-rock at last regained quality through Miles' comeback. It was Miles who reestablished line and a sense of proportion in this music, which from the second half of the seventies had become increasingly overloaded and bombastic, pleasing its followers by flaunting instrumental virtuosity. Now at long last Miles also applied his principle of simplicity to jazz-rock, removing an excess of riffs and stereotyped phrasing, in strikingly similar fashion to his modal phase at the end of the fifties when he freed jazz of a tangle of dense chordal interrelationships. Miles is not only jazz-rock's outstanding father figure; he's also its most convincing reformer.

The high points in this phase of economically played jazz-rock occurred between 1980 and 1985. During that period he produced, in pure and undistorted fashion, what was constantly promised but never really delivered in his music of the seventies: thrillingly played, vital, gripping, crisp funk. Of importance here were his various groups with drummer Al Foster (who had already played with Miles in the seventies), electric bassist Marcus Miller, and later guitarist John Scofield. They in particular concentrated funk on the essentials, exerting an enormously passionate, gripping, and concentrated impact. Two albums—*We Want Miles* (1982) and *Decoy* (1984)—were climaxes in this pared-down, economically-played funk. They set standards for group cohesion—a virtue by no means taken for granted in jazz-rock up to that time. Miles' view became a leading principle in eighties jazz-rock: "It must be a team."

Since 1984, Miles' music has been increasingly influenced by pop. He may have found inspiration in eighties pop music—Michael Jackson, Ashford & Simpson, and above all Prince—since his comeback, but it was in 1984 that Miles started to take over pop hits (including Michael Jackson's "Human Nature" and Cyndi Lauper's "Time after Time"), playing them almost literally, which didn't exactly please jazz fans. The more he turned toward the song forms of contemporary popular music, the more obviously he put his concept of lean, collectively improvised jazz-rock on the back burner.

As early as the fifties Miles had taken up popular songs and integrated them into his jazz repertoire. "My Funny Valentine" and "Autumn Leaves" were nothing but pop songs at the time, but critics have rightly shown that Davis cultivated them through the brilliant flights of his improvisations, thereby elevating them to new levels of quality. But in the eighties it seemed as if he were merely copying pop hits note for note. Miles was said to have lost his ability to make something artistically worthwhile out of the simple songs of pop music.

Yet there's no doubt that through expressive power alone, through a sound that is both lonely and triumphant, Miles does make something new out of these songs. Pianist Keith Jarrett says that Miles' achievement consists of the fact that "sound itself can say as much, if not more, than a lot of phrases." Anyone who from the sound of a single note can create the expressiveness for which others require torrents of notes doesn't need to resort to digressive improvisation. It is in those very terms that the pop Miles of the eighties must be assessed. Trombonist Jay Jay Johnson: "Miles is doing his natural thing. He's putting it in today's setting, on his own terms. If you put Miles and his new group in the studio and record them on separate mikes, and then you cut the band track and you just played the trumpet track, you know what you'd have? The same old Miles. What's new is the frame of reference."

In the eighties Miles Davis was closer to Louis Armstrong than ever before. He started his career soundwise as an antipode to Satchmo, but he seemed to want to end it as Armstrong's fellow, both humanly and communicatively. Both have broken through the division between jazz and pop, showing the way ahead. Just as Satchmo once filled the songs and hits of popular music with jazz feeling, so too does Miles Davis breathe life into pop music.

As a soloist the Miles of the eighties experienced peaks and valleys in close proximity. There were moments when his playing attained moving splendor and dazzling greatness as in "Back Seat Betty" (1982), a textbook example of how a solo should be developed in jazz-rock, or—even more impressively—in a blues ("It Gets Better," 1983) where Miles blows an enthralling long solo that sparked off a renaissance for slowly played blues in contemporary jazz. But you couldn't help hearing when Miles' playing was off form, and the fragility of his intonation was sometimes so obvious that only Davis' phenomenal sound spared him of what would have happened to other trumpeters in similar circumstances.

More important than the soloist in the eighties was Miles Davis the orchestrator and catalyst of groups. He possesses the rare gift of achieving extraordinary cohesion among a band, charging it with human and musical intensity without having to give special instructions. All the musicians who have played in his bands are astonishingly unanimous that Miles' presence is so strong that it alone is sufficient to release powers and abilities no one, least of all themselves, ever thought they had.

Miles also started playing a synthesizer more often in the eighties, but less as an autonomous instrument than as an extension of his own trumpet sound. "The synthesizer sound for trumpet is a white trumpet player's sound. Not my sound, not Louis' sound, or Dizzy's sound—a white trumpet sound. . . . And the only way I can play it is to play over it with my trumpet."

Miles' combined synthesizer/trumpet playing contributed much to the recognition that electronic instruments are most convincing when they are enriched and vitalized with "natural" sounds. That can be taken literally. With his trumpet Miles breathed life into the cold synthesizer sound.

When Miles played both instruments simultaneously—the synthesizer with his left hand and the trumpet with the right—his playing attained a striking and powerful chordal quality, inspiring or correcting his group, just like Duke Ellington used to direct his orchestra from the piano.

The most striking aspect of this comeback, however, was that Miles Davis demonstrated fresh characteristics as a human being. To the astonishment of his listeners he now gave the audience a friendly wave. He made fun of himself on stage. He demonstratively hugged his musicians after a good solo. He's now so obliging toward jazz fans and journalists that hardly anyone would think that this used to be the reclusive, contemptuous Miles. "Yes," confessed Miles to journalist Cheryl McCall, "I'm an entertainer."

An American critic wrote in 1983, "Like Picasso when he ran out of ideas, Miles has taken to enjoying poking a little fun at himself." The eighties, however, showed that Miles has by no means run out of ideas, but today he's no longer subject to the compulsion of having to change things. To be sure, he still wants to be the greatest, but it's obvious that he's in no condition for that. Hence the self-irony, the parody, and the sly flashbacks at his concerts. Picasso wasn't harmed by such an ironically retrospective phase; in fact that testified to his dignity and maturity and also brought something new by way of humor. The same is true of Miles. His music in the first half of the eighties reinvested jazz-rock with quality. And no matter what melody is touched by Miles Davis' inimitable sound, the outcome seems splendid. "Miles is a champion," said drummer Max Roach. "Champs always come back."

"You want me to tell you where I was born—that old story?" Miles once responded when he was relatively young, in the fifties. "It was in good old Alton, Illinois, in 1926. I had to call my mother a week before my last birthday and ask her how old I would be.

"There was a very good instructor in town. He was having some dental work done by my father. . . . 'Play without any vibrato,' he used to tell us. 'You're going to get old anyway and start shaking.'. . .That's how I tried to play—fast and light, and no vibrato.

"By the time I was sixteen . . . Sonny Stitt came to town with a band and heard me play. He told me: 'You look like a man named Charlie Parker and you play like him, too. Come with us.'

"The fellows in his band had their hair slicked down, they wore tuxedos, and they offered me sixty whole dollars a week to play with them. I went

home and asked my mother if I could go with them. She said no, I had to
finish my last year of high school. I didn't talk to her for two weeks. And I
didn't go with the band, either.

"I knew about Charlie Parker in St. Louis—I even played with him there,
while I was still in high school. We always used to try to play like Diz and
Charlie Parker.

"When we heard that they were coming to town, my friend and I were the
first people in the hall, me with a trumpet under my arm. Diz walked up to
me and said, 'Kid, you have a union card?' I said, 'Sure.' So I sat in with the
band that night. I couldn't read a thing from listening to Diz and Bird.

"Then the third trumpet man got sick. I knew the book because I loved
the music so much I knew the third part by heart. So I played with the band
for a couple of weeks. I just *had* to go to New York then.

"A friend of mine was studying at Juilliard, so I decided to go there, too. I
spent my first week in New York and my first month's allowance looking for
Charlie Parker.

"I roomed with Charlie Parker for a year. I used to follow him around,
down to 52nd Street where he used to play. Then he'd get me to play. 'Don't
be afraid,' he'd tell me, 'Go ahead and play.'

"You know, if you can hear a note, you can play it. The note I hit that
sounds high, that's the only one I can play right then—the only note I can
think of to play that would fit. You don't learn to play the blues. You just play.

"Would I rather compose or play? I can't answer that. There's a certain
feeling you get from playing, but never from writing, and when you're
playing it's like composing, anyway."

John Coltrane and Ornette Coleman

The jazz of the sixties—and then of the seventies and eighties—is
dominated by two towering personalities: John Coltrane, who died quite
unexpectedly in July 1967, and Ornette Coleman. One must appreciate the
difference between these two in order to realize the extent of their
influence and appreciate the scope of the expressive possibilities of the new
jazz. Neither man is a revolutionary, and if the effect of their work
nevertheless was such, this was not their wish. Both came from the South:
Coleman was born in Texas in 1930, Coltrane in North Carolina in 1926.
Both are solidly rooted in the blues tradition: Coleman more in the country
tradition of the folk blues, Coltrane more in the urban rhythm and blues
tradition.

Coltrane had a relatively solid musical education within the limits
possible for a member of the black lower middle class (his father was a
tailor). Coleman's parents were too poor to be able to afford music lessons
for him; Ornette acquired his musical tools on his own. No one told him that

a saxophone is notated differently than it is tuned. So, at the age of fourteen to fifteen—a crucial phase in his development—he played everything written "wrong" in the academic sense. Critic Martin Williams takes this to be a decisive reason for the harmonic uniqueness Coleman displayed from the start.

Whenever young Ornette played, he made a kind of music whose harmonies, sound, and instrumental technique could be placed only with difficulty within the conventional framework of jazz, blues, and rhythm and blues—that is, within the musics to which he related most in terms of style, inclination, expression, and origins. He remembered, "Most musicians didn't take to me; they said I didn't know the changes and was out of tune." He said about one of his first leaders, singer-guitarist Pee Wee Crayton, to whose rhythm and blues band he belonged, "He didn't understand what I was trying to do, and it got so he was paying me not to play." Nightclub owner and bassist Howard Rumsey recalled, "Everybody—the musicians, I mean— would panic when you'd mention Ornette. People would laugh when his name was brought up." This is placed in correct perspective if we remember that Lester Young in the Fletcher Henderson band and young Charlie Parker in Kansas City triggered similar reactions.

In contrast, Coltrane—or, as he was called, "Trane"—was accepted from the start. His first professional job was in 1947 with the Joe Webb rhythm and blues band from Indianapolis, with singer Big Maybelle. After that, he played mainly in better-known groups, mostly for lengthy periods: Eddie "Cleanhead" Vinson (1947–48), Dizzy Gillespie (1949–51), Earl Bostic (1952–53), Johnny Hodges (1953–54), until, in 1955, Miles Davis hired him for his quintet and he gained immediate fame with his solo on "Round about Midnight." It must be clearly understood: He was accepted and successful within the jazz that was accepted and successful at the time.

Ornette Coleman's emergence, however, came as a shock. He had to take work as an elevator operator in Los Angeles because the musicians would not accept him. Since his elevator was seldom in demand, he would stop it on the top floor and study his harmony books. Then, in 1958–59, producer Lester Koenig recorded the first two Coleman albums for his Contemporary label: *Something Else: The Music of Ornette Coleman* and *Tomorrow Is the Question.* A few months later, Coleman attended the Lenox School of Jazz. Many famous musicians were teaching there: Milt Jackson, Max Roach, Bill Russo, Gunther Schuller, John Lewis. Yet, after a few days of the summer courses, the unknown student Ornette Coleman had attracted more attention than all the famous teachers.

Right away, John Lewis decided that "Ornette Coleman is doing the only really new thing in jazz since the innovations of Dizzy Gillespie and Charlie Parker in the forties and since Thelonious Monk." The leader of the Modern

Jazz Quartet described the way Coleman played on his plastic alto with his friend Don Cherry, who used a miniature trumpet, as follows: "They're almost like twins. . . . I can't imagine how they manage to start together. Never before have I heard that kind of ensemble playing."

Although Coleman was not at all trying to bring about a musical revolution—he always only wanted to make his own music, and otherwise be left alone—there was suddenly the feeling in the jazz world of 1959 that this was a turning point, that a new style was beginning with Ornette Coleman: "He is the new Bird!"

The harmonic freedom characteristic of all the music played and composed by Coleman has been particularly well described by George Russell: "Ornette seems to depend mostly on the overall tonality of the song as a point of departure for melody. By this I don't mean the key the music might be in. . . . I mean that the melody and the chords of his compositions have an overall sound which Ornette seems to use as a point of departure. This approach liberates the improviser to sing his own song, really, without having to meet the deadline of any particular chord." Ornette himself feels that the rules of a music must be found within the musician himself rather than being based on harmonic principles imposed from outside. "When you get up on the morning, you have to put your clothes on before you can go out and get on with your day. But your clothes don't tell you where to go; they go where you go. A melody is like your clothes."

He called this his "harmolodic system": each harmony is, as this name suggests, established only by the melodic line. The system has influenced many other jazz musicians, such as guitarist James "Blood" Ulmer, and also the teaching at the Creative Music Studio of German-born vibraharpist Karl Berger, in Woodstock, New York.

The harmonic freedom that Coleman had achieved from the start in a manner self-evident to him, John Coltrane had to struggle for in a slow, laborious development spanning an entire decade: from the first cautious attempts at "modality" with Miles Davis in 1956 to *Ascension* in 1965.

It is a fascinating, exciting "adventure in jazz" to follow this development by way of records. In the beginning stands the encounter with Miles Davis and modality. That means: No more improvisation on constantly changing chords, but rather on a "scale" that, unchangingly, underlies the whole melodic activity. It was a first step into freedom. In spite of the tense, aware attention with which the jazz world was observing this development in all its phases, it was never made clear precisely whether Davis or Coltrane had taken the first step. This is fitting, because the step was not taken consciously. It "happened"—as something does that is "in the air."

The second phase, beginning in 1957, was the collaboration with Thelonious Monk (though Trane returned to Miles after that; only in 1960 did he permanently separate from him). Coltrane himself was best qualified to discuss Monk: "Sometimes he would be playing a different set of altered changes from those that I'd be playing, and neither one of us would be playing the changes to the tune. We would reach a certain spot and if we got there together we'd be lucky. And then Monk would come back in to save everybody. A lot of people used to ask us how we remembered all that stuff, but we weren't remembering so much. Just the basic changes and everybody tried anything they wanted to."

It was around this time that Coltrane developed what Ira Gitler named "sheets of sounds," creating the impression of metallic, glassy, crashing, colliding "sheets" of sound. This was best described by LeRoi Jones (now Amiri Baraka): "That is, the notes that Trane was playing in the solo became more than just one note following another. The notes came so fast, and with so many overtones and undertones, that they had the effect of a piano player striking chords rapidly but somehow articulating separately each note in the chord, and its vibrating subtones."

Many of the recordings that Coltrane made in the second half of the fifties for Blue Note or Prestige are exemplary for this way of playing—on Prestige, for example, with the Red Garland Trio; on Blue Note, for instance, *Blue Train*. The critic John S. Wilson wrote that "he often plays his tenor sax as if he were determined to blow it apart." In *Jazz Review,* Zita Carno coined that often-quoted sentence: "The only thing you can, and should expect from John Coltrane is the unexpected." It is one of the few statements about Coltrane that are equally true about all his stages.

The critics at that time overlooked a fact musicians probably felt instinctively—that the sheets of sounds had an immediate rhythmic effect that was at least as important as the harmonic effect: If the notes were no longer definable as eighths, sixteenths, or thirty-seconds, becoming more like quintuplets, septuplets, and nonuplets, then the symmetry of the relationship to the underlying meter was gone, too. The sheets of sounds, therefore, were a step toward substituting for the simple regularity of the conventional beat the flowing, vibrating quality of the pulse—a conception that Elvin Jones, starting in 1960, arrived at in the Coltrane Quartet, and young Tony Williams, beginning in 1963, in the Miles Davis Quintet.

When Coltrane signed exclusively with Atlantic Records in 1960, the sheets of sounds soon moved into the background—although, until his death, Trane on many occasions proved that he had not lost the technical ability necessary to play them. Instead of "shreds of sounds" and sheets of sounds, there was a strong concentration on melody: long, widely curved lines that condensed and dissolved according to an immanent, nonapparent principle of tension and relaxation. One had the feeling that Coltrane first had to supply the harmonic and rhythmic prerequisites so that he could deal more exclusively with the musical dimension that interested him most—melody. It was Coltrane the melody man who for the first time had a real hit with a large audience—with "My Favorite Things," in its original version a somewhat simple-minded waltz from a Richard Rodgers musical. Coltrane played the piece on the soprano sax with the nasal sound of a zoukra (a kind of Arab oboe). From the constant, always just slightly altered repetition of the notes of the theme, he built an accelerating monotony previously unknown in jazz, but akin to aspects of Indian and Arabic musics.

Around this time, he claimed that Eastern and Asiatic music interested him, and he proved it a year later (1961) with *Olé Coltrane* (which is also inspired by Spanish-Moorish music) on the Atlantic label. After he had moved to the Impulse label, on the momentum of his success with *My Favorite Things,* he made further records of the same orientation: in *Africa Brass* (1961) he reflected his impressions of Arab music, and in *India* (1961), with the late Eric Dolphy on bass clarinet, of classical Indian music. Just how much he admired Indian music is shown by the fact that a few years later he named his second son Ravi—after Ravi Shankar, the great Indian sitar player.

It is certainly not presumptuous to believe that Coltrane—considering that conventional tonality, stemming from European music, had meanwhile been stretched almost to the breaking point—was searching for a kind of substitute (even in the sense of emotional security) in the modes of Indian and Arab musics.

From 1960 on, Coltrane led a quartet including—with occasional substitutions or additions—Elvin Jones (drums) and McCoy Tyner (piano). The bass spot changed several times—a sign of Coltrane's continually developing conception of the basic harmonic (and rhythmic) tasks of the bassist. From Steve Davis, he went first to Art Davis, then to Reggie Workman, and finally to Jimmy Garrison—the only musician whom Coltrane retained in his quartet until the end, even after the great change of 1965. Incidentally, Coltrane was fond of using two bassists.

This John Coltrane Quartet—with, above all, Jimmy Garrison—was a perfect group. It followed the intentions of its leader with marvelous empathy, up to the crucial change in 1965. At that point, Coltrane needed a totally "free" drummer—Rashied Ali—and an equally "free" pianist—he chose his wife, Alice Coltrane.

Before that, in 1964, a record was created that for many is the apex of Coltrane's work: *A Love Supreme*—a singular, great prayer of hymnic intensity. Coltrane wrote the lyrics himself: "Let us sing all songs to God to whom all praise is due. . . .I will do all I can to be worthy of Thee o Lord. . . . I thank You God. . . .Words, sounds, speech, men, memory, thoughts, fear and emotions—time—all related. . . .they all go back to God." At the end of this prayer appear the three words that most aptly characterize the music the quartet plays to these lyrics: "elation, elegance, exaltation."

An outsider may not have expected such religious testimony from the then most discussed modern jazz musician. But Coltrane, not unlike Duke Ellington, frequently dealt with religious matters during his varied career. He said that in 1957 he experienced, through the grace of God, "a spiritual awakening." And in 1962, he said, "I believe in all religions," to which LeRoi Jones commented that music for Trane was "a way into God."

Coltrane saw religion as a hymn of praise to the cosmos that is God, and to God who is the cosmos. The psalmlike monotony that builds whole movements of the four-part *Love Supreme* on a single chord, and in this manner seems to lead from nowhere to everywhere, is for him an expression of infinity as sound. In many records made after that, Coltrane again took up religious topics, for instance, in *Meditations.* "Father, Son, and Holy Ghost" and "Love"—religious love—are two of the movements on this album.

In the meantime, the culmination of a process that had been going on for years—at first unnoticed by the jazz public—and the real jazz surprise of the winter of 1964–65 had taken place: John Coltrane, personally and musically, had joined the New York avant-garde. In March 1965, he played at the New York Village Gate in a musically, as well as socially and racially, revealing Free Jazz concert of "New Black Music," produced as a benefit performance for LeRoi Jones' short-lived Black Arts Repertory Theatre-School.

On several records, Coltrane employed the star quality of his name to help young, little-known, uncompromising free-jazz musicians reach a wider audience. And recordings made by tenor saxophonist Archie Shepp at the Newport Jazz Festival of that year were coupled with a Coltrane performance on the Impulse label. This meant the decisive breakthrough for Shepp.

A few days before the Newport Festival, on June 28, 1965, *Ascension* was produced. This was Coltrane's first record to be tonally "free." Coltrane gathered almost all the important musicians of the New York avant-garde: three tenormen—Trane himself, Pharoah Sanders, and Archie Shepp; two trumpeters, Freddie Hubbard and Dewey Johnson; two altoists, John Tchicai and Marion Brown; two bassists, Art Davis and Jimmy Garrison; and McCoy Tyner on piano and Elvin Jones on drums. Marion Brown, attempting to describe the mad intensity of *Ascension,* which at the time seemed to strain the limits of the appreciable and physically tolerable, said, "You could use this record to heat up the apartment on those cold winter days." It is hymnlike, ecstatic music of the intensity of a forty-minute orgasm.

With *Ascension* Coltrane reached a harmonic freedom Coleman had achieved many years before. However, how much more overpowering, gripping, aggressive is the freedom of *Ascension!* It is what the title implies:

an ascension into heaven, from humanity to God, taking in both—the divine and the human, the whole cosmos.

Compared to that, Ornette's freedom seems lyrical, quiet, melodious. It is illuminating that the structure of *Ascension,* consciously or unconsciously, follows a structural scheme Coleman had used five years earlier on his record *Free Jazz* (Atlantic). (This was where that term, later applied to so much of the jazz of the sixties, appeared for the first time: on a 1961 album by Ornette Coleman!) It was a collective improvisation by a double quartet, in which the Coleman Quartet (Don Cherry, trumpet; Scott La Faro, bass; Billy Higgins, drums) faced another quartet (Eric Dolphy, bass clarinet; Freddie Hubbard, trumpet; Charlie Haden, bass; Ed Blackwell, drums). From the dense complexity of collective parts rubbing against each other, a solo emerged that led to another set of collective playing, from which was born—in precisely that sense: free solos born in painful labor—the next solo.

During the years when Coltrane underwent his dynamic development, breathlessly attended by the jazz world, things became relatively quiet for Ornette Coleman. For two years, he lived in nearly total seclusion in New York.

It has been said that he played so little then because he was unable to find work. But the opposite is true: he was showered with tempting offers but did not want to play in public. He was developing his music; he composed and learned to play two new instruments: trumpet and violin. He also worked on compositions for string quartet (which he gave Béle Bartók-like sounds) and for other chamber music ensembles—among them the score for Conrad Rooks' film *Chappaqua.* The director found himself wondering if he should use music "in itself so beautiful." Rooks commissioned a new score from Ravi Shankar and Ornette's *Chappaqua*—scored for Coleman's trio, Pharoah Sanders (tenor), and a chamber ensemble of eleven musicians—was released on record in Europe only.

In early 1965, Coleman reentered public life at the Village Vanguard. Only now was the album Coleman had recorded before his voluntary retirement (in 1962 at a concert at New York's Town hall) released (on ESP). Further Coleman records were made in Europe. It was the year when *A Love Supreme,* though not recorded then, was released as well as *Ascension*—perhaps the richest jazz year since Charlie Parker and Dizzy Gillespie made their great recordings during the forties.

It was also in 1965 that Coleman went on a European tour. It was a surprise to the jazz world that he, who had turned down all offers for years, now signed a contract—accepting Joachim Berendt's invitation to appear at the Berlin Jazz Days. He arrived with a trio consisting of himself, bassist David Izenzon, and drummer Charles Moffet. At the Berlin Sportpalast he scored such a terrific success that the man who had been expected to make the hit of the evening, Gerry Mulligan, had a fit of anger. In the Stockholm restaurant Gyllene Cirkeln, Ornette recorded two albums that soon appeared on Blue Note and are comparable in lyrical beauty to Coltrane's *A Love Supreme*. Swedish critic Ludwig Rasmusson wrote in the liner notes, "The content of his music is mostly pure beauty, a glittering, captivating, dizzying, sensual beauty. A couple of years ago nobody thought so, and everyone considered his music grotesque, filled with anguish and chaos. Now it is almost incomprehensible that one could have held such an opinion, as incomprehensible as the fact that one could object to Willem de Kooning's portraits of women or Samuel Beckett's absurdist plays. Thus Ornette Coleman has been able to change our entire concept of what is beautiful merely through the power of his personal vision. It is most beautiful when Coleman's bass player, David Izenzon, plays bowed bass with him. Then, it is almost hauntingly beautiful."

A comparison of Coleman's *At the Golden Circle* with Coltrane's *A Love Supreme* shows most clearly the basic difference between the two musicians: Coleman's quiet, naturally balanced, static character versus Coltrane's dynamic nature. Both play—in the simple, naive sense of the word—beautiful music. The music of both is immensely intense. But in Coltrane's music, the dynamic nature of the intensity ranges above the static quality of beauty. In Ornette Coleman's music, the reverse is true.

That is also why it is not surprising that almost all of Coltrane's recordings are conceived from the improvisatory point of view (including his compositions!) while in Coleman's work, composition ranks above improvisation. Coleman is first and foremost a composer. There is an illuminating story—critic John Tynan tells it—that Coleman, in Los Angeles in 1958, was at a point where he simply no longer knew how to make ends meet. Filled with despair, he went to record producer Lester Koenig and asked him to buy some of his compositions. Ornette did not ask for a recording date; he only wanted to sell his compositions. He believed that to be a more promising avenue; his first thought was that the compositions would be a way out. And Ornette's first recording on the Contemporary label was made only because Koenig asked him to play the compositions on the alto saxophone.

Later, when there were heated discussions in the jazz world about the pros and cons of Ornette Coleman's music for years, it became apparent that even the critics who rejected Ornette as an improviser recognized the beauty and competence of his compositions. Colemen the composer was accepted faster than Coleman the improviser. One of the main reasons why Coleman managed to withdraw from the jazz scene for two years was that his creative genius can be satisfied for long periods by composing alone.

More often than most other new musicians, he speaks of "tunes" or "songs": "If I play an F in a tune called 'Peace' I don't think it should sound the same as an F that is supposed to express sadness." The atmosphere of the composition, in other words, the way the composer felt it, determines the atmosphere of the improvisation—a way of thinking that had become rare in jazz after Lester Young.

The fact that Coleman taught himself to play trumpet and violin is also connected with the priority of the compositional element over the improvisational. His music is supposed to be a whole. He would prefer to play everything necessary to make his music into sound himself. In an interview, he once said that he wished he was able to record all the parts himself on multitrack.

One should judge the way Ornette plays his self-taught instruments in this light. Certainly he is a perfect instrumentalist only on the alto sax. But the crux of the matter is missed if one speaks of the amateurish nature of his violin and trumpet playing. The criteria for amateurishness refer back to the "professionalism" of academic music. Ornette, however, plays the violin left-handed and tunes it as if it were played right-handed; he does not bow it, but rather beats or fiddles it with unorthodox arm movements. He is not interested in the note he might generate, but rather in the sound he can gain from sounding as many strings as possible at once. What is left of the conventional violin when Coleman plays it is only its external shape. He plays it like an independent, newly discovered instrument. And he produces exactly those effects required for his compositions. There—and nowhere else—is where the criterion lies, and that criterion is met brilliantly by Ornette's violin playing. "I can't talk about technique because it is ever-changing. That's why for me the only method for playing any instrument is the range in which it is built. Learned technique is a law method. Natural technique is nature's method. And this is what makes music so beautiful to me. It has both, thank God."

Ornette Coleman is the master of an immense compactness. This became even clearer when he (finally!) found a horn partner with whom he really enjoyed playing: tenorman Dewey Redman. Through him, Coleman found his way back to quartet music. And two musicians who had already been connected with Ornette in his early days, bassist Charlie Haden (with whom he also made great duo recordings) and drummer Ed Blackwell, joined the new quartet. The latter comes from New Orleans, where Ornette so often played in his youth, and does with the rhythm and blues patterns of the South basically the same thing Ornette did with the Texas blues: he abstracts them.

Ornette has little knowledge of the conscious structuring of a composition or an improvisation. But almost everything he plays or composes seems to be cut from the same cloth. For that reason, Coleman's recorded pieces usually are significantly shorter than Coltrane's. Listening to Coltrane meant witnessing a laborious birth. Hearing Ornette means viewing the newborn creature.

Archie Shepp commented on this phenomenon:

One of the many things [Trane] accomplished was the breakthrough into the concept that a jazz musician need not—could not—be limited to a solo lasting a few minutes. Coltrane demonstrated that a man could play much longer, and that in fact it was an imperative of his conception to improvise at great length. I don't mean that he proved that a thirty- or forty-minute solo necessarily is better than a three-minute one. He did prove, however, that it was possible to create thirty or forty minutes of music, and in the process, he also showed the rest of us we had to have the stamina—in terms of imagination and physical preparedness—to sustain these long flights.

This indeed touches on one of the more superficial among critical opinions: that the great old musicians—King Oliver, Lester Young, Teddy Wilson—were able to express all they wanted in one or two choruses of sixteen or thirty-two bars, and that it simply indicates lack of conciseness that such contemporary musicians as Coltrane (and many others since him) play such lengthy solos. In fact, the older musicians recorded short solos because records at that time usually only afforded some three minutes of music. But when they were able to play the way they really wanted, in jam sessions or clubs, they preferred, even back then, to play relatively long solos. Great music—from European symphonies to the ragas and talas of India—requires time. Only the commercial Top 40 hit is satisfied with two or three minutes.

But back to Ornette Coleman. The playing of rubato ballads, of slow pieces in a free tempo (which has become so popular in contemporary jazz from Keith Jarrett by way of Pat Metheny to Shannon Jackson and others), derives from one single point: Ornette Coleman and his celebrated 1959 "Lonely Woman." His aspiration to make his music all by himself and the periods of withdrawal from the public eye certainly say something about his problems in dealing with the world around him. John Coltrane was a builder of groups. Ornette Coleman is alone. He is filled with a deep mistrust of society. To him, agents and managers automatically are people who want to cheat him. Almost all his managers were originally his friends, but as soon as Ornette would ask them to manage him, the friendship would quickly end. His mistrust, often unfounded, would create such unpleasant situations that soon there would be a reason for his suspiciousness.

In an interview with Dan Morgenstern he said:

As a black man, I have a tendency to want to know how certain principles and rights are arrived at. When this concern dominates my business relationships,

I'm cast into schizophrenic or paranoid thinking. . . . I do not wish to be exploited for not having the knowledge or know-how required for survival in today's America. It's gotten so that in your relationships to every system that has some sort of power, you have to pay to become part of that power, just in order to do what you want to do. This doesn't build a better world, but it does build more security for the power. Power makes purpose secondary."

It fits in with his problematic relationship to the world around him that Ornette Coleman is much more concerned with communicating with his audiences at concert or club appearances than, say, John Coltrane was. Occasionally, he appears in brightly colored outfits that seem more suited to a circus performer than to an avant-garde jazz musician. Then one can sense his roots in a world where jazz musicians were trained to be entertainers.

On the other hand, John Coltrane, who certainly had an even less outgoing personality that Ornette, dealt with the world around him with quiet self-assurance.

We believe Coleman's origin in Texas and the world of country blues cannot be overemphasized. For good reason he made his first records—as a sideman, of course—in the early fifties with blues singer Clarence Samuels (who had been with the Jay McShann Band, the orchestra in which Charlie Parker got his start). Elsewhere (in the free-jazz section), we have shown that Ornette's free harmonic conception is a direct result of the harmonic freedom Southern country and blues musicians have always had.

Tenorist Archie Shepp—one of the great musicians of the new jazz—said:

It was Coleman, who, in my opinion, revitalized and refurbished the blues idiom without destroying its simplistic milieu. Far from taking it beyond its original intentions, Coleman restored [the blues] to their free, classical [African] unharmonized beginnings. I have always felt that this early work of Ornette's was much closer to the "old thing"—hoedowns, foot-tappin'—than the new. Certainly Blind Lemon Jefferson and Huddie Leadbetter must have played thirteen, seventeen, twenty-five bar blues. Regardless; no pundit would have been foolish enough to label them avant-garde.

And critic A. B. Spellman said, "Ornette's music is nothing but the blues." Ornette is a total blues musician. And if conventional jazz includes only two—or rather, since the advent of bebop's flatted fifth, three—blue notes, it can be said that Coleman has turned the whole scale into blue notes. Almost all his notes are bent up or down, off-pitch, tied, flatted, or augmented—in short, vocalized in the blues sense. Remember his statement that an F in a tune called "Peace" should not sound the same as an F in a context that is supposed to express sadness? Precisely that is a blues musician's concept. And if, after years of conventional jazz, this concept is found astonishing—because all F's, whether concerned with peace, sadness, or whatever, simply must have the identical pitch—this merely illustrates the influence of the European tradition—an influence that Ornette eliminated, at least in this realm.

The ease with which Ornette deals with free tonality has been contrasted with Coltrane's immensely tense, complex relationship to it. This became clear when, right after *Ascension,* the album *Coltrane—Live at the Village Vanguard Again* was released. At this point, Coltrane could no longer play just with the musicians who'd been with him for so many years. He founded, as we have mentioned, a new group, a quintet, with Pharoah Sanders as a second tenor sax voice, Trane's wife Alice Coltrane on piano, drummer Rashied Ali, and, as the only holdover from the old quartet, bassist Jimmy Garrison. When Coltrane plays on this record well-known themes from his earlier recordings—*Naima* or *My Favorite Things*—one feels that he loved these themes and would have preferred to continue playing them as they appeared to him as themes, if only he would have been able to express within them everything he so much wanted to express! If John Coltrane had seen a possibility of reaching, by conventional means, the degree of ecstatic heat he was aiming for, he would have continued to play, "tonally," to the end.

Coltrane hesitated for a long time. For good reason Martin Williams once called him "the man in the middle." Trane needed ten years to take the step he finally took in 1965, and that a whole generation of musicians in this era took in one day. Anybody who hears the sermonlike, sublimely swinging lines of "Naima" understands: This musician mourned for tonality. He knew how much he had lost with it. And he would have loved to return to it, had he not, during these ten years, again and again run into the limitations of conventional tonality before having been able to express all that seemed necessary to him.

It was only for the sake of increased intensity that Coltrane hired a second tenorist. In terms of physical power and the ability to bring forth the wildest and most unbelievable sounds on his instrument, the man he chose was certainly, after Albert Ayler, the most amazing tenor player in the field: Pharoah Sanders. In interaction with him Coltrane became even more intense.

Coltrane totally exhausted himself in this process and had to cancel a European tour in the fall of 1966. That is why he began to need frequent recuperation breaks. Repeatedly, during such breaks friends would anticipate that this particular one would last a year or so. But just weeks later, Trane would be on the scene again, carrying on with the tearing, ecstatic power of his jazz and love hymns.

The liver ailment doctors determined as the cause of his death may merely have added the final blow to the complete exhaustion resulting from a life led ceaselessly at the edge of humanly possible intensity.

Again and again, he seemed to be totally drained of all energy after his concert appearances. He was like a relay runner: At a certain point, he would hand the torch to Pharoah Sanders, who then had to press forward—even *more* powerfully, intensely, and ecstatically, yet without the hymnlike power of love that radiated from Coltrane.

Tragically, there was one musician among the persons close to Coltrane who had—and still has—this power of love, but she was not able to express it musically, at least not on the high level associated with Trane. In 1967, when Trane died, she had not yet emerged clearly in the jazz world, but since then, she has become the purest and clearest successor and heir to the spiritual message of John Coltrane. This is his wife—pianist, harpist, organist, and composer Alice Coltrane—or, as she was known when vibraharpist Terry Gibbs introduced her in the early sixties, Alice McLeod; or, as she now calls herself in accordance with her religious conviction, Turiya Aparna.

For her record *Universal Consciousness,* Alice enlisted the cooperation of Ornette Coleman. Thus a circle closes. Ornette shaped, or at least essentially determined, a violin sound for Alice without equal among the numerous string experiments in modern jazz, purposely avoiding the standard aesthetics of beauty and homogeneity. The four violinists are from the most diverse schools: two from concert music, Julius Brand and Joan Kalisch; one a free-jazz man, Leroy Jenkins; and the fourth a soul musician, John Blair. These four, in pieces like "Oh Allah" and "Hare Krishna," play a dense texture of sounds that combines the complexity of avant-garde concert music with traditional jazz intensity, the spiritual power of John Coltrane with the tradition of bebop and blues.

Ornette Coleman loves violins. He admires (as did Charlie Parker twenty years earlier) the great tradition of European concert music. Again and again, he has presented compositions for symphony orchestra, chamber ensembles, and string quartets—most impressively in "Skies of America," recorded in 1972 by the London Symphony Orchestra conducted by David Measham. However, Ornette Coleman remains a jazz musician, even when composing for symphony orchestra. The symphony orchestra to him is an enlarged "horn" on which he improvises.

Ironically, Coleman's admiration for strings and the wealth of harmonics produced by the sound of a symphony orchestra was also the decisive factor that led to electrical amplification of his music from the mid-seventies. For Ornette "a guitar can sound like ten violins," so he logically equipped his groups with a choir of amplified guitars. In a process of increasing compression, he ultimately ended up with two bass and two electric guitars. The instrumentation alone made Ornette's music more and more rock-oriented. And it received an additional push toward funk when drummer Ronald Shannon Jackson joined the band in 1975. Never before was

Ornette's rhythm and blues background so profoundly apparent as in his eighties Prime Time band. His albums *Dancing in Your Head* (1977) and *Body Meta* launched free funk with a big bang (see the section on "From the Eighties to the Nineties").

In view of the static and formulalike rigidities of funk, which even in jazz-rock tended to block improvisation, Ornette's musical achievement can hardly be overrated. Ornette Coleman was the first to play collectively improvised funk with his groups. He opened up funk on all levels—melodic, rhythmic, harmonic—to free improvisation. Coleman makes funk communicative. By breaking with the static elements in this music he liberates it for interaction and group thinking.

Another striking aspect of Ornette's Prime Time bands was his return to the principle of doubling instruments, as first successfully applied in the 1960 *Free Jazz* album. This time, however, there were not two equal, opposing quartets, but two trios fulfilling different roles. While the first band (Calvin Weston, drums; Al Mac Dowell, electric bass; and Charles Ellerbee, guitar) provided a foundation of impetuously "free" funk rhythms, the other trio (Jamaaladeen Tacuma, electric bass; Bern Nix, electric guitar; and Denardo Coleman, drums) commented freely on those rhythms.

Those two levels collided with enormous power and energy in the Prime Time band's collective improvisations. Above this wildly and luridly pulsating bedrock of free melodies and cooking funk rhythms floated—outshining everything else—Ornette's alto playing, in which (as if in some huge, dazzling glass) all the band's complex lines combined as a single, songlike, glowing white beam.

Ornette's encounter with Berber musicians in Morocco in 1973 (documented in a piece on the *Dancing in Your Head* album) impressed him to such an extent that from then on he had his Prime Time band play in nontempered tuning, inspired by non-Western musical cultures. Ornette speaks of music in the so-called Third World as the only avant-garde left to our century. "Nontempered instruments can arouse an emotion that doesn't exist in Western music. I mean, European music is very beautiful, but the musicians that play it don't always get a chance of expressing it that way because they have spent most of their energy perfecting the unison of playing together by saying 'You're a little flat' or . . . 'a little sharp.'" It's obvious who makes his appearance behind this love for untempered non-Western music: Ornette Coleman, the blues musician.

Many critics have complained about the thunderous volume marking Ornette's Prime Time band. But there's no doubt that Ornette's free funk cannot be experienced without this immense loudness. For Ornette knows that high volume changes sound. It elevates aspects of the sound spectrum into the realm of the perceivable, making accessible previously inaudible regions of harmonics. It is precisely because Ornette's band plays up to the limits of physically bearable storms of sound that his music discovers new tonal and expressive possibilities with whirring, shimmering overtone melodies encasing his free funk in an irridiscent net. Since the Prime Time band plays in nontempered tuning and the instruments seem to be microintervallically "detuned" among themselves, these harmonics collide with the force of elementary particles, generating new series of partials through this process of friction like a melody playing itself in an unending sequence. Where sheer volume plays such an important role, recordings have hitherto provided incomplete documentation of Ornette's free funk.

Ornette's free funk seemed piercing, shrill, and deafening to the contemporary public. In fact, as also becomes obvious in his music today, Ornette Coleman is an absolute melodist. Even at the start of the sixties when he transformed jazz with enormous revolutionary energy, Ornette was much too much of a melodist to have sacrificed the beauty of a melodic line to the energetic power of "free" noise playing. The same is true of free funk. His improvisations signify nothing less than "beautiful" music—clear, singing, wonderfully balanced alto saxophone lines. It's among the great (and unfortunate) ironies of jazz history that one of black music's greatest melodists, of all people, shocked the jazz world with his trail-blazing changes. Ornette has twice decisively influenced the development of jazz. Both times he did so (also) as a grandiose melodist.

Ornette's theory of harmolodic music says that all musical elements—melody, harmony, rhythm, tempo, metre, and phrasing—should be equal, which seemingly contradicts what has just been said. The secret of Ornette's harmolodic music ultimately entails melodization of all the musical parameters. "Harmony, movement, rhythm—they can all become a melody," said Ornette.

While Ornette Coleman was blazing new trails in free funk, his alto sax playing attained "classical" status. When he recorded the *In All Languages* double album in 1987, that was programmatic in character. Ornette devoted an entire record to the music of the celebrated, reunited "classic" quartet (with Don Cherry, trumpet; Charlie Haden, bass; and Billy Higgins, drums), while on the other disk he played contemporary free funk with his Prime Time band. Ornette subtitled the album "30 Years of Harmolodic Music," often presenting interpretations of the same pieces by both bands—for instance, "Peace Warrior," "Space Church (Continuous Services)," and "Feet Music"—thus providing fascinating documentation of his music's unbroken development and continuity.

Song X, the album that many believe to mark the highpoint in Coleman's eighties music making, came out in 1986. Characteristically, this record was created in conjunction with another great jazz melodist, guitarist Pat

Metheny, who mainly employed a guitar synthesizer here. The two of them—joined by bassist Charlie Haden and two drummers, Jack DeJohnette and Denardo Coleman—made ravishing music. Ornette inspired Pat Metheney to play the wildest and most intense lines he has ever phrased. In pieces like "Endangered Species" and "Song X," Coleman himself discovered long, singing improvisations of raging beauty—more expansive and intense than with the Prime Time band, where he usually holds back somewhat so as not to disrupt group coherence. Ornette proudly compares the intensity and spirit of this album with John Coltrane's *Ascension.*

Coltrane's music has become even more vital in the years since his death, triggering developments everywhere, from rock to jazz, in the most diverse of transitional stages.

The hymnlike element prevalent on the entire contemporary jazz and rock scene comes from Coltrane, above all from *A Love Supreme.* When the Miles Davis influence subsided during the mid-seventies, it turned out that Coltrane was now the most intensively influential musician on the jazz scene. In fact, a "John Coltrane classicism" developed that is comparable to the Count Basie and Lester Young classicisms of earlier years.

The history of contemporary jazz since 1960 has been impressively and extensively shaped by the contrasting styles of these two musicians. In the sixties both exerted an equally intense influence, but the seventies were dominated by Coltrane. In the eighties it was exactly the other way round. Now Ornette Coleman was the outstanding figure, heading the scene. Following the law regulating the swing of the pendulum, another Coltrane renaissance could be expected in the nineties.

To his friends, Coltrane was a marked man, at least after *A Love Supreme.* He already knew back then that his sounds were shaping the jazz of his times, and he suffered from this responsibility. He saw himself too strongly as a ceaseless seeker to be able to enjoy the fact that the whole jazz world now praised each of his statements as "the last word."

In answer to the question whether there would ever be an end to the development that had already led him through a half dozen different ways of playing since the mid-fifties and the Miles Davis Quintet, Coltrane told Nat Hentoff, "You just keep going all the way, as deep as you can. You keep trying to get right down to the crux."

If Ornette Coleman is the phoenix whose music from the start was revealed to us—if not in its mature form, then at least in its basic conception—as if it had sprung from the head of Zeus, then Coltrane was a Sisyphus, who again and again—from the very bottom up to the mountaintop—had to roll the hard, cumbersome rock of knowledge. And perhaps, whenever Coltrane got to the top, Coleman would already be standing there in his resplendent circus suit, playing his beautiful melodies. But the music

John Coltrane would blow then, from the top of the mountain, standing next to Ornette, was imbued with the power of the pilgrim who had reached yet another station on the long, thorny road to knowledge (or might we better say, because it was Coltrane's conviction, to God), and who knew there were many more stations to come—though in the months of exhaustion preceding his death he no longer knew how to go on.

John McLaughlin

No single musician could represent the jazz of the seventies. Jazz has become too wide. McCoy Tyner, Keith Jarrett, Chick Corea, Joe Zawinul and Wayne Shorter, Herbie Hancock, Dexter Gordon, and others are all of equal stature. And above all, Miles Davis (especially during the first half of the decade) and John Coltrane (since the late seventies) are still dominating figures. Beyond them, the jazz scene is split—into acoustic jazz on the one hand, and electric jazz on the other—actually into many more subgroupings.

And yet, there is *one* musician of that decade (and beyond it also into the early eighties) who belongs to all these groupings. He has played blues and bebop and free and fusion, and, above all, he feels bound to electric as well as to acoustic music: John McLaughlin.

The following interview took place in John McLaughlin's Paris home. McLaughlin is among those contemporary musicians who are so articulate that the interviewer merely has to give the cues, so the questions are only included if they are necessary to an understanding of the context. Further information about McLaughlin can be found in the sections on the seventies, the guitar, and the combos of jazz.

JOHN MCLAUGHLIN: I was born in 1942 in a little village in Yorkshire. My father was an engineer; my mother used to be an amateur violinist. There was always a very good atmosphere towards music in the house, which I am eternally grateful for. Classical music. The Three B's: Beethoven, Bach, Brahms. When I was about nine, my mother sent me to have piano lessons. Later we moved up to Northumberland—close to the Scottish border. Every summer the Scottish bagpipe bands used to come. Sometimes they had six or seven bagpipes, with three or four drummers—they had great drummers. Swinging in their own way. They had a big effect on me.

When I was about ten, there was the beginning of the blues revolution in England. The blues started underground among the students. One of my brothers had a guitar. He taught me three chords, and from that day on, everything was decided. I completely fell in love with the guitar. I started listening to musicians like Muddy Waters, Big Bill Broonzy, Leadbelly. [While John said this, I saw that he still had records by these musicians in his library; they were just above the record player, so he apparently still plays them.—J. E. Berendt] So I had all this music just thrown at me. It was fantastic. Incredible.

When I was fifteen, I was able to take my guitar and a little amplifier and go to a pub on a Sunday night where they had a jazz club, and I would say, "Please let me play a tune with you." And they said, "OK, come in." And they would play some very fast tunes and they would burn me out completely, but it was a very good experience. I went home and I realized I still had much to learn.

Around that time I started to listen a lot to Django Reinhardt and Tal Farlow. They were my heroes on guitar. They still are. Maybe that's why I like violinists so much—because I loved Django and Stephane Grappelli.

When I was sixteen, I went on the road with a traditional jazz band called Professors of Ragtime. This got me to London—which, of course, was the center of jazz in England. In those days there were two clubs: the Marquee and the Flamingo. They were great. Everybody met everybody there, and the attitude was that everybody could play with everybody. So this is what I did. I remember jam sessions with everybody and anybody.

I remember the Rolling Stones coming in for an audition. I didn't care much for them. They were out of tune, and I didn't think they were swinging, but at least they were playing Muddy Waters' blues tunes.

I started to play with the Graham Bond Organisation and with Alexis Korner. Alexis had everybody in his band at some point. But Miles Davis' recordings with the Gil Evans big band really did it for me. Miles crystallized a new school of music, and I immediately felt, That is my school. But I kept on playing rhythm and blues and it was great, because they were playing real jazz solos. It was blues, but at the same time it was much more than blues.

I played with Eric Clapton and Dick Heckstall-Smith and Ginger Baker and everybody, but I now must talk about Graham Bond. He meant a lot to me. I had grown up in an ordinary school where the teacher taught religion in a very dry way. He did not understand what religion—and Christianity— really means. He was not a living Christian. I never went to church, but Graham Bond—God rest his soul—really was a seeker. He was interested in the invisible things in life. He introduced me to a book about ancient Egyptian culture, and I got very interested in this because, for the first time in my life, I realized that a human being is much more than meets the eye. Later, I discovered a book by Ramana Maharshi, and the first thing I saw was a photo of Ramana Maharshi, and this was the first picture of someone I could consider to be enlightened—an enlightened human being, and it meant very much to me. I began to realize that India as a culture and as a nation has treasures waiting to be discovered.

At this time I was friends with a guitar player by the name of Jim Sullivan, a well-known pop musician. So we were hanging out together, and we both became members of the London Theosophical Society. One day he played a record of Ravi Shankar. I couldn't understand it, but there was something which grabbed me. In the notes on the jacket I read the same things I was reading in that book by Ramana Maharshi, so I realized there is a connection between the music and the wisdom. And I knew I had to listen more in order to understand this connection.

At this time I was just scuffling along. Living from hand to mouth. Impossible to make any money. So I had to do sessions: pop sessions with people like Tom Jones, Engelbert Humperdinck, and Petula Clark. Musically it was terrible, and after some time this session thing was driving me completely crazy. I had to do it in order to survive, and yet more things were happening musically that I wanted to do. Finally, one day I woke up and I said to myself, I cannot do this any more. And I got into my car and I just drove, and I didn't stop until I got to Northern England and I stayed with my mother. It was a question of sanity for me.

I didn't want to go back to London. So I decided to go to the Continent and just play the kind of music I wanted to play. The first offer I got was from Gunther Hampel in Germany, so I went there playing free music for about half a year or so.

I am very glad I had the experience with Gunther. I know, idealistically, it's right to play free music, but there is always a big "but." Because for the most part it is indulgent; this is my real opinion about free music. In order to really play it, first of all, harmonically and melodically you have to know everything, and then you have to be a real big person, a developed human being. Only a developed human being will not indulge himself. But as an ordinary human being—and that's what we mostly are—you indulge yourself. It's not making music; it's self-indulgence; it's not real.

When I was playing with Gunther, I lived in Antwerp, so I could go back to England every now and then. We had a little band with bass player Dave Holland and drummer Tony Oxley, and it was fantastic. I did a record called *Extrapolation* with Tony Oxley and John Surman on baritone and soprano saxophone. And of course we all were proud when Dave was leaving for New York to play with Miles. Imagine, an Englishman to play with Miles—it was unheard of at that time. A real coup!

A few months later, in November of 1968, I got a call from Dave. He was in Baltimore, and guess who he was with? I said, "Miles." "No," he said, "Tony—Tony Williams—and he wants to talk to you." Tony said he would like to form a band, and he would like to have me. Jack DeJohnette had played him a tape he had done with me a few months before while he was in London with Bill Evans. So I said, "When you are ready, just call me."

In early 1969 he called again. So I left the first week of February for New York. Two days later I was in the studio with Miles. That was incredible. You must understand, New York was the ultimate for any European jazz player. And to be able to go there and to play in New York—it was just unbelievable for me!

Tony Williams and Dave Holland were playing with Miles. So immediately I met everybody. Miles and Wayne Shorter and Chick Corea and Jack DeJohnette and Gil Evans! Imagine! Like a dream coming true!

I'll never forget one night in that week. Miles was talking with Louis Armstrong and Dizzy. I wish I had had a camera. The three of them together! Just to see those guys together was so beautiful for me.

On my second day in New York, Tony had to go to Miles' house to pick up some money. So I went along. Miles had a record date the day after. Miles knew that Tony would leave him in order to have a group with Larry Young on organ and me. But Miles didn't want him to leave. He loves Tony. Miles said to me, "Why don't you bring your guitar tomorrow?" Tony wasn't terribly happy about that, because suddenly there was a little competition between Miles and Tony. For me, of course, it was the ultimate. It was the last thing I could expect. But now comes the next day. Larry Young was there. And Joe Zawinul and Herbie Hancock. That I was fortunate enough to be invited, to be there at the right moment, was really nothing I could have created. It was just like a blessing.

We had a tune by Joe Zawinul—with lots of chords. Miles said, "Well, John, why don't you play it on the guitar?" I said, "Do you want all these chords? That's going to take me quite a while to work it out." And now I had my first experience with Miles' way of directing. He wanted me to play the tune with just one chord! And then suddenly everybody was waiting for me to start the tune and I didn't know what to do. I had no idea. Miles said, "Well, you know the chord." So I gave him the chord. That's all. Two chords, in fact. I started to play, and I realized the light is on; and I played the first solo, Wayne Shorter played the tune, Miles and Wayne played it together. I was confused, but I was playing on instinct. And then we played it back, and I was shocked how beautiful it was. And I realized: Joe Zawinul had brought the tune in, and Miles, in one minute, had brought the real essence, the beauty out of it. I was astonished to see how he could hear all that and just bring it out. That was one of the great things in Miles, how he brought the extraordinary out of his surroundings.

Afterwards, Miles asked me to join his group. Again, it was unbelievable for me. Imagine—I had to turn down Miles! Because it was more important for me to go with Tony Williams. I had compositions. And I realized, with Tony I would have more of a chance to play them than with Miles.

Eventually, Lifetime, our band with Tony Williams and Larry Young, was working. There was very little money involved, but musically, it was fantastic, and we couldn't believe that Columbia was turning us down. We played an audition for a guy called Al Kooper who was with Blood, Sweat & Tears. And he said no. I lost all my respect for him immediately because we were burning.

JOACHIM BERENDT: So this was your first experience with business in America? What do you think about the jazz business?

MCLAUGHLIN: I don't think they understand jazz in America. They are so far from reality. Even after eleven years in the U.S.A., I know they don't understand their own music. They don't know how to market it. In Europe and in Japan it's so much better, because people really love the music. It has always been recognized as an art form over here. In Europe, whoever does business with you deals with you on the psychology that you are an artist. But is America they don't look at it that way. Of course, there are a lot of people who love and enjoy jazz in America. But as far as the business is concerned, it's terrible. There are no festivals as you have them in Europe. So when I first encountered these problems, I was quite surprised, because I thought they would have it much more together. In fact, it was one of the shocks of my life when we made that first record with Tony Williams and when they mixed it and the sound was just terrible, and I realized they had no respect for the music and the musicians. Really, I was shocked.

BERENDT: And of course, later it turned out that everybody was blaming Tony and the musicians for the bad sound. It did a lot of harm to Lifetime. . . . However, John, I always felt you have been relatively lucky in your career—businesswise. When I look at what happened to Tony Williams, to Ornette, to Cecil Taylor, to so many others who had bad managers and agents during most parts of their careers, I really think you have been lucky.

MCLAUGHLIN: And yet I have been betrayed, people have taken money from me, and often enough I have been in very difficult positions. I'll never forget my first experience with Douglas Records. I met the man and I thought he's a real nice guy. But the first record I made for him—*Devotion,* with Buddy Miles on drums and Larry Young on organ—was a terrible experience. After I recorded it, I went on tour with Tony Williams, and when I came back, he had finished the album, mixed it, cut this out and that, and there were parts in it which I didn't recognize any more as part of our music. I was in total shock.

BERENDT: How much did they pay you?

MCLAUGHLIN: I got paid about $2,000.

BERENDT: That's all? For a famous record which was sold all over the world and which is still selling?

MCLAUGHLIN: No, not for one record. I got $2,000 for the two records I did for them—for *Devotion* and *My Goal's Beyond.* . . .

BERENDT: . . . the one with the solo side. This is the record which really established solo guitar playing in jazz—the forerunner of hundreds of solo guitar records which followed—and, in my opinion, it still is the most beautiful of all of them. . . .Well, from Douglas you went to Columbia, which is considered the best of all the companies—jazzwise.

McLAUGHLIN: Well, here I am ten years later [in 1981], and I have to leave Columbia. They have to pay me for leaving. Because they think that only electric music is worth marketing. Which I think is disgraceful to the American people. And it's patronizing. They are looking at it from a hamburger point of view.

BERENDT: Please, tell me about Sri Chinmoy, the guru you had at that time.

McLAUGHLIN: Well, just before I went to America, I started to do yoga exercises every day in the morning. I arrived in America, and being in Manhattan, I thought I had to get myself more together. So I did more exercises. I was doing one hour and a half in the morning and one hour and a half in the evening. Just yoga. So after a year of doing this I felt great physically, but I thought I was missing the interior thing. So I went to meditate with different teachers, most of them Indians. And then suddenly one day, Larry Coryell's manager introduced me to Sri Chinmoy. Immediately I felt good about him. He said some important things to me. About music and spirituality. My question was, What is the relationship between music and the spiritual consciousness? And he answered, It's not so much what you do, but what's important is the consciousness with which you do it. For instance, a street sweeper can sweep his street perfectly and at the same time have great satisfaction from doing it. He can even get enlightened. The important thing, always, is the state of your consciousness because it determines (1) how you do it, and (2) the quality of what you do, and (3) the quality of what you are. So if you are a musician and you work towards enlightenment, your music will automatically be part of it. Of course, this was a great answer, so I subsequently went to see him several times, and after a few weeks I became a disciple.

BERENDT: But a couple of years later, the jazz media made a big thing out of you leaving Chinmoy.

McLAUGHLIN: I never left him.

BERENDT: I expected that answer.

McLAUGHLIN: I will never leave him, because I love him. He is a great man, he is an enlightened man. And that's the greatest thing any human being can be, because it takes an incredible amount of work. . . . The only thing that I disagree with are the formalized things. . . . This to do and this not to do. I cannot do this because I have to go on as a musician. I have to go on tour.

Anyway, let's go back to 1971. Miles suggested I should have my own band. I had met Billy Cobham on one of Miles' dates and I looked around for a violin player. I had spoken to Jean-Luc Ponty while I was in Paris. He said no. He wouldn't want to come to America. (Two years later he did!) A few weeks later, I found Jerry Goodman. And Miroslav Vitous, the bass player, called me and said, "Joe Zawinul and Wayne Shorter are founding a group together, called Weather Report. We want you to come with us." And I said, "Well, that's really nice, but I got something to do myself." And Miroslav said, "If you need a piano player, call Jan Hammer. He is also from Czechoslovakia, and he is playing with Sarah Vaughan." So this was the Mahavishnu Orchestra: Jan Hammer, Billy Cobham, Jerry Goodman, and, of course, I had Rick Laird on bass, because I knew him from way back in England and we used to play a lot together. Right from the beginning, we had a beautiful rapport. One evening I was telling Sri Chinmoy that I got a band together and I wanted to give it a name, and he said, "Well, call it the Mahavishnu Orchestra." I said, "Mahavishnu Orchestra? This is going to take everybody out!" "Just try it anyway," he said. So we tried it, and it was great for a year. We really identified with it—with the sound and the energy. And the music was amazing. Of course, I had expected it would work, but I didn't expect a big success like that. We just worked and played and things were great.

Part of the fun was that I kept living my own life the way I wanted to. People were very interested in it. They asked me lots of questions about Sri Chinmoy and all the spiritual things—meditation and India and religion. But of course none of the other musicians went into that. Gradually, they resented it. I felt we would have worked it out, but the real problem was with Jan Hammer and Jerry Goodman. They were really heavily against it. Finally, it became a big psychosis. So we went to Japan and it didn't get better. It got worse. So when we came to Osaka, I said, "Look, why doesn't anyone say one word to me? If you have something on your mind, just say you hate me, just tell me. It's OK. Tell me and things will get better." But neither of them would say a word, and Rick Laird told them, "Why don't you tell him? You are always talking to me when he is not around." So I felt they were determined to go out, and I realized this is the end of the band. It also had to do with success. You know, success is hard to take.

BERENDT: To me, the Mahavishnu Orchestra—the first one—was the greatest of all the jazz-rock bands. Both its records were just terrific—*Birds of Fire* and *Inner Mounting Flame*. Some time later, you had a second Mahavishnu Orchestra, but I always felt you no longer reached that type of height and intensity and inspiration and density.

McLaughlin: We reached it more rarely. It did happen, I think, about two nights in a year. For me, this record *Visions of the Emerald Beyond* (with the second Mahavishnu Orchestra and a string quartet) was one of the greatest I ever made. And then I did *Apocalypse* with Michael Tilson Thomas conducting the London Symphony Orchestra.

BERENDT: But meanwhile Shakti had happened. I still remember the sensation—after all that electric high energy: you playing with those Indian guys—all acoustic music, you being the only Westerner in the group.

McLAUGHLIN: In fact, we had played together before the first Mahavishnu Orchestra had finished. I had some friends and they had a music shop and I told them, I am looking for somebody who can teach me about Indian music. So I took some vocal lessons—Indian singing—and the mrindangam player there (south Indian percussion) was L. Shankar's uncle. So I met L. Shankar, the violin player. I'll never forget when Jean-Luc Ponty arrived from California to join the second Mahavishnu Orchestra. Shankar and I had been hanging out that day, so they met—the two violinists, Shankar from India and Jean-Luc from France. And then L. Shankar started to play, and I saw that look of amazement on Jean-Luc's face—I've never seen anything like this in my life.

I was so lucky to have some lessons from Ravi Shankar and other masters of Indian music. I love India, its music and its spirituality, its religions. The spirituality *is* the music. You can't separate the two, like you can in the West.

I had met Zakir Hussain, the tabla player, at Ali Akbar Khan's school for Indian music near San Francisco. Khan-sahib, the great master sarod player, was just sitting there in his chair listening to both of us playing, and after we finished I said, I never played with anybody like that.

I did three records with Shakti. But Columbia just didn't go along with it.

BERENDT: So you went back to electric music because Columbia told you to?

McLAUGHLIN: You can't say this. You know, jazz music and Western harmonies are part of me. I cannot suppress it. Not that I have suppressed it in Shakti, but I was preoccupied with Indian music, which has its own kind of discipline. Shakti really stayed together for quite some time. So I wanted to go back to Western music. It's a part of me I cannot deny. So I really had a desire to play chords and to play with a drummer and a bass player, and that's why I made this record *Johnny McLaughlin—Electric Guitarist.* In a way it was like going back to my beginnings, and, of course, it also was a reunion with almost all the Mahavishnu players. It was like forgetting all those old problems and just playing music.

BERENDT: For many people there is almost a schism between electric and acoustic music.

McLAUGHLIN: Both are part of me. There is a style of music and a style of playing I can only do on an electric guitar, and there is another style I like to do on acoustic guitar.

BERENDT: When I presented the Mahavishnu Orchestra at the Olympic Games Jazz Festival in Munich in 1972 I considered you, more or less, a European musician, but you talked to me about New York. "It only could have happened there," you said. And: "New York makes you strong. It really is *the* jazz city." But now, ten years later, you live in Paris. And you have a

French wife. And your wife is a classical musician. And you have an apartment at the Pont Neuf in Paris. Are you coming back to your European roots?

McLAUGHLIN: In a sense, yes. I think New York has changed. America has changed. America may, at some point, enjoy a renaissance of music, but I don't know when this will happen. Right now, the situation for music is better in Europe than it is in America.

BERENDT: How do you feel about fusion?

McLAUGHLIN: I think a lot of fusion music is not true fusion. If a musician is being pushed to play a certain kind of music or if he feels he has to do something with a different beat in order to become popular, then this is basically against the spirit of music and against the spirit of jazz—that's all. The fusion has to happen inside you, otherwise it's not going to happen at all. It becomes only pseudo-fusion. There is so much pseudo-music around.

You can't say, Let's put it with a disco beat. Or let's do it with a rock beat. It won't have any weight. It won't carry any conviction. That's why I don't listen too much to that kind of music anymore. I'm not deeply touched by it. And I have to be deeply touched, otherwise it's not worth it. I want something to really grab my insides. That's the music I take along when I go on tour.

BERENDT: What do you take along?

McLAUGHLIN: I take Coltrane, Miles; I take some gypsy music. I have a cassette of a great Indian nagaswaram player. And a beautiful Indian tabla player. And I take some Chopin on the road. And some Schumann.

David Murray and Wynton Marsalis

It is the reevaluation of jazz tradition, not its negation, that has brought postmodern jazz furthest. For the first time in the history of jazz, dialogue with the past has become more important than a visionary look into the future—a dialogue in which examination of jazz's rich legacy holds more promise than utopias. There isn't, however, any single binding principle regulating encounters with jazz tradition; there are innumerably many. Nowhere else in eighties jazz does the immense range of neotraditionalism become so clearly evident as in the differences between the music of David Murray and Wynton Marsalis. Both have been influential as conservatives, even though they never labeled, let alone viewed, themselves as such. Both clarified a feeling for standards in jazz, thereby establishing new standards. After twenty years of free jazz's destruction of norms and clichés, and after ten years of fusion music's superficial formulas and mannerisms, Wynton Marsalis and David Murray endow jazz with classicism.

The first thing you notice about the sound of David Murray's tenor saxophone is its enormous robustness, weight, and intensity—a sound that tastes of rich loam and earth: rustic, effusive, brimming with wild passion and the full weight of the blues. Jazz critic Stanley Crouch extols David Murray's ability "to summon fifty years of saxophone techniques in two or three phrases, to pivot from harmonic sophistication to rhythm and blues squeals, from cleanly articulated tones to percussive blurs and blats sounds, or from swelling melody to swirls of color."

Everything that David Murray plays issues from tremendous inner intensity. His tenor saxophone seems to move in a trance—wending and climbing, bobbing and weaving a serpentine path through wildly fulminating climactic lines. This is the same abandonment and ecstasy, the same spirit possession, that can be experienced day in day out in the gospel services of black communities. "The church I come from is the Pentecostal Church of America where African rituals have been preserved and people become possessed by spirits," said Murray. "Then they speak in tongues they themselves don't understand. . . . It's the same when we've reached a certain plateau in our music. Sometimes I have the feeling that I could step out of my body and observe myself as I'm playing. I see myself playing. I don't think about it. Someone else does that."

The self-evident vitality and naturalness so characteristic of David Murray's music making contrasts strongly with Wynton Marsalis' inclination toward logic and unification. Wynton's trumpet sound radiates total purity. Not since Dizzy Gillespie has jazz trumpet been blown with such lucid mastery of instrumental technique. Some critics are even of the opinion that Wynton's technical skills exceed Gillespie's: crystal clear in sound, rounded and radiantly warm, and polished and precise in handling of line. Nonetheless, Wynton's trumpet playing is forged from an intensely focused expressiveness—a fire, but an intellectually cooled fire, similar to Miles Davis' cool radiance yet without Davis' melancholy and remoteness from the world, but overlaid with an almost scientific relationship to the blues.

Wynton Marsalis has mastered the art of moving compellingly and conclusively from one note to the next with such uncanny perfection that the listener is first amazed and then convinced, This is it! This is exactly how it must sound! Some critics contend that this highly organized mixture of mental clarity and precision is no more than a slick abstraction. In fact, there can be no doubt that this spontaneously fused crystalline containment is far superior to the efforts of those who resort to preestablished formulas, let alone composition. The concept most frequently referred to in Wynton's interviews is logic.

Wynton Marsalis comes—like Louis Armstrong and Jelly Roll Morton—from New Orleans, where he was born on October 18, 1961. His father Ellis is a well-known jazz teacher and pianist, known far beyond New Orleans. At the age of six Wynton received his first trumpet. "Miles, Clark Terry, Al Hirt, and my father were all sitting around a table in Al's club in New Orleans. . . . My father, just joking because there were so many famous trumpeters sitting there, said, 'I better buy Wynton a trumpet.' And Al said, 'Ellis, let me give your boy one of mine.' But Miles said, 'Don't give it to him. Trumpet's too difficult an instrument for him to learn.' " Fifteen years later, in the 1982 *Down Beat* readers poll, it wasn't Miles, after having made his anxiously awaited and spectacular comeback to the jazz scene in the previous year, who was voted musician of the year, but rather Wynton Marsalis—and for nothing less than "Jazz Album of the Year" and in the trumpet category. Having only entered the scene two years before, Wynton walked away with first place, while Miles had to settle for second. Since then Wynton's success in such polls has remained unbroken.

Wynton gained his musical skills at the Ben Franklin High School and the New Orleans Center of Creative Arts (NOCCA). The importance of the center for Wynton's musical development can hardly be overestimated since it upheld the venerable old Creole tradition of paying equal attention to the teaching and playing of both jazz and classical music. From the age of twelve, Wynton, unlike many other young black musicians, studied Bach alongside Bird, Corelli alongside Coltrane, and Mozart alongside Monk.

He played in guitarist Danny Barker's marching band, in funk groups, and blew first trumpet in the New Orleans Civic Orchestra. "Every year," said Wynton, "there was a competition for soloists, and the three winners then performed in youth concerts with the New Orleans Philharmonic. No one thought I had a chance. 'Who wants to hear a trumpeter play a concerto?' " At fourteen Wynton won the competition. As winner of the first prize he performed Haydn's trumpet concerto with the New Orleans Philharmonic, followed two years later by Bach's Brandenburg Concerto No. 2 in F major. His successes in the world of classical music led to appearances with the New York Philharmonic and the Cleveland Orchestra under Leonard Bernstein, Zubin Mehta, and Seiji Ozawa.

Compared with Marsalis, David Murray's musical development was completely unacademic. He was born in Berkeley, California, on February 19, 1955. Murray's mother was a respected gospel pianist. At the age of eight David started playing alto sax in the Murray family's band, which accompanied gospel services. By twelve he was blowing in a rhythm and blues group. Shortly afterward he tried his luck as a street musician, strumming a guitar à la Jimi Hendrix. At fifteen he headed an organ trio in the San Francisco area. The lineup of organ, saxophone, and drums was very popular in the black neighborhoods of the time, and the electrified, wildly cooking sounds of this particular constellation demanded an absolute maximum of physical and emotional involvement from a saxophonist. It was during this period that David Murray, inspired by Sonny Rollins, switched to tenor sax. "I knew then that I couldn't play the alto saxophone any more. It doesn't have enough substance." Murray added, "When I was growing up, everyone was trying to play all the Coltrane solos. So I told myself, 'Maybe I shouldn't study his solos because in five years all these people will sound the same.' I was right. They all sound the same."

"David Murray," wrote American jazz critic Martin Williams, "explored his horn to the extent of finding and using several notes on the top of the tenor sax that nobody knew were there before." Indeed, David Murray has uniquely developed the ecstatic overblown playing opened up by free-jazz saxophonists. Murray comes from Albert Ayler, the free-jazz tenorist who died in mysterious circumstances in 1971 after having become *the* master of overblown free playing, even though in interviews Murray time and again emphasizes (to set the record straight) his strong ties with swing tenor players Paul Gonsalves, Ben Webster, and Lester Young.

In an exciting process Murray has step by step melodized and "tonalized" Ayler's overblown playing of free jazz—characterized by spectral arcs of sound and sharpened microtonal lines—without taking away any of his music's wildness, fire, and ecstasy. It is fascinating to follow how Murray moved step-by-step from orthodox overblown playing (also known as energy playing) to ever more palpably melodic figures. His debut album *Flowers for Albert,* recorded in 1976, is still completely under the influence of Albert Ayler's eruptive cascades of sound. But within a year, in *Live at the Manhattan Ocean Club,* Murray was already pointing the way toward what he would increasingly refine and develop in the eighties, together with drummer Jack DeJohnette, with guitarist James "Blood" Ulmer, with the World Saxophone Quartet, and above all with his own groups. His overblown playing finds its way back to song forms and recognizable melodic figures. Murray possessed the nucleus of this tendency toward tonality and beat when as a twenty-year-old he came to New York in 1975 to play in the front ranks of the jazz avant-garde. "A lot of people from California have more of a melodic sense of hearing things than people over on the East Coast—musicians like Charles Mingus, Eric Dolphy, and Ornette Coleman. Ornette's not from California, but everybody from Texas is from California, really," Murray said.

Four years after David Murray moved to New York, Wynton Marsalis followed suit, enrolling in the celebrated Juilliard School of Music in 1979 in order to prepare for a concert career in classical music. In 1980, he went on a European tour with bop drummer Art Blakey's ten-piece band. Shortly afterward he became a member of Blakey's legendary Jazz Messengers and stayed with Blakey until 1982. "If it hadn't been for Art Blakey," explained

Wynton later, "I wouldn't be playing jazz. I never had the intention of doing that professionally. It was Art Blakey who gave me the chance to play every night."

Wynton's playing is a grandiose synthesis of the best that the history of the jazz trumpet can offer—from Louis Armstrong's rhythmic exuberance by way of Dizzy Gillespie's exultant high notes, Clifford Brown's warmth, Miles Davis' cool poetry, and Freddie Hubbard's powerful attack, up to Don Cherry's swirling free sounds (see the section on the trumpet). And yet everything that Wynton plays derives from his highly imaginative personality's capacity for integration. Wynton Marsalis quotes less than he paraphrases—circumscribing, refining, and cultivating by way of his own gestures and vocabulary what his predecessors have expressed, equally individually, as the truths of jazz.

Wynton Marsalis is the first musician to have mastered both jazz and European concert music in such sovereign fashion, and furthermore to find acceptance and acclaim in both worlds. Maurice André, who has himself done so much to uphold and interpret the literature of classical trumpet playing, has called Wynton Marsalis "potentially the greatest trumpet player of all time." And Ron Carter, celebrated jazz bassist, believes Marsalis to be "the most interesting young musician since the sixties."

Such enormous flexibility and diversity demand more than an exceptional twin-track talent. They require open-mindedness, a facility more frequently found in jazz than in any other kind of twentieth-century music.

Wynton Marsalis went the way that, as he stresses, "I had to go." The more difficult way of proving himself as a black musician in a world of concert music shaped by European standards, and then, after enjoying great success, withdrawing from the attractions of the classical music business. He could have pursued the career of a highly paid concert trumpeter, existing in material luxury amid conditions that were much less physically demanding. But Wynton chose jazz. "I think—I *know*—it's harder to be a good jazz musician at an early age than a classical one. In jazz, to be good means to be an individual, which you don't necessarily have to be in classical music performance." He continued: "That's the reason I had to come to the painful realization that I had to stop performing classical music before audiences. . . . I found there simply was not enough time for me to pay respects to the unarguable greatness of both European music and jazz."

It's particularly evident that the young Marsalis mastered instrumental technique to such perfection that his creative ability was overshadowed. That is especially apparent in his first recordings with Art Blakey and in his debut album *Wynton Marsalis* (1981), featuring, among others, his celebrated quintet with brother Branford (saxophone), Kenny Kirkland (piano), Charles Fambrough (bass), and Jeff "Tain" Watts (drums). Although the polished brilliance of these recordings was certainly enough to secure Marsalis a place in the history of eighties jazz, they were nonetheless plagued by tending toward the étudelike, toward virtuoso scale playing and slick eighth-note phrasing.

It's certainly not just by chance that Wynton's playing underwent a fundamental change after his mid-eighties decision to concentrate exclusively on jazz. (Since then he has only performed European concert music in studio recordings.) His playing increasingly lost its traces of slickness and became rhythmically more and more springy, refined, and spontaneous.

In the course of that development Wynton Marsalis acquired a rare mastery of rhythmic nuance. His skill in placing a note just where it's "due" is truly breathtaking. Particularly celebrated is his ability to vary the tempo and to play around the beat through deliberate *accelerandi* and *ritardandi,* clarifying and strengthening the beat by "negating" it: sometimes rushing away from the beat by a fraction of a fraction of a second, at one moment dragging slightly behind, and then again playing "on top of the beat" with razor-sharp accuracy—all this without ever losing touch with the basic meter.

This differentiated approach to rhythm goes together with the fact that Wynton Marsalis mainly revalues and updates those classic jazz styles where the lithe, flowing legato phrasing of modern jazz takes precedence over earthy, expressive sounds. To be sure, Marsalis possesses an outstanding gift for charging his playing with the entire emotional spectrum—sometimes resolute and forceful, sometimes cool and reserved, and occasionally even cheeky and mischievous—but his sound usually remains wonderfully clear, pure, and transparent. From jazz's great legacy he mainly selects elements reflecting lucidity so as not to endanger the rhythmic lines' supple flow.

Listen, on the other hand, to David Murray, and you seem to be encountering the primal forces of sound. Murray's playing, like his composition, is saturated with the earthy, raw, squeezed sounds of jazz—with the passionate vocalized wailing of archaic New Orleans jazz, with the powerfully eruptive tones of swing tenor horns, with the exciting jungle cries of the Ellington orchestra, with the throaty timbre of the blues, and with the ecstatic outbursts of free jazz that by now can almost be called traditional. David Murray thus mainly chooses and updates those elements from the legacy of jazz where the emphasis is on expressive sound production.

David Murray admires big bands. That is already apparent in the fact that the saxophonists who, after Albert Ayler, greatly influenced him often recorded with big bands: Paul Gonsalves and Ben Webster with the Duke Ellington Orchestra, and Lester Young with the Count Basie Orchestra. So it's not surprising that Murray's music, whether in smaller groups or solo concerts, is almost overwhelmingly orchestral with a "love for bigness" in sound: compact, massive, and resolute.

Throughout the eighties Murray's love of big bands increasingly led him toward composition. He has recorded many of his great works—*Flowers for Albert, Last of the Hipmen,* and *Dewey's Circle*—with all possible lineups. Each of these versions has been successful on its own terms. But the interpretations become increasingly mature, unified, and dynamic as the number of players increases. "Arrangements are like children," according to Murray. "They have to grow."

Exceptional praise has been directed toward the compositions and arrangements for his famous Octet, which made its debut appearance at New York's Public Theatre in 1978. It must certainly be ranked one of the outstanding groups within neoclassicism. Like his idol, bassist Charles Mingus, Murray had always dreamed of heading a big band. Like Mingus, he was forced by financial circumstances to make do with a medium-sized ensemble; like Mingus, Murray also made a virtue out of necessity. Whenever Murray's dream has come true and he has managed to put together a big band, critics and musicians have concurred that as a composer, Murray convinces more with medium-sized ensembles.

David Murray's mastery of disrupting stylistic norms is perhaps even more apparent in his compositions than in his tenor playing. His music is more than just a dazzling reevaluation of jazz tradition; it addresses the entire spectrum of black music: bebop, free jazz, rhythm and blues, African, soul, Swing, and right back to the cradle of New Orleans—in a synthesis that is reflective, freely interpreted, and not just a restoration of the past. His music never merely speaks through the tongues of others. They speak through him in his own voice.

Anyone who links so many influences—uniting and reassessing the work of Duke Ellington, Charles Mingus, King Oliver, Jelly Roll Morton, and Albert Ayler—runs the risk of producing a stylistic mishmash. David Murray found his own way out of that danger. The many fragments encountered in his music aren't lifeless interchangeable material. Just as in a gospel service, the calls and responses from individual members of the congregation occur independently, coming together in a process of unceasing intensification to from a multivoiced choir where every voice is a recognizable part of the whole and yet retains its own individual character. Similarly, the great range of influences in Murray's music overlap and cohere as voices with which he, like a preacher, conducts an ongoing ecstatic dialogue.

Ming, the 1980 album where Murray first presents his celebrated Octet—with Anthony Davis (piano), Henry Threadgill (alto sax), George Lewis (trombone), Olu Dara (trumpet), Butch Morris (cornet), Wilbur Morris (bass), and Steve McCall (drums)—is a key work for neoclassicism.

Here Murray for the first time put across his message—never before expressed with such shimmering color and unrestricted vitality—that "the entire legacy of jazz is avant-garde" (Stanley Crouch). Murray's music doesn't pontificate on jazz history but makes surprisingly and sensuously clear how revolutionary the collective improvisations of New Orleans jazz were, how forward-looking the jungle sounds of the Duke Ellington Orchestra, how excitingly revolutionary Charlie Parker's bebop and the Charles Mingus Band's liberation of tempo. Murray uncovers what lies at the heart of traditional elements, pointing toward the development of contemporary jazz. That was even more impressively achieved on the 1982 album *Home*, where his Octet once again mixed and fused all the great aspects of black music even more boldly and freely: gospel sounds, free jazz, Afro-Caribbean music, Delta blues, soul, etc.

Like David Murray, trumpeter Wynton Marsalis has played his way through almost the whole of jazz history, taking up and reinterpreting whatever is of relevance for his individual and critical revaluation. All the same, in this stock taking of jazz tradition he has been shaped and influenced by one musician more than any other: Miles Davis. Wynton possesses all the technical facility that Miles always desired but never attained. His conservative messages—tonality and song forms don't stand in the way of musical freedom, and a regular beat needn't be undemocratic and mechanical—come straight from Miles.

More than any other band, Wynton's groups have advanced and refined Miles' concept of "controlled freedom." His bands have attained rare mastery, particularly in playing with changing rhythms, shifting tempos, and superimposing different meters. Every new album Marsalis released in the eighties brought further intensification and refinement of rhythmic nuances. And each time you thought he had finally reached the limits of prowess, he surprised with fresh metric possibilities and new rhythmic finesse. The peaks here are *Marsalis Standard Time Vol. I* (1987), an album where he throws fresh metrical light on "standards," on great songs from American popular music; and *Live at Blues Alley* (1988).

By the end of the eighties, Wynton's concept of rhythmic density had attained such complexity that further refinement seemed scarcely possible. It is characteristic of his dynamic development and of his constantly self-critical attitude toward his own music that at this point he felt that a change of style was unavoidable. He turned away from contemporary bebop (a kind of "high energy bop" with crazily rapid tempos, aggressive rhythms, and complex metric superimpositions), which had shaped his playing up to that time, toward "simpler," more relaxed rhythms, and more traditional aspects of jazz.

This transformation, documented in the 1989 album *The Majesty of the*

Blues, had nothing calculated about it; neither was this, as some critics thoughtlessly contended, a nostalgic retrograde step. It is the logical outcome of Wynton Marsalis' musical development. After he had extensively investigated and cultivated the rhythmic foundations of his playing, timbre and melody became increasingly important in his music making.

That becomes apparent in greater use of the plunger (a rubber mute) and a more expressive, blues-related articulation—the *dirty* sounds that Wynton now explores with the accuracy and discipline he had previously devoted to bop-oriented phrasing. Since 1988, Wynton's New Orleans roots, until then concealed and only indirectly apparent in his playing, have thus increasingly moved into the foreground. Now he deliberately reflects the tradition of archaic jazz with its expressiveness: in dirges, call-and-response structures, vital melodies, exuberant rhythms, and humorous sounds—all this even though the bop element continues to be active in his music. Marsalis said:

> Everything you ever need to know is in New Orleans jazz. Duke Ellington knew that better than anybody! You have a polyphonic conception of improvisation, high stylization of the blues, a virtuosic concept of the solo, the tradition of ensemble playing with interludes and parts . . . riffs, breaks, timbral effects, a unique concept for playing the bass, tuba, saxophone, and drums—with a new instrument which never before existed: the drum set. Everything you could want is there. I guess when I was growing up I had no idea that's what it was. I just thought it was some old people in some club playing for some tourists.

There's no doubt that Wynton's musical world—even where it appears to be pure, vibrant jazz—is shaped by the aesthetic standards of European music. When American journalists Rafi Zabor and Vic Garbarini interviewed Marsalis and keyboardist Herbie Hancock for *Musician* magazine in 1985, Wynton told them, "Anybody can say 'I have emotion.' I mean, a thousand trumpeters had soul and emotion when they picked up trumpets, but they weren't all Louis Armstrong. Why?" Herbie Hancock answered first: "Because he was a better human being." And then Wynton Marsalis: "Because Louis Armstrong's technique was better. . . . Who's to say that his soul was greater than anyone else's? How can you measure soul? . . . Soul is part of technique. Emotion is part of technique. Music is a craft, man."

Zabor and Garbarini commented, "What bothered him about the notion of soul as conventionally applied is the racist subtext. Black musicians are expected to be 'soulful' and inarticulate, to perpetuate the myth of the gifted primitive whose sources of inspiration are racial and mysterious, and therefore *not his own,* which is to say he is not a conscious artist in the deific western sense of the term, and even if a genius, one of automatically the second rank." So the motor for Wynton Marsalis' musical development is this: He aspires to be an artist in the European sense of the word, recognized as someone who is *consciously* creative. That explains the vehemence with which Marsalis applies the standards of European musical aesthetics to jazz, and his exaggerated purism. Anyone who speaks so often about the seriousness and logicality of jazz must have a reason for doing so. It seems fitting that in interviews Wynton Marsalis almost never misses a chance to dismiss any spontaneous meldings of music. Whether it be world music, soul, fusion, free jazz, pop, or funk, there is hardly a direction in contemporary music that he doesn't reject.

Let's return to David Murray. For Wynton Marsalis soul is an invention of the white man aimed at degrading black music, whereas for Murray every phrase he plays is bursting with proud black soul-consciousness and soul-feeling. Marsalis' traditionalism is tinged by the standards of European musical aesthetics. David Murray's music draws its substance from acknowledgment of the African roots of black music, often to such a vital and exuberant extent that one seems to be listening to African music through a veil of jazz, soul, and blues. South African bassist Johnny Dyani (d. 1986), who liked playing with Murray, once said, "Sounds like the kind of music we play at home." Dyani conjectured that Murray had certainly "lived in Africa in a previous incarnation."

Everything that David Murray plays and composes is directly related, particularly harmonically, to the music of the black churches. In gospel services you time and again hear members of the congregation beginning to sing quite independently of one another so that various tonal centers develop simultaneously in a kind of chance polytonality. Something similar happens in David Murray's music. The natural looseness with which he attains polytonality and his mastery of free treatment of contrapuntal ideas come from the gospel churches. Free jazz only adds an intensifying element.

During the eighties David Murray's music became ever more controlled and structured. That was primarily due to Murray devoting increasing attention to composition. But his overblown tenor sax playing also grew more and more melodic. Wynton Marsalis' playing, on the other hand, has become increasingly free and spontaneous, particularly if his personal development is taken as the yardstick. His beginnings with Art Blakey in 1980 were still dominated by such great hard-bop trumpeters as Clifford Brown, Lee Morgan, and Freddie Hubbard. But on his debut album *Wynton Marsalis* he liberated (influenced by Miles Davis) hard bop from its restricted canon of formulas. And finally he gained such a liking for risks that he ended up with Don Cherry in "Knozz-Moe-King" on *Live at Blues Alley.* "Before you understand what it is to expand something, you must know what that thing actually is," Wynton said.

While David Murray has voyaged to the outer limits of the avant-garde and then retraced his way step-by-step to the legacy of jazz, Wynton Marsalis has proceeded in almost exactly the opposite direction. He started with bebop—by now viewed as the classic style of modern jazz—and has developed from that point toward ever-greater openness and freedom. To simplify: David Murray views tradition from a modern viewpoint; Wynton Marsalis, modernism from a traditional stance. David Murray is a neoclassicist, Wynton Marsalis a classicist.

THE ELEMENTS OF JAZZ

The Elements of Jazz

Sound and Phrasing

What particularly distinguishes jazz from traditional European music is sound. Crudely put, the difference is this: In a symphony orchestra, the members of, say, the string section, will wish to play their passages as homogeneously as possible. This means that each member of the section must have the same ideal of sound and know how to achieve it. This ideal corresponds to transmitted cultural standards or aesthetics: an instrument must have a "beautiful" sound.

For the jazz musician, on the other hand, it is of no particular importance to conform to a commonly accepted conception of sound. A jazz musician has his own sound. The criteria for this sound are based not so much on standardization as on emotionality and expressivity. To be sure, the latter are also found in European music. But in jazz, expression ranks above euphony, while in European music euphony is more important than expression.

Thus, one may find in jazz a tendency contradictory to the standards of aesthetics—and opposed to standarized aesthetics—but this tendency does not imply that jazz of necessity must be "unaesthetic." It does imply, however, that an artistic music is conceivable that conforms to the highest standards of jazz and yet is contrary to aesthetic conventions.

The self of the musician is clearly reflected, in the most immediate and direct fashion, in the nonstandardized sound of the great jazz improvisers. In jazz, there is no *bel canto,* no "schmaltzy" violins, but hard, direct sounds—the human voice, plaintive and complaining, crying and screaming, sighing and moaning. The instruments are expressive and eruptive, not filtered through any regulations or rules of sound. That is why the music made by a jazz player is "true" in a much more concrete sense than that made by the average player of European music. The majority of the one hundred or two hundred musicians in a large symphony orchestra probably do not feel the "titanic struggles" that occur in Beethoven's music, nor do they fully sense the secrets of form which are the basis of symphonic music. But a jazz musician, even in a big band, senses and feels, knows and understands what he plays. The lack of understanding among the "civil service" musicians in the symphony orchestras, of which so many conductors have complained (especially where modern music is concerned) is unthinkable in jazz.

Because a jazz musician's playing is "true" in a direct, naive, and "primitive" way, it may possess beauty even when it contradicts aesthetic standards. One could say that the beauty of jazz is ethical rather than aesthetic. To be able to respond to jazz means first and foremost to be able to feel this kind of beauty.

The first word the layperson thinks of when jazz is mentioned—"hot"—is not just a matter of rhythmic intensity. It is first of all a matter of sound. One speaks of "hot intonation."

The personal, inimitable sound of a great jazz musician is the reason for something that always astonishes the outsider: that the jazz connoisseur is able to recognize, after relatively few notes of music, who is playing. This certainty does not exist in classical music, where it is only with difficulty that one can guess who is conducting or playing certain parts in a symphonic orchestra.

Sound in jazz is—to give a few examples at random—the slow, expressive vibrato of Sidney Bechet's soprano sax; the voluminous, erotic tenor sax sound of Coleman Hawkins; the earthy cornet of King Oliver; the jungle sound of Bubber Miley; the elegant clarity of Benny Goodman's clarinet; the sorrow and lostness of Miles Davis or the victoriousness of Louis Armstrong; the lyrical sonority of Lester Young; the gripping, concentrated power of Roy Eldridge or the clear glow of Dizzy Gillespie.

In the older forms of jazz the shaping of sound is more marked than in the more recent ones. In the newer forms, an element that often was absent in earlier times is added: jazz phrasing. Trombonist Kid Ory, for example, played phrases that existed in circus and marching music at the turn of the century and are not necessarily jazz phrases. Nevertheless, what he plays is clearly jazz—because of his sound. Stan Getz, on the other hand—especially the Getz of the fifties—has a sound that, when isolated from its surrounding elements, is not so far removed from "classical" saxophone sound. But he phrases with a concentrated jazz feeling no symphony player could emulate.

There are modern jazz recordings (e.g., some by Jimmy Giuffre or by violinist Zbigniew Seifert) that are very close to the chamber music of modern "classical" composers. Yet the phrasing is so definitely jazz that the music is felt to be jazz even when a regular beat is not present.

Thus one notes a shift in emphasis from sound to phrasing in the history of jazz (and back, to a certain degree, from phrasing to sound with some free-jazz and postmodern players)—in a sense that will be clarified later in our final chapter.

Sound and phrasing can represent everything of importance in jazz to the extent that a jazz musician, were he to play a piece of European concert music, could transform it into "jazz"—even when playing his part note for note.

The sound of jazz and the jazz phrasing connected with it are the "blackest" elements in jazz. They lead back to the shouts of Southern plantation slaves and from there, back to the coast and the jungles of Africa. Along with swing, they are the sole predominantly black elements in jazz.

One might compare the sound that the blacks, in the formative years of jazz, coaxed from their European instruments to the situation in which the Africans deported as slaves to the New World were forced to speak European languages. It has been pointed out that the "singing" way of speaking peculiar to the southern United States can be traced back to black influence, and it is ironic that even those southerners who have no other word than "nigger" for a black person also speak in this manner. Originally, the word was nothing but the black way of saying "Negro." In the same sense, jazz sound and jazz phrasing are, or in any case originally were, nothing but the black way of playing European melodies on European instruments. And this way—like black southern speech—has penetrated the white world so completely that it has conquered audiences in this white world; it is often employed by white musicians as legitimately as by blacks.

From the vantage point of sound it becomes clear that the question of a musician's skin color remains superficial unless due regard is had for the underlying complexities. From the inner conviction that most of the creative jazz musicians were black, Roy Eldridge once claimed that he could always distinguish a white musician from a black one. Critic Leonard Feather gave him a blindfold test: Eldridge had to listen to a number of unfamiliar records and judge from them. It turned out that he frequently erred about race. In spite of this, Feather did not, as he believed, disprove Eldridge's point to show that black and white jazz musicians sound alike. He only pointed up the many sides of the problem.

On the one hand, Fletcher Henderson, black, wrote the arrangements without which Benny Goodman, white, might not have become the "King of Swing." On the other hand, Benny Goodman played these arrangements "better" with his white orchestra than Henderson did with his black orchestra—according to any standard, even that of black musicians.

Furthermore, in reverse: Neal Hefti, white, has written some of the most brilliant arrangements for Count Basie's black band. But Basie's band played them "better" than Hefti's own band, which consisted mainly of white musicians.

Finally: As early as the fifties (i.e., before the time of today's avant-garde), Charles Mingus, black, was an exponent of an experimental, deliberately abstract tendency one would almost certainly ascribe to a white rather than to a black musician—if all the generalizations we carry to the race problem made any sense. On the other hand, even before the hard-bop movement, white musicians such as Gerry Mulligan and Al Cohn again and again pointed to the importance of beat, swing, and blues; of originality, vitality, and simplicity. In other words, they did what the simplistic average judgment would sooner have expected of black musicians.

Always, there is this duality when the question of race arises in jazz—and not only in jazz. It is impossible, especially for a European writer, to do more than acknowledge both points of view.

Improvisation

A hundred and fifty years ago our ancestors went to hear Beethoven and Hummel and Thalberg and Clementi improvise richly and splendidly; and before that to the great organists—to Bach, Buxtehude, Böhm, Pachelbel; not forgetting Samuel Wesley, though he came later. Today we have to go for the same sort of musical performance to Lionel Hampton, Erroll Garner, Milt Jackson, Duke Ellington, and Louis Armstrong. I will leave you to digest the implications to be drawn from that curious circumstance.

Burnett James made these remarks in an article about improvisation in jazz.

Indeed, during the whole history of jazz, from New Orleans to today, jazz improvisation has been accomplished according to the same techniques as employed in old European music: with the aid of harmonic structures (which, however, in free jazz became so open that they are barely structured any longer).

On the other hand, from the beginning of the last century, improvisation atrophied in European music to such a degree that today even leading soloists sometimes are unable to make up the cadenzas left open to improvisation in the great classical concertos. Concert performances today are judged according to "authenticity"; that is, whether a piece of music is played or sung as the composer "meant it to be." But if, for example, we were to perform a Vivaldi concerto or a Handel sonata as the composers wrote them, we would simply be "interpreting" a bare, skeletal framework of notes. The entire improvisatory force and freedom of Vivaldi's and Handel's music—and, in general, of all of baroque and prebaroque soloistically conceived music—have been lost to the ideal of "authenticity." Arnold Dolmetsch has said that the omission of ornamentation—the improvised embellishment of the notated music—is as "barbaric" as would be the removal of the flamboyant Gothic architectural ornamentation from a cathedral with the excuse that one preferred a simpler style. The jazz musician improvises on a given harmonic structure. That is exactly what Johann Sebastian Bach and his sons did when playing a chaconne or an air: They improvised on the harmonies on which the melody was based, or embellished the given melody. The whole technique of ornamentation—the embellishment of melody—that flowered during the baroque period still survives in jazz—for instance, when Coleman Hawkins played his famous "Body and Soul." And the ground bass, organ point, and *cantus firmus* of the old music came into being to give structure to improvisation and to make it easier, in the same sense that jazz musicians today use blues chords and the blues form to give shape to their improvisations. Winthrop Sargeant speaks about harmony in this sense as a "controlling structural principle in jazz."

Of course, it is not as if the early jazz musicians had consciously taken over the improvisational techniques of the old music. They knew nothing of Bach and all these matters, and the parallels that exist here are meaningful precisely because they developed unconsciously: the result not of the same but of a related basic musical feeling. On the contrary, the parallels between jazz and old music become suspect when they are practiced deliberately and when, because similarities in improvisational methods do exist, the two forms are thrown into one pot. Nor does the relationship in conception that stands behind all this stem from the old European music. It is a conception basic to *all* musical cultures in which it is "more important to make music yourself than to listen to the music of others," in which the primeval nature of the relationship to music does not allow for any questions of interpretation or conception to arise, in which the music is judged not according to what it means but to what it is. There are such musical cultures and styles in Africa as well as in Europe, in America as well as in Asia. One might even say that almost all musical cultures anywhere in the world have this common basic conception, with the exception of the music that flowered in nineteenth-century Europe, and that still rules the musical sensibilities of the white world.

Jazz, then, has improvisation. But the problem of improvisation is not exhausted with this conclusion. It begins with it. The statement "There is improvisation in jazz" is a truism so widespread that many fans and laypeople proceed to conclude from it that if there is no improvisation in a piece, it is not jazz. Humphrey Lyttelton, the most brilliant representative of

traditional jazz in Europe, said, "In the full sense of 'composing extemporar-
ily,' that is, without preparation, improvisation has proved to be not essential
to, and practically nonexistent in, good jazz."

Most jazz improvisation is based on a theme. Usually, it is a standard song
in thirty-two-bar form—excluding the free jazz of the sixties and the more
complex song forms that came into use in the seventies and eighties—the
AABA form of our popular tunes in which the eight-bar main theme (A) is
first presented, then repeated, then followed by a new eight-bar idea, the
so-called bridge, (B). In conclusion, the first eight bars are sounded once
more. Or it may be the twelve-bar blues form, about which more will be said
in the section about blues. The jazz musician places new melodic lines over
the given harmonies of the song or the blues. This is done by embellishing
or making slight alterations in the songs or blues, (André Hodeir calls this
manner of improvising "paraphrasing") or by creating entirely new melodic
lines over the given harmonies (a manner of improvising that Hodeir calls
the "chorus-phrase").

The decorative, embellishing "paraphrase" was the main improvisatory
device of the older jazz forms. Clarinetist Buster Bailey related, "At that time
[1918] I wouldn't have known what they meant by improvisation. But
embellishment was a phrase I understood. And that was what they were
doing in New Orleans." The "chorus-phrase," on the other hand, which
creates entirely new melodic lines, is the main improvisatory manner of
modern jazz. Its possibilities are vast. Example 1 shows, in the top row, the
beginning of the song, "How High the Moon," the favored theme of the bop
era, with its related harmonies, and in rows a, b, and c three different
improvisations on it by three leading jazz musicians. One can see at a glance
that three completely different melodic lines have come into being. There is
no connection between these three lines as far as melody is concerned, but

Example 1

the connection is given through the harmonic structure of "How High the Moon": the same harmonies constitute the basis for three very different improvisations.

This example was transcribed from an RCA record that does not even give a clue to the original theme in its title, *Indiana Winter.* The three choruses (that is what improvisations on the harmonies of a theme in the number of bars corresponding to that theme are called) cited in the example were played by trombonist J. J. Johnson, trumpeter Charlie Shavers, and tenorman Coleman Hawkins.

The habits of jazz ensure that the most important jazz themes repeatedly become the foundations for the improvisations of jazz musicians. They are played day after day and night after night in hundreds of clubs and concert halls. After one hundred or two hundred choruses, a musician may arrive at certain phrases that then will crop up more and more frequently in the playing of the tune. After a while something like a "standard chorus" on the respective theme will have developed.

Many choruses have become so famous that the listener would be disappointed if the musician who made them up were suddenly to play something different. King Oliver's "Dippermouth Blues," Alphonse Picou's "High Society," Charlie Parker's "Parker's Mood," Ben Webster's "Cotton Tail," Stan Getz's "Early Autumn," Bix Beiderbecke's "Singing the Blues," Louis Armstrong's "West End Blues," Lester Young's "Song of the Islands," Chu Berry's or Coleman Hawkins' "Body and Soul," Miles Davis' "All of You," Coltrane's "My Favorite Things," and Chick Corea's "Spain"—these (written down as they came to mind) are high points one would be loath to see transplanted to other peaks, especially as one cannot be sure they would be peaks. On the contrary, such a result would be unlikely. It would be foolish to claim that choruses that are among the greatest in jazz cease to be jazz when repeated. Thus, what is created by improvising and, having proved to be of value, is repeated, also belongs to improvisation.

This concept of the once-improvised is important. It makes clear that what was once created by improvising is linked to the musician who created it. It cannot be separated from him or her, notated, and given to a second or third musician to play. If this happens, it loses its character, and nothing remains but the naked formula of notes.

At this point, the distinction between improvisation and composition becomes more differentiated. European music, insofar as it is composed, is capable of limitless reproduction by anyone who possesses the instrumental, technical, and conceptual capacities to grasp it. Jazz can be reproduced solely by the musician who produced it. The imitator may be technically better and intellectually superior but still cannot reproduce the music. A jazz improvisation is the personal expression of the improviser and of his or her musical, spiritual, and emotional situation.

In other words, the concept "improvisation" is actually inaccurate. A jazz musician who has created a chorus is at one and the same time improviser, composer, and interpreter. In jazz—even in arranged jazz, as will be shown later—these three aspects *must* be in evidence lest the music become questionable. In European music they *can* be separated without affecting the quality of the music. On the contrary: the quality may improve. Beethoven was considered a poor interpreter of his own music; others were able to play it better. Miles Davis in his formative years was, as far as technique is concerned, not an outstanding musician. Yet it is unthinkable that a technically better equipped trumpeter should have copied his phrases and, playing them note for note, have played a "better Miles Davis" than Miles himself. To express it as a paradox: Miles might have been only a fair trumpet player, but he was the greatest interpreter of his own music one could wish for. Indeed, the spiritual power of his improvisations had impact and influence even on trumpeters who were technically superior.

An improvised jazz chorus stands in danger of losing its authenticity and of becoming dishonest and untrue when it is copied by someone who did not create it. Given the multiplicity of human experience, it is inconceivable that the "other" could play from the identical situation from which the "one" improvised a chorus. The relationship between the music heard and the person who created it is more important to jazz improvising than complete lack of preparation. When copying and imitation occur without proper preparation, jazz is in greater danger than when, after hour-long, systematic preparation, phrases are created that belong to the player as expressions of artistic personality. This is the meaning of the passage from Humphrey Lyttelton quoted earlier. A musician as different from Lyttelton as Shorty Rogers means the identical thing when he said, "In my opinion all good jazz musicians are composers. I have utilized them as composers by having parts in which I merely wrote instructions and left the rest to the men to compose spontaneously, mutual instinct being the connecting link between us." (In other words, between arranger and improviser.) Misha Mengelberg, the Dutch pianist, speaks of improvisation as a process of "instant composing," thus expressing the identity of improviser, composer, and interpreter in a different way.

This identity of improviser, composer, and interpreter is what is meant when we speak of improvisation in jazz—not a wild, head-on extemporization. The identity of improviser, composer, and interpreter has to be fulfilled also by the arranger who—aside from relating what is to be improvised to what has been once-improvised—finds the real justification for his position in the fact that he can sometimes respond more satisfactorily to the demand

for the identity of improviser, composer, and interpreter than the spontaneously improvising soloist can. Jack Montrose, one of the leading arrangers on
the West Coast, said, "The jazz writer forms a unique contrast to his
colleagues in other fields of musical composition in that his ability to *write*
jazz music is a direct extension of his having acquired the ability to play it
first. He must have shared the experience of creating jazz music, the *jazz
experience.* It is my contention that jazz music bearing the stamp of true
authenticity has never been written except by composers who have first
attained this prerequisite." Elsewhere, Montrose contended that as long as
the music is the work of a jazz musician, jazz will be the result.

We shall discuss this more extensively in the next section, but for now we
propose six points that may serve as a summary of the problem of
improvisation in jazz.

1. The once-improvised is equal to improvisation.
2. The once-improvised can be reproduced by the one who produced it,
   but by no one else.
3. Both improvisation and the once-improvised are personal expressions
   of the situation of the musician who produced them.
4. The concurrence of improviser, composer, and interpreter belongs to
   jazz improvisation.
5. Insofar as the arranger corresponds to point 4, his or her function
   differs from that of the improvising-composing interpreter merely in
   terms of craftsmanship and technique: the arranger writes, even when
   writing for others, on the basis of experience as an improvising-
   composing interpreter.
6. Improvisation—in the sense of points 1 through 5—is indispensable to
   jazz; improvisation in the sense of complete unpreparedness and
   unlimited spontaneity *may* occur but is *not* a necessity.

The Arrangement

Many jazz lovers and almost all laymen believe there is a contradiction
between improvisation and arrangement. Because, in their view, improvisation is decisive, the presence of an arrangement must automatically indicate
a state of decadence since "the more arrangement, the less improvisation."

Jazz musicians—not just today, but from the start of jazz, or at least from
the great days of New Orleans jazz in Chicago—are of another opinion. They
see the arrangement not as an inhibition of the freedom to improvise but as
an aid. It is a matter of experience that the possibilities for free and unlimited
improvised solo playing are particularly enlarged when the soloist knows
what the other musicians are doing. With an arrangement, the soloist knows.
Many of the greatest improvisers—first and foremost Louis Armstrong—

have demanded arrangements. Only to a superficial observer does it appear contradictory that Fletcher Henderson on the one hand was the first jazz arranger with a precise conception, while on the other hand his orchestra offered greater freedom of improvisation than almost any other big band of its day.

In the relationship between arrangement and improvisation there is an inherent tension, which can be fertilized to an unimagined extent. Jelly Roll Morton told his musicians, "You'd please me if you'd just play those little black dots—just those little black dots that I put down there. If you play them, you'll please me. You don't have to make a lot of noise and ad-lib. All I want you to play is what's written. That's all I ask." And despite this, clarinetist Omer Simeon—long a member of Morton's bands—and guitarist Johnny St. Cyr said, "Reason his records are so full of tricks and changes is the liberty he gave his men. . . . He was always open for suggestions." This is the tension that has to be dealt with in art, and one cannot do much theorizing about it. In the early days of the Ellington orchestra, all the band members felt they were playing what they wanted; yet each note was "Ellingtonian."

Arrangements came into being as early as the formative years of jazz. Even the early jazz musicians—King Oliver, Jelly Roll Morton, Clarence Williams, Louis Armstrong—arrived through improvisation at set, repeatable turns of ensemble playing, and once their effectiveness had been tested, these turns remained. This shows how rapidly improvisation is transformed into arrangement. What was once-improvised yesterday has perhaps already become a permanent arrangement by tomorrow.

George Ball related how the New Orleans Rhythm Kings—the most successful Dixieland band between 1921 and 1925—did this kind of thing:

by predetermining definite parts for each man to play; by introduction of patterns, simple though they were, and a more even rhythmic background. Arrangements were, of course, impossible as we know them today, if only from the fact that the most important members of the melody section, Mares, Rappolo and Brunis, could not read music. [Elmer] Schoebel nevertheless spent numberless rehearsals drilling these men in their parts, which we might call arranged, although not a note of music was set down for them, and which the performers had perforce to learn by sheer memory.

Many other great groups of New Orleans and early Dixieland jazz (not to mention later ones) valued arrangements: the Hot Seven, the Memphis Five, the Original Dixieland Jazz Band, the California Ramblers—groups that have come to represent the incarnation of free, unfettered improvisation to traditional jazz fans.

Perhaps the misunderstanding arises from the fact that the term *arrangement* has not been precisely defined. There is a tendency to speak of arrangements only when something has been written down beforehand. But it is easy to see that it is actually only a question of procedure whether a certain passage actually has been written down in advance or has merely been discussed. Arrangement begins the moment something is agreed upon in advance. It is immaterial whether this is done in writing or orally. Between the agreements among the New Orleans Rhythm Kings and the complex scores of the modern big-band arrangers, who may have studied with Milhaud, Stefan Wolpe, Ernst Toch, or other great modern composers and who are conversant with the traditional European art of instrumentation, there is only a difference of degree.

Since the thirties, the expression "head arrangement" has gained currency among big bands. In the bands of Fletcher Henderson and Count Basie or in the first Woody Herman "Herd" of the forties, it was common practice to establish only the first twenty-four or thirty-two bars of a piece, the remainder was left to the improvisatory capacities of the musicians. This term also makes clear how inevitable and organic is the development from improvisation through the once-improvised to the arrangement.

Since there is no contradiction between arrangement and improvisation, the latter has not faded into the background by reason of the progressive development of the former in jazz history. Improvisation and arrangement have both developed equally. Charlie Parker, Miles Davis, and John Coltrane—and later, even more so, Albert Ayler and other free-jazz musicians—command a freedom of improvisation that King Oliver, Louis Armstrong, or Bix Beiderbecke never possessed at the zenith of traditional jazz. This can be determined quite rigorously: Often several masters of one title are recorded until recording director and musicians are satisfied. On several available versions of a given piece by Armstrong or Beiderbecke, for example, the solos vary, but they are, by and large, quite comparable; structure and line were changed only rarely. Takes by Charlie Parker, however, differ so markedly that one might say that a new piece was created each time. Of the four masters of Parker's "Cool Blues," recorded in immediate succession on the same day (only the final one was approved by Parker), three were put on the market under different titles: "Cool Blues," "Blowtop Blues," and "Hot Blues"—and to a certain degree they are all different "pieces."

Thus it is not contradictory for musicians who are members of groups dependent on arrangements to speak of improvisation as the "key word." John Lewis, the maestro of the Modern Jazz Quartet, where arrangements and composition are of decisive importance, has said, "Collective improvisation is what makes jazz singular." And clarinetist Tony Scott, who has undertaken many interesting experiments as arranger and jazz composer, said during a roundtable discussion at Newport in 1956 that jazz was more likely to progress through improvisation than through writing.

Clearly, the arrangement can only fulfill its task when the arranger lives up to the demands expressed by Jack Montrose at the end of the last section: He must be a jazz musician and a jazz improviser. In the entire history of jazz there is no exception to this basic rule. It is significant that it is not possible to speak of the arrangement in jazz without mentioning improvisation.

Insofar as the arranger has to be an improvising jazz musician, it is only a small step from arranger to jazz composer. Without doubt, the actual contradiction is not between improvisation and arrangement, but between improvisation and arrangement on the one hand and composition on the other. Because improvisation is of such importance in jazz, the music has arrangements but no compositions that are completely "composed through." Since European music, at least since romanticism, is a composed and compositionally grounded music, it has practically no improvisation aside from "aleatorics" in modern concert music (but that is a different matter, which, with its theory-laden clumsiness, casts further light on the strained attitude of the concert musicians toward improvisation!).

Thus, the "jazz composer" is a paradox. "Jazz" means improvisation, and "composer"—at least in Europe—means the exclusion of improvisation. But the paradox can be fruitful: The jazz composer can structure music in the sense of the great European tradition and nonetheless leave room for jazz improvisation. Most of all, the composer can write what he or she structures in the sense of the European tradition in a jazz manner. There can be no doubt that jazz is subordinate to European music as far as formal structure is concerned and that it might gain if mastery of form and structure becomes possible in jazz, provided nothing is lost in respect to the elements in which the singularity of jazz is contained: vitality, authenticity, immediacy of expression—in short, all that is jazzlike. From this point of view, Stravinsky's dictum that composition is "selective improvisation" acquires a much greater degree of importance for the jazz composer than it can have for the composer in the European tradition.

Since the fifties, musicians such as Jimmy Giuffre, John Lewis, Horace Silver, Bill Russo, Ralph Burns, Oliver Nelson, Charles Mingus, Carla Bley, Chick Corea, Muhal Richard Abrams, Henry Threadgill, and John Zorn have given new meaning to the term "jazz composer," with credit to both elements of the term. But only Duke Ellington, who has been jazz "composer" since the mid-twenties, stands on the level of the truly great jazz improvisers—the level of Charlie Parker, Louis Armstrong, Lester Young, Coleman Hawkins, John Coltrane, Miles Davis. . . .

Beyond all these considerations, of course, stands the kind of composer who could be found in jazz from the very start: the musician who simply writes twelve-bar blues or thirty-two-bar song themes, supplying himself and his players with materials for improvisation. This line leads straight from early musicians—Jelly Roll Morton, for example—through, say, Fats Waller in the twenties and thirties and Thelonious Monk from the forties on to the well-known improvisers of modern jazz who write much of their own material: Sonny Rollins, Miles Davis, John Coltrane, Herbie Hancock, Archie Shepp, Muhal Richard Abrams, David Murray—in fact, practically everyone who plays improvised jazz. This sort of composing is directly related to the improvisatory process, without detouring through the arrangement. Of course, there are many gradual stages—from simple sets of changes and themes merely setting up a blowing line to the complex jazz composition, formally structured and scored for many voices. All of these steps build on each other so organically that the erection of boundaries appears more or less arbitrary.

The relationship between arrangement and improvisation reflects the frequently posed question about the relationship between the collective and the individual in jazz. Jazz has been called "the music of the collective" as well as "the music of boundless individualism." But the symphony orchestra, in which a hundred musicians subordinate themselves, almost in self-sacrifice, to a single will, is collective to a much greater degree. And a disdain for rules, regulations, and laws would seem to be a prerequisite for "boundless individualism." Jazz, except for a few instances of extreme free jazz, shows no signs of such disdain.

What happens in free jazz only *seems* to follow different laws. Certainly, it has none (or only very few) of such exact written-down scores as those written by Oliver Nelson or Gerry Mulligan or Gary McFarland for the big bands. The concept of arranging actually returns to the position it had at the beginning of jazz history—to the orally predetermined arrangements of the King Oliver Band or of the New Orleans Rhythm Kings. And that same fruitful and inspiring tension between the freedom of the improvisatory principle and the order of the arrangement that existed in the other jazz styles is retained. Of course, there is, aside from that, also the kind of improvisation that entails no predetermination, in which there is no trace of arrangement whatsoever. The impression grows stronger, however, that such total lack of restraint was only a passing stage within the process of liberation during the sixties. After that, the musicians gained a much more relaxed attitude toward composition by learning to purify, structure, and disentangle the experiences of free jazz.

At any rate, since the arrangement had been growing in scope and importance for so many years, it was logical that improvisation—and finally, following the freeing of improvisation, composition as well—should do the same. With his usual cogency, Dave Brubeck summed it up: "Jazz is about the only form of art existing today in which there is freedom of the individual without the loss of group contact." This coexistence of collectivism and freedom expresses what we characterized as "the sociological situation of jazz" at the start of this book.

The Blues

Two jazz critics, a recording director, and a musician were discussing "if the blues is essential to the jazz idiom." Pianist Billy Taylor, the participating musician, said, "I don't know of one giant—early, late, mid-thirties, or cool—who didn't have a tremendous respect and feeling for the blues, whether he played the blues or not. The spirit of it was in his playing or he wasn't really a giant as far as jazz was concerned." Nesuhi Ertegun, vice president of Atlantic Records, added, "Let me ask you one question. Do you think a man like Lester Young would play a tune like 'Body and Soul' in the same way if he had never played the blues?" Billy Taylor's answer was "No." And Leonard Feather summarized: "I think what it all boils down to is that the blues is the essence of jazz, and merely having a feeling for blues means having a feeling for jazz. In other words, the chords or the notes of the chords which are essential for blues are the notes that are essential for jazz—the flat third, flat seventh, etc." To which Billy Taylor countered, "Well, I hesitate to oversimplify in that particular case because I tend to go back to the spirit. It's not the fact that a man on certain occasions would flat a certain note, bend a note or do something which is strictly a blues-type device. It's just that whatever this nebulous feeling is—the vitality they seem to get in the blues—whatever it is makes the difference between Coleman Hawkins' 'Body and Soul' and a society tenor player's 'Body and Soul'."

It becomes clear from this discussion that the blues can be defined in several ways: emotionally, racially, sociologically, melodically, harmonically, and formally. Nearest at hand and most useful at this point is the emotional definition. Leadbelly, a singer from the olden days when the blues was wholly a folk art, set down the emotional definition in incomparable fashion:

> Now this is the blues. No white man ever had the blues, 'cause nothin' to worry about. Now, you lay down at night and you roll from one side of the bed to the other all night long—you can't sleep . . . what's the matter? The blues has got you. You get up and sit on the side of your bed in the mornin'—may have your sister or brother, your mother and father around but you don't want no talk out of 'em . . . what's the matter? The blues has got you. Well you go and put your feet under the table and look down on your plate—got everything you want to eat—but you shake your head and get up and say 'Lord! I can't eat and I can't sleep! What's the matter with me? Why, the blues has got you, wanna talk to you.

Bessie Smith sings, "Nobody knows you when you're down and out." And John Lee Hooker: "I've got the blues so bad, it's hard to keep from cryin'." In "Trouble in Mind Blues" it goes, "If you see me laughin', I'm laughin' just to keep from cryin'."

This emotional definition also holds true for the blues when it is happy and full of humor, as it often is. The blues artists in whose work there are as many happy as sad blues—such as Big Bill Broonzy or later B. B. King or Otis Rush—have included themselves in this emotional definition of the blues.

Next to the emotional stands the melodic, harmonic, and formal definition. T-Bone Walker, the blues singer, has said, "You know, there's only one blues, though. That's the regular twelve-bar pattern and then you interpret over that. Just write new words or improvise different and you've got a new blues."

The blues strophe consists of twelve bars, based on the most fundamental of all chords: tonic, dominant, and subdominant.

Example 2

This twelve-bar chord structure is, exceptions aside, consistent—from the earliest blues (insofar as they already conform to the manifest blues pattern) down to the most complex blues improvisations of the modern musicians, who expand the harmonics in the most subtle way but of course without disturbing their basic function. The twelve-bar form is the standard form of blues. There are various other forms of blues that deviate from it.

The blues melodies and blues improvisations that rest on this twelve-bar chord structure derive their peculiar fascination from the "blue" notes. People previously assumed they were the product of a difficulty—of the problem that arose for the enslaved blacks deported from Africa to the New World when they had to adapt their pentatonic system (consisting of five notes) to our heptatonic scale (seven notes). In order to make the third and seventh steps of our scale accessible to their own musical sensibility, they had to flatten them. Although that can result in what traditional European functional harmonics would call "diminution," it is in principle a different process. In this process, the "diminished third" and the "minor seventh" (to use conventional musical terms that are in fact out of place here) became blue notes. That happened without recourse to the minor or major keys, which in European music govern the diminution of certain steps.

In the meantime this "theory of incapacity" seems increasingly shaky. It's not just that heptatonic systems are to be found in Africa and don't create any difficulties there. The frequency and purposefulness with which blue notes appear in early blues and jazz also indicates that these "unstable" notes were intentional right from the start, and—with black music's own sense of ecstasy—were deliberately sought as a way of increasing excitement and intensive tonal color.

Later, when the bebop musicians introduced the flatted fifth, this note, too, became a "blue" note—at first in the minor blues, then in all kinds of blues music—equal to the blue notes of the third and seventh steps.

In the blues it frequently happens that a conventionally tonic or dominant chord fall under a blue note, so that the major third may be played in the bass, and the minor third in the treble. This creates frictional sounds, which certainly can be interpreted as arising from a friction between two different harmonic systems: the chord structure, which corresponds to the European tradition, and the melodic line, with its blue notes originating in African music.

Example 3

Example 3 shows a very typical melodic line. Every other note is a blue note. The traditional blue notes at the third and seventh steps are marked by a single arrow; the double arrows indicate blue notes originating in the flatted fifth. The C chord is the basis for the whole cadence, unharmed by the constant friction. Each blue note thus stands before a "normal" note, into which the blue note resolves, so that the cadence actually is nothing but a sequence of tension and relaxation, repeated six times. The tendency in jazz to create tension only to dissolve it immediately and then to create new tension that is again dissolved here becomes particularly clear. These tensions do not have the broad span they possess in European music.

Since the blues notes are generally resolved by a note that lies one half tone lower, there is a strong tendency in the blues toward descending melodic lines, as Example 3 also shows. It is a melodic line that occurs, in this or similar form, in thousands of jazz improvisations, within and outside of blues. It also shows how all jazz is saturated with blues elements—whether an actual blues tune is involved or not.

The twelve blues bars consist of three four-bar phrases, developed in such a way that a statement is made in the first four, repeated (over different harmonies) in the following four, and a "conclusion" drawn from it in the final four.

Sara Martin sings:

> Blues, Blues, Blues why did you bring trouble to me?
> Yes, Blues, Blues, Blues why did you bring trouble to me?
> O Death, please sting me and take me out of my misery.

This threefold form, with its double question and contrasted answer, creates a finite and compact mode of expression comparable to the important "minor forms" of art, from a literary standpoint as well. The causal interconnection of form and content fulfills the highest criteria of form. It is astonishing that the highest ideal of Western art—the unity of form and content—is approximated in the "proletarian" and "Negroid" world of the blues, and so tightly and clearly that the relationship between them becomes "causal."

The finite blues form was of course not given from the start, neither musically nor textually. When looking at old folk blues, one must conclude that the threefold four-bar AAB structure was present in the beginning merely as an "idea," which was approximated and deviated from. This idea of the blues form became increasingly crystallized over the years, and today it is so pure that nonconformity to it is generally felt to be an error. But in the great, "classical" period of the blues it was no error not to conform.

Harmonically as well, there were many "errors" in the old, "primitive" blues. The singers floated with sovereign ease above certain basic chords, doing much as they pleased. Big Bill Broonzy often pointed out that to be emotionally right was much more important than to be formally and harmonically correct.

The blues singer generally fills the three four-bar phrases only up to the beginning of the third, seventh, and eleventh bar. The remainder of each phrase is at the disposal of an improvisation called a "break," a short, cadenzalike burst that sets off the preceding from the following phrase. These one and a half bars of the classic blues break are the germ cell of jazz improvisation as a whole, with its fascinating interplay of forces between the unbounded freedom of the soloist and the obligation toward the collective of players.

The blues lyrics correspond in level to their form. According to Jean Cocteau, the poetry of the blues is the only substantial contribution to genuine folk poetry in our century. Everything of importance in the life of the blues singer is contained in these lyrics: love and (often disguised) racial discrimination; prison and the law; floods and railroad trains and the fortune told by the gypsy; the evening sun and the hospital—just to mention a few of the favorite subjects of blues singers. Life itself flows into the lyrics of the blues with a surprising straightforwardness and directness to which nothing in Western poetry—and this goes for folk poetry as well—is comparable.

The majority of blues deal with love. Love is viewed, simply and clearly, as that toward which love aims, yet it is able to remain love—even when it reflects the kind of war between the sexes sociologists have found to be very frequent in the black ghettos and neighborhoods, resulting from centuries of disrupted black family structures, during and also after slavery. At a time when everyday love poetry has barely risen above the level of "Roses are red/Violets are blue," the blues reflects that lofty, unsentimental stature and strength of the emotions and the passions that we know from great literature. Not a single blues is on the housemaid level of "Too Young," and yet the blues belongs to the world of those who have supplied an entire continent with domestics, butlers, and nursemaids!

There are funny blues and fast blues. But mainly blues are the music of a first rural, then urban proletariat whose life is filled with suffering. The social origins of the blues are at least as important as the racial ones. We do not know of a single genuine, authentic blues that does not make it obvious at once that the singer is of the proletariat. It would not make sense for members of the "aristocracy" to sing the blues: They don't have the blues.

It is not without reason that references to "having" or "not having" the blues are made time and again in blues lyrics. You have to have the blues to be able to sing them. "The blues are a part of me," said singer Alberta Hunter.

From its mood and atmosphere the blues achieves continuity—something it seems to be lacking to a notable degree at first glance. It almost seems as if lack of coherence—in other words, diametrical opposition to all that stood for art in the Western sense until the end of the last century—is a mark of the blues (which, of course, also has to do with the oral tradition of the blues). Lines and verses put together from the most varied blues and songs are linked up, unconcerned with what we call narrative logic and context. Sometimes the singer himself seems to be the actor, and then a third person is acting. A moment ago the subject was a "he," and now it is a "she" . . . we were in the past, now we are in the future . . . suddenly, we switch from singular to plural.

Even those blues songs clearly created by a single person seem to show that their author was not particularly worried about continuity of content. In the "Old New Orleans Blues," although unquestionably committed to old New Orleans by title and theme, the next-to-last verse takes us to Memphis, while in the final verse the topic is the lantern swinging in the wind outside the window behind which the singer is sleeping. The "Two Nineteen Blues" first deals with the railroad and then suddenly with a streetwalker, and so forth. Dozens of blues furnish examples of this "blues discontinuity," while it seems quite difficult to find a blues in which each word follows logically from the foregoing. It would be wrong to conclude that this stems from an inability to create continuity. No, continuity is not the point. The lines and verses have an impressionistic quality. They relate to each other as do the spots of color in a painting: If you stand close, you cannot tell why there is red next to blue, or green next to orange, but as soon as you take a few steps back, it all blends into a whole. The "whole" of the blues is the mood, the blues atmosphere. It creates its own continuity. Into the blues mood flows whatever comes up—events, memories, thoughts, fancies—and out comes, always, the blues.

Everything that exists in the world of the singer goes through the blues; all is contemporaneous. Nothing can be outside. Blues singer Big Bill Broonzy tells about how when he was a boy, he and his uncle caught a big turtle:

> We drug him home and my uncle told me to make him stick his neck out of his shell. I took a stick and put it in front of him. The turtle caught hold of the stick and couldn't turn it loose. So my uncle said, "Hold his head right there and I'll cut it off." My uncle took the axe and cut the turtle's head off and we went in the house and stayed there a while. When we came back, no turtle. So we looked for him and turtle was nearly back to the lake where we caught him. We picked him up, brought him back to the house and my uncle said, "There's a turtle who is dead and don't know it." And that's the way a lot of people is today: they got the blues and don't know it.

At the beginning of the blues stand the work songs and field hollers: the simple, archaic songs sung by the blacks at work in the fields or on the levees. They were sung because it was easier to work to the rhythm of a song than without it. The rhythm had an effect on the singers, making even those perk up who otherwise would have worked sluggishly or not at all: "Lawd, cap'n, I's not a-singin'—I's just a-hollerin' to help me with my work." That's why the white man wanted to see the black sing. "A singing Negro is a good Negro," is the way French critic François Postif described the attitude of a plantation owner or prison warden.

Folk song and folk ballad, frequently in the "white" sense, joined with work song and field holler. There were the old rounds with the regular, happy repetition of a refrain of a few lines, sung by the chorus of listeners.

Blind Lemon Jefferson, Big Bill Broonzy, Leadbelly, Robert Johnson, Elmore James, Blind Boy Fuller, Rev. Gary Davis, Bukka White, Blind Willie McTell, Big Joe Williams, Sonny Terry, Brother John Sellers, John Lee Hooker, and Lightnin' Hopkins are famous representatives of blues folklore.

Most accompanied themselves on guitar, and they often are wonderful guitarists (e.g., Lonnie Johnson and Lightnin' Hopkins). Other blues singers (e.g., Sonny Terry or the late Little Walter and Sonny Boy Williamson) knew how to coax amazing sounds from a harmonica. Others recorded with well-known jazz musicians backing their folk-rooted blues vocals.

In most cases, the accompanying instrument meant more to the blues singer than mere background: It was a partner in conversation. It would inspire and excite; it could make comments in affirmation or protest; it anticipated or completed an idea.

Under no circumstances should the reader assume that we are speaking of things related to a distant past. Almost all well-known commentators on blues have consciously or unconsciously nurtured this feeling, as if they were the last of their profession with just time enough left to document a vanishing folklore art form. A feature of the white man's relationship to folklore of all kinds is that he links it to nostalgia, sentimentality, memories of the "good old days." As far as the blues is concerned, this response is wrong.

There are more blues movements and blues styles today than ever before, and they all live side by side. Not one of the old blues forms—folk blues, country blues, prison blues, archaic blues, Cajun blues—has become extinct. In fact, new ones were added: city blues, urban blues, jazz blues, rhythm and blues, soul blues, funky blues. In addition there are different styles. The most easily recognizable are Mississippi blues (rough, archaic), Texas blues (mobile, flexible, jazz-related), and East Coast blues, from Florida or Tennessee, for example (often permeated with white country and hillbilly folklore). The folk blues of Texas and of the Midwest (the so-called "territories") shaped the California big-city blues; the folk blues of Mississippi, with Memphis as the core, shaped the Chicago big-city blues. But in this case, too, the mixtures are no less interesting than the pure forms, which are illusory in the blues world, anyway—blues is by nature a mixture. The success of the Memphis blues in the sixties—of Albert King, to name one, but also of soul singers like Otis Redding—lies precisely in its combination and urbanization of elements from Mississippi and Texas.

Almost all important blues singers are at home in several forms and styles—not only in the sense that they developed from one form to the other, as from country blues to city blues and on to contemporary urban blues (e.g., Muddy Waters, Howlin' Wolf, B. B. King, Otis Rush), but also in the sense that they may practice several forms simultaneously e.g., John Lee Hooker, Johnny Shines, or Louisiana Red, who keep switching between folk, country, and city blues; or Jimmy Witherspoon, T-Bone Walker, Ray Charles, who have all frequently played with jazz musicians; or Gatemouth Brown, who mixes practically everything: blues, jazz, country, Cajun, etc.).

Since the mid-fifties, the blues has penetrated popular music to a degree unimaginable up to then. First, black rhythm and blues—the rocking music of the black South and of the Northern ghettos—led into rock 'n' roll. Bill Haley and Elvis Presley were the first white rock 'n' roll stars, but immediately following came black artists—Chuck Berry, Fats Domino, Ray Charles—who enjoyed an immense success on the white pop scene that would have been considered impossible even shortly before. By 1963, the best of rhythm and blues had become so closely linked to the mainstream of American popular music that *Billboard* magazine temporarily suspended separate listings of "Rhythm and Blues" and "Pop." Separate listing was resumed later, but the magazine kept changing its policy; it had become uncertain, and still is. Outstanding black talent is also now part of the white scene. Younger readers will hardly be able to appreciate how unusual that once would have been. The term "rhythm and blues" was only introduced in the late forties. Up to then, the term was "race records." This label makes it clear that for fifty years, black music had been played in a ghetto that was noticed by the white world only indirectly at best: by letting its own musicians degenerate, play down, drain, what in its authentic black form remained unknown to most of the white audience.

It was through musicians like Bill Haley, Elvis Presley, Chuck Berry, Fats Domino, Little Richard, and others, that the blues literally demolished the popular music of Tin Pan Alley and its babbling about schmaltzy, kitschy, dishonest feelings. If much of today's popular music is more realistic, clear, honest, and at the same time more poetic, musical, and often emotionally richer than popular music before the mid-fifties (leaving disco music aside), then this must be ascribed to the penetration of white popular music by the blues. Blues—and black music in general—has always *been* what white popular music has only recently become: realistic and full of social involvement, a commentary on the everyday life and problems of those who sang it.

What happened during the fifties was only the preparation for the "decade of rock," the phrase frequently applied to the sixties. For the United States, it was Bob Dylan; then, initially in Great Britain and later simply for the whole world, it was the Beatles—and also the Rolling Stones (who took their name from a Muddy Waters blues)—who created a new musical conscious-ness, so that artists who just shortly before had been the personification of high musical standards (think of Frank Sinatra!) within a few years became "old fogeys" when confronted with this new consciousness. The musical standards of the world of popular music demolished in the process were the symbols of the moral, social, and political standards of the bourgeois world that had created the old pop music. These standards were the real target of the new movement.

Bob Dylan, the Beatles, the Rolling Stones—they all are unthinkable without the blues. The Beatles came from rhythm and blues, particularly Chuck Berry. Dylan comes from Woody Guthrie and the American folklore at whose center stands folk blues. For half a year he lived with blues singer Big Joe Williams. It has been said that Dylan was "the first true poet of popular music." But in so saying, hundreds of black folk-blues singers who, since the turn of the century—and perhaps even earlier—have been the "true poets of popular music," are forgotten.

Both Dylan and the Beatles grew far beyond their respective bases of origin. When Dylan accompanied himself electronically for the first time (at the 1965 Newport Folk Festival), there was a storm of protest from his fans. But three years later, in 1968, he recorded his album *John Wesley Harding* with acoustic guitar and folk-blues harmonica; thus, he programmatically clarified for all his followers—and they did understand—how he viewed his musical and spiritual heritage.

There was a similar development with the Beatles. For years, they had continuously refined their rock 'n' roll heritage, sensitizing their music more and more, and had moved further and further away from the blues. In "Michelle," "In My Life," "Eleanor Rigby," and other songs, they had incorporated baroque elements; in "Yesterday" they had remembered the old Elizabethan English madrigal culture; in George Harrison's songs, they had made reference to classical Indian music. *Sgt. Pepper's Lonely Hearts Club Band* was a rock symphony. But then, in 1968, their double album *The Beatles* was released. And in this album—in reference to Chuck Berry, to early rock 'n' roll and rhythm and blues—they made it clear, as programmatically as Dylan in *John Wesley Harding,* that they knew where they came from and that they wanted their fans to know it, too. For those who did not hear, John Lennon said it once more: "If there was another name for rock 'n' roll, it would be Chuck Berry." (Berry is one of the big stars of blues and rhythm and blues.)

It has been said that the Beatles and Bob Dylan changed the musical and social consciousness of a whole generation. In this context, it is important to realize that this change of consciousness is based on the blues and would have been impossible without it. British guitarist Eric Clapton made this very clear when he said, "Rock is like a battery. Every so often you have to go back to the blues and recharge."

To be sure, from the standpoint of jazz and authentic blues, much of the blues derivations played in the rock era of the sixties and the rock 'n' roll of the fifties was inferior to the pure, uncommercialized product. But this holds true only for a minority of jazz and blues connoisseurs. For the majority, the reverse is valid: Through the blues, popular music attained a qualitative level previously unthinkable. This development continues. The stream of black music flowing into white rock and pop music is becoming wider and wider; in fact, it is already so wide that there is no, or almost no, difference anymore between black and white popular music. "Funkiness" became the fashionable be-all and end-all of commercial rock music during the seventies; funk, though, comes from the black ghetto and the blues—like rap and hip-hop ten years later.

The fact that truly black feeling entered the white world with the blues becomes apparent not only through the music, but also through the kind of dancing that goes with it.

In the world of blues—and in general in the black world, already in Africa—there has always been "open" and "individual" dancing. The actual partner of each individual dancer was and is the music: the dancer answers the music with his or her movements. In the white world, on the other hand, dancing had atrophied increasingly, as a pretext for social and physical contact for which the music merely furnished the barely noticed background. Dancing, like everything else in the rationalized white world, had to "serve a function." Dancing in the black world is done only for its own sake. The body becomes a musical instrument, as it has also for the young white rock audience from the mid-fifties on.

American blues specialist Charles Keil (to whom we are indebted in this connection) assumes that, seeing today's young people dance in the United States or in Europe, "a West African villager . . . would be delighted to see that Western men and women have at last cast aside the disgusting and lascivious practices of embracing, hugging, shuffling, and grappling in public and have adopted the vigorous, therapeutic pelvic exercise that has always been the pride and joy of his community."

At first, pure blues consciousness among white audiences and musicians was stronger in Britain than in the United States. Most of the successful British pop and rock musicians of the sixties for years had studied, imitated, and copied black blues singers and blues instrumentalists, and on that basis, they found their own styles.

Since the late fifties, there had been a true "blues movement" in Great Britain, led by a guitarist and vocalist who was born in Vienna, educated in France, and settled in England—Alexis Korner—and later also by John Mayall. One could indulge in all kinds of speculation as to why this contemporary "blues consciousness" originated in Britain rather than the United States, though the British Isles are much farther away from the creative blues centers of the American South or Chicago's South Side than are New York or Los Angeles. The question can be asked, Were there too many prejudices against black blues in the United States, and did the American music world jump on the blues wagon only when it was realized how much money British groups like the Rolling Stones—or later Led Zeppelin or John Mayall—were making on the blues?

Another point cannot be made without bitterness: It is white musicians who are making fortunes in today's British and American scenes with black blues, while the black creators of this music (with a growing number of exceptions) are still the relatively obscure voices of a suffering proletariat.

At the beginning of this section, we quoted Leadbelly: "No white man ever had the blues." For decades, the blues were thought to be the "last retreat" of black music that no white man would ever be able to penetrate. In all areas of a music originally created by blacks, whites again and again had been more successful, had made more money than the black creators: Benny Goodman and Artie Shaw in Swing, Stan Getz and Dave Brubeck in cool jazz, and all the others. Only in blues did the whites not succeed in producing really convincing sounds.

Since the sixties, parts of this "last bastion" have also been conquered. There are some white musicians who, at least as instrumentalists, can play authentic black blues. As we said, Britishers Alexis Korner and John Mayall paved the way for this, but both are still far away from the authenticity reached by the musicians following them: guitarists Eric Clapton or Rory Gallagher, then also Americans, guitarist Mike Bloomfield and Johnny Winter; or harmonica players Paul Butterfield, Charlie Musselwhite, and Paul Osher, all of whom learned in Chicago's black South Side (especially from Muddy Waters); the late guitarist Duane Allman and pianist-guitarist Dr. John; the musicians of the blues-rock group Canned Heat; and others.

Still, there is a difference. White blues—especially where it is artistically serious—is more precious, more "accurate," cleaner, less expressive, and also more vulgar, less subtle, and less flexible than black blues.

Charles Keil tells of a survey about the nature of blues and soul made by a black Chicago radio station among its audience. In the answers, again and again the word "mellow" recurred. They're "mellow," the blues and soul. And "mellow" is exactly what white blues are not; and when they become mellow, they cease to be blues.

No doubt, the "authenticity" of most white blues musicians is still relative. As soon as all these white musicians, authentic as they may sound as instrumentalists, open their mouths to sing, the illusion fades away. Then even the layman can hear who is white and who is black, and there is no bridge over that gap. Not even Janis Joplin (the singer from Texas who died in 1970 and of all white singers the one who came closest to the black sound) was able to bridge that gap. That should be remembered later, particularly when reading the sections about the white male and female singers. Not without reason, white blues player John Mayall, a man who should know and whom it concerns directly, has said, "When we talk about blues, we mean black blues. That's the real blues for us."

However, the sociological and social side of this matter should not be overlooked. The blues is black music for one thing, because the living conditions of blacks in parts of the South and in the northern ghettos are so different from those of whites, not only in degree, but more important, in essence. The late American critic Ralph Gleason speculated that to the extent that this changes, white blues musicians will gain "equality" with black blues musicians. At the beginning of the nineties it seems obvious that it will be a long time before this point is reached.

Spiritual and Gospel Song

The singer who comes closest to Bessie Smith in vocal power and expressiveness is not a blues singer but a gospel singer: Mahalia Jackson, who died in 1972. The gospel song is the modern form of the spiritual, the religious song of the blacks—more vital, more swinging, more jazzlike than the old spiritual, which frequently shows a closeness to European church music, and above all a proximity to the white spirituals of the last century (which are often overlooked by the "race-romancers").

The blues is the secular form of spiritual and gospel song. Or the other way around: Gospel song and spiritual are the religious forms of the blues. Thus it is not only in a relative, but in a literal sense that blues singer Alberta Hunter said, "To me, the blues are—well, almost religious. . . . The blues are like spirituals, almost sacred. When we sing the blues, we're singin' from our hearts, we're singin' out our feelings." And blues singer T-Bone Walker said, "Of course, the blues comes a lot from the church, too. The first time I ever heard a boogie-woogie piano was the first time I went to church. That was the Holy Ghost Church in Dallas, Texas. That boogie-woogie was a kind of blues, I guess. Then the preacher used to preach in a bluesy tone sometimes."

The visitor to a church in Harlem or on Chicago's South Side will not find a great contrast to the ecstatic atmosphere that might be found at a jazz concert by, say, Lionel Hampton. There are the identical rhythms, the same beat, the same swing in the music, and frequently, jazz-associated instruments—saxophones, electric guitars, drums, and more recently keyboards. The visitor will hear boogie-woogie bass lines and blues structures and see enraptured people beating time with their hands and feet and sometimes even dancing.

Winthrop Sargeant describes a church service in the South:

Minutes passed, long minutes of strange intensity. The mutterings, the ejaculations, grew louder, more dramatic, till suddenly I felt the creative thrill dart through the people like an electric vibration; that same half-audible hum arose—emotion was gathering atmospherically as clouds gather—and then, up from the depth of some "sinner's" remorse and imploring came a pitiful little plea, a real Negro "moan" sobbed in musical cadence. From somewhere in that bowed gathering another voice improvised a response; the plea sounded again, louder this time and more impassioned; then other voices joined in the answer, shaping it into a musical phrase; and so on, before our ears, as one might say, from this molten metal of music a new song was smithied out, composed then and there by no one in particular and by everyone in general.

Modern gospel songs are mostly composed pieces, marketed as sheet music. But these pieces are used freely in church services—certainly not quite as freely as jazz musicians treat a theme, but still as a basis for individual activity and interpretation. Leading black writers like Langston Hughes, who died in 1967, are sometimes authors of gospel lyrics. And the sheet music is often printed in larger editions than commercial tunes.

The most important gospel singer was—and will remain—Mahalia Jackson, born in New Orleans. In 1945, she became famous almost overnight with her recording of "Move On Up a Little Higher," a best seller in the category of the big hits: more than a million records sold!

Through Mahalia Jackson, the white world for the first time became familiar with the art of gospel singing on a broader scale. Actually, the whites heard only Mahalia Jackson. Gospel music still is the real underground art form of black America: a flourishing art full of power and vitality. Yet, the average white American has no idea of the wonderfully enraptured life that unfolds in the black churches each Sunday.

Under the impression of the breadth of today's jazz scene, jazz fans will have a hard time accepting the fact that there are far more gospel groups than jazz bands. To give an idea of this wealth of the gospel scene, we mention here only the most important gospel artists and groups—only those, that is, who are equal to the best jazz players and bands.

Among the female singers: Inez Andrews, Marion Williams, Delois Barrett Campbell, Bessie Griffin, Shirley Caesar, Dorothy Love, Edna Gallmon Cooke, Marie Knight, Willie Mae Ford Smith, Mavis Staple and Clara Ward.

Of the male singers: Robert Anderson, Alex Bradford, James Cleveland, Reverend Cleophus Robinson, R. H. Harris, Jessy Dixon, Isaac Douglas, Claude Jeter, and Brother Joe May.

The outstanding female gospel groups include the Davis Sisters, the Stars of Faith, the Angelic Gospel Singers, the Barrett Sisters, the Robert Patterson Singers, the Caravans, Liz Dargan and the Gospelettes, the Roberta Martin Singers, and Sweet Honey in the Rock.

The male gospel groups we should cite are the Five Blind Boys of Mississippi, the Brooklyn All Stars, the Gospel Clefs, the Gospelaires, the

Fairfield Four, the Gospel Keynotes, the Highway QC's, the Mighty Clouds of Joy, the Pilgrim Travelers, the Pilgrim Jubilee Singers, the Soul Stirrers, the Swan Silvertones, the Swanee Quintet, the Supreme Angels, and the Violinaires.

And finally, some of the best gospel choirs: the Gospel Singers Ensemble, Rosie Wallace and the First Church of Love, the Staple Singers, the Faith and Deliverance Choir, the Thompson Community Singers, Mattie Moss Clark and the Southwest Michigan State Choir, J. C. White and the Institutional Church of God in Christ Choir, Harrison Johnson and His Los Angeles Community choir, Walter Hawkins and the Love Center Choir, the Edwin Hawkins Singers, the Garden State Choir, the Brockington Ensemble, the B.C. + M. Mass Choir, and the Montreal Jubilation Gospel Choir.

Of special importance is the aged Bishop Kelsey in Washington, D.C. On some of his records, such as *Little Boy,* one hears how in the course of his sermon Rev. Kelsey gradually becomes the lead singer and how the sermon turns into the gospel singing of the entire congregation. Almost nowhere else does the flowing transition between speech and music—characteristic of black music—become so clear as in this vital passage between sermon and gospel song.

Many preachers and male gospel singers are masters of falsetto singing, which moves the male tenor or baritone voices far beyond their usual range into that of the female soprano—and even higher than that. This manner of singing was practiced in Africa for centuries as a sign of highly potent, bursting manhood. It moved from spiritual and gospel song to the blues and, far beyond that, into modern jazz (as in Leon Thomas) and into the contemporary rock and soul music of Prince and Michael Jackson. It certainly can also be perceived in the high "falsetto" playing of the post-Coltrane tenor saxophonists.

There are gospel songs with hillbilly and cowboy, mambo, waltz, and boogie-woogie rhythms. But most of all, gospel songs have a strong, full jazz beat. In gospel songs, as in blues, there is everything that can be found in daily life: elections, skyscrapers, railroads, telephones. It may appear naive to white people—with our characteristic notion of intellectual superiori-ty—when someone expresses in song the wish to talk with the Lord on the telephone, or travel to heaven in a pullman car. Yet, in the great period of European religious art, it was no different: The Flemish painters transferred the story of the crucifixion to the landscape of the Lowlands; and in the Christmas songs of Silesia, the people sing about the birth of Christ as if it had taken place in the ice and snow of their own mountains.

Spiritual and gospel songs are not, as is often thought, something belonging to history—something that existed at the beginning of jazz somewhere in the southern countryside. Quite the opposite: In the course of jazz development, they have grown more effective, more dynamic and alive. From the fifties on, gospel and soul have broken into other areas of black music on a wide front; initially into jazz. Milt Jackson, the leading vibraharpist of modern jazz, once answered the question where his particular style and soulful playing came from: "What is soul in jazz? It's what comes from inside. . . . in my case, I think it's what I heard and felt in the music of my church. That was the most important influence of my career. Everybody wants to know where I got my 'funky' style. Well, it came from the church."

In the liner notes to an early album by Ray Charles, Gary Kramer wrote, "The importance of the relationship between the religious music of the Negro and jazz is all too rarely emphasized."

Musicians such as Milt Jackson, Horace Silver and Charles generated a "soul wave" in the second half of the fifties that got its crucial impulse from gospel music and has been breaking into popular music since the sixties. Some of the most successful rock and soul singers of the sixties and seventies would be unthinkable without their gospel background: Otis Redding, James Brown, Aretha Franklin, Little Richard, Wilson Pickett, Isaac Hayes, etc.

Soul is secularized gospel music. And many of the best soul singer, even at the high points of their careers, still love to sing in gospel churches for a black audience—Aretha Franklin, for instance.

Some jazz specialists claim that gospel music was more important in the development of the contemporary sounds of rock, pop, and jazz than was the blues. As Charles Keil pointed out, "there are still at least forty store-front churches for every joint where blues or jazz is played in Chicago, the blues capital of the world."

Jazz and gospel singing are related in yet another respect: Many of the best female jazz singers got their start in church—Sarah Vaughan, for instance, who carried Charlie Parker's conception into jazz singing; or the late Dinah Washington, the successful "Queen" of rhythm and blues, who not only sang but also played piano in church; or Aretha Franklin.

The late Sister Rosetta Tharpe sang in the thirties with the Swing bands of Cab Calloway and Lucky Millinder and had a successful nightclub act, but before she became known in the jazz world she had sung in church. Afterward she again returned to gospel singing. One of the best-known composers of gospel songs—Thomas A. Dorsey—got his start in Chicago in the twenties and early thirties as a blues lyricist, singer, and pianist.

Danny Barker, the guitarist, said about Bessie Smith, "If you had any church background, like people who came from the South as I did, you would recognize a similarity between what she was doing and what those preachers and evangelists from there did, and how they moved people."

Harmony

In terms of harmony and melody, jazz does not offer much of a revolutionary nature, at least not until the beginning of free jazz in the sixties. Paradoxically, there is in this very fact a difference between jazz and concert music. In the realm of established musical culture, what is new and revolutionary is always first and foremost in terms of melody and harmony. Jazz, on the other hand, though among the most revolutionary developments in the arts in our century, is relatively traditional in respect to harmony and melody. Its newness is based on rhythm and sound.

Almost the only novel and singular thing in jazz in the harmonic domain are the blue notes. Aside from these, the harmonic language of conventional jazz—that is, of the jazz prior to and apart from free playing—is identical with that of popular dance and entertainment music. The harmonies of ragtime, Dixieland, and New Orleans jazz are—beyond blue notes—identical with the harmonies of polkas, marches, and waltzes. They are based on the tonic, the dominant, and the subdominant, and on their subsidiary functions. Bix Beiderbecke brought certain Debussy-like chords and whole-tone effects into jazz. The great Swing musicians added the sixth to the major triad, and "enriched" sevenths with ninths or even elevenths. Since bebop, passing chords ("substitutes") are placed between the basic harmonies of a piece, or the basic harmonies are extended through "alternations." Jazz musicians are (or at least were during the bebop and cool-jazz periods) proud of the developments in this realm of their music, and among them there was much talk of harmonic problems; but these problems, viewed from the position of European music, are more or less "old hat." Only very few chords with augmented or diminished fifths and ninths, characteristic mainly of modern jazz, do not exist in this form in conventional music, especially when such intervals occur in combinations. For example, harmonies occur that may have a flatted fifth in the bass and an augmented fifth in the treble, and above this one may occasionally find a diminished or augmented ninth. Example 4 show two such chord combinations, with their respective resolutions.

Example 4

Example 5 shows the first four bars of the song "I Can't Give You Anything but Love," popular since the twenties. (A) indicates the simple, almost primitive harmonies on which the jazz improvisations of that day were based, while (B) shows how the harmonies were altered in later years—during the transition from Swing to bop. No doubt the simple harmonies of (A) might just as well stem from a European folk dance. The more modern harmonies of (B) could also be employed in modern popular music.

Example 5

The development of jazz harmonies from ragtime and New Orleans jazz to bebop and cool jazz are not peculiar to jazz. They run parallel to and are "synchronized" with harmonic developments in popular music from the polka to the slickly orchestrated sounds of Hollywood movie music. André Hodeir surmises that jazz was influenced by pop music in this respect—a thought that lies near to hand since jazz musicians, who listen open-mindedly to everything they deem valid or worthy of imitation in any kind of music, heard that here was something that could be learned and applied to what seemed to them not very highly advanced in their own music. The harmonic language of jazz, according to Hodeir, is "largely borrowed." Because this is so, it is quite in accord with the main line of jazz tradition. It is peculiar to the genesis of jazz that it "borrowed" and united the best of two divergent musical cultures: European and African. Even among the first blacks who composed rags, played New Orleans jazz, and sang blues and spirituals, there were some who recognized or, at least, felt somehow that there was nothing in their own musical past that came even close to the ripe and rich harmonic expression in European music. On the other hand, there was nothing in European music that could come even close to the expressive power of "black" sonorities and to the vitality of Africa's rhythmic tradition. Thus both musical cultures contributed their "specialty."

In bebop and cool jazz, harmonies can be varied just as melodies were the basis for variations in traditional jazz. Thus Example 5 shows eight harmonies in the modern (B) version as compared to four in the old (A).

The latter only has chords which are closely related to C major. The modern version, however, creates a singable bass line that stands in contrapuntal relationship to the melodic line. The entire harmonic picture is loosened up and enriched. The chord sequence itself shows a steady succession of tension and relaxation, in terms of the tensions so important to jazz. Most of the added chords in the modern version (B) are terminal chords, having a tendency to resolve in the subsequent chord. The older version (A) shows only one resolution, in the fourth bar; the modern version shows three such processes. This, too, indicates how jazz history demonstrates an ever stronger and more intense concentration of jazzlike, tension-creating and tension-dissolving elements.

In the modern version a whole new chord structure comes into being. But this chord structure is not so new that it fails to indicate in each chord its relationship to the original harmonies. The new chords, so to speak, stand in place of the handed-down chords, which is why they are called substitutes. The tonal relationship of the whole remains as ordered and neat as one could desire.

Many laypeople and friends of traditional jazz not conversant with the harmonic vocabulary of bop at first reacted to its sounds as "atonal." Atonality, as the word itself makes clear, means that the music has no relationship to a tonal center and has no tonal center of gravity. But this is not the case in the prevalent forms of modern jazz before free music—and even there only in a relatively few instances. If many listeners cannot hear the harmonic centers of gravity, it is not because these centers are lacking, but because the listener's ear is unaccustomed to these harmonies. Indeed, harmony in music is a matter of custom. Any harmonic system, even in its most far-reaching variants, can be assimilated by the ear after a period of listening—even when the initial impression has been that of absurdity.

Altogether, the development of harmony in jazz and modern concert music shows many parallels—with jazz tending to lag considerably behind. The flatted fifth—the bebopper's favorite interval in the forties—in many respects corresponds to the tritone, which plays an important role in modern concert music: in Hindemith, Bartók, Stravinsky, Honegger, Milhaud, etc. Hindemith devoted much space to the tritone in *The Craft of Musical Composition,* one of the main theoretical works on modern concert music. In this work he states, "With increases in distance the familial relationship is loosened until at the utmost note—the augmented fourth or the diminished fifth—the tritone, it barely remains noticeable." Elsewhere Hindemith says that the tritone is indifferent to the harmonic base. Thus Hindemith feels that the flatted fifth does not destroy tonality but stands in a neutral, "indifferent," relationship to it. This is felt by jazz musicians as well. This "indifference" is the real reason for the popularity of the tritone in modern jazz. The tritone that, according to Hindemith, "neither belongs in the region of the harmonious, nor can be regarded as discordant," has renewed an old jazz tradition: the preference for the shimmering and the ambiguous, which can also be found in the blue notes of the blues. It was no accident that the flatted fifth—as its novelty started to fade—began to take on the function of a blue note. Example 3 (in the section on the blues) shows the degree to which blue notes and flatted fifths have become equivalent.

The flatted fifths and blue notes of jazz and the tritone of modern symphonic music thus do not point toward a dissolution of tonality, but toward its loosening and broadening. The presence of the flatted fifth and blue notes in jazz can be explained from the same point of view from which Hindemith explains the tritone in the new symphonic music: "Harmonic and melodic power are arrayed in opposition." Where the harmonic power is weakest—in the flatted fifth—the melodic power is strongest. And power of melodic line is what counts.

The bop musicians who were the first to use flatted fifths frequently—Charlie Parker, Dizzy Gillespie, Charlie Christian, Thelonious Monk—certainly did not have the faintest notion of the tritone or of Hindemith's *Craft of Musical Composition*. In their own way they arrived at solutions that Hindemith (whose name stands here for an entire direction in modern concert music) had derived from European musical tradition. This phenomenon, by the way, appears not only in the harmonies but also in the sound character of the music. The sounds of the Miles Davis Capitol Orchestra—in pieces like "Moves," "Budo," or "Israel"—are remarkably similar to those in Stravinsky compositions such as "Dumbarton Oaks Concerto," "Symphony in C," or other works from his classicist period.

The first few traces of the dissolution of conventional tonality began to show a couple of years after the initial phase of bebop in some jazz forms of the fifties—as in the work of Lennie Tristano, Charles Mingus, Teddy Charles, or George Russell. Russell, who wrote the famous "Cubana Be-Cubana Bop" for Dizzy Gillespie's big band in the late forties, created a system of tonality that he called the "Lydian Chromatic Concept of Tonal Organization." In many respects it resembles the scales of the old Hellenistic music. Lennie Tristano, with musicians of his school, created a freely improvised piece called "Intuition," in which Wolfgang Fortner—a well-known contemporary German symphonic composer—found tendencies toward the twelve-tone system.

Musicians like Tristano, Russell, Jimmy Giuffre, and Mingus paved the way for that sudden and explosive harmonic freedom that made jazz burst at the seams around the turn of the fifties. Free jazz, whose first outstanding representatives were Cecil Taylor and Ornette Coleman, finally rejected the laws of conventional functional harmonics. Sounds and lines rub against each other wild and hard, lending an ecstatic character to the music to a degree that goes far beyond what might have been felt as "ecstatic" in earlier jazz forms.

On the other hand, even in many of the freest jazz recordings, the music remains related to what musicians call "tonal centers." The word *tonal*, however, is not used in the sense of functional harmonics but is simply supposed to indicate certain crucial points—centers of gravity—from which the musicians take off, and to which they find their way back—or at least try, if they have not lost sight of them in the collective heat of improvisation. (In this context, see also the section dealing with free jazz.)

In the sections about Miles Davis and John Coltrane, we used the term *modal*. In the manner of improvisation created by Davis and Coltrane, the harmony is no longer determined by the constantly changing chords of a harmonic structure; every chord that corresponds to the "mode," to the scale, is allowed. This is a way of playing that has been in existence for centuries in many of the great exotic musical cultures—the Arab and the Indian cultures, for example. On the one hand, it allows harmonic freedom; on the other, it prevents arbitrariness. Modal playing also means a further Africanization of the music, away from the "dictatorship" of European harmonies toward the free harmonization that exists in many African musical cultures (not only in the Arabianized and Moslemized ones). Modalization thus creates a feeling of belonging in a dual sense: musically and racially—and in mood, too. That is the basis of its success.

The jazz of the seventies and eighties combined the freedom of free jazz with the harmonic possibilities of previous jazz styles. The new aspects it achieved in terms of harmonies were rooted mainly in the virtuosity and sovereignty with which harmonies from the most varied sources were dealt with. In pianist Keith Jarrett's playing, for example, one may find side by side, held together by modality, blues chords, Debussy-like whole-tone harmonies, traces of medieval ecclesiastical keys, baroque and romantic elements, exotic (e.g., Arab) elements; and the whole range of harmonic possibilities of conventional jazz. Often, all these elements occur in such immediate transitions that even specialists can no longer localize the sources, but they appear in an order that seems necessary and logical, although no known system could explain the necessities and logic of such an order. That is exactly where freedom is founded: no longer on freedom of tonality but rather in the mastery with which all the elements of tonality and atonality, European, exotic and jazzlike, classical and modern, are utilized. Thus, freedom also includes the freedom to be free and the opposite: to forego being free, if that is what the musician wants.

This is also how the missionary and sectarian character of the freedom of the free jazz of the sixties was overcome—a conception of freedom that condemned all nonfree playing as not only musically but also politically, socially, and morally regressive.

Melody

If one proceeds from the assumption made by modern musical theory that there is no basic difference between melody and harmony—melody is "horizontal harmony," harmony is "vertical melody"—almost everything that can be said about jazz melody has already been said in the preceding section. In the early forms of jazz there was hardly anything that could be called a "jazz" melody—with the exception of melodies containing blue notes (Example 3 in the blues section). The melodies were fundamentally similar to those of circus and march music, to the piano and drawing room music of the late nineteenth century. To the degree in which jazz phrasing gained significance, melodies began to evolve in terms of this phrasing—so thoroughly that this manner of phrasing finally changed and shaped the melodic flow itself, and something that might be called jazz melody came into being.

Jazz melody is primarily marked by its flowing character. Insofar as the melodic development is expressed in improvisation, there are no repeats, such as are often used structurally in European music. Repeats are excluded, to begin with, because the soloist mainly improvises from his subconscious, and so is unable to repeat what he has just played without first having recourse to close study of a possible recording. Repeats are part of the relationship of music to time. When a melody is repeated, it is lifted out of the flow of time. It is as if one were to bring back a span of time that has already passed in order to relive it once more. The absence of repetition in the flow of chorus improvisations makes it clear that jazz is more closely related to the realm in which music occurs—time—than is European music. The phenomenon of swing and other peculiarities of jazz also point to this. To give it pointed expression: If music—as almost all philosophies of music hold—is *the* art expressed in time, then jazz corresponds more fundamentally to the basic nature of the musical than European music.

Jazz derives one of its unique traits from the fact that it is instrumentally conceived. André Hodeir, who has expressed the most succinct ideas about the problems of melody and harmony in jazz yet published, said, "Composers in the European tradition conceive a phrase by itself and then make it fit the requirements of a given instrument. The jazz improviser creates only in terms of the instrument he plays. In extreme instances of assimilation, the instrument becomes in some way a part of him."

Since the instrument and, through it, the musician are "projected into" the melody, things like attack, vibrato, accentuation, rhythmic placement, etc., are so closely connected with a jazz melody that it may become meaningless without them. A European melody always exists "in the abstract" as well, but the jazz melody exists only in its concrete relationship to the instrument on which it is played and to the musician who plays it. It becomes nonsense (in the literal sense of the term) when it is removed from its creator and his instrument. This is the reason why most attempts to notate jazz improvisations have remained unsatisfactory. The fine points of phrasing, attack, accentuation, expression, and conception cannot be expressed in notation, and since everything depends on these subtleties, notation is largely unsatisfactory. When jazz melodies separated from these subtleties appear on note paper, they often seem primitive and banal.

In the course of jazz development, the improvisers have developed a facility for projecting subtleties into jazz that cannot be expressed in words. In order to accentuate the flowing character of jazz melody, the oppressively dotted quarter and eighth notes so typical of the jazz of the twenties have been dispensed with. Ever since the forties, this kind of punctuation has been regarded as "corny"; it can still be found in popular music, especially when nostalgia for the "good old days" is in order. (But all of a sudden there were several free-jazz musicians, most notably Albert Ayler, and then later alto saxophonist Henry Threadgill in postmodern jazz, who had fun with such "old-fashioned" march, polka, and circus elements!) Miles Davis, Lee Konitz, and Lennie Tristano have fashioned a manner of improvisation in which eighth note stands next to eighth note, almost without punctuation. Here are lines that look in transcription as "European" and "symphonic" as one could imagine. But when such lines are played by Davis or Konitz or almost any significant jazz musician today, they become the very essence of concentrated "jazzness." The jazz character no longer lies in the crude, external punctuation and syncopation of notes; it lies in subtlety of conception. That is what Fats Waller and so many other jazz musicians mean when they say, "Jazz isn't *what* you do, it's *how* you do it."

Because all these refinements (almost ephemeral but extremely important differentiations in attack, phrasing, vibrato, accentuation, etc.) were further developed, it has become increasingly possible to incorporate the beat—the rhythm section—into the melody line. More and more one can hear unaccompanied jazz solos of similarly concentrated jazz essence as a solo improvisation with a rhythm section. We noted in the section on the jazz of the seventies that Coleman Hawkins was the first to record a whole piece without rhythm accompaniment: "Picasso," in 1947. This record was the real forerunner of those long, free-swinging unaccompanied improvisations and cadenzas played by Sonny Rollins—or, for instances, in Germany by Albert Mangelsdorff—that became something of a trend during the seventies, often filled with hidden romanticism.

One could say that from the mid-fifties on, it became the jazz improviser's prime concern to play long, flowing lines without crudely external jazz effects, and nonetheless to convey real jazz intensity. This is also the source of the "flowing," "pulsating" rhythmic conception developed by such musicians as drummer Elvin Jones in John Coltrane's group or Tony Williams with Miles Davis.

It is only a step from here to the melodies of many free-jazz musicians, who in the realm of melody more than anywhere else retained all elements of post–Lester Young and –Charlie Parker jazz phrasing, in addition to an ecstatic intensity that has its roots way back in Africa. With other free-jazz musicians, the pendulum swung in the opposite direction again: away from the emphasis on phrasing to the accent on sound—in the sense of Bubber Miley's "jungle sounds," for example, of which we spoke in the section on sound.

The ability to simply let certain notes "go by the board" becomes particularly important in the organic course of a jazz melody line. Anyone who has notated jazz improvisation knows of this phenomenon, which André Hodeir has pertinently called a "ghost note." The note is here, one hears it quite clearly, and it has to be included in the notation. Yet one does not hear it because it was played but because it was *not* played; it was merely felt and hinted at. Faced with this, many a European musician has capitulated. In the spring of 1958, Marshal Brown went to Europe to recruit a big band of leading European jazz musicians for the Newport Jazz Festival. He consistently admired their high musical standards yet seldom was truly satisfied. "For example," he said, "it was difficult to find a musician who could throw away a note. Until we listened to these European musicians I had never realized that such subtleties are typical American."

The theme to be improvised on has become less and less important in the course of jazz development. The embellishment and ornamentation of the theme, so important to the old jazz, recede further into the background. They still exist in the interpretation of "ballads"—slow pieces, mostly from the realm of popular music, with melodies or chord structures that appeal to jazz musicians. Otherwise, improvisation became so free that the melody of a theme is hardly of significance. Often it cannot be recognized even at the start. Since the fifties, the jazz musician who plays fast pieces improvises not so much on a theme as on the harmonies of this theme. And thus, as Hodeir has said, the jazz variation is a "variation on no theme at all."

Example 6 clarifies the process of untying the jazz improvisation from the theme. The example is transcribed from a record by the Max Roach Quintet, *Prince Albert,* and the actual theme is Jerome Kern's "All the Things You Are." The first bars of this melody are in row a. Above the harmonies of this theme b, trumpeter Kenny Dorham and tenor saxophonist James Moody have placed a riff figure c—a new theme closer to their jazz conception. This

Example 6

theme of "All the Things You Are" is never even heard on the record. The musicians improvise on the new theme that was gleaned from the harmonies (in jazz terminology, chord changes) of "All the Things You Are," and on which in turn alternated harmonies can be based. One of these improvisations and its related harmonies can be found in rows d and e (with a flatted fifth in the fourth bar).

Clearly, this chain can be extended. A new riff can be based on the e changes, and this riff can become the basis for a different improvisation that in turn possesses alternations. The relationship to the theme is retained in all cases, and the jazz man—if he is knowledgeable—at once feels that somewhere "All the Things You Are" was the starting point.

This is radical usage of a tenet basic to all forms of music in which improvisation is alive (such as baroque music) and in which the melody (or its harmonies!) is used as material. It is not a cause unto itself, as it is in music of the romantic period. When the melody is a cause unto itself, it becomes sacrosanct. Since our musical consciousness is romanticized, we are accustomed to regarding melodies as sacrosanct, and thus many people have no feeling for the "materiality" of melody.

Johann Sebastian Bach still had this feeling. It was not the melody that played a role, as in romantic music, but what one made of it. *Executio* took precedence over *inventio:* execution came before invention, whereas the musical conception of romanticism created a mystique of invention and placed it above all else. Because Bach regarded music as working material, he was able to take melodies from other masters of his time (such as Vivaldi) and use them for his own purposes without acknowledging his source. According to contemporary conception this is plagiarism. But to Bach it seemed all right, and exactly in this sense it seems all right to jazz musicians.

Melody is the material, and so one can do with it as one wishes, with the proviso that what is made of this material should make musical sense.

The art of inventing new melodic lines from given harmonies has become increasingly differentiated in the course of jazz development. Often on older jazz recordings the improvisation actually only consists of taking the harmonies apart. Notes that in the basic chords were superimposed on one another are strung out in the melodies. The melodic movement has the flavor of cadenced triads and seventh chords. The melodies of modern jazz are more closely meshed. It no longer depends on interpreting the chord but on placing against it a contrasting, independent melodic line. This creates tension between the vertical and the horizontal, and the old jazz tendency to find possibilities for tension is thus nourished.

The jazz melody—aside from free playing—mainly obtains its structure from the twelve-bar form of the blues or the thirty-two-bar AABA form of the popular song, and in the newer stages of jazz, also from several irregular forms. There is a tendency among jazz musicians to cross over formal sections. Here, too, the indebtedness of music to time becomes clear. This crossing over the formal sections would be misread if one were to conclude that it results in a dissolution of form. The form—predetermined by the chord structure—remains intact. (It was dissolved only in certain stages of free jazz.) Not following the formal bar structure is perceived as something special and out of the ordinary. One might almost say the formal structure is accentuated by the fact that it is not accentuated. Here, too, a new possibility for creating tension has been discovered: tension between the given, retained form and the free line that swings above it.

Related to the tendency to play across structural sections and displace them unexpectedly is the preference for long melodic lines in modern jazz—lines much longer than in the older forms.

Kenny Clarke and Mary Lou Williams claim that the pioneers of bop consciously crossed bar lines so that musicians who were trying to "steal" their ideas would not be able to get themselves organized. Thelonious Monk said, "We're going to create something that they can't steal because they can't play it." Drummer Dave Tough told of the first time he walked into the place on 52nd Street where Dizzy Gillespie was playing: "As we walked in, these cats snatched up their horns and blew crazy stuff. One would stop all of a sudden and another would start for no reason at all. We never could tell when a solo was supposed to begin or end. Then they all quit at once and walked off the stand. It scared us." But, as Marshall Stearns points out, about a year later the selfsame Dave Tough was playing with Woody Herman's band some of the things that had scared him.

Independent of the structuring of four- or eight-bar sections, blues choruses, or thirty-two-bar song strophes is the natural structuring of tension and relaxation. The free-jazz musicians often went as far as to set this "natural form" in the place of predetermined structures. A collectively improvising free-jazz group creates its own form by "breathing," by moments of orgiastic intensity followed by moments of quiet and relaxation, which in turn are built up into new "climaxes." This achievement of free jazz has also proven of lasting importance for the jazz of the seventies and eighties: Even younger musicians who have returned to conventional, functional tonality as within "classicism" love to create their own "breathing" forms independent of twelve-bar, sixteen-bar, or thirty-two-bar structures. More and more, one can also hear combinations of predetermined and breathing structures.

It is illuminating that the way for this was paved by the Kansas City jazz of the thirties, the so-called "riff style": The riff creates tension, and the subsequent improvised melodic line creates relaxation. The strong, rhythmic, heavily accentuated ostinato phrases called "riffs," often only two or four bars in length and capable of being repeated until the thirty-two-bar song entity has been filled, are excellently suited to the creation of tension.

Guitarist Charlie Christian—one of the musicians who played a part in the creation of modern jazz—built up his solos in such a way that new riff elements were constantly opposed to new melodic lines. His solos are sequences of riffs and free-swinging melodic lines, the riffs creating tension, the melodic lines relaxation. Christian's manner of improvising was adopted by many musicians and has had great influence—consciously and unconsciously.

This relaxation—the moment of relief—goes further and deeper than is familiar from European music. Naturally, the aspect of tension and relaxation belongs to every organic musical art. In jazz, however, it is projected into the old call-and-response principle of African music. In the improvisations of Charlie Christian, the riffs are the "calls," the subsequent free-swinging lines the "responses." In other words, the lead singer no longer holds a conversation with the answering chorus of listeners—as in African music or in the spiritual—but the improvising soloist holds a conversation with himself. The loneliness—the "alienation"—of the creative jazz musician could never be made clearer than through this fact. Everything that goes into the give-and-take between call and response within the communion of a spiritual-singing congregation or a West African cult is now concentrated in the improvisation of a single soloist.

Of course, this thought must not be pursued too far. The principle of call and response is not projected merely in the single individual. The "call" of the riff is frequently played by the other musicians during the improvisation (which means during the "response" of the soloist), and it is possible in this way to create an intensity that carries everything with it. This intensity is rooted in concentration. Call and response no longer follow each other but are sounded simultaneously.

In the preceding discussion we have repeatedly used the word *relaxation*. To be "relaxed" has become an expression in the language of musicians as well as of jazz critics—and, as Norman Mailer has shown, an ideal in the lifestyle of jazz musicians and, in general, of people who want to be "in." From that vantage point, it has had a deep influence on the entire American lifestyle. Statements on European concert music rarely if ever use *relaxation* as a critical term.

Rhythm, Swing

Every jazz ensemble, be it large or small, consists of a melody section and a rhythm section. To the former belong instruments such as trumpet, trombone, clarinet, and the members of the saxophone family; to the latter, drums, bass, guitar, and piano—only insofar as they do not step out in solo roles of their own, of course.

There is tension between the melody and rhythm sections. On the other hand, the rhythm section carries the melodic group. It is like a riverbed in which the stream of the melodic lines flows. Tension exists not only between the two sections but within each group as well; in fact, this can go so far as to mix up the actual functions of the two sections. It is not uncommon in modern jazz that "melody instruments" take over rhythm functions while "rhythm instruments" play the melody part. In free jazz those functions are so intertwined that the separation between melody and rhythm sections often seems to have been abandoned.

Thus a many-layered rhythm is created that thoroughly corresponds to the many layers of melody found in, say, the music of Johann Sebastian Bach. To claim, as some people still do, that the rhythm of jazz is nothing but primitive pounding merely reveals that such a person disregards the fact that rhythmic possibilities are as inexhaustible as melodic and harmonic ones. The lack of such feeling is of course in line with Western musical development. Hans H. Stuckenschmidt, one of Europe's leading music critics, and thus not a man of jazz but of concert music, once spoke of "the rhythmic atrophy in the musical arts of the white race." It is oddly ironic that the oft-heard complaint of primitiveness, directed against jazz and other similar phenomena, here turns back on the world from whence it came: against the European-Western world in which there is this strange gap between admirable development of melodic, harmonic, and formal elements and, as Stuckenschmidt said, the atrophy of things rhythmic.

Not that there isn't any rhythm in European music. There are great rhythmic creations—for example in Mozart and Brahms, even more so in avant-garde concert music—but even these pale when compared to the grandiose rhythms of Indian or Balinese music, with traditions of rhythmic mastery as long and honorable as those of Western music in respect to form.

One does not have to think only of jazz when it comes to recognizing the inferiority of rhythmic elements in European music.

It is simply an inferiority of rhythmic sense. What every street urchin in the Near East can do—beat out with arms and legs on boxes and pots rhythmic structures in which three or four different rhythms are complexly entwined—is seldom possible for the percussionist of a symphony orchestra within the European tradition. In symphony orchestras, three or four different percussionists are frequently needed to achieve such complexity.

In jazz, the multiplicity of rhythms is anchored in the "beat": a regularly accented basic rhythm, the beating heart of jazz—or, as drummer Jo Jones has put it, "even breathing." This fundamental rhythm is the organizing principle. Through it, the musical happenings are ordered. It is maintained by the drummer or, in modern jazz, often only by the steady 4/4 of the bassist. This regulatory function corresponds to a European need. Certainly swing is connected with an African feeling for rhythm. But in spite of this—as Marshall Stearns has pointed out—there is no swing in Africa. Swing arose when African rhythmic feeling was applied to the regular meter of European music, in a long and complex process of fusion.

In the styles of jazz can be found certain basic rhythms, represented in simplified fashion by Example 7. This example represents the drum part. The notes in the lower row are played on the bass drum, those on the bottom on the snare drum (in the fusion example: center row), and the crossed notes on the cymbal. The carrier of the basic beat in New Orleans, Dixieland, Chicago, and Swing style is the bass drum; in bebop and cool jazz it is the cymbal. The rhythmic accents are indicated by >.

In New Orleans style and ragtime (a), the rhythmic emphasis is on the

Example 7

so-called "strong" beats: on 1 and 3, just as in march music. From here on, jazz rises to an ever-increasing rhythmic complexity and intensity. Dixieland and Chicago style (b), as well as New Orleans jazz as played in Chicago during the twenties, shifts the accents to 2 and 4, so that while 1 and 3 remain the "strong" beats, the accent now is on 2 and 4. Thus the peculiar "floating" rhythmic atmosphere from which swing takes its name was created.

Both New Orleans and Dixieland rhythms are two-beat rhythms insofar as the bass drum, carrier of the basic beat, is assigned two beats per measure. Of course there were exceptions. Louis Armstrong—always the Swing man!—requested drummer Baby Dodds to play an even four beats. Subsequently, Swing style was founded on four beats to the measure (c) but tends to emphasize 2 and 4. Up to this point, jazz rhythm had an almost staccato beat, with its concomitant punctuation: the cymbal beat in the Swing example. Bebop brings a further concentration, replacing staccato largely with legato (which is often phrased like a triplet). The rhythm becomes—as French drummer Gerard Pochonet has said—a *"son continu,"* a continuous sound. The cymbal sounds steadily—thus the *son continu.* In this *son continu* the rhythm gains the presence of an uninterrupted sound that, like a river, carries and immerses all that is happening in the music. On his other instruments—primarily on the bass drum—the drummer executes all kinds of rhythmic accents that emphasize the basic rhythm: it is not so much "beat out" as it is "encircled." Compared to this bop rhythm, the rhythm of cool jazz seems like a step backward, combining rhythmic features of Swing and bop.

At the bottom of Example 7 (e), there is a rhythm sample of fusion music (one of many possible ones!). Here the two-beat rhythm returns, in disguise. The snare drum (center row) hints at it. The bass drum accents the basic rhythm by encircling it.

For free jazz, there is no basic formula that can be notated. The beat is replaced by what many jazz musicians call "pulse": a pulsating, percussive activity so fast and nervous that single beats, standing by themselves, can no longer be perceived. The physiological shift of the beat from a correspondence to the heartbeat to the faster, more nervous, jerky throbbing of the pulse has been repeatedly pointed out by musicians and listeners (although the pulse, of course, is also based on the heartbeat; but what counts here are the different levels of awareness). Frequently, the melodic parts are played at quite moderate-medium tempo to a basic beat that, though no longer marked by any one instrument, is clearly perceived as medium-fast, while the drummer contrasts to that a frenzied, multilayered sounding of all his instruments. This certainly offers a new way of creating tension, and with stimulating results: several tempos, all different from each other, coexist next to and on top of each other! The free-jazz drummers use many rhythmic formulas that have been developed through jazz history, plus a host of new rhythms taken from African, Arabian, Indian, and other ethnic musics, occasionally also from European concert music. Many musicians for whom the freedom of free jazz not only represents a liberation from conventional harmonies, but also has racial, social, and political implications, emphasize African elements—from pride in the traditions of their own race.

It is often proposed that within free jazz, swing—that basic constituent element without which jazz is unthinkable—has ceased to exist. But what has ceased to exist is merely a certain metric symmetry. Our musical instincts used to perceive swing as rooted just in the friction between the symmetry of conventional, fundamental rhythm and the asymmetry of the various counter- and cross-rhythms that move above this fundamental rhythm and "contradict" it. Actually, what happened was that, in an even more concentrated and radical manner than when bebop rhythm was created, swing has been moved more "inward." Some contemporary musicians have learned to produce swing through phrasing (and thus to include it in the flow of the melody line) to such an extent that they find the kind of swing that depends on the mere symmetry of a steady, basic beat, or on just a steady bass beat, much too obvious, and even "primitive" and outmoded. (But since the seventies, there is also the sheer lustful joy of accenting—and overaccenting!—conventional Swing and Swing rhythms again.)

When bebop came into being, the majority of critics and fans also responded: This music doesn't swing any more! But just a few years later, when they had grown accustomed to the new rhythms, these same critics and fans said, It swings more than ever. And even Dixieland bands used bebop drummers in their rhythm sections.

Jazz of the seventies and eighties is in a similar position vis-à-vis the jazz of the sixties as, twenty years earlier, cool jazz was vis-à-vis bebop: The use of elements of earlier jazz forms is—in light of the newly gained freedom—once again held in high esteem. In addition, there are the rock elements, of which we spoke in the section about the seventies. The absence of a stylistically generally binding rhythmic principle has been even more apparent since 1980. In postmodern jazz—beyond any schematism—all the rhythmic models of jazz, and even rhythms from outside jazz, can be amalgamated and combined. The fact that even symmetrical meters and a regular beat provide opportunities for rhythmic individuality was a discovery often and gladly made in the eighties.

In these computerized times, we have come to call jazz-rock or fusion rhythms "binary," differentiating them in this way from the "ternary" ones of conventional jazz forms. Jazz-rock is based on steady eighths—a fact that explains the close relationship of rock, jazz-rock, and fusion rhythms to Latin music. Drummers like Billy Cobham and Pierre Courbois pointed this out at an early stage of the development. Conventional jazz rhythms, in contrast, are based on a triplet structure, that is, on a ternary rhythm feeling.

American jazz critic Martin Williams said:

> "Jazz" eighth notes, the "jazz" triplet: they are not the superficialities or the ornaments of a musical style. In jazz they have always been among the fundamentals. One of the unwritten (and undiscussed) laws of jazz has been that each of the great players has found his own way of pronouncing the triplet, expressed or implied—and Roy Eldridge's triplet doesn't sound like Louis Armstrong's; Miles Davis' didn't sound like Dizzy Gillespie's; Lester Young's triplet was unlike Coleman Hawkins'; and Stan Getz's is unlike Lester Young's.

This enormous abundance of individually varied rhythmic forms is among the most fascinating artistic outcomes of jazz. In keeping with the splendor of jazz's many rhythmic forms, there doesn't exist, up to the present day, any form of notation, graphic representation, and computer analysis capable of satisfactorily registering the subtlety of these rhythmic processes, which differ not just stylistically but also in terms of specific distinctions between groups and individuals.

And yet what happens rhythmically in many contemporary jazz groups is still shaped according to bebop models where the triplet feeling is most productive. They can be found everywhere in today's jazz—even in those contemporary jazz forms that are all but totally out of contact with bop in terms of sound, melody, and harmony.

The tension-filled complexity of these bop structures was clarified many years ago by Miles Davis, when he said, "Like, we'd be playing the blues, and Bird [Charlie Parker] would start on the eleventh bar, and as the rhythm section stayed where they were and Bird played where he was, it sounded as if the rhythm section was on 1 and 3 instead of 2 and 4. Every time that would happen, Max [Roach, the drummer] used to scream at Duke [Jordan, the pianist] not to follow Bird but to stay where he was. Then, eventually, it came around as Bird had planned and we were together again." Davis called this, according to Marshall Stearns, "turning the rhythm section around," and Miles added that it so bewildered him at first that he "used to quit every night."

Stearns has shown, on the basis of African recordings, that no style of jazz before free jazz was rhythmically closer to Africa than bebop. The simple, marchlike meters of New Orleans and of Dixieland were replaced by rhythmic structures in which ancient African practices seem suddenly to have come to life again.

All this took place without any direct contact between the urbanized modern jazz musician and West African rhythms. It is as if the musicians have subconsciously relived once more an evolution that their ancestors had gone through centuries ago—or conversely: as if they have shaken off habits rooted ultimately not in their own, but in European tradition, becoming increasingly "free," rediscovering, consciously *and* unconsciously, their true rhythmic heritage. This is also supported by the fact that in free jazz—as with drummers Sunny Murray and Rashied Ali—there was a further "Africanization" of jazz rhythms.

As early as the fifties, Art Blakey traveled to West Africa to become acquainted with old African rhythms. Even earlier, in the late forties, Dizzy Gillespie had hired the conga drummer Chano Pozo, who was still a member of an African sect in his native Cuba, where West African traditions remained alive to a much greater degree than in North America.

Meanwhile, what used to be the exception has almost become the rule on a host of jazz recordings: Frequently, percussionists who are exponents of Africanizing rhythms—Latin Americans and Africans—are included in the rhythm sections of jazz groups. No longer do we have to face a flaw that used to be so prevalent in earlier combinations of jazz and African rhythms—a rhythmic gap.

But all these remarks are insufficient. It may be possible to write down and notate the most complex rhythms by Max Roach or Art Blakey—or today, Tony Williams, Billy Cobham, and Jack DeJohnette—only to discover that what has been written down and copied is merely a miserable skeleton of what the music really sounded like. You see, it swung, and swing cannot be notated. It cannot even be grasped in words. "It's a real simple thing," said Jo Jones, "but there are some things you can't describe, some things that never have been described. . . . The best way you can say what swinging is, is you either play with a feeling or you don't. It's just like the difference between receiving a genuine handshake or a fishy one."

Jo Jones thinks that the difference between jazz and European music lies in swing. In European music—"that approach to music is scientific"—the musician plays the notes that are placed before him or her. If one is sufficiently musical and has studied music, one can play the required parts. But in order to play jazz it is not sufficient to be musical and to have studied music long enough. Here lies the problem of all the jazz courses at conservatories and music schools, where jazz musicianship supposedly is taught. Surely much can be learned there. Almost all important representatives of modern jazz have studied music, and it is part and parcel of a good musician that he should know and understand his craft. But the decisive part cannot be taught: swing. One can hardly say what it is.

In the course of jazz development swing became ever more far-reaching and concentrated. According to André Hodeir,

The phenomenon of swing should not be regarded as the immediate and inevitable result of a confrontation between the African rhythmic genius and the 2/2 beat. What we know about primitive jazz excludes the hypothesis that swing sprang into being like a spark at the collision of two stones. Pre-Armstrong recordings reveal, on the contrary, that swing was merely latent at first and took shape progressively over a long period.

The aspect of tension and relaxation belongs to swing. Jo Jones said, "Another thing about rhythm is that when an artist is performing on his instrument he breathes in his normal fashion, and he has a listening audience that breathes along with him."

Steadiness of natural conditions of breathing create the uniqueness of swing. There are never two possibilities. "The only way I can describe swing," said ragtime pianist Wally Rose, "is it's the kind of rhythmic movement where you can place a note where and when it is due. The only thing that keeps you together is when the whole band meets on this beat, meets on the split second you all think the beat is due. The slightest deviation from that causes tension and frustration."

Swing gives jazz its peculiar form of precision, which cannot be compared with any kind of precision in European music. Conductors and composers of symphonic music have been among the first to admit this. The difference between the precision found in Count Basie's band and the precision of the best European orchestras—jazz as well as symphonic—is due to the fact that Basie's precision stems from swing, whereas the other kind of precision is the result of academic drill. Basie's musicians feel that the note is due, and since they all feel this at the identical moment, and form the basis of swing, everything is precise in a direct, unfettered way. The kind of precision gleaned from academic tradition, on the other hand, is neither direct nor unfettered.

To swing belong, furthermore, the multiple layers of rhythm and the tension between them—the displacements of rhythmic accents and all that we have said about them. This displacement is called "syncopation" in European music. But the use of this term in jazz reveals an essential misunderstanding of the nature of jazz. In European music syncopation signifies a clearly defined shift of emphasis within the bar. The accent falls precisely at the midpoint between two beats. In jazz the displacements of accent are freer, more flexible, and more subtle. The accent can now be anywhere between two beats—precisely where the musician feels it is "due." This accent moves away from the beat but simultaneously stresses it, so it is termed "off-beat."

It must be clear by now: Swing is not the task of a drummer who has to "swing" the soloists. A jazz musician who does not swing—all alone and without any rhythm section—is no jazz musician. Thus the considered opinion of many modern musicians that it is almost as possible to swing without a drummer as with one: "The drive that creates the pulsation has to be within yourself. I don't understand why it should be necessary to have someone else drive you," said Jimmy Giuffre. Nat Hentoff remarked, "The ability to swing must first be contained within each musician. If he is dependent on a rhythm section . . . he is in the position of the rejected suitor who can't understand that one must be capable of giving love if one wishes to receive it."

It becomes increasingly clear that such paraphrases, by the musicians themselves or by sympathetic critics, are more satisfactory elucidations of the phenomenon of swing than "exact" explanations made by musicologists who have no feeling for swing. It is particularly unedifying to see swing explained as off-beat accentuation, which is so often the case. Off-beats—in other words, the accentuation away from the beat—do not of necessity produce swing. Most non-Western ethnic music and even modern pop music (even it doesn't swing) is full of off-beats.

Equally unsatisfactory is the attempt (frequently found in writings on jazz) to equate jazz's triplet feeling with the phenomenon of swing. Certainly there are connections, but the mere fact that many jazz musicians (say, John Coltrane, Eric Dolphy, or David Murray) have largely or completely abandoned triplet phrasing and yet swing with the greatest of ardor, intensity, and vitality speaks against an identity between jazz triplets and swing.

Some of the most concise thoughts concerning swing have been expressed by the Swiss musicologist Jan Slawe. In his *Versuch einer Definition der Jazzmusik,* in the context of rhythm and meter, he states:

> The main concept of jazz theory is "formation of conflict"; originally, these formations of conflict were rhythmic in nature, existing in the antagonism between simultaneously executed, different segments of music-filled time. . . . The fundamental nature of swing is expressed in the rhythmic basis of the music as a whole. . . . in particular, swing postulates a regularity of time in order to simultaneously be able to negate it. The particular nature of swing is the creation of rhythmic conflicts between the fundamental rhythm and the rhythm of the melody; this is the musical-technical cornerstone of jazz.

But these definitions, too, remain unsatisfactory. Meanwhile, so much has been written about swing that one might tend to accept once and for all the dictum that swing cannot be verbally expressed. Maybe this is because swing involves a feeling for time for which there is no precedent in European music. Ethnology has shown us that the African's sense of time—and, in general, that of "primitive" peoples—is more holistic and elementary than the differentiated time sense of the Westerner. Swing developed when the two concepts of time met. In all the polyrhythms of African music, often much more complex than those of jazz, there is still no swing—as is the case in European music. One might assume that its nature is rooted in the overlapping of two different conceptions of time.

Musicology knows well that music may occur in two different conceptions of time. Stravinsky called these "psychological" and "ontological" time. Rudolf Kassner spoke of "lived" and "measured" time. These two kinds of time cannot be equalized in those aspects of our being that count most: One second of pain becomes an eternity, and one hour can be but a fleeting moment in a state of happiness. This is of significance to music. Music is art in time, as sculpture is art in space, and painting the art of the plane. But if music is art in time, we may ask which time: psychological or ontological, relative or absolute, lived or measured?

This question can be answered only in respect to one particular musical style. It has been said that the relationship between lived and measured time is of considerable formative consequence to music. Thus romantic, and particularly late romantic, music is almost exclusively an art of lived, psychological time. Private and subjective experience of time is primary here. On the other hand, the music of a Bach is almost exclusively in measured, objective, ontological time, related in each note to the movement of the cosmos, to which it is of no concern whether a minute seems to us like an eternity, or eternity like a minute.

The question is, Which is the time of swing? And here it becomes clear why Westerners must "leap over the shadow of their time sense" if they want to find out about swing. For there can be no doubt that swing is related to both levels of time at once—to measured, objective time and to lived, psychological time. By the same token, it is also related to both an African and a European sense of time. Swing is rooted in the awareness of a simultaneously desperate and joyous inability to find a common denominator for lived and measured time. More precisely: A common denominator for lived and measured time has been found, but the listener is aware of a duality—in other words, he or she is aware of swing.

THE INSTRUMENTS OF JAZZ

The Instruments of Jazz

The Trumpet

The trumpet has been called the "royal instrument of jazz" because its sound is so piercing and brilliant that in almost all ensemble passages in which a trumpet takes part, the lead almost automatically is assigned to it. This happens in the New Orleans collective as well as in the ensembles of the big bands, which are almost always dominated by the trumpet section.

With the trumpet belong, the cornet, on the one hand—particularly in the older forms of jazz—and, the fluegelhorn, on the other—in the newer styles. In the early days of jazz, "trumpet" almost always meant cornet. Later on, there were few cornetists, probably because the trumpet offers greater range and technical possibilities. Nevertheless, cornetist Rex Stewart ranks as one of the greatest technical virtuosos of the "trumpet" up to the beginnings of bop. Other technically able "trumpeters"—mainly in the realm of Dixieland—stayed with the cornet, among them Wild Bill Davison and Muggsy Spanier. In modern jazz the cornet is used by, among others, Nat Adderley and occasionally also by Clark Terry; in free jazz by Bobby Bradford and Butch Morris. In some modern forms of jazz, however, the fluegelhorn became popular due to its round, flowing sound. There are fluegelhorn players in jazz who manage to lend their instrument a saxophonelike suppleness, and who yet are able to preserve the brilliance of the brass sound. Among the best fluegelhorn players are Art Farmer, Thad Jones, Jimmy Owens, the Dutch player Ack van Rooyen, Canadian-born Kenny Wheeler, who lives in England, and Clark Terry again.

The first generation of jazz cornetists is that of Buddy Bolden—the legendary progenitor of New Orleans jazz, who regrettably played before the time of recorded jazz music—and his contemporaries, active around the turn of the century and immediately thereafter. They played jazz or similar music—we might call it ragtime and march music with hot intonation. To this generation belong Freddie Keppard, Emmanuel Perez, Bunk Johnson, Papa Celestin, and primarily King Oliver, whose recordings provide rich material for study. They have that rough, earth-bound, hard sound, still lacking the triumphant tone that Louis Armstrong gave to the jazz trumpet.

Tommy Ladnier links this sound to a strong and expressive blues feeling, accentuated primarily in the lower registers of the instrument. Initially, Ladnier stems wholly from Oliver. In the twenties, he traveled as far as Moscow, billed as "Tommy, the talking cornet." Ladnier, born in 1900, belongs to Louis Armstrong's generation, but one feels inclined to place him earlier in terms of musical conception. We have spoken of Armstrong in a special section. He did not switch from cornet to trumpet until 1928. Armstrong is the measure for all jazz trumpeting up to this day.

Among the musicians who played most à la Armstrong were Hot Lips Page, Teddy Buckner, and Jonah Jones. Page, who died in 1954, was active in the Kansas City circle of musicians from the late twenties to the mid-thirties. An exceptional blues player, he sometimes played so much like Armstrong that he could be mistaken for him. As a singer, too, he was astonishingly close to Armstrong.

Now, back to the first generation of white trumpet (and cornet) players, beginning with Nick La Rocca, founder of the Original Dixieland Jazz Band. His cornet in a way retained the sound of the circus trumpeters of the turn of the century, in paradoxical contrast to his preposterous claims that he and his white orchestra had been the first jazz band.

In the realm of the old Dixieland, but considerably more musical and differentiated, was the trumpeting of Sharkey Bonano. He and Muggsy Spanier are among the white trumpeters who frequently are counted by traditional jazz fans among black New Orleans rather than white Dixieland. Spanier, who died in 1967, made the first Chicago-style recordings in 1924 with his Bucktown Five. In 1939 he had a short-lived band—Muggsy Spanier's Ragtime Band—that made a deep and lasting impression with its musicianly and original Dixieland music. In 1940 he made records with Sidney Bechet, accompanied by guitar and bass only, that are a kind of "chamber music" of traditional jazz.

Along the line originating from La Rocca, but more polished and musical, are Red Nichols and Phil Napoleon, two musicians representative of "New York style." This term is common usage for the music of the white jazz musicians in New York during the twenties and early thirties, who did not have the privilege of steady, stimulating contact with the New Orleans greats, as did their colleagues in Chicago. On the other hand, they were often ahead of them in terms of academic training, technique, and craftmanship. Comparison between Nichols and Bix Beiderbecke illuminates this point: Nichols' blowing was perhaps even more clean and flawless than Bix's, but he could not approach Bix where sensitivity and imagination were concerned. Both Napoleon's Original Memphis Five and Nichols' Five Pennies found great favor with their kind of "purified" jazz, especially with commercial audiences.

Bix Beiderbecke brought elegance and cool sensitivity to the sound of the jazz trumpet. He had more followers than any other white trumpeter of his time. Bunny Berigan, Jimmy McPartland, and Bobby Hackett are among these. The Bixian conception can be pursued well into cool jazz. Many solos by Miles Davis, and even more by Chet Baker, sound as if Beiderbecke's Chicago style had been "transformed" into modern jazz—although, of course, there is no direct link between Bix and Miles.

Stylistically, the most significant of Beiderbecke's followers was Bobby Hackett, who died in 1976. Hackett was a genuine master of the art of playing standards, the great songs of popular music in America. His "traditional" jazz playing was spiced with many harmonic and rhythmic experiences from much more "modern" periods of jazz.

Rex Stewart, although not a Beiderbecke successor, copied some of Bix's solos during the years when Beiderbecke was the talk of all jazz musicians, mainly—with the Henderson band of 1931—Bix's celebrated "Singing the Blues," one of the most famous trumpet solos in jazz history.

With Stewart we arrive at a group of trumpeters who might be described as "Ellington trumpets." These are first and foremost the "jungle-style" trumpeters.

The first in this group was Bubber Miley, who died in 1932 and who gave the Ellington band of the twenties the characteristic coloration that until this day is associated with Ellington. Bubber was first influenced by King Oliver: If one recalls Oliver's most famous solo—"Dippermouth Blues"—it illuminates how direct the link is to Miley's famed solo on Ellington's first version of "Black and Tan Fantasy," which Bubber cocomposed.

Ellington remained interested in the retention of the "Miley color." Stewart, Cootie Williams, Ray Nance, Clark Terry, and others had to see to this during various epochs in Ellington's career. Cootie Williams plays growl trumpet with particular expressiveness and strength. He is the soloist on one of Ellington's most significant recordings, *Concerto for Cootie* (1940). Stewart, who died in 1967, has often been admired for the lightness and assurance with which he could play at even the most rapid tempos—and very expressively, at that.

An element of Stewart's style was the half-valve technique: the valves of the trumpet are pressed down only halfway. Clark Terry transplanted this style of playing into modern jazz. He has created a unique, completely personal style and is perhaps the only modern trumpeter prior to free jazz who did not become enmeshed in the back-and-forth between Dizzy Gillespie and Miles Davis. And, above all, Terry is master of intelligent musical humor.

All trumpeters mentioned up to now actually belong to the immediate Armstrong school. In contrast to this school stands what might be called, for simplification, the Gillespie school. It, too, is a product of what had come before. The Gillespie tradition actually begins long before Dizzy, with Henry "Red" Allen. Allen, who died in 1967, took King Oliver's place in the Oliver band when it was taken over by Luis Russell in 1929. In his playing, the shift in emphasis from sonority to phrasing was indicated for the first time—if only in spurts. When compared to his contemporaries, Allen plays more legato than staccato, in a more flowing manner, connecting rather than separating his phrases.

The tendency toward this kind of playing becomes more marked with a group of trumpeters who came after Allen: Roy Eldridge, Buck Clayton, and Harry Edison. Eldridge became the most important exponent of his instrument between Armstrong and Gillespie. Fluidity now became an ideal for jazz trumpeters. The saxophone is the most "fluid" of jazz instruments, and here was revealed for the first time the impact of the saxophone on the sonority of modern jazz. Eldridge once said, "I play nice saxophone on the trumpet." He later abandoned this saxophone emphasis in his playing, but it remained an active influence.

Buck Clayton and Harry Edison, finally, play the most gentle and tender trumpets of all the Swing musicians. Edison earned his nickname "Sweets" because he loved to eat anything sweet. But his nickname applies also to the supple tenderness of his playing. Harmonically speaking, he is the most "modern" trumpet before Gillespie, while Clayton still tends more toward traditional harmonies. Both were among the star soloists of the classic Count Basie band of the late thirties. In the fifties, Edison became a busy Hollywood studio musician who participated in recording sessions with stars like Frank Sinatra and later in New York in jazz and rock productions. No other trumpeter so completely expresses the sensitivity of modern jazz in the idiom of Swing style.

Clayton is frequently mentioned when Ruby Braff's antecedents are under discussion. Braff is a unique stylistic phenomenon: a trumpeter of the jazz generation of the fifties who took his cues not from Dizzy or Miles, but from the trumpeters of the earlier jazz tradition—a perfectionist of the Swing cornet, full of grace and charm in Swing and Dixieland. In the seventies he co-led a quartet with guitarist George Barnes, whose Swing was characterized by a floating weightlessness. This Swing tradition is still alive, as in Warren Vaché, who, although prominent only since the end of the seventies, remains very much indebted to it in everything he plays.

Jazz trumpeters began early to make use of the stimulating effects of the highest registers of the instrument, playing far above conventional trumpet range. As with everything else in the history of the jazz trumpet, this, too, begins with Louis Armstrong. But Charlie Shavers, an unusually brilliant all-round Swing trumpeter, was the musician who most influenced the high-note specialists: "Cat" Anderson and Al Killian with Duke Ellington, and eventually Maynard Ferguson, who became known as a member of Stan Kenton's orchestra. Kenton scored with the record sales of Ferguson's skyscraper-climbing escapades, but the critics were almost unanimously antagonized by the tastelessness of this way of playing. Later, Ferguson showed that he is a musician with real jazz feeling and tremendous swing, mainly with his wildly swinging big bands, which he led in the late fifties in the United States, later in Great Britain (more about that in the section on the big bands).

With astonishing ease and assurance, Ferguson plays things other trumpeters would consider impossible. Most of all he does not just scream and screech when playing at skyscraper heights; even up there he hits each note accurately and phrases musically. Not until the end of the seventies did he meet with a real competitor in this field: Cuban-born Arturo Sandoval, who further develops Ferguson's high-flight trumpeting with fiery élan and captivating relaxation, linking (when playing in the Irakere big band until 1981 and then in his own groups) this form of high-note playing with Dizzy Gillespie's bop brilliance.

Dizzy Gillespie based his style of playing on the instrumental achievements of Eldridge and on the stylistic contributions of the other bop pioneers: antipodal to Armstrong and yet only comparable to him in power and brilliance. Gillespie, too, has been discussed in a separate section.

Just as all trumpeters of traditional jazz come from Armstrong, so do all modern trumpeters stem from Gillespie. The four most important in the forties were Howard McGhee, Fats Navarro, Kenny Dorham, and young Miles Davis. The early death of Fats Navarro was as lamented by the musicians of his generation as Bix Beiderbecke's passing had been mourned by the musicians of the Chicago period. Fats' lithe, assured playing was a forerunner of the style practiced by the generation of hard bop since the late sixties, combining the melodic arcs of Miles Davis with the fire of Dizzy Gillespie. In his autobiography *Beneath the Underdog,* Charles Mingus makes Fats Navarro into an emblematic figure of modern jazz.

Miles Davis began as a Dizzy imitator, just as Dizzy had begun by imitating Eldridge. But he soon found his own, completely new style. Miles is the founder and chief representative of the second phase of modern jazz trumpeting: lyrical arcs of melody in which the sophistication of simplicity is admirably cultivated, even less vibrato than Dizzy—and all this with a tone less glowing than loaded with coolly smoldering protest. After Davis, the development of jazz trumpeting is contained in the interplay between Dizzy and Miles, frequently spiced with a shot of Fats Navarro (into whose place Clifford Brown later stepped). Kenny Dorham (who died in 1972) proved himself to be a musician in this mold who by no means received the recognition due his talent.

Chet Baker, Johnny Coles, and Art Farmer are all stylistically close to Miles Davis, but only Chet (who died in 1988) was directly influenced by Miles. Baker played his way to sensational success with his solo on "My Funny Valentine," recorded in 1952 with the Gerry Mulligan Quartet. For a short time he dominated all jazz polls. His phrasing is so supple that he occasionally was chided as "feminine." Today that would be a compliment. No other trumpeter, apart from Miles, captured the phenomenon of loneliness and sadness so movingly as Chet Baker (who also made a name for himself as a vocalist). Every note he played was like parting from a good friend. It often seemed as if he were "singing" rather than blowing his trumpet, with such a floating, melancholy lightness that when he put aside his horn to sing the voice seemed a logical continuation of his trumpet playing.

On muted trumpet, Art Farmer, who lived in Europe for many years, combines liquid mobility with soulful expressiveness and strong jazz feeling. Art, along with him Johnny Coles, are the only modern trumpeters who can equal the lyrical intensity of Davis without imitating him—in their own unmistakable ways. And it is indeed illuminating that just these two trumpeters, who are above any attempt at copying Miles, come closer to him in expressiveness than all the many musicians directly influenced by him. Art Farmer also emerged in 1952 from the same Lionel Hampton band that brought to light modern jazz's most highly praised trumpeter next to Miles Davis: Clifford Brown, who died in 1956 in a tragic automobile accident. "Brownie," as he was called, further developed the playing style of Fats Navarro. In many respects, he—and, of course, Navarro—are the "fathers of the hard-bop trumpet." The black musicians untouched by cool jazz had continued to play bop in the first half of the fifties. Only hardly anybody took notice. It was Brownie's success that initiated the breakthrough of hard bop. After his untimely death, a Clifford Brown myth developed, comparable to the Beiderbecke legend. Clifford Brown's influence was also apparent in seventies neobop and—more strongly still—eighties classicism. There's scarcely a trumpeter in these two styles who didn't relate to Brown's mellow sound, harmonic flexibility, and austere phrasing.

The musical experience of cool jazz in the first half of the fifties and the vitality of the bop of the forties merged in hard bop. Donald Byrd, Thad Jones, Lee Morgan, Bill Hardman, Nat Adderley, Benny Bailey, Ira Sullivan, Yugoslavian Dusko Gojkovic, Ted Curson, Blue Mitchell, Booker Little, Freddie Hubbard, and Woody Shaw are all trumpeters in this mold.

Donald Byrd combined a certain academic solidity with so much professional flexibility that he became one of the most frequently recorded trumpet players of hard bop. In the seventies, he was successful in funk jazz, even though many critics objected to it. Byrd is one of the great teachers of jazz. Thad Jones, an exceptional arranger, was co-leader of the Thad Jones–Mel Lewis Big Band until 1979. He stems from the Basie Orchestra, and he blew some of his first remarkable solos in the then experimental-sounding Jazz Workshops of Charles Mingus. Lee Morgan, who died in 1972, worked with Dizzy Gillespie's big band in the mid-fifties, and, as an eighteen-year-old, was featured extensively by Dizzy. He became (as a member of Art Blakey's Jazz Messengers) a frequently recorded hard-bop musician.

Among other creative hard-bop trumpeters living in Europe is Benny Bailey, who has won many friends with his great, full sound—a true trumpet stylist and, in addition, one of the best lead trumpeters one could wish for in a big band. If Bailey were living in New York, he would probably be as busy as Clark Terry, because his particular combination of inimitable improviser and perfect studio and section musician is rare.

The development of the trumpet, as far as it took place within "tonal" jazz, brought little that was stylistically new up to the late eighties—aside from an astounding perfecting of bop fire, which occurred in two thrusts forward: first in neobop at the end of the seventies and then in eighties classicism. After the much too early death of the very promising Booker Little in 1961 (who had made some of his most beautiful recordings with Eric Dolphy), Freddie Hubbard and Woody Shaw became by far the best-known representatives of the transition from hard bop to neobop. Hubbard is the most brilliant trumpeter of a generation of musicians who stand with one foot in hard bop and the other in fusion music. He played as inspiredly in Max Roach's ensemble as, for example, in a studio band Friedrich Gulda put together, as well as on numerous records under his own name that vividly reflect the development of jazz from hard bop through free playing of the sixties to the electric sound of the seventies. Many critics have deplored the stereotyped character of Hubbard's jazz-rock and fusion productions. For years, he kept wavering between making convincing jazz music and more commercially oriented records. Only in the eighties, in wonderful duo recordings with Woody Shaw and in albums with his own groups, did Hubbard really find a way back to his bop roots.

Woody Shaw (who died in 1989), on the other hand, has been going his own way without making compromises as the most inspired trumpeter of neobop. He produced great work both with Eric Dolphy and in the band that Dexter Gordon headed during his triumphant 1976 comeback. He far outstripped anyone else in successfully integrating the outcome of modal jazz into bop, conclusively making improvisation with pentatonic scales (so beloved of modal players) bop-conscious and bop-accessible. At the start of the eighties he headed a much lauded quintet with a front line consisting solely of brass—trumpet and trombone (Steve Turre).

In neobop, therefore, bop and modal jazz flow together with John Coltrane as the absolutely outstanding influence. Jack Walrath, Jimmy Owens, Jon Faddis, Swiss-born Franco Ambrosetti, Lew Soloff, Hannibal Marvin Peterson, Terumasa Hino, and Randy Brecker represent the younger generation of such trumpeters. Over the years a number of them have taken up neobop alongside other styles, developing it further.

Randy Brecker, for example, became known as a fusion stylist (and will later be considered as such), but he also blows an unusually dynamic and vital neobop trumpet. In his powerful way of creating a climax he transposes elements from jazz-rock to neobop, particularly impressively when playing during the eighties with Brazilian pianist Eliane Elias. Lew Soloff is a phenomenon: an excellent big-band specialist who made a name for himself in both the Thad Jones–Mel Lewis big band and in the orchestra created by Gil Evans with whom he was closely linked for almost twenty years. He particularly likes the metallic, bronze register of the trumpet, and he is a specialist in making surprising changes of register. Jack Walrath from Montana, who played and served as an arranger in Charles Mingus' last band, blows his neobop trumpet with great sarcasm and tongue in cheek. Jon Faddis is one of neobop's most reliable lead trumpeters, endowing big bands with unusual brilliance. In addition he's a dazzling Dizzy Gillespie-inspired high-note virtuoso, who found his own style in the eighties.

Terumasa Hino gave up a successful career in his native Japan in order to live in New York. In Japanese *hino* means "burning from a fire within," and that's the way he plays. No other trumpeter born outside the United States can compare with his power and blast. In the course of the seventies he became interested in jazz-rock. Hannibal Marvin Peterson, who was first presented by Gil Evans, has mastered the entire range of jazz from Bessie Smith to Coltrane with so much energy and power that in the mid-seventies *The New York Times* dubbed him the "Muhammed Ali of the trumpet."

The fascination once again exerted by the entire phenomenon of the new bebop, particularly on younger musicians, becomes apparent once you realize how many jazz musicians took up and further developed this style during the eighties. Wynton Marsalis, Terence Blanchard, Wallace Roney,

Marlon Jordan, Philip Harper, Roy Hargrove, Brian Lynch, and Tom Harrell are the most important trumpeters within classicism, reassessing jazz tradition in the light of bop. What is striking about these trumpeters—to a greater degree than neobop trumpeters—is the eclectic way in which they relate to almost the entire history of tonal jazz trumpet playing, coupled, however, with one dominant influence: a blending of the cool Miles Davis line with Clifford Brown's springy and warm hard-bop concept.

Wynton Marsalis' dominance in the realm of the classicist trumpet has already been covered in the section devoted to him and David Murray. When Wynton left Art Blakey's Jazz Messengers in 1982, he was succeeded by a nineteen-year-old trumpeter who also came from New Orleans and who had also been trained at the New Orleans Center for Creative Arts (NOCCA): Terence Blanchard. His style displays strong affinities with the crescent city's melodies and rhythms, and a special love for the Mardi Gras music of the New Orleans carnival. It is also accompanied by profound awareness of the African roots of black music. With his mellow, full tone, Blanchard has gained much recognition in the quintet he led together with alto saxophonist Donald Harrison. Tom Harrell, who played with Horace Silver and Phil Woods, is the great lyricist of classicist trumpet playing—an expert in subtly placed notes with a rare sense of economy and balance in a realm that often inclines toward technical pyrotechnics. He doesn't seem to play a single note too many. Wallace Roney from Philadelphia blows a powerful Miles-inspired trumpet with an unmistakable dark, metallic timbre. He's so much in demand among classicists that in 1986 he was simultaneously a member of both Art Blakey's and Tony Williams' groups, which demonstrates his range: sovereignly revealing both the conservative wing of classicism with its leaning toward hard bop and also the style's contemporary trend.

But bebop trumpeters from the middle and older generation have also attracted renewed, and hardly to be anticipated, interest. That is especially gratifying in the case of Red Rodney and Ira Sullivan, both of whom are particularly responsive to the music of Charlie Parker. Sullivan also plays the tenor saxophone. Rodney is a veteran of the great Jimmy Dorsey, Les Brown, and Woody Herman big bands.

Now, let's move on to free playing; to do so we have to go back in time. Don Cherry, the ground-breaking, free brass player, blows a cornetlike "pocket trumpet"—more or less a child's trumpet. When he became known in the late fifties as a member of the Ornette Coleman Quartet, he seemed to most critics merely a good friend of Ornette's who also happened to play the trumpet. Since then, he has become a "poet of free jazz" of great, intimate, glowing expressiveness, commended even by so strict a critic as Miles Davis. During the mid-sixties, Cherry moved to Europe (he has since returned to the States), where he made notable achievements—in a twofold sense. On the one hand, he created particularly unusual realizations of new large-orchestral jazz that excel over all other attempts in this direction with their melodiousness and charm. On the other hand, he became an exponent of "jazz meets the world"—of the incorporation into jazz of elements of the great exotic musical cultures. Cherry assimilates Balinese, Indian, Tibetan, Arabic, and Chinese elements, often not only on his trumpet but also on various flutes and other instruments.

The immensity of Cherry's importance is illustrated by the fact that all other free-jazz trumpeters stood in his shadow for years—Lester Bowie, Clifford Thornton (who has made a name for himself on the valve trombone, too), Bobby Bradford, Leo Smith, and Butch Morris, among the black musicians; Don Ellis and Mike Mantler among the whites; and Toshinori Kondo among the Japanese.

Ellis, who died in 1978 and who became known in the late fifties as a member of George Russell's sextet, scored a sensational success at the 1966 Monterey Festival, where he introduced his new big band. He played a custom-made "quarter-tone trumpet" that allows for the finest tonal nuances (before him, the Czech trumpeter Jaromir Hnilička had already employed such an instrument, stimulated by the quarter-tone music of Czechoslovakian composer Alois Hába).

Leo Smith discovered the magic of silence and the rest for free jazz, making that the basis for his own notation (deviating from the standardized European system), which he calls "rhythm units." Smith's multilayered compositions seeking new sounds also made an essential contribution to the structuring of free jazz in the seventies.

The rediscovery of tradition is to be found in all styles of playing, from the new bebop to free trumpeters. Lester Bowie, who emerged from the AACM circle in Chicago, is in some respects the initiator of the neoclassical style of trumpet playing. With his growl solos he sounds like an avant-garde Cootie Williams. His ability to shape and change trumpet sounds seems inexhaustible. He once said, "The history of our music does not just go back to 1890 or to New Orleans. It goes back thousands of years! We try to express this with our music."

From Roots to the Source was thus the name Bowie gave to his early eighties band, forming a bridge between Africa, gospel songs, and contemporary jazz. Since the mid-eighties his Brass Fantasy (eight brass instruments and a drummer) has delighted with adaptations of rhythm and blues hits and pop songs—from Fats Domino to Whitney Houston, full of exuberance, wit, and sardonic joyousness.

Following on from Lester Bowie's achievements, the trumpeters of neoclassicism—Olu Dara, Baikida Carroll, Herb Robertson, Rasul Siddik,

Stanton Davis, and Paul Smoker—developed their own playing. Strikingly many adherents of this performance style—contrasting with modern playing's inclination toward brilliance and clarity—upgraded the earthy, speechlike sounds of archaic jazz, transforming them in contemporary presentations. Olu Dara, who previously played with Henry Threadgill and David Murray, has been particularly and impressively successful there. He blows the most melodic trumpet in neoclassicism. Mississippi reminiscences flow time and again into his inspired blues-saturated solos.

Closely linked with that return to the trumpet sounds of archaic jazz is an astonishing (and until then scarcely expected) renaissance in playing with mutes. Herb Robertson, who became known during the eighties in groups with alto sax player Tim Berne, is a master of muted playing. Many trumpeters only use a single mute during a solo. Robertson deploys an entire arsenal, brilliantly changing them in the course of his solo. He inspires postmodern jazz with the whole range of jungle and plunger sounds, from Bubber Miley to Rex Stewart.

After Don Cherry the most persuasive trumpeter in world music is Jon Hassell, who comes from Memphis and has worked with such minimalist musicians as La Monte Young and Terry Riley. Hassell "dematerializes" the trumpet as no other player does. Not a gram of brass, not a gram of metal vibrates in his playing. Instead there is a stream of floating sounds and whispered notes whose breathy impact is closer to a voice than the blaring sounds of a trumpet. Stimulated by Miles Davis and ethnic music, he studied with Pandit Pran Nath, the Indian singer, transposing this song style onto his electronically distanced trumpet and utilizing the same microtonal, richly ornamented lines. Together with keyboardist Brian Eno he developed a concept of "Fourth World Music" uniting high-tech computerized sounds of the "First World" with the vital magical melodies and rhythms of the "Third World"—particularly impressively in an encounter with the Farafina group of African drummers from Burkina Faso in 1988.

Let's turn to European trumpeters. Starting off from free jazz, in the sixties they quickly developed a style of their own, often with a striking liking for *melos* as is indicated by the fact that during the seventies many moved on from free jazz into other directions. The most important are Kenny Wheeler and Harry Beckett in England, Enrico Rava and Paolo Fresu in Italy, Tomasz Stanko in Poland; and in Germany Manfred Schoof and Herbert Joos among the older generation, and Markus Stockhausen among the younger.

The best known, covering the widest musical range, is Kenny Wheeler: from free jazz to the aestheticized playing many jazz fans associate with the ECM record label. He combines crystal-clear lucidity of sound with poetry and romantic passion. Almost equally versatile is Manfred Schoof: from the traditional big band to the free jazz of the Globe Unity Orchestra, from bebop to a gentle, beautiful aesthetic. Schoof's trademarks are "skidding sounds," as musicologist Ekkehard Jost called his rapid, overlapping streams of sound, flowing together in virtuoso fashion.

Enrico Rava is master of *melisma,* certainly in the Italian tradition with its full sound and fervent intensity—a specialist in supercharging beautiful melodies as is also documented by his love of Brazilian music. Tomasz Stanko is a unique figure: one of the very few trumpeters in the world who gives solo concerts, unbacked by a rhythm section, offering an impressive wealth of expression and sounds.

Herbert Joos, who became known as a soloist with the Vienna Art Orchestra, blows his new jazz fluegelhorn with great fluency and suppleness. No other European trumpeter so sensitively creates lyrical, fine-spun tone poems where he electronically distances his trumpet sound in a great variety of natural-sounding ways.

Markus Stockhausen, son of composer Karlheinz Stockhausen, phrases his free trumpet improvisations with an inwardly directed intensity unusual in this sphere. His trumpet lines are close to the New Music, reflecting enormous composure and concentration.

Among the trumpeters who have incorporated rock elements, Randy Brecker, Eddie Henderson, Chuck Mangione, and Danish player Palle Mikkelborg require special mention. In the seventies, Mangione, with his catchy music, was particularly successful on the American college and university circuit. Palle Mikkelborg, who is also active as an arranger, Europeanized the Miles Davis concept in exemplary fashion, lyrically moderating the angry, rebellious fusion Miles and imbuing his music with a romantic glow without reducing the pressure. Mikkelborg is one of the very few trumpeters after Miles who has found his own style on the wah-wah pedal. His use of other forms of electronic distancing is also particularly sensitive. The regard Mikkelborg enjoys is revealed too by the fact that he succeeded in winning Miles—otherwise not a friend of guest appearances— for participation in the 1985 Copenhagen recording of the *Aura* suite dedicated to Davis.

Randy Brecker—also an outstanding fluegelhorn player—became known through his work in Art Blakey's Jazz Messengers and in the Horace Silver Quintet. He probably is the trumpeter best versed in a technically complex kind of electric jazz. He is one of the busiest New York studio musicians, so he really knows about jazz rock: "Playing trumpet is often difficult in rock because you have to compete with all that electricity," he said. "Certain elements of jazz have come to rock, but rock people still can't improvise on the level of a jazz artist. As a jazz musician, you feel like yourself. As a rock musician, you feel like a star."

The Trombone

The trombone began as a rhythm and harmony instrument. In the early jazz bands it was hardly more than a "blown bass." It supplied an additional harmonic background for the melody instruments—trumpet and clarinet—above which they could move, and it stressed the rhythmic accents. In big bands, the trumpets and trombones form the brass section, which stands opposite the reed section, the saxophone group. Both, brass and reeds together, form the horn section, whose counterpart and partner is the rhythm section.

In view of the substitute-bass role the trombone had to play in the marching bands of early New Orleans, it can be said that the style of the first jazz trombonist worth mentioning was already a sign of progress. This style is called "tailgate." The name stems from the fact that the trombonist took up more space than other musicians on the band wagons—the carts on which the bands rode through the streets of New Orleans on festive occasions—and had to sit as far back as possible, on the tailgate. There he had room to work his slide. The tailgate position made possible effective, glissandolike fills placed between the melodic phrases of the other horns. Kid Ory, who died in 1973, was the most important representative of this style.

A trombonist of very personal conception within the New Orleans tradition is Charlie Green. Bessie Smith liked his accompaniments—as in "Empty Bed Blues"—which gives an indication of his style: blues trombone full of extrovert, earthy sounds. He was a kind of Tommy Ladnier of his instrument.

The first jazz musician to play musically conceived, expressive, and melodically rich solos on the trombone was Jimmy Harrison, who died in 1931. Critics have called him the most important trombonist in the realm of the older styles. He was one of the leading soloists in Fletcher Henderson's band. And he was the first to at least come close to, if not yet attain, the biting sound of the trumpet on the trombone.

Miff Mole is in many respects a white "counterpart" of Jimmy Harrison. Perhaps he lacked the former's mighty inspiration, but he was a flawless technician, and by his playing rather than Harrison's the white musicians of the day were made aware of the fact that the trombone was about to achieve "equal rights." Miff's trombone was an important voice in the Original Memphis Five led by Phil Napoleon, and along with the latter and Red Nichols, he made up the "triumvirate" of memorable New York–style brass musicians.

The Chicago-style trombonists were also influenced by Mole—for instance, Tommy Dorsey and Jack Teagarden. Dorsey evolved in the thirties into the "Sentimental Gentleman," leader of a successful big band and eventually hardly a jazz musician anymore. Yet he always remained a player of great technical ability and soulful feeling. Teagarden was one of the few traditional jazz players who were especially respected by the cool jazz musicians of the fifties for his controlled, expressive sound and his supple lines. Bill Russo—a former Stan Kenton arranger and an excellent trombonist himself—praised him as "a jazzman with the facility, range and flexibility of any trombonist of any idiom or any time; his influence was essentially responsible for a mature approach to trombone jazz." Teagarden—or Big T, as he was called—was Louis Armstrong's favorite trombonist. Together, they played and sang on some of the most spirited and enjoyable duo recordings in jazz. Both as singer and instrumentalist, Teagarden was a blues man with a very modern, reflective attitude toward the blues.

There is a Duke Ellington group among the trombones as well, although they are not as closely related, stylistically, as the Ellington trumpets. These are Joseph "Tricky Sam" Nanton, Juan Tizol, and Lawrence Brown. Tricky Sam is *the* great man of growl trombone. Juan Tizol (coauthor with Ellington of the famous "Caravan," considered to be the most important early Latin jazz tune, though there were already Latin elements in Jelly Roll Morton's "New Orleans Blues" and in W. C. Handy's "St. Louis Blues" around the time of World War I) does not play the slide trombone, as do most jazz trombonists, but the valve trombone. He plays it softly and sweetly, and occasionally becomes a trifle saccharine. His sound has been compared to that of a cello. Lawrence Brown, stylishly melodic and sometimes not very intense, is a musician of strong personal warmth with a preference for tuneful (sometimes almost sentimental) melodies.

Benny Morton, J. C. Higginbotham, Vic Dickenson, Dickie Wells, and Trummy Young are the great trombonists of Swing style. Their playing shares a vibrant vehemence. Morton, Wells, and Dickenson were all heard with Count Basie's band. Morton had previously worked with Fletcher Henderson. His playing has an intense, blueslike quality—something on the order of a Swing fusion of Jimmy Harrison and Charlie Green. Dickie Wells has been described as a musician of "romantic imagination" by André Hodeir. He is a romanticist not in the sense of overblown pathos but in terms of a forceful, imaginative sensitivity. Much of this romanticism is contained in the incomparable vibrato of his trombone sound.

J. C. Higginbotham was the most vehement, powerful trombone of the Swing period—his tone sometimes reminiscent of the earthy, tight sound known in the twenties as "gutbucket" trombone. Sometimes he played with an abrupt explosiveness, as if the trombone had been struck rather than blown. Vic Dickenson has a lusty, pleasing sense of humor that sometimes seeps into even his slow solos. With his appealing and singable ideas, he is among those Swing musicians who, across all boundaries of style, enjoyed a remarkably active career well into the seventies. Dan Morgenstern once wrote about Dickenson, "When he picks up his trombone he tells you a story that's personal through and through. His horn seems to be an extension of his body. The complete ease with which he masters it makes the instrument, which actually is a bit cumbersome, appear like the embodiment of elegance."

Trummy Young is to the trombone what Roy Eldridge is to the trumpet—a fulcrum linking Swing and bop ways of playing. From 1937 to 1943 he was one of the principal soloists in the Jimmie Lunceford band. His "Margie" was a particular success from that period. Louis Armstrong brought Trummy Young into his All Stars in 1952 as the replacement for Jack Teagarden. With this group Trummy popularized—and sometimes banalized—his style.

Directly linked to Trummy Young, in terms of tone related to the vehement verve of Swing trombonists like Benny Morton or J. C. Higginbotham, is the trombonist who created modern trombone style and remains its personification: J. J. Johnson. Before discussing him, we must mention a white trombonist, Bill Harris, master of a brilliant virtuoso technique. Harris was a member of Woody Herman's band from 1944 to 1946, again from 1948 to 1950, and later played with Herman again from time to time. His solo on "Bijou," recorded with Herman in the mid-forties, was the most admired trombone solo of the time. His personality was marked by the contrast between the piercing, springy style of his fast work and the polished, studied vibrato of his slow solos. The contrast is so pronounced one might think two musicians were involved, if one did not know that Harris, with his slightly professorial looks, was responsible for both. Next to J. J. Johnson, Harris, who died in 1973, was for years the strongest influence on trombonists.

J. J. Johnson became to trombonists what Dizzy Gillespie is to trumpet players; what he plays is not just bop trombone but also "trumpet-trombone." He plays his instrument with that brilliant glow long associated with the trumpet; no other trombone player before him accomplished this feat. Contrast to this the muted playing of J. J.: earthy, tight, reminiscent of Charlie Green's blues trombone but with all the mobility of modern jazz. Johnson went through the same development as Gillespie: from the nervousness of bop to great sobriety and quiet sovereignty. J. J., also an outstanding arranger, went to Hollywood in the late sixties to start a new career as film and television composer and arranger. When bebop returned in the eighties, he started again to play solo trombone—even *more* mature and mellow than during the period of his great success. This maturity shows in his statements, too: "A change in art shouldn't take place for novelty's sake, as in fashion. New styles in music or painting or poetry should result from a new style of thinking in the world. The next style in music will come from the heads and hearts of real artists and not from opportunists."

Kai Winding is the white counterpart of J. J. Johnson. Independent of J. J., he found a style often so reminiscent of J. J. that time and again they were mistaken for each other. It must be counted among the marvels of jazz that two musicians as different as Winding and Johnson should have arrived at similar styles. Kai, born in Denmark, was a member of Benny Goodman's band and later came to the fore through his playing with Stan Kenton; thus he was first and foremost a big-band musician. J. J. Johnson, from Indiana, black, combo-man of the bebop groups, came to the fore through his playing on 52nd Street.

Ten years later, among the musicians of hard bop, Curtis Fuller, Jimmy Knepper, Julian Priester, Garnett Brown, and Slide Hampton (also notable as an arranger) are especially worthy of mention. Fuller is particularly typical of the Detroit generation of hard bop, and he is also a specialist in rapid lines, notable for their full-toned fluidity and lightness. Jimmy Knepper, associated for many years with Charles Mingus, blows a "piercing," vital trombone style in which Swing and bop elements are equally alive. Knepper and Garnett Brown are all-round trombonists who master everything from conventional big-band work to avant-garde experimentation. Julian Priester became known primarily through his work with the pianoless Max Roach Quintet of the sixties. He blew a tasteful jazz-rock trombone—from 1970 to 1973 in the Herbie Hancock Sextet, later in his own groups—and then returned in the eighties to acoustic music making, particularly impressively in recordings with bassist Dave Holland. Slide Hampton, with his octet of 1959, "modernized" the classic Miles Davis Capitol Band of 1949, giving it a touch of soul. For years Slide lived in Europe, playing in the most diverse groups, from quartet to big band. He was connected with the great tenorman, Dexter Gordon, in a very fruitful cooperation that initially took place in Europe in the sixties. Ten years later, in the United States, Slide Hampton was also the man behind the most impressive mass trombone effort in jazz so far: his *World of Trombone,* recorded in 1979, with no fewer than nine excellent trombonists, among them Janice Robinson and Curtis Fuller.

J. J. Johnson and Bill Harris had an almost inestimable influence on all trombonists who came after. Frank Rosolino stems primarily from Johnson. His typically Italian feeling for effects, his temperament, and his sense of humor often stood out in Stan Kenton's 1953–54 band. In his countless appearances and recordings, he remained a bebop man until his tragic death in 1978. Carl Fontana plays without Frank's striving for effects, but with great flexibility and feeling for harmonic subtleties. He, too, is a big-band musician and emerged from the bands of Kenton and Woody Herman.

Further trombonists of this line are Frank Rehak and Eddie Bert—the latter a particularly temperamental Bill Harris–influenced improviser.

Rehak, Bert, Al Grey, Bill Watrous, and, most of all, Urbie Green are flexible trombonists, able to cope with any style or demand. Urbie, who became known through his work in the Benny Goodman band of the fifties (during which stint he often stood in for Benny) has said, "My playing has been compared to almost every trombonist who ever lived. The reason probably is that I had to play in so many different styles—Dixieland, lead à la Tommy Dorsey, and later, modern jazz." To this flexibility, Al Grey adds the aspect of humor, which has always had an especially live tradition among the trombonists—from tailgate style through Vic Dickenson and Trummy Young up to Albert Mangelsdorff and Ray Anderson, whom we will discuss later. Grey is a big-band veteran: from Benny Carter and Jimmie Lunceford to Lionel Hampton and Dizzy Gillespie up to Count Basie.

Among the most significant trombonists of the sixties are Jimmy Cleveland, the previously mentioned Curtis Fuller, and Bob Brookmeyer. Cleveland is a "super J. J.," whose brilliant tromboning often seems almost explosive, especially since this explosiveness is combined with the fluency of a saxophone in the most natural way.

Valve trombonist Bob Brookmeyer, on the other hand, is a musician of modern Lester Young classicism, who "cooled off" the tradition of his hometown, Kansas City, in quite a remarkable way. With Jimmy Giuffre, he recorded an album entitled *Traditionalism Revisited* that demonstrates the classicist position: the jazz tradition viewed from the standpoint of modern jazz long before that became fashionable in postmodern jazz. Here famous old jazz themes—such as Louis Armstrong's "Santa Claus Blues" and "Some Sweet Day," King Oliver's "Sweet Like This," Tommy Ladnier's "Ja-Da," and Bix Beiderbecke's "Louisiana"—are transported into the world of modern jazz. Since the seventies Brookmeyer has made a name for himself as an excellent arranger: first in the Thad Jones–Mel Lewis orchestra, then in its eighties successor, the Mel Lewis Orchestra.

Among the trombonists of the younger generation who carry on, refine, and play the J. J. Johnson tradition in a contemporary way are Janice Robinson, Bruce Fowler, Tom Malone (who plays thirteen instruments besides the trombone), and Jiggs Whigham, who lives in Europe, heading the Jazz Department of the Cologne Music Academy. Glenn Ferris and Brazilian Raoul de Souza have taken this playing style into jazz-rock, funk, and fusion, in many records that are highly electronicized. With his disco-oriented music, de Souza achieved a success comparable, among trombonists, to Tommy Dorsey's in the thirties.

In free jazz, Grachan Moncur III, Roswell Rudd, and Joseph Bowie, among others, gained prominence—all musicians who widen and inflect the sound spectrum of their instrument, including noise elements in their music. Roswell Rudd deserves special attention in this field as he has a certain Dixieland and blues approach to his tonally free excursions. Through the vocal qualities Rudd incorporates in his playing, he discovered the folk music of the world: "Suffice it to say that vocal techniques I had associated at one time only with the jazz singers of my own country were revealed to be common to the oldest known musical traditions the world over. What I had always considered the epitome of musical expression in America, the blues, could be felt everywhere in the so-called 'folk world.' "

Rudd is connected with soprano saxophonist Steve Lacy in a particularly fruitful partnership. Characteristically, both got into free playing directly from Dixieland, skipping the stages in between. Joseph Bowie incorporated the free jazz trombone in the realm of free funk, particularly vitally in the eighties with his band Defunkt.

Actually, the trombone scene—more so than any other instrument, with the exception of the clarinet—atrophied during the sixties. Some of jazz's best trombone players, among them J. J. Johnson, Kai Winding, and Bill Harris, were practically absent from the scene. In the jazz polls, no instrument had fewer entries than the trombone. In this situation, European trombone players, somehow, took over: Paul Rutherford in Great Britain, Eje Thelin in Sweden, and, most important, Albert Mangelsdorff in West Germany. They developed new styles of playing, creating a lively, flourishing trombone scene again.

Mangelsdorff emancipated the long lines of alto player Lee Konitz—under whose influence he began in the fifties—in a gradual and seemingly necessary process, becoming ever freer harmonically, until they were "freed"—in the exact sense of the word. Since the beginning of the seventies, Mangelsdorff has been developing a technique that permits him—as the first trombonist in jazz—to play "chords" on his instrument. By blowing one tone and simultaneously singing another, usually higher, tone, Mangelsdorff gives the vocal tone the sound quality of the trombone. Taking these two tones as his starting point, Mangelsdorff creates—simultaneously!—three-, four-, and five-tone chords by playing with the combination tones generated through the friction between the blown and sung tones. This deliberate use of "multiphonics"—multivoiced sounds on an instrument that usually only produces single notes—wasn't specifically discovered by free-jazz players in the sixties. Performers of traditional jazz, such as tenor saxophonist Illinois Jacquet in the forties, knew about them. But nowhere has the art of multiphonic playing been so cultivated and advanced as in free jazz. More among saxophonists than trombonists, multiphonics, with such tenor players as Pharoah Sanders, Dewey Redman, or Archie Shepp, often became more important than the de facto blown notes.

Mangelsdorff made many of his best records with important American drummers like Elvin Jones, Alphonse Mouzon, and Shannon Jackson. In his long solo appearances—without rhythm section—he manages to keep audiences attentive to his music through the wealth of his ideas and sounds. Since the sixties, his name constantly appears in the leading spots of the American jazz polls, even though he does not live in the United States. (Generally, Europeans achieve this kind of recognition in America only if they decide to live there.) In 1980, Mangelsdorff was voted the world's best trombonist in the annual *Down Beat* critics' poll.

Even if Mangelsdorff is left out of account, the European trombone scene—with its striking love for experimenting with multiphonics—is richer than the American. Eje Thelin from Sweden and Conrad Bauer from [East] Germany have developed, independently of Mangelsdorff, a similarly sovereign soloistic and chord-based approach to the trombone.

Worthy of mention among the second generation of European free-jazz trombonists are Günter Christmann from [West] Germany, Willem von Manen from the Netherlands, Johannes Bauer from [East] Germany, and, above all, his previously mentioned brother Conrad. Conrad Bauer probably plays the most flowing free-jazz trombone. Going against all the conservatory rules, he has developed a new way of playing that is smooth without being cold, and operates, through circular breathing, with long-held, unbroken sounds that are inwardly varied and developed. Like Mangelsdorff he is a master of polyphonic playing; but whereas Mangelsdorff fosters and refines the tonal aspect of multiphonics, Bauer uses them as "free" tone colors, which can exert an almost noiselike impact.

The younger European trombonists include Dutch Wolter Wierbos, English Annie Whitehead, French Yves Robert, and Austrian Christian Radovan, who made his name with the Vienna Art Orchestra. Wierbos' playing is particularly impressive. He energetically and grippingly opens up the tradition of free-trombone playing to the stylistic amalgams of postmodern jazz, effectively incorporating rock and bebop sounds as well as the growl techniques of swing trombonists.

Since the seventies, the trombone scene has been revitalized in America in the realm of contemporary mainstream (mainly through Bill Watrous) and in free jazz, especially through George Lewis, who was first introduced by Anthony Braxton. Watrous blows with fantastic power and brilliance and with astounding technical virtuosity. Lewis, who belongs to the AACM, has studied philosophy, especially the German philosophers Heidegger and Husserl. The level of abstract thinking required for that can also be felt in his music. Lewis is also interested in computer music and other electronic sounds: "With the synthesizer, you have a whole new source of available sounds, rhythms, timbres, and colors. It's just a matter of organizing them rhythmically. I want to be able to do everything with it on the same level as on my trombone."

The eighties brass renaissance was characterized by an ongoing trombone revival in postmodern jazz, with stylists like Ray Anderson, Steve Turre, Craig Harris, Frank Lacy, Art Baron, Dan Barrett, and Robin Eubanks. The most vital of these players is Ray Anderson, who was also first presented by Anthony Braxton but lacks his abstractness. Anderson is a stylist full of drama and wild passion, who transposes the gruff, emotionally loaded sounds of the tailgate and gut-bucket trombone into the language of new jazz. He's a strong player of gripping melodic lines and reminds us that one element has been more important in the history of the jazz trombone than in that of any other instrument (and it has certainly been part of the nature of the trombone from the start): humor. In the eighties Anderson also, together with bassist Mark Helias, jointly headed the Slickaphonics free-funk band.

If anyone has ever demonstrated the rewards to be gained from playing a trombone as if it were a percussive instrument, then that's Steve Turre from Omaha, Nebraska. His brilliantly articulated rhythmic lines carry on from where Jay Jay Johnson stopped, but his playing also reveals the influence of saxophonists and trumpeters: Charlie Parker, John Coltrane, Miles Davis, and Woody Shaw (in whose quintet Turre played until 1985). Turre, also an arranger, is one of the few trombonists to have completely mastered pentatonic playing, which is very difficult in terms of slide technique.

Craig Harris blows the most muscular, powerful trombone in postmodern jazz. He is a master of overblowing and circular breathing, and he has never confused awareness of tradition with lack of a spirit of experimentation. Harris has played with Sun Ra and David Murray and has been influenced by Ellington trombonists Tricky Sam Nanton, Lawrence Brown, and Juan Tizol as well as by African and Australian music. He and his Tailgaters Tales band organized a benefit concert for New York's homeless, and his "Shelter" suite is concerned with the same issue. "The hungry and homeless are the product of both highly developed and underdeveloped states. They challenge all social systems. Their number grows daily. We can no longer afford the luxury of turning our backs. They exist from Bombay to Broadway, from Ethiopia to the Upper East Side. My music expresses what they have moved in me," Harris said.

Robin Eubanks from Philadelphia has found a completely individual stylistic niche in a realm between bop trombone and free-jazz trombone. His phrasing, inspired by saxophonist Wayne Shorter, is characterized by great harmonic freedom. Of all the trombonists in postmodern jazz, he perhaps possesses the richest stylistic palette. His dark, powerful sound has exerted formative influence in a variety of directions: in altoist Steve Coleman's free funk, in the bop of Art Blakey's Jazz Messengers, in the neoclassicism of the Dave Holland Quintet, and in McCoy Tyner's modality. Eubanks said, "If you look at very different kinds of music from varying viewpoints, you discover what they have in common, which you would otherwise miss from a *single* viewpoint."

The Clarinet

In all stages of jazz development, the clarinet has been a symbol of interrelation. The function of the clarinet in the old New Orleans counterpoint, filling in the space between the contrasting trumpet and trombone and entwining them like ivy, is characteristic for its position. Not coincidentally did the clarinet have its greatest period during the Swing era, when jazz and popular music were largely identical.

Alphonse Picou (1879–1961) was the first clarinetist from New Orleans whose style became known. His famous chorus on "High Society" is one of the most copied solos in jazz history. Down to this day, almost every clarinetist who plays "High Society" is quoting Picou—just as every trombonist who plays "Tin Roof Blues" is quoting from George Brunis' solo with the New Orleans Rhythm Kings, or playing it entire.

The second important clarinetist from old New Orleans is George Lewis—though his influence was felt much later, in the New Orleans revival of the forties and fifties. Lewis (1900–1968) participated in New Orleans jazz life from the time he was sixteen. In the thirties, he worked on the docks until the New Orleans revival movement in the forties carried him to worldwide fame. In the music recorded by George Lewis then and in the fifties (initially with trumpeter Bunk Johnson, later with his own bands staffed with the best New Orleans–style musicians) the listening public, which was inundated with amateurish or commercialized New Orleans and Dixieland records, was reminded of the really authentic New Orleans jazz. Lewis's tenderly fragile clarinet playing, as in his classic "Burgundy Street Blues," on his many long, worldwide concert tours found admirers in many countries, including Japan.

It points up the multiple layers of jazz development that the great triumvirate of the jazz clarinet, Johnny Dodds–Jimmie Noone–Sidney Bechet, preceded Picou and Lewis in recording, while in a certain sense building musically and stylistically on their way of playing. Picou, Lewis, and, of course, Bechet, actually were merely the final representatives of a style cultivated in old New Orleans by many other Creole clarinetists. As late as 1964, on the island of Martinique, Joachim Berendt heard an eighty-year-old man play at a fair who sounded virtually like Sidney Bechet, and yet he had never heard the name of that great clarinetist. On the other hand, Bechet, when he came to Paris and was introduced to music from Martinique, played many pieces of Martiniquan folk music as if they were—as they actually could be—old Creole dances from New Orleans.

But back to the triumvirate: Dodds-Noone-Bechet. Noone is best known for the gentleness and sublety of his tone. Compared to him, the improvisations of Johnny Dodds seem almost wild and brutal. Dodds, a master of the lower register of his instrument, was Louis Armstrong's preferred clarinetist during the time of the Hot Five and Hot Seven recordings. Bechet, finally, of whom we shall speak again in the soprano section, is the embodiment of the jazz *espressivo.* The strong, moving vibrato of his clarinet produced a sound recognizable even to the jazz layperson. In France, where Bechet lived during his final years (he died in 1959), he was as popular as any *chanteur.* And even when much in his playing seemed to have become mannered, it was one of the especially moving human experiences in jazz to see this white-haired, dignified man from old New Orleans play amid the young Dixieland existentialists in Saint-Germain-des-Près.

In Paris, too, Albert Nicholas, the last great New Orleans clarinetist, made his home (he later moved to Switzerland, where he died in 1973) playing in a clearly "clarinetistic," technically masterful style that in the fifties became somewhat Bechet-like, yet always retained that wealth of ideas and mobility that Bechet often seemed to have lost in the final years of his life. Nicholas, also a Creole, emerged from the orchestras of King Oliver and Luis Russell, while the Bechet of the twenties is primarily represented by records made with the Clarence Williams Blue Five. In the thirties Bechet recorded with his own New Orleans Feetwarmers. Among his most important clarinet recordings are those he made with pianist Art Hodes in the forties.

Nicholas—along with Omer Simeon and Barney Bigard—belongs to what might be called the third generation of the jazz clarinet. Omer Simeon was Jelly Roll Morton's favorite clarinetist, while Barney Bigard became known mainly through the flowing, supple solos he recorded as a member of Duke Ellington's band from 1928 to 1942, and with Louis Armstrong's All Stars from 1946 to 1955, as one of the few jazz musicians who spent considerable time with both of these giants. Bigard, who died in 1980, was a sorcerer of melody, playing with strong feeling and with dynamics almost equal to those of Benny Goodman.

Bigard, though indebted to the New Orleans tradition, in his great period already belonged among the Swing clarinetists. Before going on to these, we must recapitulate the history of the white jazz clarinet. It begins with Leon Roppolo of the New Orleans Rhythm Kings, that famous white group of the early twenties. Roppolo is one of the Beiderbecke types so frequent in jazz who seem to burn themselves out in their music and their lives. The most important of his successors in the realm of Chicago style are Frank Teschemacher, Jimmy Dorsey, and Pee Wee Russell. All three played with Bix Beiderbecke. Teschemacher, who died in 1932, loved to connect and smear his notes, perhaps subconsciously feeling that this would make him sound more like a black musician. He was a great influence on the young Benny Goodman. Pee Wee Russell, who died in 1969, preferred the lower registers of the clarinet. He played with a vibrato and way of phrasing that puts him in a similar relationship to Lester Young and Jimmy Giuffre as Bix Beiderbecke seems to be to Chet Baker. Willis Connover dubbed him the "poet of the clarinet."

Finally, Mezz Mezzrow, a musician who gained renown through his friendship with the French jazz critic Hugues Panassié, must be mentioned among the Chicago clarinetists. From the standpoint of technique, he was mediocre, and as an improviser he often had to limit himself to stringing triads together. Still, he played with a feeling for the blues surprising in a white musician of his generation. "The race," Mezzrow wrote, "made me feel inferior, started me thinking that maybe I wasn't worth beans as a musician or any kind of artist, in spite of all my big ideas." Mezzrow's most important contribution is not so much his clarinet playing as his autobiography *Really the Blues,* in which the flavor of Chicago in the twenties, and even more, of Harlem in the thirties and forties, has been so well captured that even Henry Miller expressed his enthusiasm.

It may be part of the instrument's nature that traditional jazz elements have stayed alive for the clarinetists way into the seventies and eighties, much more so than for most players of other instruments. This is true, for instance, for Bob Wilber, initially inspired by Bechet, and for Kenny Davern. Both combine the warmth of traditional playing and a contemporary kind of elegance. Wilber once said, "I felt then [in the fifties] and even more so now that there's a *oneness* about jazz. Style shouldn't be a barrier between musicians."

But back to the thirties: The clarinetist of whom the layperson thinks first when jazz clarinet is mentioned is Benny Goodman. He, too, stemmed from the circle of Chicago style. He is the "King of Swing" whose scintillating and polished clarinet playing is the reason why the clarinet and the Swing era are largely synonymous. "B. G.," as he is known, was one of the great stylists of jazz, a musician of superlative charm, spirit, and gaiety. His clarinet playing is associated in equal degrees with his big-band recordings and those he made with various small combos: from the Benny Goodman Trio, with Teddy Wilson at the piano and Gene Krupa on drums, through the quartet in which Lionel Hampton first found public recognition, to the Benny Goodman Sextet in which guitarist Charlie Christian helped pave the way for modern jazz. In terms of expression, Goodman (who died in 1986) accomplished on the clarinet almost everything other instruments could not achieve until the advent of modern jazz. But he did this—and here is the heart of the matter—without the harmonic finesse and rhythmic complexity of modern jazz. This may be one reason for the disadvantageous position occupied by the clarinet in modern jazz. On the other hand, B. G. is a master of subtleties. His dynamics range smoothly, like those of no other clarinetist, from softest pianissimo to jubilant fortissimo. Particularly astonishing is the skill with which Goodman manages to play even the softest notes and still, even when playing with a big band, capture the attention of the listeners in the very last row of a large concert hall.

Other well-known clarinetists of the Swing era were Artie Shaw and Woody Herman, both of whom had big bands to celebrate their clarinets in Goodmanesque fashion. Jimmy Hamilton, Buster Bailey, and, indirectly, Edmond Hall were also influenced by Goodman, as were all clarinetists who played alongside and after him—except Lester Young and the modern clarinetists who stem from him. Hamilton has played solos with Duke Ellington that are softer and more restrained than even Goodman. If the theories of the jazz racists were correct, one would have to conclude— comparing Hamilton and Goodman on purely aural evidence—that the former was white and Goodman black, though the opposite is true. During the fifties, Hamilton evolved into an important clarinet voice in modern jazz, and it is regrettable that his name was so rarely mentioned in the same breath with Buddy DeFranco, Tony Scott, and Jimmy Giuffre. In the eighties he played in the Clarinet Summit, that imposing clarinet quartet whose members (apart from himself: Alvin Batiste, John Carter, and David Murray) with ease embrace four generations of clarinet playing—from Swing by way of bebop and free jazz to neoclassicism.

Edmond Hall, who died in 1967, was the most important black Swing clarinetist and, alongside Benny Goodman, the towering Swing stylist on this instrument. He had a sharp, biting tone that often stands in contrast to Goodman's suppleness. During the forties and fifties, Hall played with Eddie Condon's New York Dixieland bunch.

It is indicative of the organic rightness of jazz evolution that the approaches to the playing of different instruments have evolved on a parallel course. Nearly every instrument has its Roy Eldridge or Charlie Parker. The "Eldridge" of the clarinet is Edmond Hall; the "Parker" of this instrument became Buddy DeFranco, the first clarinetist who could outdistance Benny Goodman in terms of technique. He is an improviser of vital force, which led impressario Norman Granz to team him with Lionel Hampton and other great Swing musicians on numerous recordings. The brilliance of his playing is of such clarity it has sometimes been regarded as "cold." It is one of the paradoxes of jazz that the playing of so "hot" and basic an improviser as

DeFranco should have impressed so many listeners as cold. It symbolizes the difficult, almost hopeless situation of the clarinet in modern jazz that so brilliant a musician as DeFranco finally resigned himself to taking over the direction of the Glenn Miller Orchestra "for reasons of economic survival ... playing tiresome music and adding nothing to his own development," as Leonard Feather put it. In the eighties he played jazz again with great success—in recordings with pianist Oscar Peterson as well as with vibraphonist Terry Gibbs with whom he headed a quintet. Here at last he found the artistic challenge his playing demanded.

It does not contradict Buddy DeFranco's position as the "Charlie Parker of the clarinet" to point out that a European musician was the first, strictly speaking, to play bebop on the clarinet. This was the Swede Stan Hasselgard. Benny Goodman made him a member of his sextet in the spring of 1948, the only clarinetist he ever tolerated alongside himself. A few months later, in November of the same year, Hasselgard was fatally injured in an automobile accident. Hasselgard was the second European jazz musician of stylistically creative consequence. The French gypsy guitarist Django Reinhardt, who had a considerable influence on almost all jazz guitarists between the late thirties and the late forties, was the first.

After DeFranco's "coldness," the "warmth" of Jimmy Giuffre seemed even stronger. Initially, Giuffre played almost exclusively in the low register of his instrument—the so-called Chalumeau register. He has on occasion pointed out that he did this because he was technically unable to do anything else. In fact, making the transition from low to high register fluently is the greatest problem involved in playing this instrument.

Giuffre's technical handicap became a stylistic identification. The dark warmth of his playing at last seemed to embody what had been missed for so long: a modern clarinet conception somehow corresponding to the "Four Brothers" sound of the tenor saxophonists. But Giuffre played his clarinet much as Lester Young had played his twenty years before—on the few recordings Pres had then made on this instrument: in 1938 with the Kansas City Six, and around the same time with Count Basie's band. Many experts do not doubt that Lester, had he played it more often, would have become as important on the clarinet as he was on the tenor. Lester himself said he played clarinet so rarely mainly because he could not find an instrument that suited him.

The paradox of the situation is that cool jazz actually has only two clarinetists whose playing corresponds to the cool conception in a narrower definition—Lester Young and Jimmy Giuffre—whereas among the tenor saxophonists the Lester Young sound was multiplied to such a degree that Lester Young, the tenor man, seemed to be living in a world of mirrors. Indirectly, however, a few tenor men have extended the cool Lester Young conception when occasionally playing clarinet: Zoot Sims, Buddy Collette, and others. But this was usually perceived only as a surprising side effect, not as a genuine style—as, for example, Sims' way of playing tenor. Much later, in the early seventies, a musician who had come to attention through Miles Davis' *Bitches Brew,* Benny Maupin, reminded us on clarinet and bass clarinet that the quiet balance of the Lester Young heritage can be particularly attractive even among the electronicized contemporary jazz sounds.

But back to Giuffre. During the second half of the fifties, he moved away from his preference for the low register of his instrument, probably because the success of his dark-toned playing forced him to play clarinet so much that he overcame his technical handicap. Since the sixties, Giuffre has stood out as a sensitive musician, presenting a restrained, chamber-music-like cool free jazz.

Two other important musicians who took up the struggle with the difficult position of the clarinet in jazz are the German Rolf Kühn and the American Tony Scott. From 1956 to 1969, Kühn lived in the United States, and John Hammond called him "a new Benny Goodman" then. Leonard Feather found that "Kühn had the misfortune to enter the jazz scene at a time when his chosen instrument had suffered an apparently irreversible decline in popularity. Had it not been for these circumstances, he might well be a major name in jazz today." In the sixties and seventies Kühn incorporated a lot of modern impulses, at first from Eric Dolphy and later elements of fusion music.

Tony Scott is a true "jam session" musician, one of the few still extant, with an immense drive to play and, above all, with the "loudest sound of all clarinetists" (Perry Robinson). He is a genuine clarinetist who feels the music through his horn, undisturbed by the unfavorable stylistic situation of the instrument. "I don't like funerals," said Scott when it seemed in the late fifties that the jazz clarinet was finally laid to rest. "That's why I went to Asia."

In Asia, Scott inspired and trained dozens of musicians. What all those "Americans in Europe" accomplished together, Scott achieved almost alone in the much more extended Asian territory. From Taiwan to Indonesia, from Okinawa to Thailand, he passed the message of genuine jazz on to a whole generation of young jazz musicians. Since the beginning of the seventies, Scott has been living in Rome.

Of course, the dilemma of the clarinet—that it simply didn't seem to fit into the "saxophonized" sound of modern jazz—was not solved by Scott's flight to Asia. A solution was initiated by the great avant-gardist Eric Dolphy, who died in Berlin in 1964—however, not so much on clarinet as on bass clarinet.

Never before had the bass clarinet been a true jazz instrument. Dolphy turned it into one—with searing, wild emotional expression and also with a physically immense power that gave his listeners the feeling that he was not playing the traditional bass clarinet, which had always appeared somewhat old-fashioned, but rather a totally new instrument that had never been heard before. (Harry Carney, baritone saxophonist with Duke Ellington, and a few others had occasionally used the bass clarinet in more conventional contexts.)

Dolphy's way of playing the bass clarinet quickly found followers, particularly in Europe where many musicians (mostly saxophonists) also blow bass clarinet. Dutch-born Willem Breuker; John Surman from England; Germans Gunter Hampel and Wollie Kaiser; and Italian Gianliugi Trovesi have further developed Dolphy's legacy in their own way.

For most musicians, however, the bass clarinet remained a secondary instrument, probably because Dolphy had expressed, with a hitherto unattained intensity, almost everything that can be said there. Only Michel Pilz, Michel Portal, and Louis Sclavis have been able to give such complete expression to themselves on the bass clarinet that they concentrated on this instrument right from the start. Strikingly, they all come from the rich Francophone traditions of clarinet playing: Pilz from Luxembourg and Portal and Sclavis from France. As an expert in overblown playing whose furious lines contrast miraculously with the gentleness and warmth of his tone, Michel Pilz plays nothing but bass clarinet, and he has brought Dolphy's legacy into the ecstatic free collective improvisations of the Globe Unity Orchestra. Multi-instrumentalist Michel Portal comes from the concert hall and New Music, having worked with Pierre Boulez, Luciano Berio, and Karlheinz Stockhausen. As a bass clarinetist he links the dancelike impulse and the joyous liveliness of southern French folk music with free jazz's explorative awareness of sound. He also often works with attractive electronic transformations. Louis Sclavis from Lyon, cofounder of the ARFI (Association pour la Recherche d'un Folklore imaginaire), became known for his impressive performances with the Workshop de Lyon and the La Marmite Infernale orchestra.

Sclavis, who blows other clarinets alongside the bass instrument, is master of an "imaginary folklore": music that's sometimes cheerful and bucolic, and then once again dark and abrasive, sounding strangely folklike and yet containing hardly any original ethnic material—music full of the angularities of rock dynamics, digital wit, and the élan of free jazz. Folklore here develops out of the imagination, as a brilliantly devised free arena for creative sensibility. Sclavis excitingly enriches his clarinet playing with percussive accents, "drumming" entire melodies on the instrument by making virtuoso musical use of the clattering sounds of the keys or reed.

Among the Americans who should be mentioned in this context are Doug Ewart, Hamiet Bluiett, David Murray, John Purcell, and Marty Ehrlich. Murray discovered poetic, lyrical colors and emotions on the bass clarinet, fascinatingly contrasting with his elementally vital tenor sax style. Bluiett plays the alto clarinet whose appearance often leads to it being mistaken for the bass instrument. He attracted attention in the eighties with the Clarinet Family, to date the most colorful and opulent concentration of clarinet sounds in jazz: eight clarinetists and a rhythm section, reflecting and updating the instrument's entire history from New Orleans to free jazz.

John Purcell, who became known in Jack DeJohnette's and Muhal Richard Abrams' groups, is—like Anthony Braxton (still to be discussed)—one of the few real multi-instrumentalists. He phrases with equally remarkable expressiveness and steadiness on the bass clarinet, and also oboe, English horn, and the soprano and tenor saxophone so that no distinction can be made between primary and secondary instrument. Marty Ehrlich is almost his equal: a musician who can cope with all styles in postmodern jazz and whose love of rich colors and contrasts is to be heard in his bass clarinet, as well as in his alto sax and flute phrasing.

Beyond that the mainstream also flowed into the music of the seventies and eighties through such clarinetists as Bobby Jones (who died in 1980), Dick Johnson, Bill Easley, Richard Stolzman, Swedish-born Putte Wickman, and, particularly brilliant, Eddie Daniels. Jones, who came to the fore in his work with Charles Mingus, occasionally seemed like an "Edmond Hall of the seventies," with Hall's swinging expressiveness but greater, more contemporary flexibility. In 1988, Putte Wickman made ambitious duo recordings with bassist Red Mitchell. He cultivates the charm of the swing clarinetists while spicing it with a refreshing and bolder modern harmonic openness.

Most successful of all in the eighties was Eddie Daniels, who started out as a tenor sax player and won a reputation as an experienced studio musician. The clarinet became his chief instrument in 1985. A year later the readers of *Down Beat* chose him as the best clarinetist (and in following polls, too)—a category that, unlike any other, had been absolutely dominated for decades by the grand old masters of the instrument. Daniels—a "Wynton Marsalis of the Clarinet," according to Leonard Feather—further developed Buddy DeFranco's concept of the bop clarinet in unique fashion, with enormously supple, flowing lines bubbling over with a wealth of ideas and a special feeling for the music of Charlie Parker. "The clarinet has the widest range of all woodwinds. It has one of the warmest sounds. . . . It's been the most neglected instrument since the bebop era primarily because it is one of the hardest," said Daniels.

The fact that the clarinet experienced a timid comeback in the eighties was also partly thanks to Daniels. But more important still have been performers coming from "free" playing, which they often developed in a variety of directions. Anthony Braxton, Don Byron, J. D. Parran, Perry Robinson, German Theo Jörgensmann, Hungarian Lajos Dudas, and, most important of all, John Carter made people almost forget the instrument's shortcomings—its lack of tonal sharpness and physical presence—by using the clarinet's rich register for a shimmering palette of highly diverse sounds.

Multi-instrumentalist and composer Braxton is a masterly player of the entire spectrum of clarinets from the soprano to the contrabass, creating iridescent abstract sounds that to many listeners seem complicated despite their having attained worldwide success in the seventies.

Perry Robinson has played with the Jazz Composers Orchestra and Roswell Rudd, with Charlie Haden and Sunny Murray, with Gunter Hampel, and with Dave and Darius Brubeck; all those names testify to his universality. Already in the seventies he took free jazz, cool jazz, bop, swing, and rock to that postmodern style that was to become a matter of course in the eighties. "We want to be able to play any kind of music and yet we want to be ourselves," he said. "The clarinet, it's incredible, because you have these different sounds. The only frustrating thing about it that has to be overcome somehow is that it's too small; it won't carry the weight when you're trying to get through. I made a study of it, and I learned a lot of things about sound, about overblowing."

Theo Jörgensmann transposed the open expressiveness of free playing into bop and modal jazz—as a specialist in making surprising changes of register, utilizing with particular sensitivity his instrument's dark warm register reminiscent of Jimmy Giuffre. In the eighties, Jörgensmann headed the CL-4 clarinet quartet, discovering unusual sounds in the borderline area between jazz and New Music. Also playing with CL-4 is Lajos Dudas, who comes from classical concert music. He's a much appreciated stylist in Europe, esteemed for the delicacy and tenderness of his playing with free tonality.

Don Byron and J. D. Parran are remarkable neoclassical clarinetists. Byron unites Tony Scott's explosive fervor with Jimmy Hamilton's subtle harmonic refinement. As a black clarinetist he refreshes jazz tradition (viewed from a free standpoint) with the rich legacy of Klezmer music—with the Jewish music of emigrants from Eastern Europe as further developed in America. Parran, who came out of the Black Artist Group in St. Louis, has played with pianist Anthony Davis and violinist Leroy Jenkins.

Lastly is the musician whom one first thinks of in connection with outstanding contemporary clarinet playing: John Carter. A Texas companion of Ornette Coleman who only became famous in the eighties, Carter is a sparkling, subtle melodist within tonally free jazz whose playing is deeply rooted in the great tradition of the jazz clarinet. He has enriched

contemporary clarinet playing with creative new sounds, with exciting
whirling sounds (based on circular breathing) and unusual disaltered chords
that extend into the region of polyphonic playing. Carter is a magician of the
flageolet. Where other clarinetists take an easier way, noisily overblowing
their instrument, Carter does something much more difficult. He plays
elastic, absolutely sure notes—tonally free and in tempered tuning, up to
three octaves above the instrument's normal range. In the eighties, Carter
also became an important composer, a master of extended form who
achieved a rare balance between notated and improvised parts. His *Roots
and Folklore: Episodes in the Development of American Folk Music* marks
a peak of unification. This composition, consisting of five suites documented
on five records, stands alongside Duke Ellington's *Black, Brown & Beige* as
probably the most successful and creative tone poem depicting over two
hundred years of black culture in America: from deportation and slavery by
way of emancipation and rural black folklore to the urbanization of modern
blacks.

The Saxophones

The ideal jazz instrument is an instrument that can be as expressive as the
trumpet and as mobile as the clarinet. The instruments of the saxophone
family combine these two qualities, which are in extreme opposition where
most other instruments are concerned. That is why the saxophone is
important to jazz. But it became important only at the start of the thirties.
One can hardly speak of a New Orleans saxophone tradition. The few
saxophonists active in New Orleans were looked upon with the expressions
reserved today for sousaphone or theremin players, regarded as odd
characters rather than musicians. Generally, the saxophone belonged to
sweet bands and popular dance music rather than jazz. During the days of
Chicago style, things changed. It is noteworthy that the New Orleans
Rhythm Kings were without a saxophone when they came to Chicago from
New Orleans in 1921; yet when they obtained the engagement at Friar's Inn
that was their springboard to fame, they were urged to include a saxophone.
The saxophonist stumbled and staggered about amid the collective
ensemble of the Kings, and never really found his place. As soon as the band
quit the job at Friar's Inn, he was let go.

Since no jazz tradition existed for the saxophone, the clarinet tradition
had to do for jazz-minded saxophonists. The importance that the saxophone—primarily the tenor—has achieved in modern jazz immediately
becomes clear when one realizes that at the outset of its jazz career, the
saxophone was played more or less like a peculiar sort of clarinet, whereas
since the fifties jazz clarinetists often have had a tenor-sax approach to their
instrument.

The saxophones range downward from soprano (and sopranino) through alto, tenor, and baritone to bass (and contrabass). The most important in jazz are the first four.

Adrian Rollini played Dixieland and Chicago-style music on the bass sax with its hollow, somewhat burping sound, with great agility and basically with the same intention that motivated Boyd Raeburn to use the instrument as the lowest voice in the sax section of his modern big band: to give depth and bottom to the sound spectrum. Joseph Jarman and Roscoe Mitchell use the bass sax in free jazz, creating similar "honking," exotic sounds as those produced at the beginning of the saxophone development in old New Orleans on the other saxophones. The bass sax has nevertheless remained an outsider instrument.

The Soprano Saxophone

The soprano saxophone continues where the clarinet leaves off, because of its loudness, for one. It has the most disproportionate history of all instruments in jazz, even more disproportionate than the violin. In the beginning, there was only Sidney Bechet. Today, there are hundreds of sopranoists. A tenor man is no longer acceptable in countless big bands and studio orchestras if he does not double on the soprano. In fact, things have been somewhat reversed since the seventies: Often the soprano became the main instrument and the tenor the second one.

For decades, we were told that soprano sax was used so rarely because of the difficulty in playing it "clean." Its high notes necessarily sound "out of tune." Today, however, we know that this is the very advantage of the instrument: The "dirtiness" of sound, which has been of great importance in all phases of jazz history, is an integral part of the soprano. One could almost say that the soprano tends to flatten each note, to turn it into a "blue note," to turn the whole scale "blue." This is a tendency imminent from the start in folk blues and the archaic jazz forms. The three classical blue notes of jazz are compromises with the European harmonic system. Actually, the music of the African and the African-American tends toward slanting each individual tone, toward not accepting a note as it is, toward reinterpreting each note as a personal statement. The soprano does all this in an exemplary manner: It "Africanizes." The thesis that this is its actual strength can even be verified in a test: There are sopranoists who have managed to produce "clean" sounds in spite of all the technical difficulties of the instrument—Lucky Thompson, for example, who in the sixties transferred the perfect beauty of his tenor sound to the soprano. But he has remained relatively unsuccessful, in spite of the high degree of sophistication of his playing. He is admired, but fails to truly excite and move.

Sidney Bechet is the Louis Armstrong of the soprano saxophone—he has

Armstrong's majestic expressiveness. During the span of his rich life, which led from the New Orleans of pre–World War I days to the Paris of the fifties, he changed—gradually at first, but then more and more decidedly—from clarinet to soprano sax. It has been said he did so because with advancing age the soprano became easier for him, since it requires less air for full-volume play. His main reason, however, was that the soprano makes possible a wider range of expression, and the maximum of *espressivo* was Bechet's main goal. For good reason he has been called the forefather of the great ballad tradition of jazz. For the outsider, this tradition begins with Coleman Hawkins' "Body and Soul" in 1939. But actually, it began much earlier—with Sidney Bechet (and, of course, like all things in jazz, with Louis Armstrong!).

Bechet had only a few soprano students: Johnny Hodges, Don Redman, Charlie Barnet, Woody Herman, Bob Wilber—and in a certain sense, even in the Coltrane era, Budd Johnson and Jerome Richardson. They all applied their Bechet experiences to the stylistic periods to which they belonged. Hodges, the most famous soloist of the Duke Ellington Orchestra, was devoted to expressiveness in a way similar to Bechet. But the soprano solos he played with Ellington in the twenties and thirties seem pale compared to the power of his alto sound. Hodges gave up the soprano altogether after 1940. Perhaps he also felt that playing the soprano would always keep him somewhat in the shadow of the great Bechet, to whom he was indebted in many ways. Toward the end of his life, when the soprano sound became fashionable, Ellington wanted Hodges to give it another try, but there was not time. Hodges died in 1970.

The close proximity between Hodges and Bechet in this aspect is made clear by Woody Herman: If he derives from Hodges as an alto player, he stems from Bechet as a soprano man.

John Coltrane was also among Bechet's students on this instrument. Joachim Berendt knows that from personal experience: Around the turn of the fifties into the sixties, Coltrane repeatedly had him send him soprano records by Bechet, especially from his French period, so he could study them. With his solo on "My Favorite Things" in 1961, Coltrane created a sweeping breakthrough for the soprano sax (see also the section on Coltrane).

The development of the soprano saxophone again displays the continuity of growth so very characteristic of jazz: from New Orleans—from Sidney Bechet in this case—to the modern and complex creations of Coltrane and Wayne Shorter and to their "students" and contemporaries.

Coltrane retained the expressiveness and "dirtiness" of Bechet. But for Bechet's majestic clarity, which is reminiscent of Louis Armstrong, he substituted an Asiatic meditativeness. Coltrane's soprano sound calls to mind the shenai of northern Indian music, the nagaswaram of the music of southern India, and the zoukra of Arabian music. His soprano sound virtually demands modality. It becomes particularly clear at this point what modality actually is: the equivalent in jazz to the "modes" of Arabic music and the Indian ragas.

Without Coltrane's soprano work it is hard to conceive of the whole Asiatic movement in jazz—not only in the area of the soprano, but transcending to all other instruments. This is particularly true of those instruments that, since the sixties, have increasingly been incorporated into jazz or were imbued with a new approach: violin, flute, bagpipes, oboe, English horn, etc. In fact, we must say that these instruments were incorporated into jazz or experienced changes in approach precisely because Coltrane's way of playing the soprano became the great example.

Still, Coltrane was not the first to play a modern type of jazz on the soprano sax. The first musician to do so was Steve Lacy. We have already mentioned his peculiar development in the section on the trombone, in connection with Roswell Rudd. He moved from Dixieland directly to free jazz, bypassing the usual way stations of bebop and cool jazz. Quite to the contrary, he did not discover bop until after he had been playing free jazz. In 1952, he played Dixieland with musicians like Max Kaminsky, Jimmy McPartland, and Rex Stewart; in 1956, he played with Cecil Taylor; and in 1960, with Thelonious Monk. He is one of the few horn players—and probably the only white among them—who fully understood and assimilated Monk.

The stations of Lacy's development—Kaminsky, Cecil Taylor, Monk—indicate his originality. He is the first well-known soprano saxophonist in jazz who made the soprano his main instrument right from the start without deriving his way of playing from the clarinet, tenor, or alto sax. He can express himself so completely on this instrument that he doesn't need any other. Only in the eighties did Lacy find a fellow stylist, Jane Ira Bloom, who is completely his equal in that respect. Lacy, who has lived in Paris since the sixties, stands outside the three main currents in soprano playing: Sidney Bechet, John Coltrane, and Wayne Shorter. He was the first to produce sounds by blowing "in reverse": not by blowing into the instrument, but by sucking air "backward" through the horn. Many others have since adopted this way of playing. Bruce Ackley, known for his work with the ROVA Saxophone Quartet, was one of the few musicians who could advance Lacy's brittle, angular playing in the eighties. And Canadian-born Jane Bunnett sensitizes Lacy's concept with especially rounded and supple linear constructions.

Leonard Feather surmises that Coltrane first became interested in the soprano saxophone through Steve Lacy. This is suggested by the fact that before Lacy joined the Thelonious Monk Quartet, Coltrane had played with Monk. The club in which Monk then could be heard regularly was the Five Spot in New York, the meeting place of the in-group of jazz. No doubt Coltrane must have heard Lacy there.

"My Favorite Things," as we have said, became a hit. Soon, big bands and studio orchestras jumped on the soprano bandwagon. The range of the saxophone section was extended. Some arrangers became specialists in incorporating soprano sounds into this range: Oliver Nelson, Quincy Jones, Gil Evans, Gary McFarland, Thad Jones, and, later, Toshiko Akiyoshi.

The soprano not only took up the legacy of the clarinet; in a certain sense it was also heir to the tenor saxophone. Since free jazz, many tenor men love to "overblow" their instruments in a way reminiscent of the falsetto sound of blues and gospel vocalists, driving into the range of the alto and soprano sax. In this way the tenor becomes "two or even three instruments in one": tenor, alto, and even soprano. This tendency to play "high" has always been part of jazz. A hot way of playing is frequently achieved by playing high, in a way which prompted the German ethnomusicologist Alphons Dauer to suspect that the term *hot* actually was derived from the French *haut*—high. It is obvious that the overblown tenor saxophone is a very ecstatic, intensive instrumental sound on the one hand, but that it is musically rather limited on the other. No doubt, the soprano continues where the overblown tenor leaves off. In this way a tenorist who overblows the instrument and also plays the soprano commands the entire range, from the lowest tenor tones to the flutelike heights of the overblown soprano saxophone. Thus it is no surprise that there is a host of soprano players who were initially specialists of falsetto tenor, among them Pharoah Sanders, Archie Shepp, Roscoe Mitchell, Joseph Jarman, Sam Rivers, and Englishmen Evan Parker and John Surman (whose main instrument at first was the baritone and who first used the soprano only as a "falsetto baritone," until he made an increasingly decisive switch from baritone to soprano). Further discussion of the musicians whose main instruments are tenor, alto, or baritone will be found in the chapters dealing with those instruments.

Other important soprano saxophonists after Coltrane include altoist Charlie Mariano and tenor players Dave Liebman (who in 1980 decided to devote himself full-time to the soprano sax), Roland Kirk (who included the sopranolike manzello among his various instruments), Zoot Sims, René McLean, and, most important of them all, Wayne Shorter (who influenced many of those previously named).

Shorter, who came out of one of Art Blakey's Messenger groups, became known as *the* saxophonist of the Miles Davis Quintet from 1964 to 1970. *In a Silent Way* of 1969 was the first record on which he played soprano. Apparently, he and the producers thought this to be such a minor point that not even the personnel identifications on the record indicate his soprano contribution. But the jazz world immediately noticed and listened. *Bitches Brew*, produced a year later, is unthinkable without Shorter's soprano sound. His soprano playing made such a strong impression on Miles Davis that Miles from that time onward no longer engaged any sax players who couldn't also play soprano, which often resulted in horn players who had started with tenor and alto having to learn the soprano as well. Shorter aestheticized Coltrane's legacy. Miles plus Trane = Shorter; that is, Shorter combines Coltrane's meditativeness with Miles's lyricism. His soprano sound has, in a way, the expressiveness described in the beginning of the chapter on Miles Davis: loneliness, forlornness, "the sound floats like a cloud." As a soprano player (more perhaps than as a tenorist!) Shorter ranks among the truly great improvisers in jazz. The tone alone implies the music and the complete musical personality of the improviser.

Shorter loves Brazilian music. One of his masterpieces is the transformation of "Dindi"—one of the earliest bossa compositions, dedicated by Antonio Carlos Jobim to the late Sylvia Telles, the first singer of bossa nova—into an exciting, hymnal free-jazz excursion, which yet retains in every note some of the Brazilian tenderness. Shorter was part of Weather Report, one of the most successful of all fusion groups from its beginnings in 1970 until its dissolution in 1985. Amid all the electronics of this group, his characteristic sound is often hard to pick up, but Shorter definitely is a main force behind the soprano's rise to the spot of most favored horn in jazz-rock and fusion music. In his own diverse bands of the eighties, he has presented jazz-rock with complex intertwinings of melody. Some of the musicians who have blown the soprano in records with fusion, rock, and funk music are Ernie Watts, Tom Scott, Ronnie Laws, Grover Washington, Kenny G. (alias Gorelick), Bendik (alias Bendik Hofseth), George Howard, Bill Evans (no relation to the pianist with the same name), and, in Europe, chiefly Barbara Thompson from England.

As a soprano saxophonist Wayne Shorter has been just as influential as John Coltrane and Sidney Bechet. Of the many soprano sax players who followed the Shorter line in the eighties, the most important are Branford Marsalis (a year older than his brother Wynton), Greg Osby, and, above all, the previously mentioned Jane Ira Bloom. No saxophonist has so sovereignly transposed, and further developed, the loneliness and forlornness of Shorter's soprano sax sound into jazz classicism as Branford Marsalis. Branford's warm and tender soprano also made a decisive contribution to the poetic impact of Sting's pop music.

If Sting headed the best-integrated pop band of the eighties, he ultimately owes much to Marsalis, who, like the other jazz players in Sting's band (pianist Kenny Kirkland, bassist Daryl Jones, and drummer Omar Hakim), staked the openness and warmth of musical dialogue against increasing mechanization and computerization in the pop sector. Greg Osby, who also plays alto sax, encapsulated and abstracted Shorter's concept particularly effectively in recordings with drummer Jack DeJohnette and pianist Michele Rosewoman. Jane Ira Bloom is, after Steve Lacy, one of the only players who right from the start has been able to express herself exclusively on the soprano saxophone. She first attracted attention in vibraphonist David Friedman's band, displaying rare poetic power in her courageously linear style. In her playing the frontiers between composition and improvisation blur. And she uniquely employs electronics, delicately coloring the soprano sound by way of pitch shifter, digital delay, and vocoder without overwhelming her instrument's gentle natural harmonics.

Some of these players, and even more so those belonging to free jazz, make it especially clear that the soprano comes closer to an African sound and intonation than the other saxophones. Important free players to gain attention as sopranoists can be found mainly in and around the AACM: Anthony Braxton, Joseph Jarman, Roscoe Mitchell, as well as Oliver Lake and Julius Hemphill. Occasionally, Jarman produces that typical growl sound that Sidney Bechet so movingly employed in the lower registers to create his blues and ballad renditions. Hemphill dedicated one of his works to the West African Dogon tribe, which lives in total seclusion in Burkina Faso, making references not only to the music but also to the mythology of this tribe.

In Europe, British-born Evan Parker, inspired by Coltrane and yet beyond the Coltrane school, developed a "free" way of playing that exceeds all received ideas about how the soprano sax should sound. Parker blows the soprano like a new instrument that's just been invented. No other soprano saxophonist can match his wealth of ideas in modeling harmonics. He's a master of circular breathing and, stimulated by Scottish bagpipes and non-European music, has developed a multivoiced way of playing that goes beyond the limited blocklike impact of many multiphonic performances to achieve polyphonic interweavings.

But the "pure" Bechet legacy also remains alive, touched more by Swing than by Coltrane and Shorter. It is represented in an exemplary manner by Bob Wilber and Kenny Davern, on individual records as well as in their joint *Soprano Summits* since 1975.

"Pure" soprano playing, in the vein of the contemporary aestheticism, is especially cultivated by Norwegian Jan Garbarek and Paul Winter, but also in unaccompanied duos and chamber-music-like formations by some of the musicians named earlier, such as David Liebman. Particular attention has been aroused by the clear and yet melancholy sound of Jan Garbarek, who, despite his somewhat mannered style, has influenced both European and American colleagues.

The Alto Saxophone

The history of the alto saxophone actually begins in the Swing period. To the clarinet triumvirate Jimmie Noone–Johnny Dodds–Sidney Bechet of the twenties corresponds a duo of altos that set the pace for everything played on this instrument during the thirties: Johnny Hodges and Benny Carter.

The Duke Ellington musician Johnny Hodges, who died in 1970, was a melodist of the rank of Armstrong or Hawkins. His warm, expressive vibrato and his way of melting notes in erotic glissandos made the Hodges sound one of the best-known instrumental signatures in jazz. Dark, tropical warmth seems to lie in this sound, which may occasionally approach sentimentality on slow pieces. At faster tempos, Hodges remained the great, gripping improviser he had been since joining Duke Ellington's band in 1928.

Among the many Hodges disciples, Woody Herman for many years was one of the best known. Herman (d. 1987) blew Hodges-inspired solos that stood in pronounced and sometimes amusing contrast to the more modern conceptions of the young musicians in his band.

Benny Carter is Hodges' opposite. Where the latter loves melancholy and earthiness, Benny Carter has a buoyant clarity and airiness. During the forties Carter settled in Hollywood, where he started a second career as arranger and composer for film and television studios. Carter is one of the most versatile musicians in jazz, of equal importance as alto saxist, arranger, and orchestra leader, and also a notable trumpeter, trombonist, and clarinetist. We shall have more to say about Carter in the chapter on big bands.

The maturity of the Hodges-Carter constellation seems all the more astonishing when one considers how few notable alto players preceded them. There was Don Redman, who as an arranger had a great impact on the development of the big-band sound of the twenties and early thirties and who played occasional alto solos with his bands; and then there was Frank Trumbauer among the Chicago-style musicians, who recorded with Bix Beiderbecke. Trumbauer did not play the E-flat alto, but its relative, the C-melody saxophone.

After Hodges and Carter, the whole development of the alto saxophone is concentrated on one towering personality: Charlie Parker. In the section dedicated to him and Dizzy Gillespie, we have attempted to clarify his singular position. Parker possessed both Hodges' emotionality and Carter's clarity. His importance was so great initially that there was hardly another bop altoist worth mentioning. The sole exception was Sonny Stitt, who vacillated between alto and tenor, and who, strangely enough, developed independently of Parker a Bird-like alto style of great clarity and bluesy expressiveness.

There was one realm that stayed relatively free from bebop way into the fifties: "jump," a style of playing (and dancing!) popular in Harlem and other big-city ghettos. Three of its outstanding players were alto saxophonists: Earl Bostic, Pete Brown, and Johnny Hodges. The latter was—mainly in those few years of his career when he was not a member of the Ellington band—a player of dynamic jump rhythms, as in records with organist Wild Bill Davis. In the late forties, long before the great rock 'n' roll era, Bostic scored hits of rock 'n' roll proportions with his *Flamingo* and other records. And Pete Brown found a way of playing in which the contrast between old-fashioned staccato and the modern conception is unintentionally (and sometimes intentionally) humorous.

While all the other instruments during the great days of bop produced important musicians in addition to the leading representative on the respective horn, the alto saxophone (apart from Sonny Stitt) had to wait for the start of the cool era for a considerable figure to emerge: This was Lee Konitz, who came out of the Lennie Tristano school. The abstract, glittering alto lines played by Konitz around the turn of the forties on his own and Lennie Tristano's recordings later became more singable, calmer, and more concrete. Of this change, Lee said that then "I played more than I could hear"; he'd feel better when "I really can hear what I'm playing." In the meantime, Konitz has absorbed and incorporated into his music many of the jazz elements since then—and some of Coltrane and of free jazz—and yet he has always remained true to himself. He is one of the really great improvisers in jazz. In the seventies he gained special attention with a unique nonet. After that he increasingly became a sensitive specialist in high-quality unaccompanied duos as principally documented in recordings with such pianists as Harold Danko, Hal Galper, and Michel Petrucciani, and also with trombonist Albert Mangelsdorff.

After Charlie Parker and Lee Konitz, the development of the alto saxophone takes place in the interplay between them. Art Pepper found his way toward a mature, Parker-influenced style of deep emotionality. Pepper, who spent more time in jails and reformatories than outside them, is an especially distressing example of the disastrous effect that heroin has had on the lives of some jazz musicians. He tells about it in his autobiography, *Straight Life,* which appeared in 1979 and initiated his comeback. The book is a moving document of the depressing conditions under which so many jazz musicians have to live. He died in 1982.

Paul Desmond (d. 1977) was a particularly successful figure of the Konitz line as altoist in the Dave Brubeck Quartet—and surely the most significant jazz talent in this well-known group: a lyricist of the alto sax.

The most significant altoists of West Coast jazz were Bud Shank, Herb Geller, and Paul Horn. Shank was one of the first jazz musicians to play with one of the great masters of classical Indian music. As early as 1961 he was recording with sitar master Ravi Shankar. Herb Geller, who moved to Germany, has much of the clarity of Benny Carter, but of course it is a Carter style that is touched by what came afterward, especially by Bird.

The power of Parker's personality gains full clarity when it is realized that the Bird influence—after the ideas originating with Konitz had been digested—did not recede during the late fifties but rather increased steadily: Lou Donaldson with his strong blues emotions; Cannonball Adderley, who until his death in 1975 was highly successful with the soul and funk-inspired music of his quintet; Jackie McLean, who joins Parker's blues feeling with a freer, less restrained expressiveness; Sonny Criss, who combined the archetypical world of the old blues tradition with that of Charlie Parker; Charles McPherson, who stems from the Detroit hard-bop circle; Gigi Gryce and Oliver Nelson, who are also outstanding arrangers (Nelson died in 1975); and, finally, Frank Strozier and James Spaulding, who both mark the transition to free jazz—all of them have, in the final analysis, their roots in Charlie Parker. This is true of Phil Woods, too: No other altoist transformed the Charlie Parker heritage so consistently into contemporary jazz. Swiss critic Peter Rüedi called him (in 1972) "the most complete alto player in today's jazz." It is significant to note that this completeness is shaped by the awareness of all the way stations Woods passed through in twenty-five years: Lennie Tristano's institution, Jimmy Raney's cool jazz, George Wallington's bop, Dizzy Gillespie's and Quincy Jones's big bands. . . . Since the end of the seventies Woods has found in Richie Cole an altoist from the younger generation who carries on in the realm of neobop from where the older man stops, thus underlining the continuity of the Parker heritage up to the present. Cole combines effervescent joy in playing with burning intensity.

While Bird's way of playing still dominated the scene, Ornette Coleman appeared at the Lenox Jazz School, which was under John Lewis' direction, in the summer of 1959. In the section devoted to him, the musical revolution this towering musician instigated is discussed in detail. The fact that he—as is true of all genuine innovators—did exactly what was "in the air" is significantly illustrated by other musicians taking similar roads at about the same time, or just after him, without being directly influenced by him. Among the alto saxophonists in this group, we should particularly mention Eric Dolphy, who died in 1964, but whose influence still affects today's scene. Dolphy (who based his playing somewhat more on functional harmonics than Coleman) came out of Chico Hamilton's and Charles Mingus' groups and made recordings of lasting value with trumpeter Booker Little and with his own groups. With his emotionally charged intonation, the wild, free flight of his ideas, and his great intervallic leaps, he created effects on a par with those of Ornette Coleman. The degree to which free playing was "overdue" is also demonstrated by the fact that in Great Britain Jamaican-born Joe Harriott developed—around 1960 and independently of Coleman and Dolphy—a high-quality free bop that never gained the recognition it merits.

The breakthrough created by Ornette Coleman and Eric Dolphy had an especially liberating effect on the alto players. Among the first to be affected were John Tchicai, Jimmy Lyons, and Marion Brown (who combines the virtuosity and the clarity of a man like Benny Carter with the possibilities of free jazz), followed by Byard Lancaster, Carlos Ward, and from the AACM Anthony Braxton, Joseph Jarman, Roscoe Mitchell, Henry Threadgill, and John Purcell, as well as Julius Hemphill and Oliver Lake, both from the Black Artist Group in St. Louis.

Brown's development is typical: from a "wild" free player when he entered the scene in the mid-sixties to a musician who now commands the entire stylistic range of his instrument. Dan Morgenstern wrote of Oliver Lake, member of the World Saxophone Quartet, that he sounded "like Dolphy into Hodges." His music is shaped by inimitable feeling for the unity of black music—whether in the context of his avant-garde quartet or in his Jump Up band inspired by reggae melodies and West African dance rhythms. "It's all the same thing: dealing with the blues," said Lake.

Jarman and Mitchell are founding fathers of the Art Ensemble of Chicago (which are mentioned in the combo section). The former has combined his far-ranging improvisations with modern black poetry; the latter developed into an outstanding solo performer on unaccompanied alto saxophone with a fragile, economical style of playing.

Having similarly wide stylistic range in their playing are the following non-Americans: Japanese-born Akira Sakata, Englishmen Trevor Watts and Mike Osborne, German Ernst Ludwig Petrowsky, and South African Dudu Pukwana with his exciting combination of Bantu music and Bird.

More than anyone else, Anthony Braxton has introduced thousands of people all over the world, who would never have heard such sounds without him, to the music of the jazz avant-garde.

Braxton's main instrument is the alto saxophone, but he also plays clarinet, sopranino, bass clarinet, contrabass clarinet, flute, alto flute. Said Braxton, "I consider myself a composer first and an instrumentalist second."

Anthony Braxton the jazz improviser comes from Charlie Parker and Paul Desmond; Braxton the composer has been shaped by Schönberg, Anton Webern, John Cage, and Johann Sebastian Bach: "Listening to Desmond led me to Konitz. And listening to Bird led me to Ornette."

The degree to which Ornette Coleman shapes the contemporary alto saxophone scene also becomes apparent in the fact that his influence within neoclassicism has not declined but rather increased. It's striking how many alto saxophonists—far more than other horn players—have also made a name for themselves as composers, here also clearly following on from Coleman. Above all: Henry Threadgill, Julius Hemphill, John Zorn, and Tim Berne. Threadgill and Hemphill have exerted an impact within the inner circle of neoclassicism, while Zorn and Berne further developed Coleman's legacy in the stylistically ramified realm of postmodern jazz.

Henry Threadgill, who became known for the transparent music of the Air trio, excited attention in the eighties with his Sextet, which is in fact a septet with doubled drum parts. In the 1988 *Down Beat* poll, critics mentioned him in no fewer than eleven categories, including alto saxophonist, flutist, baritone saxophonist, big-band leader, composer, and arranger. His dark, dramatic alto playing stresses the instrument's vocal qualities with concentrated originality. His Sextet compositions are full of morbid, somber, ironic tanginess—melodies incessantly circling around what Threadgill calls "the beauty of death—I can't think of anything more beautiful." Threadgill, an expert in imperceptible linking of composition and improvisation, seamlessly unites the legacy of free jazz with New Orleans dirges and funeral marches, with Ellington and Mingus. "The total vocabulary is valid, you don't throw away anything," said Threadgill. Nevertheless, "Tradition is a background of ingredients; in itself it's nothing. If you can't make something out of it, the world can do without it."

John Zorn began as a radical saxophonist in noise music, producing unusual sounds from an arsenal of over sixty saxophone and clarinet mouthpieces as well as various bird calls (geese, ducks, etc., used as hunting decoys). He later developed into a sensitive alto player whose homage to forgotten masters of hard bop—Kenny Dorham, Sonny Clark, and Hank Mobley—contributed more to their rediscovery than those who should really have been responsible: the classicists.

As a composer Zorn is a master of musical fragmentation. He atomizes music. He smashes it into rapidly changing disparate blocks of sound that catapult the listener within fractions of a second from one musical world to the next, nevertheless wonderfully linking them at a superordinate level: from the trash rock of Hüsker Dü to Edgar Varese's sound collages, from music for animated films to Stockhausen, and from Japanese koto music to Ornette Coleman.

In the seventies Julius Hemphill was a kind of multimedia specialist, working with actors and dancers, with film, video, and theater. He brought the Texas saxophonist's throaty, squeezed timbre into neoclassicism and wrote most of the World Saxophone Quartet's compositions until leaving the group in 1990. Tim Berne carries on from where Hemphill stops—as a rich melodist whose cutting, splintered sound at last liberates free jazz from the necessity of endless sequences of solos, shimmeringly intensifying and integrating what is stylistically disparate, inclusive of rock rhythms and psychedelic guitar sounds.

Steve Coleman and Greg Osby also belong in this contest of postmodern alto saxophone playing. Coleman is in fact the musical intelligence behind a Brooklyn-based initiative that became famous at the end of the eighties, calling its music M-BASE (Macro Basic Array of Structural Extemporization). Critics have vainly struggled to find a common stylistic denominator within M-BASE, but this program entails unrestricted stylistic openness as upheld by postmodern jazz, founded (as the name indicates) on the basic idea that real musical freedom is only possible within clear structures. Steve Coleman is the most rhythmically vital of all postmodern alto sax players. He has developed a highly complicated, powerful free funk, which breaks through the static forms of jazz-rock and superimposes asymmetrical melodies and rhythms that lead to greater flexibility; yet it possesses the motor power and drive of original street funk. Coleman went particularly far in abstracting from the legacy of Charlie Parker, especially thrilling in the neoclassicism of the Dave Holland Quintet. Greg Osby, who first came to the fore with Jack DeJohnette and also belongs to the M-BASE circle, worked independently of Coleman in developing a similarly angular, asymmetrical way of playing—to such an extent that he is sometimes mistaken for Coleman, even though his sound is darker and warmer, and his playing permeated by love of Wayne Shorter and Japanese music.

In the realm of fusion and jazz-rock, David Sanborn, Ernie Watts, Kenny G., and Chris Hunter have attracted particular attention alongside Elton Dean and Ian Ballamy in England and Sadao Watanabe in Japan. Sanborn is especially influential. Even in the context of beautiful, smooth melodies, his lines preserve the characteristic cry of rhythm and blues. Sanborn has inimitably "saxophonized" the vocal style of Stevie Wonder (with whom he played at the start of the seventies), assimilating Stevie's characteristically impassioned mordents and appoggiaturas.

Beyond all that there still flows—even for alto saxophonists—the mainstream, no longer nourished just by the Swing style but also by bebop and Coltrane. This is represented by John Handy, Paquito D'Rivera, Arthur Blythe, Eric Kloss, Charlie Mariano (who mainly lives in Germany), and British-born Nigel Hitchcock, as well as musicians more closely associated with eighties classicism: Donald Harrison, Bobby Watson, Ed Jackson, Kenny Garrett, and Jim Snidero. D'Rivera, who comes from the Cuban band Irakere and has lived in the United States since 1980, plays the hottest postbop alto sax, amalgamating Cuban music and Bird with his volcanic temperament. Donald Harrison is singularly symptomatic of many alto players who have expanded Bird's legacy in conjuction with strong Coltrane influences. In the quintet he heads together with trumpeter Terence Blanchard, he has extended the harmonic basis of bop's message particularly strongly, incorporating polymodal, bitonal, African, and Indian elements. Bobby Watson, who, like Harrison, first played with Art Blakey's Jazz Messengers and then founded the 29th Street Saxophone Quartet, enlivens classicism with his courageous, light-footed sunny lines full of high spirits. The enormously powerful Arthur Blythe outstandingly exemplifies the fact that in eighties jazz it was traditionalists rather than avant-gardists who dominated the scene. In 1990, he became a full-time member of the World Saxophone Quartet. Blythe developed Parker's legacy particularly originally, but he was also influenced by Johnny Hodges and Ornette Coleman—an excitingly expressive musician whose phrasing (cuttingly sharp and with a penetrating vibrato) impressively brings a modern style of playing into jazz's great alto sax tradition.

The continuing impact of Parker's legacy becomes ironically clear in the fact that Frank Morgan, a musician from the second generation of bebop, was astonishingly successful in the mid-eighties: He's a passionate stylist who keeps the Bird flame burning with throaty expressiveness.

In European postmodern jazz of the eighties, the alto saxophonists—Wolfgang Puschnig from Austria, Dutch-born Paul van Kemenade, Switzerland's Urs Blöchlinger, and Roberto Ottaviano from Italy—are remarkable. By way of contrast to their American colleagues, they often grapple with jazz history from loving distance. Wolfgang Puschnig, a founding member of the Vienna Art Orchestra, is a true original whose phrasing is characterized by joy in playing and intelligent wit. He has maintained an unmistakable profile despite the many styles he has touched on: from world music with the Korean Samul Nori percussion group to an avant-garde duo with keyboardist Roland Mitterer, from the Pat Brothers advanced jazz-rock to Air Mail's contemporary jazz. In 1988, he made ambitious duo recordings with Carla Bley, Jamaaladeen Tacuma, Bob Stewart, etc. Blöchlinger plays a roguish, humorous free bop where his profound respect for jazz's great legacy is demonstrated in his ironic breaches with the faith.

Perhaps Charlie Mariano from Boston possesses the widest range of styles of all alto sax players. That may surprise American readers since Mariano has said, "My American career came to an end when I went with Toshiko to Japan in 1962." Mariano got started in 1941, still under the influence of Johnny Hodges. He played with Charlie Parker, initially forming his style after Bird. In the mid-fifties he was in the Stan Kenton orchestra, and in the early sixties with Charles Mingus. Then he went to Japan with Toshiko Akiyoshi, his wife at that time. There, and in Malaysia and India, he learned and worked on Indian music. Under the influence of Coltrane and Indian wind instruments, he took up the soprano saxophone and studied the nagaswaram, a kind of south Indian oboe. In the early seventies, he finally returned to Europe, opening himself up to the more ambitious and musicianly forms of jazz-rock. His development hasn't stood still over the course of forty years, and it is still continuing.

The Tenor Saxophone

> "The best statements Negroes have made, of what their soul is, have been on the tenor saxophone."—Ornette Coleman

The evolution of the tenor saxophone is the reverse of that of the clarinet. While the latter begins with a wealth of brilliant names and then seems to ebb off into a decrescendo—albeit a wavy one—the history of the tenor sax is one imposing crescendo. At the beginning stands a single man. Today there are so many tenor saxists that it sometimes becomes difficult even for the expert to survey the subtleties that distinguish them. We have said before that the sound of modern jazz was "tenorized", which it actually was after Lester Young, until in the course of the late sixties it was "guitaricized" and later "electronicized." "The tenor saxophone is such an expressive instrument" said Michael Brecker, "that everyone sounds different on it."

The single figure at the beginning is Coleman Hawkins. Until the end of the thirties, all jazz tenor playing took its cues from him: from his dramatic melodic structures, his voluminous sonority, and his rhapsodic improvisations. A Hawkins pupil then was quite simply anyone who played tenor. The most important are Chu Berry, Arnett Cobb, Hershel Evans, Ben Webster, Al Sears, Illinois Jaquet, Buddy Tate, Don Byas, Lucky Thompson, Frank Wess, Eddie "Lockjaw" Davis, Georgie Auld, Flip Phillips, Charlie Ventura, and Benny Golson. Chu Berry came closest to the master. During the second half of the thirties, while Hawkins was in Europe, he was a much sought-after musician, the man who first came to mind when a tenor was needed. One of his most famous solos was on "Ghost of a Chance." Arnett Cobb was a member of the Lionel Hampton band in the early forties. His playing can best be characterized by the way he was advertised after quitting Hampton: "The Wildest Tenorman in the World." Hershel Evans was Lester Young's opposite in the Count Basie band. Though Lester was the greater musician, Evans played the most renowned tenor solo in the old Basie band: "Blue and Sentimental."

"Why don't you play alto, man?" Evans used to tease Lester. "You got an alto sound." And Lester would tap his forehead: "There are things going on up there, man. Some of you guys are all belly." Basie found the contrast between the styles of Lester and Hershel so effective that he saw to a similar contrast in most of his bands from then on. In his fifties band, for instance, these roles were taken by the "two Franks": Frank Foster representing the "modern" trend, Frank Wess the Hawkins school. Later, Lockjaw Davis took Wess' place. Davis is a typical "Harlem" tenor, with hard, striking presence. Later in his career, Foster gained fame as an arranger, and in 1986, two years after Count died, he took charge of the Basie Orchestra.

Before Hershel Evans, there was a tenor man in Count Basie's first Kansas City band whose place he took: Buddy Tate. When Evans died in 1939, Buddy returned to Basie. Later he dropped into comparative obscurity, until the mainstream wave of the fifties and sixties brought him renewed attention. For many years, he led his own band in Harlem, enriching the style of the classic Harlem big bands (as played in the old Savoy Ballroom) with modern rhythm and blues tendencies. Tate and Arnett Cobb (d. 1989), the two "Texas Tenor Men," are among the few musicians of their generation who even in the late eighties were still active.

Don Byas became known primarily for his "sensuous" vibrato and ballad interpretations. He played with Basie, was one of the first Swing musicians to work with the then young bebop people, and made his home in Holland from the late forties on.

Ben Webster, who died in Europe in 1973, was two things: a musician with a throaty, harsh vibrato on fast pieces, and a master of erotic, intensely felt slow ballads. Of all the musicians of the Hawkins school, he has had the strongest influence—on many musicians of modern and postmodern jazz as well. In the early forties, Webster was a member of the Ellington orchestra, with which he recorded one of his most famous solos—"Cotton Tail." Al Sears took Webster's chair with Ellington in 1943. His stylistic bent is indicated by a rhythm and blues piece, "Castle Rock," that he wrote for Johnny Hodges and became a hit. Later Paul Gonsalves (d. 1974) became Ellington's featured tenor in the Webster tradition. Gonsalves' marathon tenor displays were legendary: fast, torrid runs in flowing motion, almost free from repeated notes and honks, yet more exciting—and musically more logical—than many solos played by tenor men whose honking ecstasy was outside the realm of music. Ellington took care to always have a musician who could take the spot of the great and, in the final analysis, unreachable Ben Webster.

A stylistic phenomenon is Benny Golson: a tenorist and arranger who emerged from the Dizzy Gillespie band of the mid-fifties and played with all the young modern musicians at the time. Nonetheless, he is cast in the mold of the rich, mature ballad style of Byas-Webster-Hawkins. "Out of the Past" is the title of one of Golson's most beautiful pieces, and out of the past, full of sadness and long-lost magic, are his tenor improvisations and melodious compositions. After a period when little was heard from this "jazz romantic," he reappeared, further matured, in the eighties—especially in the reestablished Jazztet that he co-led with trumpeter Art Farmer.

Illinois Jacquet, finally, is perhaps the "hottest," most exciting musician of the Hawkins school. Long before the modern free-jazz tenorists, he was able to extend the range of his instrument into the extreme heights of the flageolet. Jacquet came from Lionel Hampton's band, where he played his famous solo on "Flyin' Home." He is also renowned for his triumphs with the early tours of Norman Granz's Jazz at the Philharmonic. Jacquet said, "Granz owes the worldwide success of JATP to me!"

Georgie Auld, Flip Phillips, and Charlie Ventura are the leading white tenor men of the Hawkins school—the first two via Ben Webster. For years, Flip Phillips was used as an effective crowd-pleaser with the Jazz at the Philharmonic troupe. But in Woody Herman's band in the mid-forties, and later also on records and in concerts, Phillips has played excellently structured ballads with a polished and "reduced" Hawkins sound. Charlie Ventura became known through the medium-sized groups he led on and off from 1947 into the fifties. During the bop era he performed under the banner of "Bop for the People" and contributed much to the popularization of bop.

Bud Freeman, the tenor voice of Chicago style, who touched Lester Young in his earliest period, preceded Coleman Hawkins. Bud, still active in the eighties (he died in 1991), became the most compelling Dixieland tenor—a state of affairs that did not prevent him from studying with Lennie Tristano in the fifties.

With these musicians we have for the present exhausted the Hawkins chapter of tenor history. Lester Young became the great man of the tenor in the forties, and particularly in the fifties, but then, tension between Hawk and Pres has remained alive—to the degree that a renewed predominance of the Hawkins tradition could be detected among the tenorists of the Sonny Rollins school after the late fifties.

What fascinates tenor players about Hawkins is, first of all, his big, strong, voluminous tone. What fascinates them about Lester Young are his lyrical, sweeping lines. Simplified, the tension that underlies the history of the tenor sax is the tension between Hawkins' sonority and Lester's linearity. This tension is already present in some of the tenor players who have been mentioned as representatives of the Hawkins line—Byas, Gonsalves, Phillips, and Ventura. To these must be added a group of tenor men who, stylistically speaking, are firmly in the Lester camp but show a noticeable tendency toward the Hawkins sonority. Gene Ammons, who died in 1974, is the most important. The son of boogie-woogie pianist Albert Ammons, he was in the Billy Eckstine and Woody Herman bands of the forties and moved into the limelight through the "battles" (those popular contests between two practitioners of the same horn) he fought with Sonny Stitt (on tenor!). He has the biggest, mightiest tone outside the Hawkins school: "Big as a house, a fifteen-story apartment dwelling, and very vocal, too," said Ira Gitler, who compared his playing with the blues singing of Dinah Washington.

Otherwise, the tenorists of the Lester Young school may be grouped—in much simplified terms—in two sections: the musicians who have linked Lester's ideas to the ideas of bop, and the school of modern Lester Young classicism, in which the bop influence receded in proportion to the youth of the musicians. The most important tenorists of the "Lester Young plus bop" direction are Wardell Gray, James Moody, Budd Johnson, and Frank Foster, as well as the forerunners of Sonny Rollins whom we shall mention later.

James Moody, altoist and flutist as well as tenor man, was one of the more remarkable musical personalities of the bop era, often filled with a rollicking humor that was replaced by maturity and mellowness during the seventies. Dizzy Gillespie hired him for his quintet in 1960 and again in 1980. Budd Johnson (1910–1984) emerged from the most influential big bands of the bop era—Earl Hines, Boyd Raeburn, Billy Eckstine, Woody Herman, Dizzy Gillespie—and was probably the only musician to play in all these great bands. Under this influence, he repeatedly reoriented his approach to playing to contemporary trends. He belonged to the handful of musicians of his generation who dealt with the musical movements of the seventies and eighties.

Wardell Gray, who died in 1955 under mysterious circumstances (his body was found in the desert near Las Vegas), was a musician of supreme importance. He had Lester's linearity, the phrasing of bop, and his own distinctive hardness of attack and sparkling mobility, all joined in convincing stylistic unity. It is fitting that such genuine Swing musicians as Benny Goodman and Count Basie were attracted by Gray but became aware of stylistic conflict when he began to play in their combos or bands. "The Chase," that characteristically titled tenor battle recorded in 1947 by Gray and Dexter Gordon (who is of similar importance and will be discussed later), still ranks among the most exciting musical contests in the history of jazz.

It should be noted that, initially, there were only a few tenor players who could be considered bebop musicians (in a strict sense). Wardell Gray, James Moody, Sonny Rollins (in his early career), Dexter Gordon, and Allen Eager were the only ones at the time. Lester Young's stature was still too great to allow a different development. Even a man like Sonny Stitt, who was, on alto, pure bop, clearly showed the Lester Young influence when he changed to tenor saxophone. In fact, up to the middle of the fifties, Lester's—not Charlie Parker's—importance for the tenor scene continued to grow!

Wardell Gray occupies a central position between the two tenor movements of the fifties: the "Brothers" and the Charlie Parker school led by

Sonny Rollins. In the former, Lester Young celebrated his real triumphs. The abundance of names belonging to this Lester Young classicism will be categorized according to the manner in which the Basie-Young tendency has made itself increasingly felt. At the beginning of our list the bop influence is noticeable—Allen Eager, Stan Getz, Herbie Steward, Zoot Sims, Al Cohn, Bob Cooper, Buddy Collette, Dave Pell, Don Menza, Jack Montrose, Richie Kamuca, Jimmy Giuffre, and Bill Perkins. A remarkably large segment of these musicians either have worked with Woody Herman or are more or less connected with the California jazz scene. That is where the "Four Brothers sound" developed in 1947. "We had a band," Stan Getz said "in the Spanish section of Los Angeles. A trumpeter named Tony de Carlo was the leader, and we had just his trumpet, four tenors and rhythm. We had a few arrangements by Gene Roland and Jimmy Giuffre." Roland and Giuffre, in other words, created the Four Brothers sound. The four tenors in this band were Getz, Herbie Steward, Zoot Sims, and Jimmy Giuffre.

At the time, Woody Herman was about to form a new band. He happened to hear the four tenors and was so taken with the sound that he hired three of them: Sims, Steward, and Getz. In place of the fourth tenor he put Serge Chaloff's baritone, to add warmth to the tenor combination. The new sound was made famous by a piece written for Herman in 1947 by Jimmy Giuffre. It was called "Four Brothers"—thus the name of the sound. Along with the Miles Davis Capitol sound it became the most influential ensemble sound in jazz up to Miles Davis' *Bitches Brew*, and even after that it remained effective. Its warmth and suppleness symbolized the sound ideal of cool jazz.

In the years to follow, a succession of tenorists passed through the Four Brothers sax sections of various Herman bands. The first was Al Cohn, who took Steward's place as early as 1948. Then came Gene Ammons, Giuffre, and many others, down to Bill Perkins and Richie Kamuca. Getz, who from the start of the Brothers counted as the *primus inter pares*, made some combo recordings (for Prestige) in 1949 with Sims, Cohn, Allen Eager, and Brew Moore in which the Four Brothers sound was celebrated by five tenorists.

The following passage by Ira Gitler—a critic with particular affinity for the modern tenor scene—will give an impression of the fine distinctions among these tenor players:

> An excellent example of inner differences in a similar area can be found in examining the work of Zoot Sims and Al Cohn and comparing it to the playing of Bill Perkins and Richie Kamuca. In the broad sense, all would be considered modernists in the Basie-Young tradition, but Sims and Cohn, who were originally inspired by Lester Young, grew up musically in the forties when Charlie Parker was at his peak and his influence at its most powerful. Although they do not play like Parker, they have been affected somewhat stylistically and very much harmonically.

Kamuca and Perkins (active from the fifties) who for inspiration go back to the Pres of the Basie period and also to the Brothers (Sims, Cohn, Getz) are only touched by Bird through osmosis from the Brothers, and since it is twice removed, the traces are intangible.

The Parker traces are strongest in Allen Eager, as shown by the splendid, stimulating solos he played with the Buddy Rich big band around 1945. Getz is the towering figure in this school, an improviser in the sense of truly great jazz improvising and altogether one of the outstanding white jazz musicians. He is a virtuoso who can play anything possible on the tenor sax. It is this technical element that distinguishes him from most of his Brothers colleagues and their sophistication of simplicity (which in a sympathetic way, hides the fact that these players, too, are masters of technique). Stan became known mainly through his ballad interpretations. Nonetheless, during the fifties, he had a Parker-inspired affinity for very fast tempos. Some of the most exciting recordings of his career were made in 1953 at the Storyville Club in Boston with guitarist Jimmy Raney and at a 1954 concert at the Shrine auditorium in Los Angeles with trombonist Bob Brookmeyer.

In 1961 when bossa nova, with its poetic, charming songs from Brazil, entered the United States, Getz was introduced to this music by guitarist Charlie Byrd, just returned from Brazil. Initially with Byrd, later without him, he scored a number of great hits with Brazilian music.

It has been said so many times that Getz was inspired by the bossa nova and that he "owes everything" to it, that it is necessary to point out that earlier there had been a reverse influence: from cool jazz (where Getz has his roots) to the Brazilian samba. Only from the interaction between cool jazz and samba did the bossa nova emerge. Thus, a circle was closed when Getz "borrowed back" (as he himself expressed it) Brazilian elements. This may be one of the main reasons for the fascination of his "Brazilianized," melodic cool-jazz transformations, although some creative Brazilian musicians called these recordings falsifications or bastardizations. It is interesting to remember that the characteristic switch from the choralelike *cantilena* to intensely rhythmic passages, so typical of Brazilian music, also existed in a different form in Getz's cool improvisations from the early fifties on, long before the emergence of bossa nova.

Since the mid-sixties, after the bossa nova wave died down, Getz combined his classicist Lester Young legacy with some harder, more expressive ingredients, originating mainly in Sonny Rollins. The expressive range of this great jazz musician became continuously even more universal and towering. He died in 1991.

Zoot Sims is considered the most swinging of the Brothers. He is an untrammeled, vital improviser with a certain knack for emphasizing the upper ranges of his instrument, lending to his tenor an occasional alto sound. Characteristically, he has played alto, too; later, under the influence of Coltrane, he also played soprano with very personal inflections. Al Cohn (d. 1985) mirrored the *conscious* turn toward Basie-Young classicism—not only in his playing but also as arranger and leader on many recordings. The little twists and turns he gives to his smooth Lester Young tone make his playing especially expressive. For several years Cohn and Sims co-led a two-tenor quintet that—within the confines of their similarity—gained attractiveness from their subtle dissimilarity.

Most of the remaining musicians on our list of Lester Young classicists are representatives of West Coast jazz. Jimmy Giuffre's tenor playing has something of the quality of his clarinet—a great affinity for cool, "distilled" blue notes. His is a Young classicism based on a keen knowledge of modern "classical" chamber music and a deep love of folk melodies. Buddy Collette is one of the few black musicians in West Coast jazz, but his black roots are shown more by his alto playing, veering toward Parker, than by his relatively polished tenor sound. And Don Menza, who also is an excellent big-band arranger (for Buddy Rich, for instance), is among those who carried the Four Brothers sound close to Sonny Rollins in the seventies and eighties.

There is a European who belongs in this illustrious list of otherwise American players: Austrian Hans Koller. He began in the early fifties in Lee Konitz's line, was impressed by Sims and Cohn, and later, through Coltrane, developed his own expressive conception.

Several musicians will not fit into either of the categories into which we have attempted to divide the Lester Young tenors. Among them are Paul Quinichette, Brew Moore, and Warne Marsh. Brew Moore, who died in 1973, belongs in Lester's immediate vicinity, without the detour via fifties tenor classicism. Warne Marsh is a product of the Tristano school. Marsh (d. 1987) was said to play "tenorized" Lee Konitz, but he does have his own fluid style, which became so up-to-date again in the seventies and early eighties that Marsh was able to attract much attention with his duet records with musicians many years his junior, such as Pete Christlieb and Lew Tabackin.

So far, it might seem as if the contest between the ideas of Hawkins and Young in the evolution of the tenor sax had ended with complete victory for Young. This picture became blurred in the course of Sonny Rollins' overwhelming influence during the second half of the fifties. Rollins the improviser became so important one tended to mention him right after Miles Davis. Nonetheless, neither Sonny himself nor his way of playing were "new" in the strictest meaning of the word. From 1946, he played with many important bop musicians: Art Blakey, Tadd Dameron, Bud Powell, Miles Davis, Fats Navarro, Thelonious Monk, and others. His style involves combining Charlie Parker lines with the voluminous sound of Coleman Hawkins—which Sonny developed into his very own, angular, edged, immensely individual sound—plus that slight Lester Young influence that hardly any tenor player since Pres can completely escape.

This combination, which appeared so novel in the second half of the fifties, was *comme il faut* during the bop years. Not only Sonny Rollins played that way then. Sonny Stitt, and, most of all, Dexter Gordon are musicians of this lineage, related in many respects to the previously mentioned Lester-plus-bop line (James Moody, for instance). Gordon was *the* bop tenor man, with all the quicksilver nervousness belonging to bop. In 1944, in a recording of Billy Eckstine's big band ("Blowing the Blues Away"), Gordon and Gene Ammons founded the musical practice of "battles" and "chases" of which we have spoken already in this chapter. (More about Gordon is given later in this section.)

That Sonny Rollins nevertheless achieved primary importance so suddenly was due less to his innovations than to the temperament and vitality he brings to his improvisations—in short, to his stature. Thus, he can afford to treat the harmonic structures on which he improvises with an astonishing lack of constraint and great freedom, and often indicate melody lines only with widely spaced staccato notes, satirizing and ironicizing them in this manner. It is a freedom similar to that of Thelonious Monk's piano improvisations. Both Monk and Rollins are New Yorkers, and there's that typically quick and dry New York sense of humor in their music. "Sonny Rollins fears nothing," said the French tenorist Barney Wilen at a time when he was one of the many young musicians of the Rollins school.

This school remained alive in the eighties. Rollins, who visited India and studied yoga and Asian religions, now makes most of his records in the fusion vein. This displeases the jazz purists, but they overlook the fact that Rollins retains more bop elements in the realm of jazz-rock than any other musician. He still displays his most important asset: his sound, and his (occasionally somewhat sarcastic) humor. His family has roots in the Caribbean. Again and again, he has composed and included in his music calypsos, and Latin themes and rhythms in general. In the eighties, he amazed audiences with unaccompanied solo appearances in which he blew breathtakingly long improvisations.

Before turning to John Coltrane and the musicians of his school, we have first to mention a number of tenor players who are more or less independent of both the Rollins and the Coltrane schools—even though some of them may, in the course of their careers, have received impulses particularly from John Coltrane. They are Wayne Shorter, Hank Mobley, Johnny Griffin, Yusef Lateef, Charlie Rouse, Stanley Turrentine, Booker Ervin, Teddy Edwards, Roland Kirk, Clifford Jordan, Bobby Jones, Jack Montrose, and others.

In that group Wayne Shorter is the player who developed most imposingly: from the hard bop of Blakey's Jazz Messengers, where he made a name for himself at the end of the fifties by way of the second Miles Davis Quintet's controlled freedom, to the multielectronic sounds of the legendary Weather Report jazz-rock combo. His brittle, restrained, and yet full sound mediates distance to perfection. Shorter's trademark is an abstract shimmering quartal melody directed against conventional harmonic models but nevertheless preserving the foundations of tonal playing. That's probably why Shorter's work from the sixties—especially in the celebrated second Miles Davis Quintet—made a strong impression on the eighties tenorists of classicism. As a composer he has created more lasting modal works than any other musician, pieces whose complicated simplicity has fascinated and challenged musicians up to the present day: "Nefertiti," "Footprints," "Yes or No," "Masqualero," etc. Shorter plays as he composes: economically and circumspectly. There isn't a note too many. According to Miles Davis, "Wayne tells splendid stories."

Hank Mobley has a velvety tone that hangs like a veil over his long, seemingly self-perpetuating lines. Stanley Turrentine applies a "rocking soul" approach to the "jumping" lines of Ben Webster and Coleman Hawkins. The late Booker Ervin, who first became known through his association with Mingus, was one of the most solid improvisers of the early and mid-sixties with a marvelous wealth of blues-inspired and vehement swing. Johnny Griffin, with his melodic, humorous improvisations, has enthused many an audience.

Yusef Lateef stems from the Detroit circle of modern bop musicians. As early as the fifties, he became the first jazz musician to try to incorporate elements from Arabic and oriental musics into jazz, making inspiring, exciting recordings on which he (aside from tenor) blows such instruments as diverse flutes of often exotic origin, oboe, and bassoon (used only rarely in jazz). Most of these musicians have been active for a relatively long time span—from the early fifties until today—proving that they are playing a kind of music that is, in the best sense of the word, "timeless," independent of passing fashions.

And then, there is Roland Rahsaan Kirk: a blind musician who came to Chicago from Columbus, Ohio, in 1960, with three saxophones hanging around his neck, sometimes playing them all simultaneously—and, on top of that, a flute and about a dozen other instruments—blowing on a siren between choruses.

Kirk, whose death in 1975 was mourned by the entire jazz world, was one of the most vital, most communicative of the modern jazz musicians. He was like the old folk musicians who packed up their bundle and wandered through the world. And, no doubt, he was a symbol of many things that have occurred in jazz during these years: sophistication rising from roots, naiveté from a genuine childlike attitude, sensitivity from vitality. Said Kirk, "People talk about freedom, but the blues is still one of the freest things you can play."

For Kirk, jazz was "black classical music." In his compositions and improvisations, he deliberately elevated this tradition into a program, not in the sense of historicizing backward looks, but quite to the contrary by incorporating it into the sounds of the seventies. A few times he played with pop and rock groups: "I just want to play. I'd like to think I could work opposite Sinatra, B. B. King, the Beatles, or a polka band, and that people would dig it." Roland Kirk based his work on so many of the great black musicians—Duke Ellington, Charles Mingus, Sidney Bechet, Fats Waller, Don Byas, John Coltrane, Clifford Brown, Lester Young, Bud Powell, Billie Holiday, etc.—that it may be stressed: Kirk played on the black tradition as if it were an instrument long before that became a matter of course in postmodern jazz. He said, "God loves black sound."

A distinction of many of these musicians—certainly of Sonny Rollins and Roland Kirk—is their relationship to rhythm. They play beyond the rhythm with the same free sweep that characterizes their approach to harmony; but since on the one hand they move far away from the basic beat while on the other never losing contact with it, they develop an intense, exciting rhythmic tension in which the real stimulation of their playing resides. In this respect, too, Rollins continues Charlie Parker's heritage. "Charlie Parker's Successors Play Tenor" said the headline in a French jazz magazine as the Rollins influence reached its peak in the late fifties.

At this peak the Rollins influence changed over into the perhaps even more engulfing John Coltrane influence. Coltrane (see the section devoted to him and Ornette Coleman) became the teacher and master of most of the tenorists of the sixties, seventies, and the eighties as well—and not only of the tenorists.

The Coltrane "students" can be classified into two groups (similar to the groupings of the players of other instruments): those within the boundaries of tonality and those outside (with all the intermediate shades that must be called expressly to mind in such a generalized classification). Among the former the Coltrane model is stronger and more immediately perceptible, whereas the latter see Coltrane's impulses as "liberation" only in general terms, bringing their own individuality into play that much more clearly.

Members of the first group are musicians as diverse as Joe Henderson, George Coleman, Charles Lloyd, Joe Farrell, Sam Rivers, Billy Harper, and others. Henderson led the great bop tradition exemplarily into the jazz of the post-Coltrane era. He has the darkest, "blackest" sound on the entire bop-oriented tenor scene. Farrell couples the power of a more conservative tenor style with contemporary sensitivity, which certainly was one reason why Chick Corea repeatedly used him for recordings. Charles Lloyd led a group in the late sixties that was one of the forerunners of the jazz-rock bands. Harper, who has been incorporating elements of gospel music, carries on John Coltrane's message in a hymnlike manner, both musically and spiritually. Like George Coleman, Sam Rivers played with Miles Davis during the sixties and with Cecil Taylor later on. Something like a father figure to the New York avant-garde in the seventies, he bridges over to the next group of tenor players.

Archie Shepp, Pharoah Sanders, Albert Ayler, John Gilmore, Fred Anderson, Dewey Redman, Frank Wright, Joe McPhee, Charles Tyler, as well as—among the younger generation—David Murray, Chico Freeman, and David S. Ware stem from the camp of the "free tonal" (to some ears even "atonal") avant-garde jazz. Shepp, an especially devoted, "angry" free-jazz man in the beginning, has meanwhile come to infuse the traditions of Coleman Hawkins, Ben Webster, and Duke Ellington with the experiences of free playing. "My sax is a sex symbol," Shepp once said.

Albert Ayler, who often appeared with his trumpet-playing brother, Don Ayler, had a different motto: "We play peace." Ayler's involvement was less political than religious, even philosophical. In the freedom of his tenor breaks, Ayler (who developed his style more or less independently of Coltrane) referred back to tradition in an especially peculiar, folk-music-like manner, incorporating march and circus music of the turn of the century, folk dances, waltzes and polkas, or the dirges—the music of the old New Orleans funeral processions. Ayler, who died in 1971 at the age of thirty-four (his body was found in New York's East River after he had been missing for twenty days), was "in many ways closer to [the old sound] of Bubber Miley and Tricky Sam Nanton than to Parker, Miles, or Rollins," said Richard Williams. "He brought back to jazz the wild, primitive feeling which deserted it in the late thirties. . . . His technique knew no boundaries, his range from the lowest honks to the most shrill high harmonies being unparalleled."

Pharoah Sanders is the tenor man bursting with musicianly and physical power whom John Coltrane engaged in 1966 as the second horn player of his group, in order to grow through his challenge. Like others among the newer tenorists, he extends the range of the tenor sax, by means of overblowing, into the highest registers of the soprano. For a couple of years, Sanders stereotyped and banalized his way of playing, but since the late seventies it has become obvious again that Trane knew why he chose him.

Around the turn of the decade from the sixties to the seventies, Dewey Redman finally became the congenial musicial partner whom Ornette Coleman—and later also Don Cherry—had been seeking for so long. He was one of the first players to have sung into the instrument while blowing it, intensively vocalizing and emotionalizing the tenor sound. Old and New Dreams is the name of the group Redman co-led with Cherry in the seventies and eighties, and that is exactly what they are presenting: new dreams of an old and basically timeless black tradition.

Then came neoclassicism with David Murray (see the section devoted to his work) providing a decisive impulse. Other important tenorists who reflect and modify the legacy of free jazz within the framework of a traditional way of playing include Chico Freeman, George Adams, Bennie Wallace, John Purcell, Ned Rothenberg, and Edward Wilkerson. All of them—except for Wallace—have strong links with Coltrane's music but their playing is so individual that they eclectically reflect and integrate a large number of other tenor styles against that background. Freeman is a particularly intensive "inside-outside" player, "inside" implying that Freeman knows his tradition and "outside" that he ventures into free sounds. Freeman's special characteristic is that he often employs both approaches simultaneously rather than alternating between them. Chico learned such inside playing from his father, Von Freeman, who is also a tenorist, and the outside aspects come from his links with the AACM, the avant-garde group from his home city, Chicago.

George Adams, who became known through Charles Mingus and Gil Evans, allows his vital, throaty improvisations to explode with such wildness in the horn's upper register that they time and again evoke the falsetto singing of gospel and blues, with the same intensity and ecstasy of expression. In fast pieces he builds on Coltrane and Albert Ayler's overblown glissando style; in slow pieces he follows on from Ben Webster's velvety ballad sound.

Tennessee-born Bennie Wallace was one of the few eighties tenorists who developed an individual style independently of the overpowering Coltrane influence. Wallace comes from Rollins, whose vehement and sardonic sound he has transformed with rhapsodic élan into an original musical language. Wallace blows what seem to be strange lines full of crazy intervallic leaps, moving in a flash from the highest flageolet register right down to the depths and back again, incorporating influences from Don Byas, Eddie "Lockjaw" Davis, and the hoarse sounds of rhythm and blues tenorists in this resourceful playing.

The free tenor style found particularly fertile soil in Europe. Some of these tenorists play in a style totally their own. Willem Breuker from Holland, already mentioned as a bass clarinetist, exerted a liberating influence—with his burlesque humor and clownlike music theater—in the mid-seventies when European free jazz was marked by unspoken dogmas and exaggerated seriousness. He satirizes and defamiliarizes nineteenth-century popular music—polkas, operettas, waltzes, marches, tangos—and his parodies sometimes also become joyfully ironical attacks on the world of the avant-garde. He has been called the "Kurt Weill of jazz." German-born Peter Brötzmann blows his tenor clusters with an intensity usually only found among black musicians, yet in a way that critics have time and again felt to be "German." Richard Williams, the English critic, even used the word "teutonic." Evan Parker from England has perhaps gone further than any other European tenorists in exploring overblown sounds. He has genuinely created a new style: abstract and minimalist, fluently melodizing the falsetto without any recognizable influence from John Coltrane and Ornette Coleman.

Among the tenorists in the realm of post–free jazz who sovereignly structured and molded the freedom gained, Anatoly Vapirov and Vladimir Chekasin from the Soviet Union, France's André Jaume and Sylvain Kassap, Swiss-born Hans Koch, and Germany's Alfred Harth and Sibylle Pomorin are remarkable. Vapirov, who now lives in Bulgaria, transposes the gentle, soft saxophone sound of European concert music into free jazz, showing particular interest in the music of the Second Viennese School. His "Lines of Destiny" (1985), dedicated to Alban Berg, is the most successful meeting to date between a jazz musician and the sounds of a string quartet. Kassap is an exciting mixer of styles absolutely in accordance with the principles of postmodern jazz. Folklore, minimal music, free jazz, rock, and advanced European concert music make contact here in a kind of simultaneity of the disparate. Alfred Harth imbues the somber visions and splintered sound collages of no wave with an unusual poetry and tonal warmth—without depriving the music of any of its charged protest and exciting provocations. Pomorin made a name for herself playing with pianist Irène Schweizer and the Reichlich Weiblich women's orchestra.

The number of good European tenorists, who have in their own way carried forward the Coltrane legacy, has by now become so great that we can only mention the most important here: Alan Skidmore, Steve William-son, and Mike Mower from England; Poland's Tomasz Szukalski and Leszek Zadlo; Swedish-born Lennart Aberg and Bernt Rosengren; Juani Aaltonen from Finland; Frenchman François Jeanneau; and Germany's Heinz Sauer, Gerd Dudek, Wollie Kaiser, Günter Klatt, and Christof Lauer. Skidmore, who became known with the European Jazz Quintet and the S.O.S. trio, reflects the modality of middle-period Coltrane in his passionate linear playing. Szukalski adds Polish folk music's dancelike element to Coltrane's language. Zadlo and Lauer are emotionally enormously powerful stylists whose playing is deeply founded in the great black tenor tradition. In the realm of world music, Aberg has distinguished himself—in recordings with the Rena Rama and Oriental Wind groups—with succinct and sensitive arches of melody. Jeanneau loves droll lineups and unusual sound textures. Dudek fosters Coltrane's power within a sensitive, withdrawn style. Kaiser, who comes from the Cologne Jazz House Initiative, is the real compositional force behind the Kölner Saxophon Mafia. His expressive and energetic phrasing combines unruliness and great capacity for empathy. Sauer has recorded a moving tribute to Duke Ellington, and demonstrated in an album with George Adams that he is the well-known American tenorist's equal.

Let's move on to the musicians influenced by rock and fusion. They include Wayne Shorter, Argentinian Gato Barbieri, Tom Scott, Wilton Felder, Mike Brecker, and in the younger generation Bill Evans (not related to the pianist of the same name), Bob Berg, and Gary Thomas. The best known is Wayne Shorter, whose roots are in both Sonny Rollins and Coltrane. Nevertheless, Mike Brecker has exerted even greater influence on tenor playing in jazz-rock with his lightning lines shooting up to the flageolet register. Parallel to that he linked acoustic and electric playing to become a fiery, harmonically flexible neobop stylist, infusing the Coltrane legacy with the motor élan and impact of rock-oriented styles. Brecker thus calls his music "electric bebop." In fact he is one of the few tenorists in the tonal sphere whose development of the Coltrane tradition is so original that they have formed an unmistakably individual style of their own. That's why Brecker's sound—crystal clear, metallically cutting, and yet full of radiant warmth dynamically rising and falling—has become a determining color in postmodern jazz's tenor playing.

The extent of Brecker's impact on the eighties tenor scene is also shown by the fact that his influence is even increasing the more tenorists turn away from jazz-rock and take up neobop. Among the many tenorists inspired by Brecker, ensuring by way of the "Brecker bridge" that the Coltrane legacy stays alive, the most important are Bob Mintzer, Bob Malach, Larry Schneider, Bob Berg, Tony Dagradi, British-born Tommy Smith (who played with vibraphonist Gary Burton), Norwegian Bendik Hofseth (who made his name with the Steps Ahead group), and Tony Lakatos from Hungary. Bob Mintzer and Bob Malach are studio musicians (and also important as big-band leaders and arrangers) who can cope with all technical and stylistic demands, in their own way processing Brecker's vocabulary in both jazz-rock and the progressive mainstream.

The other white tenorist who, alongside Brecker, exerted particular influence in the seventies and eighties is Jan Garbarek from Norway. Garbarek dramatically cooled, elegized, and aestheticized the ardent "cry" of free-jazz tenorists—above all the late Coltrane, but also Albert Ayler and Archie Shepp. His playing, rich in pauses, expresses both sorrow and joy. Garbarek's tenor saxophone cries but doesn't lament. His lines open up areas of absolutely magical expansiveness—dream images interweaving elements of Scandinavian folk, free jazz, and Asian music rituals to create enraptured beauty. Garbarek is basically the only European tenor saxophonist who has also influenced the American scene, which is all the more remarkable since his work has moved astonishingly far from the African-American roots of jazz, stressing instead the sources of European music, especially of Scandinavian folk music.

Proceeding to neobop, we must first retrospectively discuss a senior figure in jazz whose name has already been mentioned several times in this section: Dexter Gordon, who died in 1990. Dexter, a musician whose wealth of ideas seemed inexhaustible, belongs to the generation of great bebop musicians. John Coltrane talked of Dexter as having been one of the few players who influenced him. Gordon in turn later took over elements of Coltrane's style. Like so many American jazz musicians, Dexter Gordon, disappointed by the U.S. scene, went to Europe at the start of the sixties and lived first in Paris and then in Copenhagen. For years he was one of the central figures on the European jazz scene. In 1976—as previously mentioned in another context—he returned to New York for a short engagement and thereby became *the* catalyst for bebop's comeback. Ten years later he played the main part in Bertrand Tavernier's film *'Round Midnight,* which uses elements from the lives of Bud Powell and Lester Young in a fictitious story set in fifties jazz clubs. Gordon's performance, as both actor and musician, made a considerable contribution toward *'Round Midnight* being the first feature film to present a sensitive and undistorted picture of jazz musicians' lives and problems at that time. In the eighties, too, Dexter exerted a lasting influence on the tenor scene. His majestic sound and way of phrasing slightly behind the beat transmit mounting excitement to the highest degree.

Bop-oriented music has been played by so many musicians since the mid-seventies that here too we can only mention the most important: Ricky Ford, Branford Marsalis, Courtney Pine, Carter Jefferson, Bob Berg, Billy Pierce, Ralph Moore, Jean Toussaint, Don Braden, Ralph Bowen, and Todd Williams. Characteristically, most of them underwent a development that got under way in the second half of the seventies with neobop (the bebop revival), and then extended in the course of the eighties to the rich stream of classicism into which there flowed, alongside bop as the chief component, many other influences (for the most part more modern): modal jazz, Coltrane, Shorter, and sometimes even elements from early free jazz and even the prebop era.

Ricky Ford, who became known through playing with Charles Mingus, probably has the most complete tenor voice in classicism. He is capable of summarizing within a single solo the great tradition of black tenor playing—from Coleman Hawkins by way of Don Byas, Ben Webster, and

Dexter Gordon to Sonny Rollins—while always remaining unmistakably and totally himself. Among classicist tenor players Ford is basically the only one who has been able to completely escape the overwhelming influence of Coltrane, pursuing instead the Rollins line with a love for Dexter Gordon. Branford Marsalis, first presented by Art Blakey, phrases equally imposingly. He too is much influenced by Rollins, but Marsalis is a more modern and contemporary player than Ford, reflecting Coltrane, Wayne Shorter, and Joe Henderson alongside Rollins.

Both Ford and Marsalis are masters of quotation, and yet the contrast between their ways of playing could hardly be greater, exemplifying the enormous range of tenor playing in classicism. The difference becomes immediately apparent if you realize that Ford delights in mixing all the many great tenor styles, allowing them to flow together and blend joyously within a single piece, while Marsalis quotes as a *totality*. From solo to solo, from piece to piece, Marsalis reflects and develops a complete saxophone style as a whole. The spontaneity and quality of his interpretations elevate them above any superficial suspicion of copying. Branford Marsalis' best recordings are in the quartet format where he shows himself to be a lively, exciting, sonorous stylist. Conceptually he derives from Wayne Shorter, soundwise from Sonny Rollins and Ben Webster.

Courtney Pine, the black tenorist from England, is a phenomenon: a player who so effusively and energetically emotionalizes the Coltrane legacy that his lines explode climactically—from passion rather than calculation—into sounds reminiscent of such free jazz tenorists as Albert Ayler and Archie Shepp. He unites humor with a profound feeling for the melodies and rhythms of Caribbean music.

The timelessness of the great black tradition nowhere becomes so convincingly apparent as on the tenor saxophone represented by musicians like Dave Liebman, Sal Nistico, Pete Christlieb, Odean Pope, John Stubble-field, Joe Lovano, Billy Drewes, Lew Tabackin, and many others who have already been mentioned (including the tenorists in the first Coltrane group and classicism). Tabackin, by the way, offers an interesting contemporary reflection of Sonny Rollins, whereas in the music made by most of the others John Coltrane remains vital in an endless variety of ways. Together with most classicist tenor players and adherents of the Brecker style, this group of musicians represents a Coltrane classicism, which got under way in the seventies and even intensified in the eighties. For over a quarter of a century tenorists have lived off the legacy of John Coltrane's music, which nevertheless time and again offers astonishing and hitherto unsuspected openings for individuality.

On the other hand, even good old Swing is back again. After all that has been said in this section, it almost goes without saying that the front man for the young Swing generation is a tenor player: Scott Hamilton, already mentioned in the section on seventies jazz.

The Baritone Saxophone

For decades, Harry Carney represented the baritone saxophone, more monopolistically than any other jazz musician ever represented any other instrument. In 1926 Duke Ellington received permission from the Carney family to keep sixteen-year-old Harry in the band, and from that point until Duke died in 1974 Carney remained with Ellington. Five months later, Carney, who was almost synonymous with the history and the sound of the Ellington orchestra, died too. Carney was to the baritone what Coleman Hawkins was to the tenor—of equal power, volume, and expressivity. He played his instrument with all the dark force and roughness it embodies. "No baritone player should be scared of the noise his horn can make. Carney isn't scared," said Pepper Adams, a baritonist of the generation that in the late fifties took up the Carney tradition again. Until the mid-forties, Carney ruled royally over the baritone scene. Aside from him there was only Ernie Caceres, who managed to play Dixieland on the cumbersome horn, and Jack Washington, who provided a similarly professional and powerful foundation for Basie's sax section as did Carney for the Ellington band—without, of course, Carney's brilliance and stature.

Then came bop. And paradoxical as it might seem to play the nervous, mobile phrases of bop on the big horn, suddenly there was a whole row of baritonists. Serge Chaloff, who came from a Russian-Jewish family, was first. He applied to the baritone all the new things played by Charlie Parker—as Buddy DeFranco did on the clarinet and J. J. Johnson on the trombone. Chaloff is among the musicians who played big-band bop with Woody Herman's important 1947 band. Ten years later—when the original Brothers section was reconstructed for a recording date—he had to be taken to the studio in a wheelchair. A few months later, he was dead of cancer.

The restless expressiveness of Chaloff's baritone was smoothed out into cool sobriety by Gerry Mulligan. Mulligan began quite *à la Chaloff* in the combos of Kai Winding and Chubby Jackson toward the end of the forties. He worked in the big bands of Claude Thornhill and Elliot Lawrence and was one of the important participants in the Miles Davis Capitol sessions, also as an arranger. From 1951 on, he became the increasingly influential baritone voice of Basie-Young classicism. Mulligan is of great importance as baritone saxophonist, arranger, band leader, but most of all as a catalytic personality. Few modern musicians are so firmly rooted in the "mainstream" of the Swing era. His "meetings" on record (Verve) with such Swing musicians as Harry Edison, Ben Webster, and Johnny Hodges are impressive proofs of this. The famous pianoless quartet that first made the name Mulligan popularly known in the early fifties and will be discussed in our combo section was organized on the West Coast. Though he himself didn't want to be called a West Coast man, he had lasting influence there. Since the end of the sixties, Mulligan has repeatedly taken the place of altoist Paul Desmond in the Dave Brubeck Quartet for different lengths of time.

The true baritone sound of West Coast jazz came from Bob Gordon, who—fatally injured in an automobile accident in 1955—was an improviser of sweeping vitality. He, too, was a musician of Basie-Young classicism. The records he made with tenorist-arranger Jack Montrose are among the most memorable combo recordings in West Coast jazz.

Influenced more by Charlie Parker and the other great bebop musicians than by his own baritone colleagues on the East Coast, and later in Europe, Sahib Shihab developed into a baritonist who has received much too little recognition. Shihab plays his instrument with power and conviction, often also with ironic humor, totally free of any mannerisms, and beyond the three modern "baritone styles" signified by the names Chaloff, Mulligan, and Pepper Adams.

Another excellent bebop baritone saxophonist is Cecil Payne, who has played a lot with Dizzy Gillespie. In the fifties and sixties, Charlie Fowlkes earned himself a solid reputation as a lively musician among the players with whom he made music firmly grounded in the healthy Basie tradition.

However, the man who got the whole new wave of interest in the baritone saxophone rolling is Pepper Adams (d. 1986). Before him, it seemed as if the possibilities of the baritone had been exhausted with Mulligan and the musicians of his generation and that the only thing yet to come could be an increase in perfection. This opinion was blown down by Pepper Adams' "sawing" sound. Pepper emerged in 1957 from the Stan Kenton band. There he was nicknamed "The Knife." Drummer Mel Lewis said, "We called him 'The Knife' because when he'd get up to blow, his playing had almost a slashing effect on the rest of us. He'd slash, chop, and before he was through, cut everybody down to size." Adams is one of the musicians who ebulliently negates the belief that one can distinguish between "black" and "white" in jazz. Prior to the appearance of his first photographs in the jazz magazines, almost the entire European critical fraternity thought him to be black. They were supported in this opinion by the fact that he comes from Detroit, the Motor City, which is the birthplace, physically and musically, of many black musicians of this style. Said Pepper, "Hawkins made a tremendous impression on me." Since Pepper Adams came onto the scene, he has been the most powerful baritone voice in bebop and hard bop, as he was in the neobop of the eighties.

Meanwhile, however, there is a whole generation of excellent baritone players in the different fields of contemporary bebop—among them Ronnie

Cuber, Charles Davis, Bruce Johnstone, Bob Militelo, Jack Nimitz, and, especially brilliant, Nick Brignola. Most of them have worked in big bands, above all in Woody Herman's orchestra, which has been something like a breeding ground for good baritone players in modern jazz, from Chaloff in the forties to Brignola in the seventies. The latter has been neobop's outstanding voice on the baritone saxophone since the end of the seventies.

Among the musicians inclined toward free playing, only two baritonists became internationally known during the sixties: Pat Patrick as a member of the Sun Ra Arkestra and, in Europe, Briton John Surman, whom Japanese critics of those days called "the most important baritone saxophone player of the new jazz." At the start of the seventies the soprano saxophone became more important for Surman, but then in the eighties he once again concentrated on the baritone sax. With his vivid glissandos and swirling sounds, Surman has expanded the tonal range of the baritone—previously thought to be limited—into the overblown regions of tenorlike playing and beyond. Up there he sounds sharp and raw, while in lower registers he emanates a gentle, warm, full sound. Since the mid-seventies his music has become increasingly meditative under the influence of a variety of elements: English and Scandinavian folk music, the polyphony of British sacred music, and the ostinato patterns of minimalism.

Amazingly few baritone players emerged from sixties free jazz. Surman explains that the baritone—much more than other saxophones—naturally inclines toward certain standard phrases and effects, and in absolutely free playing it is strikingly liable to clichés. Only in the course of the seventies and eighties did the baritone scene start moving again with musicians like Henry Threadgill, Mwata Bowden, Fred Ho (formerly Houn), Seppo Paakkunainen from Finland, German-born Bernd Konrad, and, above all, Hamiet Bluiett. Threadgill has been associated with both the free jazz of the Air trio and the neoclassicism of his own sextet. He plays his baritone with impressive ease as if it were a flute, and he is indeed also a convincing stylist on the flute. As a Chinese-American Fred Ho has developed a special feeling for linking African-American and Asian musical styles. His melodic playing is characterized by powerful pentatonic lines. According to Ho, "Many Chinese songs have a quality very similar to the blues." Bernd Konrad links vital jazz feeling with the ambitious formal and structural consciousness of the new concert music.

Hamiet Bluiett, who emerged from the Black Artist Group, dominates the realm of neoclassicism as a baritone saxophonist with a sovereignty matching Harry Carney's dominance of Swing and Gerry Mulligan's of cool jazz. He commands what is probably the most powerful baritone sound since Carney. He blows his horn with a vibrating intensity at sound levels usually associated with big-band baritonists, but Bluiett has marvelously adapted his voluminous timbre to combo playing, first in free jazz and later in neoclassicism, and above all in the World Saxophone Quartet (still to be introduced). Independently of Surman he has gained exceptional virtuosity in overblowing the baritone sax, driving it up three octaves above his instrument's normal range, full of the characteristic smears and growls of the blues. Bluiett phrases with an alert awareness of the African roots of black music. He isn't simply a "free player." He, like so many neoclassicist musicians, plays "everything": free and blues, bop and Swing, Dixie and soul, commanding all those styles as if they were *one* music, which in fact is what Bluiett feels.

Saxophone Groups

Nowhere is the idea of open musical dialogue, characteristic of jazz, so clear-cut as in a saxophone quartet. And nowhere is that concept so completely, harmoniously, and vitally realized as in the World Saxophone Quartet (WSQ). In fact, its members really do sound like four people talking together in an ongoing exchange of overlapping statements and counter-statements. Certainly such dialogue is a key concept on the playing of "pure" saxophone groups. Since that concept can be implemented much more clearly and with much greater tonal homgeneity within the chamber-music-like context of a saxophone ensemble than in other "pure" groupings, there was a remarkable boom in saxophone groups during the eighties. When saxophonists David Murray, Julius Hemphill, Hamiet Bluiett, and Oliver Lake set up the World Saxophone Quartet in 1976, they were on their own. Even without a rhythm section they swung more intensively and vitally than some good jazz groups with bass and drums. Today dozens of saxophone ensembles in jazz do just that. Under the influence of the World Saxophone Quartet, the eighties were so enriched by these saxophone ensembles—sometimes even going so far as to include other reeds and even flutes—that such groups require a section onto themselves rather than being dealt with under combos.

The World Saxophone Quartet is jazz's most important and influential saxophone ensemble. But it wasn't the first. Long before the saxophone quartet was introduced into jazz, such groups existed in European (especially French) concert music. Their influence on the development of jazz ensembles was, however, astonishingly minimal. The jazz saxophone quartet arose out of the inner laws and logic of black improvised music. In the beginning—as so often in jazz—was Duke Ellington. As early as the late twenties, Duke time and again featured his saxophone section in a way that went far beyond what was usual in the jazz of the day. Already with "Hot and Bothered," recorded in 1930, the Ellington orchestra's saxophone section acquired such presence and autonomy that it seemed less a functional part of the band than a single newly invented solo instrument. Then in 1947 came the Four Brothers sound in the Woody Herman Orchestra, accompanied by further concentration on the purely "saxophonic" in jazz. The Four Brothers' use of four saxophones shaped even the least detail in the orchestral sound, even the structuring of themes and arrangements. If anyone seeks the nucleus of the four-voiced saxophone quartet style, it is to be found here in the homogenous, transparent sound of the Four Brothers Band (and in the various combo recordings the Brothers saxophonists made without the big band).

So far as we know, the first all-saxophone group in jazz (without a rhythm section!) came, however, from Europe—from England, where in 1973 tenorist Alan Skidmore, baritone and soprano saxophonist John Surman, and altoist Mike Osborne formed the SOS group. The trio's free improvisations were still very much under the spell of the novelty of such an instrumental combination. The extent to which the idea of saxophone groups was in the air at that time is revealed by the fact that a year later Anthony Braxton recorded his *New York Fall, 1974* album, already featuring Julius Hemphill on the alto, Oliver Lake on the tenor, and Hamiet Bluiett on the baritone. This is the earliest jazz recording of a saxophone quartet, and indeed it already expresses that spirit of permanent dialogue that would become so important for later saxophone ensembles (such as the Rova Saxophone Quartet, which cited this very recording as a reason for setting up). The *Saxophone Special* album—with Steve Lacy (soprano) and fellow saxophonists Trevor Watts, Evan Parker, and Steve Potts—dates from the same year.

Yet such precursors did nothing to change the fact that pure saxophone groups remained a curiosity in jazz. It was the World Saxophone Quartet that finally succeeded in making this "unusual" and "exotic" grouping an institution and even an autonomous instrumental genre. With its vital jump playing full of wildly exciting riffs—transposing the collective improvising of free jazz into swing and rhythm and blues, into bebop and New Orleans jazz, Ellington and Mingus—the World Saxophone Quartet makes exemplarily clear what counts in such an ensemble. Here every player possesses an unmistakable, completely individual sound, and yet in collective improvisation they meld as *one* voice that goes far beyond what the sum of four parts can achieve.

Since there is no rhythm section in a saxophone quartet (the saxophonists themselves must fulfill that function), such an ensemble generally makes greater demands of the players' phrasing than a band with bass and drums. The World Saxophone Quartet pointed the way there. In its first concert—at Southern University in New Orleans in December 1976—the quartet was still backed by a rhythm group. But then financial difficulties forced the group to appear without bass and drums. From that moment the four musicians have so vitally and intensively transferred the beat to the saxophone lines, swinging so much to the point, that no one would think of asking what's happened to the rhythm section.

The Rova Saxophone Quartet, founded at San Francisco in 1977, became the most important jazz saxophone quartet alongside the WSQ. This ensemble (Larry Ochs, Bruce Ackley, Jon Raskin, and Andrew Voigt, who was replaced in 1988 by Steve Adams) demonstrates complexity and subtle inventiveness in the quest for new saxophone sounds. They perhaps even surpass the World Saxophone Quartet in that respect, but come nowhere near the older group's vitality and power. Compared with the WSQ's earthy, vehement playing, their music seems cool and abstract. Nonetheless, it is unusually rich and gripping. In its complex interweaving lines, which come from free jazz (above all Anthony Braxton), the Rova Saxophone Quartet links the spontaneous and the notated so artistically that even experts have difficulty in distinguishing between where composition ends and improvisation begins. How completely the musicians can give expression to themselves in this quartet also becomes apparent from the fact that until the end of the eighties none of them felt any urge to make recordings outside the Rova context.

Of all such groups the 29th Street Saxophone Quartet (with Bobby Watson, Jim Hartog, Ed Jackson, and Rich Rothenberg) produces the most catchy melodic phrasing. In its gripping contrapuntal lines the jaunty zest of bebop rhythms attractively encounters the hard-driving melodies and rhythms of street music—funk, rap, soul, and hip-hop. Whatever a saxophone quartet needs, the 29th Street Saxophone Quartet has it: balance and homogeneity. Tenorist Rich Rothenberg said, "In a big band the whole sax section is supportive, but here each of us is a section in and of ourselves."

Among the other important saxophone quartets that have in their own way refined the WSQ approach are the Your Neighborhood Saxophone Quartet, Itchy Fingers, and the Hornweb Saxophone Quartet from England; Position Alpha in Sweden; and the Kölner Saxophon Mafia in Germany. The Your Neighborhood Saxophone Quartet (with Steve Adams, Tom Hall, Bob Zung, and Allan Chase) cultivate, in chamber music style, the great saxophone tradition established by Swing orchestras from Basie to Ellington. The humorous improvisations of Itchy Fingers (Mike Mower, Martin Speaks, John Graham, and Howard Turner) offer a crazily fascinating kaleidoscope of styles, with Latin, pop, bebop, funk, and jazz-rock interweaving and superimposing to create ever-changing patterns. Position Alpha bursts onto the saxophone ensemble scene with anarchic wit plus punk wildness and gloom, but its phrasing also demonstrates a special liking for the sea shanties of Swedish folk music. The Kölner Saxophon Mafia represents an emphatically European variant of the jazz saxophone ensemble with a love of extended formal structures and complex harmonies, but at the same time the players groove compellingly, as is shown in a recording with the Elima percussion group from Zaire.

It is important to realize that the development of pure saxophone groups particularly demands new ways of playing the low instruments. The baritone saxophone serves, often a harmony instrument, to carry the ensemble, and yet it must satisfy the requirement of being a fully functional and equal member of the group. Hamiet Bluiett's lines have helped shape the way the baritone is played in such saxophone groups: pulsating, forward-driving riffs, which nonetheless are time and again broken up like solos within ensemble playing. Following the model of Bluiett's improvisations—with the instrument the center of gravity on the one hand and a fully equal solo voice on the other—the baritone has been further developed in saxophone groups by many musicians: Jon Raskin, Jim Hartog, Tom Hall, Joachim Ullrich, and Steve Adams.

All the saxophone ensembles mentioned here "celebrate" a wealth of new, unusual sounds that no one would have been able to foresee ten or twenty years ago—a development that will continue in the nineties.

The Flute

As recently as the fifties, the flute ranked among "miscellaneous instruments." But in proportion to the decline of the clarinet came the flute's ascendancy. At least since the late fifties, this instrument has taken the position of playful, airy, triumphant heights on jazz recordings that had been the domain of the clarinet during the Swing era, to which, since the mid-sixties, was added another "clarinet successor": the soprano sax under John Coltrane's influence.

Still, the flute has only a relatively short tradition in jazz. The earliest flute solo we know of is by Alberto Socarras in "Shootin' the Pistol," a 1927 recording of the Clarence Williams Orchestra. Socarras' main instrument was the saxophone, and his flute phrasing still has the angularity and stiffness of a musician who came from European concert music. Wayman Carver was the first jazz flutist who really has to be taken seriously. In "Sweet Sue," a 1933 recording of Spike Hughes and His All-American Orchestra, Carver plays with a suppleness that seems astonishingly modern. Chick Webb, too, occasionally used a flute in his orchestra of the early Swing era. But back then, the instrument still was a curiosity. Strange how suddenly this state of affairs changed when, in the early fifties, the appearance of a half-dozen jazz flutists—literally overnight—established the instrument in jazz.

The first musician to record modern flute solos with a direct, vital bop feeling was tenor player Jerome Richardson. Immediately after him, Frank Wess and Bud Shank stepped into the limelight. Wess (mentioned in the tenor saxophone chapter) was in Count Basie's orchestra. And in this band, whose name stands for Swing *par excellence,* he played the flute—still thought to be alien to Swing by many jazz fans—with the natural ease of his saxophone.

Wess symbolizes the breakthrough that led to the acceptance of the flute. The flute has difficulty in making itself heard, so it only had a real chance of getting across in the post–Lester Young era when people became generally aware of supple, springy, modern jazz phrasing taking precedence over expressive sonority. Lester Young is the "main culprit" in this shift of accent from sonority to phrasing, and thus jazz flutists are initially shaped in his mold. Wess illustrates this point almost ironically. As a tenorist, he clearly is of the Hawkins tradition; as a flutist, he is just as clearly of the Young line. Wess recorded some of his most interesting flute solos on a date with Milt Jackson (vibraphone), Hank Jones (piano), Eddie Jones (bass), and Kenny Clarke (drums): *Opus de Jazz.*

Bud Shank was the most important West Coast flutist. He emerged from Stan Kenton's band, where, in 1950, he had already recorded an interesting flute solo showing Latin influences, "In Veradero." Later, his duets with Bob Cooper, into which Max Roach drummed swing, stirred much discussion. A strong Arabic and oriental tendency is detectable in Yusef Lateef, on flute as on his numerous other instruments. Aside from the usual concert flute, he has used a whole store of other, exotic flutes: Chinese bamboo flute, a flute of Slovak folk origin, cork flute, the Arab nai flute, Taiwan flute, and a ma ma flute he constructed himself.

Other good jazz flutists are Sahib Shihab, James Moody, Herbie Mann, Sam Most, Buddy Collette, Paul Horn, Rahsaan Roland Kirk, Joe Farrell, James Spaulding, Eric Dixon, and Sam Rivers. It should be noted here that many of these musicians are saxophonists first and foremost and play the flute as a second instrument. This is true, for instance, of tenor and alto player James Moody (whom we have mentioned in the tenor section) who came out of the first bop circle of the forties. Although the flute is only one instrument among others for him, he has been considered one of the best jazz flutists for thirty years—a bebop man par excellence also on this instrument.

For a long time, the most successful jazz flutist was Herbie Mann. He incorporated many different ethnic elements into his jazz recordings: Latin, Brazilian, African, Arabian, Jewish, Turkish; and in the seventies and eighties, of course, rock, and finally even fusion.

Herbie Mann won the Reader's Poll of *Down Beat* magazine—*the* authoritative popularity poll of the jazz world—from 1957 to 1970—thirteen years! To everyone's surprise, Hubert Laws took over this spot as best-liked jazz flutist with a real classical sound. He has successfully attempted to create a number of jazz adaptations of classical music (compositions of Bach, Mozart, Debussy, Stravinsky, and others), but he has also made many jazz-rock and fusion records.

Paul Horn, who became known in the second half of the fifties for his work with the Chico Hamilton Quintet, in the early seventies made unaccompanied flute recordings in the Taj Mahal, on which the flute sounds echo back from the hundred-foot dome of the marvelous edifice "like a choir of angels" multiplied a hundredfold, as in an acoustic hall of mirrors: meditational mantras transformed into flute music. The success of this Horn record, *Inside,* was so great that it was later followed by a second one, this one recorded in the burial chambers of Egyptian pyramids (among them the famous Cheops pyramid). Horn later became a universal flutist within world music. He traveled through China and the Soviet Union and convincingly absorbed various ethnic flute techniques—Indian, Tibetan, Chinese, and Japanese—in his playing of the European concert flute. The "duets" he recorded with the songs of whales also attracted great interest.

New flutists keep coming. The reservoirs seem inexhaustible. More and more saxophonists choose the flute as a supplementary horn only to discover one day that it has become their main instrument—as has occasionally happened to James Moody.

A special place is occupied by the outstanding avant-garde player Eric Dolphy, who died in 1964. His influence as an alto and bass clarinet player was felt immediately, from the early sixties on, while on flute the importance of his message was not realized by other musicians until the mid-seventies. The genius of his ideas already included all of what "jazz flute" means on today's scene. His flute "message"—quite in contrast to what he expressed on his other instruments—was one of lightness and airiness. For people who knew Dolphy the man, there is reason to feel that his flute playing expressed more of his humanity, his soft-spoken gentleness and amiability, than the bursting expressivity of his alto style and the pain-filled eruptions of his bass clarinet improvisations.

Strangely enough, the first to understand and elaborate on Dolphy's flute style were European musicians. They distinguish themselves through an awareness of classical traditions—musicians like the Bulgarian Simeon Shterev, Czechoslovakian Jiří Stivin, German Emil Mangelsdorff, Briton Bob Downes, and Dutchman Chris Hinze. Downes, who has also stepped out as a composer of contemporary ballets, belongs to the realm of classics as much as to jazz. Hinze plays mainly jazz-rock. Mangelsdorff has an especially full, rich sound. Stivin, also an excellent composer and altoist, is a virtuoso with Bohemian musicians' roots. Shterev commands the whole rich musical heritage of his Balkan homeland.

Many of the flutists named above cultivate the "overblowing" technique where, through simultaneous blowing and singing or humming, two voices become audible (often through the resultant combination tones, even three or four voices)—creating jazz intensity of an astonishing degree. Anybody who knows the flute from classical music (from baroque music, for instance) may not immediately think of the flute as an instrument that lends itself to jazzlike intensity in the same terms as, say, the tenor saxophone. Only by way of the technique of overblowing has it gained this intensity, and only in that way could it have achieved its success on today's scene.

The first jazz musicians to overblow the flute as early as the mid-fifties, were Sam Most and Sahib Shihab (whom we discussed in the section on baritone saxophone). Ever since the sixties, this technique has been employed by a growing number of flutists, most intensely, most hot by Rahsaan Roland Kirk who when overblowing the flute didn't just sing into the instrument, like his predecessors, but also spoke, shouted, and screamed. He sometimes seemed to explode in a dozen different directions with the many different sounds he created simultaneously while blowing the flute (and, at the same time, blown through the nose, his so-called nose flute).

A master of overblowing is Jeremy Steig. He was the first flutist to structurally incorporate air and functional and finger noises into his music, while Kirk still used them mainly to increase ecstatic vitality. Steig recorded some highly interesting chamber-music-like duos with bassist Eddie Gomez.

Flutists in the actual jazz-rock field are, among others, Dave Valentin, Tom Scott, Gerry Niewood, and the two jazzwomen Bobbi Humphrey and Briton Barbara Thompson. Dave Valentin, who studied with Hubert Laws, plays sunny, bright lines that derive their optimism and relaxation from the supple rhythms of Latin American, particularly Brazilian, music. It may be presumed that the flute horizon of jazz will widen further in the coming years.

The flute does not exist: no instrument is more universal. The history of the flute begins symbolically with Pan, the Greek god of the shepherds and of "the whole," the god who gives a soul to "everything." Every musical culture on earth has developed its own particular types of flutes. To the degree to which jazz musicians incorporate the musical cultures of the world do they discover flutes. Joachim Berendt once did a record date with Don Cherry to which Cherry brought thirty-five different flutes—among them a Chinese shuan flute made from ceramic, a Latin American Maya bird flute, a Bengali flute, a bamboo flute, a metal flute (in B flat), a plastic flute in C, American Indian flutes, Japanese flutes, etc.

The flute has always been an instrument with a special affinity for world music—as early as the fifties through Yusef Lateef and Bud Shank, later particularly impressively through Paul Horn, and in the seventies, for instance, through Brazilian Hermeto Pascoal, who overblows the flute with truly passionate intensity.

Among the important musicians, all greatly influenced by Eric Dolphy, who play free flute (in that universal sense of free that evolved within neoclassicism) are Douglas Ewart, Henry Threadgill, Oliver Lake, Prince Lasha, Lloyd McNeil, Gary Thomas, Canadian-born Jane Bunnett, and, most important of all, James Newton. No other jazz flutist has so individually and unmistakably reworked and developed Dolphy's legacy. Newton possesses the most powerful flute sound—penetrating, mellow, and full but never loud despite the power involved, emanating a magic and spiritual energy reminiscent of shakuhachi flute players. One of the few jazz musicians whose main instrument is the flute, Newton has mastered the art of overblowing almost unsurpassably. He often blows, at the same time as the sung tones, contrapuntal lines that move completely independently of the vocal part. "A lot of the things I play where I use my voice are related to the way the brass instruments would growl in the Ellington orchestra," said Newton.

Newton recorded what he believes to be his most beautiful album (*Echo Canyon*) in Echo Canyon, New Mexico, a huge natural amphitheater formed by erosion, playing with the echoes thrown back from many directions as if answering partners standing everywhere on the edges of the canyon, and incorporating the sounds of nature—birds, coyotes, stones falling into the depths—into his performance.

Contemporary mainstream is played on the flute by, among others, George Adams, Steve Slagle, Robin Kenyatta, Dwight Andrews, Jerry Dodgion, Steve Kujala, and Kent Jordan. Jordan blows the piccolo flute with stupendous virtuosity within the realm of classicism, emancipating this instrument, hitherto mostly serving a coloristic function, especially impressively. Once in a while, Lew Tabackin, co-leader of the Akiyoshi-Tabackin Big Band, produces sounds reminiscent of Japanese shakuhachi flutes in his amazing virtuoso flute excursions played in a quartet or his big band. Tabackin remarked, "No wonder. With my wife being Japanese, you absorb these sounds automatically."

But one of the greatest shakuhachi players in Japan (perhaps the greatest of them all), Hozan Yamamoto, has also played this immensely expressive bamboo flute—probably the most expressive instrument of the worldwide flute family—in a jazz context with his own kind of mastery. He has done so with, for instance, singer Helen Merrill and percussion player Masahiko Togashi.

Tabackin is also part of those sections consisting of four or five flutes that have produced some of the most interesting and novel sounds of the Akiyoshi-Tabackin Big Band. In an earlier edition of this book we surmised that one day combinations of this sort involving several flutes would exist in jazz music. Now they do exist, and they seem so rich and differentiated that, now that the ice is broken, it is to be hoped that other jazz composers and arrangers will also try their hand at them.

The Vibraphone

Percussion instruments (instruments that are struck or hit) tend to be used primarily as rhythm instruments. If such instruments additionally offer all kinds of melodic possibilities, it can be assumed that they would make ideal jazz instruments. In this sense, the vibraphone is an ideal jazz instrument. The fact that so vitally rhythmic a musician as Lionel Hampton incorporated it in jazz—or at least helped to do so—points in this direction. If it nevertheless has been slow to assert itself, it may be due to its inability to allow for the production of a hornlike jazz sound. The sound of the vibraphone can only be influenced indirectly, by way of its electrically adjustable vibrato, or by foregoing any electrical adjustment, or through the force—or sensitivity—with which it is struck.

Lionel Hampton and Milt Jackson are the outstanding vibraphonists of the jazz tradition. Hampton is a volcano of energy who, like hardly anyone else, can carry thousands of people to a trancelike state of ecstasy by the sheer power (and, of course, showmanship) of his playing and performing. He loves to have a big band with trumpet, trombone, and sax sections behind him. His big bands often pound away without consideration for intonation, blend, or precision, but Lionel Hampton, the vibraphonist, derives from the rhythmic riff orgies of his big bands even more inspiration and fire and power than he possesses on his own.

Hampton and, a couple of years before him, Red Norvo introduced the vibraphone to jazz at the beginning of the Swing era. Their music demonstrates with exemplary clarity the contrasting possibilities open to the jazz vibraphone. To simplify somewhat, the vibraphone can be played in two ways: like a percussion instrument or like a piano. Hampton phrases percussively, Norvo pianistically. That is already apparent in their instrumental backgrounds. Hampton came from the drum set to the vibraphone, Norve from the xylophone. Norvo developed in a remarkably open way from Chicago style through Swing, bebop, and cool to contemporary jazz—with a special sensitivity for small chamber-music-like jazz groups.

As Hampton's vibraphone career had started with Louis Armstrong, so Milt Jackson's began in 1945 with Dizzy Gillespie, in his ground-breaking bebop big band. From 1951 onward Jackson was a member of the Modern Jazz Quartet, which originated as the Milt Jackson Quartet and to begin with was hardly more than the combination of Milt Jackson's vibes and a rhythm section. The Milt Jackson Quartet became the Modern Jazz Quartet under the influence of John Lewis, and it has sometimes been said that the shape and form given by Lewis to this ensemble restricted Jackson's flow of ideas and improvisatory freedom. The fact is, however, that Jackson has played the most beautiful solos of his career as a member of the Modern Jazz Quartet. As so often happens in jazz, the tension between the rigidity of the arrangements and the freedom of improvisation did not hinder the artist but rather inspired him.

Milt Jackson's improvisations deserve the adjective "flowing," more than any other kind of jazz. A provocative element of Jackson's playing is the seemingly unconscious way in which he makes the most complicated harmonies seem natural and organic. That is also one of the reasons why he is one of the great ballad players in jazz. Already in the mid-fifties, Jackson was one of the first soul musicians. However far vibraphonists may have developed away from Milt's style, whoever plays vibraphone in modern jazz speaks of him with respect and admiration.

Of course, Jackson is not the only vibraphonist of his generation; others are Terry Gibbs, Teddy Charles, Cal Tjader, Vic Feldman, and the somewhat younger Eddie Costa, Tommy Vig, Lem Winchester, Larry Bunker, Charlie Shoemaker, and Mike Mainieri. Gibbs became known through his brilliant solo work with the Woody Herman band of the late forties. Even in later years, he remained interested in big bands and in the contrast between his vibraphone and the big-band sound. Cal Tjader's blend of jazz phrasing with mambo, conga, bolero, cha-cha-cha, and other Latin rhythms is a valid and intelligent development and sophistication of Cuban jazz, as initiated by Dizzy Gillespie, Chano Pozo, and Machito in the great days of bop. Teddy Charles belongs among those musicians who, in the fifties, were already expanding tonality and preparing the way for free playing.

Lem Winchester, who died in 1961, was the first to display a feeling for the glittering, oscillating sound quality of his instrument, at first only in initial intimations. In the ensuing years, this manner of playing became more and more pronounced through musicians like Gary Burton, Walt Dickerson, Tom van der Geld, and Bobby Hutcherson. These are the players who after years of an unchallenged Milt Jackson reign have revolutionized the style of their instrument as dramatically as has happened only to the bass during this timespan. These musicians accomplished what Ornette Coleman had wanted to see replace the "old rules of playing": "a continuous exploring of all possibilities of the instrument." They found that the flittering, oscillating quality of sound that we mentioned in connection with Lem Winchester fits their instrument better than simply "a continuation of standard bop by means of the vibraphone."

Gary Burton plays with a fascinating combination of tender, floating lyricism and great virtuosity. No other vibraphonist has so comprehensively revealed his instrument's pianistic possibilities. He has developed further than anyone else the ability to play with three or four mallets simultaneously, creating chordal effects similar to those of pianist Bill Evans, who influenced him. Another influence was the country and hillbilly music of his home state, Indiana. Burton joins all these elements into a new, independent whole so securely that he has become successful far beyond jazz. It was Burton, too, who initiated the contemporary trend toward playing without a rhythm section and who led this trend to its first big triumphs.

Walt Dickerson has transferred ideas of John Coltrane to the vibraphone. He is another vibraharpist who loves exploring new sounds, and he, too (like all these other players of the vibraphone), is an impressive improviser without accompaniment. But the real "star" among the more recent vibraphonists (since the late sixties) is Bobby Hutcherson. He began his career with Archie Shepp's free jazz and also played jazz-rock, before developing in the eighties into an outstanding classicist performer on the vibes. Hutcherson took Milt Jackson's legacy furthest, masterfully incorporating Coltrane and the new vibraphone sound. He's an enormously complete player unifying in his lines the possibilities open to the instrument, both percussive and pianistic. His skill in overcoming the vibraphone's lack of flexibility and mechanical predisposition, characterizing this instrument more than any other employed in jazz, is thrilling. And he's also a magician of touch, excitingly diverse in the art of giving emotional shape to a piece and "molding" the sound. "It's not the note itself that counts", Hutcherson said, "it's the story you tell in the note." Steve Nelson is a young vibraphonist who pursues Hutcherson's way of playing within the realm of classicism.

Tom van der Geld is the most sensitive, most tender player among the new vibraphonists. Once in a while his improvisations sound as if the bars of his instrument were set vibrating not by being struck with mallets, but by a mild, warm wind. David Friedman has a brilliant, gripping sound, occasionally like a "Lionel Hampton of the eighties," with a pronounced fondness for surprising technical effects. Off and on, he includes a second vibraphonist (and marimba player), David Samuels, in his group, "multiplying" the vibraphone sound in this way. What Friedman and Samuels play together sometimes sounds like an entire "metallophone ensemble," reminiscent to a certain extent of Balinese music. Austrian-born Werner Pirchner produces never previously heard sounds from his specially constructed "tenor vibes."

Strikingly few vibraphone players became interested in the sounds of jazz-rock and fusion music. Among them are Roy Ayers, Dave Pike, Mike Mainieri, Ruth Underwood, and Jay Hoggard. Mainieri electrified the vibraphone, with fluctuating success.

Radically new ways of playing have been discovered by two German musicians who have made their home in the United States: Gunter Hampel and Karl Berger. Hampel (who has also distinguished himself as flutist, clarinetist, bass clarinetist, and pianist) is the more sensitive of the two;

Berger (who heads the Creative Music Studio in Woodstock, NY) is the more dynamic, with bop roots that he has been developing in the direction of a wide and deep interest in world music. With his different groups, Hampel has created mesmerizing webs of sound, combining the vibraphone with flutes and saxophones played in the high registers.

A synthesis of all these tendencies has been created by four American players, who on the one hand play free and on the other command the entire tradition of their instrument: Bobby Naughton, Gust William Tsilis, Khan Jamal, and, above all, Jay Hoggard. Jamal made free-funk recordings with Ronald Shannon Jackson's Decoding Society. Hoggard is an enthrallingly emotional neoclassicist improviser who possesses a fine sense for discovery of tonal parallels between, on the one hand, the vibraphone and, on the other, related instruments in ethnic music. In his playing he resorts to African balafone techniques or the metallophones of Balinese Gamelan music. Since the mid-eighties he has inclined toward jazz-rock, but his appearances there are less expressive.

There were three main trends in eighties vibraphone: percussiveness in the Lionel Hampton tradition, as exemplified by Jay Hoggard and David Friedman; the iridescent sensitivity initiated by such players as Gary Burton, Lem Winchester, Walt Dickerson, and Gunter Hampel, and carried on by Tom van der Geld and Khan Jamal; and, above all, as a balancing element mediating between those two ways of playing, the legacy of Milt Jackson, which lives on in the suppleness of Bobby Hutcherson and Steve Nelson.

The Piano

Since the history of jazz begins with ragtime and ragtime was a pianistic music, jazz begins with the piano. Yet the first bands on the streets of New Orleans had no pianos—perhaps because pianos could not be carried around, but perhaps also because the piano could not produce the jazz sound that seemed essential to the early hot players.

The history of jazz piano is acted out between these two poles. The piano offers more possibilities than most other instruments used in jazz. It is not limited to playing one note at a time, as are the horns. It cannot only produce rhythm but can also harmonize this rhythm. It cannot only state the harmonies, as can the bass, but also connect them with other musical possibilities. But a horn line is more intense than a piano line.

In summary, we find that, on the one hand, the more the pianistic possibilities of the piano are exploited, the more the piano seems overshadowed by the hornlike, intense phrasing of jazz blowers. On the other hand, the more the pianist adopts the phrasing of the horns, the more he or she relinquishes the true potential of the instrument—up to a point that can represent "pianistic suicide" for anyone familiar with pianistic virtuosity in European music.

Art Tatum and Bud Powell (who was too great to be capable of such "pianistic suicide," though it did exist within the piano school he represents) signify the extremes of this last dichotomy. These extremes have been sharpened since the eighties of the past century, when Scott Joplin began to play ragtime in the Midwest. Joplin was a "pianistic" pianist. In many respects he played his instrument clearly within the conventions of the romantic piano tradition. (See the section on ragtime.)

Since New Orleans bands had no use for pianistic piano players, and since a hornlike piano style had not yet been "discovered," there was hardly one pianist in the jazz bands of old New Orleans. But there were pianists in the saloons and the bars, in the "houses" and cabarets—pianists in abundance. Every house had its "professor," and the professor was a pianist. He played ragtime piano. And even when he played blues and stomps and honky-tonk piano, ragtime was always in the background.

The great professor of New Orleans piano was Jelly Roll Morton, who died in 1941. Morton played ragtime piano with awareness of the marching bands on the New Orleans streets. Filled with pride at his certainly considerable accomplishments, he became almost paranoid: "I have been robbed of three million dollars all told. Everyone today [1939] is playing my stuff and I don't even get credit. Kansas City style, Chicago style, New Orleans style—hell, they're all Jelly Roll style."

The professors, the honky-tonk and "barrelhouse" pianists, existed in New Orleans not only before and during the period of the actual New Orleans style, but also after, into our times. However, only a few of them gained fame beyond the limits of the Delta City—for instance, Champion Jack Dupree, Huey "Piano" Smith and Professor Longhair (who died in 1980). Fats Domino (mentioned in the blues section and later again in the vocalists chapter), who stood at the center of the rock 'n' roll movement of the fifties, emerged directly from this tradition. Indeed, in the chapter dealing with jazz vocalists, we shall discuss the fact that New Orleans created styles twice in the history of black music—not only during the era of New Orleans jazz, but also fifty years later in rhythm and blues and in rock. The New Orleans piano professor bridges these two fields. Jelly Roll Morton made New Orleans jazz with his band; Fats Domino or Professor Longhair made rhythm and blues and rock 'n' roll. Although separated by half a century, they all belong to the same professor and honky-tonk tradition.

Ragtime as played in the Midwest by Scott Joplin was clearly different from ragtime in New Orleans as played by Jelly Roll Morton, but both were music in which one could feel the elements of rag—the elements of "ragged time." Soon, there was ragtime in New York, and again it was different from the piano sounds in the Midwest and in New Orleans. From New York ragtime developed the great era of the Harlem jazz piano. But even if Scott Joplin played in Sedalia, Missouri, from the 1890s, and Jelly Roll Morton named 1902 as the year he "invented" jazz, and the first ragtime pianists played in New York and Harlem around 1910, this still does not prove that the line of evolution led directly from Sedalia over New Orleans to Harlem. Styles, as we have mentioned, develop when the time is ripe, independently of causal schemes of evolution.

James P. Johnson, who died in 1955, was the first important Harlem pianist. He was a schooled musician; from the beginning there were many academically trained musicians among the pianists, in contradistinction to the players of other instruments. James P. Johnson had studied with a pupil of Rimsky-Korsakoff, and late in his career, during the thirties, he composed a series of symphonic and quasi-symphonic works.

With Johnson is revealed for the first time an aspect of jazz piano at least as important as all the brilliant solo achievements: the art of accompaniment, the art of adapting oneself to a soloist, stimulating and giving him or her a foundation on which to build. Johnson did this in unsurpassed fashion for Bessie Smith—on "Preachin' the Blues" or "Backwater Blues," for instance.

Harlem of the twenties was a breeding ground for jazz piano. Duke Ellington related, "Everybody was trying to sound like the 'Carolina Shout' Jimmy [James P. Johnson] had made on a piano roll. I got it down by slowing up the roll. . . . We went out every evening regardless of whether we had money or not. I got a big thrill when I found Willie The Lion Smith [one night]. . . . We made the rounds every night looking for the piano players."

Willie The Lion Smith is another great pianist of the Harlem tradition of the twenties—a master of charming melodies, which he set off with the mighty rhythm of his left hand.

The Harlem pianists—Johnson, Smith, Ellington, Luckey Roberts, and young Fats Waller—played for "rent parties" and in "cutting contests," all part of the whirling jazz life of Harlem. At the rent parties, jazz was a means of getting up the rent for one's apartment in a friendly atmosphere, and the cutting contests were play-offs among the leading pianists, ending only when one man had definitively "cut" all the others. The most characteristic of their various styles was called stride piano. "Stride" means a constant, swinging alternation of a bass note (played on one and three) and a chord (played on two and four). The switch between the low bass note and the higher chord involves a further step, a stride.

The most important pianist to come out of this Harlem tradition was Fats Waller, who died at thirty-nine in 1943. Louis Armstrong said, "Right now, every time someone mentions Fats Waller's name, why, you can see the grins on all the faces." Fats was two men: one of the greatest pianists in jazz history and one of the funniest and most entertaining comedians of popular music—both of which he managed to combine with inimitable relaxation.

"Livin' the Life I Love" was the theme of his life and his music. He did not always bring it off; for all his comic sense, he still suffered when the public seemed to appreciate his showmanship more than his music. Gene Sedric, Fats' tenor man said:

> Fats was sometimes very unhappy about his music. You see, he was appreciated for his showmanship ability and for that amount of piano that he played on records, but very few of Waller's record fans knew how much more he could play than what he usually did on records. He didn't try to prove anything by his singing. It was a matter of fun with him. . . . Yet he wanted to do great things on organ and piano—which he could do.

Elsewhere, Sedric said, "As for the record sessions, it seems like they would always give him a whole lot of junk tunes to play because it seemed as if only he could get something out of them."

As composer, Waller wrote some of the most beautiful jazz themes, equally agreeable to all styles. "Honeysuckle Rose" and "Ain't Misbehavin' " are the most important. "Waller," said Coleman Hawkins, "could write tunes as fast as he could play the piano."

As a pianist, Fats had the strongest left hand in traditional jazz—a left hand that could replace not only a rhythm section but a whole band. He was altogether an "orchestral" pianist; that is, his piano sounded rich and full like an orchestra. Quite relevantly, the most orchestral of all jazz pianists, Art Tatum, invoked Waller: "Fats, man—that's where I come from. . . . Quite a place to come from, too!"

The other great pianist to come from Fats Waller is Count Basie. Basie told of his first meeting with Fats: "I had dropped into the old Lincoln Theater in Harlem and heard a young fellow beating it out on the organ. From that time on, I was a daily customer, hanging on to his every note, sitting behind him all the time, fascinated by the ease with which his hands pounded the keys and his feet manipulated the pedals."

Even later, one could sometimes still hear in the piano solos Basie played with his band that he came from Fats Waller. He played a kind of "economized" Fats: an ingeniously abstracted structure of Waller music in which only the cornerstones remain—but they stand for everything else. Basie became one of the most economical pianists in jazz history, and the way he manages to create tension between often widely spaced single notes is incomparable. Many pianists have been influenced by this: Johnny Guarnieri in the Swing era and during the fifties, John Lewis, the maestro of the Modern Jazz Quartet, in whom one senses behind Basie's unconscious economy of means a sage knowledge of all that economy and abstraction imply in music and art. When musicians like Basie or John Lewis leave open spaces in their improvisations, it is more than just empty space; it is a medium of tension and relaxation every bit as important as any note they play.

However, another stream of jazz piano development flowed into Count Basie: the stream of great boogie-woogie pianists. Basie not only plays "economized" Fats Waller, but economized boogie as well.

In the early days, the ragtime and Harlem pianists always looked down a bit condescendingly on the "poor boogie-woogie piano players." Chicago became the center of boogie-woogie. Whereas Harlem rent parties and cutting contests jumped to the sound of stride piano, their counterparts on Chicago's South Side rocked to the beat of blues and boogie piano. Boogie-woogie, too, has its roots in the Midwest and Southwest, down to Texas. From Texas comes one of the few remarkable pianists who in the seventies and eighties still played genuine, uncommercialized boogie and blues piano: Sam Price. Memphis, St. Louis, and Kansas City were important boogie-woogie towns. Memphis Slim, who came from Memphis (d. 1988 in Paris), is among the more recent masters of boogie. He made a name for himself primarily as a blues shouter. There are many blues singers in the black sections of northern and southern cities who accompany themselves with convincing boogie-woogie piano, or even are outstanding boogie soloists—for example, Roosevelt Sykes, Little Brother Montgomery, and above all, Otis Spann (who died in 1970).

The boogie-ostinato—the sharply accented, continuously repeated bass figures—may have developed in the South from the banjo or guitar figures with which the blues singers accompanied themselves. Anyhow, blues and boogie belong together since their origin. The first boogies were played as blues accompaniments, and to this day almost all boogies are in the twelve-bar blues pattern. Often, the difference between blues and boogie is anything but distinct; as might be pointed out here, the notion that all boogie-woogie is fast and bouncy is an erroneous generalization. It is just as false as the idea that all blues are slow.

If the search for the origins of boogie-woogie takes us beyond the early banjo and guitar blues accompaniments, we arrive at a time when the differentiation between Latin American (rumba, samba, tango, etc.) and North American (ultimately jazz-influenced) music was not yet so distinct. Jimmy Yancey, the "father of boogie-woogie," and other boogie pianists have based some of their pieces on the bass figures of Latin American dances—Yancey's "Lean Bacon Boogie," for example, is based on a tango figure. In the last analysis, boogie is a sort of "arch-rhythm" of black music, which is why one encounters it again and again in modern times—as "in disguise" in rhythm and blues of the fifties, in soul music of the sixties, or in Muhal Richard Abrams' piano improvisations of the seventies and eighties, of course often in an alienated, abstract manner. That authentic boogie-woogie can still be alive and effective became apparent when a number of British rock and blues musicians formed Rocket 88 in 1978 on the occasion of the fiftieth anniversary of boogie-woogie (in 1928 Pinetop Smith had recorded his "Pinetop's Boogie-Woogie," which gave the whole style its name). Rocket 88 included, among others, Rolling Stones drummer Charlie Watts, British boogie team George Green and Bob Hall (on two pianos), as well as Alexis Korner, the father of British blues. Equally vital are the recordings made in the eighties by German-born Axel Zwingenberger together with blues singer Big Joe Turner and vibraphonist Lionel Hampton. All these musicians played boogie-woogie with the same cooking intensity that heated up the old boogie joints of 1920s Chicago.

At that time, Jimmy Yancey, Pinetop Smith, Cow-Cow Davenport, and Cripple Clarence Lofton were the first important boogie-woogie pianists. Yancey was originally a tap dancer, which might have inspired his eight-to-the-bar playing.

Most brilliant of the boogie-woogie pianists was Meade Lux Lewis, who died in an automobile accident in 1964. His "Honky Tonk Train Blues," first recorded in 1929, achieved legendary fame. In the mid-thirties, when the Negro audience for whom boogie-woogie had been played in the twenties on Chicago's South Side and elsewhere had long since gone beyond this style, the white world began to warm up to it. At that time, jazz critic John Hammond searched for Lewis and found him as a car washer in a suburban Chicago garage. At New York's Cafe Society Hammond brought him together with two other pioneers of boogie-woogie piano: Albert Ammons and Pete Johnson. The records made by these three masters of boogie at three pianos are among the most exciting examples of boogie-woogie.

The third branch of pianistic development—hornlike piano playing—was the latest to evolve. Earl Hines has been called the first musician of this direction; in any case he is its most important pathbreaker. His playing has been called "trumpet style piano"; the mighty octave movements of his right hand sounded like a translation of Louis Armstrong's trumpet lines to the piano. But Hines (d. 1983) was a musician in his own right, filled with energy and humor and revealing musical and human development even in his old age. He is one of those fascinating personalities of jazz who have become legends in their own time.

No piano can sound "like a horn," but Hines is the founder of a school whose pianists realized lines—little by little at first, but more and more generally later—that may not have attained a hornlike expression but surely the contours of hornlike phrases. This school leads via Mary Lou Williams,

Teddy Wilson, Nat "King" Cole, and, of special importance, Bud Powell, up to countless pianists of contemporary jazz.

Of special interest is Mary Lou Williams, since she lived through this entire school and developed parallel to it. Mary Lou (who died in 1981) is surely the most important female figure in the whole history of instrumental jazz. She began to play around 1927, in the blues and boogie-woogie style of the day. In Kansas City she became arranger and pianist for the Andy Kirk band. She wrote a number of arrangements—for Kirk, Benny Goodman ("Roll 'Em"), and Duke Ellington ("Trumpets No End," which is an arrangement of Irving Berlin's "Blues Skies")—that cannot be left out of any history of jazz. As a pianist she evolved through Swing and bop into a mature representative of modern jazz piano, which caused some to say that this "First Lady of Jazz" had no style of her own. She herself said with justified assurance:

> I consider that a compliment, although I think that everyone with ears can identify me without any difficulty. But it's true that I'm always experimenting, always changing, always finding new things. Why, back in Kansas City I found chords they're just beginning to use now. What happens to so many good pianists is that they become so stylized that they can't break out of the prison of their styles and absorb ideas and new techniques.

She demonstrated this openness toward new developments as recently as 1977, when she played a noted duo concert with the best-known player of free-jazz piano, Cecil Taylor.

In the Swing style of the thirties the Earl Hines direction is embodied first of all in Teddy Wilson. He connects it with the format of the great black Swing horn players and with the elegance and affability that Benny Goodman brought to the jazz of that day. Wilson, as a member of the Goodman combos and as leader of his own ensembles, participated in some of the best and most representative combo recordings of the Swing era. During the thirties, he influenced almost every pianist—including Mel Powell, Billy Kyle, Jess Stacy, and Joe Bushkin. Bushkin, of course, was also influenced by the "grand old man" of all jazz pianists: Art Tatum. Marian McPartland has transferred the elegance of Wilson—with whom she recorded a duo album—to the contemporary scene, incorporating many of the musical insights since then. She is one of those players who in the course of their lives keep growing in format and stature.

Everything created in the course of the history of jazz piano up to the time of his renown—the mid-thirties—comes together in Art Tatum, with the addition of a pianist virtuosity that has been compared to that of the great concert pianists, such as Rubinstein or Cherkassky, and that before him was unheard of in jazz. The cadenzas and runs, the arpeggios and embellishments of the virtuoso piano music of the late nineteenth century are as alive in his playing as is a strong feeling for the blues, which he demonstrates in, say, his recordings with blues singer Joe Turner. Nurtured on the piano techniques of the nineteenth century, Tatum shows a certain preference for the salon pieces of that time—such as Dvořák's "Humoresque," Massenet's "Elégie," and others of this genre, which didn't always satisfy the highest of artistic demands. But it is characteristic of the high esteem in which Tatum is held by almost all jazz musicians that a storm of protest arose when French jazz critic André Hodeir brought up this question of taste. Even musicians who otherwise could not be moved to write took pen in hand to send in glowing defenses of Tatum.

Tatum, who died in 1957, was a soloist—period. Aside from a few combo recordings with all-star personnel or the previously mentioned sessions with blues singer Joe Turner, he was accustomed to playing solo or with his own trio. Tatum continues to be influential—as on French pianist Martial Solal or Adam Makowicz from Poland, and indirectly also on dozens of piano players who today play virtuoso solo piano. In this sense it might be said that Art Tatum's universal piano approach experienced real triumphs in the seventies and eighties, over twenty-five years after this great musician's death.

After Tatum, the counterplay between the pianistic and the hornlike conceptions of jazz piano becomes particularly marked. Bud Powell, who died in 1966 under tragic circumstances, was the primary exponent of the hornlike approach and, in general, the most influential pianist of modern jazz. At eighteen, he had already played with Charlie Christian and Charlie Parker at Minton's. He has been called the "Bird of jazz piano," and he was similarly tormented and threatened as a human being. After his creative period, from the mid-forties to the early fifties, he spent more than half his time in asylums. During this relatively long time he often was only a shadow of the greatness he displayed in those few years when he actually created the modern piano style.

The problem of Powell is an intensification of the problem of the jazz musician in general: the problem of the artist who is creative within a socially and racially discriminatory world whose aggressiveness and lack of sensibility cannot possibly be borne by those artists who are neither willing nor able to play the game.

Powell created those sharply etched lines that seem to stand free in space like glowing metal that has hardened. Yet Bud is also a romanticist, whose "Glass Enclosure" (an original composition) or whose ballad interpretations—for instance, "Polkadots and Moonbeams"—have the gentle charm of Robert Schumann's "Scenes from Childhood." This tension between the hardness of his hornlike lines and his romantic sensibility is always present, and perhaps it was this tension between two ultimately incompatible extremes that also contributed to the tragedy of this wonderful musician. Lennie Tristano said of Powell that he got "the piano past being the piano. There's hardly anything anybody could say about Bud Powell which could emphasize how great he was."

From Tatum comes the technique; from Powell, the style. Tatum set a pianistic standard that for a long time seemed unattainable. Bud Powell founded a school. Thus, there are more pianists in modern jazz who are "Powell students" than there are "Tatum students." Descended from Tatum are first of all Billy Taylor, Martial Solal, Hank Jones, Jimmy Rowles, Phineas Newborn, and Oscar Peterson (who, of course, are also influenced to a certain degree by Bud Powell and other pianists). Jones combines bebop and Tatum, leading this combination to ever greater maturity—since the seventies also in impressive solo appearances. Solal possesses French brilliance and Gallic humor and esprit. Sometimes the wealth of his ideas and intimations explodes like fireworks.

When in the course of the seventies Polish pianist Adam Makowicz came to the fore, it became apparent how strong the Tatum tradition still is. Makowicz plays a very concertlike, Chopinesque kind of Tatum style. Guided by John Hammond, the greatest talent scout of jazz, he moved to New York in 1978, where he stated, "What I am learning here is mainly rhythm." John Colianni, who came from the Lionel Hampton Orchestra during the eighties, established himself during the Swing revival as a young, highly promising Tatum-oriented pianist.

The most successful pianist of the Tatum school, however, is Oscar Peterson; time and again he has pointed out how strongly indebted he feels to Tatum. Peterson is a swinger of immense energy and gripping attack. In the seventies, when he started to give solo concerts (without the small groups with whom he had appeared until them), it could be heard that the Harlem pianists had also left their mark on him: Fats Waller and James P. Johnson with their mighty bass lines, who in turn are the ancestors of Tatum. In the meantime, Peterson has formed a school of his own. One of the pianists in this school is Monty Alexander, who combines an attack *à la* Peterson with the charm of his native Jamaica.

From Bud Powell come Al Haig, George Wallington, Lou Levy, Lennie Tristano, Hampton Hawes, Claude Williamson, Joe Albany, Dave McKenna, Japanese émigré Toshiko Akiyoshi, Eddie Costa, Wynton Kelly, Russ Freeman, Harold Mabern, Cedar Walton, Mose Allison, Red Garland, Horace Silver, Barry Harris, Duke Jordan, Kenny Drew, Walter Bishop, Elmo Hope, Tommy Flanagan, Bobby Timmons, Junior Mance, Ray Bryant, Horace Parlan, Roger Kellaway, Roland Hanna, Les McCann, Austrian Fritz Pauer, and a legion of other pianists, including representatives not just of neobop (where many of those mentioned here are also to be found) but of contemporary classicism, too.

Al Haig, Duke Jordan, and George Wallington played in combos on 52nd Street during the formative years of modern jazz. Lennie Tristano (who died in 1978) is the head of the previously mentioned Tristano school, which had such great importance at the time of the crystallization of cool jazz. He played long, sweeping, sensitive melodic lines (often almost in the sense of Bach's linearity) over complex harmonic structures. As Lynn Anderson put it, "He was the first piano player to spontaneously improvise extended chord stretches . . . . He was the first to improvise counterpoint. . . . Another of his innovations was his conception of bypassed resolution, so that harmony does not always move in the way you think it should." Tristano anticipated the harmonic freedom of free jazz by as much as ten years.

Tristano's influence reaches across many styles. Among those pianists who have paid allegiance to him are Don Friedman, Clare Fischer, and, above all, Bill Evans; among the younger ones are Alan Broadbent, Connie Crothers, and Ken Werner, all of whom show how alive the Tristano influence still is.

Russ Freeman and Claude Williamson are the main pianists of West Coast jazz. Hampton Hawes, who also lived on the West Coast (he died in 1977), does not fit in the West Coast bag. He had a strong blues and Charlie Parker feeling, which was very much rooted in his black heritage. Mose Allison (see also the section on vocalists) represents an intriguingly direct connection between old blues and folk songs and modern Bud Powell piano. Red Garland is a hard-bop pianist who sparkles with ideas. He became known through his work with the Miles Davis Quintet in the mid-fifties. After he left Davis, his place was taken first by Bill Evans (of whom more later) and then Wynton Kelly. Kelly, and even more so Junior Mance, Les McCann, and Bobby Timmons, belong to the funk- and gospel-inspired hard-bop pianists. Timmons's compositions "Moanin'," "This Here," and "Dat Dere," written in the late fifties when he was in Art Blakey's Messengers and Cannonball Adderley's quintet, became highly successful. In the early seventies, Les McCann combined his soul piano conception, which he had presented with great success in the fifties, with contemporary electric sounds.

Ray Bryant is a master of expressive, highly rhythmicized blues lines, into which he time and again incorporates powerful boogie elements. Tommy Flanagan, a musician of the Detroit hard-bop generation, has found a delicacy in the "hardness" of hard bop that few others have. His duo album *Our Delights,* recorded with Hank Jones in 1978, is one of the most beautiful duo piano records in all of jazz. Barry Harris has always been designated a "genius" by the musicians to come out of Detroit. He was the strongest and most individual personality behind the Detroit jazz scene and a highly respected teacher of many musicians. Horace Silver has extended the Powell heritage particularly convincingly—to a funk and soul-inspired playing style, coupled with an audacious sense of form and affable vitality, which has become a success formula for himself and his quintet.

Thelonious Monk, who died in 1982, also belongs among the hornlike pianists. He was one of the important musicians from the in group of the bop creators, but his influence was realized only from the second half of the fifties on. Monk, a pioneer of modern jazz from Minton's, played "*al fresco*–like," widely spaced, often barely indicated lines. In terms of the dissolution of the phrase as a unit and harmony as a functional system, he went further than almost anyone before free jazz. His great harmonic freedom was rooted in knowledge and in a strong and original creativity. Much of what leads to Ornette Coleman, John Coltrane, Eric Dolphy, and all the other avant-gardists of jazz was heard for the first time in his music—anchored in a strong blues feeling and saturated with a mocking, burlesquing sense of humor. Monk's own themes, with their rhythmic displacements and irregular structures, are among the most original themes in modern jazz. Monk plays "composer's" piano. His angular, bizarre improvisations are certainly spontaneously invented, but they don't consti-tute chains of association detached from the theme. They are in fact so closely linked with his compositions, pursuing them so "logically," that they themselves seem "composed." Monk has seldom been successfully imitated on the piano—probably because his piano style entails continuation of composition (by other means) rather than jazz virtuosity as such.

The first musicians to take up Monk's musical language, further develop-ing it in personal fashion, were Randy Weston, Herbie Nichols (d. 1963), and Mal Waldron. Weston, who besides Monk names Ellington as a model, lived in North Africa for years, where he also worked with Arab music. Nichols played in traditional and blues bands before he had an opportunity to present his bizarre and novel compositions. He was one of the true originals of jazz piano. Mal Waldron had great success in Japan during the seventies. His way of playing was referred to as "telegraph style": his phrases sounded like "long-long-short-long," like a mysterious Morse code. Waldron was the last accompanist for the great Billie Holiday. He developed an increasingly individual style in which "space" is very important.

As especially successful pianist was Bill Evans, who died in 1980. Evans was one of the few white musicians accepted within the narrower circles of hard bop; yet his style was completely different from that of other hard-bop pianists, much more sensitive and fragile. In today's terms, he was the first "modal" pianist. He might be designated a "Chopin of the modern jazz piano," with the eminent skill—without comparison in jazz—to make the piano sound in a way that places him (in terms of sound) in the vicinity of a pianist like Rubinstein. It is no wonder that such a unique and interesting combination of heterogeneous elements has been successful in commercial terms as well (in the Bill Evans Trio). Evans' work with other musicians—with Miles Davis or bass player Scott LaFaro, for instance—said German pianist Michael Naura, shows him to be "a musician who seems to register his environment in an almost spiritualistic manner. Only someone capable of total devotion can play a piano like that."

Bill Evans revolutionized the jazz piano trio, a genre that dates back to the twenties. To simplify somewhat, before the Evans Trio was formed in 1959, jazz piano trios played "two-dimensionally." On the one hand, the piano dominated and led; on the other hand, the rhythm section of bass and drums had the task of establishing the appropriate foundation. The Bill Evans Trio, however, was the first jazz piano group to play "three-dimensionally." Now each instrument in the trio could assume a leading role, which meant that bassist Scott LaFaro was by no means restricted to playing walking lines (with four quarter-notes to the bar). He also phrased lines that were melodically and rhythmically independent of his supporting function. Paul Motian similarly developed a way of playing that extended time-keeping (marking the beat) and opened up additional melodic possibilities for the drums.

It is illuminating that Evans has been a point of departure for a whole line of pianists. Don Friedman on the East Coast, with his sensitive and clear piano improvisations, and Clare Fischer on the West Coast, who also has made a name for himself as an arranger, were the first, later followed by such younger players as Fred Hersch, Italian-born Enrico Pieranunzi, and Michel Petrucciani, a particularly impressive French performer. Fred Hersch is an Evans-oriented pianist of great linear clarity. His contrapuntal playing, with its long arches of melody ignoring formal divisions, inspired many musicians in the eighties mainstream, including Charlie Haden and Jane Ira Bloom.

When Michel Petrucciani moved from Paris to America in 1981, only a few European jazz specialists knew about him. Then, at the age of eighteen, he played with saxophonist Charles Lloyd, and later with Lee Konitz and Jim Hall. Since then his concert appearances have been among the most moving occasions at all the big jazz festivals. When the dwarflike pianist, who has to be carried to the piano stool, starts playing, he develops Evans' vocabulary so vitally and with such joy in risk taking that you'd think he is presenting a "percussionized" Evans, expanding his precursor's sensitivity with fiery élan. It is fitting that Petrucciani—whose improvisations also reflect Art Tatum, Maurice Ravel, and Claude Debussy—should have started out as a drummer.

But seventies and eighties aestheticism would also have been inconceivable without the Evans touch. Chick Corea, Keith Jarrett, Paul Bley, Steve

Kuhn—"Evans is the father of them all," according to Michel Petrucciani. In the eighties there existed (as will be shown) a Bill Evans classicism.

Jaki Byard holds a special position. He emerged from the Mingus group, and on the one hand plays very modern, nearly free improvisations with abrasive sounds; but on the other hand, he is rooted in the stride piano of the twenties. As early as the fifties, he was a musician with that total grasp of the black tradition, which Mingus and Roland Kirk set up as an ideal.

There are a few musicians who do not fit into the system we have tried to use in classifying the pianists. They should be discussed now, before going on. As a member of Lionel Hampton's band, Milt Buckner (who died in 1977) created a "locked hands style"—with intertwined, parallel octave movements—that has a strong, stimulating effect. He sometimes sounded as if he were transferring a whole trumpet section in all its sweeping brilliance to the piano.

British-born George Shearing incorporated Buckner's style into the sound of his quintet. Combined with the bop lines of Bud Powell, he developed this style into a success formula, but he also has a Chopinesque sensitivity.

Characteristically, the most sensational success has been enjoyed by the two pianists who are least definable in terms of schools: Dave Brubeck and Erroll Garner. Brubeck has incorporated a wealth of European musical elements, from Bach to Darius Milhaud (with whom he studied), in his playing—elements that in his music seem to be enveloped within a certain romanticism. The question whether Brubeck "swings" has been debated for years. Critics and musicians have attacked him for "pounding" the piano. But Brubeck is a marvelously imaginative and individual improviser. He and his alto saxophonist Paul Desmond mutually inspired one another almost in the intuitive way of sleepwalkers. Brubeck often finds his way to moving climaxes. The way in which he builds to these climaxes over wide stretches and seemingly "shores up" to them is unique and original.

Since Fats Waller, there has been no pianist whose name was so synonymous with happiness and humor as that of Erroll Garner, who died in 1977. Garner is also comparable to Fats—and to Tatum—in his orchestral approach to the piano. He sovereignly commands the entire keyboard. *Concert by the Sea* is the title of one of his most successful records; the title is appropriate not only because this concert was recorded on the Pacific Coast, but also because Garner's piano cascades bring to mind the roar of the sea. Garner was a player of fascinating relaxation. When he played, the listener sometimes felt that the beat had been delayed too long, but when it came, you knew it fell just where it belonged. Also masterful were Garner's introductions, which—often with cadenzas, often also with humorous intimations—seemed to delay the start of the theme and the beat further and further. Garner's worldwide audiences applauded enthusiastically when pianist and audience finally arrived "back home" again, in the well-known melody and the even better-known "Garner beat," with its even "trotting" quarter-note chords in the left hand.

Garner was so singular and original that only two pianists are really related to him: Ellis Larkins and Ahmad Jamal. Larkins played some of the most beautiful piano accompaniments in jazz history, on a record of Ella Fitzgerald singing Gershwin. The younger Jamal occupies a curious position, evaluated in sharply contrasting fashion by musicians and critics. While most of the latter hardly consider him more than a gifted cocktail pianist, many musicians—primarily Miles Davis—have called him a towering "genius." Jamal's timing and combination of embellishment and economy are masterly. Gunther Schuller believes that Miles's high regard for Jamal is mainly due to the fact that the Davis of the fifties adopted certain ways of embellishing and, to a certain degree, his sophisticated simplicity from Jamal, and that Miles' great success began with this adoption.

The next step in the development was taken by Cecil Taylor, in a manner that had not been thought possible by even the most farsighted critics. In his clusters, racing across the entire keyboard of the piano, swings the world of Bartók's "Mikrokosmos." Martin Williams claims that Taylor transforms modern concert music into the idiom and technique of jazz as surely as Jelly Roll Morton transformed John Philip Sousa's marches.

Taylor himself has pointed out that he feels more at home in his own black tradition—above all, in Duke Ellington—than in European music. If you listen to him carefully, you can detect in his playing dozens of elements from the history of black piano music: blues cadenzas and bop phrases and boogie basses, but all of them as if they were encoded in clusters, only intimated, estranged, abstract, and—as soon as they are sounded—transformed into the next element in the gushing stream of idea after idea. His intensity consists not just of racing across the keyboard; it is fed by, as he put it, "the magical lifting of one's spirits to a state of trance. . . . It has to do with religious forces"—in the sense of the African tradition.

There are musicians who have placed Taylor's influence above that of Ornette Coleman. In any case we must remember that Taylor was already introduced at the 1957 Newport Festival, after he had learned his trade in the groups of Swing musicians like Hot Lips Page, Johnny Hodges, and Lawrence Brown, and thus chronologically stands before Coleman. The actual, overwhelming aspect of Taylor's improvisations lies in the physical power with which he plays. German pianist Alexander von Schlippenbach, strongly influenced by Taylor, has pointed out that any other pianist would be capable of generating such burning and bursting intensity for only a few minutes, and that it is incredible that Taylor is able to keep up such playing for an entire evening in long concerts or club appearances.

Cecil Taylor is the outstanding pianist in free jazz, but there are—independently of him or coming from him—an abundance of other pianistic possibilities in this field. First the American musicians. Important free-jazz pianists (who often developed in other directions) are Paul Bley, Carla Bley, Ran Blake, John Fischer, Sun Ra (famous mainly as the leader of his free big band), Dave Burrell, Bobby Few, Borah Bergman, Marilyn Crispell; and then, already as a bridge to neoclassicism, Muhal Richard Abrams, Don Pullen, Anthony Davis, Amina Claudine Myers, and Geri Allen. We can discuss only a few of these pianists in detail.

In the sixties, Paul Bley played free jazz with humor and affability. Later he became an aesthete whose still, fragile lines seem to freeze in time like ice crystals. Ran Blake and Carla Bley are especially sensitive players. Ran, who has been influenced by Thelonious Monk, is a master of estranging standard tunes by the great writers of American popular music. He tears, shreds, and abstracts these tunes, transplanting them to a new musical world diametrically opposed to their original world (which certainly involves a sociocritical process). Carla Bley (more about her in the big-bands chapter) became known mainly as a player of her own tender, delicate compositions, perhaps the most original jazz compositions this side of Thelonious Monk. "Escalator Over the Hill," the "chronotransduction" Carla created with writer Paul Haines, is the first successful piece of postmodern jazz, which matured as early as 1971 to that colorful polystylism and category-transcending eclecticism that was to become a matter of course only ten years later in the eighties. The linguistic creation "chronotransduction" illuminates the point: time and space are being transcended in a musical and poetic sense.

Borah Bergman endowed free jazz piano with lightness and elasticity. He possesses, as one critic said, "increased power and strength in his left hand." Often his left-hand lines sound as if they were played with both hands. Bergman thus attains total equality between the two hands. The most interesting and original advancement of the Cecil Taylor line in the eighties came, however, from a woman: Marilyn Crispell. Crispell, who first worked with Anthony Braxton's group and studied at Karl Berger's Woodstock Creative Music Studio, unites Taylor's enormous energy with Coltrane's spirituality. Like Taylor she came from classical concert music to jazz, and like Taylor she also studied at the New England Conservatory in Boston. But Crispell plays more lyrically, pointillistically. She breaks up Taylor's blocklike clusters and momentum into free, highly intense contrapuntalism, spiritually rather than materially inspired by baroque music, and Bach in particular. Crispell causes energy-charged particles of ideas to collide within fractions of seconds, and yet she does so with the sovereign and refined assurance of a postfree musician who has found the way from "controlled chaos" to more formally unified structures.

Muhal Richard Abrams is the "chief" (although he would object to that term) of the frequently mentioned AACM: one of the first pianists who deliberately moved on from free jazz to neoclassicism, incorporating the entire black tradition from ragtime and boogie onward into free playing. Amina Claudine Myers, who is also linked with the AACM, plays free music out of the ancient tradition of blues and spirituals. The most vital and wildest pianist among the neoclassicists is, however, Don Pullen, who made his name in a quartet with tenor saxophonist George Adams. Pullen has uniquely melodized cluster playing and made it tonal. He phrases impulsively raw clusters with his right hand and yet embeds them in clear, harmonically functional tonal chords simultaneously played with the left hand. Independently of Taylor he has developed an entirely individual cluster technique. Unlike Taylor he doesn't *strike* such clusters, but rather uses the knuckles and side of his hand in sweeping across the keys, producing glissandolike, quasi-melodic streams of sound perpetuating the rawness and directness of the blues. *Evidence of Things Unseen* (recorded in 1983) is perhaps the most successful piano solo album produced in the eighties.

Anthony Davis is a cool, aware player, who was also influenced by romantic and classical music (particularly chamber music) that he heard in the parental home. He is the most distinctive musician in a generation that discovered, within the realm of "free" jazz, the importance of composition for their playing. "I would like everything I play to be linked with what went before and what will come afterwards," he told Francis Davis, the U.S. critic. "Even when I'm improvising freely, I'm still thinking compositionaliy. . . . It amounts to the same thing."

Michele Rosewoman sensitively brought the percussiveness of Afro-Cuban rhythms, dating back to the ancient rituals of Yoruba culture, into neoclassical piano playing. Geri Allen from Detroit has attained particular pianistic originality in pursuing the postmodern principle of mixing styles. Equally at home in the neoclassicism of James Newton and Oliver Lake or Steve Coleman's free funk, Allen mainly comes from Cecil Taylor and Thelonious Monk, her long mysterious tone poems, possessing the droll magic of distant fairy-tale worlds, also provide exemplary illustration of multilayered jazz piano playing. They give voice to the romanticism of Chick Corea (still to be introduced), the percussiveness of African balafone music, Count Basie's art of playing with pauses, and Ellington's feeling for tonal color. Above all, Allen plays the most complex bass figures and ostinatos in contemporary jazz piano—full of tricky changes of rhythm and effective displacements and dissonances, accompanied by a strong feeling for the African roots of black music. Her piano often sounds like a "mbira with 88 keys," like a giant westernized African thumb piano.

But Taylor's message has also fallen on fruitful soil in Europe and Asia. There the important free pianists include Yosuke Yamashita and Aki Takese from Japan; Englishman Keith Tippett; Dutch-born Misha Mengelberg; Belgian Fred van Hove; Germans Alexander von Schlippenbach, Bernd Koeppen, and Ulrich Gumpert; Swiss-born Irène Schweizer; Russians Vyacheslav Ganelin (immigrated to Israel in 1987) and Sergey Kuryokhin; and Giorgio Gaslini from Italy. Here too only a few musicians can be mentioned.

U.S. critics have accused Yosuke Yamashita of imitating Cecil Taylor, but he derives his ritualistic power and intensity (reminiscent of Taylor) from the Japanese rather than the American tradition, drawing on a centuries-old culture of fervency. Aki Takase merges filigrain style with a high degree of esprit and humor. At the end of the eighties her duo appearances with Portuguese singer Maria Joao constituted a highpoint at the important European jazz festivals. Keith Tippett plays a free jazz much influenced by ethnic music where ostinato patterns and meditative structures, magical in their impact, are of considerable importance. His Centipede orchestra, bringing together fifty-one musicians from rock and jazz who recorded the *Septober Energy* album in 1971, was one of the crucial (and yet too little appreciated) seventies jazz groups extending beyond established frontiers. Misha Mengelberg, who attracted attention as head of the Instant Composers' Pool, is inspired by Thelonious Monk and Herbie Nichols. He plays free jazz full of idiosyncratic, eccentric humor. His duo with drummer Han Bennink, reflecting the spontaneous happenings of fluxus art, is among the longest lasting of European free-jazz combos. Alexander von Schlippenbach heads the Globe Unity Orchestra, the first and longest lasting European free-jazz orchestra (established in 1966), which has held together through the eighties. Musicologist Ekkehard Jost calls Schlippenbach's sounds "rasping structures": highly energetic and unusually dense sounds, concentrating on color and rhythm. Irène Schweizer is at the communicative, tranquil center of many women's ensembles in jazz such as the Feminist Improvising Group, but her astonishing richness of interaction also acts as a sovereign focus for performances with male musicians. Her phrasing is characterized by a high degree of percussiveness. Vyacheslav Ganelin was from 1971 until its dissolution in 1989 the main musical and dramatic force behind the Ganelin Trio, which developed a completely individual form of free interaction in the Soviet Union. This group cultivated an often parodistic, stylistic openness consciously directed against all of free jazz's dogmas, pursuing an ironical dialectic rooted in Soviet tradition.

In any case, jazz piano playing is becoming more and more individualized—not only on the free side of Cecil Taylor but also among nonfree players. Among the latter there are also a number of pianists who defy categorization. Andrew Hill, originally from Haiti, has infused African elements from his Caribbean homeland into modern piano compositions and improvisations. "Really listen to the avant-garde, and you can hear African rhythms. You hear the roots of jazz," he said. The fact that the African, black nature of jazz not only is not being suppressed as the music's development continues, but on the contrary gains increasingly concentrated and valid prominence as the black music of America progressively throws off the shackles of European musical laws, becomes impressively clear in musicians like Hill—and also in Muhal Richard Abrams, Don Pullen, Geri Allen, and others.

Even more direct in his relationship to Africa is Dollar Brand, a musician from Capetown, South Africa. Pianistically, his playing may be not much more than self-sufficient, but the spiritual strength of the emotions he gets across is amazing. Dollar's father belonged to the Basuto tribe, his mother to the Bushman tribe. Brand fuses this heritage with a deep knowledge of Ellington and Monk, but also with the songs and chorales of the Dutch and Low German Boers who colonized his South African homeland.

In 1983, Herbie Hancock topped the international hit parades with "Rockit," with rhythm tracks devised by bassist Bill Laswell and keyboardist Michael Beinhorn. That was not only the greatest instrumental hit in eighties pop music but also considerably influenced the rise of hip-hop. And yet Hancock, despite his successes in funk and pop, has always remained a jazz man.

Herbie Hancock has progressively turned to "commercial funk" music— hardly jazz anymore—yet the jazz world keeps considering him one of its own, not only because his Blue Note records *Empyrean Isles* and *Maiden Voyage* from the sixties are among the few convincing tone poems jazz has brought forth, aside from Duke Ellington. They are "tone paintings of the sea" comparable to Debussy's "La Mer" in concert music. Hancock is one of the important musicians who became known through their work in the Miles Davis Quintet in the sixties. His own sextet (1971–73) presented one of the most interesting and musically most demanding solutions to the entire problem posed by electronics in jazz. The fact that Hancock didn't lose his jazz feeling even after he changed over to commercial funk became apparent with the group V.S.O.P. that he led for a few concert tours during the second half of the seventies (with Freddie Hubbard, Wayne Shorter, Tony Williams, and Ron Carter—all on acoustic instruments). And it became even more apparent when he appeared with Chick Corea on two grand pianos—a great, worldwide concert event that also appealed to those who normally would not have attended such a concert but were lured by the names Hancock and Corea, well known from their commercial and electric recordings. Since then, Hancock switches between the "acoustic" and "electric" camps, successful as few others are—a musician who has developed his own unmistakable style in both spheres. In 1986, he won an Oscar for his film score in Bertrand Tavernier's 'Round Midnight.

Chick Corea is another musician from the Miles Davis circle. Interestingly enough, before getting into fusion music he played free jazz. At the start of the seventies he headed Return to Forever, one of the groups in which jazz-rock attained a never-to-be-repeated peak scarcely before the style had got going. Corea is an affable musician with a fondness for childlike fairy-tale moods. He knows Bartók, loves Latin American and Spanish music, and is an outstanding composer. Critics have compared his charming tunes with famous piano pieces of the nineteenth century (with Schumann and Mendelssohn) but have failed to notice the imminent, highly sensitized jazz tension with which Chick Corea fills his romanticism. Far from being an unusual phenomenon today, this "filling" of romanticism with modern tension became very contemporary. It can also be found in the work of other important pianists of the seventies and eighties—for example in Keith Jarrett, Richie Beirach, Stu Goldberg, Art Lande, Denny Zeitlin, Warren Bernhard, Walter Norris, Bob Degen, Ken Werner, Norwegian Bobo Stenson, Dutchman Jasper van't Hof, Makoto Ozone from Japan, German Wolfgang Dauner, Briton John Taylor, and, years before this trend began, Steve Kuhn. The first player who filled romanticism with modern tension was Bill Evans. Beirach's music often has the lovely simplicity of folk songs; his record company has presented him mainly with such aestheticized music. But he is also a dynamically powerful player of more far-reaching piano possibilities. That, too, is often a part of romanticism: an attitude of moderation and often even self-sufficiency.

Romanticism without moderation is the main characteristic of the most successful pianist of this kind and the most successful jazz pianist of the seventies: Keith Jarrett. He is a "pianistic totalizer" whose fingers—and, above all, head and heart—command almost everything ever played on a piano. His solo concerts are musical voyages not only through several centuries of piano history, but also through many landscapes of an ever more complex human psyche.

After giving up one-man appearances for a year and a half in order to distinguish himself as an interpreter of classical piano music (from Mozart by way of Bartók to Bach), Jarrett returned to solo jazz in 1985. "I came to know the world of classical musicians and saw almost nothing but frustration among those people—the higher their ranking, the more cultivated the frustration."

Jarrett has the ability to make his piano "sing," to such an extent that his playing gains a hymnlike and almost sacral quality. It was Coltrane who introduced hymnlike elements into jazz, but Jarrett is unrivaled in cultivating and transposing this dimension into metaphysical realms. His secret lies less in the melodies and harmonies he plays than in the quality of his playing. This often spiritual quality is linked with the fact that not since Bill Evans has there been another pianist with such a differentiated touch, an ability to "give life" to the notes, ranging—as critic Peter Rüdi says—across the entire spectrum: "from harp-like arpeggios barely floating above silence to screaming, stinging fandango lines drawn with finger-breaking expressiveness." That's why Jarrett followers such as George Winston and Liz Story probably seem dreary and banal—they only imitate the surface without approaching the quality, which also involves "touch." On the other hand, both Jarrett's public appearances and his music possess something of the Wagnerian mannerisms of certain late-romantic artists who seem to breed an atmosphere of devotion by admiring themselves.

All of the pianists in this "romantic group" are part of the already mentioned Bill Evans classicism, which developed out of the rediscovery of tonality and beat in the seventies and eighties. That is documented not only in the playing of such younger pianists as Michel Petrucciani and Fred Hersch but also in many jazz groups themselves. During the eighties more and more piano trios built on the achievements of the Bill Evans Trio. Especially successful was the Keith Jarrett Trio, which offered unusually fresh and melodically mature interpretations of standards, the great timeless melodies of American popular music. A similarly homogeneous and contemporary continuation of Evans' concept came from Chick Corea and his Akoustic Band.

Behind all these styles and streams, in fact feeding them all, flows the mainstream (in the sense of that main development line of jazz history that leads from bebop via Coltrane to contemporary music): Here, McCoy Tyner is the towering figure, in the seventies the number one pianist in most jazz polls of the world. He is the essence of jazz in the most powerful, swinging sense of that word. "McCoy Tyner plays piano like a roaring lion," said critic Bill Cole.

Tyner became known in the early sixties as the pianist of the classic John Coltrane Quartet. In the meantime (we have talked about it), the whole scene—jazz, jazz-rock, fusion, pop—has become unthinkable without Coltrane. And yet, today McCoy Tyner represents the Coltrane tradition more validly than any other musician. In fact, Tyner *is* that tradition: quietly serving, filled with seriousness and religiousity.

The first Tyner album voted "Record of the Year" (more would follow) was *Sahara* in 1972. In connection with it, McCoy quoted the Arabian historian Ibn Khaldoun: "This desert is so long it can take a lifetime to go from one end to the other, and a childhood to cross at its narrowest point." This quote is characteristic, because for McCoy Tyner, all of music is "a journey of the soul into new, uncharted territory." He said, "I try to listen to music from many different countries: Africa, India, from the Arabic world, European classical music. . . . All kinds of music are interconnected."

It is an enigma to other pianists how McCoy Tyner manages to get so much power out of the piano. Cecil Taylor's piano is similarly powerful, but he plays free music, where it is easier to reach that kind of energy level. Other pianists may pound the piano keys as hard as they can, and they would sound only half as powerful as McCoy. "You've got to become one with your instrument," he explained. "Like, you start learning an instrument—and at first the piano is nothing but an instrument. But after a while it becomes an extension of yourself, and you and your instrument become one."

It must be this "union" with his instrument that has enabled McCoy Tyner to find his own characteristic sound on the piano—very much in line with the great jazz horn players. Naturally, this is much more difficult on the piano than on a horn. McCoy is one of the few piano players who have done this successfully, which, he says, is one of the reasons why he does not use electric instruments: "Electric music is bad for your soul."

Many pianists are influenced, directly or indirectly, by Tyner: Hal Galper, John Hicks, Hilton Ruiz, Jorge Dalto, Michel Camilo, Henry Butler, JoAnne Brackeen, and from Germany, Joachim Kühn, the European pianist who has incorporated McCoy Tyner's style most convincingly.

Among these, JoAnne Brackeen has become especially successful. *Mythical Magic* is the title of one of her records—which is exactly what one feels when listening to her music: a ritual of mythical-magical power. Brackeen played with Art Blakey and Stan Getz and later with Joe Henderson prior to appearing in solo performances and with her own groups. She studied with Lennie Tristano—one of the many students in whom this great jazz teacher brought out their own identity. (Said Lennie, "Teaching is an art—as much as playing.")

JoAnne Brackeen was the first person to create a new image of the woman in jazz: the woman as a jazz musician—simply a jazz musician, without asking whether this musician is a man or a woman—and yet still a woman who will not let herself be exploited by men and by a male-dominated society, or even by the male-chauvinist music business; the woman and jazz musician who does not feel the need to escape from the implications of her situation into glamor or into flirting with the supposedly inescapable female inferiority in the man's world of jazz, or (as was somewhat the case with Mary Lou Williams) into religious faith. All this has never existed so purely, so totally, and so convincingly as with JoAnne Brackeen. She is the first representative of a new type of female jazz musician, who does not merely talk about emancipation but *is* emancipated.

Of course, the spirit of Coltrane and Tyner can be also felt, directly or filtered, among those piano players who are affiliated with contemporary neobop and eighties classicism. Onajee Allen Gumbs, Kenny Barron, George Cables, Mickey Tucker, Jim McNeeley, and Mark Soskin, and then—leading to the realm of classicism—Mulgrew Miller, James Williams, Kenny Kirkland, Jason Rebello, Benny Green, David Kikoski, Renee Rosnes, Kirk Lightsey, Marcus Roberts, and Larry Willis—each with his personal approach and, of course, influenced not only by McCoy but by other musicians, too. This is the largest stylistic grouping of contemporary pianists, particularly since they are directly related to those players whom we have mentioned as members of Bud Powell's school.

Classicist pianists, however, make the Powell legacy more dynamic by subjecting it to modern styles of piano playing (McCoy Tyner, Herbie Hancock, Bill Evans) and individualizing it by way of a large number of mixed forms. Mulgrew Miller, who played with Art Blakey and Tony Williams, is especially successful at this bop-oriented "style mixing." Miller emotionalizes the classicist jazz piano with his vital attack and a balanced sense of musical climaxes: sparkling, agile, impressive lines full of unexpected turns. Kenny Kirkland, who made a name for himself in Wynton Marsalis' quintet, produces a clear, gentle, supple sound brilliantly contrasting with his playing's vehemently dynamic possibilities of intensification. Marcus Roberts unites elegant contemporary bop-oriented lines with the complex harmonic foundations of Duke Ellington and Thelonious Monk.

A large number of European players also belong in this context of progressive contemporary bop—in fact, so many that we can mention only three pronounced individualists here: Britons Stan Tracey; as a real virtuoso, Gordon Beck; and the Spaniard (or as he would call himself: Catalonian) Tete Montoliu. Montoliu once said, "Basically we Catalonians are all black." And that's the way he plays—perhaps the "blackest" of the European pianists, and yet rooted in the tradition of his native Catalonia, whose folk songs he has given moving interpretations. Tracey has occasionally been called a "British Thelonious Monk," but he is more than those words can express. His humor is typically British, full of understatement and intimations and often of sarcasm, too.

Organ, Keyboards, Synthesizer

The organ: Originally, it was the dream of exalted church music, resounding in hallowed cathedrals, the "royal instrument" of the European tradition (Ligeti: "the largest prosthesis in the world").

The realization of this dream was the starting point of the organ in jazz. It began with Fats Waller.

John S. Wilson wrote, "Like the inevitable clown who wants to play Hamlet [Fats] had a consuming desire to bring to the public his love of classical music and of the organ." And Waller himself, in reference to a Chicago music critic who had written that "the organ is the favorite instrument of Fats' heart, and the piano only of his stomach," said, "Well, I really love the organ. . . . I have one at home and a great many of my compositions originated there."

To be sure, the organ was also the instrument of escape for Fats Waller: It symbolized a world—a distant, unattainable world—in which the artist is accepted solely on the basis of his musical abilities, without racial or social prejudice and also without regard for his talents as showman and entertainer. If one hears the organ records made by Fats Waller—such as his famous version of the spiritual "Sometimes I Feel Like a Motherless Child"—one encounters an element of sentimentality that makes it clear that Waller had only a fuzzy notion of the world into which he wanted to escape.

The instrument that Fats Waller truly loved was the great church organ of the European tradition, the pipe organ. Once, in Paris, he had an opportunity to play the organ in the cathedral of Notre Dame. It was, as he put it, "one of the greatest moments in my life."

Fats Waller passed his love for the organ on to his best-known pupil—Count Basie, whose organ playing is (almost) as light and spare as his piano style. Basie, however, played the electric organ because it had become obvious in the meantime that the pipe organ can be used in jazz only with great difficulty. The pipes sound too slowly because the distance between the console and the pipes is too long and mechanically involved. That's why it is very hard to swing on a pipe organ. "On a normal pipe organ," Clare Fischer said, "the lag is about half a beat behind, which plays hell with your mind when you're trying to play rhythmic music. It makes it impossible to play jazz."

It was Fischer who in 1975 made probably the most swinging (and musically most interesting) pipe organ recordings, on a small "chamber organ," where the distances the air column has to travel are relatively short. Among the Europeans, Belgian Fred van Hove has developed his own style of playing (free) jazz on a pipe organ, with gigantic sound columns and imposing clusters. The rich free duets recorded by Hans Günther Wauer, cathedral cantor at Merseburg, Germany, and drummer Günther "Baby" Sommer have also been much praised.

Meanwhile, and in a general sense, the term *organ* in jazz refers to the electric organ, in any of the many different types available on the market.

From Count Basie and Fats Waller many organists have been inspired to use the instrument for a kind of rhythm and blues. Wild Bill Davis and Milt Buckner were the first. In America's black neighborhoods the organ is a particularly popular instrument together with guitar or tenor saxophone (in both cases with drums but without bass, since the bass lines can be played with the organist's feet or on the instrument's bass register). Among the organists who still play such a variant of rhythm and blues—twenty years after Wild Bill Davis and Milt Buckner while incorporating much that has happened, musically and stylistically, since then—are Jack McDuff, Johnny Hammond, Don Patterson, Lou Bennett, Richard "Groove" Holmes, Lonnie Smith, Jimmy McGriff, Charles Earland, and many others. Shirley Scott has brought some of the relaxation and amiability of Erroll Garner to this way of playing. Since Ray Charles (who also plays organ) became successful, not only the blues, but also the soul and gospel element of the black churches has become significant for practically dozens of organ players.

A host of rock organists have taken over the traditions of rhythm and blues and of gospel music—among others, Stevie Winwood (in his early phase), Al Kooper, and the black, particularly soul-oriented musicians Billy Preston and Booker T. Jones.

Musicians like Richard "Groove" Holmes, Jimmy McGriff, Charles Earland, Booker T., Billy Preston, and many others bring to mind that the technique of playing the Hammond organ was already well developed in the gospel churches when it was only in its infancy in jazz. It is important to note that for both black and white audiences, the organ implies a totally different musical background for each. For both, the organ may come from church. But "church" for black listeners is associated with the cooking sounds of the gospel churches, while white listeners might have Johann Sebastian Bach in mind.

We have gone somewhat ahead in time to clarify the position of the blues and soul tradition in jazz organ playing. Before the road was free to travel by all the organists coming after Wild Bill Davis and Milt Buckner, Jimmy Smith had first to appear on the scene. Smith did for the organ what Charlie Christian had achieved for the guitar; he emancipated it. Only through him did the organ gain equal footing with the other instruments in jazz. Probably his most important record, made in 1956, is an improvisation on Dizzy Gillespie's "The Champ." Nobody had accomplished this before: achieving effects on the organ reminiscent of a big band—in this case of the most exciting Dizzy Gillespie big band of the late forties—by employing a high, overpowering dynamic range built on wide, steadily rising arcs of sound.

Smith can also be compared to Christian because he was the first consciously to play the organ like an electronic instrument, similar to Christian's transition from acoustic to electric guitar. Certainly, Wild Bill Davis, Milt Buckner, and others played Hammond organ before Jimmy Smith. But they played it more like a piano with an electric organ sound. It was left to Smith to realize that the electric organ is an independent, new instrument that has only the keyboard in common with the piano or the conventional organ. Indeed, the realization that electronics do not simply amplify an instrument but rather make of it something new, took a long time to be generally accepted. Electronics, we emphasize again, meant a revolution—for organs, guitars, violins, bass, and other instruments.

During the sixties and seventies, Smith made many commercial pop-jazz recordings of doubtful value. But that does not detract from his historic achievement: He made the organ a vehicle for jazz improvisations of the highest artistic quality.

Smith came on the scene in 1956. Nine years later came the next step in the development of the organ, through Khalid Yasin (at that time still known as Larry Young). Yasin, who died in 1979, played the organ in the spirit of John Coltrane. It is illuminating that he became well known at the moment when Smith, through continuous repetition of blues and soul clichés, more and more seemed to have become a roaring "Frankenstein of Hammond Castle." Understandably, organists and audiences initially became enraptured with the instrument's immense range of dynamics, its fortissimo possibilities. Yasin discovered the potential of the organ played pianissimo.

Yasin belongs to the generation of musicians that carried the Coltrane legacy into advanced rock. It is regrettable that he never got to enjoy great commercial success. But his influence is omnipresent in the organists of modern jazz and rock. It is especially notable in the two British players Brian Auger (who, like Yasin, also made recordings with Tony Williams) and Mike Ratledge (of the group Soft Machine).

In Europe, Frenchman Eddie Louiss (whose family comes from Martinique) has developed the Coltrane influence into an individual, hymnlike, singing, triumphant style, with some Caribbean-Creole overtones. Interesting organ sounds have also been created during the seventies and eighties by musicians like Carla Bley, Amina C. Myers, Clare Fischer, Joey DeFrancesco, Cuban Chucho Valdez (from the Irakere group), English-born John Taylor, Wojciech Karolak from Poland, Germany's Barbara Dennerlein, and, especially originally, Arturo O'Farrill. But in general it must be said that organ playing in jazz has been stagnating since Khalid Yasin. This is so mainly because since the turn of the sixties, a new group of musicians has developed who do play the organ but whom we hesitate to call organists in the sense of the term as used so far in this section. For them, the organ is one instrument among several others: acoustic and electric piano, synthesizer, clavinet, and such accessories as wah-wah pedal, fuzz, vibrator, Echoplex and Echolette, phase shifter, ring modulator, etc. These musicians are referred to as "keyboard artists." And indeed, the only thing all the instruments they play actually have in common is the keyboards.

Joe Zawinul, a prototype of these new keyboard players, sits at the center of half a dozen different instruments, like an astronaut in the cockpit of his spaceship, surrounded by a mass of electronics that can hardly be increased. Almost ironically, the good old sound of the acoustic piano is also there, produced by a Yamaha *electric(!)* grand piano.

Joe Zawinul's importance for synthesizer playing in jazz can hardly be overemphasized since he led the way in completely transcending the instrument's mechanical, technical, and electronic rigidities. Zawinul "humanizes" the synthesizer. Of all synthesizer players he produces the most organic sounds, full of warm, mellow, rich colors.

Before Zawinul, Paul Bley, Richard Teitelbaum, Sun Ra, and Wolfgang Dauner wrested unfamiliar tonal colors and sounds from the synthesizer within sixties free jazz—more exciting and stimulating than much that followed in jazz-rock and fusion. And yet it certainly wasn't just chance that almost none of the many sounds they discovered were sufficiently satisfying to retain their interest for any length of time. The synthesizer thus gained a tendency toward tonal arbitrariness. Revealingly, all those musicians, except for Teitelbaum, time and again changed over to the piano. Among the early jazz synthesizer players, working electronically in the tonal sphere, were saxophonist Oliver Nelson and Dick Hyman. Viewed from today, their somewhat timid presentations suffered from a striking tonal poverty. Only Joe Zawinul, surmounting the two extremes of synthesizer playing—tonal arbitrariness and tonal poverty—gave the instrument an autonomous and fully matured sound aura. That's why Zawinul is as important for jazz synthesizer playing as Jimmy Smith is for the organ. His preeminence is confirmed by the fact that he cannot be assigned to either of the two basic ways of playing the instrument (soon to be discussed here) but is equally influential in both. Later, after the breakup of Weather Report in 1985, Zawinul succumbed in his unaccompanied solo appearances to a tendency toward striving for effects.

Since the first generation of synthesizers could only be played monophonically, performers phrased vehemently as soloists, creating long digressive phrases in the same way as guitarists link long chains of single notes. Among the soloists who gained an international reputation for this style are the following keyboardists (who naturally mastered other ways of playing, and later developed in different directions): Chick Corea, Jan Hammer, George Duke, Barry Miles, Mike Mandel, Patrice Rushen, Bob James, Richard Tee, Dave Grusin, Joe Sample; and among the younger generation, Wladislaw Sendecki from Poland, Brazilian Eliane Elias, Cuban-born Gonzalo Rubalcaba, Denmark's Kenneth Knudson, and Django Bates from England.

Two keyboardists, Chick Corea and Jan Hammer, have been particularly successful in the sphere of solo synthesizer playing. Corea has cultivated the rich, warm tonal colors of the "Minimoog" in his fine-spun, imaginative interweavings of line. Among the great paradoxes of keyboard development is Corea's utilization in the eighties of sinfully expensive, highly refined digital equipment for "imitating" that "cheap," simple Minimoog analog sound that he unmistakably made his own at the start of the seventies. "Advances in keyboard technology," said a well-known keyboardist, "don't guarantee an improvement in actual sound quality. Many older analog synthesizers have characteristic sounds and personalities unmatched by today's digital dream machines."

Jan Hammer, who became known through the Mahavishnu Orchestra, played "the best jazz-rock guitar" (Wolfgang Dauner) on the Minimoog in the first half of the seventies, with distortions *à la* Jimi Hendrix. In the keyboard realm Hammer is the real master of pitch bending (achieved through manipulating a wheel or stick alongside the keyboard), which permits smaller and more subtle tonal nuances than the half tones usually available on a keyboard. Hammer later commercialized and trivialized his music.

Herbie Hancock stands apart from this "soloistic group." He mainly made his name in jazz-rock as a soloist on the electric piano and clavinet while remaining strikingly restrained on the synthesizer. Nevertheless, Hancock merits prominence among the pioneers of synthesizer playing. He produced the most refined rhythmic superimpositions and intermeshings of electronic sound. The intensity of sound mixtures and the funkiness his sextet attained between 1971 and 1973 still serve as a model even today.

Herbie Hancock is an inventor of playing textures on keyboards. Toward the end of the seventies, solo playing became hackneyed. Musicians regarded endless synthesizer lines as being superficial and egomaniacal. More and more keyboardists, helped by the emergence of polyphonic synthesizers, all of a sudden turned to inventing refined sound textures, patterns, and layerings. Solo playing wasn't, of course, completely re-nounced but clearly moved into the background. The important players of such textures, alongside Herbie Hancock and naturally Joe Zawinul, are Wayne Horvitz, Lyle Mays, Geri Allen, Adam Holzman, John Irving III, Kenny Kirkland, Mitchell Forman, Clyde Criner, Harold Budd, German-born Rainer Brüninghaus, and, from Britain, John Surman, John Taylor, and Brian Eno. Wayne Horvitz most strikingly fragments and distances the cool, metallic, glasslike, and dark sounds characteristic of digital synthesizers such as the highly popular Yamaha DX7. Compared with the horrendously expensive technology employed by other keyboard greats, he uses cheap and simple equipment—and yet produces more exciting and more stimulating sounds than people employing keyboard "altars" costing hundreds of thousands of dollars.

Lyle Mays, who is deeply rooted in jazz tradition, plays particularly vividly: pastellike, delicately dense superimpositions of chords and sounds permeated with unsentimental romanticism and melancholy, like a sensitive electronic pendant to Bill Evans' piano music. Mays can also develop highly contrapuntal drama, and he played a great part in the sound of Pat Metheny's music. He has played with Metheny since 1976, and it's scarcely possible to distinguish which elements in the Metheney Band come from Mays and which from the guitarist. The fact that Mays' own projects have been less convincing demonstrates the quality and inwardness of this "musical symbiosis." John Surman is a specialist in "sequencing"—the development of complex patterns, repeated as often as wished, which he likes to overlay with long saxophone improvisations. Rainer Brüninghaus has impressively transposed the repetitive patterns of Balinese gamelan and minimal music into synthesizer playing.

The wave of keyboard artists that has been inundating the scene since the early seventies has produced surprisingly few individualists. Musicians with a sound unmistakably their own can be counted on two hands.

And yet, the electronic keyboard instruments are indispensable for today's jazz, as we have shown with what we said about electronics in the chapter about jazz styles. We live in an electronic world, which implies electronic sounds, which in turn imply electronic keyboards. It also is a phenomenon of volume; electronic instruments can be heard better because they are easier to amplify and to control. In a way, the sound of the electric piano is to that of its acoustic sister instrument what the vibraphone is to the marimba; it is clearer, more sparkling, more precise—i.e., more percussive. That is certainly one of the main reasons why the electric piano made its breakthrough so swiftly.

Carla Bley has pointed out that the lack of individualism has to do not only with the instruments, but also with the record industry: "There is such a trend toward superclean sound in the industry that all these things will become depersonalized. They are trying to get rid of personalities, to make everyone sound like a million other people. Maybe that's so people can be replaced by other people and nobody will have the industry over a barrel."

This situation is even more paradoxical when you consider that the synthesizer offers millions of different sounds, making it the perfect tool for personal expression. "Keyboard players are confronted with almost too many options when it comes to formulating an identifiable sound," said Adam Holzman. The wealth of variety that the synthesizer offers is also its most crucial problem: It is too easily used for pure effects, cheap sound imitations and incongruous playing around with the sound. "There are a number of keyboard synthesizer players who don't have a lot of technical means but have these programs," said John McLaughlin. "And today's factory programs are becoming so complex and interesting, software development is snowballing, but these people with slight means are able to get a good sound and get by. From the playing point of view, we have to distinguish the difference. It's one thing to play sounds, and it's another to play and *play.*" It is the dialectic of the great instruments in the history of music that they offer their players resistance. Personalities grow with the resistances they meet and deal with. And exactly because the electronic instruments make many things so easy—because they initially level out resistance— individuality is difficult to achieve on them.

It fits into this picture that keyboard artists mainly play fusion music, in other words a kind of music primarily produced from a commercial point of view. This music is not only supposed to be successful as fast as possible; most of it is also supposed to be off the market again soon in order to make room for new "products." And it also fits this picture that, interestingly enough, those musicians who found a personal expression on keyboards had already developed this personality on the acoustic piano—musicians like Kenny Barron, Barry Miles, and Bill Evans. The latter succeeded in realizing the entire rich and brilliant sensitivity of his acoustic piano on the electric instrument as well.

Nowhere is the latent inferiority complex of the keyboard scene so apparent as in the meaningless but understandable attempt to produce electronic emulation of the natural harmonics familiar to us from the venerable old instrumental tradition. An imitation syndrome shapes the synthesizer scene considerably. All creative synthesizer players in jazz are characterized by their surmounting of this syndrome.

If we say that a saxophonist has an individual sound, that's a mighty understatement. In reality great jazz saxophonists avail themselves, whether consciously or not, of a multitude of the most differentiated, nuanced sounds. The sound spectrum inclusive of the buildup and decay of tones is constantly changing. Every modification of embouchure, every change in the air column or lip tension, every nuance of phrasing (whether loud or soft, deeper or higher, legato or staccato) transforms the parameters of saxophone sound. There doesn't as yet exist any synthesizer capable of producing all those enormously complex sound processes.

The synthesizer doesn't justify its musical existence by copying natural harmonics. That is only meaningful for the record industry, which can thereby rationalize away studio musicians, but it has become apparent that the industry can't ever do so completely. Every new musical instrument demands a new way of playing and an aesthetic of its own. In the realm of the synthesizer, only the initial stages of such an aesthetic are apparent. "The instrument is a lot further ahead than most of the players," said British rock synthesizer player Rick Wakeman. "The technology is racing ahead of the musicians."

The synthesizer, developed by R. A. Moog in the late fifties, gained sudden popularity in 1968 through the worldwide success of Walter Carlos' record *Switched-On Bach,* which presented electronic versions of some of Johann Sebastian Bach's compositions. Here, the electronics simulated the original instrumental voices; there were hardly any signs yet of a truly autonomous use of the new sounds and new instrumental possibilities. The first artists, besides Carlos, to experiment with the synthesizer in an effort to create really new and original sounds were not jazzplayers but musicians of different types of music—for example, John Cage and Terry Riley.

In jazz, the new possibilities of the synthesizer that make up its actual attraction were used most creatively by players like Paul Bley, Sun Ra, Richard Teitelbaum, George Lewis, Joe Gallivan, Pete Levin, and by the German Wolfgang Dauner. These musicians have refuted the argument leveled so often against the synthesizer, and against electronics in general, that they sound mechanical and "inhuman." This was done most convincingly by Sun Ra through the boiling intensity of his synthesizer improvisations, and also by a player like Terry Riley through his spirituality, and by Richard Teitelbaum through his very personal intellectual level.

There are constant additions on the synthesizer and accessory market. Specialists have pointed out that even after thirty years the development is only in its beginning stages. There is a new kind of jargon that goes along with electronics. Insiders use it as a sort of ritual language: pink noise, white noise, phasing, sawtooth sound, sequencer, shatter, quadrophone, sinus tone, trigger, trigger impulse, low-pass, high-pass, tape-pass, and so on.

In the meantime, the synthesizer scene has become so extensive that almost every instrument can now employ MIDI (musical instrument digital interface) for operating a synthesizer without using a keyboard. On the one hand, the time has long passed when keyboardists were alone in using synthesizers. Now guitarists (by way of the guitar synthesizer), saxophonists (through EWI or Pitchrider), trumpeters (through EVI), drummers (through Simmons), etc., also preside over an abundant world of synthesizer sounds. On the other hand, the electronic sounds of wind, string, and percussion instruments have become so similar to keyboard sounds that the electronic scene largely seems to be "keyboardized" even when that isn't the case. This development sometimes even takes on paradoxical aspects when instruments with natural harmonics imitate electronic sound generators that previously served to copy such instruments. Nonetheless, some musicians have been able to employ these new technologies creatively. (We consider the guitar synthesizer and the synth-drums in the sections on the control instruments.)

The electronic scene has become even more complex through the development of samplers—digital equipment for storing sounds, making it possible to record, store, and then call up and use sounds at whatever pitch required by way of control equipment, such as a keyboard. The real attraction of samplers is that musicians can now employ the sounds of instruments they cannot play in terms of the technical skills involved. "I can't play drums at all," said guitarist Henry Kaiser, "but thanks to microcomputer technology it becomes possible for me to play things and express myself musically in ways I couldn't before." Among the keyboardists who have taken playing with samplers beyond the usual imitation of natural harmonics to the point of individual musical creativity are Peter Scherer, Wayne Horvitz, Austrian-born Wolfgang Mitterer, and Heiner Goebbels from Germany.

Musicians have shown that the trend toward automation in the keyboard realm occurs at the expense of expressiveness and spontaneity. That's probably why computer music—which is used much more effectively in the New Music—hasn't been well received in jazz. Improvisation can't be preprogrammed. Even the "human error" included by way of contingency generators is based on a program and thus is far inferior to the spontaneity of human playing.

The most convincing deployment of computer music in jazz came from Richard Teitelbaum and, above all, George Lewis, who allowed a computer with interactive software to react to the impulses of a free-jazz soloist.

Every synthesizer player needs knowledge of programming in order to achieve a personal sound. However, the confrontation with algorithms, envelopes, oscillators, etc., brings aspects of mathematics and engineering into the creative musical process, obstructing the principle of intuitive, spontaneous discovery of sound, so important in jazz. The synthesizer enforces a "technocratization" of musical thinking. That tendency is even more apparent in the second generation of digital synthesizers. Since the programming of synthesizers has become a laborious science of its own, many keyboardists have their sounds made to measure by program writers. Herbie Hancock, for instance, first called on Patrick Gleeson, creator of the music for Coppola's film *Apocalypse Now.* These programmers are by now so important that in fusion music they receive credit on albums just like the musicians involved. It is certainly not just chance that creative keyboard-players—musicians like Joe Zawinul, Sun Ra, Lyle Mays, Wayne Horvitz, and Wolfgang Mitterer—exclude the programmer as middleman and search for new sounds themselves.

Finally, let's return once more to the organ. Outside the realm of jazz, although with clear repercussions on it, an organ style has developed that goes beyond Larry Young: the music of Terry Riley. Riley's music cannot be categorized—neither as jazz nor as rock nor as avant-garde concert music—but it has influenced musicians from all these fields (Don Cherry, for example, or the British group Soft Machine or composer Steve Reich, to mention three names from three fields). Riley is far from playing the organ with the kind of technical brilliance and loudness taken for granted among contemporary organists. He plays at a low volume, carefully, moderately, as a sort of aid to meditation. His music is supposed to be felt more than heard. It is music as much for the aura of a person as for his ears. Riley's music is modal, but it is not so much Coltrane's modality—even though "jazz ears" may perceive it as such—as it is the modality of Asia, above all of Indian ragas. And yet it is Western music, played on modern Western electronic instruments. Riley's music has been called "minimal music," since it hardly seems to change. The listener has the impression that the same tonal movements are constantly being repeated; but in the course of these repetitions, imperceptible changes take place, so that at the end of a Riley piece something new, something different is reached, while the listener is still under the impression of hearing the same tonal movements, phrases, and sounds with which the piece began a long time ago. Riley's phrases are "mantras" that develop and grow in meditation—hardly noticed by the meditating subject—and begin to be effective in a spiritual world, according to their own laws. Riley has dematerialized the organ—certainly a significant accomplishment with an instrument that just a short while before (as with Jimmy Smith and Jack McDuff or with rock players like Keith Emerson or Rick Wakeman) had seemed to be one of the most material, robust, and solid of all instruments. But he also brought the organ back to where it had been before it became electronic: to the spiritual realm—not, however, to a regressive spirituality, but rather to one that progresses into new spaces not only of sounds but of consciousness.

The Guitar

The history of the modern jazz guitar begins with Charlie Christian, who joined Benny Goodman in 1939, and began to play in the Minton circles shortly thereafter. He died in 1942. During his two years on the main jazz scene, he revolutionized guitar playing. To be sure, there were guitarists before him; along with the banjo, the guitar has a longer history than any other jazz instrument. But it almost seems as if there are two different guitars: as played before Charlie Christian and as played after.

Before Christian, the guitar was essentially an instrument of rhythm and harmonic accompaniment. The singers of folk blues, work songs, and blues ballads accompanied themselves on guitar or banjo. In the whole field of jazz prehistory—the field of the archaic, West African–influenced folk music of the southern slaves—the guitar (or banjo) was the most important and sometimes sole instrument. This was the beginning of the tradition that singers like Leadbelly and Big Bill Broonzy carried into our time, playing

rich and long melodic lines that jazz guitarists per se discovered considerably later.

The surveyable history of the jazz guitar begins with Johnny St. Cyr and
Lonnie Johnson. Both are from New Orleans. St. Cyr was an ensemble player,
with the bands of King Oliver, Louis Armstrong, and Jelly Roll Morton in the
twenties; while Johnson, almost from the start, concentrated on solo work.
The contrast between the rhythmic chord style and the solo-type,
single-note style that dominates the evolution of the guitar is emphasized
from the very beginning in St. Cyr and Johnson.

The supreme representative of the rhythmic chord style of playing is
Freddie Green, the most faithful of all Count Basie band members, from
1937 until the Count's death in 1984. (Green himself died three years later.)
Indeed, what is meant by the concept "Basie" is in no small degree to
Freddie Green's credit: the tremendous unity of the Basie rhythm sections.
Nowhere else in jazz did rhythm become "sound" to the degree it did with
Basie, and this sound, basically, is the sound of Freddie Green's guitar. He
hardly ever plays solos or is featured, yet he is one of the most dependable
guitarists in jazz history. Green is the only guitarist who surmounted the
breach created by Charlie Christian as if there had been no breach at all.
Green, by the way, has a very prosperous successor on today's rock,
jazz-rock, funk, and soul scene: Cornell Dupree, who plays the kind of
dependable rhythm guitar that Green has played for six decades in the Basie
band. His playing, of course, is enriched by the many developments in the
music since then.

Lonnie Johnson was the main influence on Eddie Lang, the most important
Chicago-style guitarist, and he also made duet recordings with him. Lang
came from an Italian background and reflects the tendency toward the
cantilena and the *melos* of the Italian musical tradition noticeable in so
many jazz musicians of Italian origin. The other important Chicago-style
guitarist is Eddie Condon, more influenced by St. Cyr, purely a rhythm
player and, until his death in 1973, the tireless guiding spirit of the
Chicago-style scene in New York.

If you had heard everything played by these guitarists well into the second
half of the thirties, and then had gone to Europe to hear Django Reinhardt,
you would have understood the appeal that Django had. Django came from
a gypsy family that had trekked through half of Europe and was mainly at
home in Germany and Belgium (where he was born). Django's playing
vibrates with the string feeling of his people—whether they play violin, like
the Hungarian gypsies, or flamenco guitar, like the Spanish gypsies of Monte
Sacre. All of this, combined with his great respect for Eddie Lang, came alive
in Django Reinhardt's famed Quintet du Hot Club de France, consisting
solely of stringed instruments: three guitars, violin, and bass. The melan-

choly strain of the ancient gypsy tradition lent a magic to Reinhardt's music; down through his last years (he died in 1953), he found his greatness in slow pieces. Often the very titles of his compositions capture the enchanted atmosphere of Django's music: "Douce Ambiance," "Mélodie au crépuscule," "Nuages," "Songs d'automne," "Daphne," "Féerie," "Parfum," "Finesse." In 1946, none other than Duke Ellington took Django Reinhardt on an American tour.

Django was the first European whose influence could be felt on the American scene, in countless guitarists. In fact, even a nonguitarist like pianist John Lewis named Django as a man who had influenced him through the climate of his music. Lewis named his composition "Django," one of the Modern Jazz Quartet's most successful pieces, in memory of Reinhardt. And even in the eighties, many guitarists showed allegiance to Reinhardt—in the United States, for instance, Earl Klugh, mandolin player David Grisman (see "Miscellaneous Instruments"), Larry Coryell; in Europe, French guitarist Christian Escoudé, Boulou Ferré, and Bireli Lagrene (all three from gypsy families), as well as the splendid and absolutely original Belgian guitar virtuoso Philip Catherine. It was above all Philip's sound that made Charles Mingus call him "Young Django."

The phenomenon of Django has often been cause for amazement. How was it possible for such a musician to emerge from the European world? In all probability, the only possible explanation—if one is not satisfied with the statement that Django simply was there—is sociological: European gypsies were in a social situation comparable to American blacks. Again and again, ethnic minority groups have been the sources of great jazz musicians: in the United States—besides blacks—Jews and Italians; and in the Europe of the thirties and forties, particularly Jews. Here too it once again becomes clear that authentic jazz, undictated by the music business, is a cry for freedom, whatever the racial environment and whatever the style.

Django's position as an outsider is somewhat related to that of Laurindo Almeida, a Brazilian musician of the rank of the great concert guitarists, such as Segovia or Gomez. Almeida employed the Spanish guitar tradition within jazz initially, in the late forties, as a member of Stan Kenton's band. The solos he played on some of Kenton's recordings emanate more warmth than almost anything else in the cold and glittering music of that phase of Kenton's development. Since the seventies, he has been one of the L.A.4, with altoist Bud Shank, bassist Ray Brown, and drummer Jeff Hamilton. They have been quite successful with their mixture of classical and Latin American music plus jazz.

Another guitarist who loves to mix different kinds of music is Charlie Byrd, who lives in Washington. He really is in command of everything that can be expressed on the guitar, from Bach to Brazilian bossa nova.

The connection of the Iberian baroque guitar tradition with the modern age (and also with a West African rhythmic feeling coming from the Yoruba tradition) was made even more convincing by the great guitarists of Brazil. The three best known are Baden Powell, Bola Sete, and Egberto Gismonti. Powell is the most original and rhythmically most dynamic of them. Sete, who has been living in the United States since 1960 and who played with Dizzy Gillespie, names Reinhardt and Segovia as his important influences. In the seventies, Gismonti appeared with Norwegian saxophonist Jan Garbarek and American bassist Charlie Haden. They played a kind of music that transcends style and geographical borders—world music in the best sense. As a writer, Gismonti has developed his own kind of chamber music, which intelligently combines classical and Latin American (especially Brazilian) music.

But back to Django Reinhardt (who also featured, in a totally different cultural environment but in a similar process of acculturation, many Ibero-Spanish elements). The melodic lines he initially played on unamplified guitar seemed almost to cry out for the technical and expressive possibilities of the electrically amplified guitar. Charlie Christian gave the electric guitar such renown that almost all guitarists switched from acoustic to amplified instruments at the turn of the thirties. Yet Christian was not the first to play amplified jazz guitar. First came George Barnes and Eddie Durham, the arranger, trombonist, and guitarist in the bands of Jimmie Lunceford and occasionally Count Basie. The earliest electric guitar solo we know of on record was played by Durham in Lunceford's 1935 version of "Hittin' the Bottle." In Basie's 1937 recording of "Time Out," the contrast between Freddie Green's rhythm acoustic guitar and Durham's solo electric guitar is charming. More recent guitarists as well—for example, Tal Farlow in the fifties, John McLaughlin in the seventies, or Pat Metheny in the eighties—have frequently made use of the possibilities for contrast between electric and acoustic guitar. As far as Durham and Barnes are concerned, however, they did not yet know how to exploit fully the potential of the electric guitar. They continued to play it as if it were the old acoustic instrument, only electrically amplified—as in the seventies many pianists initially approached the electric piano as if it were a grand, but with an electric sound. An outstanding musician was needed to recognize the new possibilities of the electric guitar. Charlie Christian was that man.

Christian is comparable to both Lester Young and Charlie Parker. Like Young, he belongs to the Swing era and to the pathbreakers; like Parker, he belongs to the creators of modern jazz.

Christian is the outstanding soloist on some recordings made privately at Minton's around 1941: "Charlie's Choice" and "Stomping at the Savoy."

These records were later issued publicly and must be regarded as the first of all bebop records.

Christian charted new territory in terms of technique, harmony, and melody. Technically, he played his instrument with a virtuosity that seemed incredible to his contemporaries. The electric guitar in his hands became a "horn" comparable to the tenor sax of Lester Young. His playing has been described as "reed style"; he played with the expressiveness of a saxophone.

Harmonically, Christian was the first to base his improvisations not on the harmonies of the theme but on the passing chords that he placed between the basic harmonies.

Melodically, Christian smoothed out the tinny staccato that almost all guitarists prior to him had employed into interconnected lines that radiated some of the atmosphere of Lester Young's phrases. Not surprisingly, Christian had played tenor sax before becoming a guitarist.

Whoever comes after Charlie Christian has his roots in him. To begin with, there is the first generation of "post-Christian" guitarists: Tiny Grimes, Oscar Moore, Irving Ashby, Les Paul, Bill de Arango, Barney Kessel, and Chuck Wayne. The most important is Barney Kessel, who, as a member of the Oscar Peterson Trio and with his own groups, made many Swing-oriented recordings in the United States and in Europe. Strange how that which had seemed revolutionary in Christian appeared in Kessel, since the end of the fifties, conservative and not very daring. In the early fifties, Les Paul had an immense commercial success with recordings in which he overdubbed different sounds and tracks of electronically manipulated guitar voices. At the time, these techniques were put down in jazz circles as "extramusical trickery." Only from today's vantage point is it clear that—long before Jimi Hendrix and all the others about whom we will talk later—Les Paul was the pathbreaker of modern electronic manipulation of sound. That is why, more than twenty years after his big successes, many young guitarists still refer back to him.

If Kessel could be designated the most rhythmically vital guitarist of the jazz of the fifties, Jimmy Raney is harmonically the most interesting and Johnny Smith the one with the most subtle sound. But before Raney and Smith comes Billy Bauer. He emerged from the Lennie Tristano school, and in the early fifties played the same abstract, long lines on the guitar that Warne Marsh played on tenor or Lee Konitz on alto. With Konitz, Bauer made duet recordings—just guitar and alto sax—among them, the slow, deeply felt "Rebecca"—one of the first duets in modern jazz that, even at that time, pointed toward the rich duo culture that evolved from the seventies. Jimmy Raney is also indebted to the Tristano school, but his melodies are more concrete and singable. Where Bauer played "dissonant" chords and pointed leaps in which the thresholds are barely exploited,

Raney featured richly nuanced harmonies, whose interrelatedness seems rounded, logical, often almost inevitable. Johnny Smith unfolded these harmonies to the last note. A whole universe of satiated, late-romantic sounds evolved—the world of Debussy's *L'Après-midi d'un faune* brought into jazz; a fatigued, decadent faun who relaxes in the warm sun of late summer . . . or in "Moonlight in Vermont." The mood of this ballad has never been more subtly captured than by Johnny Smith.

All this comes together in Tal Farlow. Farlow initially stems from Raney, but with his big hands he had possibilities quite different from those of Raney, who only played single-finger style. After Tristano, and before Sonny Rollins, hardly any jazz musician swung such long, ceaseless, seemingly self-renewing lines above the bar lines of choruses, sequences, and bridges as Farlow. But these are not the abstract lines of Tristano; they are the concrete lines of early jazz classicism. It is regrettable that Farlow has withdrawn so much from the scene. Only George Wein, the jazz impresario, managed to lure him into occasional, albeit highly successful, appearances during the seventies. In the early eighties, he was reunited very successfully with Red Norvo, on records and in person.

Beyond the Bauer-Raney-Farlow constellation, yet inspired by it, stand the other guitarists of modern jazz: Jim Hall, Herb Ellis, Les Spann, Gabor Szabo, Grant Green, the early George Benson, Kenny Burrell, Larry Coryell, and finally the most significant, Wes Montgomery. Jim Hall—with his beautifully melodious, tuneful improvisations—gained renown, initially, through his work in the Chico Hamilton Quintet and in Jimmy Giuffre's trio; Herb Ellis, through his long cooperation with Oscar Peterson. Ellis often combines the stylistic elements of Christian with a shot of blues and country music (in which he has roots).

Jim Hall, when less and less was heard from the other great cool-jazz guitarists (Farlow, Raney, and Bauer), became a master of delicate, sensitive guitar improvisations that have long left behind the confines of cool jazz and, since the seventies, can be considered the truly ageless jazz guitar style. In this sense, Hall, who in the eighties made wonderful duo recordings with bassist Ron Carter, has become *the* timeless jazz guitarist par excellence.

Detroit-born Kenny Burrell could be designated *the* outstanding hard-bop guitarist, but he has grown in the most diverse directions, on electric as well as Spanish guitar. The steadiness of his improvisations is appreciated by many musicians. He has played with Dizzy Gillespie, Benny Goodman, Gil Evans, Astrud Gilberto, Stan Getz, and Jimmy Smith—which proves his versatility and openness.

The late San Francisco critic Ralph Gleason said that Wes Montgomery, who died in 1968, was "the best thing to happen to the guitar since Charlie

Christian." Wes was one of three musical Montgomery brothers from Indianapolis (the others are pianist-vibraphonist Buddy and bassist Monk), who first became known in San Francisco. He combined a fascinating, at the same time almost inconceivable octave technique with hard and clear self-restraint, in statements in which the blues and the Charlie Christian tradition figured prominently—even when he moved into pop-jazz, as he did frequently during the last years of his life.

Wes Montgomery's development exemplifies the way in which so many jazz musicians become subject to the marketing process of the industry. His producer, Creed Taylor, produced him strictly from a market point of view, with string orchestras and commercial tunes. He did not even allow him to play the kind of music really near and dear to him on every third or fourth album, which would have been the least you could have expected, as critic Gary Giddins once remarked. In 1962, Wes said in a *Newsweek* interview, "I know the melody and you know the melody—so why should I turn around to lay the melody?" But only a few years later, he did nothing but play melody. Toward the end of his life, Wes said, "I'm always depressed by the result of my playing."

Wes Montgomery's legacy was carried on by many musicians, but especially so by two players who are diametrically opposed to each other: Pat Martino and George Benson, the latter in a commercial direction, the former in the opposite. Martino is one of the great outsiders on the contemporary guitar scene; he is one of the few players who have not only copied Wes Montgomery's octave technique but have made their own style out of it. George Benson, at first solidly within the great black guitar tradition, in the course of the seventies became the guitar superstar with recordings selling in the millions. Along with Herbie Hancock he was at that time the bestselling musician of modern jazz. Singer Betty Carter commented in a *Rolling Stone* interview, "It's like George Benson . . . the way he can play, why does he have to sound like Stevie Wonder to make money?" And Benson himself said, "I'm not there to educate an audience; I'm there to play for them." It is Benson's singing, of course, that made him so popular on records.

But we have advanced too far. In the meantime, a "guitar explosion," as the British *Melody Maker* called it, had taken place—a widening of the guitar scene by a factor of hundreds, if not thousands, within the span of a few years. Up to that point, the tenor sax had been the major instrument, now suddenly it was the guitar. Even psychologists have dealt with this phenomenon. Both instruments, they claim, are "gender symbols"—the tenor being a male symbol, the guitar, with its shape reminiscent of the human female figure, a female one.

Three musicians were the actual igniters of the sixties' guitar explosion, each in a different field of music: Wes Montgomery in jazz, B. B. King in blues, and Jimi Hendrix in rock.

B. B. King (more about him also in the section on the seventies) is the father of all guitar playing in rock and popular music of the sixties and seventies. He "rides" on the guitar sound: He lets it approach, jumps in the saddle and bears down on it, spurs it on and gives it free rein, bridles it again, dismounts, and jumps on the next horse: the next sound. It was King who fully realized the development that began with Charlie Christian: the guitar sound grew increasingly longer, was further and further abstracted from the instrument. Of course, this development began in fact before Christian; at the moment when first the banjo, then the guitar were used in African-American music. It leads straight from the metallic chirpings of the banjo in archaic jazz (so brief in duration one often could barely hear them), through Eddie Lang and Lonnie Johnson, who (still without electric potential) waged a constant battle against the brevity of their sounds, and via the saxophone style of Charlie Christian and the great cool guitarists of the fifties, to B. B. King—and from him, as we shall see, on to Jimi Hendrix. This development has a single goal: the continuous, determined elongation and the related individualization and malleability of the sound (which, however, as it became easier and easier to realize technically and electronically, finally began to lose its attraction). The aim of this development—the fact that one can do almost whatever one wants with the sound of the guitar, more so than with any other instrument—may have been the main reason for the immense progress and popularity of guitar playing in the sixties and seventies.

In the sixties and early seventies, B. B. King represented the apex of a development that points back to the history and prehistory of the blues. A particularly significant role in the transformation of the rural blues guitar into the "riding" guitar phrases of B. B. King was played by T-Bone Walker, who died in 1975. As we mentioned in the blues section, the South Side of Chicago has been a center of the blues tradition—with guitarists like Muddy Waters, Jimmy or "Fast Fingers" Dawkins, Buddy Guy, and Otis Rush. There is a white guitarist who stems from the Chicago school of guitar playing, influenced greatly by Muddy Waters, and who stands solidly in this tradition: Mike Bloomfield. About Otis Rush it is said that he carries on where B. B. King left off, playing the King style even harder and more charged with electric and emotional tension. Among the guitarists bridging the gap to rock are Albert King, Albert Collins, Jimmy Johnson, Luther Allison, Stevie Ray Vaughan, and, particularly successfully in the eighties, Robert Cray. Said Collins, "I wanted to play jazz. I wanted to sound like Kenny Burrell. . . . I've been known as a blues player, but I wanna be more than a 'rock-blues' guitarist." Cray epitomizes the new blues musician: a stylist who doesn't only play "down home" blues but is also a master of contemporary soul, funk, and rock, making clear their links with the source: the great legacy of black music.

The third great musician who, with Wes Montgomery and B. B. King, ignited the guitar explosion is Jimi Hendrix. Hendrix—born in 1947 as a "black Indian" in Seattle, Washington, died in 1970 in London as a world star—is surrounded by a halo of myths. Among instrumentalists, he was the real genius of the rock age of the sixties. The exact cause of his death is still not entirely clear. An overdose of heroin, said the sensationalist press; suffocation in his own vomit was the coroner's verdict. "I don't know whether it was an accident, suicide, or murder," is what his friend, musician Noel Redding, said. And it is still unclear where all the money, certainly millions, that Jimi had earned with his music went.

Hendrix was the musical symbol of the counterculture of the sixties, comparable only to Bob Dylan. At the legendary Woodstock Festival, he shredded the American national anthem, but what he really meant was America itself. He ripped the anthem with machine guns, tore it to shreds with bomb explosions and the sound of children moaning.

Hendrix had strong links with jazz. Critic Bill Milkowski points out that at the end of his career the guitarist had grown weary of rock's simple forms and was devoting more attention to jazz. Hendrix jammed with Roland Kirk and later even with Tony Williams. He dreamed of a big band with vocal backing. Preparations were being made for working with Gil Evans when Hendrix unexpectedly died.

Hendrix has been dead for over twenty years, and there are half a hundred books about him. There are complicated analyses of his playing technique: his use of wah-wah pedals and whammy bars; how he used rings and bottle necks and occasionally even his teeth; how he played not only on his guitar but also "on" his amplifier, with switches and controls; how he retuned his instrument, fast as lightning, in the middle of a song, employing totally unusual tunings; the way he seemed to drum his guitar rather than pick it; the way he played with his own feedback, waiting for it and then answering it, returning it to the amplifier, as if asking questions that he then would try to reply to, which would lead to further questions. Often it seemed as if the feedback was his real partner, more so than the rhythm sections that never really satisfied him.

Jimi's actual accomplishment was to open the music to electronics. Electronics became his instrument, while the guitar served only as a control device. He was the first to explore the wide, unfathomable land of electronic sounds, the first to play "live electronics"—more than all of those who use this catch phrase today—and the first to transform electronics into music with the instinct of a genius, as if plucking the strings of an instrument made of waves, rays, and currents. Whatever can be called electronics in today's music—in jazz, jazz-rock, fusion, rock, and pop—come from Jimi Hendrix. And that applies to guitarists as much as to electric piano and synthesizer players, and even to horn players who use electronics, as long as they employ them as more than a gimmick or a gag.

Jimi Hendrix spoke of his guitar as his lover. He got high just from playing it. But he also beat it, destroyed it, burned it—on stage. It was love and hate at the same time, a kind of sadism that was also masochism, as if someone were losing his mind, a lover who could neither give nor receive true love.

So these are the pillars of today's guitar playing: Wes Montgomery, B. B. King, and Jimi Hendrix. Many guitarists have built their structures on these pillars, but none as brilliantly as John McLaughlin. His range extends from folk blues and Django Reinhardt through the great guitarists of the fifties—in particular Tal Farlow—to the Indian sitar (see also the sections about jazz of the seventies, McLaughlin himself, and the combos of jazz).

McLaughlin has played the most diverse kinds of music—free jazz in Europe (with Gunter Hampel, for example), fusion with Miles Davis, highly electronicized music with his Mahavishnu Orchestra, Indian music with his group Shakti, solo guitar and duets with French guitarist Christian Escoudé. But whatever he plays cannot be thought of separate from his spirituality. "God," he said, "is the Master musician. I am His instrument."

McLaughlin's 1983 trio recordings with Al DiMeola and Spanish flamenco guitarist Paco de Lucia are an exhilarating feast of acoustic guitar playing, taken on the highly electronized fusion scene as a sign. Legions of "pure" acoustic guitar ensembles emulated the example set by this trio. Less successful was the reestablishment of the Mahavishnu Orchestra whose highly charged sounds seemed anachronistic in the eighties.

The guitar scene continues to explode. In order to get an even halfway correct picture, we can form the following groupings (remembering that they all blend into one another): rock, jazz-rock and fusion, folk jazz, free, free funk, no wave, cool, traditional, and neobop classicism.

Most directly rooted in Hendrix (and in the blues) are the rock players whom we can only mention summarily in this context: Eric Clapton, Duane Allman, Carlos Santana (who is influenced by Latin music and who has made recordings with McLaughlin), Jeff Beck, Adrian Belew, Robert Quine, Prince, and, perhaps the most individualistic rock guitarist of them all, Frank Zappa—to name only a very few.

In diametrical opposition stand those players who have transposed the tradition of the cool guitarists from the fifties to today's jazz. The most important of them, the one who was already active during those years, is Jim Hall, whom we discussed earlier. "The quiet American" is what *Melody*

Maker called him when he appeared in London. And Hall himself has said, "Even though I never got to work with Lester Young, that's the sound I try to get from my guitar."

Other guitarists who deserve mention in this context are Hungarian-born Attila Zoller, Canadian Ed Bickert, and Americans Howard Roberts, Doug Raney (the son of Jimmy Raney, whose tradition Doug carries on), and Jack Wilkins. Zoller was initially indebted to the Lennie Tristano school. As the first among the guitarists, he transferred the long, singable melody lines he had learned back then into the freer realm of the new jazz, as in his collaborations with pianist Don Friedman. Zoller is a master of sensitive, romantic restraint, and it is hard to understand why a man of such talent is still known only to insiders. Bickert made recordings with Paul Desmond, the "poet of the alto saxophone," and Bickert's style is just as "poetic." Wilkins, perhaps the most talented of the younger guitarists of this direction, has become known through his work in trombonist Bob Brookmeyer's group.

Let's move on to the largest grouping, the jazz-rock and fusion guitarists. This grouping incorporates extreme positions: rock and blues on the one hand, cool and bebop on the other. This extensive group of jazz-rock guitarists falls into two almost diametrically opposed categories, with of course constantly fluctuating boundaries. On the one side the emphasis is on virtuoso playing with its sweeping gestures and expansive improvisations. That realm is predominantly shaped by older players who still phrase in the spirit of new departures and the striving for peak technical achievement that characterized early jazz-rock: musicians such as Joe Beck (who was chronologically the first), Larry Coryell, Eric Gale, Earl Klugh, Al DiMeola, Lee Ritenour, Allan Holdsworth from England, Holland's Jan Akkermann, and Finland's Jukka Tolonen. Younger masters have also pursued virtuosity in the eighties: most importantly Stanley Jordan, Kevin Eubanks, Robben Ford, Scott Henderson, Frank Gambale, Bireli Lagrene from France, and Germany's Michael Sagmeister.

Larry Coryell was already playing fusion music in the mid-sixties, when nobody even knew the term, in the Gary Burton Quartet and in the group Free Spirits. His major influences were Jimi Hendrix and John McLaughlin: "Jimi is the greatest musician who ever lived, as far as I'm concerned." But then he added, "I hate him, because he took everything away from me that was mine." And about John McLaughlin: "McLaughlin heard me in England, and I still hear some of my own style coming back at me. Then, when he came to the United States, I started listening to him. It's a two-way street." Coryell hails from Texas, which is his third major influence: "If you listen to me carefully, it must come through that I'm from Texas."

With keyboard player Richard Tee, drummer Steve Gadd, and the already mentioned Cornell Dupree on rhythm guitar, Eric Gale formed the successful group Stuff. At the outset of his career, Al DiMeola recorded a wonderful duet album, transcending all musical cultures, with the great Spanish flamenco guitarist Paco de Lucia; but he never subsequently fulfilled the promise of this duet. His brilliance, albeit very superficial, nevertheless continued to fascinate. Lee Ritenour probably is the busiest guitarist on the Los Angeles fusion scene. Allen Holdsworth, who emerged out of Soft Machine, has impressively transposed Coltrane's "sheets of sound" into jazz-rock guitar playing. With his IOU trio at the start of the eighties he made an important contribution toward a new, more economical concept of jazz-rock. Stanley Jordan revolutionized the technical aspect of guitar playing. As a street musician in New York his tapping technique attracted such attention that George Wein presented Jordan in the 1984 New York Jazz Festival. Since then Jordan's unaccompanied performances have been among the main attractions at all the big jazz festivals. Jordan doesn't pluck his guitar. He gets the strings to sound by tapping with the fingertips of both hands on the fingerboard just as if it were a piano keyboard. In fact Jordan says he developed this technique so as to attain the "orchestral" capacities of a pianist.

Jordan certainly wasn't the first person to develop "tapping" (also known as "hammering"). He was preceded by Jimmy Webster (who in addition wrote a guide to this way of playing), Eddie Van Halen, David Torn, and Adrian Belew. Those guitarists, however, used tapping merely as ornamentation and one playful method among many others, whereas Jordan is the first person to make this technique into the basis for his playing—with such rich polyphonic interweavings that you get the impression that two guitarists are playing here rather than one.

Critics have put Jordan on the same level as Wes Montgomery and Jimi Hendrix, but up to now Jordan has only revolutionized guitar playing technically, not stylistically. People also regret the thinness of his sound and the problems created by trying to integrate his polyphonic concept, so fascinating in solo appearances, into a group.

So much for the representatives of deliberately virtuosic jazz-rock playing. The other group of guitarists puts the emphasis on deliberately economical use of the guitar with less lavish, more concise phrasing, concentrating on what is essential. The early representatives of this way of playing included Larry Carlton, Steve Khan, Terje Rypdal from Norway, and German-born Volker Kriegel and Toto Blanke. But most of the stylists within this group come from the second and third jazz-rock generations, and their deliberately economical playing is a reaction to their precursors' overemphasis on virtuosity. Their number includes Pat Metheny, John Scofield, Hiram Bullock, Mike Stern, David Torn, and Japanese-born Kazumi Watanabe. Terje Rypdal paints pictures on his guitar, reminiscent of the fjords and dark mountain lakes of his Norwegian homeland. Hiram Bullock, first presented by David Sanborn and Gil Evans, plays a jazz-rock guitar full of droll humor and witty harmonic deviations. Steve Khan was also among the first fusion guitarists, but in the eighties he played purified jazz-rock that had shed all unnecessary pomp. His quartet with bassist Anthony Jackson, drummer Steve Jordan, and percussionist Manolo Badrena exerted an astonishing (and much too little remarked) reformist influence on the new jazz-rock. Mike Stern, who became known through Miles Davis, phrases flowing legato lines precisely on top of the beat, thereby gaining unusual drive and power. David Torn mixes Hendrix's wild, distorted sounds and Allan Holdsworth's complex harmonic sense, much influenced by ethnic music.

By far the most important musicians in this group are, however, Pat Metheny and John Scofield. Metheny is a magician of melody. He plays songlike, mellifluously sensitive, well-rounded lines, constantly renewing themselves from within and extending over a great dynamic range. His improvisations are founded on harplike, floating electric guitar sounds rich in harmonics—on his celebrated "Chorus sound," named after the device that duplicates the note being played at an octave's distance (as Wes Montgomery used to do "manually"). It's one of the most copied sounds of the eighties, but no one masters it so completely as Metheny. With other guitarists the Chorus sound is an effect; with Metheny it becomes an art. It is in his rare ability to make synthetic sounds seem "natural" that Metheny demonstrates such sensitivity. Critics have found fault with the cloying character of his music and the rococolike ornateness of his arrangements, much colored by Brazilian music (particularly through singer Milton Nascimento). Even amid their tropical extravagance of weltschmerz, kitsch, and sweetness Metheny's improvisations uphold that love of clarity, homgeneity, and balance that have brought him a following of millions. Of all the jazz-rock guitarists he is the most sophisticated harmonically. His wealth of melody seems inexhaustible.

Pat Metheny was also the first person to play the guitar synthesizer like an autonomous new instrument, beyond all sounds imitative of keyboards and unlike his otherwise more ethereal playing: angular, biting, penetratingly intense sounds. In "Endangered Species" (1986), a recording from Ornette Coleman's album *Song X,* Metheny gained an ecstatic element.

Metheny's playing of the guitar synthesizer fulfills the jazz guitarist's dream of greater physical presence. The first step involved was the changeover from banjo to guitar. Then came Charlie Christian's use of the electric guitar, and next Hendrix's elongation of guitar sound. And now with Pat Metheny the instrument (but only on the guitar synthesizer) attains a new, augmented dimension of tonal penetration that actually achieves (rather than merely strives for) a hornlike impact. Other musicians playing the guitar synthesizer include John McLaughlin, John Abercrombie, Bill Frisell, and Harry Pepl from Austria. The extent to which Metheny's improvisations uphold both jazz tradition (bebop, Jim Hall, and Wes Montgomery) and the country music of his home state Missouri became clear when he recorded—together with tenorists Dewey Redman and Mike Brecker, bassist Charlie Haden, and drummer Jack DeJohnette—the *80/81* double album, one of the most beautiful eighties jazz recordings.

John Scofield, who became known through playing with Billy Cobham and Miles Davis, transmits a strong feeling for bebop into the jazz-rock context. He unites the legato feeling of Jim Hall and Wes Montgomery with B. B. King's biting blues and funkiness. Scofield, who also presented himself as a splendid neobop stylist, phrases jazz-rock with a warmth and ardor that helped move this often cool realm, dazzling with technical skills, toward an unanticipated revival, with soulful, inventive improvisations. In the three years when he played with Miles Davis he wrote a great deal of creative music for the trumpeter. Scofield was as important for the "funky Miles" as Wayne Shorter had been for his compositions in the sixties.

Scofield's wealth of unusual intervallic leaps and original runs influenced numerous eighties guitarists including Leni Stern, Mitch Watkins, French-born Marc Ducret, and John Schröder from Germany.

In some ways folk-jazz guitarists are related to jazz-rock players. That becomes particularly apparent in the music of Steve Tibbetts from Minneapolis. His magical sound paintings range from highly electronic, distorted, rocklike guitar sounds to the meditative acoustic tones of ethnic music (mainly Indian and Japanese). Independently of Hendrix he developed his own way of playing with extreme feedback. Considering how deeply rooted the guitar is in the ethnic music of many cultures, the existence of these folk-jazz guitarists is not surprising. Apart from Steve Tibbetts they include such different musicians as Alex de Grassi, William Ackerman, Leo Kottke, Ry Cooder, John Fahey, and Michael Hedges. Hedges plays a steel-string guitar and particularly relishes harplike, "open" string sounds full of a percussive quality.

Proceeding to the free guitarists, the first musician to play free-jazz guitar in the sixties was Sonny Sharrock, who played with Pharoah Sanders, Don Cherry, and the punk jazz group Last Exit. He was followed by Michael Gregory Jackson, James Emery, Eugene Chadbourne, Briton Derek Bailey, and Germans Hans Reichel, Uwe Kropinski, and Helmut "Joe" Sachse. Probably the most radical of these free players is Bailey; working on his instrument in all imaginable ways, he is one of the most original players on the European free-jazz scene.

James Blood Ulmer, who made his name in Ornette Coleman groups, has been more successful than anyone else in making the transition from free jazz to free funk. His concise, refractory, deliberately spluttering lines build a bridge from free jazz to funk, concretizing the former and musicalizing the latter. Ulmer's motto: "Jazz is the teacher; funk is the preacher."

Among the other important free-funk guitarists are Kelvyn Bell with his striking emphasis on "wiping" phrasing, Jean-Paul Bourelly who transposes Hendrix's sound into the unruly language of free funk, Bern Nix, Charles Ellerbee, and Vernon Reid.

Particularly original new sounds in the eighties came from the no wave guitarists, the players who most consistently pursued the demolition of stylistic categories in postmodern jazz. Although their origins are in free jazz, they transcend that by making numerous other fragments collide in their playing: punk and ethnic music, avant-garde and rock, minimal music and folk. Among the interesting guitarists here are Arto Lindsay, Henry Kaiser, Fred Frith, Elliott Sharp, Rhys Chatam, Franco-Canadian René Lussier, and German Caspar Brötzmann. Arto Lindsay makes the guitar sound like "a collapsing twenty-story glasshouse." He shaped such splintering, crashing, somber sounds when working with the Golden Palominos and alto saxophonist John Zorn; but Lindsay also commands the supple melodiousness of the music of Brazil where he grew up. In Henry Kaiser's playing the guitar is transformed (with assistance from computers, MIDI, rhythm machines, and other digital aids) into a "crazy" turbulent orchestra. There Kaiser batters and bends extremely disparate musical styles—Korean music and Delta Blues, Vietnamese traditions and punk, Captain Beefheart and Ali Akbar Khan—in such original fashion that these apparent extremes gain a degree of relationship. Fred Frith played no wave with the group Henry Cow as early as 1968 when that term didn't yet exist. He's an expert in collages, contrasting a broad spectrum of unfamiliar guitar sounds. René Lussier plays imaginary folklore full of droll humor. His lines often meticulously follow the course of linguistic patterns. Hence the vocal quality of his playing.

Diametrically opposed to the free and no wave players, to use another pair of contrasts, are the guitarists who remained connected with the Swing tradition. Among them are George Barnes (who died in 1977) and Bucky Pizzarelli, who formed a wonderful guitar duet; Cal Collins; Chris Flory, and the best known of them, Joe Pass. In the early seventies, Barnes co-led a quartet with Ruby Braff, in whose stylistic mold both he and Pizzarelli belong. Pass made recordings with many of the important jazz people of Norman Granz's Pablo label, among them Ella Fitzgerald and Oscar Peterson. He is a master of ballad playing as well as of swinging jam sessions. Like tenor man Scott Hamilton and trumpeter Warren Vaché, Collins is part of the new Swing movement that has been crystallizing since the end of the seventies.

Finally, the contemporary mainstream—which extends from bebop by way of Coltrane to classicism, where the all-dominant influence of Wes Montgomery lies—developed further within a large number of individual styles. John Scofield, Emily Remler, Bruce Forman, Joe Diorio, Joshua Breakstone, Peter Leitch, Henry Johnson, Rory Stuart, and others are among those who are a part of this mainstream. The best known is the already-mentioned Scofield whose trio—together with Steve Swallow (electric bass) and Adam Nussbaum (drums)—set standards for guitar groups in eighties jazz classicism, with its angular rock-and blues-imbued neobop improvisations integrated to an extent never previously experienced in such guitar trios.

Last of all, however, three particularly individual musicians, who don't fit into any of the leading groups, must be mentioned: John Abercrombie, Ralph Towner, and Bill Frisell. Since the mid-seventies Abercrombie has developed into a poet of contemporary guitar playing. He phrases sensitive, airy lines full of a chamber-music-like quality. His trio—with Marc Johnson (bass) and Peter Erskine (drums)—also attracted great attention in the eighties, illuminating the great timeless classics of American popular music in the spirit of the Bill Evans Trio. On the guitar synthesizer he plays massive, penetrating blocks of sound, which constitute a powerful contrast to the fragility of his actual guitar lines.

Ralph Towner, leader of the group Oregon, began as a pianist and still plays the instrument. His guitar style is molded by this piano element. Towner studied in Vienna, and he admits to not being quite sure which side he is more indebted to: European music—in particular music from Vienna, that is, Viennese classicism, romanticism, and avant-garde (Schönberg, Webern, etc.)—or jazz. "I wasn't on the jazz scene until I got a classically oriented technique on the guitar. . . . I do find acoustic instruments more sympathetic than electric instruments. . . . I treat the guitar quite often like a piano trio. If I'm playing alone, it's almost like a one-man band approach," he said.

In eighties postmodern jazz Bill Frisell is the guitarist with the greatest range: from Eberhard Weber's aestheticism to the free funk of the Power Tools trio, from the Bass Desires quartet's contemporary mainstream to John Zorn's noise music. No other guitarist negates the harsh percussive moment that occurs when striking a string so completely as Bill Frisell. His lines seem to come out of nothingness and to vanish back there again—floating sounds becoming louder and softer, a pearly chain of mellow legato notes sliding like wax dripping from a candle. Frisell played the clarinet before moving to guitar. Characteristically, it is the warm, wafting sounds of woodwind that made an unmistakable mark on his original style. Frisell "breathes life" into the jazz guitar. His lines combine elements of Jim Hall, Jimi Hendrix, and the pedal-steel guitarists of Country Music he heard in his home state of Colorado, creating one of the most original guitar styles in postmodern jazz.

The guitar has come a long way—from the African banjo to the instrument of John McLaughlin and Bill Frisell, from folk blues to the guitar synthesizer. Like the flute, the guitar is an archetypical instrument. The Greek god Pan, the Indian god Shiva, and Aztec gods have blown on flutes; angels and Apsaras (the female heavenly beings of Hindu mythology) have played guitars.

The Bass

In 1911, Bill Johnson organized the Original Creole Jazz Band, the first real jazz band to go on tour from New Orleans. He played bowed bass. In the course of a job in Shreveport, Louisiana, he broke his bow. For half the night, he had to pluck the strings of his bass. Ostensibly, the effect was so novel and interesting that the jazz bass has been played pizzicato ever since.

This tale, told by jazz veterans from New Orleans, is probably an invention, but it has the advantage of reflecting much of the spirit of those years. Thus, it is "true" on a higher level. On the everyday level, it is true that the string bass had much competition from the tuba in old New Orleans. The tuba tradition was so strong that even thirty years later, many of the great Swing bassists—such as John Kirby and Red Callender—still played tuba.

The bass provides the harmonic foundation for the jazz ensemble. It is the backbone of a jazz group. At the same time, the bass has a rhythmic task. Since bop, the four even beats to the measure played by the bass (called "walking bass") are often the only factor keeping the basic rhythm firm. Since the plucked string bass can fulfill this rhythmic function with more precision than the blown tuba, bass replaced the tuba at an early date. Thirty-five years later, the electric bass has established itself next to the "acoustic" contrabass. The evolution thus moves from tuba via stand-up bass to electric bass guitar. In the course of this development, the rhythmic impulse has become shorter, sharper, more precise. At the same time, on the other hand, the sound has become less personal and direct. Many of the great bassists have pointed out that the acoustic bass is such a sensitive, highly developed instrument that it will never be replaced by modern electronics. In the meantime it has become apparent that the stand-up bass has an ideal median position between the two extremes of the tuba on the one hand and the electric bass guitar on the other, because it fulfills the needs of sound and rhythm optimally.

All bassists of traditional jazz refer back to Pops Foster. Foster worked with Freddie Keppard, King Oliver, Kid Ory, Louis Armstrong, Sidney Bechet, and all the other New Orleans greats. He can easily be identified by his "slapping" technique (today also called "slap technique"). This way of letting the strings snap back against the fingerboard of the bass—rejected by the bassists of the fifties as a sign of extreme technical inability, but used again by the free-jazz bassists to increase sound and intensity—gave Foster's playing much of its rhythmic impact. During the thirties, Foster was chosen several times as the "all-time bassist" of jazz. In 1942 (the year when Jimmy Blanton, the man who had "emancipated" the bass, died) he went to work for the New York subway system but resumed his playing career when the traditionalist revival began. He died in 1969.

John Kirby and Walter Page are the great bassists of the Swing era. Kirby, who emerged from the Fletcher Henderson band in the early thirties, was leader of a small group in the late thirties that cannot be omitted from the history of the jazz combo. Walter Page (who died in 1957) was a member of the classic Basie rhythm section, which was shaped by the sound of Freddie Green, already mentioned in the guitar section. Jo Jones, this rhythm section's drummer, says that it was Page who really taught him to play in Kansas City: "an even 4/4."

Further Swing-era bassists who should be mentioned are Slam Stewart and Bob Haggart. Stewart is best known for the way he sings in octaves with his *arco* playing: the humming effect of a bee, which can be very amusing if not heard too often. Later, Major Holley also played in a similar manner, but Holley sings in unison with his bowing.

Generally speaking, the history of the bass can be approached from the same point of view as that of the guitar. As modern guitar history begins with Charlie Christian, so the story of modern bass starts with Jimmy Blanton. Both Christian and Blanton stepped onto the main jazz stage in 1939. Both died of lung disease in 1942. In two short years, both revolutionized the playing of their respective instruments, made "horns" of them. This function was established as clearly in the duo recordings made by Blanton in 1939–40 with Duke Ellington at the piano as it was by Charlie Christian with Benny Goodman during the same period. The Ellington band of the early forties is considered the best band of Ellington's career primarily because Jimmy Blanton was on bass. He gave the Ellington Band an especially high degree of rhythmic-harmonic compactness. Blanton was twenty-three when he died. He made the bass a solo instrument.

From Blanton stretches the impressive line of modern jazz bassists. Oscar Pettiford is the second. Soon after the death of Blanton he became Ellington's bassist. And as Duke had recorded duets with Blanton's bass, he now made quartet recordings with Pettiford on cello. Harry Babasin was the first jazz cellist, but Pettiford was the man who gave the cello its place in jazz. The road from the deeper sounds of the bass to the higher range of the cello seemed a natural consequence of the evolution of the bass from harmonic to melodic instrument. Since then, there have been other bassists, too, who have chosen the cello as secondary instrument, as did the late Doug Watkins, and later Ron Carter, Peter Warren, and Dave Holland until finally, in today's jazz, the cello has become an autonomous solo instrument. Musicians like Abdul Wadud, Diedre Murray, Hank Roberts, Tristan Honsinger, Kent Carter, and Frenchman Jean-Charles Capon play it. (For more details, see the section "Miscellaneous Instruments.")

Pettiford, Ray Brown, and Charles Mingus are the great post-Blanton bassists. Pettiford, who died in Copenhagen in 1960, played on 52nd Street in the mid-forties with Dizzy Gillespie, really disseminating the new "Blanton message." In the fifties, he was the busiest bass player on the New York scene. Several times during his career Pettiford organized big bands for recording purposes. His mobility on the bass was consistently amazing. He knew how to create tones on the bass that sounded as if he were "talking" on a horn. There may be more perfect bassists, but nobody could "tell a story" as O. P. could. In the two years before his death, when he lived in Europe (first in Baden-Baden, then in Copenhagen), he had a strong and lasting influence on many European musicians. (And if the author [Berendt] is permitted a personal word of gratitude here, I should like to say that I have not learned more from any great jazzman than from those night-long talks and record-listening sessions with O. P., who always considered it a special challenge to spread the "message," as he called it, of jazz.)

Ray Brown is considered the most dependable and swinging of bass players in classical modern jazz. He was featured in a bass concerto, "One Bass Hit," recorded by Dizzy Gillespie and his big band in the late forties. Brown is the preferred bassist for Norman Granz's record productions. Compared to the technical stunts of contemporary bassists, he may not be one of the modern virtuosos; but his unerring way of infusing swing and relaxation into a band still is unbeatable today.

Charles Mingus, who died in 1979, is of overriding significance, not only as a bass player, but also as a band leader. Mingus, who called jazz "black classical music," had an especially keen awareness of the black musical tradition, long before that became the norm, and he really lived this tradition. In the early forties, he briefly played traditional jazz with Kid Ory. Then he joined Lionel Hampton, whose best band—that of 1947—gained much from Mingus' arrangements and personality. Through his work with the Red Norvo Trio in 1950–51, he won renown as a soloist. Subsequently, he increasingly turned his attention to breaking new paths for jazz, never fearing powerful and exciting harmonic clashes. There was probably more collective improvisation in the Mingus groups of the fifties and early sixties than in any other significant jazz combo of that time. As a bassist, Mingus led and held together the many different lines and tendencies that took shape within his groups with the certitude of a sleepwalker. More than any other musician, he paved the way for the free, collective improvisations of the new jazz. The duets of Mingus on bass and the great avant-gardist Eric Dolphy on bass clarinet offer some of the strongest emotional experiences in all of jazz.

The triumvirate Pettiford-Brown-Mingus seems even more brilliant when seen in the light of a host of other outstanding jazz bassists of that generation, among them Milt Hinton, George Duvivier, Percy Heath, Tommy Potter, Curtis Counce, Leroy Vinnegar, Red Mitchell, Paul Chambers, Wilbur Ware. . . .

Duvivier and Hinton are "musicians' musicians," highly regarded by musicians for their assurance and dependability but less known to the general public. Percy Heath has become a much admired musician through his sovereignly supportive playing in the Modern Jazz Quartet. Leroy Vinnegar turned the California-based rhythm sections built around Shelly Manne upside down, insofar as Shelly found many melodic potentials in the drums, while Leroy's bass delivered the rhythmic foundation that made the swing felt. He, and before him Curtis Counce, who died in 1963, and later Monty Budwig, Carson Smith, and Joe Mondragon were among the most frequently recorded bassists on the West Coast. Red Mitchell is a wonderful soloist who phrases with saxophonelike intensity and mobility. In the seventies he had a fabulous comeback, particularly with Japanese audiences. The late Paul Chambers, one of Miles Davis' bassists, had the expressiveness and vitality of the Detroit hard-bop generation. He was also a master of bowed bass, and played *arco* with intonation and phrasing reminiscent of Sonny Rollins' tenor sax. His rounded, supple lines maintain an ideal balance between a supportive function and a melodically "emancipated" way of playing, thus radiating classicality to a particular degree. It is fitting that the bassists within modern classicism have time and again referred to Chambers. Wilbur Ware, who died in 1979, was a unique soloist and the chosen bassist of Thelonious Monk—probably the most empathetic Monk ever had.

With Chambers and Ware, we have arrived within the circle of hard-bop bassists: Jimmy Woode (who emerged from the Duke Ellington band, and since has become one of the most indispensable "Americans in Europe"), Wilbur Little, Jymie Merritt, Sam Jones, the late Doug Watkins, Reggie Workman, and others belong to this group. Some of them have been pathbreakers for the development that was carried out by Charlie Haden and Scott LaFaro: the second phase of the emancipation of the bass, after the first one associated with Jimmy Blanton and Oscar Pettiford.

Scott LaFaro, tragically killed in a 1961 auto crash at twenty-five, was a musician on the order of Eric Dolphy, creating new possibilities not from disdain for the harmonic tradition but from superior mastery of it. Hearing LaFaro improvise with the Bill Evans Trio makes clear what the bass has become through its second emancipation: a kind of superdimensional, low-register guitar whose sound has so many diverse possibilities as would have been thought impossible for the bass only a short time before, but that still fulfills the traditional functions of the bass. Said bassist Dave Holland, "The bass has become something like the fourth melody voice in the quartet. Wasn't Scott LaFaro the major reason for that?" John Coltrane's bassist Jimmy Garrison, who died in 1976, developed Scott LaFaro's "guitar sound" into a "flamenco guitar sound"—for example, in the long solo which he plays at the beginning of the 1966 recording of Trane's hit, "My Favorite Things." Perhaps even more amazing technically was the bass work of David Izenzon (who died in 1979) in the Ornette Coleman Trio during the mid-sixties. He presented his "guitarlike" bass sounds with the drive of a percussionist.

Since the turn of the fifties, Haden has frequently worked with Ornette Coleman, and he was—in the beginning perhaps even more so than Don Cherry—an essential partner of Coleman. His Liberation Music Orchestra, for which Carla Bley writes arrangements, expands not only musical but also political consciousness: music conceived as the guiding torch of freedom, using themes and recordings from East Germany, Cuba, the Spanish Civil War, and the Latin American liberation movements.

Haden revolutionized the harmonic concept of bass playing in jazz. He was the first bassist who consistently avoided playing *changes* or following preestablished harmonic schemes, but instead created a solid harmonic foundation out of the passage of independent melodies. In technical terms Haden isn't a virtuoso. His virtuosity lies on a higher level—in an incredible ability to make the double bass "sound out." Haden cultivates his instrument's gravity as no one else in jazz: with an unfathomably dark resonance and an earthiness of timbre, endowing even apparently "simple" lines with an affecting quality. He is a master of simplicity, which is among the most difficult things to achieve.

These, then, are the "headwaters" from which the bass mainstream flows through the sixties, seventies, and eighties—with musicians like Richard Davis, Ron Carter, Gary Peacock, Steve Swallow, Barre Phillips, Eddie Gomez, Marc Johnson, Cecil McBee, Buster Williams, Cameron Brown, Mike Richmond, Avery Sharpe, Neil Swainson, Ed Schuller, Charnett Moffett, David Friesen, Glen Moore, Rob Wasserman, Hungarian-born Aladar Pege, Henry Texier and Didier Levallet from France, Germans Günter Lenz and Thomas Heidepriem, Swedish Palle Danielsson, Denmark's Niels Henning-Ørsted Pedersen and Mads Vinding, and George Mraz and Miroslav Vitous from Czechoslovakia.

Because of this wealth of players, we can give special mention to only a few. Richard Davis is perhaps the most versatile of all bassists. He is one of those universalists who have mastered with equal perfection everything from symphonic music to all kinds of jazz, all the way from bop to free playing. Ron Carter became known through his work with Miles Davis. He is an improviser with such a wealth of ideas that, as critic Pete Welding put it, it "occasionally seems as if he is playing duos with himself." And he's also a master of "note bending"—sensitively sliding and bending the tone. Coming from the acoustic bass, he has mastered a wide range of instruments: first the cello, and since 1976 a "piccolo bass"—an instrument of baroque music—in cellolike tuning. Carter plays the piccolo bass, which is to the contrabass approximately what the violin is to the viola, with the brilliance and lightness of a pizzicato concert violin and, at the same time, with the drive of a jazz player like Oscar Pettiford. It is fascinating how, in the quartet he led from 1977 to 1980, his piccolo bass and the conventional acoustic bass (initially played by Buster Williams, later by others) complemented each other, creating the impression that the group employed a single eight-string bass—probably the richest bass sound on today's scene. Ron Carter in a *Down Beat* interview:

> The term "liberation of the bass" has such negative overtones to it—it means that someone has been in bondage up to this point. . . . I've never felt inhibited in what I was trying to play. I didn't necessarily feel that I was a bass in a rhythm section that played behind or accompanied a soloist, that my function was just a function. . . . Since the music the electronic bass is predominantly used in is so different from the acoustic bass, it's like comparing apples and oranges. I don't see the electric bass as having any major input in regard to the development of the upright bass at any time.

Gary Peacock, Steve Swallow, and Europe-based Barre Phillips are particularly sensitive and immensely flexible bassists. Eddie Gomez is the most resplendent player extending the virtuoso Scott LaFaro line. For eleven years he was bassist in the Bill Evans Trio. Charles Mingus appointed Gomez, a Puerto Rican, as stand-in when the bandleader's state of health prevented him from playing in recordings. Gomez phrases on the bass as if he were playing an oversized cello. His emancipated playing with its brilliant singing sound reaches up to the highest registers. He also "percussionizes" bass playing: his *pizzicato* lines seem to be "drummed." Gomez is a master of plucking the G string by way of an abrupt, sideways flicking of the finger, creating a tearing, splitting sound—similar to the slap technique but more supple because the string doesn't smack against the fingerboard.

Particularly worthy of notice among bassists from the younger generation influenced by Gomez are John Patitucci, who made a name for himself with Chick Corea, and Dieter Ilg from Germany. Patitucci unites the Gomez technique with an especially virtuoso legato style. Ilg has time and again been engaged for the European tours of trumpeter Randy Brecker's group.

Marc Johnson is the ideal trio bassist on the current scene, as in the Bill Evans Trio or the John Abercrombie Trio. He is a master of anticipation, of inducing and introducing harmonic changes. With his group Bass Desires he made a decisive contribution toward his instrument gaining unexpected acclaim in eighties jazz-rock. Among the other bassists who have brought the warmth and relaxation of upright bass playing into a jazz-rock-oriented context, giving the style an unanticipated boost, are Charnett Moffett, Lonnie Plaxico, Steve Rodby, and Frenchman Bruno Chevillion.

Charnett Moffett, son of drummer Charles Moffett, played in Wynton Marsalis' band at the age of sixteen. Since then he is viewed as one of the most flexible bassists on the contemporary scene—from a traditional mainstream player *à la* Ray Brown by way of extension of the Paul Chambers tradition within classicism to the fusion sounds of Stanley Clarke (still to be introduced).

Cecil McBee and Buster Williams cultivate and update the Coltrane tradition on the bass in a way similar to McCoy Tyner on the piano. David Friesen and Glen Moore have come to the fore in the sphere of world music with a number of chamber-music-like recordings: Friesen, for instance, in a duo with flutist Paul Horn with an absolutely original sound produced by a self-constructed "Oregon bass," and Moore in the group Oregon. Aladar Pege, bass teacher at the Hungarian National Conservatoire in Budapest, has been extolled for over fifteen years now as a "simply incredible bass miracle in terms of playing technique." His performance at the Jazz Yatra at Bombay in 1980 so moved Charles Mingus' widow that she gave him one of her husband's basses as a present. Since then Pege has several times taken the place of the great Mingus in the Mingus Destiny group. Miroslav Vitous was a founding member of the first Weather Report in 1971. He's a specialist in unconventional bowing, even up to the highest, elegiacally "singing" flageolet reaches. Avery Sharpe has been McCoy Tyner's favorite bassist since 1981, matching the pianist's percussive intensity. He ironically calls himself a "frustrated drummer."

The most-recorded bassist in Europe is the Dane Niels-Henning Ørsted Pedersen. During the last two decades, whenever an American soloist on tour in Europe needed a bassist, Niels-Henning was almost always the musician to get the call. In this way, he came to play with Bud Powell, Quincy Jones, Roland Kirk, Sonny Rollins, Lee Konitz, John Lewis, Dexter Gordon, Ben Webster, Oscar Peterson, and dozens of other famous musicians.

Ørsted Pedersen summarized the situation of the bass on today's scene in the following way:

> The bass has become more and more independent as an instrument. In the older jazz there was a very strong connection between instrument and solo, and

it's my opinion that a solo should not be determined by the instrument. What I like today is that you've left the point behind where you have technical difficulties; there's no reason to be impressed by anything, just go for the music.

In a countermovement to the "emancipated" playing of the sixties and seventies, many eighties bassists returned to fundamentals. Instead of going for agile, solo-type lines as in the "cello school of bass playing" (Branford Marsalis), they concentrated on their instrument's powerful deep dimension. In their striving for melodic flexibility, many bassists may have made their instrument more quickly playable—by working with pick-ups (contact microphones) that brighten the sound or by lowering plucking strength—but they often achieved a thinner tone and a less succinct sound.

That's where the eighties "fundamentalists" of bass playing set to work. They consciously reflect the deep sound quality of the bass, its gravity and supportive weight, while their interest in solo flexibility somewhat recedes. Strikingly, most such players come from the sphere of classicism (or at least closely related to it, alongside other ways of playing). They include Bob Hurst, Reginald Veal, Lonnie Plaxico, Charles Fambrough, Ira Coleman, and Santi DeBriano. Bob Hurst in particular convincingly cultivates the bass's natural harmonics with that warmth and suppleness present in the instrument's wood. In recordings with Wynton Marsalis and Tony Williams he seems like a "Ray Brown of classicism," but he also shines in the rhythmic challenges of free funk, for instance when playing with altoist Steve Coleman. Lonnie Plaxico is an enormously supple, powerful bassist who has performed with such different drummers as Art Blakey and Jack DeJohnette.

Beyond the mainstream, we find—as with the other instruments—players of free music on the one hand, and fusion and jazz-rock players (who mostly use the electric bass) on the other. (Here, too, one must realize that, particularly today, many musicians have become so versatile that they can belong to the most diverse stylistic camps. We will list them in the groupings where they are most often found.) Important free bassists are Buell Neidlinger, Peter Warren, Sirone, Henry Grimes, Alan Silva, Malachi Favors, Dave Holland, Fred Hopkins, John Lindberg, Rick Rozie, William Parker, Briton Brian Smith, Japanese Yoshizawa Motoharu and Katsuo Kuninaka, Austrian Adelhard Roidinger, Norwegian Arild Andersen, Italian Marcello Mellis, Dutchmen Arjen Gorter and Maarten Altena, Germans Peter Kowald and Buschi Niebergall, South African Johnny Dyani, and Joelle Leandre from France. Musicians like Neidlinger, Sirone, and Silva belong to the first generation of free players. Neidlinger and Sirone worked with Cecil Taylor, Silva with Sun Ra's orchestra. Malachi Favors plays bass in the Art Ensemble of Chicago. Arild Andersen could be called an especially "romantic" player. Yoshizawa Motoharu's immensely intense bass is deeply rooted in the Japanese tradition, as was Johnny Dyani's (d. 1986) in the tradition of his native South Africa. Maarten Altena and Peter Kowald have particularly persisted in breaking with the principle of ongoing rhythm demanded of conventional bass playing.

Neoclassical players follow on directly from free bassists, absolutely in accordance with the style-surmounting principles of postmodern jazz. They are headed by Dave Holland, and then come Fred Hopkins, Mark Helias, Anthony Cox, John Lindberg, Lindsey Horner, Mark Dresser, Jaribu Shihad, and Swiss-born Martin Schütz. Dave Holland has moved on from being a seventies bassist specializing in free timbres to becoming a majestic bass voice of neoclassicism. No one since Mingus has so convincingly demonstrated what a bass player can achieve within traditional forms if he deliberately turns these upside down, rhythmically and harmonically, as Holland and his celebrated Quintet do. He is a master of unexpected rhythmic and harmonic resolutions. Fred Hopkins is the bassist in Air and the Henry Threadgill Sextet. Of all neoclassical bass players he possesses the fullest sound, resonating powerfully—as a critic once said—"like a giant suspension bridge of dark wood." Mark Helias started with Anthony Braxton, and from that avant-garde stance has worked step by step backward through the legacy of jazz. His lines are so flexible and full of ideas that they unfold particularly well when not backed by other harmony instruments. Anthony Cox, who first played with the bands around James Newton and Muhal Richard Abrams, is an unusually elegant, supple stylist with a strong sense of the African roots of black music. John Lindberg played with Anthony Braxton and now belongs to the String Trio of New York. Mark Dresser, first presented by Anthony Braxton and Ray Anderson, has an especially homogeneous, natural sound and has made marvelous recordings with the Arcado string trio.

It took years for electric bass players to solve the problems they had with their sound—the dull, somehow always empty tone of the instrument. Their dilemma was this: On the one hand, the electric bass had more flexibility, its sound (and volume!) fit better into electric groups; on the other hand it lacked expressivity and didn't sound "human" but technical. The first player to initiate a change in the early seventies was a rock bassist: Larry Graham of Sly and the Family Stone. He did something that bass teachers of the academy would strictly forbid: He played, incredibly percussively, with his thumb. In the black rock and rhythm and blues production of Motown Records, this thumb style became something like a trademark: the bass played with such intensity that its strings occasionally hit the wood of the instrument, just like the old New Orleans slap bass. Stanley Clarke combined this thumb style with Scott LaFaro's technique (and was immensely successful with his fusion music). LaFaro's technique had already been used on the electric bass by Steve Swallow. His wiry, brittle, and yet full sound and his melodious lines constitute one of the most unmistakable styles in the realm of the electric bass, unfolding with great sensitivity in his performances with Carla Bley. The problem was solved, however, by Jaco Pastorius from Florida, who became famous overnight in 1976 when he played with Weather Report but who died tragically early in 1987. The significance of Pastorius' playing for the electric bass is comparable to Charlie Parker's importance for the (alto) saxophone. On his fretless instrument he combined the thumb approach and LaFaro's flexibility with an octave technique previously associated with guitarist Wes Montgomery but considered out of reach for bassists. He added as well an iridescent flageolet technique and virtuosic chordal playing. Pastorius thereby became the real "bass sensation" of the seventies. Only through him did the electric bass gain complete emancipation. All of a sudden the electric bass possessed what Oscar Pettiford had made the chief criterion for all jazz bass playing: "Humanity, expressivity, emotionality, the ability to tell a story." Said Pastorius, "I play the bass as if I were playing a human voice. I play like I speak. I like singers."

If there's a high point in the consistently high-quality development of the jazz-rock group Weather Report, then it was in the time from 1976 to 1981 when Pastorius played there. As arranger, composer, and producer, he constituted (to a greater extent than Wayne Shorter) the ideal creative counterpart to Joe Zawinul. Zawinul admits that he asked the unknown Pastorius, after hearing him for the first time on a tape, whether he could also play the electric bass. "He was playing so fast and so fluid, unlike any electric player at that time, that I thought it was an upright bass."

Among the other important electric bassists we must first mention four musicians who predate the development just discussed: Jack Bruce, Chuck Rainey, Eberhard Weber, and Hugh Hopper. Jack Bruce was a member of the celebrated group Cream, which in the sixties was involved in then-new sorts of jam sessions and blues-inspired rock improvisations. Even though he was closely linked with the British rock scene, Bruce made several recordings with jazz musicians, including Charlie Mariano, Carla Bley, and Kip Hanrahan. Eberhard Weber developed—independently of Jaco Pastorius—a singing, "humane" way of playing the electric bass. His pervasively warm sound floats with the lightness of an imaginary choir. Weber has talked about his sense of allegiance to the European tradition, bringing elements from that tradition (above all from Romanticism) and also from Steve Reich's minimal music into his own playing and that of his group Colours. Hugh Hopper was linked with Soft Machine. Alphonso Johnson is a particularly elegant, versatile, much-employed performer on the West Coast fusion scene.

All electric bassists after Pastorius refer to Jaco in the same way as all saxophonists after Charlie Parker relate to Bird. Correspondingly long is the list of musicians who individually cultivate Pastorius' legacy: Will Lee, Abe Laborial, Jeff Berlin, Mark Egan, John Lee, Percy Jones, Tom Barney, Marcus Miller, Bill Laswell, Victor Bailey, Gerald Veasley, Daryl Jones, Jeff Andrews, Kim Clarke, Lincoln Goines, Denmark's Bo Stief, Swedish-born Jonas Hellborg, Lawrence Cottle and Phil Mulford from England, and Spaniard Carlos Benavent.

Jeff Berlin is the only electric bassist Bill Evans ever allowed to play with him, matching the pianist's sensitivity. During the seventies Bo Stief was the most sought-after electric bassist on the European scene. Hellborg has attracted attention as both a sensitive duo partner with John McLaughlin and a performer of punk jazz. He is a highly virtuoso player who cultivates Pastorius' legacy with refined chordal playing, almost "pianistic" in its fullness. Victor Bailey followed Pastorius in Weather Report in 1981 and is also his equal in virtuosity even though, unlike Jaco, he plays a bass with frets. Gerald Veasley, who came from the bands of Odean Pope and Joe Zawinul, phrases percussive, intense, jagged lines, playing the electric bass like "an African drum orchestra." John Patitucci, who became known through playing with Chick Corea, has particularly advanced phrasing on the relatively rare six-string electric bass, making use of the entire tonal register and harmonic range of an instrument that is so difficult to master. Even before Patitucci, Anthony Jackson drew attention to the possibilities open to the six-string electric bass with a profoundly deep dryness of sound, which made him much in demand among many other musicians including Steve Khan and Gerry Mulligan.

Jaco Pastorius brought virtuoso electric bass playing to a high point and, some musicians believe, its apogee for the moment. At the start of the eighties, at any rate, emphasis on solo virtuoso performance seemed played out. More and more bassists concentrated on their instrument's earthy, robust, supportive qualities, paralleling in striking fashion developments in the sphere of the double bass. However, similar outcomes often arise independently of one another, as was the case here. The return to the earthiness of the electric bass resulted from the laws inherent in the instrument itself. Two musicians showed the way ahead, leading to completely different outcomes: Marcus Miller and Bill Laswell. Miller economized and pared down the Pastorius legacy, bringing it back to the foundations. "I analyzed all his solos, man, and it opened up a whole new world for me. I got my basic chordal training from listening to his records." Miller's supple, springy rhythms optimize swinging intensity in the realm of the electric bass. In his concentration on the essentials he's a fellow spirit to Miles Davis, which a musician with Miles' nose immediately recognized. He engaged Miller not only as bassist in his band (the most supple electric bassist Miles has ever had in a band) but also as producer, composer, and arranger for three albums (*Tutu*, 1986; *Siesta*, 1987; and *Amandla*, 1989), a privilege only previously accorded Gil Evans. Critics in fact noticed similarities in the way Miller and Evans arrange. According to Miller, "The bass is there to supply a foundation for the rest of the music. The guys who excite me most are the guys who can supply the foundation and still be interesting."

Bill Laswell, who is also a successful producer and supplied the rhythm tracks for Herbie Hancock's hit "Rockit," minimalizes the Pastorius approach by way of the vibrant vehemence and brusqueness of punk. But he also allows elements from rap, reggae, and free jazz to flow into his music. He phrases somber, low lines full of "dirty" timbre and weight. His band Material was one of the most important eighties no wave groups. He later played free jazz with heavy metal influences in the Last Exit band. "I don't want to have the bass competing up on top with guitars and brass," Laswell said. "I want to feel the bass as a foundation."

Among the other electric bassists who deliberately make the Pastorius style more plain and elemental are Daryl Jones, Lonnie Plaxico, Jeff Andrews, Lincoln Goines, Kim Clarke, and German Alois Kott. Daryl Jones combines a fat, robust sound with a feeling for paring down, so that he acted as an unshakeable anchor in the Miles Davis and Sting bands. Kim Clarke became known through her playing with the group Defunkt and with George Gruntz.

Outside the Pastorius school, although much stimulated by Jaco, are the free-funk bassists: Jamaaladeen Tacuma, Melvin Gibbs, Albert MacDowell, Kevin Bruce Harris, and Amin Ali. All these musicians, except for Harris, can be assigned, more or less closely, to the circle around Ornette Coleman's harmolodic music. Jamaaladeen Tacuma (formerly known as Rudy Mc-Daniel) was for long linked with Coleman's Prime Time band, and he was involved in the *Dancing in Your Head* recording. Tacuma changed the role of the electric bass. Most electric bassists play static riffs, but Tacuma opens them up into free tonality, bringing about an unceasing process of melodic renewal by continuing and modulating the initial melody. Tacuma thus succeeded in simultaneously providing a foundation and being equally important as melodic soloist. Ornette Coleman called him the "master of the sequence." Melvin Gibbs, who emerged from Ronald Shannon Jackson's Decoding Society, produces metallic, angular, vehemently forward-thrusting lines. Kevin Bruce Harris is close to altoist Steve Coleman's rhythmically complex, interlocking world of free funk.

Jazz has made the bass, the "clumsy elephant" of the symphony orchestra, into a highly sensitive instrumental voice commanding the whole range of expressive possibilities—to a point where bassists like Rick Rozie, Jaco

Pastorius, or David Friesen can successfully play solo concerts that are filled with musical tension and beauty. When you consider that Pastorius can handle Charlie Parker's "Donna Lee"—a tune that has driven many a horn player to exasperation—as if it were the easiest thing in the world, then you start to realize what kind of development the jazz bass has gone through since the days of Jimmy Blanton.

At the conclusion of this bass section, let's once again quote the veteran bassist Ray Brown:

> Take a guy like myself, who's been playing the bass since he was fourteen. I've seen this instrument go from a slapped, two-beat instrument into complete freedom with people like Stanley Clarke.... I have been cast in situations where the guy says, "You're free." I said, "Wait a minute. I don't know if I want to be free," I've talked to kids who don't know anything but freedom. They don't know what it's like to play time and enjoy it.... And yet, I like what's happening to the bass. Some of the young people I have heard play the bass like a guitar and it's fantastic. But I also still enjoy going someplace and seeing somebody playing time with a good sound—that will never be replaced! It's like a heartbeat.

The Drums

To the person raised in the tradition of European concert music, jazz drums initially appear to be noise-making devices. But, paradoxical as it may seem, this is because the drums serve this very purpose in European music. The timpani parts in Tchaikovsky or Richard Strauss, in Beethoven or Wagner, are "noisemakers" insofar as they are intended to create additional intensity and *fortissimo* effects. The music "happens" independently of them; the musical continuity would not break down if they were left out. But the beat of the jazz drum is no mere effect. It creates the space within which the music "happens": the musical continuity would sometimes be disrupted if there were no chance of constantly "measuring" it against the beat of a swinging drummer. Jazz rhythm, as we have already shown, is an ordering principle.

It was no accident that there were no drum solos in the early forms of jazz; indeed, there were no drummers then with developed individuality. Concerning early jazz history, we know of Buddy Bolden and Freddie Keppard and the Tio family; we know of trumpeters, trombonists, even violinists; but we hardly know anything of drummers. Since the beat was the ordering principle (and only that!) the drummer had no task but to mark the beats as steadily as possible, a task that was performed the worse the less neutrally (i.e., the more individually) he drummed. Only later was it discovered that an additional element of the tension so important to jazz could be gained from the individuality of a drummer—without loss to the ordering function. Quite the contrary: unvaried, metronomic regulation developed into organically nuanced artistic order.

At the beginning stand Baby Dodds and Zutty Singleton, the great drummers of New Orleans. Zutty was the softer, Baby the harder. Zutty created an almost supple rhythm; Baby was vehement and natural—at least in the terms of that day. Dodds was the drummer in King Oliver's Creole Jazz Band, later with Louis Armstrong's Hot Seven. He can be heard on many records with his brother, clarinetist Johnny Dodds. Baby was the first to play breaks: brief drum eruptions, which often fill in the gaps between the conclusion of a phrase and the end of a formal unit or which set off solos from each other. The break is the egg from which drummers—primarily Gene Krupa—hatched the drum solo.

Oddly enough, white drummers initially expressed more strongly the tendency toward accentuating the weak beats (2 and 4) so characteristic of jazz. The first two are the drummers of the two famous early white bands: Tony Spargo (Sbarbaro) of the Original Dixieland Jazz Band and Ben Pollack of the New Orleans Rhythm Kings. Pollack later founded one of the first larger jazz-oriented dance bands in California (1925) in which many musicians who began in Chicago style—among them Benny Goodman, Jack Teagarden, and Glenn Miller—first became known. In the late twenties, Ray Bauduc held the drum chair in the Pollack band. Ray is one of the best white drummers in the New Orleans–Dixieland tradition.

Within the Chicago-style circle "white" drumming developed in a different direction: toward virtuoso play with rhythm, in which the play occasionally became more important than the rhythm. The three most important Chicago drummers were Gene Krupa, George Wettling, and Dave Tough. George Wettling was the only one who remained true to the musical tradition of Chicago style until the end of his life (he died in 1968). Wettling was also a gifted abstract painter. He remarked that jazz drumming and abstract painting seemed different to him only from the point of view of craftsmanship: in both fields, he felt rhythm to be decisive. To someone who expressed amazement that Wettling should be both abstract painter and jazz drummer, he conveyed his own surprise that he should be the only one active in both spheres, since in his opinion they belonged together. George Wettling was one of those fascinating personalities who demonstrate the unity of modern art simply through their work.

Gene Krupa, who died in 1973, became the star drum virtuoso of the Swing era. "Sing Sing Sing," his feature with the Benny Goodman band, in which he played a long solo (in part with Benny's high-register clarinet soaring above him), drove the Swing fans to frenzy. Technically, Krupa was topped only by the drummers of modern jazz. He was the first who dared to use the bass drum on recordings in the twenties. It had been the practice to dispense with recording this part of the drummer's equipment, due to the danger that its reverberations would cause the cutting needle to jump on the still rather primitive recording equipment.

The most important drummer of the Chicago circle is Dave Tough, who died in 1948. He, too, was a man who knew something about the unity of modern art—if not as a painter, then as a would-be writer. Throughout his life, he flirted with contemporary literature as Bix Beiderbecke had flirted with symphonic music. Tough was one of the most subtle and inspired of drummers of his time. To him, the drums were a rhythmic palette on which he held in readiness the right color for each soloist. He gained his greatest fame around 1944 as the drummer in Woody Herman's "First Herd." He helped pave the way for modern jazz drumming, as did Jo Jones with Count Basie's band, and it is interesting to note how a white and a black drummer arrived at similar results more or less independently of each other.

More about Jo Jones later, but let us point out that here is a fact vividly illuminating the element of inevitability in jazz evolution. Aside from Baby Dodds, the white Chicago drummers hardly drew much from other black drummers. Even though there were constant relations with black musicians, one could say that for twenty years "white" and "black" drumming in the main developed independently of each other. Nevertheless, the two evolutionary branches arrived at similar results. Dave Tough prepared the way for the new style in Tommy Dorsey's band, which he joined in 1936. At this time, Jo Jones was doing basically the same thing with Count Basie.

Jo Jones developed under the influence of the great black New Orleans and Swing drummers. Along the line leading from Baby Dodds to Jo Jones, there are four important drummers. The most important is Chick Webb, whose elemental power conjures up a giant rather than the crippled, dwarfish man he actually was. Chick Webb and, among white drummers, Gene Krupa were first in the line of the "drummer leaders," big band leaders whose instrument was drums. This line was later continued brilliantly by Mel Lewis, Buddy Rich, and Louie Bellson. Webb was a drummer with a magnetizing aura. There are recordings of his band in which his drums are barely audible, and yet each note conveys the excitement that emanated from this amazing man.

Big Sid Catlett, Cozy Cole, and Lionel Hampton follow Webb. Big Sid (d. 1951) and Cozy (d. 1981) are Swing drummers par excellence. Cozy made his first recordings in 1930 with Jelly Roll Morton. In 1939, he became the drummer with Cab Calloway's band, in which he was frequently featured in solos. In the late forties, he was the drummer in Louis Armstrong's best All-Star group, and in 1954 he founded a drum school with Gene Krupa in New York.

Cole and Catlett were for a long time considered the most versatile drummers in jazz, equally in demand for combo or big-band work, for New Orleans, Dixieland, and Swing recordings (and Catlett even in a few records important in the history of bop)—in other words, in all the different fields in which other drummers specialized. Catlett was with Benny Carter and McKinney's Cotton Pickers in the early thirties, then worked with Fletcher Henderson. At the turn of the thirties, he was Louis Armstrong's preferred drummer. "Swing is my idea of how a melody should go," he said—not a scientific definition, but a statement that the musicians of the time, and jazz fans of all times, have understood better than all the fancy theories.

The difference between traditional and modern drumming becomes clear when one compares Cozy Cole and Jo Jones. Both are great musicians, but Cole is completely absorbed in the beat, staccato fashion, and relatively unconcerned with musical shading of what the horns are playing. Jones also creates an imperturbable, driving beat, but in more legato fashion, carrying and serving the musical happenings. The Count Basie rhythm section in its classic period (with Jones' drums, Freddie Green's guitar, Walter Page's bass, and Basie's piano) was known as the "All American Rhythm Section."

Jo Jones is the first firmly committed representative of the even four-bar unit. He said, "The easiest way you can recognize whether a man is swinging or not is when the man gives his every note its full beat. Like a full note four beats, and a half note two beats, and a quarter note one beat. And there are four beats to a measure that really are as even as our breathing. A man doesn't swing when there's anticipation." Kenny Clarke followed this dictum through: The even four beats became the *son continu*—the ceaseless sounding of the rhythm. The basic beat was displaced from the heavy, pounding bass drum to the steadily resounding ride cymbal.

Clarke, the drummer of the Minton circle that included Charlie Christian, Thelonious Monk, Charlie Parker, and Dizzy Gillespie, is the creator of modern drum technique. It seems to us that he is often overlooked in this capacity by jazz friends in the United States, perhaps because he lived in Paris from 1956 until his death in 1985 and became the respected father figure of all the many Americans in Europe. Max Roach, of course, has developed this manner of playing to its most complete maturity. He is the prototype of the modern percussionist: no longer the more or less subordinate "drummer" who must beat out his even 4/4, but an accomplished musician who has studied, generally is able to play an additional instrument, and often knows how to arrange. It is almost the opposite of what used to be: Once, drummers almost always were the least schooled musicians in the band; today they are often the most intelligent, as interesting in personality and education as in their playing. Roach once said, "To do with rhythm what Bach did with melody." This was not just meant as an impressive slogan; jazz rhythm has literally achieved the multilinear complexity of baroque play with melodic lines.

Roach was the first to drum complete melodic lines. There are private recordings, made at the historic bop sessions at the Royal Roost in New York in the late forties, on which Roach, in dialogue with Lee Konitz, consistently completes phrases Konitz has started. You can sing along with Roach's drumming just as well as with Konitz's alto playing. And vice versa: What Lee plays on alto is rhythmically as complex as what Max plays on the drums. The drums are no longer exclusively a rhythm instrument, and the alto sax is no longer just a melody instrument. Both have enlarged their range in a complex joining of what earlier could more readily be distinguished as "melody," "harmony," and "rhythm" than today. Thus, Roach could manage without a piano in his quintet of the late fifties. His sidemen vividly said, "He does the piano player's comping on the drums."

Roach has effectively destroyed the belief that jazz can swing only in 4/4 time. He plays entire drum solos in thorough, accurately accented waltz rhythm and swings more than many a musician who limits himself to 4/4. And he superimposes rhythms tightly and structurally, almost as in polyrhythmic conterpoint, such as 5/4 over 3/4. Roach does all this with a lucidity and restraint that gives meaning to his expression "I look for lyricism." No one has proved more clearly than Roach that lyricism—poetic lyricism—can be conveyed through a drum solo. His *We Insist! Freedom Now Suite* is one of the most moving jazz works dedicated to the black liberation struggle in America.

Max Roach founded entire drum ensembles—in 1970 the M'Boom group: ten drummers of percussionists superimposing rhythm with a complexity and differentiation that make the phrasing of similar groups in modern concert music seem naive and clumsy.

Of all the players of the bebop generation, Max Roach developed furthest and opened himself stylistically most imposingly. He is the only drummer to have been involved in the trail-blazing recordings of no fewer than three jazz styles: in the 1945 Charlie Parker Quintet shaping bebop, in the 1949–50 Miles David Capitol Orchestra forming cool jazz, and in the mid-fifties Max Roach–Clifford Brown Quintet opening the way for hard bop. His group at the end of the seventies was one of the germ cells for the neobop scene. And at the start of the eighties he also demonstrated his powers of rhythmic and melodic communication in "free" duo concerts and recordings with musicians like Archie Shepp, Anthony Braxton, and Dollar Brand. The dialogues he undertook with avant-garde pianist Cecil Taylor, recorded live at a New York concert in 1979, are among the most exciting duo experiences jazz has to offer. Said free-jazz drummer Jerome Cooper,

"Before this concert I thought that Max Roach was the king of bebop drummers. Now I know he's the king of the drummers."

Meanwhile, it has become obvious: The drums became a melody instrument . . . or more precisely, became a melody instrument *as well.* Certainly the drums did not suddenly give up their rhythmic function. Through the increasingly complex, more musical conception of rhythmic function, the melodic function arose by itself. Logically and inevitably, the drums went the way of all the instruments in and around the rhythm section. First came the trombone, which had only furnished the harmonic background in New Orleans; Kid Ory began, with his tailgate effects, and Jimmy Harrison completed, with his solo work with Fletcher Henderson, the emancipation of the trombone. Then came the piano, which insofar as it was used at all in New Orleans bands, was purely a rhythm-and-harmony instrument. Earl Hines emancipated it: not relinquishing the rhythmic-harmonic function but opening the way toward a hornlike one. Guitar and bass went a similar way. The evolution of the guitar from Eddie Lang to Charlie Christian is one of increasing emancipation. On the bass, Jimmy Blanton brought about this emancipation with one stroke. And finally, Kenny Clarke and Max Roach made the drums an "emancipated instrument."

The interest expressed by Roach and the bop musicians in drumming and in Cuban rhythms (which also are in principle West African) thus appears logical. Art Blakey was the first jazz drummer to go to Africa, in the early fifties, and study African rhythms and incorporate them into his playing (see also the section on percussion). He has made duet recordings with the Cuban Bongo drummer Sabu that are a constant interplay between jazz and West African rhythms; *Nothing But the Soul* (1954) is the characteristic title of one of these recordings. (It was the first time that the word *soul* was used in a jazz title; a couple of years later it designated a playing style in jazz, and later in rock and in pop music.) In the late fifties (i.e., before Roach) Blakey put together whole percussion orchestras: four jazz drummers (Jo Jones among them) and five Latin drummers, using all kinds of rhythm instruments and playing together under the slogan "Orgy in Rhythm." And, of course, once the drums were emancipated—that is, once they have acquired melodic possibilities from the complexity of the rhythms—orchestras of percussionists had to become possible, just as there are orchestras made up of brass players or saxophonists.

What is characteristic about these efforts is the fact that the African influence has continually gained in importance for jazz drummers. Many theoreticians and ethnomusicologists believe that the African heritage was strongest in the original jazz forms and has been lessened ever since. In reality, however, jazz instrumentalists—and mainly drummers, in parallel with their growing political and sociological awareness and identification—have infused more African elements into jazz since the days of free jazz than the instrumental, urban jazz music from New Orleans via Chicago to Harlem ever had to show.

Since the fifties Art Blakey has done more for up-and-coming musicians than all the conservatories, music colleges, and clinics with all their theories and seminars taken together. So many musicians emerged out of his diverse Jazz Messengers groups—a "university" of *lived* rather than pontificated jazz intensity—that only the most important can be mentioned here: Wayne Shorter, Lee Morgan, Freddie Hubbard, Woody Shaw, Keith Jarrett, Chick Corea, JoAnne Brackeen, Mulgrew Miller, Curtis Fuller, Slide Hampton, Bobby Watson, Terence Blanchard, Donald Harrison, Wynton and Branford Marsalis, Wallace Roney, and Robin Eubanks.

Blakey is the wildest and most vital of all the jazz drummers to emerge from bop. His rolls and explosions are famous. Compared to this, Max Roach seems more subdued and intellectual. Philadelphia-born "'Philly' Joe Jones (d. 1985) merged the two approaches. He played with the explosive vehemence of Blakey, but he also had elements of Max Roach's musical cosmopolitanism. Even more "sophisticated"—in the refined sense this word has acquired in the terminology of jazz musicians—is the playing of Joe Morello. He had the maturity, if not the vitality, of Max Roach, with a nearly somnambulistic feeling for the improvisations of his colleagues. Morello joined the Dave Brubeck Quartet in 1957. Through him, Brubeck gained a rhythmical awareness that he had lacked before. Ten years later, Alan Dawson replaced Morello for a while. Dawson also taught percussion at Berklee College in Boston, the most famous of jazz schools. He combines intellect and spirit with a swing and drive that hark back to the great drummers of the jazz tradition. Particularly integrated into melodic play is the drum work of Connie Kay with the Modern Jazz Quartet (see also the chapter dealing with jazz combos).

The drummers of hard bop—Art Taylor, Louis Hayes, Dannie Richmond, Pete LaRocca, Roy Haynes, Albert Heath, and (although he has gone far beyond hard bop) Elvin Jones, to mention only the most important—link back to Blakey and Roach. Dannie Richmond (d. 1988) was the only musician to remain affiliated with Charles Mingus for a considerable time. In the combo chapter, we will point out how important he was for the togetherness of Mingus' music (and in the seventies and eighties for the continuation of his legacy). Roy Haynes gave the successful, bossa-nova-influenced Stan Getz Quartet of the sixties its true jazz feeling. Roy possesses that certain hipness so important not only for the music but also for the jazz musician's life-style. He made recordings in the seventies that are heard as jazz-rock rhythms by fusion fans but that can be perceived as ironic questionings of jazz-rock, too. Elvin Jones—the third member of the family from Detroit, which gave us two other remarkable talents in pianist Hank and trumpeter-composer Thad—plays a kind of "superbop" that musicians felt to be a new way of "turning the rhythm around"—after all that has already been done in this area by Charlie Parker and Kenny Clarke. In a period when one could hardly imagine that further concentration and compression of the rhythmic happenings in jazz were possible, Elvin Jones and his cohorts proved that the evolution continues. There has been further development, too, in the field of "encircling" the basic rhythm. The less the drummers play "on" the beat and the more they play "around" it, the more elemental is the perception of the basic rhythm—almost paradoxically. "It's less, and yet more," said John McLaughlin about Elvin Jones.

Before we can attempt to show where this development has led, we must refer to a number of drummers who stand outside the realm of these tendencies and represent a basically timeless modern Swing approach, in which new developments are less of a stylistic nature but tend more toward even greater professionalism and perfection. *The* main representative of these drummers is Buddy Rich (d. 1987), a *ne plus ultra* of virtuoso technique. His astonishing drum solos and no less astonishing personality were highlights of the big bands of Artie Shaw, Tommy Dorsey, and Harry James, as well as of his own brilliant big bands. At a drum workshop at the 1965 Newport Festival, he "stole the show" from all the other drummers—and among them were Art Blakey, Jo Jones, Elvin Jones, Roy Haynes, and Louie Bellson. However, Rich often gives one the impression that he is a great vaudeville artist—a circus artist who performs the most breathtaking *salti mortali* without a net—rather than a genuine jazz musician in the sense of Roach, Blakey, or Elvin Jones. It certainly is of psychological interest that Buddy Rich was born into a family of vaudevillians.

Louie Bellson, also an excellent arranger, put *two* bass drums in the place of one, and played them with an agility comparable to the footwork of an organist. During his years with Duke Ellington (1951 to 1953) the band gained a new, typical "Bellson" sound. Ellington's Sam Woodyard retained the two bass drum setup, and fifteen years later double bass drums became standard equipment for many rock drummers.

The name Denzil Best stands for a way of playing known as "fill-out" technique. Kenny Clarke, Max Roach, and Art Blakey "fill in" the musical proceedings, placing their accents wherever they deem appropriate. This is the "fill-in" technique. But Best "fills out" the musical space evenly, placing no (or hardly any) accents but stirring his brushes continuously on the snare drum, and thus creating his own special *son continu* swing. This, too, is an end result of the legato evolution initiated by Jo Jones and Dave Tough. After the great success of the George Shearing Quintet around 1950, where Best was a member, his way of drumming has been copied in hundreds of modern cocktail-lounge groups.

From Dave Tough descend a number of excellent big-band drummers, such as Don Lamond, Dave's successor with Woody Herman, or Tiny Kahn, who died much too young and also was a gifted arranger whose themes are still being played. Other drummers of this lineage are Gus Johnson, J.C. Heard, the late Osie Johnson and Shadow Wilson, as well as Oliver Jackson, Grady Tate, Mel Lewis, Sonny Payne, and Rufus Jones.

Wilson, Gus Johnson, and Payne were Jo Jones' successors in the Basie band, a lineage continued into our present time by Butch Miles and Dennis Mackrel. Heard participated in many of Norman Granz's Jazz at the Philharmonic tours and is in some respects a "modernized" Cozy Cole or Sid Catlett. Grady Tate is much in demand for modern Swing recordings. Mel Lewis (see also the big bands chapter) has turned the great big-band drum tradition of men like Chick Webb, Dave Tough, or Don Lamond into a contemporary art.

On the West Coast, Shelly Manne took a step that was as logical as Art Blakey's, though it led in the opposite direction. Manne is the absolute melodist among jazz drummers. His way of playing is spare and subtle, spirited and animated, but frequently quite removed from what swing means in terms of the line leading from Webb to Blakey. On the other hand, Manne has shown that he can swing—as in the famous quartet recording of "The Man I Love" (with Coleman Hawkins and Oscar Pettiford) from the mid-forties, or in the many combo recordings he made on the West Coast—from the fifties until his death in 1984, when he began to include fusion elements, too. He became well known through many dozens of records that made the term "West Coast jazz" a trademark.

The "in group" of New York jazz—that small elite from whence almost everything important in jazz originates—has gone even further. Its development leads from Elvin Jones (here we tie up with the paragraph in this section where we first mentioned this outstanding drummer) via Tony Williams to Sunny Murray, and from there to Billy Cobham.

Elvin took the *son continu* that began with Kenny Clarke to the extreme limits of what is possible within the framework of a symmetrical meter. He went to the extreme limits, but not beyond. When Coltrane wanted him to go further, Jones resigned from the Coltrane group in an act of great inner consequence. He was replaced by Rashied Ali, in whose playing the meter initially was totally dissolved (but who has since returned to recognizable meters). Jones, however, has remained one of the great, independent jazz drummers even up to the nineties—a musician who refers to Coltrane on the drums as convincingly as does McCoy Tyner on the piano.

Meanwhile, in 1963, Miles Davis had hired Tony Williams (only seventeen at the time) for his quintet. Williams arrived—from a different point of origin—at a similar reduction of the jazz beat to a nervelike vibration and swing. In the section about jazz rhythm, we spoke of the fact that there is a certain physiological parallel to this reduction: from heartbeat to "pulse." Thus, a new physiological level, heretofore virtually blocked to musical approaches, was made accessible. The physiological level of great classical music was breathing; that of "classic" jazz reflects the heartbeat, that of the new jazz the pulse. Williams' trademark became his hi-hat accentuation of all quarter notes—four beats to the bar, completely unlike many drummers who only close the hi-hat (two cymbals clashed by way of a foot pedal) on the second and fourth beats.

Before all this, however, three drummers who had worked with Ornette Coleman since 1959 had already shown that the "liberation" of the rhythm does not mean a liberation from the function of the drummer. These three were Billy Higgins, Ed Blackwell, and Charles Moffett (who has been described as a "Sid Catlett of free jazz"). Blackwell is from New Orleans, and he has said that he sees no contradiction between what the drummers of his hometown have always been doing and the new conception. In general terms, it is important to realize that Higgins and Blackwell—to a certain extent also Moffett—played mainly metrically with Ornette. It only sounded "revolutionary," while it was "traditional" at the same time. Higgins and Blackwell have remained significant jazz drummers, the former in countless record sessions on the West Coast, the latter in his work with, for instance, Don Cherry and Dewey Redman.

The most extreme representative of the possibilities of free-jazz rhythm, however, was and still is Sunny Murray. In a radical fashion, the marking of the meter is here replaced by the creation of tension over long passages. When Murray was with Albert Ayler in the mid-sixties, especially when Ayler was playing folk-music themes, there were clearly perceptible metric pulses in the horn melodies, but Murray just didn't seem to consider them. He played above—and often enough even against—the meter with pulsating beats that seemed to be collecting energy, and suddenly he broke out into wild rolls utilizing the entire spectrum of his instrument. "Murray," wrote Valerie Wilmer, "seems obsessed with the idea of strength and intensity in music."

There can be no doubt that Murray's music swings with an immense density and power. It swings without beat and measure, meter and symmetry—all that which only recently was thought indispensable to swinging—simply by virtue of the power and flexibility of its tension arcs. One is tempted to wonder whether this fact might not call for revision of all previous swing theories, because this way of playing creates tension, too; in fact, it increases tension, in an ecstatic sense, far beyond anything previously known. And swing in earlier jazz can be subsumed under this, too: swing as an element of tension building.

Murray said, "I work for natural sounds rather than trying to sound like drums. Sometimes I try to sound like car motors or the continuous cracking of glass."

Obviously, Murray is not the only drummer of this kind. Other drummers of the "first generation" of free jazz are Milford Graves, Beaver Harris, Barry Altschul (in the beginning of his career), as well as the previously mentioned Charles Moffett and Rashied Ali—and (worthy of special attention) Andrew Cyrille, who gave important rhythmic impulses to Cecil Taylor from 1964 to the mid-seventies. He played with Illinois Jacquet as well as with West African drum groups from Ghana and is conversant with the different kinds of European percussion music. At the risk of oversimplification, he could be called "the intellectual" among free-jazz drummers.

Cyrille captured the attitude of many of these drummers to swing:

> "Swing" is the natural psychic response of the human body to sound that makes a person want to move his or her body without too much conscious effort. . . .
> In a more abstract sense, "swing" is completely integrated and balanced sound, forming a greater, spirituallike, almost tangible magic sensibility of being—the conscious knowledge that something metaphysical is happening.

This "first generation" of free drummers was the point of departure for a second and third generation, of whom we will speak later.

Rock rhythm is not very flexible. In some respects, it returned to Cozy Cole and Sid Catlett of the thirties; it reverted the accent away from the cymbals and back to where it had been—to the bass drum and the tomtoms. Thus, it cannot react as easily and effortlessly to the soloists' playing as a rhythm "played on top." But it is clearly defined. One can always tell where "beat one" is, which occasionally was no longer possible in the playing of jazz drummers in the sixties.

The task of the new type of drummer to gain significance since the beginning of the seventies was, in other words, to merge the emotionalism and communicative power of rock with the flexibility and complexity of jazz. The drummers who first accomplished this—and, in a certain sense, are still accomplishing it most perfectly today—are Tony Williams, Alphonse Mouzon, and Billy Cobham. We have already mentioned Williams. He long played the "freest" rhythms in the realm of jazz-rock, and he was only later surpassed in this respect by Ronald Shannon Jackson. His playing accordingly first tended in two directions: toward both the avant-garde and jazz-rock. Since the mid-seventies Williams' playing has returned to a traditional context. But even when he plays nothing but "pure" neobop and classicism, something of his development is still apparent. Compared with his delicate, filigrain style in the sixties, which was more cymbal-based, his drumming today is more massive, more angular, more drum-oriented, but still undiminishedly sensitive.

Billy Cobham accomplished his path-breaking contribution in John McLaughlin's first Mahavishnu Orchestra. He led his own groups after that, but he hasn't reached the level of his Mahivishnu playing. Mouzon's development shows a similar problem. He was, on the one hand, a founding member of Weather Report and, on the other, one of McCoy's Tyner's sidemen in the early seventies, playing "acoustic" jazz in the Coltrane tradition—both of these styles on the highest level. During the late seventies Mouzon repeatedly said that he considered himself not a jazz but a rock musician; the rock world, however, obviously has problems accepting him as one of its own, because his playing is too complex and too demanding for a rock context.

The panorama of contemporary jazz-rock and fusion drummers built on the foundation laid down by Williams, Cobham, and Mouzon, is so wide that, again, only a few can be named: Steve Gadd, Peter Erskine, Lenny White, Gerry Brown, Steve Jordan, John Guerin, Paul Wertico, Dan Gottlieb, Al Foster, Terry Lyne Carrington, Omar Hakim, and Dennis Chambers. Among the Europeans of this group (even though they play with a kind of "European understatement" that differentiates them from their more aggressive American colleagues) are Dutchman Pierre Courbois, the French-Italian Aldo Romano, and Fredy Studer from Switzerland.

Steve Gadd, known through his work with Stuff and Steps Ahead, was the most successful and most demanded studio drummer of the seventies and eighties. Developing Tony Williams' style, he created the "dry" studio sound that served hundreds of drummers as a model. In the eighties, Gadd's precise and clever style was refined and taken further by Dave Weckl. Lenny White from Jamaica (strikingly many jazz-rock drummers—including Billy Cobham—come from the Caribbean area) was involved in Miles' 1969 *Bitches Brew,* and he also played with Larry Coryell and Chick Corea. Peter Erskine, who was in Stan Kenton's big band, helped solve Weather Report's protracted rhythmic problems when he was with the group from 1976 to 1982, forming in conjunction with Jaco Pastorius one of jazz-rock's most creative rhythm sections. Erskine's successor in Weather Report was Omar Hakim, a master of complex hi-hat figurations.

If there's been something akin to a musical axis in Miles' seventies and eighties bands, then it's the link between the trumpeter and Al Foster from 1972 to 1985. Miles' belief in an ongoing beat found its ideal counterpart in Foster's imperturbable timing. They were so attuned to one another that Foster often foresaw and initiated unexpected transitions between Davis' pieces, implementing such developments with sleepwalking ease. More than almost any other musician, Foster carried a swing feeling into jazz-rock rhythms, and he also integrated elements of the New Orleans tradition (such as its march rhythms, which have a uniquely supple quality compared with brisk Prussian marches) into that context.

Terri Lyne Carrington, who played with Wayne Shorter, brought sensitivity to the hard, jagged rhythms of jazz-rock without diminishing their motor power and directness. Dennis Chambers became known for playing with John Scofield and Miles Davis. John Guerin, Paul Wertico, and Dan Gottlieb are distinguished by a special filigrain style.

Most of these musicians have also taken a close look at rhythm machines and drum computers; but revealingly they've either combined such electronic equipment with performances utilizing the conventional drum set, or they've decided totally in favor of the drum kit. Not because, as some people maintain, a drum computer can't swing. It certainly can if expertly programmed. The trouble, however, is that the results lack that very spontaneity and spirit of communication that make a drummer so indispensable in jazz.

Pierre Courbois was a significant influence on the entire European scene in the early seventies with his group Association P.C., but he has since grown away from this style of music. This is true also of several other players we have named: for instance, Peter Erskine (to whom we'll return later) and Lenny White, who first played fusion with Chick Corea's group Return to Forever, but then also bebop and even experimental bop with Heiner Stadler.

Jon Hiseman, Robert Wyatt, John Marshall, Bill Bruford, and Simone Phillips are part of the British scene. Hiseman drums in the successful United Jazz and Rock Ensemble. As early as the late sixties, Robert Wyatt, in the British group Soft Machine, was creating a network of sensitive rhythms that were ahead of what most other drummers on the early jazz-rock scene were able to play then, even in America.

Bill Bruford is a master of synthesizer drum playing. He drums on pads instead of skins, on flat rubber pads where an impact creates an electrical impulse triggering a synthesizer. In his Earthworks group Bruford thereby achieves melodic and sonic effects that virtually match those of a keyboardist. Talk of playing drums "melodically" thus takes on a more tangible reality, opening up completely new chordal, harmonic, and sonic possibilities for drummers.

Aldo Romano has developed a "very French" style of jazz-rock playing, full of *joie de vivre* and a lightness pleasantly contrasting with the more powerful drumming of jazz-rockers. Fredy Studer from Switzerland is a specialist in sensitive and subtle jazz-rock rhythms with a great feel for differentiated cymbal sounds. Mark Nauseef has linked jazz-rock elements with world music in original fashion. He's an expert in magical sound images in which meditative floating sounds—influenced by Indian, Tibetan, and Balinese music—coalesce with rock drive and the openness of free jazz.

The "daddy" of European jazz-rock drummers is Ginger Baker. After he became world famous in the sixties in the blues-rock group Cream, he spent several years in Nigeria studying African percussion music. Later, he tried a comeback but did not succeed, because (like his colleague on bass, Jack Bruce) Baker has power and musical fire but has not been able to keep up with the playing standards meanwhile achieved.

Similarly diverse is the panorama of free drummers whose second and third generations lead into neoclassicism. These players include Phillip Wilson, Don Moye, Steve McCall, Barry Altschul, Pheeroan Ak Laff (officially Paul Maddox), Thurman Barker, Bobby Battle, Warren Smith, and, among younger musicians, Reggie Nicholson, Tani Tabbal, and Gerry Hemingway. Strikingly, all of these drummers, despite their ties with free jazz, have increasingly found their way back to playing above a meter, an ongoing beat. That doesn't mean that the freedom previously gained has now been renounced, but rather that it is implicit in more traditional playing and resonates as an amplifying experience. Wilson, Moye, and McCall are close to the AACM, even though Wilson changed to a different kind of music at the end of the sixties. He played in the Paul Butterfield Blues Band but later returned to free music when his AACM colleagues finally gained recognition in the United States in the second half of the seventies. During the eighties he performed with Lester Bowie's Brass Fantasy. His knowledge of the diversity of African-American rhythms seems inexhaustible. Moye, linked with the Art Ensemble of Chicago, makes particularly impressive use of the African legacy of black music with an impulsive drum style ritualistic in its impact. Steve McCall (d. 1989) lent a light and breezy quality to the rhythms of the trio Air. Barry Altschul had already played free bop with Circle when that term didn't yet exist. He's a master of rim shots, and the way he creates intensity and tension by his very restraint is inimitable.

Turning to the European scene, we must first mention the "daddies" of free drumming there: the Swiss Pierre Favre and Dutchman Han Bennink, the former perceptive and sensitive, the latter vital and gripping. More than any other drummer today, Favre is able to produce percussion "sketches" so vividly that one can almost "see" them as pictures: a Sunday morning in Switzerland or a young girl on her way to school. While Bennink's sound is especially convincing and developed on the skins, Favre is particularly impressive on cymbals, gongs, and other metal percussion instruments. Even before their American colleagues, both Favre and Bennink utilized the rich arsenal of percussion instruments employed today by so many drummers: instruments of Africa, Brazil, Bali, Tibet, India, and China. Favre and Bennink can certainly be considered founders of something like a European percussion lineage. From that lineage stem the Swiss Peter Giger, Reto Weber, and Marco Käppeli; Italian-born Andrea Centazzo; the Finn Edward Vesala (who has also studied Balinese music); Briton Tony Oxley (who has constructed his own set of instruments, including electronic sound sources); as well as Germans Paul Lovens (who became known through his involvement with the Globe Unity Orchestra), Detlef Schönenberg (who played in one of the most interesting seventies European duos, with trombonist Günther Christmann), and Günter "Baby" Sommer.

Günter "Baby" Sommer is the outstanding drummer in European postfree jazz. He is a master of magical intensity and enormous drive with a captivating sense of breaks and rests accompanied by an almost "Prussian sense of order," that is time and again dialectically disrupted. Sommer is the most melodic drummer in the sphere of freely improvised music. He has extended his drum set by adding kettle drums, tubular bells, and other percussion instruments, producing such clear and finely-meshed sounds that you sometimes forget it's a drummer playing here.

In the Soviet Union Vladimir Tarasov has developed an individual free style independent of the European free-jazz tradition. He also plays in symphony orchestras and was a member of the Ganelin Trio until its dissolution in 1987. His playing is particularly percussive. Tarasov links the pulse techniques of free jazz with traditional swinging phrases, marches, circus music, and Lithuanian folk music, ironically disrupting all of those elements in a multitude of ways.

Finally, we must mention the Japanese free drummers Masahiko Tagashi, Shota Koyama, and Takeo Moriyama. Togashi plays "spiritual" percussion music in which can be found elements from the Japanese musical and spiritual tradition, including Zen. There is hardly another percussionist today in whose music "space"—the emptiness between the beats—has such significance and is filled with so much content. Moriyama and Koyama are very wild and intense players, with a kind of intensity that is fed not only from blacks but also from traditional Japanese sources.

An important step beyond all these drummers—Americans, Europeans, and Japanese—was taken around the turn of the seventies by Ronald Shannon Jackson. One of the musicians at the 1980 Moers Festival in Germany said, "In a sense, Ronald is doing what Elvin Jones did in the early seventies. As Elvin emancipated the bop rhythms then, so Ronald Jackson is emancipating the rock and funk rhythms today." Jackson is the main free-funk drummer—not only because of his new, impressive polyrhythms but also because he has managed to transmit these polyrhythms to his compositions and to the music of his group, Decoding Society.

What is new about free funk is first of all, as in usually the case in jazz, the rhythm. This links the physical directness and power of jazz-rock with the independence and flexibility of free playing. Motor drive plus pulse: No one has driven that formula to such shattering intensity in climaxes of rhythmic energy as Ronald Shannon Jackson. He first became known through playing with Albert Ayler, Ornette Coleman, and Cecil Taylor. At the start of the eighties he made some trail-blazing recordings with his Decoding Society, particularly influenced by Coleman's harmolodic music, but later never regained the high level of that time. In the Last Exit band he played a heavy-metal-oriented free jazz.

Other important free-funk drummers include Calvin Weston, Cornell Rochester, Mark Johnson, and Paul Samuels. Weston and Rochester have played with guitarist James Blood Ulmer. Mark Johnson, who is linked with the music of altoist Steve Coleman, specializes in highly complex rhythmic changes. Paul Samuels belongs to the band set up by alto and soprano sax player Greg Osby.

Like free-funk drummers, noise music and no wave percussionists similarly extend and update the treasure trove of experience gained in free jazz. David Moss is the most important representative of that direction. He drums something of the aggressiveness of punk and the harshness of avant-garde rock into the differentiated pulsations of free jazz. Moss is a master of the noise collage, one of the most imaginative of today's creators of sounds, incorporating toms, gongs, cymbals, balloons, toys, vocal effects, and all possible and seemingly impossible generators of sound. This man has so much sound within himself that he only need roll up a piece of paper and music comes into being.

The "hostile" camps of jazz-rock and free music are reconciled in the field of drumming, too, by the players of contemporary mainstream (also the reason why an especially large number of them have been in the limelight of both styles): Billy Hart, Stu Martin, Clifford Jarvis, Al Foster, Peter Donald, Adam Nussbaum, Woody Theus, Freddie Waits, Horacee Arnold, Wilbur Campbell, Mickey Roker, Terry Clarke, Frank Butler, Jake Hanna, Jeff Hamilton, Bob Moses, Paul Motian, Joe LaBarbera, Elliot Zigmund, Ignacio Berroa, Ronnie Burrage, Jon Christensen from Norway, Swiss-born Daniel Humair (who lives in France), Poland's Janusz Stefanski, Austrians Wolfgang Reisinger and Alex Deutsch, and Germans Thomas Alkier and Wolfgang Haffner, and others.

Billy Hart is an immensely empathetic drummer, one of the most intensive as well as swinging on the scene today, who plays a kind of "sensitized Elvin Jones." Also having their base in Elvin Jones are Eddie Moore, Janusz Stefanski, Woody Theus, and Al Foster.

Stu Martin (d. 1980) came out of Quincy Jones' band of the early sixties. He commanded a particularly wide musical spectrum, including even

Eastern European and Jewish music. Freddie Waits, Horacee Arnold, and Wilbur Campbell are members of the Max Roach percussion group mentioned earlier. Mickey Rocker was Dizzy Gillespie's favorite drummer in the seventies. Jake Hanna and Jeff Hamilton are true Swing men, referring back to the music of the great classic Swing tradition. Ignacio Berroa has transferred Cuban percussion rhythms to the jazz drum set particularly infectiously. Daniel Humair is the "most swinging" of all European drummers—a musician who very much enjoys communicating, and whose inventive, springy playing is also appreciated by American stylists.

Three of these drummers have played with Bill Evans, and all are characterized by the sensitivity of Evans' music: Paul Motian, Elliot Zigmund, and Joe LaBarbera. Motian is another drummer in whose music space—the space between notes—plays a distinct role; he, too, received impulses from Asian percussion techniques.

Jon Christensen from Norway also belongs in this group of especially sensitive and adaptable drummers. He is a master of finely meshed "binary" rhythms, which are based—unlike the rounded "triplet" playing of most jazz drummers—on units of twos.

No other drummer, however, dominated eighties jazz so sovereignly and originally as Jack DeJohnette, who influenced many of the previously mentioned players. He is the most complex drummer on the contemporary scene, and his group Special Edition points toward new directions for jazz. DeJohnette has both: Tony Williams' filigrain and Elvin Jones' vitality. He calls his music multidirectional and open to an imposing range of styles, and that characterizes his impressive range of playing: jazz-rock, reggae, free jazz, neobop, aestheticisism, blues, etc.

Jack DeJohnette's drum playing possesses an almost orchestral abundance of colors and rhythmic movements. One of the most fascinating moments in jazz is provided by the experience of how DeJohnette dissolves the beat into complex "four-voiced" polyphonic patterns, allowing the rhythmic focus to move around the entire arsenal of his drum set in the same way as the leading voice migrates between instruments in a polyphonic piece. It's revealing that DeJohnette started out as a pianist; he has also appeared on recordings as such.

DeJohnette is also an outstanding writer, but in contrast to most other drummers, his works do not immediately reveal themselves as "drummer's compositions." Indeed, a certain type of very obvious "drummer's writing" has been prevalent in almost all tunes composed by drummers so far—from Sid Catlett and Cozy Cole to Billy Cobham and Alphonse Mouzon.

Jack DeJohnette is the "father" of postmodern drum playing. From DeJohnette comes (and he is the source of reference for) the new type of percussionist who by now plays, develops, and integrates so many styles—far beyond the degree of versatility and technical competence always demanded of drummers—that he can no longer be assigned to any single category.

The most important among such drummers at the start of the nineties are Peter Erskine, Joey Baron, Bobby Previte, Marvin "Smitty" Smith, and Ralph Peterson, Jr.. Erskine, who has made recordings with such groups as Steps Ahead and Bass Desires but also with guitarist John Abercrombie, unites great power with delicate responsiveness. His range of rhythmic coordination is especially captivating. Joey Baron is linked with the bands of alto saxophonist Tim Berne and guitarist Bill Frisell. Bobby Previte is a specialist in somber surrealistic tone poems incorporating elements from ritualistic Asian drum techniques—Tibetan, Japanese, and Korean. Marvin "Smitty" Smith has worked with David Murray, Wynton Marsalis, Sting, Sonny Rollins, Steve Coleman, Hank Jones, and Art Farmer, and was a member of Dave Holland's celebrated Quintet. He has a particularly warm, deep, and dark sound, which partly results from his playing the bass drum with two foot pedals instead of one. Ralph Peterson, Jr., sovereignly drums away the schism between the "hostile" trends in the new traditionalism—classicism and neoclassicism—as if there had never been a breach.

Compared with the colorfulness of such postmodern drummers, the representatives of classicism seem more concerned with stylistic rectitude, which has led some people to charge them with "purism." In fact, however, classicist drummers—Jeff "Tain" Watts, Kenny Washington, Carl Allen, Tony Reedus, Eddie Gladden, Victor Lewis, Cindy Blackman, Lewis Nash, Herlin Riley, Winard Harper, and Mark Mondesir from England—beat similarly eclectic rhythms, just like other contemporary drummers except that classicists constantly refer back to bop-oriented rhythms. They reflect and modernize all the rhythms that have existed from Max Roach and Art Blakey by way of Philly Joe Jones to the refinements of Elvin Jones and Tony Williams. Nevertheless, their playing is fundamentally different from that of bebop drummers. They drum more powerfully, explosively, and communicatively, out of the experience of a generation that has not only experienced bop but also free jazz, rock, and jazz-rock. The drums accordingly intervene, moving from an accompanying role to near-equality with the soloists.

Jeff "Tain" Watts, who made his name with Wynton Marsalis' band, is such a drummer, "filling" bebop with controlled freedom and the entire spectrum of music between the new jazz and jazz-rock. He's been called a "lexicographer of drum styles" and has expanded bebop vocabulary through deliberately asymmetrical polyrhythms. Victor Lewis and Tony Reedus came from the central groups in neobop around trumpeter Woody Shaw and saxophonist Dexter Gordon. Cindy Blackman, who played with Wallace

Roney, follows on from Tony Williams just as Kenny Washington does from Max Roach.

It is strange how the development of the drum has taken place in pairs, from the beginning until today. We discussed how Jo Jones came up with results in the thirties in Count Basie's band that were quite similar to those reached independently by Dave Tough with Tommy Dorsey. Among the bop drummers, there is on the one hand "wild" Art Blakey and on the other intellectual Max Roach. During the sixties, Elvin Jones stood in opposition to Tony Williams. Or among the free drummers: "racing" Sunny Murray here and complex Andrew Cyrille there. Or in Europe: dynamic Han Bennink and sensitive Pierre Favre. Similarly poised in opposition among the drummers on the contemporary scene are Billy Cobham (or, if you wish, Shannon Jackson) and Jack DeJohnette. In fact, this polarity can be found right from the beginning of drum development, even in New Orleans: "wild" Baby Dodds on the one hand and Tony Spargo, who incorporated European elements into the music of the Original Dixieland Jazz Band, on the other. ("European elements" back then, however, meant marching band and circus music.)

The Percussion Instruments
(Cuban, Salsa, Brazilian, African, Indian, Balinese)

The percussion instruments used to be side instruments for the drummers. However, in the course of the sixties, the store of percussion instruments became so immense that a new type of musician, the percussion player, evolved. The percussionist must be distinguished from the drummer, even though there are countless drummers who are *also* percussionists, and vice versa.

Initially, most of the percussion instruments came from Latin America: claves, chocallo (also referred to as shaker), guiro (also named gourd or, in Brazil, reco reco), cabaza, maracas, quijada, cencerro (or more simply, cowbells), guica, bongos, conga, timbales, pandeira, and so on. Then other instruments were added, from India, Tibet, China, Japan, Bali, and Africa (where most of the Latin American percussions originated anyway). Airto, the renowned Brazilian percussionist, spent years before his move to the United States traveling through Brazil—through the Amazon jungle, the dry Northeast, and the Matto Grosso prairie—where he collected and studied about 120 different instruments.

The father of all percussionists relevant to the modern jazz scene is *Chano Pozo* from Cuba (his complete name was Luciano Pozo y Gonzales). He infused Cuban rhythms into Dizzy Gillespie's big band of 1947–48 and thereby became the great catalyst for so-called "Cubop." The creator of this music, however, is Dizzy Gillespie, the only jazz improviser of his generation who could improvise as comfortably on Latin rhythms as on jazz rhythms (often favoring the former because he considered them less "monotonous").

Some of the tunes the Gillespie band recorded with Chano Pozo— "Cubana Be-Cubana Bop," for instance, or "Manteca," "Woody'n You," "Afro Cubano Suite," or "Algo Bueno"—are bacchanals of rhythmic differentiation. Chano Pozo died in a stabbing in 1948 in East Harlem's Rio Café. There have been rumors that he was slain because he had made public—and thus desecrated—the secret rhythms of the Nigerian Abaquwa cult, to which he had belonged in Cuba. The rhythmic power of this mysterious Cuban conga player is illuminated by the fact that Gillespie, though he often employed several Latin American percussionists at one time, never again was able to achieve the effects he had reached with Chano Pozo alone.

The percussion players can best be grouped according to where they, their instruments, or their styles come from. In this way, we have percussionists with Cuban (and, later, Puerto Rican), Brazilian, African, and Asian roots. Those are the groupings to which most percussionists belong. There are others from Mexico (active mainly on the West Coast of the United States), Trinidad, Jamaica, Haiti, and other countries.

The Cuban wave reached its first high point between the late forties and the mid-fifties. Not only did Dizzy Gillespie play Cuban rhythms again and again, but so did the favorite white big band, Stan Kenton's: in 1947, for example, with their successful version of "The Peanut Vendor," in "Chorale for Brass, Piano and Bongo," or in the "Fugue for Rhythm Section" with bongo player Jack Costanzo. Later, Kenton used Carlos Vidal on conga, Machito on maracas, and others in pieces like "Machito," "Mambo in F," "Cuban Carnival," and "Cuban Episode." In 1956, Kenton devoted to Latin (and above all Cuban) music a grand suite: "Cuban Fire," written by Johnny Richards and featuring six Latin percussionists.

The Latin bands enjoying the greatest recognition in the jazz world of the fifties were, in New York, the orchestra of Machito (alias Frank Grillo) with the inspired and jazz-experienced arranger and trumpeter Mario Bauza (who had done arrangements also for Chick Webb's and Cab Calloway's bands) and that of timbales player and arranger Tito Puente; and on the West Coast, the band of Perez Prado, with Kenton-like brass effects and a new kind of rhythm, the mambo—the first Latin dance to originate in the States (influenced by Mexican rhythms). "Rumba with jitterbug" is how *Down Beat* defined the mambo, which was quite a hit in the mid-fifties.

It was Machito who frequently played and recorded with jazz musicians— first with Charlie Parker (starting in 1948) and later with Brew Moore, Zoot Sims, Stan Getz, Howard McGhee, Herbie Mann, and others. Machito's alliance with Parker was instigated by jazz impresario Norman Granz, mainly because Cubop was a widespread fashion back then. Parker was not nearly as accomplished on Cuban rhythms as Gillespie. Above all, it was Machito who nurtured the realization in the jazz world that it is wrong simply to add a Latin percussion player to a conventional jazz rhythm section—as was usually the case then (and often later). Instead, complete Cuban rhythm sections must be formed where the Latin percussionists are conversant with jazz and the jazz drummers with Latin American music. Such a group usually would employ several Latin percussion players, and the bassist has to command the bass lines of Latin music with as much ease as those lines he normally would play.

Among the significant Cuban percussionists of those years were conga players Carlos Vidal, Candido, and Sabu Martinez, and bongo player Willie Rodriguez. They made recordings with many jazzmen: Vidal with Stan Kenton, for instance; Candido with Gillespie; Sabu (d. 1979) with Gillespie and Art Blakey.

On the West Coast, the vibraphonist and bongo player Cal Tjader has worked since 1954 on an intelligent and spirited combination of jazz with Latin music, often revealing Mexican elements. Tjader came from the George Shearing Quintet of 1949. Jazz critics have written a lot about the peculiar sound of this group, but the Shearing Quintet was also important in terms of rhythm, as a jumping-off point for a number of Latin percussionists who later became known through their own recordings: timbales player Willie Bobo, conga player Mongo Santamaria, and conga and bongo player Armando Peraza.

During the late fifties, Cuban music lost considerably in attractiveness. A second wave came in the seventies in the shape of salsa, which since then has been sustained not only by Cuban musicians but also by players from Puerto Rico and other Latin American countries. Its centers are where most of these ethnic groups are concentrated in the United States: New York and Miami. *Salsa* means "sauce" and has been defined as "Cuban plus jazz," with elements of blues and rock. Fania Records has been quite successful in bringing together salsa and jazz musicians for studio dates and also for large concerts, as in New York's Yankee Stadium and in Madison Square Garden. Among the best-known "Fania All Stars" are Mongo Santamaria, Ray Barretto, Larry Harlow, Willie Colon, and the musical director of Fania Records, Johnny Pacheco. He patterned the All Stars primarily on the Cuban *conjuntos* (medium-size ensembles composed of percussionists and horn players). Pianist and bandleader Eddie Palmieri (who was inspired first by Bud Powell, later by McCoy Turner) created a salsa concerto style with pieces in larger forms, earning him the title of a "Duke Ellington of salsa."

Conga player Mongo Santamaria has been the most influential Cuba-style percussionist for more than thirty years, with a host of recordings in the fields of Cuban as well as jazz and rock music (plus all imaginable mixtures). He wrote the jazz standard "Afro Blue," which has been recorded by such musicians as John Coltrane, Dizzy Gillespie, and Cal Tjader, among others. Santamaria also scored the first real salsa hit in the mid-sixties with his version of Herbie Hancock's composition "Watermelon Man." Since that time his music has been studied by Latin percussionists (and also by many jazz drummers) as diligently as Chano Pozo's work was studied in the forties and fifties. Also of great significance is timbalero Willie Bobo, who has made records with, among others, Miles Davis, Stan Getz, and Cannonball Adderley.

Meanwhile, there is a whole generation of Latin musicians born not in Cuba or Puerto Rico or elsewhere in Latin America, but in New York, mostly in the Barrio district of East Harlem. Ray Barretto, Johnny Pacheco, and Eddie Palmieri are among this group of players. As can be easily understood, these musicians have an additional interest in North American music, particularly jazz. But the dictum that you have to be a Latino to play outstanding Latin music still holds—with a few exceptions. The first such exception was Cal Tjader, whose heritage is Swedish (certain non-Latin elements can be perceived in the "coolness" of his music).

Birger Sulsbrük from Denmark and drummer Don Alias were others. Sulsbrük has even managed, as a European, to assimilate Cuban rhythms so completely that he is recognized by Latino musicians. Alias is Anglo, but grew up with Cubans; he is not only an excellent jazz drummer but also a brilliant conga player. The successful fusion drummer Billy Cobham, who has played with the Fania All Stars, has a highly developed feeling for Latin music. Cobham hails from Panama and thus, like many other Panamanian musicians, has two cultural roots, Anglo and Latin.

The rule that only a Latino can play convincing Latin music is true not only for percussionists but also (though less strictly) for horn players. Trumpeter Fats Navarro, who died in 1950, and tenorist Sonny Rollins were among the first important jazz improvisers on Latin rhythms. Navarro came from a Florida Latino family; Rollins (though born in New York), from a family from the Virgin Islands. Navarro played especially well over Cuban rhythms. Rollins, as composer and also as improviser, infused the amiable charm of Caribbean music, particularly of calypso music from Trinidad, into jazz long before today's tendencies in that direction. On the other hand, since the sixties, it has become more and more obvious that a growing number of non-Latin horn players are interested in Latin music.

Nowadays, there is a vast number of mixtures of Latin American and North American music: "Latin rock," "Latin soul," "rock salsa," in dozens of different combinations. After the mambo, the boogaloo was the second Latin dance to be created in the United States—the latter, however, with English lyrics, not Spanish like the mambo. The boogaloo is a mixture of mambo with rock 'n' roll and, depending on who is playing, with undercurrents of jazz and blues. An especially successful, highly differentiated combination of rhythms from the spheres of rock and Latin music (above all salsa) was created on the West Coast during the early seventies by Carlos Santana, who originally came from Mexico. The rock group Earth, Wind and Fire is so successful mainly because it includes conga and timbales players, producing a ravishing mixture of soul (or gospel) elements with salsa rhythms. Percussionist Ralph MacDonald (born in Harlem in a family of Trinidad calypso musicians) has become successful with his "Latin fusion," including also aspects of the African tradition.

A new quality has been brought into Latin music since the start of the eighties by two musicians: by the New York–based exile Cuban and Congalero Daniel Ponce and by percussionist, trumpeter, and arranger Jerry Gonzalez. Ponce, a particularly striking and powerful percussionist, is unequalled in the way that he breaks with the self-indulgent and often almost clichéd patterns of the salsa scene. He has played contemporary "Cuban jazz" with altoist Paquito D'Rivera as well as no wave with Bill Laswell and hip hop with Herbie Hancock, and he was involved in Kip Hanrahan's style-crossing musical encounters.

Hanrahan's projects in the eighties were in fact also a launching pad for many other percussionists including Milton Cardona, Nicky Marrero, Puntilla Orlando Rios, and, the youngest and most promising of them all, Giovanni Hidalgo from Puerto Rico, who commands what is probably the most virtuosic conga technique on the contemporary scene.

Jerry Gonzalez already belongs to the second generation of Latino musicians who grew up in New York. The intermingling of "Latin American" and "U.S. American" influences has by now gone so far that neither, as was once the case, dominates at the expense of the other. His Fort Apache Band, which infectiously brings together the great legacy of Afro-Cuban rhythms with the modern jazz tradition's wealth of experience (from Thelonious Monk by way of Bud Powell to Miles Davis), attracted special attention in the eighties.

A specialist in Caribbean rhythms—especially those from Martinique, his father's birthplace—is French-born Mino Cinelu. He has played in Miles Davis' bands and Weather Report. Apart from excelling on the entire arsenal of percussion, he is also a master of impelling, delicate triangle figurations.

Poncho Sanchez has linked Afro-Cuban elements with the contemporary mainstream in some endearing recordings, demonstrating that vital Latin colors are also possible on the American West Coast—far away from the salsa center of New York.

Latin rhythms are almost ubiquitous on the jazz and rock scenes, certainly also because, as we have shown, rock and fusion rhythms are basically latent Latin rhythms. John Storm Roberts (to whose book *The Latin Tinge* we are indebted in this context) quotes salsa bandleader Ray Barretto: "The whole basis of American rhythm . . . changed from the old dotted-note jazz shuffle rhythm to a straightahead straight-eighth approach, which is Latin." Or, to put it more precisely, it is ambivalent, referring to rhythms from North America as much as to those from Latin America.

"Salsa" has become a sort of catch phrase that should be used with caution. No longer does it refer only to Cuban rhythms, but also to the bomba from Puerto Rico, the meringue from Santo Domingo (which was particularly popular on the eighties New York Latin scene), the Songo from the Caribbean, and to other dances and rhythms from the Caribbean and Mexican sphere. In a 1977 *Down Beat* interview, Mongo Santamaria pointed out that some of these rhythms still are *"nañigo,"* that is, "coming from secret religious cults."

Let's move on to Brazil. The interest of the jazz musicians in Brazilian music was instigated by guitarist Charlie Byrd, who went there in 1961. A year later, in 1962, he recorded the album *Jazz Samba* with Stan Getz, including the famous song "Desafinado" written by Joao Gilberto and Antonio Carlos Jobim. The Grammy Award for this tune was not given to Charlie Byrd but to Stan Getz, because Byrd's guitar solo was cut from the version shortened for single release! As a result of this, Charlie Byrd's decisive contribution was neglected, and from that point on Getz stood at the center of the bossa nova wave. The Brazilian musicians defined the bossa as "samba plus cool jazz." A first hint of the potential of Brazilian music was given on the West Coast as early as 1953 by the album *Brazilliance,* recorded by a quartet featuring Brazilian-born guitarist Laurindo Almeida and alto saxophonist and flutist Bud Shank (the two are still collaborating in this field).

But the percussive side of Brazilian music was realized on the American scene only 1967, when Brazilian percussion player Airto Moreira and his wife, singer Flora Purim, moved to New York. Airto was involved in two tunes on Miles Davis's pathbreaking album *Bitches Brew.* Along with the many other impulses this record gave rise to, it caused the in-group of jazz musicians to become aware of Brazilian rhythms. Many leading jazz groups since the seventies have used Brazilian percussionists, among them Chick Corea, McCoy Tyner, Dizzy Gillespie, Weather Report, Pat Metheny, Armando Marçal, and others. The percussionists in these groups were (and still are) Airto, Dom Um Romao, Paulhino da Costa, Guilherme Franco, and one of the most sensitive and flexible players, Nana Vasconcelos. Mainly because of his fusion recordings and the albums he made with Flora Purim, Airto became the real initiator of the percussion wave that hit the scene at the beginning of the seventies. Nana is a real master of the berimbau, an instrument that looks like a bow and arrow: a single metal string stretched over a staff is played with a coin, using a coconut pressed against the player's body as resonator and modulator. On this simple instrument, which comes from Bahia, the "New Orleans of Brazilian music," Nana has discovered a fascinating wealth of expressive possibilities. On one of his records, he makes "body music," employing no instruments but using his entire body as a percussion instrument, producing the most diverse sounds with his hands, fingers, and feet on his chest, stomach, and trunk, as well as on his arms, legs, and shoulders.

Another interesting percussion instrument from Brazilian music is the cuica, an open drum with a pipe inside that is rubbed, mostly with a moist cloth, producing a strange "giggling" sound. More than any other country in Latin America, Brazil has an immense wealth of these different instruments, and a vast number of them—typical of Brazilian music—directly connect the rhythmic and the melodic elements.

The Brazilian rhythms are softer, more supple, more elastic, and less aggressive than the Cuban ones. That's why the Brazilian percussion players have been able to create a perfect integration of jazz and Latin rhythms, so perfect that often the constituent elements—jazz here, Brazilian there—can no longer be singled out. Another reason why this could be achieved is the fact that there are stronger ties between the basic rhythm of Brazilian music, the samba, and that of North American jazz than between jazz and Cuban rhythms. The fascination of combinations of jazz with Cuban music lies in the tension between the two, which creates power, aggressiveness, explosiveness. Combinations of jazz and Brazilian music fascinate through their softness and suppleness and an almost unnoticeable blend of their rhythms which creates elegance and charm.

Guilherme Franco has demonstrated that in especially masterly fashion. In the seventies as a member of the Coltrane-inspired McCoy Tyner group (and later with Keith Jarrett), he established an enormously flexible unity between jazz and Brazilian rhythms.

In the course of the growing new awareness of their African roots, many American jazz musicians have adopted African percussion instruments, rhythms, techniques, and musicians. The forerunner of this development was Art Blakey, who on his record *Orgy in Rhythm* was already forming entire drum orchestras as early as the fifties. Wayne Shorter once said: "Dizzy Gillespie's thing was Afro-Cuban. Then Art Blakey took off the Cuban and said 'Afro' and the whole jazz world understood." A Blakey record released in 1962 is entitled *The African Beat;* it employs, among others, the following musicians with their African instruments: Solomon Ilori (African talking drum), Chief Bey (conga, telegraph drum, double gong), Montego Joe (bambara drum, double gong, corboro drum, log drum), Garvin Masseaux (chekere, African maracas, conga), James Folami (conga), and Robert Crowder (batá drum, conga). Later, Max Roach and others formed similar percussion groups.

The first African percussionist to gain recognition in the jazz world, as early as in the beginning of the sixties, was Nigerian Olatunji, who also worked with John Coltrane. For his recording dates, he employed musicians like Clark Terry, Yusef Lateef, and George Duvivier. For years, his composition entitled "Uhuru"—the Swahili word for "freedom"—with lyrics by the Nigerian poet Adebayo Faleti, was the "in song" of the New York musicians and music fans, even in United Nations circles, interested in African problems and the liberation struggle of African peoples.

Since the seventies, percussionists like Kahil El'Zabar, Don Moye (from the AACM circle), and Mtume (made known by Miles Davis), as well as the aforementioned Ralph McDonald, have referred directly to African rhythms. El'Zabar, leader of his Ethnic Heritage Ensemble, plays the mbira: the old African "thumb piano," which, in a slightly different version, is also called kalimba and, in other parts of Africa, nsimbi or zanza.

Two highly respected Haitian drummers are Ti-Roro (who died in 1980 and was connected with Haitian voodoo cults) and his somewhat younger colleague, Ti-Marcel. Ti-Roro once said that a person cannot understand Haitian (and that means African) drumming without realizing that drums and drummer are "two different beings." The "loa"—the sacred spirits—do not speak to the drummer, but to the drums. A drum must be "baptized", and for the ceremony it is dressed like a baby. The drums are fed and put to bed at night. They have their own will, which can be quite contrary to that of the drummer—to such an extent that they refuse to "talk" to their player on certain days or under certain circumstances. Ti-Roro: "If you don't consider your drums as 'beings,' you can play technical tricks on them at best, but not meaningful music."

The next group of percussionists we have to consider are those with Asian roots. The most satisfying integration of Indian rhythms with jazz was achieved by Indian tabla player Zakir Hussain. The son and student of famous tabla drummer Alla Rahka, Hussain grew up with jazz from the beginning: "I heard Charlie Parker when I was twelve. My father made records with Buddy Rich and Elvin Jones, and he also worked with Yusef Lateef. Thus Indian music and jazz came together for me by themselves." Hussain made ground-breaking recordings with John Handy and Ali Akbar Khan as well as in John McLaughlin's group Shakti. In a way, he integrated Indian tabla rhythms and sounds as perfectly into jazz as did Guilherme Franco (and others) in terms of Brazilian rhythms.

Among the other Indian percussionists who have worked with jazz musicians are Trilok Gurtu, Badal Roy (with such players as Miles Davis), Ramesh Shotam (with Rabih Abou-Khalil), and T. A. S. Mani. The latter plays the mrindangam, a transverse drum with two skins. He is director of the Karnataka College of Percussion, which introduced the great tradition of southern Indian music into encounters with saxophonist Charlie Mariano.

American-born Collin Walcott (who died in a car crash in 1984) is, after Don Cherry, the most outstanding stylist in world music. He achieved celebrity in his performances with Oregon and the Codona Trio (with Cherry and percussionist Nana Vasconcelos). As an American musician, he is up to now the only non-Indian player of the tabla (and also sitar) to have gained an international reputation as a stylist. Walcott studied the tabla with Alla Rahka and the sitar with Ravi Shankar. His particular achievement consists in having opened up classical Indian tabla playing to other Asian and also African, Brazilian, and Oriental rhythms and drum techniques. Walcott's exceptional musicality is characterized by the fact that with this (as he put it) "nonidiomatic" way of playing, he was able to assimilate and transmit more of the spirit and greatness of non-European cultures than other musicians no matter how refined their imitations.

Walcott's successor in Oregon in 1986 was Trilok Gurtu from Bombay, not only an excellent tabla player but also a very good jazz drummer, a combination that would have been unthinkable a few years previously. Gurtu has also made recordings with Don Cherry and Charlie Mariano. He has an unusual talent for shadings of dynamics.

In view of the cosmopolitan, world music spirit of today's jazz, it goes without saying that percussion techniques from other musical realms and cultures have also been incorporated into jazz. Andy Narell (an unusually flexible improviser) and Othello Molineaux (who was consistently employed by Jaco Pastorius) brought steel drums from Trinidad into the jazz context. Okay Temiz has carried the rhythms of his native Turkey into jazz with his group Oriental Wind. Karl Berger is of the opinion that "Turkish music is world music *par excellence,* because in it Asian, European, and African sources come together."

Swedish-born Bengt Berger studied balafone techniques in Africa and together with his Bitter Funeral Beer Band made impressive recordings combining jazz with ritual burial music from Ghana. And with Mahama Konaté from Burkina Faso there at last exists an African master of balafone playing who is also active in today's jazz, playing with trumpeter Jon Hassell.

Glen Velez, who first worked with Steve Reich and Paul Winter, is a
phenomenon. Just a few years ago it seemed impossible that a percussionist
should devote himself exclusively to something so specialized as the
tambourine (also known as the frame-drum), and yet Velez generates such
a wealth of rhythms and sounds from the frame-drums he has collected from
many cultures (the bodhran from Ireland, the Brazilian pandeira, the Afghan
doira, the Arab duff, the North African bendir, and the kanjira from southern
India) that he fills entire solo albums with them.

The impact and the "totality" of percussive rhythms from many countries
of the earth becomes clear when you realize that Weather Report, the most
successful fusion group until its dissolution in 1985, employed one or more
percussionists in addition to the drummer during most of that decade. The
first percussion player in the group was also the first with Miles Davis and
Chick Corea: Airto. After him come Dom Um Romao, Alejandro Acuna,
Manolo Badrena, Alyrio Lima, Muruga (the latter not only on Latin American
but also on Moroccan and Israeli drums), and Jose Rossi from Argentina—
musicians, in other words, who belong to or have mastered the most diverse
musical cultures.

Another characteristic of this totality of percussive rhythms is that a new
type of percussionist has evolved. He or she is no longer indebted to one of
the different musical cultures, but rather feeds on many of them. Musicians
like Kenneth Nash, Sue Evans, Armen Halburian, Ayibe Dieng, J. A. Deane (an
expert in electric percussion), Arto Tuncboyaci, Denmark's Marilyn Mazur,
German-born Christoph Haberer, and others belong in this category.

A modern percussion player uses dozens of different instruments. Each
has its own tradition and demands its own playing technique. It is no longer
anything out of the ordinary that a percussionist commands Cuban and
Brazilian instruments as well as Indian and Tibetan ones, and Turkish and
Moroccan. In order to play them congenially—or at least professionally—
musicians have to be familiar with the way they were originally played in
their native cultures. That's how universal jazz has become today.

It would be a misunderstanding to consider all that has been discussed in
this chapter a radically new development. It is new in a gradual sense at best.
The tendency for the jazz musician to include and incorporate anything he
or she is confronted with has been immanent from the beginning of jazz.
Many of the things discovered by jazz in the past few years and decades
simply were not known by the early jazz musicians, for example, Indian
music. But Latin American music was known from the start. The main reason
why New Orleans was the most important city in the development of jazz
was because it not only is the southernmost city in the North American
cultural sphere but also the northernmost city of the Latin American—Latin
and Creole—cultural sphere. Both converged there almost as intensely as in

Miami or New York's Barrio today. The "Latin tinge" Jelly Roll Morton spoke of in respect to his "New Orleans Blues" was from the start more than just a tinge. It was an integral part of jazz, because the black rhythms of both North and South America were based on African rhythms—mainly from the same African cultures and, above all, from the Yorubas. It is important in this context that African rhythms and instruments were less tainted, kept purer and more alive, in the Latin sphere (above all, in Cuba, Haiti, and Brazil) than in North America, where they underwent stronger changes and mutations, mainly because the white masters suppressed the black heritage of their slaves. At the risk of oversimplification, it can be said that Latin music is "Africanized European dances and melodies," whereas North American music can be considered "Europeanized African rhythms."

John Storm Roberts has shown that "the Latin ingredients in early New Orleans jazz are more important than has been realized." He writes that Papa Laine, leader of the first known white jazz band, had a trumpeter at the turn of the century named "Chink" Martin, whose parents were Spanish and Mexican. In interviews, Martin said that Royal Street between Dumaine and Esplanade (a central point in New Orleans' old French Quarter) had been inhabited mainly by Spanish and Mexican people. Jelly Roll Morton never saw a duality of only black and white elements, but from the beginning a trinity: "We had Spanish, we had colored, we had white . . ."

"Spanish" in old New Orleans is what we would call "Latin" today. Jelly Roll Morton went so far as to claim that the "Spanish tinge" was the essential ingredient that differentiated jazz from ragtime. New Orleans author Al Rose believes that ragtime came into being when black bands tried to play Mexican music. And the old journal, *New Orleans,* surmised that the word *jazz* was a bastardization of the Mexican expression *"Musica de jarabe."* We don't have to take all these speculations at face value, but they point to the significance of Latin elements in old New Orleans—a significance neglected by most jazz historians to date.

The Latin elements are not only significant to the music of old New Orleans but also to the New Orleans of today. Contemporary New Orleans rock, by people like Fats Domino, Professor Longhair, Allen Toussaint, Dr. John, the Neville Brothers and others is (as we pointed out in the piano section) different from Northern rock music because it is Latinized and Creolized: a "combination of offbeat Spanish beats and Calypso downbeats," as Professor Longhair put it. This, then, is a constant element in the musical tradition of the city. It points not only toward Mexico and Cuba but directly toward the Spanish history of New Orleans—all part of the same cultural sphere, encompassing Cuba and Mexico as well as the entire Creole realm right down to Trinidad and French Guiana.

It has also become clear that in this field (as in all the others) jazz developed according to the law under which it came into being. Everything was *in nuce*—was already potentially present—in the early forms of jazz.

The Violin

What had happened to the flute during the fifties has come true for the violin since the end of the sixties: All of a sudden, it was at the center of attention—there was talk of a "violin wave." This seems particularly paradoxical in view of the inferior role the violin had previously played in the history of jazz. Though the violin is by no means new to jazz—it is as old as the cornets of New Orleans—its softness of sound long kept it from playing an equal role in the swinging consortium of trombones, trumpets, and saxophones.

Early New Orleans and ragtime bands frequently included a violinist, but only because it was a nineteenth-century custom to have a violin in that sort of a band. The violinist in the old New Orleans orchestras was the counterpart of the "stand-up fiddler" of Viennese *Kaffeehaus* music. As late as the fifties, this *Kaffeehaus* tradition still cast its shadow over the jazz violinists. As soon as they were no longer "modern," they wound up where their instruments (as far as jazz was concerned) came from: in commercial music.

The first important violinist in jazz was Joe Venuti. Rediscovered in the decade preceding his death in 1978, the "old man" generated an amazing vitality, outplaying many of the younger violinists—a phenomenon breaking through all generational boundaries, comparable to Earl Hines among the pianists. One of his specialties was a kind of bow technique that would have filled "venerable" conservatory teachers with horror. He often removed the pin from the frog of the bow, wrapping the bow hair around all four strings of his violin, and holding the stick under the body of the instrument, thereby producing unusual chords. Eddie South, born in Louisiana in the same year as Venuti (1904; died in 1962), never achieved Venuti's fame. South, who had ties to the European scene as early as the twenties, spent time in Paris during the thirties and played there with Django Reinhardt and Europe's most important jazz violinist, Stephane Grappelli. An amazing recording made by these three is the "Interprétation swing et improvisation swing sur le premier mouvement du concerto en ré mineur pour deux violons par Jean Sebastian Bach." Here, South and Grappelli play the main segment of the first movement of the Bach D-minor concerto for two violins, with Reinhardt taking the orchestra part on guitar. This recording is one of the earliest, and perhaps the most moving, testimonies to the admiration so many jazz musicians have for Bach's work. During World War II, the German occupation authorities in Paris melted down all available copies of this record as a particularly monstrous example of "degenerate art" (*Entartete*

Kunst). Fortunately, a number of copies in private hands survived, and the recording was later reissued.

Stephane Grappelli is the "grand seigneur" of the jazz violin with a very French sort of amiability and charm. From 1934 on, he was, with Django Reinhardt, a key member of the famous Quintet du Hot Club de France, the first important combo in European jazz. During the German occupation, he lived in England. During the late forties and after, he played with many well-known European and American musicians in Paris. Then he faded from the scene for a while; but when the "violin wave" started in the late sixties, he made a true comeback. Among his most beautiful recordings are those the seventy-year-old Grand Old Man made with musicians half his age—for example, with Larry Coryell, Philip Catherine, and Gary Burton.

In the meantime, in the United States—beginning with his 1936 record of "I'se a Muggin' "—Stuff Smith had become the great jazz violinist. He was the first to use electronic amplification. With the sovereignty of a master, he ignored all the rules of the conservatory. A well-bred concert violinist might cringe at Stuff's violent violin treatment, but he achieved more jazzlike, hornlike effects than any other player prior to today's "violin wave." Smith, who died in Munich in 1967, was a humorist of the caliber of Fats Waller. During the second half of the thirties, he led a sextet on 52nd Street in New York with trumpeter Jonah Jones that combined jazz and humor in a wonderful way. In the fifties, Norman Granz teamed Smith's violin with the trumpet of Dizzy Gillespie.

For years, Ray Nance, who died in 1976, was a trumpeter in Duke Ellington's orchestra and also played occasional violin solos. But on violin he played mostly moody, sentimental melodies, while his trumpet solos belong with the great examples of the genre in jazz. On the other hand it is an illustration of the growing importance of the jazz violin that the instrument became increasingly essential to Nance in the years before his death. Now, in smaller groups, he played happy, swinging violin solos that showed his roots in terms of style and phrasing to be where he originated as a trumpeter as well: in Louis Armstrong. Claude Williams (who also played guitar for Count Basie) emerged from Andy Kirk's Clouds of Joy. He has transmitted to our own times the charm and humorous lightness of Swing violinists, in recordings with Jay McShann and in his own name.

Interestingly enough, it was a European who initiated the great success of the violin in the new jazz: Jean-Luc Ponty, born in 1942, the son of a violin professor, really and definitely electrified the violin. His position is thus the same as Charlie Christian's among guitarists, Jimmy Smith's among organists, or Jaco Pastorius' among bassists.

Ponty, who studied classical violin (he was a first-prize winner at the Conservatoire Nationale Supérieur de Paris), began with true jazz recordings, as in *Violin Summit* with Stuff Smith, Stephane Grappelli, and the Dane Svend Asmussen. He moved to the United States in 1973, where he played first with Frank Zappa, then in John McLaughlin's second Mahavishnu Orchestra. In the late seventies, Ponty developed the impulses he had received there into his own kind of fusion music: "Lighter, warmer, more romantic and more accessible" (Tim Schneckloth) than McLaughlin, which made him successful with a wide audience extending beyond the actual realm of fusion. But he also developed a tendency, as *Down Beat* put it, to become "quite predictable" and "corral both his playing and arrangements into the most narrow of bags." Ponty uses a vast number of accessories to produce the electronic sounds on his violin and his music has become a case of constant brinkmanship between extramusical effects and high musical quality.

As the musician who actually initiated the contemporary interest in the violin—with his jazz recordings around the turn of the sixties—Ponty became indirectly responsible for the comeback of the music of veteran masters Venuti and Grappelli.

Around the same time as Ponty, Don "Sugar Cane" Harris became known, only to disappear from the scene again, regrettably, after a couple of years. As Ponty stems from the classical violin tradition, Harris comes from the blues. For years he toured the United States with Johnny Otis' Blues Show, where he acquired his funky blues style.

But the list of extraordinary contemporary violinists only begins with Ponty and Harris. Immediately after, and in part also parallel to them, come Mike White, Jerry Goodman, Poles Zbigniew Seifert, Michal Urbaniak, and Krzesimir Debski, as well as John Blake, Darol Anger, Marc O'Connor, French-born Didier Lockwood, Pierre Blanchard, and Dominique Pifarely, Indians L. Shankar and L. Subramaniam, and, in the realm of free jazz, Leroy Jenkins, Ramsey Ameen, Billy Bang, Charles Burnham, Ali Akbar, Terry Jenoure, Mark Feldman, and Phil Wachsman from England.

White made Coltrane-inspired recordings with Pharoah Sanders. Goodman is an especially eclectic player, uniting jazz-rock, country, and hillbilly music, the Nashville sound, Mingus, gypsy and classical music. Urbaniak plays a very personal kind of fusion music often revealing traces of the folk music of his native Poland. Since the mid-eighties he also plays MIDI violins triggering synthesizers. Darol Anger and Marc O'Connor have uncovered, far from all academic traditions, the "white" folk roots (hillbilly, blue grass, Nashville sound) of their instrument, the former in recordings with Alex DeGrassi and William Ackerman, the latter with mandolin player David Grisman and the jazz-rock group Dregs.

Of particular significance is Zbigniew Seifert, whom critic Patrick Hinely compared directly to John Coltrane: "What links Seifert and Coltrane, besides total dedication to their instruments, is a quality one might call 'controlled drift' or 'responsible freedom.' In both men's music, there is no way you can tell what is going to happen next, but you can trust them to take it all the way to the edge."

And from Seifert himself: "What I play on the violin, I imagine being produced by the saxophone. I admire Coltrane and try to play as he would if his instrument were the violin. That's probably the reason that I avoid playing my instrument in the usual way, with all the well-known effects." And McCoy Tyner said at the 1976 Berlin Jazz Days, "I've never heard a violinist like him before!"

Seifert is among the outstanding Polish jazz musicians who have made their country one of the most interesting jazz nations in the world. His music lives in the tension between his classical roots and his love for Coltrane. There is, in other words, a Zbigniew of chamber music and one who is "Trane-like." Seifert made recordings with Eddie Gomez, Jack DeJohnette, John Scofield, Joachim Kühn, Cecil McBee, Billy Hart, Charlie Mariano, and others. Toward the end of 1978, only a few weeks before his tragic death early in 1979, the members of the group Oregon, who had just become acquainted with his style, invited him to the studio. The resulting record, *Violin,* was dedicated to his memory.

The jazz world had just lost Zbigniew Seifert when another European jazz violinist arrived on the scene and was immediately hailed as "the new Zbiggy": Didier Lockwood, who comes from France, the classical land of great jazz violinists. The first of them was Michel Warlop, as early as in the late twenties. When Django Reinhardt and Stephane Grappelli made their first big-band jazz recordings in the early thirties, it was with an orchestra led by Warlop. When Warlop concluded in 1937 that Grappelli was a greater violinist than himself, he gave him one of his violins as a present. By doing so, he initiated a tradition. And since then the most promising French jazz violinist has been presented with the Warlop violin. Grappelli passed it on to Ponty. In early 1979, Ponty and Grappelli decided that Didier Lockwood had become worthy of possessing Warlop's instrument. It was handed on to Lockwood at a Paris concert.

Said Lockwood, "No other violinist has moved and influenced me more than Zbigniew Seifert." In Lockwood's music, too, the Coltrane tradition remains alive, but he is more interested in fusion music than Seifert was. He possesses an elegance and charm matched by only a very few musicians on today's fusion scene. Krzesimir Debski, Pierre Blanchard, and Dominique Pifarely impressively extend Seifert's legacy—Debski in his group String Connection, Blanchard in recordings with Martial Solal and Lee Konitz, and Pifarely in his playing with Mike Westbrook and Eddy Louiss.

It is remarkable that Coltrane has had such a strong influence on violinists.

However, his legacy led to quite different results with players like Ponty, Mike White, Seifert, and Lockwood. It resulted in yet another style in Philadelphia-born John Blake, who was first presented by McCoy Tyner as a member of his group and has played with Grover Washington. Blake is an improviser with the burning power of the saxophonists who could be heard in Tyner's groups during the seventies; he has a noticeable interest in black soul and funk music.

It is fitting that with the opening up of jazz toward Indian Music, two significant Indian violinists have become successful on the jazz and fusion scene: L. Shankar and L. Subramaniam, the former known through his work in John McLaughlin's Shakti, the latter through recordings with Larry Coryell, Herbie Hancock, Maynard Ferguson, John Handy, and Ali Akbar Khan. Both Shankar and Subramaniam hail from the same families of southern Indian musicians; that means they belong to the Carnatic musical culture of India (the other being the Hindustani, in the northern part of the country). Subramaniam currently possesses the title "Violin Chakravarti" ("Emperor of the Violinists"), a title given to only one violinist in each generation.

The outstanding and far too little-known violin voice of free jazz is Leroy Jenkins. His clusterlike, "pounded" violin sounds have a kind of manic drive. Especially in the 1970s, Jenkins used the violin as percussion instrument or noise producer, without scrupling about the traditional rules of violin and harmony. Ramsey Ameen became known in the late seventies through his work with Cecil Taylor, and Billy Bang and Charles Burnham through the String Trio of New York. Akbar Ali played with Ronald Shannon Jackson. Terry Jenoure became known for her sensitive playing in clarinetist John Carter's group, and later she phrased free funk with Leroy Jenkins. Mark Feldman is able to play with equal ease the frenetic music of John Zorn and Tim Berne and the stately jazz-influenced classical music of Anthony Davis. He has made thrilling recordings with the Arcado String Trio. But it is Billy Bang who, after Leroy Jenkins, offers one of the most original violin voices in the new jazz. He plays his instrument with an unusually virtuosic bow technique and that raw "percussive" attack more concerned with natural-ness and blues quality than with so-called "classical" norms. He has also recorded a highly interesting solo violin album that shows that, even on an instrument with a tradition as great and old as that of the violin, new ways of playing can still be found.

The extent to which rhythmic and tonal self-assurance has increased among jazz violinists can also be indirectly seen in the fact that a "wave" of jazz playing and improvising string quartets has broken onto the jazz scene, in an astonishing parallel development to the rise of "pure" saxophone quartets. Stylistic openness and an imagination that defies categorizations are shared by such groups as the Kronos Quartet, the Black Swan Quartet, the Turtle Island String Quartet, the Soldier String Quartet, and the Modern String Quartet (with German-born Jörg Widmoser). The Kronos Quartet, which has held together since 1977 (David Harrington and John Sherba, violins; Hank Dutt, viola; and Joan Jeanrenaud, cello), phrases particularly impressively. For years it has been one of the most highly esteemed groups in modern concert music, and Terry Riley and Phillip Glass are among the many composers who have written for it. The Kronos Quartet may not improvise, but it has so "disrupted" the "comfortable" image of the string quartet (with the sounds of Jimi Hendrix's "Purple Haze," James Brown's "Sex Machine," and pieces by Ornette Coleman, Bill Evans, and Thelonious Monk) and so advanced a new sensibility that jazz musicians have frequently worked together with Kronos: Steve Lacy, Max Roach, Anthony Braxton, Cecil Taylor, etc.

No other instrument in jazz has as many European players as the violin. Among the violinists mentioned in this section, there are eleven Europeans (plus sixteen Americans and two Indians). In addition, the American players Eddie South, Stuff Smith, and Alan Silva all lived in Europe for extended periods; and "Sugar Cane" Harris, L. Subramaniam, and Billy Bang made some of their most important recordings in Europe. The irony is the fact that the very first of the well-known jazz violinists, Joe Venuti, was European by birth. Venuti used to claim that he had been born of Italian parents on the Atlantic Ocean, en route to America. But when Joe was in his seventies, he admitted that he was born in northern Italy, near Lago di Como, where Venutis still live to this day.

Miscellaneous Instruments

For fifty years, until about 1950, only a relatively small "family" of instruments was employed in jazz. They were basically the same instruments that had been used in early New Orleans jazz: two instruments from the brass group (trumpet and trombone), saxophone and clarinet from the reed group, and, of course, the rhythm-section instruments—drums, bass, guitar, and piano.

Nevertheless, there have been shifts in emphasis within jazz instrumentation—to such a degree that the entire history of jazz can be viewed in terms of shifting emphases placed on particular instruments. In this scheme, the piano would stand at the beginning; it ruled the ragtime period. Then the trumpet blew its way to the forefront: first in New Orleans, where the "Kings of Jazz" always were trumpeters (or cornetists), then in the great Chicago period, when trumpeters like King Oliver, Louis Armstrong, and Bix Beiderbecke came to the fore. The Swing era was the time of the clarinet. And with the appearance of Lester Young and Charlie

Parker, the saxophone became the main instrument—initially tenor, then
for a while alto, and after that tenor again. In the early seventies, finally,
electronics became the determining sound factor—first in the shape of the
electric guitar but soon to such a degree that the electronic sound has
frequently become more important than the original sound of the
instruments electronically amplified or manipulated. Only in eighties jazz
was it impossible, because of the multitude of values, to find a single
instrument dominating the scene.

There have been three major changes in jazz instrumentation: first,
through the Lester Young–initiated switch of jazz consciousness from
sonority to phrasing; then, as we indicated, through electronics; and, finally,
through the opening of jazz to world music.

After Lester Young had cleared the path for the recognition that the jazz
essence was no longer tied, for better or worse, to sonority, jazz could be
played on practically any instrument offering possibilities for sufficiently
flexible, clear jazz phrasing. Thus, instruments were "discovered" for jazz
that previously had hardly ever (or never) been in jazz use. The flute, the
French horn, and the violin are examples of this phenomenon. Saxophonist
Rufus Harley from Philadelphia has shown that you can convincingly
improvise jazz on the Scottish bagpipes. Trombonist Steve Turre blows
absolutely modern and captivating jazz solos on conch-shells. And with
Christian Marclay the record player becomes a jazz instrument. The
wildness of his scratching (moving records rhythmically forward and
backward while the needle is in the groove) and the rough and humorous
subversions of his sound collages sound like a punky counterpart to the
music of John Zorn.

While some of these instruments could be summarily discussed under the
heading "Miscellaneous Instruments" in prior editions of this book, they
have since become so important that they require chapters of their own:
flute, violin, organ and keyboards, percussion instruments.

Another motive behind this ongoing process of discovering new instruments for jazz is the musicians' interest in sound. In the chapter "The
Elements of Jazz" it was shown that sound is an indispensable jazz element,
and in the course of jazz history, the interest in sound has grown
continuously. There are musicians and groups today for whom involvement
in and joy of sound seem to have become of paramount importance.

Discovering new sounds has been a crucial motivating factor for jazz
musicians. In the late sixties it seemed as if electronics were especially
suited to take over this function. But then it became clear that precisely the
"oversupply" of sound possibilities in electronics (we discussed this in the
section on organ and keyboards) caused problems regarding individuality
and personal style. As we have seen, the chief aim of the interest in sound is

to arrive at a *personal* expression. That is why, paradoxically, the sound consciousness associated with electronics led to a revival of acoustic jazz from the late seventies on.

But let us return to the topic of "miscellaneous instruments." Many of them are used as secondary instruments, and we have mentioned them where a certain musician's primary instrument was discussed: the cello in connection with bassist Oscar Pettiford; the bass clarinet introduced by Eric Dolphy in the clarinet section; oboe and bassoon in connection with Yusef Lateef in the tenor and flute sections. There we also discussed Roland Kirk, who in addition to all his other instruments played two archaic saxophones, used mainly in turn-of-the-century Spanish military bands: the stritch and the manzello.

How the limits of jazz instrumentation have expanded becomes clear when one hears the harp improvisations of Alice Coltrane. In the fifties, Corky Hale from the West Coast and Dorothy Ashby from New York had already attempted to play in a jazz vein on this instrument. (A curiosity: The first traceable jazz harp was played by Caspar Reardon in 1934, on Jack Teagarden's recording of "Junk Man" [with Benny Goodman], and after that by Adele Girard in Joe Marsala's "Jazz Me Blues" [with Eddie Condon and Joe Bushkin!].) But only the modality of the new jazz seems to have cleared the way for this difficult instrument, which has to be constantly retuned. Alice Coltrane was the first to develop a *jazz-harp* sound into something more than just a curiosity.

A step beyond Alice Coltrane was taken by Zeena Parkins, who became known in the no wave circle around John Zorn, Elliot Sharp, and Wayne Horvitz. Parkins plays splintered clusters of punk-inspired restlessness, so radically electronically alienating the sound of her harp that she literally "picks to pieces" the romantic aura that is associated with this instrument more than any other musician.

For long the accordion played no part in jazz, even when as early as 1930 Charles Melrose played an accordion solo with the Cellar Boys: "Wailing Blues" with Bud Freeman and Frank Teschemacher. But all the accordionists who followed him—Buster Moten (in the Bennie Moten Orchestra), Joe Mooney (who headed a swing quartet in the second half of the forties), Mat Mathews, and Art van Damme—could only partially diminish the instrument's rigidity and its innate imprecision of phrasing (which is similarly problematic on the pipe organ since both are reed instruments). Astor Piazolla made remarkable duo recordings with baritone saxophonist Gerry Mulligan, intertwining the tango and jazz.

But only in the eighties did the accordion become an absolutely valid jazz instrument. Two musicians brought that about: Argentinian-born Dino Saluzzi (on the bandoneon) and New Yorker Guy Klucevsek (on an arsenal of the most diverse types of accordion). Saluzzi emancipates the tango from its schematic aspects by enriching the essence of this music—its rebellious melancholy—with the openness and vitality of the whole of Argentinian folklore: with Indian melodies and European waltzes, with the candomblé rhythms of the enslaved Africans transported to South America, with the milongas of rural gaucho folklore, and also with the romantic and impressionistic music of the nineteenth century. Through such bandoneon players as Saluzzi, Juan José Mosalini, and Luis DiMatteo—tango musicians who, together with and following on from Piazzolla, expand the range of world music—Argentina has now found its way onto the music scene (as Brazil did long before).

Guy Klucevsek, who made a name for himself playing with John Zorn, produces the most uncharacteristic of sounds on the accordion. He is a master of really fast tonal breaks and unaccustomed changes of register, conjuring up intense, strange sounds on his instrument, which sometimes take on a fairy-tale-like and folkloristic character—sounds that you might expect from keyboards but scarcely from an accordion.

Two instruments have come full circle: harmonica and tuba. In old New Orleans, the tuba, as mentioned, was a kind of forerunner of the string bass. Today, musicians like Howard Johnson, Don Butterfield, Bob Stewart, Joe Daley, Earl McIntyre, and in Europe Peter Kowald, Larry Fishkind, and Pinguin Moschner are playing tuba solos of almost trumpetlike agility. Blues singer Taj Mahal used an entire tuba section as accompaniment on one of his records. Howard Johnson briefly led a tuba band in the seventies. Bob Stewart blows lines of exceptional melodic and rhythmic complexity. Since one tends to forget the man who initiated this whole development, it should be pointed out that as early as the fifties, in Los Angeles, bassist Red Callender, Charles Mingus' teacher, incorporated the tuba into the then-dominant West Coast sounds. Later came Ray Draper, who in the second half of the fifties played striking tuba solos in the hard bop bands of Max Roach, Donald Byrd, and John Coltrane.

The harmonica is the "harp" of the folk-blues singer. The two Sonny Boy Williamsons, as well as Sonny Terry, Junior Wells, Shakey Jake, Little Walter, Big Walter Horton, James Cotton, Carey Bell, Whispering Smith, and many others have played marvelously expressive "talking" harmonica solos—usually in the blues groups that existed (and continue to exist) in the South or on Chicago's South Side. Nevertheless, this instrument was always afflicted with the stigma of a certain folklorelike primitiveness. Belgian Toots Thielemans liberated the harmonica from this affliction. He plays it with a mobility and wealth of ideas reminiscent of the great saxophonists of the cool-jazz era.

Since the emergence of electronic amplification, the harmonica has been given equal rights in the family of instruments. it has also made inroads in contemporary blues-rock music where it is played by white musicians like Paul Butterfield or John Mayall in the style of the great black blues "harp" men. Magic Dick has contributed exciting harmonica solos in a pure rock context. Stevie Wonder has combined Thielemans's refinement with the "harp" sound of the old blues. Mauricio Einhorn has incorporated the Thielemans sound into his native Brazilian music, adding the specific Brazilian rhythm feeling.

Next are such instruments as French horn, oboe, English horn, and bassoon. Their "fathers" (in terms of jazz) were, as early as the fifties, Julius Watkins and Yusef Lateef. Watkins played the French horn on recordings with important musicians like Kenny Clarke, Oscar Pettiford, and Quincy Jones, reaching a remarkable jazzlike intensity difficult to find on this difficult instrument. Watkins is the "Charlie Parker of the French horn." His lyrical phrasing and a wealth of ideas going beyond the horn's normal range have influenced all contemporary players of the instrument: Vincent Chancey, Sharon Freeman, and John Clark (all of whom have played with Carla Bley), and Peter Gordon (with Jaco Pastorius). *The* French horn voice in contemporary jazz is, however, Tom Varner. On an instrument where intonation is so difficult, he phrases impetuous but outstandingly relaxed free-bop lines whereby free is represented by lack of prescribed chord changes and bop by a regular swinging beat.

Lateef—who is as outstanding on tenor sax, flute, oboe, and bassoon as he is on diverse exotic instruments such as the argol (an Egyptian kind of oboe)—was the precursor, even before Coltrane, of the opening up of jazz to world music. In the fifties, tenorist Bob Cooper played oboe and English horn on West Coast jazz recordings, including some with Max Roach on drums. Perhaps the most interesting bassoon solos in today's jazz are by Frank Tiberi. Paul McCandless has come to the fore in the group Oregon on oboe and English horn; he is a musician with roots in the romantic tradition of these instruments. Django Bates has attained an almost trumpetlike fluency on the rarely used tenor horn.

Let's move on to some miscellaneous string instruments. The mandolin is so engulfed by the serenade sound of Italian mandolin groups that it might seem paradoxical that it has made its way into jazz. But it has happened—characteristically at first by way of musicians close to country and western and bluegrass music (who, at the same time, are real "Swingers"): Tiny Moore and Jethro Burns. The latter made his first mandolin recordings as early as the forties, with Bob Wills's Texas Playboys. In a modern context, guitarist John Abercrombie (especially convincing in his quartet recordings with McCoy Tyner) and above all David Grisman have employed the mandolin. Grisman, who celebrated successes at the start of the eighties with what he calls his "dawg music," creates string sounds that seem like a contemporary counterpart of Django Reinhardt's Quintet du Hot Club de France. Lebanese-born Rabih Abou-Khalil, who lives in Munich, plays the oud, the Arab lute, with captivating lightness in the realm of world music.

The "fathers" of cello playing in jazz have already been mentioned in the section about the bass. But it was up to Abdul Wadud (who has recorded with quite a few AACM musicians), David Darling, and Hank Roberts to realize the full potential of this instrument in today's jazz—Darling with romanticizing and aestheticizing sounds and a lot of overdubbing, Wadud with convincing jazz feeling and an astonishing talent for improvisation (and yet complete awareness of the classical and romantic cello tradition). Indiana-born Roberts "vocalizes" the cello most intensively, not only figuratively with an absolutely hymnlike sound but also in actual fact. He often complements his cello line with the elegant force of his singing voice, which, like his cello playing, is electronically transformed in a multitude of ways (with a harmonizer, digital delay, headphone microphone, etc.). Another outstanding cellist in the mainstream of today's jazz is Jean-Charles Capon from France. Free jazz on the cello is played by Irene Aebi (especially in Steve Lacy's group), Diedre Murray (in the Henry Threadgill Sextet), David Eyges, and Tristan Honsinger. The latter's radically uncompromising playing brings to mind Derek Bailey's guitar style. Tom Cora has represented the cello in the no wave context with bizarre distancing of folklore melodies.

The horizon of instruments was extended even further by the exotic instruments that became available in the course of the opening up of jazz to the other great musical cultures of the world. Don Cherry, for example, has used instruments from Lappland, Africa, Tibet, India, China, and elsewhere. Han Bennink occasionally uses the dhung, a giant Tibetan Alpine horn. Collin Walcott, Bill Plummer, and others have played the Indian sitar for jazz records. Saxophonist Charlie Mariano studied the nagaswaram, an oboelike instrument from southern India, for years, first in the city of Kuala Lumpur, then in a small Indian village. He has created a unique union of Karnatic (south Indian) spirituality and the Coltrane tradition.

One of the most interesting among these musicians is Stephan Micus, a "world musician" in the full sense of the word. Micus commands a zither from Bavaria, bamboo flutes from Japan, a rabab from Afghanistan and instruments from Bali, India, and Tibet—plus a Scottish bagpipe. For years, he traveled in Asia, studying these instruments. He plays them with a profound internationalization of their tradition and spirituality, uniting their sounds in a musical river that makes the stream of inner consciousness audible. In the section on jazz in the eighties, we discussed a new type of musician who plays world music. Many players who represent this type have been mentioned. But hardly anyone represents it in so ideal, so visionary a way as Micus. The inner space of sounds in search of which so many musicians dared to venture into electronics: Micus not only imagines it, he realizes it—not with electronics, but on instruments thousands of years old.

In conclusion we must mention two stylists who don't play any instrument in the traditional sense of the word: Kip Hanrahan and Hal Willner. The "instrument" they do play is the recording studio. One could call them—to adapt a term from the visual arts—"conceptualists." That is precisely what they are—shapers of concepts and creators of contexts for ideas, who are much more comprehensively and profoundly active than is demanded by the role of the usual record producer. Both are masters in bringing about encounters where stylistic divisions are spectacularly surmounted. In his record projects Willner even succeeded in uniting musicians from such "hostile" camps as jazz, pop, chansons, rock, and European concert music. This produced two of the eighties' most original and trail-blazing monuments. *That's The Way I Feel Now,* recorded in 1984, is devoted to Thelonious Monk, the incomparable pianist and composer, with fascinating Monk interpretations by such diverse players as John Zorn, Donald Fagen, Arto Lindsay, Joe Jackson, Randy Weston, Bobby McFerrin, Carla Bley, Johnny Griffin. The other album is devoted to Kurt Weill: *Lost in the Stars,* recorded a year later, with unusual interpretations by Lou Reed, Phil Woods, the Armadillo String Quartet, Carla Bley, Tom Waits, Charlie Haden, Sting, Dagmar Krause, and so forth.

Kip Hanrahan, an expert in musical confrontations, even goes a step further in his projects. Here the most divergent of musical worlds collide even more directly and immediately. High friction is generated when the cream of the New York Latin scene encounters no wave musicians, rock singers, contemporary jazz makers, Caribbean guitarists, soul musicians, etc. "It's not always putting things together. Sometimes it is putting things apart," Hanrahan said. "I mean, if you have musicians who always play the same things together, you would have to build an obstacle, so that they would have to dismantle their normal way of communicating and build another thing. Sometimes I try very hard to set up a way in which there are tensions between the bands, so that the tensions themselves become the music." Paradoxically, Hanrahan's projects, aiming at contrast and surprising oppositions—his "aesthetic of confrontation"—have led to some of the most homogeneous and successful results in eighties jazz. Some critics think that his double album *Desire Develops an Edge* (Hanrahan: "The clearest articulation of myself") is for the eighties what Carla Bley's *Escalator over the Hill* was for the seventies. Kip Hanrahan tears down barriers between musical ghettos, bringing together what is apparently incompatible. Here that is successful to the utmost degree because Hanrahan doesn't attempt to bring diverging musical styles closer but looks for what they have in common, within their differences.

THE VOCALISTS OF JAZZ

The Vocalists of Jazz

The Male Singers

Before jazz, there were blues and shouts, work songs and spirituals—the whole treasury of vocal folk music sung by both black and white in the South. There was what Marshall Stearns has called "archaic jazz." From this music jazz developed. In other words, jazz developed from vocal sources. Much about the sounds peculiar to jazz can be explained by the fact that horn blowers imitate the sounds of the human voice on their instruments. This becomes obvious in the growling sounds of trumpets and trombones in the orchestra of Duke Ellington, for example, or in Eric Dolphy's bass clarinet.

On the other hand, jazz today is so exclusively an instrumental music that its standards and criteria derive from the realm of the instrumental, even the standards of jazz singing. The jazz vocalist handles his voice "like an instrument" like a trumpet or trombone or, today especially, a saxophone. Thus the criteria important to European vocal music, such as purity or range of voice, are inapplicable to jazz. Some of the most important jazz singers have voices that—according to "classical" criteria are almost ugly. Many have a vocal range so limited that it would hardly encompass a Schubert song.

The dilemma of jazz singing can be expressed as a paradox: all jazz derives from vocal music, but all jazz singing is derived from instrumental music. Significantly, some of the best jazz singers (at least among the males) are also players—above all, Louis Armstrong.

In the literature of jazz, critics of the most diverse persuasions mean to be laudatory when they say of an instrumentalist—such as alto saxophonist

Johnny Hodges—that his sound "resembles that of the human voice." On the other hand, nothing more flattering can be said of a singer than that he or she knows how to "treat the voice as an instrument."

Only one domain is beyond this dilemma of jazz singing: the blues. But precisely this makes the vicious circle clear. For decades, almost all jazz singers who found favor with the general public were outside the stream of real blues, whereas the first-rate singers of authentic blues and gospel—at least until the big success of blues in rock music from the sixties on—were hardly known. This breakthrough began as early as the late fifties with Ray Charles, a real blues singer in the tradition of folk blues and gospel, who was accepted by the whole world of modern jazz and found a wide audience beyond both blues and jazz. It has been rightly said that no one did more to assure the return of the blues to the common consciousness of America than Ray Charles in the fifties. But Charles was only the final link (at that time) in an unending chain of blues singers whose earliest representatives disappear somewhere in the darkness of the South of the past century. And simultaneously, he was the first link in the still growing chain of black singers who sing authentic blues and yet have great success even with white audiences.

The first well-known representatives of this blues folklore are probably Blind Lemon Jefferson, a blind street musician from Texas, and Huddie Leadbetter (called Leadbelly) who served time in Angola State Penitentiary in Louisiana, first for murder and a few years later for manslaughter. From them, the line runs via Robert Johnson, who came from Mississippi and was poisoned in Texas, to Big Bill Broonzy and Son House and the many blues singers who made Chicago the blues capital of the United States (though all are natives of the South): Muddy Waters, Little Brother Montgomery, St. Louis Jimmy, Sunnyland Slim, Sonny Boy Williamson, Little Walter, Memphis Slim, Howlin' Wolf and many others. John Lee Hooker, who lives in Detroit, also belongs here. Almost all the blues singers are also excellent guitarists. And when they play piano, they accompany themselves with exciting boogie-woogie bass lines. (Other important folk-blues singers are mentioned in the blues section.)

In an unending stream, over the decades, more and more new blues singers became known as they migrated from the South to the cities of the North and West. There are two main streams in this great blues migration and two main states: Mississippi and Texas. Mississippi-born blues people generally migrate to Chicago; those from Texas go to California. The two streams differ musically, too. The Mississippi stream is rougher, "dirtier"; the Texas stream softer, more flexible and supple. It was the Texas stream that merged with the Midwestern big bands during the Swing era, leading to Swing blues and jazz blues. But here, too, there are, of course, all imaginable kinds of crossings and mixtures.

The blues was as alive in the eighties as it was during the twenties and thirties. Since the sixties, a new generation of blues singers has appeared, filled with the consciousness of race and social protest that can be found in many contemporary jazz musicians as well. Members of this new blues generation include singer–harmonica player Junior Wells, singer-guitarists Buddy Guy, Albert King, Albert Collins, Otis Rush, as well as Taj Mahal and Robert Cray, who have found success with contemporary rock audiences. They no longer hope—as did Trixie Smith and many other 1920s blues vocalists, filled with the despair and irony that coexist in the blues—that some day "the sun will shine in their back door." (The irony is in the avoidance of the front door!) Rather, filled with sense of self, they demand—like singer-pianist Otis Spann in 1967—"I Want a Brand-New House."

When Joachim Berendt visited Angola State Penitentiary in the summer of 1960, he heard several young blues singers every bit as good as the well-known Chicago names—among them Robert Pete Williams, who was later released and made a name for himself in blues circles prior to his death in 1980. The day before his visit, there had been a thunderstorm. One of the prisoners told Berendt he had nearly been struck by lightning. He was still under the spell of the fear that had possessed him. Berendt suggested that he might someday write a blues about his experience—and right away, he strummed a few chords on his guitar and improvised his "Lightning Blues." The surprise was the lyrics, which reflected his experience in intensely realistic expression. These blues lyrics are the real "jazz and poetry." Here the difference between "jazz" and "poetry" is one of terminology, not substance.

One of the most successful singer-guitarists of authentic big-city blues for more than twenty years now is Mississippi-born B.B. King, a cousin of Bukka White, one of the great old folk-blues men. In the 1966 edition of Leonard Feather's *Encyclopedia of Jazz*, it is stated that King "would like to see Negroes become unashamed of blues, their music." Indeed, King himself has been an essential factor in the fulfillment of this wish, though (especially in the middle class) there still are many blacks who look down on blues as rustic, primitive, and archaic, and want to dissociate themselves from it. The black American will have found the road to full awareness of his own identity—and thus to true equality—only when he takes as much pride in the blues as a German does in Beethoven or an Italian in Verdi.

From the start, the borderline between folk blues as a realm distinct from jazz and the domain of jazz itself has been fluid. A number of singers who are authentic blues singers have been counted as belonging to the jazz world at least as much as to the world of blues. The first of these, and founder of this vocal Swing tradition, was Jimmy Rushing, who died in 1972. Rushing, from

Oklahoma (a state that always was within the sphere of Texas blues influence) became *the* blues singer par excellence of Swing style. He was the first not to sing "on the beat," as the folk-blues people did, but in front of or behind the beat, to "sing around" the rhythmic centers and counter them with his own accents, thus creating greater tension. During the thirties and forties, Rushing was Count Basie's singer, and his singing was the exact vocal expression of Basie's instrumental theme of those years: "Swingin' the Blues." Other singers of this brand are Jimmy Witherspoon, who lives in California, and Big Miller from Kansas City. In the Basie band of the fifties, Joe Williams took the place of Rushing. He is a fine musician, who on the one hand endows his ballads with a blueslike intensity and on the other sings the blues with the sophistication of a modern jazzman.

Big Joe Turner (d. 1985) from Kansas City is the blues shouter of boogie-woogie. In the thirties he worked with the great boogie pianists; a generation later, he had a second round of success—as did many other bluesmen—with the emergence of rock 'n' roll, creating one of its biggest early hits, "Shake, Rattle and Roll."

One, or even two, steps further is Leon Thomas, combining the blues tradition with the music of the post-Coltrane era in free, cascading falsetto improvisations, for which he also found inspiration in ethnic music, such as the songs of Central African pygmy tribes. Thomas shows the acute political awareness of the new blues generation in a particularly exemplary manner: "How much does it cost to fly a man up to the moon? I think of the hungry children that I see every afternoon."

The line that leads from Blind Lemon Jefferson through the South Side of Chicago to the modern blues of Otis Rush and B.B. King is the backbone of all jazz singing. This line could be designated the "blues line" of jazz singing to differentiate it from the "song line." But it is important to see the continuous, intensive interrelationship between these two. This is illustrated by the first and most significant singer of the "song line," Louis Armstrong. Armstrong's music remains related to the blues even when it is not blues—and in the orthodox sense of the word, it rarely is. Armstrong's singing has come to exemplify the basic conception involved not just in jazz but in the whole of pop, rock, and soul music: emotion and personal expression taking precedence over any kind of traditional standards.

Some years ago, on the occasion of an Armstrong visit, the *London Times* noted, "Of course, this voice is ugly when measured against what Europe calls beautiful singing. But the expression which Armstrong puts into his voice, all the soul, heart, and depth which swing along in every sound, make it more beautiful than most of the technically perfect and pure, but cold and soulless singing in the white world of today."

Trombonist Jack Teagarden (who died in 1964), sang some of the most humorous and spirited vocal duets in jazz with Armstrong. Teagarden was a master of "sophisticated" blues singing and was so as early as in the thirties, long before the ironic sophistication of the blues became "modern" in the late fifties. Later, in a more modern field, one finds in Woody Herman a similar sophistication, tasteful and musicianly, but not as expressive as Teagarden or the great black vocalists.

Most male singers who have maintained a position in the realm of jazz *per se* have been instrumentalists. The others who began somewhere within jazz or close to it have gone over to commercial music: Bing Crosby, Frankie Laine, Perry Como, Matt Dennis, and the musically outstanding Mel Tormé. Wavering between jazz and commercial music, Tormé tries to combine both; he belongs among the best and most swinging interpreters of the songs by America's great popular composers. Appropriately, Nat "King" Cole was a first-rate jazz vocalist as long as he was mainly a pianist. Later, as he became a successful singer in the commercial field, his piano playing and his jazz interest were pushed further and further back. Nevertheless, his jazz roots and a certain jazz *espressivo* remained noticeable in his singing up to his death in 1965. His influence has extended over a whole generation of singers between Ray Charles and Stevie Wonder. This is one reason why American commercial music is the world's best: so many of the popular stars have a jazz background and "paid dues" in jazz before attaining commercial success. (Outside the vocal realm, Glenn Miller, Harry James, and Tommy and Jimmy Dorsey are examples of this.)

The jazz instrumentalist, as we said, is especially qualified also to be a good jazz singer. Examples of this can be cited not only from the times of Hot Lips Page and Jack Teagarden, but also from today: drummer Grady Tate, trombonist Richard Boone, tenor saxophonist George Adams, guitarist George Benson, and trumpeters Chet Baker and Clark Terry are notable singers in their stylistic area—Terry with lots of joy and humor, Boone with a combination of traditional blues and contemporary satire, Baker with an almost "feminine" kind of fragility, Benson (he, too!) with a lot of the King Cole tradition, Adams with the masculine attack known from his tenor playing.

In the forties Billy Eckstine was to male singers what Sarah Vaughan was to the females. Eckstine had the greatest vocal gift since Louis Armstrong and Jimmy Rushing. He belonged to the bop circle around Gillespie and Parker and was so full of enthusiasm for their music that he took up an instrument—the valve trombone. "Jelly, Jelly" was the big (and still popular) hit by "Mr. B.," relating bebop to the blues tradition.

With Billy Eckstine we have reached bop, and we should mention Babs Gonzales (who died in 1979), whose fun-filled group Three Bips and a Bop was successful in the late forties and who later—as the writer of

"Oop-Bop-A-Da," for instance—was one of bebop's entertaining voices; Earl Coleman, whose sonorous baritone was once accompanied by Charlie Parker; and Kenneth "Pancho" Hagood and Joe Carroll, who both worked with Dizzy Gillespie. Carroll reminded people of Dizzy in mobility of voice and sense of humor. Of course, one must not forget Dizzy Gillespie himself when speaking of bop vocalists. Dizzy's high-pitched, slightly Oriental-sounding voice corresponds as closely to Dizzy the trumpeter as Satchmo's voice corresponded to *his* trumpet. Jackie Paris carried the bop vocal conception into cool jazz. Oscar Brown, Jr., who worked on Max Roach's "Freedom Now Suite," is a singer, nightclub artist, and lyricist. Johnny Hartman is a "musicians' singer," whose supple, flowing phrasing (as in his ballad recordings with John Coltrane) has been much admired by connoisseurs. Bill Henderson and Mark Murphy sing with a healthy, Basie-inspired mainstream conception; the latter has put a whole era of jazz into song with ravishing sophistication. Mose Allison transforms, in a totally personal style, black and white blues and folk songs into his own compositions with a modern soul character. In fact, when soul singing became an "in thing" in the sixties and seventies, some white singers who didn't know the black tradition at all referred to white Mose Allison—who, to be sure, comes from an overwhelmingly black town in Mississippi and has absorbed black folk music since childhood. Ben Sidran carries the characteristic Allison style into the realms of jazz-rock and fusion.

No doubt the yield of great male jazz singers—aside from the blues singers and Louis Armstrong—is not impressive. This fits our conception of the jazz vocal dilemma. Jazz singing, beyond blues, is the more effective the closer it approximates instrumental use of the voice. The female voice has the greater potential in this respect. It certainly is characteristic that quite a few male singers have had voices that seemed deformed by nature or at least sounded unusual—beginning with Louis Armstrong. Often deformation increases expression.

Also from the realm of bebop stems a development that led to a highly successful vocal group, the Lambert-Hendricks-Ross Ensemble. Eddie Jefferson, as early as at the start of the forties, was the first to equip recorded jazz solos with his own lyrics. He was followed by King Pleasure (who owed his big hit "Moody's Mood for Love" to Eddie Jefferson from whom he took over this solo rendition of James Moody's 1953 recording) and British-born Annie Ross (whose song "Twisted," based on a tenor improvisation by Wardell Gray, was a hit in 1952). Jon Hendricks carried this approach to its peak. He was the actual "poet of the jazz solo," a "James Joyce of Jive," as *Time* magazine called him. Dave Lambert (who died in 1966) had arranged and recorded a group vocal in 1945 with Gene Krupa's big band, "What's This?", which was the first recorded bebop vocal. So in a sense, Dave

Lambert, Jon Hendricks, and Annie Ross belonged together musically even prior to forming Lambert, Hendricks and Ross in 1958. The trio began with vocalizations of Count Basie records and went on from there to develop an entertaining, spirited vocal ensemble style that has remained unique, vocalizing the entire spectrum of modern jazz. When these three sang solos by Charlie Parker, Lester Young, Sonny Rollins, Miles Davis, Oscar Pettiford, John Coltrane, and others to Jon Hendricks' lyrics, one had the feeling that this was what all those great musicians had wanted to say. When Annie Ross returned to England in 1962, Ceylon-born Yolande Bavan took her place until the trio finally broke up in 1964. Hendricks, however, and Eddie Jefferson (who died in 1979), carried on this style—Hendricks also in a musical based on the much-lauded "Evolution of the Blues" he had created for the Monterey Jazz Festival, Jefferson in an inspired collaboration with the alto player Richie Cole.

But the "song line," as we called it, of male jazz singing also continues to develop. It has been carried into our times by singers like the aforementioned Mark Murphy, as well as by Bob Dorough, Joe Lee Wilson, Gil Scott-Heron, Lou Rawls, Tony Middleton, and Tom Waits. Murphy and Dorough sing songs by the great composers of American popular music with the special intensity of contemporary jazz. Wilson is the male singer of the New York avant-garde; he worked with Archie Shepp and Rashied Ali, among others. Scott-Heron is a poet of the ghetto with an acute political and social consciousness. With his hoarse voice, seemingly "eaten up by rust," Tom Waits establishes impressive musical memorials to the outlaws and down-and-outs for whom the American dream has become a nightmare.

We have mentioned the strong influence of Brazilian music on modern jazz, so we ought to name some of the singers from that country: first the two great "father figures" of modern Brazilian music, Antonio Carlos Jobim and João Gilberto; later, among the younger vocalists, Edu Lôbo, Gilberto Gil, Caetano Veloso, and above all Milton Nascimento. They all possess that melodic enchantment and poetry that makes Brazilian music so unmistakable, the younger ones also with a more contemporary manner and socially critical approach. Nascimento's instrumental falsetto singing—floating way up in the heights, "angelically" dreamy and at the same time unusually expressive—attracted astonishingly many followers in jazz, influencing Pedro Aznar, David Blamires, and Mark Ledford (all three in the Pat Metheny Band), Delmar Brown (in the Gil Evans Orchestra), and guitarist Michael "Gregory" Jackson.

Al Jarreau became the most successful and most frequently named singer of the seventies. He says that he took his cues from Billie Holiday and Nat King Cole and especially from the Lambert-Hendricks-Ross trio. That connection is even visible: When Al sings his saxophonelike phrases, he

moves his fingers and his hands as if he were playing some imaginary
instrument—just the way Jon Hendricks used to do years ago. Jarreau's
throat produces an entire orchestra of sounds: drums and saxophones,
trumpets and flutes, congas and basses—all from the mouth of one man,
from the lowest bass to the highest falsetto, as if he had a dozen or more
different male and female voices at his disposal. Later Jarreau went the way
of so many male jazz vocalists, but his inimitable jazz feeling remains
apparent even in his commercial successes as a pop and rock singer. Anyone
who thought that Jarreau's vocal skills could scarcely be exceeded
discovered otherwise at the start of the eighties with the appearance of
Bobby McFerrin. McFerrin disposes over an arsenal of vocal possibilities that
no other male singer can match. Bobby was the son of an opera singer, began
as a pianist, and was influenced by Jon Hendricks, Ornette Coleman, Herbie
Hancock, and above all Keith Jarrett. He sustains unaccompanied solo
concerts for hours. In a cappella singing McFerrin's wealth of expression is
most completely revealed, using his hands to drum the beat on his chest and
changing vocal registers so quickly as to create an impression of polyphony.
You think that everything is sounding out at the same time: deep bass lines,
highest falsetto parts, accompanying voices, the rhythmic sizzling of hi-hat
patterns, guitar riffs, and "blown" sounds—all enriched with a panorama of
sounds for which you would have to invent a new vocabulary to capture
their novelty and unfamiliarity. With Bobby McFerrin the entire body
becomes an orchestra. "Other people have to project their sensations and
feelings through an instrument," said McFerrin, "but a singer only has to
open his mouth." McFerrin achieves this striking multitude of possibilities
by singing not just during exhalations (as normal vocalists do) but also when
he is breathing in, thereby surmounting the handicap of disruptive pauses
for taking breath, a technique that he is the first jazz singer to employ
consistently.

Strict jazz fans took amiss McFerrin's hit "Don't Worry, Be Happy," but for
the singer that was the greatest success in his career. For weeks he
dominated the international hit parades exclusively through the power of
his voice alone. He sang all the parts by way of playback in a realm where
synthesizers, computers, and other electronic equipment usually set the
style. McFerrin commented with the jazzman's usual vividness, "I'm my own
walkman."

Strikingly associated with development of modern male jazz singing is
ever-greater use of the voice as an instrument. The importance of the lyric,
of the sung text, clearly recedes into the background. Bebop vocalists still
aligned their singing with the horns, mainly saxophones and trumpets,
which they not infrequently imitated. With Jarreau and McFerrin, however,
the "entire" palette of orchestral instruments is opened up for the voice:

bass, flute, percussion, guitar, saxophone, drums, etc. On the other hand, the songs of Eddie Jefferson and Jon Hendricks—as sung "copies" of famous jazz solos—may be instrumental in character but they are still very closely linked with texts. For Al Jarreau and Bobby McFerrin, the instrumental aspect predominates to such an extent (except in their pop vocals) that the sung text is of little significance.

English-born Phil Minton has most consistently opened up male jazz singing to the possibilities of noise: squeaking, screeching, groaning, moaning, raving as if he were driving all these "deformed" sounds to the limits of "white noise," but nevertheless organizing and refining them with such musicality that he became the singer most in demand in European free jazz and no wave.

Two other singers who, like Minton, stand beyond the song line, forming a "noise line," are guitarist Arto Lindsay and drummer David Moss—Lindsay with the protest-charged, eruptive rage of punk, and Moss with the childlike curiosity of the playful inventor of sounds.

We have said a great deal about the tradition of black music in this book. Among the instrumentalists, the avant-garde musicians—like those from the AACM circle—are often the ones who maintain this tradition. The situation is quite different with the vocalists. Especially among the female singers, avant-garde musicians have almost nothing to do with the tradition. Here, the black tradition is largely cultivated in a field outside of jazz—the area of pop music. This was already under way with the successful soul singers of the sixties (unthinkable without Ray Charles): Otis Redding leading on by way of James Brown (whose cry, "Say it loud, I'm Black and I'm Proud!" did more for the new self-confidence of the black masses than all the words of people like Eldridge Cleaver, Rap Brown, or Stokely Carmichael) and Marvin Gaye ("Save the World—Save the Babies—Save the Children!") to Stevie Wonder, and Prince. What these vocalists sing is, very much in the sense intended by Charles Mingus and Roland Kirk, "black music"—in fact, in particular with Stevie Wonder, "black classical music." Wonder has been compared as a composer with Duke Ellington. His albums, some of them consisting of several records—*Songs in the Key of Life, Hotter Than July,* and *Journey through the Secret Life of Plants*—are suitelike compositions conceived as large works with an inner coherence; they summarize and recapitulate today's stock of black music in a way similar to Ellington. Wonder is a musician of fascinating universality and flexibility. He is a composer and arranger as well as a singer, plays almost every imaginable instrument on his records, and commands all the modern studio techniques: overdubbing, all kinds of synthesizers and sound manipulators, etc., as if the studio with all its electronic gadgetry were an additional instrument on which to play music (which, in fact, it is).

The Female Singers

The history of female blues singing starts later than male blues singing. No
female singers from "archaic" times are known to us. Folk-blues singers like
Blind Lemon Jefferson, Leadbelly, or Robert Johnson did not have female
counterparts; nor do their contemporary successors. The simple, rural
world of folk blues is dominated by man; woman is an object.

This changed as soon as the blues moved into the big cities of the North.
At that time—in the early twenties—the great era of classic blues, whose
"mother" was Ma Rainey and whose "empress" was Bessie Smith, began. In
the section on Bessie, we discussed the classic blues period in detail. Singers
like Bertha "Chippie" Hill, Victoria Spivey, Sippie Wallace, and Alberta
Hunter carried on the message of classical blues, while Big Mama Thornton
incorporated it into rhythm and blues. But it is important to note that in the
late twenties the musical climate was already changing, shifting the accent
away from the blues and toward the song.

The first female singers important in this field (who are worth listening to
even today) are Ethel Waters, Ivie Anderson, and Mildred Bailey. Ethel
Waters was the first to demonstrate, as early as the twenties, the many
possibilities for jazz singing in good commercial tunes. Ivie Anderson
became Duke Ellington's vocalist in 1932 and remained for almost twelve
years; Duke called her the best singer he ever had. Mildred Bailey, of
part-Indian origin, was a successful singer of the Swing era with great
sensitivity and mastery of phrasing. She was married to Red Norvo; and with
him, Teddy Wilson, and Mary Lou Williams she made her finest recordings.
Her "Rockin' Chair" became a hit of considerable proportions; it was a blues,
but an "alienated," ironic blues.

The songs of the female singers in this "song line" were—and are—the
ballads and pop tunes of "commercial music," the melodies of the great
American popular composers—Cole Porter, Jerome Kern, Irving Berlin,
George Gershwin—sometimes even tunes from the "hit parade," all sung
with the inflection and phrasing typical of jazz.

In this area, improvisation has retreated to a final, irreducible position.
The songs must remain recognizable, and of course the singers are
dependent upon the lyrics. But in a very special sense there can be
improvisation here, too. It lies in the art of paraphrasing, juxtaposing,
transposing—in the alteration of harmonies, and in a certain way of phrasing.
There is a whole arsenal of possibilities, of which Billie Holiday, the most
important figure in this branch, had supreme command. Billie was the
embodiment of a truth first expressed by Fats Waller (and after him by so
many others): In jazz it does not matter so much what you do, but *how* you
do it. To pick one example among many: In 1935, Billie Holiday recorded

(with Teddy Wilson) a banal little song, "What a Little Moonlight Can Do," and what resulted was a completely valid work of art.

Billie Holiday sang blues only incidentally. But through her phrasing and conception, much that she sang seemed to become blues.

Billie Holiday made more than 350 records—among them about seventy with Teddy Wilson. She made her most beautiful recordings in the thirties with Wilson and Lester Young. And in the intertwining of the lines sung by Billie Holiday and the lines played by Lester Young, the question which is lead and which is accompaniment, which line is vocal and which instrumental, becomes secondary.

Billie Holiday is the great songstress of understatement. Her voice has none of the volume and majesty of Bessie Smith. It is a small, supple, sensitive voice; yet Billie sang a song that, more than anything sung by Bessie Smith or the other female blues singers, became a musical protest against racial discrimination. This song was "Strange Fruit" (1939). The "strange fruit" hanging from the tree was the body of a lynched Negro. Billie sang this song as if she were stating a fact: That's the way it is. Any blues by Bessie Smith, even a simple, everyday love song, was sung with more emphasis and pathos than this: the most emphatic and most impassioned musical testimony against racism to become known before Abbey Lincoln's interpretation of Max Roach's "Freedom Now Suite" of 1960.

Charm and urbane elegance, suppleness and sophistication are the chief elements in the understatement of Billie Holiday. These elements can be found everywhere—for example, in "Mandy Is Two" (1942), the song about little Mandy, who is only two years old but already a big girl. And this is expressed so straightforwardly and warmly! How simple and unpretentious it is! Nothing rings false, as is the rule with commercial ditties attempting childlike naiveté. It is almost inconceivable that something seemingly destined by every known law to become kitsch could be transformed into art.

Billie's singing had the elasticity of Lester Young's tenor playing, and she had this elasticity prior to her first encounter with Lester. Billie was the first artist in all of jazz—not just the first woman or the first jazz singer—in whose music the influence of the saxophone as the style and sound-setting instrument became clear. And this took place, only seemingly in paradoxical fashion, before the beginning of the saxophone era, which actually only began with the success of Lester Young in the early forties. The "cool" tenor saxophone sound is apparent already in Billie Holiday's first recording— "Your Mother's Son-in-Law," made in 1933 with Benny Goodman. It can be said that because of Billie Holiday, modern jazz had its beginning in the realm of singing earlier than in the field of any instrument.

It had its beginning with Holiday also because she was the first to realize—certainly subconsciously—that not only was her voice the instrument but also the microphone. Holiday was the first vocalist to understand that a singer using a microphone has to sing in a totally different way from one not using a mike. She humanized her voice by "microphonizing" it, thus making subtleties significant that had been unknown in all singing up to that point—in fact, that had been unnecessary, because they could not have been made audible.

The life story of Billie Holiday has been told often and even more often has been effectively falsified: from servant girl in Baltimore through rape and prostitution to successful song star, and through narcotics all the way downhill again. In 1938 she worked with Artie Shaw's band, a white group. For months she had to use service entrances, while her white colleagues went in through the front. She had to stay in dingy hotels and sometimes couldn't even share meals with her associates. And she had to suffer all this not only as a black but also as the sole woman in the band. Billie felt she had to go through all this to set an example. If it could work for *one* black artist, others could make it too. She took it . . . until she collapsed.

Before that, she had appeared with another great band, that of Count Basie, and had suffered the reverse kind of humiliation, possibly even more stinging than what she had to endure in Shaw's band: Though Billie was as much a black as any of Basie's musicians, her skin color might have seemed too light to some customers and it was unthinkable at that time to present a white female singer with a black band. At a theater appearance in Detroit, Billie had to put on dark makeup.

In the last years of her life—she died at the age of forty-four in 1959—Billie Holiday's voice was often a mere shadow of her great days. She sang without the suppleness and glow of the earlier recordings; her voice sounded worn, rough, and old. Still, even then her singing had magnetic powers. It is extraordinary to discover just how much a great artist has left when voice and technique and flexibility have failed and nothing remains except the spiritual power of creativity and expression. To hear this on recordings made by Billie Holiday in the fifties is an almost eerie experience: a vocalist devoid of all the material and technical attributes of her profession who still remains a great artist.

Billie Holiday stands at the center of great jazz singing. After Holiday comes a host of female singers whose common denominator was, and still is, their application of Billie's accomplishments to the particular stylistic field to which they belong.

Before that, however, Ella Fitzgerald must be discussed. She also stems from the Swing era. But Ella, born in 1918 and thus only three years younger than Billie Holiday, is not only a great Swing vocalist but also one of the great voices in all of modern jazz. No other female singer—and hardly any other jazz musician—commands a wider range of music. In the thirties, her big hit "A-Tisket, A-Tasket," done with the Chick Webb band, was a naïvely playful song dressed up in the Swing sounds of the day. In the forties, her scat vocals (to be considered later) on such themes as "How High the Moon" or "Lady Be Good" led to the core of bop. In the fifties, Ella developed a mature ballad conception. Her interpretations of the "songbooks" of the great American songwriters—Gershwin, Kern, Porter, Berlin, Arlen—are among the lasting documents of American music. From the sixties to the eighties she has retained supreme mastery of all the different styles through which she has lived and sung.

Even today, no matter how much she may have changed during all these years, Ella still has some of the simplicity and straightforwardness of the sixteen-year-old girl who was discovered in January, 1934, in an amateur contest at Harlem's Apollo Theatre—as were so many other great jazz talents (for example, her greatest competitor, Sarah Vaughan). The "prize" Ella won back then was a "short" engagement with Chick Webb's band, but the engagement did not end even with Webb's death five years later. In 1939, Ella took over nominal leadership of the Webb band for a while.

June Christy was the voice of Stan Kenton's band, and the warm, human climate of her singing won her many friends time and again, even when one could not go along with her all the way as far as intonation was concerned. June Christy replaced Anita O'Day with Kenton in 1947. Anita is still, after forty years, considered to be the "greatest white female jazz vocalist in classic modern jazz," with a musical assurance of virtuoso caliber and great improvisational capacity.

Even more important female vocalists came from the circle surrounding Charlie Parker and Dizzy Gillespie: Sarah Vaughan, Carmen McRae, and somewhat later, because she initially was with Lionel Hampton's band, Betty Carter. Like so many jazz singers, Sarah Vaughan received her first impulses in a gospel church. She said, "You have to have a little soul in your singing, the kind of soul that's in the spiritual. . . . It's a part of my life." In 1943, she became the singer of Earl Hines' band; in 1944, of Billie Eckstine's. Both bands were "talent cradles" for the important bebop musicians of those years, and Sarah knew immediately: "I thought Bird and Diz were the end. I still do. I think their playing influenced my singing."

Sarah Vaughan was the first real jazz singer with a vocal range equal to that of an opera singer. Her rich, dark contralto brought a new sound into jazz singing. Her ability to change this sound in the most diverse manner and to literally charge it with emotional content surpasses anything done by any other female jazz singer.

Sarah Vaughan's stature is so towering that other singers of her generation remained in her shadow. This is particularly regrettable with Carmen McRae (who was once married to Kenny Clarke, the creator of bebop drum style). She is also one of the great individualists of modern jazz singing. Especially impressive is the way Carmen sounds so "definitive." Nat Hentoff once compared her with a "sternly exotic figurehead over the cutwater of a New England whaling ship," referring both to her personality *and* to the powerful individualism of her singing.

McRae's junior by eight years, Betty Carter was recognized only relatively late by the jazz world as belonging among the great bop singers. Only in the course of the seventies did she become an embodiment of bebop singing—in fact, of jazz vocalizing in general. Betty Carter upholds the standards, the great songs of American popular music, by fragmenting and adapting them in the most subtle and original fashion. Even though you're never in doubt about what song this is, you nevertheless think she's inventing, here and now, a completely new piece. Her interpretations are peppered with atmospheric transformations and unexpected changes of mood, with explosive fluctuations of rhythm and sudden variations of tempo. Yet they are all presented with the sovereign assurance of a musician who has carried forward and further developed the best of classical jazz singing by women from Billie Holiday by way of Ella Fitzgerald to Sarah Vaughan, creating an absolutely individual language of her own.

Other female singers of this generation are Chris Connor, Jackie Cain, Dakota Staton, Ernestine Anderson, Abbey Lincoln, Helen Merrill, Carol Sloane, Nina Simone, Nancy Wilson, and Sheila Jordan. Ernestine Anderson's comment, "If I had my way, I'd sing true like Ella and breathe like Sarah Vaughan," is in many ways the musical creed of most of them: They want to sound like Ella Fitzgerald in terms of expression and like Sarah in terms of phrasing, though some of them also want it the other way around, combining Ella's phrasing with Sarah's expression.

Jackie Cain first became known in Charlie Ventura's band. With her husband, pianist-arranger Roy Kral, she forms the most perfect vocal duo in jazz history—spirited, pleasant, humorous. Helen Merrill is a much underrated singer. She has often been accompanied by John Lewis, the former leader of the Modern Jazz Quartet, and indeed has some of his sensitivity and sophistication. Nina Simone's is an especially passionate voice in the struggle for black dignity and identity, a struggle she supports as a woman, singer, pianist—as an entire human being. She once referred to the blues as "racial memory," and this memory is the source for her songs, however modern they may sound. Another voice in the black struggle is that of Abbey Lincoln, especially in songs by Max Roach, her former husband, whose "Freedom Now Suite" she sang with poignant and moving emotion. Sheila Jordan is of special significance. She has "emancipated" song singing, thus paving the way for all the female vocalists in free jazz whom we will discuss later. Sheila became known through her work with George Russell—above all, in the grandiose, satirical "You Are My Sunshine," a spoof full of sharp cynicism.

Once more, we have to backtrack: In his uncompromising endeavors to use the human voice as instrumentally as possible, Duke Ellington first employed Adelaide Hall, then Kay Davis, the former in the twenties, the latter in the forties. Kay Davis's voice was used as a kind of coloratura above the orchestra, often scored in parallels with clarinet, creating a fascinating meshing of sounds. Later, this combination of a jazz voice with the sound of an ensemble or full band was used by others, but few remember that this, too, began with Duke.

One result of the instrumental conception of jazz singing is the development of scat vocals: stringing together "nonsense" syllables with complete absence of lyrics. Louis Armstrong "invented" scat singing way back in the twenties; the story goes that he hit upon it when he forgot the lyrics while recording. Anita O'Day, June Christy, Sarah Vaughan, Carmen McRae, Dakota Staton, Jackie Cain, Annie Ross, Betty Roché, Betty Carter, and others have created excellent scat vocals; but the mistress of this domain, often also referred to as "bebop vocal," still is Ella Fitzgerald. Both vocalizing and scat singing necessarily led to today's "free" singing (to be discussed later).

To be sure, there is also a "blues line" among the female vocalists, which refers back to the blues singers mentioned at the beginning of this section. The last of the great classic blues singers, Alberta Hunter, made some wonderfully expressive recordings in 1980—at age eighty-five!—which is even more astounding when you realize that it was Alberta who wrote "Down Hearted Blues," Bessie Smith's first hit, in 1923! In the twenties, she sang with Louis Armstrong, Sidney Bechet, and Fletcher Henderson. She died in 1984.

Among the female singers, too, the blues proves to be the constant element of black music, always changing but always the blues, whose message is passed on from one generation to the next. Among those who have done so are Helen Humes (with Count Basie in the late thirties; she, too, unusually expressive until her death in 1981), Dinah Washington (who died in 1963), Betty Carter (who began with the blues as Dinah Washington's successor in Lionel Hampton's band), Ruth Brown, LaVern Baker, Etta Jones, Koko Taylor, and many others. Dinah Washington was called the "Queen of the Blues." She, too, had her start in gospel music, and these gospel roots remained audible in many of her blues recordings. Her sardonic humor, sometimes even cynicism, gave her performances an additional dimension.

Janis Joplin carried the art of classical blues into rock. Almost nothing she sang can be thought of without Bessie Smith; yet Janis' singing always sounded harder, cruder, louder, more obtrusive. She was driven by a fierce will to live and love, up to her untimely death in 1970, which prompted the media to all sorts of wild speculations. Joplin's singing made particularly clear how many white performers—often even those who appear "authentic" in their relationship to black music—have vulgarized and coarsened the message of their black models.

In the course of the sixties, the heritage of the black spiritual and gospel tradition entered even more strongly into the mainstream of female singing. The white world had become conscious of this heritage through the recordings of Mahalia Jackson, who died in 1972, but Mahalia was only one of the many wonderful singers of black religious music. Others are Dorothy Love Coates, Marion Williams, the late Clara Ward, Bessie Griffin (see the section on spirituals).

When the gospel tradition finally made its way into popular music, soul music came into being. Its representatives are singers like Tina Turner, Diana Ross, Chaka Kahn, and, above all, Aretha Franklin. Aretha is the daughter of Rev. C. L. Franklin, the preacher of New Bethel Baptist Church in Detroit. From childhood on, she heard the rousing gospel songs in her father's church. When she was able to carry a tune, she joined the church choir; and at twelve or thirteen, she became a soloist. As her first important influence she named Mahalia Jackson; later, she pointed in particular to the significance of jazz musicians in her musical development: Oscar Peterson, Erroll Garner, and Art Tatum. Aretha herself is also a good, soul-inspired pianist.

Aretha's hit records are among the best that seventies and eighties pop music has to offer, but one of her recordings is of exceptional interest from a jazz point of view: "Amazing Grace," recorded in 1972 at the New Temple Missionary Baptist Church in Los Angeles, in front of and with the congregation. It is nothing less than a swinging, ecstatic gospel service. This was not only a homecoming to the musical and spiritual world from which she originates—that alone would have meant much—but a conscious, jubilant rediscovery of her own roots. She repeated that affirmation with the 1987 double album *One Lord, One Faith, One Baptism*, another gospel service recorded in the New Bethel Baptist Church, Detroit.

It is only a short step from the female vocalists just mentioned to those in fusion and on the borderline between jazz and fusion. There are so many singers of the most diverse directions in this field that they can be named here only summarily: Phoebe Snow, Dee Dee Bridgewater, Ricky Lee Jones, Bonnie Herman (the rich, "sensual" voice of the vocal group Singers Unlimited), Marlena Shaw, Ann Burton, Jean Carn, Lorraine Feather, Gayle

Moran (known through her recordings with Chick Corea), and Janis Siegel (from the Manhattan Transfer vocal ensemble).

Betty Carter pointed out in the seventies that it's almost impossible to be a female jazz singer today: "I guess, I'm the last of the Mohicans. It's understandable: jazz singing is not profitable. Young singers tend toward commercial singing—and let's face it, it's one way or the other: if what you're singing becomes commercial, it's no longer jazz." Many of the singers we just named have discovered this—often quite painfully. One example is Dee Dee Bridgewater. She became known with the Thad Jones–Mel Lewis big band in the early seventies and made some breathtaking records, some of them along avant-garde lines, such as a duet with bass player Reginald Workman. Meanwhile, Bridgewater has all but left the jazz world.

Among folk singers, too, there are some of interest to the jazz scene. Just as the black singers refer back to the gospel, soul, and blues tradition, so the folk singers have their roots in white Anglo-American music. The two representatives of this direction of most interest from a jazz viewpoint are Judy Collins and Joni Mitchell. Collins did a superb job of incorporating the wistful songs, cries, and signals of whales into her song, "Farewell to Tarwathie." Mitchell's album *Mingus*, released in 1979, is the most beautiful, moving memorial to this great jazz musician to date. Critics have called Mitchell's singing much too ethereal and fragile to have anything to do with Mingus' music, yet this very fact makes it clear how far Mingus' message carries. Mitchell has always been fond of employing jazz musicians on her studio dates, among them bassist Jaco Pastorius and drummer Don Alias. Just how much she is associated with jazz is illustrated by her statement that the most important record in her musical development was the Count Basie album by Lambert, Hendricks and Ross.

What the tradition of Anglo-American folk music is to singers like Collins and Mitchell, the samba tradition (which, in turn, is rooted in West African Yoruba music) is to the Brazilian singers. Flora Purim became the most famous in the northern hemisphere because she moved to the United States in 1968. But back home in Brazil there are even more impressive voices, practically unknown in the States or in Europe: Ellis Regina and Maria Bethânia—the former having Ella Fitzgerald's flexibility, the latter Billie Holiday's emotional energy.

Purim and her husband, percussionist Airto Moreira, were at the center of a "Brazilian movement" on the American scene of the seventies. Flora was first introduced by Stan Getz and Gil Evans, then by Chick Corea (in his first Return to Forever group of the early seventies). One of her most beautiful recordings is *Open Your Eyes, You Can Fly* (1976), the entire record being a triumphant song of liberty. One senses that the song mirrors personal experience. Flora had just been released from prison where she had been put on a drug charge that was never proven.

Tania Maria sings Latin-colored scat vocals with a supple feel for Brazilian rhythms, all in unison with her piano playing.

Flora Purim leads us to our final grouping of female vocalists: those who sing free music. The first to do so, as early as the sixties, were American Jeanne Lee and Norwegian Karin Krog. Then came the British singers Norma Winstone, Julie Tippetts, and Maggie Nicols: Polish Urszula Dudziak: American Jay Clayton; Holland's Greetje Bijma; Russian-born Valentina Ponomareva; Uschi Brüning from the German Democratic Republic; Greek-American Diamanda Galas; and American Lauren Newton. These singers have extended the "voice as an instrument" into realms that would have seemed inaccessible only a few years ago. Singing to them is not only vocalizing songs, but everything else: screaming, laughing, and crying; the moaning of sexual experience and childlike babbling. The entire body, from the abdomen to the sinuses and the skull, becomes an instrument, a vibrating source of sounds, a "body of sound." The entire range of human—and specifically female—sounds is employed; nothing human or organic seems to be alien to it. These singers are unrestrained in the way they scream, moan, and belt out whatever fits the particular song, the mood, or the atmosphere; and yet this lack of restraint is only an apparent one, because all these sounds have to be formed, mastered, and musically integrated in order to become meaningful.

"The voice as an instrument"—this expression can be used sensibly only in relative terms. What seemed a ne plus ultra of instrumental vocalizing in the twenties with Adelaide Hall in Duke Ellington's band was surpassed by Ella Fitzgerald in the forties, by Indian singer Yma Sumac in the fifties, by Jeanne Lee and Karin Krog in the sixties, by Urszula Dudziak in the seventies, and by Lauren Newton and Diamanda Galas in the eighties. In their time, each of these voices was hailed as the unbeatable final stage of the development—and that's the way it will continue to be.

Jeanne Lee has become known primarily through the artful musical textures she weaves in the group of her husband, multi-instrumentalist Gunter Hampel. Her singing flows from a musical as much as from a literary feeling. Jeanne has vocalized modern poetry. There is no other singer with her acute and detailed sense for words, listening and following the sound of each word, each single syllable. Karin Krog made one of her most beautiful albums in a duo with tenorist Archie Shepp. As paradoxical as it may sound, the young woman from cool Scandinavia and Shepp with his highly developed consciousness of black music play together in perfect empathy.

For the sake of a few tunes, band leader Don Ellis had Karin Krog flown in from Oslo to Hollywood. Said Ellis, "There is no singer in the States who could have done what she does." Norma Winstone combines the experiences of the new jazz with classical song forms, above all the ballad. She has done so particularly impressively in the group Azimuth, with pianist John Taylor (Norma's husband) and trumpeter Kenny Wheeler.

Julie Tippetts's career went against the current. She didn't move from jazz to pop music, but from pop to free jazz. In the second half of the sixties, singing as Julie Driscoll, in recordings with organist Brian Auger—including her hit "This Wheel's on Fire"—she was one of the most frequently heard and most sensitive and musically flexible of female rock singers. In the seventies, it often seemed as if she (now under the name Julie Tippetts) was hiding from her old identity in a music of a most demanding and complex kind of abstractness. Maggie Nicols, who became known for her work with pianist Irene Schweizer, specializes in deliberately "hyped-up," "agitated" vocal acrobatics, driven with enormous inspiration right up to the very top of her alto voice. Polish-born Urszula Dudziak electronicizes her voice, and she "percussionizes" it. She channels her voice through a number of different synthesizers and uses a custom-built electronic percussion instrument. An American critic wrote, "Imagine that the 'Girl from Impanema' comes from Warsaw instead of Rio and is now living in New York—then you'll have an idea of how she sounds."

Jay Clayton's singing is clearly influenced by techniques of vocal alienation found in advanced concert music, accompanied, however, by an inimitable jazz feeling. Together with Jeanne Lee, Lauren Newton, Urszula Dudziak, and Bobby McFerrin, she formed (at the start of the eighties during the New Jazz Meeting Baden-Baden) Vocal Summit, perhaps the most original and "complete" vocal ensemble on the contemporary scene. Uschi Brüning has recorded witty and exciting duos with saxophonist Ernst Ludwig Petrowsky. Valentina Ponomareva from the Soviet Union vocalizes with an unusual feel for the impact of sounds—veiled, mysterious, magical. Greetje Bijma from Holland has a vivacious talent for improvisation. In Noodband's free funk she produced ravishingly strident sounds full of sensitivity. Lauren Newton from Oregon, who made a name for herself with the Vienna Art Orchestra, commands what is perhaps the largest range of styles among all these singers. She has studied baroque music as well as modern concert music—Schönberg and Ligeti, for instance—and she includes all these experiences in an immensely light and witty kind of improvisation that sparkles with fresh ideas. Said Lauren, "I can dare to do things in jazz that you just wouldn't think of doing in modern concert music.

Jazz gives you more freedom, but jazz is also more demanding." Diamanda Galas (from San Diego) starts where other singers usually leave off. Immediately, without requiring any time to arrive, she reaches a level of almost insane, shocklike intensity, assaulting her listeners' ears with her screams and vocalized eruptions. She is like a raving bacchante from Greek mythology transposed into modern times (and indeed she does have a Greek family background!) And if one Diamanda isn't enough for you, she's singing to multiple tapings of her own voice.

Years ago, jazz singing (as strictly defined) was said to be dying. It really was difficult during the seventies to find a young woman singer who simply sang swinging jazz music, in the vein of Mark Murphy or Bob Dorough among the male vocalists. At the start of the eighties, however, female vocalists experienced an astonishing renaissance as part of jazz classicism (as we had predicted in the previous edition of this book, suggesting similarities to the situation when some critics rushed to write off big bands only to be surprised by a wave of new, vital groups).

What is special about this comeback for mainstream singing is the versatility of these women vocalists (sometimes concealing a degree of stylistic uncertainty). The important singers—all individually following on from Betty Carter and developing the mainstream, often in conjunction with other styles inclusive of fusion and contemporary jazz—are Cassandra Wilson, Dianne Reeves, Diane Schuur, Carmen Lundy, Michele Hendricks, Portugal's Maria Joao, Italian-born Tiziana Ghiglioni, and Gabriele Hasler from Germany.

Diane Schuur made some compelling recordings in 1987, mainly blues, with the Count Basie Orchestra headed by Frank Foster, uniting the robustness of Dinah Washington with Ella Fitzgerald's agility and childlike playfulness. Dianne Reeves, who played with Clark Terry, sings with particular feeling for West African, Caribbean, and Brazilian rhythms. Carmen Lundy, sister of bassist Curtis Lundy, "romanticizes" the legacy of female jazz singing (principally Sarah Vaughan and Betty Carter), making it dreamy and comfortable. Maria Joao extends bebop singing by way of "free" lines—her tonal palette has an astonishing range—and also feeds from the roots of Portuguese folk music. And Gabriele Hasler writes her own songs and texts with increasingly mature female self-assurance, uniting unusual awareness of tradition (especially Betty Carter) with a feel for "free" forms.

The most promising and probably most important of these singers is, however, Cassandra Wilson whom a New York magazine called the "Ella of the nineties." Her counter-alto possesses something of the smokiness and robustness of women singers in her home state of Mississippi, and she also commands the most imposing range of style: from free funk with Steve

Coleman by way of neoclassicism with New Air (successor to the celebrated Air Trio) to standards à *la* Betty Carter.

All that marks an astonishing change from the seventies. At that time Betty Carter had to speak of herself as "the last of the Mohicans." By now her "message" is being passed on by so large (and ever increasing) a "tribe" of young female vocalists that no one would think of asking whether jazz singing had died out.

THE BIG BANDS OF JAZZ

The Big Bands of Jazz

It is difficult to determine where big bands begin. What a moment ago was New Orleans music in the next moment has become big-band jazz, and we stand at the doorstep of the Swing era. In "The Chant" by Jelly Roll Morton's Red Hot Peppers (recorded in 1926), there are traces of big-band sounds, though the idiom is purest New Orleans jazz. And when King Oliver yielded his band to Luis Russell in 1929, the orchestra, though it had scarcely changed, turned from a New Orleans group into a Swing band. How fluid these transitions were can be clearly seen in the case of Fletcher Henderson. The real big-band history of jazz begins with him. From the early twenties through 1938, he led large orchestras and exerted an influence comparable only to Duke Ellington. (We are omitting Ellington from this section because his music and his spirit run through nearly all stages of big-band jazz; an entire section about Duke may be found in the first part of the book.)

At the outset, Fletcher Henderson played a kind of music that differed little from the New Orleans music of the time. Between 1925 and 1928, he fittingly made records under the name of the Dixie Stompers. Slowly and almost imperceptibly, sections were formed, joining related instruments in groupings. From that point on, the sections were to be the characteristic of the classical jazz big bands. Among the first "sections" were the clarinet trios. They can be found in Henderson and in Jelly Roll Morton as well, and, of course, in Duke Ellington. The development from the nine or ten men Henderson had at the start—a personnel that today would be called a combo, but then was the ultimate in "bigness"—to the typical ensemble work of the compact trumpet, trombone, and saxophone sections of the height of his career, is smooth and barely perceptible.

Fletcher Henderson and the Beginning

Fletcher Henderson had a real instinct for trends. He was not a man like Ellington, who spearheaded evolution. He followed, but not without giving format and content to what the trend happened to be. It is fitting that he did not retain his musicians for long periods of time, as Ellington did, but changed personnel frequently.

Henderson, who died in 1952, was a great arranger; there are experts who rate him as the most important arranger of traditional jazz, next to Duke Ellington. At any rate, he and Duke were the first who knew how to write for big bands with a sure feeling for jazz improvisation.

The versatility of the Henderson band was great. Around 1930, a program might have consisted of Jelly Roll Morton's old "King Porter Stomp," "Singin' the Blues," with Rex Stewart soloing à la Beiderbecke; a number featuring the big sound of Coleman Hawkin's tenor sax or the fluent trombone of Jimmy Harrison; then perhaps a showpiece from the repertoire of the old Original Dixieland Jazz Band such as "Clarinet Marmalade"; and finally "Sugar Foot Stomp," patterned on King Oliver's famous "Dippermouth Blues," with Stewart playing Oliver's original trumpet solo. And in between, some real stomp numbers tailored to the taste of the Harlem audience (a taste that since then has changed, if at all, only in terms of an even stronger beat and—related to this—a preference for the traditional rhythm and blues elements), pieces like "Variety Stomp" or "St. Louis Shuffle"; and now and then also one of the commercial tunes of the day, such as "My Sweet Tooth Says 'I Wanna' But My Wisdom Tooth Says 'No.' "

Henderson always had an amazing knack for using the right soloists. Musicians who played in his band have been mentioned in almost every section on instruments in this book. Among the most important are alto saxophonists Don Redman and Benny Carter; tenorists Coleman Hawkins, Ben Webster, and Chu Berry; clarinetist Buster Bailey; trumpeters Tommy Ladnier (the one with the blues sound), Rex Stewart, Red Allen, Roy Eldridge, and Joe Smith; trombonists Jimmy Harrison, Charlie Green, Benny Morton, and Dickie Wells; drummers Kaiser Marshall and Sid Catlett; and Fletcher's brother Horace Henderson, who played piano (as did Fletcher) and often lent his name to the band. Many of these musicians later became band leaders, most prominently, Redman and Carter.

Don Redman is one of the names that might well be offered in answer to the oft-asked question about the most underrated musician in jazz history. "I changed my way of arranging after hearing Armstrong," he said. From 1928 on he made recordings with McKinney's Cotton Pickers; from 1931 to 1940 (and intermittently after that until his death in 1964) he led his own band. Many of the musicians who played with Henderson have also been with

again, he used black musicians in his band: Billie Holiday, and trumpeters Hot Lips Page and Roy Eldridge. The indignities these musicians had to suffer during the successful tours of the Shaw band have been touched on before, when speaking of Billie Holiday.

Three white Swing bands are outside the Henderson-Goodman circle in certain respects: the Casa Loma Band, and the orchestras of Bob Crosby and Charlie Barnet. Glen Gray's Casa Loma Band was a hit with the college crowd before Benny Goodman. In the stiffness of its arrangements and its mechanical ensemble playing, it was a forerunner of the Stan Kenton band of the late forties—the band for which Pete Rugolo was the arranger and that was connected with the "progressive jazz" slogan. Gene Gifford was the "Rugolo" of the Casa Loma Band. He wrote pieces which then seemed as imposing and compact as did the Kenton "Artistry" recordings fifteen years later: "White Jazz," "Black Jazz," "Casa Loma Stomp."

Bob Crosby played Dixieland-influenced Swing, pointing back to the Ben Pollack band (which he took over in 1935) and the New Orleans Rhythm Kings, and ahead to the modern brand of commercialized Dixieland music. He had an ideal Dixieland rhythm section consisting of Nappy Lamare (guitar), Bob Haggart (bass), and Ray Bauduc (drums). Since the late sixties, the World's Greatest Jazz Band has been bringing the old Bob Crosby tradition back to life.

Charlie Barnet founded his first big band in 1932 and led bands almost continuously until the sixties—bands that were all shaped by Barnet's strong feeling for the music of Duke Ellington. Perhaps it is fair to say that Barnet's relationship to Ellington corresponds to that of Goodman to Henderson. "Cherokee," recorded in 1939, was the theme song of the Barnet band, also used as a theme by dozens of radio programs the world over.

The Black Kings of Swing

Fletcher Henderson not only influenced most of the successful white bands of the thirties but himself led the first successful Harlem band. This concept, the "Harlem" band, became a stamp of quality for jazz bands, just as the word "New Orleans" is a stamp of quality for traditional jazz. Even Benny Goodman had the desire to play for the expert and excited—and exciting—audiences of Harlem, which had made the Savoy Ballroom into a famous center for music and dance in the Swing era. In 1937, Goodman played a musical battle with the then most popular band in Harlem, that of Chick Webb—and lost! Four thousand people jammed the Savoy Ballroom, and five thousand more stood outside on Lenox Avenue to witness this friendly battle.

From Henderson the Harlem line leads straight through Cab Calloway, Chick Webb, and Jimmie Lunceford to Count Basie and the various Lionel

Hampton bands; and beyond these to the bebop big bands of Harlem in the forties and finally to the jump bands of the fifties à la Buddy Johnson; or to the back-up band for Ray Charles' appearances.

Cab Calloway, the comedian of scat singing, took over a band in 1929 that had come to New York from the Midwest: the Missourians. From then on through the late forties he led consistently good bands of which the later ones are important primarily for the musicians who played in them: Ben Webster, Chu Berry, Jonah Jones, Dizzy Gillespie, Hilton Jefferson, Milt Hinton, Cozy Cole.

Tiny, hunchbacked Chick Webb presided over Harlem's Savoy Ballroom. Duke Ellington said, "Webb was always battle-mad, and those guys used to take on every band that came up to play there. And most times they did the cutting, regardless of the fact that half the time the other bands were twice the size. But the unforgettable and lovable Chick ate up any kind of fight, and everybody in the band played like mad at all times." Gene Krupa, who was "drummed out" by Webb while with Benny Goodman, said, "I was never cut by a better man." And pianist-arranger Mary Lou Williams remembered, "One night, scuffling around Harlem, I fell in the Savoy. After dancing a couple of rounds, I heard a voice that sent chills up my spine. . . . I almost ran to the stand to find out who belonged to the voice, and saw a pleasant-looking, brown-skinned girl standing modestly and singing the greatest. I was told her name was Ella Fitzgerald and that Chick Webb had unearthed her from one of the Appollo's amateur hours."

Of at least equal importance was Jimmie Lunceford, orchestra leader par excellence. Through him "precision" started to gain ever-increasing significance in the playing of large jazz bands. From the late twenties until his death in 1947, he led a band whose style was mainly developed by arranger Sy Oliver, who also played trumpet in the band. This style is marked by a two-beat "disguised" behind the 4/4 Swing meter, and by the effective unison work of the saxophone section, with its tendencies toward glissandos. Both the Lunceford rhythm and the Lunceford sax sound were widely copied by commercial dance bands in the fifties, most of all by Billy May. The Lunceford beat was so potent in its effect that the general designation of "Swing" did not seem to suffice. The Lunceford beat became "bounce." Lunceford's music "bounced" from beat to beat in a way that emphasized the moment of "lassitude," as Erroll Garner did, for example, in his piano playing. Oliver's section writing was the first really new treatment of the sax section since the work of Redman and Carter. From this developed the first typical orchestra sound—aside from Ellington's growl sounds and the clarinet trios of Fletcher Henderson's and Ellington's bands. Such sounds and tricks of instrumentation, which stuck to a band like a trademark and made it identifiable after just a few bars, now became increasingly popular.

With Count Basie, the stream of Kansas City bands merges with that of the successful Harlem bands. To Kansas City belong the Bennie Moten band (which Basie himself took over in 1935); the bands of Jay McShann and Harlan Leonard, in both of which Charlie Parker played; and, prior to these, primarily Andy Kirk and His Twelve Clouds of Joy. All were blues- and boogie-oriented, with a well-developed riff technique, using short, reiterated blues phrases as themes or to heighten tension, or employing such riff phrases as contrasting elements. Andy Kirk's pianist and arranger was Mary Lou Williams, and it was mainly due to her influence that the Kirk band developed beyond the simple blues-riff formula of the other Kansas City Bands.

At first (and in some of his recordings until his death in 1984), Basie retained the Kansas City blues-riff formula, but he made much more than a formula of it. In it, he found the substance that gives his music (which in the course of the years has absorbed many of the elements brought forth by the evolution of big-band jazz) its power. Basie led big bands from 1935, with but a few short interruptions. In the Basie bands of the thirties and forties the emphasis was on a string of brilliant soloists: Lester Young and Hershel Evens (tenors); Harry Edison and Buck Clayton (trumpets); Benny Morton, Dickie Wells, and Vic Dickenson (trombones); and the previously mentioned "All American Rhythm Section." In the modern Basie bands, the emphasis is on an effortless, resilient kind of precision, but of a sort that develops in the most natural way from swing. It has been said that Basie is "orchestrated swing." The Basie band of the fifties also had good soloists: trumpeters Joe Newman and Thad Jones; saxophonists Frank Foster, Frank Wess, and Eddie "Lockjaw" Davis; trombonists Henry Coker, Bennie Powell, and Quentin Jackson; and, last but not least, Basie himself, whose sparing piano swings a band as no other pianist can.

In the seventies, Basie presented recordings with arrangements by Bill Holman and Sam Nestico. Basie's indestructible "Swing machine" consisted of trumpeters Sonny Cohn, Frank Szabo, and Bobby Mitchell; trombonists Al Grey, Curtis Fuller, and Bill Hughes; saxophonists Eric Dixon, Bobby Plater, and the late Jimmy Forrest and Charlie Fowlkes. Freddie Green was still lending the band his unmistakable guitar sounds; and with Butch Miles, Basie had again found an outstanding Swing drummer.

Above all, Count made a number of excellent combo recordings: jam sessions with Eddie Lockjaw Davis, Joe Pass, Clark Terry, and Benny Carter; quartet efforts with Zoot Sims; a date with blues singer Joe Turner; and, especially remarkable, a trio album featuring Basie the pianist.

Count Basie achieved what only Duke Ellington has otherwise managed. He became an institution. This institution hasn't been forgotten since the Count's death, thanks in particular to two musicians from the Basie orchestra who have brought it forward into our own times: first, in 1985 and 1986, Thad Jones; then when Jones became too ill to carry on directing the orchestra (he died soon afterward), Frank Foster. Both perpetuated the Basie tradition with that relaxation that is today still this orchestra's trademark, making sensuously accessible what the Count signifies for jazz: a symbol of swing pure and simple.

Woody and Stan

Elements of the Swing era have remained more important for the styles of modern big bands than for the improvisations of individual soloists. In 1936 Woody Herman became front man for a collective of musicians from the disbanded Isham Jones orchestra. Swing *à la* Benny Goodman was the last word then. Nevertheless, Herman did not play conventional Swing but blues. He called his band The Band That Plays The Blues. "The Woodchopper's Ball" was the band's most successful record. When the war broke out, the band that played the blues began to dissolve, but soon thereafter the brilliant line of Herman Herds began. The First Herd was perhaps the most vital white jazz band ever. "Caldonia" was its biggest hit. When Igor Stravinsky heard this piece on the radio in 1945, he asked Herman if he could write a composition for his band. Thus the "Ebony Concerto" came into being: a piece in three movements in which Stravinsky, in his own way, combines his classicist ideas with the language of jazz. And though most jazz people might not like the piece (because it does not "swing"!), it should be said that the "Ebony Concerto" is by far the best "jazz-inspired" composition so far written by one of the great classical composers of the twentieth century.

Bassist Chubby Jackson was the backbone of the First Herd. The drummers were first Dave Tough, then Don Lamond. Flip Phillips was on tenor; Bill Harris established himself with one stroke as a significant new trombone voice with his solo on "Bijou"; John La Porta played alto; Billy Bauer, guitar; Red Norvo, vibraphone; and Pete Candoli, Sonny Berman, and Shorty Rogers were among the trumpets—in short, a star lineup which no other jazz band of the time could match.

Indicative of the spirit of this band is Chubby Jackson's recollection that the musicians frequently would congratulate each other on their solos after a night's work.

In 1947 came the Second Herd. It grew into the Four Brothers Band, mentioned in our sections on the tenor sax and saxophone ensembles. This, too, was a bebop band—with Shorty Rogers and Ernie Royal (trumpets); Earl Swope (trombone); Lou Levy (piano); Terry Gibbs (vibraphone); the previously mentioned tenor men, and singer Mary Ann McCall. "Early Autumn," written by Ralph Burns, was the big hit of the Four Brothers sound.

George Wallington's "Lemon Drop" was characteristic of the Second Herd bop music.

In the fifties came the Third and Fourth Herman Herds and so on; the transitions are blurred. Herman himself once said, "My three Herds? I feel as if there'd been eighty." Ralph Burns wrote a "book" (i.e., library of arrangements) for the Third Herd in which the Four Brothers sound became the trademark of the band. (This had not been the case in the actual Four Brothers band, where the typical Brothers section of three tenors and one baritone was used alongside the traditional five-voiced sax section with the alto as lead.)

In spite of all the talk about the end of the big bands, Woody Herman's music has swung so successfully through the sixties, seventies, and eighties that even his closest followers have stopped counting Herds. Herman adapts the more musical rock themes to his big-band conception—pieces like the Doors' "Light My Fire" or Chick Corea's Latin hit "La Fiesta." And he discovered a fascinating new arranger: New Zealand–born Alan Broadbent, a musician who studied at the Berklee School in Boston and with Lennie Tristano and who proves that even today new, exciting sounds can be generated from the tried and true big-band instrumentation. In 1986 Herman undertook a "50th Anniversary Tour" (thereby outstripping even Count Basie as big-band leader). He also managed to keep his band together after discovering that its manager had embezzled money, leaving debts of millions of dollars. Woody Herman died in poverty in 1987.

Stan Kenton, who died in 1979, has also led various bands of differing styles, and so more space must be devoted to him than to any single bands. Perhaps the most typical Kenton piece is "Concerto to End All Concertos"— typical in title as well. It opens with poorly copied Rachmaninoff-like bass figures by pianist Kenton. The whole late-romantic musical climate lurks behind these figures, along with the notion that sheer size and volume equal expressive power—this seemed to be the peculiar Kentonian world of ideas. From this climate sprang Kenton's first well-known piece, "Artistry in Rhythm," in 1942. It was followed in subsequent years by a series of other "Artistries": in Percussion, in Tango, in Harlem Swing, in Bass, in Boogie. Arranger Pete Rugolo is often linked with this effect-laden and elaborate style, but Kenton himself clearly had already established the "Artistry" style when Rugolo, then still in the army, first offered him an arrangement in 1944. Rugolo, who studied with Darius Milhaud, the important modern French composer, is primarily responsible for the second phase of Kenton's music, "Progressive Jazz" in the narrower sense, even more powerful and elaborate, laden with massive chords and multilayered clusters of sound. During the late forties—the main period of Rugolo's influence—Kenton was enormously successful. His soloists led in the jazz polls: drummer Shelly Manne; bassist Eddie Safranski; tenorman Vido Musso; trombonist Kai

Winding; and most of all, singer June Christy. Hers was the most engaging voice in the band.

In 1952–53 came the most significant Kenton band from a jazz standpoint. Kenton seemed to have forgotten some of his past and decided to make a swinging music, perhaps not directly influenced by Count Basie, but nevertheless extremely well suited to a time in which the Basie spirit had come to life to a degree that hardly anyone in jazz could escape it. Kenton had many gifted soloists in this band, and the emphasis was on swinging solo work as never before in Kenton's career. Zoot Sims and Richie Kamuca played tenors; Lee Konitz was on alto; Conte Candoli on trumpet; Frank Rosolino on trombone. Gerry Mulligan wrote such arrangements as "Swinghouse" and "Young Blood," and Bill Holman, obviously inspired by Mulligan, furnished artfully simple examples of sections employed in contrapuntal ensemble play. Bill Russo maintained the Kenton tradition of a highly demanding music based on complex section interplay.

In the following years, Kenton involved himself more and more deeply in work at American colleges and universities. He established "Kenton Clinics," in which he and his musicians acquainted thousands of young students with the fundamentals of contemporary jazz, particularly of big-band music. In the process, Kenton did not shrink from personal sacrifices, often furnishing arrangements and musicians free of charge or below usual rates. "Stan is the driving force in jazz education in America," said Dr. Herb Patnoe of De Anza College in California.

Toward the end of the sixties and in the early seventies, Kenton experienced a comeback hardly anyone had expected. He surrounded himself with young, contemporary musicians with whom he played more direct, simple, and straightforward music than in his "Progressive" and "Artistry" periods, if still with the Kentonian power and his own incomparable pathos. He recorded some of his best later work at concerts held at universities, such as Redlands and Brigham Young.

In the meantime, Kenton had severed relations with Capitol Records, the label with which he had been affiliated since the start of his career, and began to market his records by mail on his own "Creative World of Stan Kenton" label. This prompted an entire wave of independent record companies to distribute their records in the same way. Experience has shown that mail order often can reach customers faster, more simply, and more effectively than conventional marketing methods, which, even after ninety years of jazz, seem unable to serve demanding jazz record buyers.

The Bop Big Bands

In the meantime, bebop had arrived, and there were various attempts at big-band bebop. The first signs could be discovered in the Earl Hines big band of the forties. The great pianist, identified with the trumpet style of piano in Louis Armstrong's second Hot Five, led big bands almost uninterruptedly from 1928 to 1948—along lines in which Harlem Jump and bop could merge smoothly. Billy Eckstine, a Hines alumnus, made the first deliberate attempt to play big-band bop when he formed a band in 1944. He and Sarah Vaughan were the vocalists (see the chapter on singers). Dizzy Gillespie, Fats Navarro, and Miles Davis successively played in the band—the three most important modern trumpet voices; Art Blakey was on drums; and the saxophones at various times included Charlie Parker, Gene Ammons, Dexter Gordon, and Leo Parker.

In 1947, the orchestra had to disband, but by then Dizzy Gillespie, who for a time had been musical director of the Eckstine band, had brought about the final transformation of bop into big-band jazz. Gillespie, Tadd Dameron, John Lewis, and Gil Fuller furnished the arrangements. Lewis was at the piano, Kenny Clarke on drums, Milt Jackson on vibraphone, Al McKibbon (later Percy Heath) on bass, James Moody and Cecil Payne among the saxes; and Chano Pozo added the incredibly exciting Cuban rhythms so characteristic of this band—rhythms that remind one of the Machito band, which must be cited among the important big bands of the time. It was the witches' cauldron in which the mixture of Cuban rhythms and jazz phrases was most thoroughly brewed. Its musical director was Mario Bauza, also known as a trumpeter (working with Chick Webb and others), who engaged a number of arrangers for the great jazz orchestras (out of the Cab Calloway and Chick Webb bands) to work for the Machito band. Bauza thus became the real originator of salsa big bands. At times, its horns would consist of North American musicians and the rhythm section of Cubans (see also the section about the percussion instruments). In fact, one of Dizzy's reasons for hiring Chano Pozo (and, later, other Cuban percussionists) was that he wanted to capture the excitement of Machito's music.

Gillespie was in the process of forming his big band when President Truman warned the Japanese in the summer of 1945 that they must surrender or experience "ultimate destruction." When the first atomic bomb was dropped, the Gillespie band was just about ready to play. This fact takes on almost ghostly symbolism when listening to a piece like "Things to Come." This is the Gil Fuller "Apocalypse in Jazz" mentioned in our Parker-Gillespie montage, with its jabbing, hectic, decaying phrases.

It is illuminating that the accents of "Things to Come" were not taken up again until twenty years later, in the big-band attempts of free jazz.

A string of bands worth mentioning existed in the realm between Kenton and Herman. Les Brown provided dance music, but it was so sophisticated and musical that jazz fans, especially jazz musicians, often responded to it.

Claude Thornhill played his calm, atmospheric piano solos amid a big-band sound that inspired the conception of the Miles Davis Capitol Orchestra in the late forties.

Boyd Raeburn led a band in the mid-forties that in many respects paralleled Kenton's. "Boyd Meets Stravinsky" was a representative title. Soloists such as pianist Dodo Marmaroso, bassist Oscar Pettiford, and drummer Shelly Manne (on one occasion even Dizzy Gillespie) brought much jazz feeling to the complex arrangements by, among others, George Handy and Johnny Richards. The latter wrote the arrangements for Dizzy Gillespie's 1950 recordings with strings—the most jazz-oriented string arrangements created up to that time—and in the mid-fifties he put together a band that attempted to extend the ideas of Progressive Jazz. The Richards band featured huge, piled-up blocks of sound and focused on irregular meters.

Basie as Basis

In the mid-fifties, the conviction that there is a contradiction between swing and elaborate production effects that cannot be bridged beyond a certain point seemed to gain ground everywhere. This conviction is quite in line with what we have called "Basie classicism." Big bands of this persuasion make music beyond experimentation. Maynard Ferguson, who emerged in 1950–53 from the Kenton band, organized his "Dream Band" in the mid-fifties for an engagement at Birdland in New York. It really was a dream band. Every musician in it was a famous exponent of his instrument, and all these musicians had the same musical ideal: to play swinging, blues-based jazz, vital and musically interesting in equal measure. Jimmy Giuffre, Johnny Mandel, Bill Holman, Ernie Wilkins, Manny Albam, Marty Paich, and others furnished the arrangements. Eventually, Maynard decided to form a permanent band instead of a studio orchestra whose members were unable or unwilling to leave New York. He found a bunch of excellent young musicians who made a brand of big-band jazz as fiery and wild as Woody Herman's First Herd, yet more clearly rooted in the language of modern Basie-Young classicism. "Fugue," written by trombonist-arranger Slide Hampton for Ferguson, is perhaps the most swinging fugue yet to have emerged from jazz.

Ferguson lived in Great Britain during the sixties (where he also led a successful band), but in the seventies he had a commercial comeback in America. Ferguson said, "I'm not interested in nostalgia. You have to move along with the times . . . you just have to take and use the current rhythms. In the so-called golden era of the big bands, the great bandleaders of the day all played the better tunes of the day—so why not now?" And so Ferguson plays contemporary pop tunes in jazz-rock arrangements filled with effects that hardly elicit applause from the jazz crowd but reach a large young audience.

But back to the fifties, when Basie's influence was stronger than Ellington's. Shorty Rogers made a kind of Basie jazz with a West Coast conception, full of original, spirited inventiveness. Arranger Quincy Jones, bassist Oscar Pettiford, trombonist Urbie Green, Boston trumpeter Herb Pomeroy, and others made big-band recordings in which the Basie influence is strongly apparent.

Quincy Jones called his first orchestral album—with such marvelous soloists as Art Farmer (muted trumpet), Lucky Thompson and Zoot Sims (tenors), Phil Woods (alto), Herbie Mann and Jerome Richardson (flutes), Jimmy Cleveland (trombone), Milt Jackson (vibraphone), Hank Jones and Billy Taylor (pianos), and Charles Mingus and Paul Chambers (bass)—"This Is How I Feel About Jazz." He wrote in the liner notes that the music reflected his feelings about "the less cerebral and more vital or basic elements contained in jazz."

Jones always had a great liking for Europe. In 1959 he brought to the Old World the first modern American big band to be permanently based in Europe. The band was to supply the music for the show *Free and Easy,* but the show folded. With great difficulty Quincy managed to keep the band together for a time with work in Paris, Sweden, Belgium, and Germany. Among the members were Phil Woods, Sahib Shihab, Budd Johnson, and Jerome Richardson in the sax section; Quentin Jackson, Melba Liston, Jimmy Cleveland, and Sweden's Ake Persson in the trombone section. The music was moving and healthy, simple and honest; in many ways the most enjoyable big-band jazz of the turn of the fifties next to Ellington and Basie. To be sure, Quincy offered nothing very new. But he perfected the old, and made it shine as hardly anyone managed to do. Too bad that Jones, after his band returned from Europe and continued to work for several months in the United States, gave up fighting for its survival in the face of the lack of commercial possibilities.

Meanwhile, Jones has become one of Hollywood's most successful producers of pop music (Michael Jackson, Brothers Johnston) and film and television composers. One can feel the jazz tradition in everything he writes and produces, and occasionally a big-band or fusion record by Quincy is released, joining commercialism and jazz quality with a cleverness and "hipness" totally Quincy's own.

Of similar interest in this context are the big-band recordings of Gerry Mulligan—almost like a "sophistication" of Basie, but with much additional contrapuntal work. Around that same time, Bill Holman was the first to attempt something on the order of a big-band realization of hard bop, with intense and concentrated arrangements of such bop themes as Sonny Rollins'

"Airegin." A little later (in 1960), there was, for the first time, a big band of "funk" and soul and gospel jazz, if only for recording purposes: tenor man Johnny Griffin's "Big Soul Band" with arrangements by Norman Simmons.

On the West Coast during the sixties, Gerald Wilson came to the fore with a big band that found great admiration among musicians. Wilson, who had written arrangements for Lunceford, Basie, Gillespie, and other important orchestras, also did not want to "prove anything new," but rather summed up with power and brilliance the "mainstream" of the development of orchestral jazz up to that time.

Gil Evans and George Russell

The one man whose big-band jazz really seemed "new" in this period was Gil Evans (d. 1988). Gil, who emerged from the Claude Thornhill band, wrote for the Miles Davis Capitol Orchestra. He once again teamed up with Davis in 1957, to produce those warmly glowing, impressionist orchestral sounds discussed in the Miles Davis section. The Evans band became the big-band realization of Miles Davis' trumpet sound. Occasionally—regrettably much too seldom—Evans also created similar sounds for other soloists, among them trumpeter Johnny Coles and guitarist Kenny Burrell.

Later, Evans—meanwhile a gray-haired veteran by the early seventies—also opened himself to free music and even to the compositions of rock guitarist Jimi Hendrix. But Gil, who broke up the classic big-band sections in a very sound-conscious way, is not a "diligent" arranger as, say, Quincy Jones is. He lets his music ripen within himself and seldom writes anything finished and final. Even during recording sessions, he often whittles away at changes and reconstructs entire compositions and arrangements. In many cases, his music is born while it is being played—almost in the sense of the early Ellington. That is why there are, regrettably, far too few records by this incomparable musician who until his death was closely linked with Miles Davis. In the eighties Evans, the great laissez-faire arranger, collected together a big band (the Monday Night Orchestra) with the best jazz musicians at New York's Sweet Basil club every Monday night, offering them every possible freedom to improvise. The musical outcome—freer and "more open" than anything the then over seventy-year-old Gil Evans had ever achieved during his rich career—is among the best orchestral music ever produced in the realm of jazz-rock.

The other great loner among arrangers is George Russell, already mentioned several times. He also emerged from the jazz revolution of the forties. During the fifties, Russell created his "Lydian Chromatic Concept of Tonal Organization," the first work deriving a theory of jazz harmony from the immanent laws of jazz, not from the laws of European music. Russell's concept of improvisation, "Lydian" in terms of medieval church scales yet chromatic in the modern sense, was the great pathbreaker for Miles Davis' and John Coltrane's "modality." Russell came to Europe for the first Berlin Jazz Days in 1964, and subsequently lived in Scandinavia where he notably influenced the music of Terje Rypdal, Jan Garbarek, and others. Today he teaches at the distinguished New England Conservatory in Boston. With European as well as American musicians, he has created numerous works that are as individual, as different from the mainstream of what most of jazz arrangers write, as the works of Gil Evans.

Free Big Bands

Meanwhile, free jazz had entered the scene, and the question was, What does the new, free jazz sound like when played by big bands?

The musician who stood out most clearly in the transition from tonal to free tonal orchestral jazz was bassist Charles Mingus with his big-band concerts. These infrequent concerts occasionally bordered on chaos in terms of organization and yet produced results—above all, exciting collective improvisations—that moved the jazz world for years to follow.

The most highly praised big band of Mingus' career was probably the band with which he recorded his 1971 album, "Let My Children Hear Music." Mingus commented:

Jazz is black classical music. . . . Let my children hear music, for God's sake—we've heard enough noise. . . . Now I, myself, came to enjoy the players who didn't only just swing, who invented new rhythmic patterns, along with new melodic concepts. And those people are Art Tatum, Bud Powell, Max Roach, Sonny Rollins, Lester Young, Dizzy Gillespie, and Charlie Parker, who is the greatest genius of all to me because he changed the whole era around. But there is no need to compare composers. If you like Beethoven, Bach or Brahms, that's okay. They were all pencil composers. I always wanted to be a spontaneous composer.

In 1965, composer (and pianist) Carla Bley and trumpeter-composer Mike Mantler presented their Jazz Composers Workshop first in New York and then at the 1965 Newport Festival.

From this, the Jazz Composers Orchestra evolved, with soloists such as Don Cherry, Roswell Rudd, Cecil Taylor, Pharoah Sanders, Larry Coryell, Charlie Haden, Gato Barbieri—in general, the cream of the New York avant-garde—under Mike Mantler's direction. If one realizes how difficult it is to find an audience for such avant-garde productions in the United States—definitely much more difficult than in Europe—he or she can speak of Mantler's personal contribution with only the greatest respect.

The Jazz Composers Orchestra was also involved in the Jazz Opera, "Escalator Over the Hill," by Carla Bley and Paul Haines, which was mentioned in the section on pianists. In the meantime Carla Bley had become increasingly prominent with medium-sized groups of her own. Her compositions and orchestrations are imaginative collages of swinging jazz elements and national anthems (ridiculed, of course!), of world music and children's songs and massive clusters—all this permeated with sensitive, often socially critical humor (as in a piece she wrote in 1980, after Ronald Reagan had been elected to the U.S. presidency).

During the eighties Carla Bley made many recordings with smaller ensembles, usually sensitized fusion music but not compositionally ambitious like her work in the seventies. Her sensitive and delicate duos with bassist Steve Swallow are particularly remarkable. Unforgettable are the arrangements she created, mainly outside her own band, during this period: for Charlie Haden's Liberation Music Orchestra; for Hal Willner; for Nino Rota's "8½" where she "celebrates" (with much melancholy) and simultaneously sardonically parodies Italian fairground, march, and circus music; and for Thelonious Monk's "Misterioso" where tenorist Johnny Griffin's lines fall like a "Bebop Light" in the gloom of strange, punky, weird sounds.

The other, perhaps even more important name in free big-band jazz is Sun Ra. As early as the mid-fifties, Sun Ra, who had learned his trade thoroughly as relief pianist with the Fletcher Henderson band of the late forties, had formed a big band in Chicago, incorporating percussive and other sounds totally new for the time—sounds that their composer and creator perceived as "cosmic sounds," as "music of the outer galaxies" and of the "Heliocentric Worlds." On one of his album covers, Sun Ra had himself depicted with Pythagoras, Tycho Brahe, and Galileo.

Sun Ra's music is more than just avant-garde, free big-band jazz. It certainly is that, but behind it stands the whole black tradition: Count Basie's Swing riffs and Duke Ellington's saxophone sounds; Fletcher Henderson's "voicings"; old blues and black songs; African highlife dances and Egyptian marches; black percussion music from South, Central, and North America and from Africa; Negro show and voodoo ritual; trance and black liturgy—celebrated by a band leader who strikes one as an African medicine-man skyrocketed into the space age.

Sun Ra's music is even more free from the sections common to conventional big bands than that of Gil Evans or the Jazz Composers Orchestra. The instruments play together in ever-changing combinations. Especially notable are the saxophone players of the Sun Ra Cosmic Arkestra, among them John Gilmore, Marshall Allen, Pat Patrick, and Danny Davis. Their saxophone and woodwind sounds are as new and revolutionary as Benny Carter's saxophone sections were in the early thirties. The Arkestra includes, among other rarely used instruments, original constructions by band members, such as the "Sun Horn," as well as oboe, bassoon, bass clarinet, English horn, violin, viola, cello, and a group of dancers, occasionally even a fire-eater.

Sun Ra's compositions have titles like "Next Stop Mars," "Outer Spaceways Incorporated," "Saturn," "It's After the End of the World," "Out in Space," etc. Many uninitiated listeners have smirked at such titles and at the show Sun Ra puts on as naïve. They joke about the dancers and acrobats Sun Ra has jumping all over the stage or about a film he has shown with his music: Sun Ra as a Christ figure, a dozen times in twenty minutes. They mock the glittering "Saturn gowns," "galaxy caps," and "cosmic rosaries" that the Sun Ra musicians and dancers wear. Occasionally, the culmination of a Sun Ra show involves a telescope that the master sets up next to his organ, and through which he searches for his "home planet Saturn" during special "cosmic climaxes."

But naïveté does not exist where black art is concerned. It did not exist when the chorus girls of the Cotton Club in Harlem during the twenties took · on the hullaballoo of white Broadway musicals, accompanied by Duke Ellington's jungle sounds; it does not exist when the preacher of a black Revivalist church expresses his hope that his parishioners may "go to Heaven tonight! right now! by subway"; it did not exist when Louis Armstrong sang "I Hope Gabriel Likes My Music." It existed only in the heads of white critics; and while they diagnose him as a naïf or even a charlatan, they say nothing about Sun Ra's music—and definitely nothing about the man Sun Ra—but a lot about themselves. Sun Ra's music, to LeRoi Jones, is the most precise expression of ancient black existence today. And Sun Ra himself said, "I paint pictures of infinity with my music, and that's why a lot of people can't understand it."

In 1988 the *Down Beat* critics poll ranked the Sun Ra Orchestra in first place following all the leading bands.

Unlike the United States, Europe offers a mass of free big-band jazz—by Alexander von Schlippenbach, for instance. His "Globe Unity" evolved from the 1965 New Jazz Meeting Baden-Baden and was only given a chance for a short life span back then. Yet it is still playing its arrangements, which often satirize the jazz tradition while at the same time paying tribute to it, and its wild collective improvisations. Schlippenbach's Berlin Contemporary Jazz Orchestra, founded in 1988, is more interested in compositional and formally structured possibilities. As composers (alongside himself) for this big ensemble the pianist won over Carla Bley, Misha Mengelberg, Willem Breuker, Kenny Wheeler, and others. The gap between free jazz and modern concert music is bridged by the London Jazz Composers Orchestra of bassist

Barry Guy, who structures his music almost in the sense of classical compositions.

John Coltrane's pathbreaking "Ascension" and the preceding double-quartet record "Free Jazz" by Ornette Coleman (both cited in the section on Coleman and Coltrane) have been key experiences for many free big bands. Here the form was created: exciting, hectic collective improvisations, from which emerges a solo that in turn intensifies to the point that the next collective improvisation (which, again, will "give birth" to a new solo) comes into existence. This form has been further developed by others—differentiated, sublimated, and structured—with especially personal results indicating future directions by musicians like Anthony Braxton (with his Creative Music Orchestra), Karl Berger (with his Woodstock Workshop Orchestra), Leo Smith, Roscoe Mitchell; and in Europe by Willem Breuker, Misha Mengelberg, Mike Westbrook, Keith Tippett, and Ulrich Gumpert.

Anthony Braxton's Creative Music Orchestra links particularly far-reaching abstractions and distancings with allusions to bebop and march music. From Karl Berger comes some of the most interesting and integrated big-band realizations of world music. Leo Smith has opened up orchestral "free" jazz, sensitizing it to "space," pauses, and stillness. Willem Breuker is *the* master of parody. Following on from Kurt Weill and Hanns Eisler he distances the popular music of the nineteenth and early twentieth centuries—marches, opera and operetta, polkas, waltzes, tangos—filling it with farcical burlesque humor, often accompanied by his Kolektief's turbulent music theater. Misha Mengelberg's Instant Composers Pool Tentet present this principle of parodistic exaggeration in a "more relaxed," compositionally less determined (less "drilled") context. His droll, idiosyncratic compositions have become the ICP Tentet's trademark. Keith Tippett is a specialist in massive, magical agglomerations of sound where spirituality, and occasionally also African melodies and rhythms, play a central part. At the start of the seventies his fifty-one-player Centipede Orchestra achieved some powerful, innovative crossovers between jazz, rock, and modern concert music. Mike Westbrook, on the other hand, is a master of large-scale orchestral refurbishings of European tradition, from Rossini by way of Stravinsky to Brecht/Weill. He also makes considerable use of theater and literary texts (William Blake, Goethe, Wilhelm Busch, etc.). Westbrook has particularly convincingly transferred Ellington's compositional principle of long, expansive suites to the European scene. People have justly talked of him composing a "Europeanized Duke". [East] German pianist Ulrich Gumpert and his Workshop Band make especially impressive use of elements of European popular music (marches, waltzes, and polkas) but also of swing and bebop rhythms, diversely disrupting and satirizing them through "free" music.

Rock Big Bands

There were three main currents in the big-band jazz of the early seventies:

1. Continued development of free big-band jazz
2. Continued development of conventional big bands, utilizing contemporary themes and tendencies
3. So-called "rock big bands"

And of course there were widely varying combinations of the three.

Let us first discuss rock big bands, ensembles like Blood, Sweat & Tears, Chicago, Dreams, or The Flock. The word *big* should actually have been put in quotation marks because we are here dealing mostly with groups of seven to eleven members—in other words, relatively small according to the conventions of big-band jazz. Still, it became customary to call them "big bands," because with the help of electronics they show tendencies to play in "sections." Keep in mind, too, that the big jazz band, in its early stages, also consisted of no more than eight to eleven musicians. Quite possibly, an evolution could have come full circle here. At least theoretically, there was a possibility for a while that the rock big band was standing at the beginning of a development similar to that of the jazz big band from the twenties on, but the reality was otherwise.

Rock big bands frequently strike the listener as being strangely stiff and inflexible, reminiscent in many respects of Stan Kenton during the forties. Since so many young big-band rock musicians have emerged from the university and college bands shaped by Kenton and his clinics, one might perhaps find a connection here.

The musical results often are in grotesque contrast to the effort involved. Unlike most other forms of rock, its big bands have failed to utilize and sophisticate tradition, particularly the jazz tradition. On the whole, their horn parts are hardly more than orchestrated guitar riffs. The use of horns is often so primitive that the impression is that beginners who do not have the slightest idea of the mysteries of orchestral arrangement, neither in jazz nor concert music, are at work here.

Until the second half of the seventies, only Frank Zappa had found in rock music—in real rock, that is—musical avenues which reach the level and complexity of big-band jazz. Significantly, Zappa did not start with jazz or blues or rock, as did all the others. In interviews he has repeatedly said he was prompted to become a musician by the works of Edgar Varese, the great modern composer who as early as in the twenties treated and solved many problems relevant to modern classical music in the fifties and sixties: problems of noise integration, electronics, percussion, collage techniques, musical density, etc. In the early fifties, Zappa, then unknown and unnoticed, attended the *Kurse für Zeitgenössische Musik* (Courses in Contemporary Music) in Darmstadt, Germany, where many of the composers who have so radically changed the contemporary avant-garde music scene lectured or studied: Boulez, Stockhausen, Nono, Zimmermann, Ligeti, Henze, Kagel, Berio, etc. That is the world that shaped Zappa—and that he longs for even today, though you are not supposed to notice. Thus his eccentricity, his bizarre humor, his pose are at once ironic and sincere. In this day and age, doesn't he seem like a Don Quixote struggling against windmills? And doesn't he love to appear this way?

Many critics feel that with the album *The Grand Wazoo,* released in 1972, Zappa's music reached its culmination. The production is said to show influences by—we will simply list the names—Miles Davis, John McLaughlin, Manitas de Plata, Gil Evans, Kodaly, Prokofieff, Stravinsky, Kurt Weill, etc. Critic Harvey Siders calls one of the pieces from *The Grand Wazoo* one of the "most successful weddings of jazz and rock in the book."

Big Bands Forever: The Seventies and Eighties

Anyone who realizes how few convincing rock big-band records have ever appeared, and on the other hand takes into account the excellent productions featuring the conventional big-band setup released in growing numbers from the early seventies on, certainly cannot speak of the "end of big bands." Many outstanding leaders and arrangers have proven that the big band still has noteworthy possibilities. Among these musicians are Don Ellis, Buddy Rich, Louie Bellson, Thad Jones–Mel Lewis, Oliver Nelson, Doc Severinsen, Toshiko Akiyoshi–Lew Tabackin, and—in Europe—Kenny Clarke–Francy Boland and Chris McGregor and his Brotherhood of Breath. In addition, there is a whole line of arrangers and band leaders who have been active for decades and have kept their music alive as times changed—among them Woody Herman, Count Basie, Maynard Ferguson, and so on.

The scope of contemporary big-band music has become so broad because on the one hand new possibilities are continually being discovered, while on the other nearly all the possibilities that have been discovered in forty years of big-band history have remained alive.

Don Ellis (who died in 1978) came out of the George Russell sextet of the early sixties and later studied Indian music with Hari Har Rao. He was especially interested in using new meters and rhythmic sequences. Other musicians, to be sure, had employed asymmetrical meters in jazz before Ellis—Thelonious Monk and Max Roach, then Dave Brubeck and Sonny Rollins, and as early as in the thirties, Fats Waller and Benny Carter. But nobody went as far as Ellis, who said, "I reasoned that since it was possible to play in a meter such as a 9, divided 2-2-2-3, it would then be possible to play in meters of even longer length, and this led to the development of such meters as 3-3-2-2-2-1-2-2-2 (19). To arrive at this particular division of 19, I tried many different patterns, but this was the one that swung the most. The longest meter I have attempted to date is a piece in 85."

Some of Ellis' meters look like mathematical equations—for instance, the blues in 11 that Ellis played as three times $3\frac{2}{3}/4$ with natural, swinging ease. Ellis once said, ironically, that if his orchestra had to play a traditional 4/4 beat, one had best explain it to the band as "5/4-1," otherwise it would be no fun.

Buddy Rich (d. 1987), on the other hand, did not experiment at all. His big band "celebrated" his spectacular drum artistry effectively. An evening with the Rich Big Band was show business in the conventional sense, but in its utmost perfection. The band's repertoire included evergreens, classic jazz themes, originals, and good contemporary tunes.

Another famous drummer who made big-band recordings in the seventies and eighties is Louis Bellson. He does not appear so much as the star in the center, but takes on a functional role on drums in order to present musicianly convincing arrangements (frequently his own) that combine the great big-band tradition with, sometimes, the seventies' rock atmosphere.

Many of these bands—those of Rich, Bellson, and Maynard Ferguson, for example—recruited and still recruit their musicians among the graduates of jazz courses at American colleges and universities. In a sense, it can be said that with the fine training of these young musicians, the bands tend to reach an even higher professional level than most of their forerunners. There is nothing in terms of technique they cannot handle. They are unbeatable readers and can play higher and faster than ever. But strangely enough, what often is lacking is the magic goal of the jazz musician: individuality. A basic problem of music education is revealed here: individuality cannot be taught. It has to grow organically, like a plant. In our modern world of media, with radio and television programs all sounding alike, the plant called "individuality" has a hard time thriving. The American educational system, a model for the world, and its jazz educators should address themselves more strongly to this problem.

But we have to backtrack once more by a couple of years—to Europe. Here, the Clarke-Boland Big Band proved how alive the big-band tradition can be even when no concessions are made to the *Zeitgeist.* In the sixties, under the co-leadership of drum patriarch Kenny Clarke and Belgian arranger Francy Boland, some of the best-known American expatriates— among them trumpeters Benny Bailey, Art Farmer, and Idrees Sulieman; saxophonists Herb Geller and Sahib Shihab—united with European musicians of the caliber of Swedish trombonist Ake Persson, German trumpeter Manfred Schoof, and British sax men Ronnie Scott and Tony Coe. The band's second drummer was a British musician similar to the famous Clarke not only in playing, but also in name: Kenny Clare. He impressively supplemented Clarke's musicianship and stylistic feeling with his professional dependability, occasionally also disguising a lack of stamina in Clarke, the grand old master.

For years, pianist Boland's arrangements were considered the "most traditional contemporary big-band arrangements" on the jazz scene. Especially characteristic of this are the albums *Sax No End* (with tenorists Johnny Griffin and Eddie Lockjaw Davis) and *Faces* (with musical portrait sketches of the band members). It is too bad that just when the orchestra was becoming successful with a larger audience in the early seventies, it disbanded.

About that time, Peter Herbolzheimer formed his Rhythm Combination & Brass. All through the seventies and eighties, this was Europe's most professional big band—certainly making many concessions to fads of the day, but again and again showing a high degree of musicianship and a swinging power generated by some of the best musicians in Europe and a few American guests.

The musically most convincing of all more recent big bands was, for most of the seventies, the Thad Jones–Mel Lewis Orchestra. For many years, it played New York's Village Vanguard every Monday night. Without making compromises with the rock spirit of the times, the two coleaders, trumpeter, composer, and arranger Thad Jones and drummer Mel Lewis, managed to appeal to a large audience and to create an orchestral jazz that, as swinging as it was in the traditional sense, was full of sounds and ideas never heard before. Jazz from all periods—including the jazz of the sixties and the music of John Coltrane and the post-Coltrane era—merged in the compositions and arrangements, furnished mainly by Thad Jones and played by an elite troupe of New York's finest musicians. Thad Jones' compositions and arrangements are full of wonders, scintillating with ideas and surprises, full of contrasts and unexpected changes of course, opening up new harmonic, melodic, rhythmic, and also technical worlds without losing sight of the big-band mainstream.

Regrettably Jones and Lewis separated in 1979. For seven years Jones headed the Danish Radio Big Band in Copenhagen, one of the most swinging in Europe today. Then in 1985, a year after the Count's death, Jones took charge of the Basie Orchestra. A year later he was also dead. Contemporary jazz thus lost one of its most important composers and arrangers.

It was Mel Lewis who most vitally carried on the tradition of the New York band through the eighties until his death in 1990, adding new arrangers such as Bob Brookmeyer and Bob Mintzer. Thad Jones' unmistakeable "composer's touch" is still to be felt: not only in his well-known, sensitively swinging pieces, presented time and again, but also in everything the band otherwise played.

Meanwhile, however, another orchestra had made its breakthrough, the Toshiko Akiyoshi–Lew Tabackin Big Band in Los Angeles. Most of the critics voted it the number one big band from 1978 to the first half of the eighties. The orchestra gets its stamp from the compositions and arrangements of Japanese-born pianist Toshiko Akiyoshi. She said, "When I look back and analyze what I've done, I find that in many cases I seem to have had a tendency to write in what you might call layers of sound. In other words, I will have one thing, then I will hear another that goes along with it. It's just like a photograph with a double exposure, you know?" Characteristic of Akiyoshi arrangements are the wealth and refinement of harmonic color. Particularly original is a five-part flute section that Toshiko formed with members of her orchestra, with her husband Lew Tabackin taking the lead voice. She has also been successful in widening the scope of the sax section by adding different kinds of flutes and clarinets in new and original combinations. In some of her pieces, she has drawn on Japanese tradition, for example, on *gagaku,* the ancient court music of the Japanese emperors.

The stream of the great big-band tradition continues to flow. Many orchestras all over the world are a part of it. Some of the more important ones are Jaki Byard's Apollo Stompers, Ed Shaugnessy's Energy Force, Nat Pierce and Frank Capp's Juggernaut, Rob McConnell's Boss Brass, Charli Persip's Superband, the Bob Mintzer Big Band, the Illinois Jacquet Orchestra, and the American Jazz Orchestra (headed by pianist John Lewis).

All in all, clearly a comeback of tradition can be found on the big-band scene since the early eighties. It is no longer free-jazz orchestras or rock big bands, but the conventional big-band instrumentation (four trumpets, four trombones, a five-piece saxophone section, with minor deviations, alterations, and additions) that today again is the focal point of big-band attention—forty years after the period when there first was talk of the "death" of the big bands.

And finally, there are also big bands that put rock elements to creative use, without the stiffness and lack of inspiration we talked about earlier.

The most important of such ensembles was Gil Evans Monday Night Orchestra (see the section on Evans); but Bob Moses, the Jaco Pastorius Big Band, Edward Wilkerson's Shadow Vignettes, and in Europe the United Jazz & Rock Ensemble, England's Loose Tubes, and Young Power from Poland have also vitalized and expanded jazz-rock with the palette of contemporary jazz feeling. Drummer and composer Bob Moses, who played with Gary Burton and Pat Metheny, creates out of an unusually picturesque tonal imagination. He writes less in "movements" than in "textures"—gentle, pastel-colored, shimmering layers of sound in which there lives the magic of

African and Indian music, permeated by the motoric élan of jazz-rock (mainly Miles) and modern jazz (Gil Evans, Monk, but also much Ellington). The titles of pieces on his much-praised albums *When Elephants Dream of Music* (1982) and *Visit with the Great Spirit* (1983) already reflect something of his music's exceptionally visual impact: "Black Orchid," "Lava Flow," "Machupicchu," and "Visit with the Great Spirit." In his Shadow Vignettes Edward Wilkerson—who is already part of the AACM's third generation and one of the few stylists within that musician's organization to remain based in their home city, Chicago—links elements of street music (from rap by way of funk to hip-hop) with the African roots of black music.

Since its establishment in 1975 with such musicians as Barbara Thompson, Charlie Mariano, Albert Mangelsdorff, Eberhard Weber, and Jon Hiseman, the United Jazz & Rock Ensemble (initiated by pianist Wolfgang Dauner) has been the most popular and successful big European orchestra. The reason is that the Ensemble endows orchestral jazz-rock with something only seldom to be found in that sphere: warmth and communicativeness, and melos without affected pathos. Loose Tubes, on the other hand—the twenty-one-head group around keyboarder Django Bates—whirls with turbulent wit through a colorful "chaos" of styles, interweaving South African music, Weather Report, bebop, Arab music, country and western, and free jazz, expressing sheer joy in life. Young Power, the eighteen-piece orchestra headed by Polish flutist Krzystof Popek, has transposed Ornette Coleman's "harmolodic" concept of free funk into especially powerful and expressive multistyle realizations.

But even beyond the integration of rock elements, there are a multitude of results outside the conventional big band lineup. The significance of David Murray's big ensembles within neoclassicism has already been covered in the section devoted to the saxophonist. But even more important in that context was probably the work of pianist, composer, and AACM initiator Muhal Richard Abrams. He has most consistently drawn on the entire palette of "classical" big-band sounds for free jazz: following the roots of black music from Duke Ellington by way of Benny Carter, Don Redman, and Fletcher Henderson, and then further through archaic jazz back to Africa—all of which is to be felt in his abstractly shimmering compositions, nevertheless saturated with enormous feeling for the blues. Astonishingly, Abrams' orchestrations, based on compositional structures and traditional big-band know-how, produce a more modern and vital impact than many a "free" orchestra still radically assailing all the musical norms. Anthony Braxton: "In Muhal's music I hear voices about the future—from the ancients."

Two other unusual orchestras came from Europe in the eighties: the Vienna Art Orchestra, established in the Austrian capital by Swiss composer

Mathias Rüegg in 1977, and Pierre Dørge's New Jungle Orchestra. With neo-Dadaist wit and a portion of "Viennese mockery," the Vienna Art Orchestra reflects European and American traditions as being of equal stature: Mozart and Mingus, Satie and Ellington, Stravinsky and Basie, with multitudinous references to Alpine folklore (predominantly the *Ländler*). Masterly too is the high degree of amalgamation of composition and improvisation, which often results in the ensemble's long suites. The Vienna Art Orchestra has become the leading European big band in postmodern jazz, acclaimed on numerous tours not least because of its "unity," which is not just musical but also human. This success has been achieved together with such soloists as American singer Lauren Newton (who performs with even greater freedom and relaxation here than in her own groups) and flugelhorn player Herbert Joos. As a composer Rüegg is pointing European big-band jazz in new directions. He has gone furthest, beyond all superficial parody, in developing the art of quotation, and yet he is completely himself in every note he writes. His "wit" and wealth of ideas seem inexhaustible.

Equally far removed from the usual big-band sound is Danish guitarist Pierre Dørge's New Jungle Orchestra whose "open" way of playing in conjunction with African and Asian melodies and rhythms sounds like a uniquely vital and effervescent orchestration of Don Cherry's concept of world music. Most of the arrangements are by Dørge, who traveled to Gambia and Nepal to study music there, but saxophonist John Tchicai also writes for the orchestra with such soloists as Harry Beckett, Johnny Dyani (d. 1986), and percussionist Marilyn Mazur.

Of importance too is Irakere, headed by pianist-composer Chucho Valdés. The group became known in 1979 through CBS Records' *Havana Jam* in Cuba, and since then it has attracted worldwide attention. Irakere plays "Cuban jazz" along the lines sketched earlier in connection with the Machito band, but even more exciting, engaging, contemporary than the Cuban bands in the United States. Chucho Valdés' "Missa Negra" is a ritual of black music that refers at the same time back to Africa and ahead to a new type of Latinized big-band sound. But Irakere actually represents only the tip of an iceberg: Cuba is full of such music. The American-Western European world simply has not yet realized it.

Lastly, one other big-band scene should be mentioned that also is "underground"—in both senses of that word: all the big bands at America's high schools, colleges, and universities. There are hundreds of big bands of all imaginable (and certainly also some unimaginable) shadings. These orchestras form the vital "underground," the basis, for tomorrow's professional big bands. Some of them are good enough to bear comparison with some of the best-known big bands of today. If you know this scene, with its volcanic vitality, you have to laugh when someone asks if big bands are dead.

THE JAZZ COMBOS

The Jazz Combos

Jazz is initially a music of small ensembles. Jazz was a combo music long before the word *combo* existed. This word came into being when it became necessary to distinguish between big bands and small groups. Before that, any jazz band was automatically a combo. If one did not know from hindsight what would evolve from the bands of Fletcher Henderson and Duke Ellington in the twenties, these ensembles, too, could be regarded as "combos."

Since jazz from the start has been an art of small ensembles, a history of combos must be written differently from a history of big bands. Since practically every jazz man has played in combos, such a history would turn into an endless listing of names. The required selective principle rests in the fact that a combo should be more than merely a group of musicians who have come together to play. By way of the Modern Jazz Quartet and John Lewis, "integration" has become a key term in jazz criticism. Here indeed is the key to our history of the combo in jazz. Integration means that everything belongs to a whole, that all elements are subordinate to one main idea.

In this sense, Dave Brubeck made a relevant statement about the combo situation: "The important thing about jazz right now is that it's keeping alive the feeling of the group getting together. Jazz, to make it, has got to be a group feeling." This describes what we have referred to as the sociological situation of jazz—as at the beginning of the section dealing with Swing style and in that about the arrangement. Jazz is at once music of the individual and music of the collective. No other art has attained both in such extreme measure. In such simultaneity the sociologist may find philosophical, political, and historical aspects. With jazz, this simultaneity of the individual and the collective of—if you will—freedom and necessity, has acquired musical aspects for the first time. Rarely can jazz be seen so clearly as a legitimate artistic expression of our time as in this point. And since this is so, the combo history of jazz is almost something like a concentration of jazz history per se.

In the selective sense in which we wish to present combo history, Jelly Roll Morton's Red Hot Peppers (1926 to 1930) and Louis Armstrong's second Hot Five with Earl Hines (1928) are the first significant jazz combos. Morton was the first to map out pieces from beginning to end and give them the stamp of a formative personality. Armstrong's Hot Five recordings achieved integration through the telepathic rapport between Louis and his musicians, above all pianist Earl Hines.

Orrin Keepnews writes in the liner notes to a Morton album:

> This is complex, intricate music. The musicians reputedly did not play from written scores but each number was preceded by perhaps a half-hour of studying the tunes, deciding on the placements of solos, memorizing the basic arrangements. It is the definitive answer to anyone who would claim that jazz is deficient in counterpoint or in depth of musical structure. It is a remarkable combination of improvisation and arrangement. . . . These are all talented musicians, but nevertheless, the voice that is heard here, the single, unified sound, is Morton's. This is the mark of his greatness.

In the Armstrong Hot Five with Hines (they consisted of six and sometimes even seven musicians) and in the Morton Red Hot Peppers we see for the first time a coming together of elements that previously had only existed separately: the collective improvisation of the old New Orleans bands in which soloistic achievement, and the individuality of the improviser in general, had barely begun to develop; this soloistic achievement itself; and, lastly, the conscious or intuitive creation of form through an outstanding personality.

The Swing Combos

What the thirties brought was, compared to this, initially a step backward. In 1935 Benny Goodman formed his Benny Goodman Trio. It became the germ cell and model not only for all the other Goodman combos—the Quartet with Lionel Hampton and eventually the Sextets with Charlie Christian and Cootie Williams—but also for all the combos that developed as "bands within bands" in all the important large orchestras. Thus, Artie Shaw formed his Gramercy Five with himself on clarinet and first Billy Butterfield and then Roy Eldridge on trumpet. Tommy Dorsey, Bob Crosby, and Jimmy Dorsey formed Dixieland combos within their big bands. Chu

Berry recruited his Stompy Stevedores primarily from the ranks of Cab Calloway's band, of which he was a member. Count Basie's band had its Kansas City Six and Seven and Woody Herman his Woodchoppers.

The most important of these "bands within the bands" originated in the Duke Ellington orchestra. Trumpeters Cootie Williams and Rex Stewart, clarinetist Barney Bigard, and altoist Johnny Hodges all made recordings in which the atmosphere of Ellington's music was, amazingly, projected into ever-changing small instrumental combinations. The "Ellington spirit" served as the integrating factor. It was so strong that even some records made by Lionel Hampton with musicians drawn mainly from this band acquired a noticeable Ellington aura.

The opposite of the integration that permeates the recordings made by the Ellington musicians can be found in the recording groups put together by Teddy Wilson from 1935 on. In a sense, these groups should not be mentioned here, in view of our selective combo principles. Here solo follows solo, but precisely on this account it is amazing how often the musical climate creates its own unity—especially when Billie Holiday and Lester Young are among the participants. In a record like *Easy Living* (1937) there is certainly nothing "integrated," and yet, from first note to last, we are in the unifying climate created by the tune, the lyrics, and the way in which Billie Holiday sings and the musicians, obviously, feel with her.

It is remarkable how the turning point in jazz evolution, which came toward the end of the thirties and beginning of the forties, not only involved the harmonic, melodic, and rhythmic innovations of the bop musicians but also initiated new concepts of integration. In 1938 bassist John Kirby formed an ensemble that in every respect made Swing music in the best sense of the term, yet it was a combo in a sense that did not become the rule until the fifties. With Kirby—and with the King Cole Trio as well—begins the real "integration" line of combo history that leads through the Art Tatum Trio and the Red Norvo Trio to the characteristic combos of the fifties and sixties: the Gerry Mulligan Quartet, the Modern Jazz Quartet, the Jimmy Giuffre Trio, the Max Roach–Clifford Brown Quintet, the Miles Davis Quintet, the Horace Silver Quintet, Art Blakey's Jazz Messengers, the various Charles Mingus groups, the Ornette Coleman groups, and further on to Weather Report and John McLaughlin's Mahavishnu Orchestra, and still further (in the eighties) to the World Saxophone Quartet, the David Murray Octet, the Wynton Marsalis Quartet, and the Henry Threadgill Sextet, and so forth.

Kirby's "Biggest Little Band in the Land" created airy, complementary frameworks of sound within which trumpeter Charlie Shavers, clarinetist Buster Baily, altoist Russell Procope, and pianist Billy Kyle improvised pretty and pleasing solos. The band had a clearly identifiable sound. It was the first ensemble to find success as a completely integrated combo in the sense that the Gerry Mulligan Quartet or the Modern Jazz Quartet achieved it fifteen years later.

Many of these successful later combos sprang up on the West Coast, and perhaps it is fitting that the combo that, alongside Kirby, initiated this whole development also started there: the King Cole Trio. It is the first combo of the modern piano-trio type: not merely a pianist accompanied by a rhythm section, but three instruments constituting a single entity. The Nat "King" Cole Trio was formed in 1940, with Oscar Moore on guitar and Wesley Prince on bass. Later, Cole had guitarist Irving Ashby and bassist Johnny Miller. But in the course of the forties, the success of Cole the singer gradually began to overshadow the pianist, until Nat gave up his trio and became a singer of popular songs.

Bop and Cool

In the meantime, bop had arrived. The Charlie Parker Quintet, with Miles Davis on trumpet, set the standard for both the music itself and for the format of the combos who played this music. For the first time it was again as it had been in the old Dixieland jazz: music and structure belonged together. Then it had been the free counterpoint of trumpet, trombone, and clarinet over a two-beat rhythm; now it was trumpet and saxophone in unison over the new legato rhythm. This unity of music and structure remained obligatory for the combos of hard bop: Art Blakey's Jazz Messengers, the Horace Silver Quintet, the Clifford Brown–Max Roach Quintet; and, above all, from the mid-fifties to the end of the sixties, the Miles Davis Quintet; and then again (that's how durable this structure has proven) in seventies and eighties neobop and classicism, in groups like Dexter Gordon's, Woody Shaw's, Wynton Marsalis', and many others.

It is only natural that in the course of this long time span many musicians have tried to widen and vary song and group structures, while at the same time preserving their basic format. In the mid-fifties, pianist Horace Silver was especially successful in this respect through the individualistic construction of his themes. Thus, he might use two twelve-bar blues phrases, follow them up with an eight-bar bridge taken from song form, and then repeat the blues phrase, thus combining blues and song form; or he might combine a fifteen-bar main theme with a sixteen-bar interlude— "even though it's not even, it sounds even," as Horace has said—and so on in many similarly conceived compositions. If today's music, even in the more demanding forms of rock, has often become free of the schematic nature of the conventional thirty-two-bar song form, this is due in no small measure to Silver, who was the first to pave the way for this development. To be sure, there were unique forms deviating from conventions even in the early days of jazz—as in Jelly Roll Morton's music or in William Christopher

Handy's (e.g., "St. Louis Blues")—but awareness of this had meanwhile been buried. Horace Silver unearthed it.

A number of years before the first Silver success in this field, around the turn of the forties, Lennie Tristano had already refined and abstracted the Parker format. He also had two horns, but they were both saxophones—Lee Konitz (alto) and Warne Marsh (tenor)—and to this he added a third hornlike line through Billy Bauer's guitar. In the Lennie Tristano Sextet could be found a very mobile linearity, moving over highly differentiated harmonies. After bop had broadened the harmonic material, Lennie Tristano "widened" the line—in the conscious conviction that jazz musicians had been concerned enough with harmonic problems for years and that the time had come to strengthen this awareness of line and melody. There were recordings such as "Wow," with a vigor that only hard bop would return to the general jazz consciousness in the late fifties; but above all there was a thoughtful, inspiring coolness with something of the atmosphere of the medieval cloisters in which scholastic debates were held at dusk.

Even before Tristano, bop musicians had attempted to broaden the structure of the Parker Quintet, in terms of sound. Primarily, Tadd Dameron, James Moody, and Charlie Ventura were involved in this effort—Dameron in his recordings for Blue Note, for which he used such musicians as trumpeter Fats Navarro and tenorists Wardell Gray and Allen Eager; James Moody with his significant and much-too-neglected recording of "Cu-Ba" (also on Blue Note); and, most successfully, Charlie Ventura with his Bop for the People combo, in which vocalist Jackie Cain and pianist Roy Kral (later to become her husband) sang humorous, spirited vocal duets. All this culminated in the Miles Davis Capitol Orchestra. In it, sound became definitively established as a structuring element. (In the Davis section, the ensemble is discussed in detail.)

What followed consists of manifold combinations and developments of these three elements: the harmonic, connected with the name of Charlie Parker; the element of sound, for which Miles Davis' Capitol Orchestra created an ideal; and the element of integration, for which the John Kirby Band and the King Cole Trio had already broken ground.

On the West Coast, for example, Shorty Rogers with his Giants and Gerry Mulligan with his Tentette made recordings that further perfected the sound of the Davis Capitol Orchestra, though sterilizing it a bit in the process. Later, Rogers reduced the Giants to the size of a quintet and created polished West Coast music within the Parker format, as did drummer Shelly Manne. He is one of the few West Coast musicians flexible enough to keep his own musical concept alive by continually reorienting himself in the changing musical stream until his death in 1984.

On the East Coast, J. J. Johnson and Kai Winding found an impressive solution. They joined their two trombones in a quintet; thus on the one hand they preserved the two-horn format of bop and on the other discovered a structuring sound in the subtleties of differentiated trombone tones. This structure was so intriguingly simple that it was frequently copied. Winding himself did it—after the original combo disbanded—by combining four trombones instead of two. Al Cohn and Zoot Sims followed suit, combining two tenors—and on occasion, two clarinets—instead of trombones. Phil Woods and Gene Quill did something similar when they teamed up on alto saxophones. Tenormen Eddie "Lockjaw" Davis and Johnny Griffin projected the idea into the world of hard bop around the turn of the fifties. In the early seventies, drummer Elvin Jones transplanted this concept of the "duplicated instrument" into the post-Coltrane era, using two tenor players. And in Jack DeJohnette's Special Edition, this principle of "horn doubling" became particularly vital in eighties jazz.

First High Points of Integration

As early as the late forties, vibraphonist Red Norvo formed a trio with guitarist Tal Farlow and bassist Charlie Mingus that basically established the concept of "chamber jazz." In light, relaxed, transparent interplay, the lines of vibraphone, guitar, and bass flowed into, opposite, and around each other. If Norvo, as a representative of the older jazz generation, didn't play quite as "modern" as Farlow and Mingus, the twofold stylistic plateau thus created lent an added charm. The linear function Norvo had assigned to the bass of Mingus (later Red Mitchell) was adopted in Gerry Mulligan's successful Quartet from 1953 on. Gerry did away with the piano, let the changes be indicated by a single bass line that took on additional contrapuntal significance, and set the lines of his baritone sax and Chet Baker's trumpet above that. After Chet Baker (who became famous almost overnight through his playing in this quartet) had made himself independent, valve trombonist Bob Brookmeyer or trumpeters Jon Eardley and Art Farmer took his place. In a manner that has been described as "busy," Mulligan played contrapuntal countermelodies or riffs on his baritone behind the improvisations of the second horn in his quartet. So it became apparent that even the riff—one of the most rudimentary of jazz elements—could be used structurally in terms of modern combo integration. Of course, after some time it became obvious that the more one became used to the surprising sound of this quartet, the more clearly the formulalike nature of its music was revealed. So Gerry Mulligan, who is not only a great musician but also a far-sighted man, enlarged his quartet to a sextet. And it is this lineup to which he has returned again and again.

The most often cited of all these combos is pianist John Lewis' Modern Jazz Quartet, with Milt Jackson, vibraphone; Percy Heath, bass; and first

Kenny Clarke, then Connie Kay, drums. Founded in 1951, disbanded in 1974, and then reestablished in 1981, it is by far the longest-lived combo in jazz history. Lewis, one of the melodically most gifted of all jazz composers, found much stimulation in the contrapuntal art of Johann Sebastian Bach. At the beginning, he often took over classical forms almost literally—above all in "Vendome," a precise and knowledgeable version of a baroque invention, with the one difference that in the place of the "episodes" in the form of the invention are put improvisations by the members of the Modern Jazz Quartet. Later, Lewis discovered contrapuntal possibilities more germane to jazz than to old music. As he said, "In the little piece entitled 'Versailles,' which also used a 'classical' form—the fugue—as a model, I don't feel that this has anything to do with the model, the best-known examples of which are Bach's. We have started to work on some new concepts of playing which give freer rein to the creativity of the improviser and yet produce an even stronger form." In those terms, Lewis also worked on an incorporation of the percussion part into the linear and contrapuntal play of his quartet. His percussionist, Connie Kay, was equipped with a whole arsenal of auxiliary rhythm instruments: finger cymbals, triangles, small Chinese drum, etc. And if drum instrumentation in general has become increasingly enlarged since the sixties, Connie Kay was among those who gave this direction its first impetus.

Characteristic of Lewis' jazz-minded relationship to baroque music are these thoughts, expressed by him in connection with his suite "Fontessa": "'Fontessa' is a little suite inspired by the Renaissance Commedia dell'Arte. I had particularly in mind their plays, which consisted of a very sketchy plot and in which the details—the lines, etc.—were improvised."

The MJQ—as Lewis' combo is abbreviated—had gone through a clearly perceivable development. During the sixties, the Bach elements became rare, but this was compensated for by a much more swinging jazz intensity. Lewis' "Django," for example, became less and less melancholy in the successive recordings available, and more and more swinging and intense.

The MJQ had great influence. Even in the hard-bop combos with their Parker Quintet structure, one suddenly could detect echoes of John Lewis' will to form. And even Oscar Peterson, whose trio at first was a kind of modernized King Cole or Art Tatum Trio, has paid respect to John Lewis' integration principle.

A similarly long development was undergone by the Dave Brubeck Quartet, formed in 1951, after Brubeck had first gained experience with a highly interesting octet (1946) and a trio (1949). Brubeck has probably had more hits than any other jazz musician of his generation, yet—and certainly because of this—he has been harshly criticized; but Brubeck has charisma, which has carried him from one success to another (see the piano section).

Brubeck's most important partner was Paul Desmond, a "poet of the alto saxophone," whose improvisations have been valued much more highly by critics than Brubeck's piano playing. When Desmond withdrew in the late sixties, Gerry Mulligan stepped into his place. Mulligan has always been an immensely swing-oriented, "busy" improviser, and it is obvious that through his participation the until then somewhat pastoral, cool Brubeck Quartet definitely became a more intense, "hotter" group.

From Hard Bop to Free

We have already mentioned hard-bop combos in connection with the Charlie Parker Quintet. It is apparent that an evolution toward greater integration took place here as well. Even the most vital hard-bop group, the Jazz Messengers—thrust forward by Art Blakey's wild percussion work—tends to have at least one (sometimes even two) musical "integrator" in the sense of the function of John Lewis within the MJQ, if in hard-bop terms. Horace Silver, then Benny Golson, Bobby Timmons, Wayne Shorter, Cedar Walton, Bobby Watson, Wynton Marsalis, etc., had this function with Blakey, whose groups have been of central significance right into the eighties. (More about contemporary bop and classicism later in this section.)

Marvelous integration is also a characteristic of the various groups Max Roach has led since his work with Clifford Brown and Sonny Rollins in the mid-fifties—ensembles partially with full, rich three-part horn sounds, without piano; later with pianist Ron Mathews and trumpeter Freddie Hubbard; frequently also with Roach's then wife, Abbey Lincoln. Max's main work, "The Freedom Now Suite," is exemplary not only for content but also in structure.

The second Miles Davis Quintet (1964–68)—with Wayne Shorter (saxophone), Herbie Hancock (piano), Ron Carter (bass), and Tony Williams (drums)—combined a maximum of integration with a maximum of individual expressivity. This Quintet made exemplarily clear that jazz involves a musical dialogue: an ongoing exchange of ideas both serving the whole and making individual demands. On the one hand, the group still improvised with "time" (i.e., over a regular beat, which was, however, interpreted very freely), but on the other, without the regulating principle of "changes" (prescribed harmonic successions) that had exclusively determined jazz improvisation until the end of the fifties. It's fascinating when listening to the Quintet's records to follow how this principle of "time but no changes" almost inevitably led to an ever-greater degree of interaction and integration between the musicians, culminating in a "togetherness" only comparable with Louis Armstrong's Hot Five, with the Charlie Parker Quintet, with the John Coltrane Quartet, and with the Ornette Coleman Quartet.

From the point of view of our combo-selection principle, it is important also to see that the concept of "modality," introduced by Miles and John Coltrane, creates a high degree of connection, and thus integration. The integration factor here is the "scale"—no longer many, continuously varying chord changes, but only a single chord (or very few chords).

John Coltrane transplanted this principle into "freer" jazz, in a sense shown in the section about him (and elsewhere throughout the book). One of the most beautiful recordings of the "classic" Coltrane Quartet—with McCoy Tyner on piano and Elvin Jones on drums—is the famous *A Love Supreme,* which combines spiritual fervor with formal completeness in a way not heretofore achieved in jazz. This group, with its high standards of improvisation and interplay, with the lasting value of its themes (composed mostly by its leader) and its "togetherness," was still a model for many jazz groups way into the eighties.

Among the groups that paved the way for the new jazz, three are important: the Jimmy Giuffre Trios of the fifties, Charles Mingus, and George Russell. In the early fifties, Jimmy Giuffre recorded his "Tangents in Jazz," in which the drummer, as percussionist, is drawn into the melodic and structural development of the music to such an extent that a continuous beat is largely dispensed with. In the trio organized by Giuffre in 1954 there was no drummer at all, and one may surmise that this outcome was near at hand: Once the drums are used more or less as melody instrument, there surely must be other instruments capable of serving this purpose better. In this trio, Giuffre used guitarist Jim Hall and bassist Ralph Peña. Giuffre went one step further when he joined with valve trombonist Bob Brookmeyer in a trio without a rhythm section—two horns plus guitar in an exhilarating web of lines that elaborated on both chamber music and folk music.

Even more important for further developments were the various groups led by George Russell from the second half of the fifties on—above all, his sextets with musicians like trombonist Dave Baker, multi-instrumentalist Eric Dolphy, and trumpeter Don Ellis. In the freely swinging modality of Russell's music a hymnic tone is achieved—a tone that reached a larger audience only years later through John Coltrane's *A Love Supreme*—but also shows an aspect of abstraction which often seems like a premonition of Anthony Braxton's work.

The most important pathbreaker for the new jazz, however, was Charles Mingus. As we discussed earlier, his music returned the feeling of collective improvisation to jazz. To be sure, there has always been collective improvising in jazz, but ever since jazz had given up the three-part New Orleans counterpoint, the emphasis had shifted to solo improvisation, the work of single players accompanied by a rhythm section. Through Mingus, improvising became collective again and to an extent unknown since the days of New Orleans jazz, which was not only indicative of a process in music but also in society. It is no accident that the revolutionary Mingus recordings we are referring to were made around the turn of the fifties (i.e., immediately preceding the new awakening of social and political awareness in the sixties). Again and again, jazz has anticipated and heralded such social developments. "Polyphonic music says: We," is what Theodor Adorno, the philosopher, once wrote. In those terms, New Orleans and Dixieland jazz on the one hand, and Charles Mingus and the free, collective jazz of the sixties and seventies on the other, all say "we." The music of the great individuals—of, for instance, Charlie Parker, Lee Konitz, and, earlier, Coleman Hawkins and Lester Young—says "I."

Among Charles Mingus' most important recordings are "Better Git It in Your Soul," "Goodbye, Pork Pie Hat," "Open Letter to Duke," "What Love" (with Eric Dolphy), "Ysabel's Table Dance" (with Clarence Shaw, trumpet), and "Solo Dancer" (with Charlie Mariano). Drummer Dannie Richmond played a crucial part in the success of almost all of Mingus' productions. With the assurance of a sleepwalker he kept up with his leader's many tempo changes (still rather new and unusual in jazz at the time), and thus held the music together.

Ornette and After

Aside from Lennie Tristano's "Intuition" and "Digression" (which, in 1949, were lone precursors of much later developments), the Ornette Coleman Quartet of 1959–60 was the first group to play "free" yet from the start meet the integration criteria of this section. Appearing at a New York club, the Five Spot, Coleman and his trumpeter Don Cherry enraptured audiences night after night for months. The many musicians always present in the audience were fascinated by the precision with which Ornette and Don entered in unison after their long, free solo excursions, though it wasn't recognizable to the majority of even the specialists why they came in at this particular spot and not somewhere else. One of the musician-listeners said then, "You can't hear it, but there is no doubt: Ornette and his men know what they're doing. In a couple of years, everybody else will know it, too" (which of course, has become true). Bassist Charlie Haden had an especially integrating effect in his group, with his totally free bass lines that dispensed with conventional harmonies yet created connection and structure. The integrating factor within the Coleman quartet was communication pure and simple.

A few years later, Ornette did away with the second horn, forming a trio. It may certainly be surmised that he himself took on the roles of trumpeter and violinist—however much he was criticized in them—in addition to his alto work because he needed further sound colorations but nevertheless wanted to mold the music of his group as directly and immediately as possible. Only toward the end of the sixties did Coleman succeed in finding another congenial horn partner in tenor saxophonist Dewey Redman.

From Coleman and Coltrane spring all the free-jazz groups that emphasize the collective experience of their music to an extent heretofore unknown. Dismayed by the isolation of the individual in modern society, these musicians feel that their improvisations unite them to a degree "as otherwise, among humans, only love can do" (Don Cherry). Cherry's piece "Complete Communion," realized in 1965, first in Paris and then in New York, indicates this concept of "total communication" even in its title.

Other groups that compensated for the isolation of the individual expressing himself without restraint (which is where a music that knows no harmonic or formal ordering factor may easily lead), with much stronger and more intensely personal collective relationship, were the Archie Shepp Quintet with trombonist Roswell Rudd; the New York Art Quartet with altoist John Tchicai (and also with Rudd); the Albert Ayler Quintet; and in Europe the Brötzmann/van Hove/Bennink Trio (with tenorist Peter Brötzmann, pianist Fred van Hove, and drummer Han Bennink), drummer John Stevens' Spontaneous Music Ensemble, and the Manfred Schoof Quintet.

The Seventies

Between the early seventies and the early eighties, the combo situation has been similar to that of the big bands. There are four streams and various cross-connections between them:

1. The combos playing along the lines of contemporary mainstream jazz, among which the hard-bop and neobop groups occupy a special place, of growing significance around the turn of the seventies
2. The groups playing free music around Chicago's AACM
3. The jazz-rock and fusion groups, whose development was initiated by Miles Davis' *Bitches Brew*
4. Chamber-music-like groups, who further refine the tradition of the Red Norvo Trio or the Jimmy Giuffre Trio. The prototype of these is Oregon with Ralph Towner (guitar and piano), Paul McCandless (oboe and English horn), Glen Moore (bass), and Collin Walcott (sitar, tabla, percussion). In a sense, Oregon constitutes *the* culmination of integrated, chamber-music-like jazz playing in all of jazz history so far. Similar coherence was achieved by pianist Keith Jarrett's two quartets: both the American group (with Dewey Redman, saxophone; Charlie Haden, bass; and Paul Motian, drums) and the "European" (with saxophonist Jan Garbarek, bassist Palle Danielsson, and drummer Jon

Christensen). The American ensemble was more powerful and hard-driven but also closer to the ideas of world music, whereas the phrasing of Jarrett's "European" quartet was more elegiac, impressionistic, and balladlike.

Neobop

Among the groups of the mainstream of the seventies, there are, on the one hand, those whose "first editions" were formed twenty years ago (and thus have been mentioned already) and on the other, newly formed ensembles. Of course, the groups whose leaders had formed ensembles in the fifties have integrated the subsequent musical experiences as much as those groups that were first formed in the seventies. For this reason, we list both kinds of groups together: Art Blakey's Jazz Messengers, the Dizzy Gillespie Quintet, the Max Roach Quartet, the Cannonball Adderley Quintet, McCoy Tyner's group, the Phil Woods Quartet, and Herbie Hancock's VSOP. Most of these are groups with ever-changing lineups. McCoy Tyner is a central figure among them, as a source of strength and inspiration for the entire scene.

In all these groups, the bop character is alive, but this character has gained a new significance since the turn of the seventies that not even farsighted observers had expected. It initially appeared as if bebop were slowly fading away, but suddenly the exact opposite seemed to be occurring: bop was coming back with full force. Neobop of the seventies (of which we have repeatedly spoken) produced a host of new groups. Towering above them all are the combos of the great veteran tenorist Dexter Gordon, the initiator of this whole movement. Also of great importance was the Quintet formed by trumpeter Woody Shaw (d. 1989), which made a decisive contribution toward reconciling bebop and modal playing (the latter still viewed at that time as tending toward free performance). Shaw so successfully introduced modality (improvisation over scales) into the language of bebop that a style over thirty years old suddenly sounded refreshingly different, contemporary and topical.

The AACM

As early as 1961 pianist Muhal Richard Abrams founded the Experimental Band in Chicago, a free-jazz orchestra that gave rise (formally in 1965) to the AACM, the Association for the Advancement of Creative Musicians—a grouping of musicians that has had much significance, not only musically, but also in terms of consciousness in the self-identification process of black musicians. The AACM first met with real success in Europe, aside from the much too limited local resonance it found in Chicago. In the late sixties, in a deliberate reaction against the lack of interest in free music on the part of the American public (and against its political and social implications!), some of the most important AACM musicians moved to Paris—among them saxophonists Joseph Jarman and Roscoe Mitchell, trumpeter Lester Bowie, bassist Malachi Favors, and multi-instrumentalist Anthony Braxton. From there, the Art Ensemble of Chicago quickly became known all over Europe. Since Jarman, Mitchell, Bowie, and Favors did not have a regular drummer (Phillip Wilson, Don Moye and Steve McCall worked only briefly with the group), they soon began to play percussion themselves: Bowie on the bass drum and Mitchell, Jarman, and Favors on the entire range of various percussion instruments that, around that time, became customary in the new jazz. In this way, the percussion parts—played alternately by musicians whose main instruments were trumpet, saxophone, and bass—were integrated completely in the melodic activity. This was also a crucial contribution of the Art Ensemble of Chicago. Don Moye has been the band's drummer since 1969. The increased level of percussive intensity is also indicated by the fact that the other AEC musicians continue to play percussion parts alongside their usual instruments.

As far as we know, there has never been a jazz combo that had so many different instrumental colors at its disposal as the Art Ensemble. On their European tours, the four musicians carried whole busloads of instruments. Particularly versatile are Mitchell (who plays alto, soprano, tenor, and bass saxophone; clarinet, flute, piccolo, sirens, whistles, bells, steel drum, congas, gongs, cymbals, etc., etc.) and Jarman (whose instruments include sopranello; alto, soprano, and tenor sax; alto clarinet; oboe; flute; piano; harpsichord; guitar; marimba; accordion; vibraphone; and several dozen percussion instruments). With this instrumentation, the AACM players made numerous records in France, Germany, and Great Britain, including the first big-band realization of AACM music, at the 1969 New Jazz Meeting Baden-Baden.

The majority of the American jazz audience became aware of the significance of the AACM almost ten years later. It was a slow process, beginning with Anthony Braxton's success and resulting in many AACM musicians being rated in top positions of the 1979 *Down Beat* critics' poll.

In the meantime, another group rooted in the AACM had been formed: Air (Henry Threadgill on saxes and flutes; Fred Hopkins, bass; Steve McCall, drums, who was succeeded in 1982 by Pheeroan akLaff). This trio, established in 1971, is one of the few avant-garde bands where oneness isn't just proclaimed, but all the instrumental parts really do flow together in complete equality. *Air Lore,* the 1979 album with ragtime compositions by Scott Joplin and New Orleans pieces by Jelly Roll Morton, was the most courageous and undisguised declaration (at that time absolutely unprecedented) of a seventies avant-garde group's indebtedness to the great legacy of jazz.

Of course, there has also been combo music on a high level by other AACM musicians (and also by members of a similar grouping founded in St. Louis, BAG, as well as by musicians close to these two groupings). These include players like saxophonist Oliver Lake; trumpeter Leo Smith; Muhal Richard Abrams, the great innovative spirit of the AACM; and the best-known AACM musician, Anthony Braxton. Braxton came to the fore particularly with his quartets, which included trombonist George Lewis, later his colleague Ray Anderson, and in the eighties pianist Marilyn Crispell, in a gradual process of abstracting music to the limit.

The attitude of most of these musicians toward tradition is illuminated by a motto formulated by the players of the Chicago Art Ensemble: "Ancient to the future." This not only means (in the Western rationalistic sense) "pointing toward the future from the ancient past," but it also refers (in the sense of ancient concepts of African mythology) to a "suspension of time." Said Abrams, "My thoughts . . . are my . . . future . . . now and forever . . . symbolizing . . . the past . . . present . . . and future . . . in the eternal now." This is an African thought. Or Asian. Definitely not Western.

It fits in with the initially mentioned process of sensitization that Muhal Richard Abrams should have influenced the musicians of the AACM not just in terms of music. Trombonist George Lewis said that he was even prompted to his extramusical studies—mainly German philosophy—by Muhal. And Joseph Jarman stated that before meeting Abrams he had been "like all the rest of the 'hip' ghetto niggers" on the streets of Chicago's South Side. Quite possibly, his future would have been bleak, as it is for so many young people trapped in the ghettos. But then he met Muhal, and his life acquired a sense of direction. It seems that Abrams, who remained more or less in the background for years, was much more interested in furthering the careers of other AACM musicians than his own. Only since the second half of the seventies—in fact, after his appearance at the 1978 Montreux Festival—has he found the recognition as a pianist and composer that other, much younger AACM players had gained earlier.

Jazz-Rock and Fusion

The integration of jazz and rock—long awaited, often prematurely announced during the sixties, and accomplished by Miles Davis' *Bitches Brew*—shaped the style of the best-known (and best-selling) jazz groups of the seventies. The groups that broke ground for this development in the United States and in Britain have already been discussed in the section on the seventies. The outstanding jazz-rock and fusion groups of the decade were Weather Report, Larry Coryell's Eleventh House; John McLaughlin's Mahavishnu Orchestra; Lifetime, led by drummer Tony Williams; Chick Corea's Return to Forever; Herbie Hancock's Sextet of the first half of the seventies; the Pat Metheny Quartet; trumpeter Ian Carr's Nucleus and saxophonist Barbara Thompson's Paraphernalia in Britain; the Association P.C. of drummer Pierre Courbois and keyboard player Jasper van t'Hof's Pork Pie in Germany and the Netherlands; Magma in France; and, finally, the groups of guitarist Volker Kriegel.

In the early seventies, it was mostly former Miles Davis players who carried forward the development beyond *Bitches Brew.* They include soprano and tenor saxist Wayne Shorter; keyboard players Joe Zawinul, Chick Corea, and Herbie Hancock; drummer Tony Williams; guitarist John McLaughlin, etc.

Some of the first steps in this direction—surprising in light of how little was to follow from this great musician as composer and arranger—were taken by Wayne Shorter with his two albums *Super Nova* and *Odyssey of Iska.* Shorter is the only hornman (on tenor and soprano) on both records; with him are guitarists, bassists, a vibraphonist, percussionists. The *Odyssey of Iska* is the mythical journey of a black explorer—a Nigerian Ulysses— who becomes a symbol of the human soul. Shorter said about the album, "Perhaps you can relate the enclosed [music] to the journey of your own soul."

"Odyssey of Iska" is an impressive "tone poem" in jazz, calling to mind the Herbie Hancock tone poems mentioned in the piano section. And, indeed, since Hancock's "Maiden Voyage," there has been an increasing tendency toward compositions in larger forms, complete within themselves, toward suites and tone poems. This is reflected, for instance, by Zappa's *Grand Wazoo* (mentioned in the big-band section) or by *Zawinul,* released around the same time as Shorter's two records: "Impressions of Joe Zawinul's days as a shepherd boy in Austria. . . . A tone poem reminiscent of his grandfather's funeral on a cold winter day in an Austrian mountain village. . . . Zawinul's first impressions of New York when he arrived here as a boy on a ship from France."

Great things were expected from the start when Joe Zawinul and Wayne Shorter founded the group Weather Report in 1970. In the first Weather Report, Miroslav Vitous played bass and Alphonse Mouzon drums, but elemental Mouzon and intellectual Vitous did not fit together. During most of the seventies, the rhythm players of the group kept changing, until a consolidation was reached toward the end of the decade when bassist Jaco Pastorius became the most important member of the group next to Zawinul, while Shorter no longer seemed to function as co-leader. Shorter's friends have often regretted that he was featured so rarely on the various Weather Report albums in solos commensurate with his significance as an outstanding saxophonist.

No doubt, after Miles' *Bitches Brew* and along with John McLaughlin's

Mahavishnu Orchestra, Weather Report is the most important and the most influential group in fusion. But time and again "WR" polarized the scene, until its dissolution in 1985. After publishing a devastating review of its album *Mr. Gone* in 1979, *Down Beat* was inundated for months with letters from fans and adversaries of the group. The review of *Mr. Gone* said, in part, "Weather Report has done to jazz in the seventies what Paul Whiteman did to it in the twenties. . . . Like Whiteman, Weather Report has overorchestrated its sound. Where Whiteman's band made hot jazz saccharine, Weather Report has made experimentation sound processed. . . . By not taking chances they have nothing to lose, but conversely they have nothing to gain."

Zawinul, on the other hand, emphasizes that his Weather Report music is embedded in the tradition of jazz, above all, in bebop. His most famous composition is "Birdland," named after the legendary jazz club on Broadway, which in turn was named for Charlie Parker. Around the turn of the fifties, Zawinul was in the Birdland almost daily. Twenty years later, in 1980, he said, "The old Birdland was the most important place in my life." In fact, the bop element, albeit veiled and transposed into electronic music, is to be felt during all the stages of Weather Report's development.

Herbie Hancock (see also the piano and keyboards sections) had left Miles Davis before *Bitches Brew*. In 1972, he created the record *Crossings* with its rich electronic instrumentation (electric piano, melotron, Moog synthesizer), into which three horns are interwoven: Benny Maupin (soprano saxophone, alto flute, bass clarinet, piccolo), Eddie Henderson (trumpet), and Julian Priester (trombone). With his electronics and the three horns, Hancock achieved sounds reminiscent of Gil Evans' rich orchestral palette. "Quasar," the title of one of his pieces, is representative of the music: mystical, primordial cosmic explosions, in which time seems to be standing still.

Drummer Tony Williams had also left Miles Davis in 1969 to devote himself more intensely to the integration of jazz and rock than seemed possible to him with Miles at the time. The different ensembles he formed under the heading of Lifetime were advanced jazz-oriented rock groups, whose integration problems Williams failed to solve—less for musical than for psychological reasons. Only one Lifetime could satisfy the strict principle of integration applied in this section: the first Lifetime with guitarist John McLaughlin (who here assembled the experience he needed for his Mahavishnu Orchestra) and organist Larry Young (aka Khalid Yasin). This produced cooking, wildly surrealistic improvisations, opening up to jazz-rock a sense of freedom and an avant-garde consciousness that was only to return in eighties free funk.

Later versions of Lifetime—and Weather Report and the Mahavishnu

Orchestra, too—illuminate particularly well the complexity of the musical and human (and technical!) mechanisms of such groups. It is truly a stroke of luck when such organisms produce great music: a string quartet has it much easier.

The process of attrition to which jazz-rock and fusion groups are subject can also be seen in Chick Corea's music. In the opinion of most critics, of the various groups he has led—at first under the name Return to Forever—the first of 1972 (with singer Flora Purim, percussionist Airto Moreira, saxophonist and flutist Joe Farrell, and bassist Stanley Clarke) was by far the best. It was one of the happiest, lightest products of seventies jazz. But his later groups have also retained the playful, communicative aspect so characteristic of Corea's music.

Possibly the most dense, artistically most satisfying fusion music so far has come from guitarist John McLaughlin, with his Mahavishnu Orchestra—here, too, with the first (1971–72) of the Mahavishnu groups (with Jan Hammer, keyboards; Billy Cobham, drums; Jerry Goodman, violin; and Rick Laird, bass). Nowhere else has it been demonstrated so convincingly, what astounding, liberating, delightful, and spiritual effects fusion music can create.

The tunes by the first Mahavishnu Orchestra had titles like "The Dance of the Maya," "A Lotus on Irish Streams," "Sapphire Bullets of Pure Love," "Meeting of the Spirit," "Awakening," "Sanctuary," and "Vital Transformation," characterizing the meditative spirit at the core of those pieces. To the strength of this meditative spirit belonged (which only seems to be a paradox) the high volume at which this music was played; it brought forth a kind of stillness precisely by virtue of being so overpowering. The Mahavishnu music created a "cathedral of sounds" that admitted nothing but these sounds.

One negative result of the density of this music was that within a short time the musicians had worn each other out in personal and musical tensions and conflicts, causing the group to break apart. With his later Mahavishnu groups, McLaughlin never again reached the level of this first orchestra. From 1976 on, he began to appear with the outstanding Shakti group (see the section on world music in this chapter).

After moving to Paris at the end of the seventies, McLaughlin reestablished closer links with his European roots, in sensitive jazz-rock pieces colored by romantic and impressionistic music. An eighties revival of his Mahavishnu Orchestra was less successful.

There was something frightening about the process of wear and tear involved in jazz-rock and fusion. Never before in the history of jazz had anything similar occurred. Basically only a single new group of artistic stature developed during the second half of the seventies: the Pat Metheny

Band with keyboardist Lyle Mays. With its melodic, poetic playing and its warm, sensuous, glowing electronic timbres, it reached a public of millions. The Pat Metheny Band commands an almost "symphonic" feel for a great range of dynamic shadings. No other jazz-rock group constructs such rounded, expansive, and far-reaching arches of tension. On the other hand, Metheny's music has been charged with a leaning toward kitsch and pathos, overprettification and excessive polish. Nevertheless, the legacy of jazz tradition—alongside much Brazilian music and a touch of country and western—also remain apparent in everything the Metheny Band plays. Other groups (such as Spyro Gyra) brought fusion so close to commercialized funk and muzak that it was often difficult to tell the difference. They are concerned with creating products for the market to such an extent that they themselves become throw-away products.

The Eighties

The eighties brought such a high degree of stylistic overlapping and amalgamation that only very broad and oversimplified generalizations can be made about five strands of development that shaped the combo scene. They were accompanied by a multitude of superimpositions and interlinkings.

1. *Classicism:* groups refining, through a broad range of styles, the development that started in the seventies with neobop
2. *Neoclassicism:* reflecting and updating elements of traditional jazz in the light of "freer" ways of playing
3. *Free funk:* expanding funk and jazz-rock by adding aspects of avant-garde styles
4. *World music:* amalgamating ethnic music from all parts of the world with contemporary jazz
5. *No Wave:* structuring, differentiating, and extending avant-garde jazz by combining it with punk, heavy metal, ethnic music, minimal music, and many other stylistic elements. The outstanding groups in this category have centered around alto saxophonist and composer John Zorn. Nowhere else does musical disruption sound so logical as with Zorn: a master of rapid changes between musical genres and styles from the most diverse of geographical and historical backgrounds. His groups nevertheless attain an incomparable degree of integration in their abrupt, rapid-motion-like, foreshortened playing around with musical fragments and quotations.

Classicism

Classicist groups don't simply copy bebop, as some people claim. For a start, they seem more integrated than the typical forties bebop band. The reason is to be found in the rhythm section's new way of playing, particularly the drummer: more aggressive, wilder, harsher, and—of particular relevance with regard to our criterion of integration—more interactive and communicative. In that context classicist groups don't reflect a single style. They work on the entire jazz tradition viewed in the light of bebop.

Art Blakey and his diverse Jazz Messengers have acted as the classicist movement's backbone. Although never essentially changing his hard-bop concept throughout the seventies and eighties, Blakey gave young musicians so much freedom that his Jazz Messengers became a real springboard for the groups that refine and extend bop-oriented playing multistylistically: the Wynton Marsalis Band, the Branford Marsalis Quartet, the Terence Blanchard–Donald Harrison Quintet, the Mulgrew Miller Band, the Wallace Roney Group, and even in some respects the eighties' Tony Williams Quintet playing "swinging" pure jazz (where many young ex-Messengers musicians gained additional experience). Strikingly, all these groups put the emphasis—as a deliberate countermovement to the hypertrophied results of jazz-rock and fusion—on the concept of musical integration. The "key" to such playing is what is viewed as a "classical" law governing jazz: A band can only sound good when every individual musician phrases "as if he were playing through all of the band's instruments" (Stanley Crouch).

The two most successful combos in that respect have been the Wynton Marsalis Group and the Terence Blanchard–Donald Harrison Quintet. Wynton Marsalis is one of the few trumpeters who can produce coherence and rich communication within a group merely through the lines he plays. But members of his group—including pianist Marcus Roberts, bassist Bob Hurst, and drummer Jeff "Tain" Watts—also made their contribution to a togetherness that has stimulated numerous other classicist groups.

Like the Marsalis groups, the Terence Blanchard–Donald Harrison Quintet refines and differentiates in its own particular way the "message" transmitted by the celebrated second Miles Davis Quintet. It plays "controlled freedom" on a bop foundation but, unlike the Miles group, adds a powerful shot of New Orleans tradition whose African, Spanish, and French *tinge* very much comes to life in this quintet.

In general it's striking how many classicist musicians come from New Orleans. Never since the twenties—since Louis Armstrong, Jelly Roll Morton, and Sidney Bechet—have musicians from the Crescent City exerted such lasting influence on the current jazz scene as during the eighties. For the second time in the history of jazz New Orleans has been a source of renewed energy: with such musicians as trumpeters Wynton Marsalis, Terence Blanchard, and Marlon Jordan; saxophonists Branford Marsalis, Donald Harrison, and Tony Dagradi; flutist Kent Jordan; bassist Reginald Veal; drummer Herlin Riley; and the players in the Dirty Dozen Brass Band.

The latter perform in the archaic tradition of the New Orleans marching bands, with Mardi Gras exuberance and *joie de vivre*. But the Dirty Dozen Brass Band does something that was previously strictly tabu among such groups in the Crescent City. It plays funk, bebop, jump, and soul arrangements—all with contemporary drive at unusually fast speeds for brass bands. That had never happened before: After the funeral dirge and burial of a corpse, a brass band returned to the city to the bebop sounds of Charlie Parker's "Bongo Beep." "Right from the start the other brass bands told us that wouldn't work," said trumpeter Gregory Davis. "When we were in a street parade and the people in front played marches, we struck up with Thelonious Monk's 'Blue Monk' or with pieces by Charlie Parker, Miles Davis, or Duke. . . . They came to us afterward and said, 'Man, you shouldn't play such stuff in parades.' "

In the meantime there are dozens of New Orleans brass bands that play like that: the Rebirth Brass Band, the Pair-A-Dice Brass Band, the All Stars Brass Band, etc.—all part of an astonishing revitalization of the venerable tradition of New Orleans brass bands in a dialogue with modern jazz. That too is the achievement of the Dirty Dozen Brass Band.

Viewed overall, it is questionable whether eighties classicism would ever have exerted such influence on playing styles and the jazz scene if crucial impulses hadn't come from Crescent City musicians. Jazz has certainly come full circle. New Orleans is back.

Neoclassicism

By the start of the eighties the AACM groups (and the closely connected Black Artists Group) had structured and formally organized free jazz to such an extent that the label "avant-garde" became invalid. Traditional forms of playing, often concealed or merely ironically referred to in free jazz, then became simply essential. The freedom that had once been gained wasn't, however, renounced but rather differentiated, refined, and enriched.

Among the important groups that update the great legacy of jazz tradition, making it contemporary by way of "free" styles, are the World Saxophone Quartet, the David Murray Octet (see the section on David Murray), the Arthur Blythe Quartet, Lester Bowie's Brass Fantasy, the George Adams–Don Pullen Quartet, the Tim Berne–Herb Robertson Quintet, the Chico Freeman Group, and the Dave Holland Quintet.

Perhaps the most unified neoclassicist band is the World Saxophone Quartet (see also the section on saxophone ensembles). What welds the quartet so closely together are two integrating factors that generate mounting intensity within the band's vital jump style. The WSQ gains its unusual degree of unity from constant interaction between, on the one hand, the fundamental freedom underlying its collective improvisation and, on the other, the unifying principle provided by riffs (the unceasingly repeated figures, derived from swing and rhythm and blues bands, which both support a soloist and provoke his efforts).

The World Saxophone Quartet's influence is also demonstrated by the fact that the group did more than inspire an entire wave of saxophone ensembles. If in the eighties there have been hundreds of bands where musicians playing the same instruments came together to form "pure" groups (string ensembles, brass bands, etc.), and if more and more groups play without a rhythm section so that the instrumentalists themselves become responsible for beat and meter, then it was the World Saxophone Quartet that made such developments possible.

The Henry Threadgill Sextet (in fact a septet) has grappled with the New Orleans tradition particularly intensively, reflecting and transforming the music of the start of the century—dirges, marches, and archaic blues, full of dark, sarcastic, and both joyous and morbid sounds. Henry Threadgill achieves unity within his group (with trombonist Craig Harris, cellist Diedre Murray, and drummer Pheeroan Ak Laff) through his compositions rather than his interventions as soloist. He ingeniously embeds his musicians' improvisations in the notated parts simultaneously performed by other players so that the compositional elements seem to be natural continuations of the solos.

The Dave Holland Quintet has so artistically extended the Mingus tradition with rhythmic and melodic asymmetries that the listener scarcely hears what complexities are involved in completely integrated playing.

"A golden constant" within this trend—and yet much of what the band plays points the way ahead—comes from Jack DeJohnette's Special Edition. He calls his music "multidirectional," stylistically open to all sides, with probably the most imposing range on the contemporary scene: contemporary jazz, bebop, modalism, impressionism, jazz-rock, free jazz, funk, reggae, etc. Something of Jack DeJohnette's integrative power, not just as a drummer but also as band leader and composer, is revealed by the fact that many famous jazz musicians have sometimes played more economical and focused solos in Special Edition than in their own groups: Arthur Blythe, David Murray, Chico Freeman, Greg Osby, Gary Thomas, and others.

World Music

World music, initiated in the sixties by John Coltrane and then taken up by many groups in the seventies, experienced high points of integration around 1980. Catalyst in chief has been trumpeter Don Cherry with his various bands. His poetry and magic accompanied many of the groups playing world music and inspired even more (basically all of them): above all, Codona (with tabla and sitar virtuoso Collin Walcott and Brazilian percussionist Nana Vasconcelos), Old & New Dreams (with tenorist and musette player Dewey Redman and drummer Ed Blackwell), and Nu with altoist Carlos Ward. Of importance in Europe were the groups around Charlie Mariano, the grand old master of saxophone playing, American drummer Mark Nauseef's band, Bengt Berger's Bitter Funeral Beer Band in Sweden, and the group around Lebanese-born Rabih Abou-Khalil who plays the oud, the Arab lute.

The first successful implementations of world music took place in the seventies, particularly impressively in Shakti, established by John McLaughlin in 1976 as an astonishing change of direction after the electronic high-energy phase of the Mahavishnu Orchestra. The four musicians in Shakti—John McLaughlin (guitar) and three Indians including violinist L. Shankar and tabla virtuoso Zakir Hussain—played gentle acoustic music. This was an encounter between jazz and both Indian music (from the south as well as the north) and Indian spirituality and religiosity, at a level of perfection even surpassing another important musical constellation: the earlier cooperation between Ali Akbar Khan, the Indian sarod player, and altoist John Handy, celebrated for his playing in Charles Mingus' groups.

Shakti was criticized for an "abrupt break" with John McLaughlin's Mahavishnu music, but the guitarist's dedication to Indian music and spirituality was already apparent during the Mahavishnu period. Above all, Shakti's music was similarly rich and as interwoven as the Mahavishnu performances. According to John McLaughlin, "India is part of my home on this planet . . . India is a part of me, not only physically but also psychologically." That also becomes clear from the names of the two bands. Mahavishnu means "divine compassion, power, and justice" and Shakti "female creative intelligence, love, and beauty."

Just as the Charlie Parker Quintet with Dizzy Gillespie brought together the prototypes of bebop, so too did the Codona Trio ideally unite the progenitors of contemporary world music: both Don Cherry (on trumpet, numerous flutes, and the African doussn' gouni long-necked lute), and American sitar and tabla virtuoso Collin Walcott, as well as Brazilian percussionist Nana Vasconcelos. Walcott once said, "I first studied African music, and then Indian. Before that I did American Swing. Moving between them I only had to take a very short step." That's just how Codona sounds. Three musicians here build bridges between musical cultures and continents—between Brazilian, African, Arabian, Tibetan, and Indian music—with such poetry and playfulness as if they had never been separated in any way.

Established in 1970 by four former members of the Paul Winter Consort, Oregon with its sensitive, introspective, acoustic playing marks the high point to date in chamber-music-like integration in jazz. The four musicians play over eighty different instruments: Ralph Towner (guitar, trumpet, piano, French horn, etc.), Collin Walcott (tabla, sitar, percussion, etc.), Paul McCandless (oboe, English horn, soprano sax, bass clarinet, etc.), and Glen Moore (bass, violin, flutes, etc.). Hence the wealth of melodies and tonal color with which this band plays world music par excellence, combining ethnic music from all over the globe with romantic, impressionist, and contemporary concert music as well as free jazz and folklore.

After Walcott's death in 1984, Oregon never recovered the unity and magic the quartet had achieved with the sitar and tabla virtuoso, but even today the group's great chamber-music-like sensitivity still captivates. Its music has become more percussive with Trilok Gurtu from India, and the use of electronic instruments (various synthesizers and drum machines) opens up additional dimensions of tonal coloring.

Strikingly, the integrative high points in world music came at the start of the eighties with groups like Shakti, Oregon, Codona, and Old & New Dreams. In the meantime, jazz groups have so much accepted world music that they no longer deliberately seek to amalgamate elements from different musical cultures but instead allow world music to enter postmodern jazz as one element among many others. It's only in rock, with the ethno-pop wave, that the idea of world music still possesses that aura of newness it had in jazz twenty years ago. World music has become an established force in the rock business, but wherever ethnic music flows into rock or pop, that derives—whether consciously or not—from the pioneering work and the advances achieved by such jazzmen as John Coltrane, Don Cherry, and Collin Walcott.

Free Funk

When jazz-rock's problems with integration became ever more obvious at the mid-seventies, little hope seemed left for this style. All that suddenly changed in 1977 with the appearance of Ornette Coleman's *Dancing in Your Head:* a cooking, bubbling brew of rock rhythms, free jazz, and North African music, the first satisfactorily unified realization of free funk. But only at the start of the eighties was Ornette's "message" understood, taken up, and refined by other jazz groups.

All free-funk ensembles are thus directly or indirectly linked with the music of Ornette Coleman's groups. In that respect, the part played by Ornette in free funk is indeed very reminiscent of Miles Davis' influence on seventies jazz-rock. Directly from Coleman's "harmolodic" Prime Time Band came Shannon Jackson's Decoding Society, the James "Blood" Ulmer Group, and the Jamaaladeen Tacuma Band. But other musicians who haven't played with the altoist are also linked with Coleman's music: the Steve Coleman Band, Ray Anderson's Slickaphonics, Defunkt (around trombonist Joseph Bowie), the Greg Osby Group, and the Gary Thomas Band.

Critics have reproached Coleman for turning away from free jazz, but his "harmolodic" music has only changed since the sixties to the extent that the Prime Time Band now implements this concept in a contemporary framework of rock-oriented and electronic music. They are the same great collective improvisations of a "harmolodic" nature. All the musical developments involve elaboration and modulation of a *single* melody—but without being bound in terms of key, functional harmony, or meter, or even by any reference to the unifying tonal system provided by Western tempered tuning. The "cement" that holds the band together is communication by way of the initial melody. All the players' actions are based on that, even in their wildest "free" moments.

Whereas Ornette Coleman's Prime Time Band has achieved free funk's most melodically integrated performances, Ronald Shannon Jackson's Decoding Society stands for the most rhythmically impulsive solutions. In the first half of the eighties (but later seldom) Shannon Jackson and his group succeeded in creating integrated combo jazz by "melodifying" the polyrhythmic patterns of his drumming and transferring them to the ensemble playing. The James "Blood" Ulmer Groups have transposed the language of the blues and their archaic precursors into particularly robust free funk, giving vent to raw expression and unrestrained vitality. The Steve Coleman and Greg Osby bands break through the rigidity and symmetry of funk and rock rhythms, "opening" them up by way of complex angular lines. Free-funk groups have made jazz-rock more communicative and interactive by linking it with elements from free jazz. The outcome is that such ensembles are often more integrated and "together" than the usual jazz-rock bands. On the other hand, it became ever more apparent during the second half of the eighties that the rock beat can only be "emancipated" to a limited extent. Otherwise this music loses precisely what characterizes it: its "groove," its physical directness.

TOWARDS A DEFINITION OF JAZZ

Towards a Definition of Jazz

Jazz is a form of art music that originated in the United States through the confrontation of blacks with European music. The instrumentation, melody, and harmony of jazz are in the main derived from Western musical tradition. Rhythm, phrasing and production of sound, and the elements of blues harmony are derived from African music and from the musical conception of American blacks. Jazz differs from European music in three basic elements, which all serve to increase intensity:

1. A special relationship to time, defined as "swing"
2. A spontaneity and vitality of musical production in which improvisation plays a role
3. A sonority and manner of phrasing that mirror the individuality of the performing jazz musician

These three basic characteristics, whose essentials have been—and will continue to be—passed on orally from one generation to the next, create a novel climate of tension. In this climate, the emphasis is no longer on great arcs of tension, as in European music, but on a wealth of tension-creating elements, which continuously rise and fall.

A history of jazz could certainly be written from the point of view of the three jazz characteristics—swing, improvisation, and sound/phrasing—and their relation to each other. All these characteristics are important, to be sure, but their relationships change, and these changing relationships are a part of jazz evolution.

That jazz sound and jazz phrasing stand in dialectic opposition has been pointed out already. In old New Orleans jazz, phrasing still largely cor-

453

responded to European folk and circus music. On the other hand, typical jazz sonority was particularly highly developed here. Later, this kind of sonority came to be regarded as exaggerated. No major musician in any phase of jazz has had a purely European sonority; nevertheless, jazz sonority and the sonorities of European music occasionally have come very close. By way of compensation, jazz phrasing has become increasingly important. Thus, modern jazz, since cool jazz, is as far removed from European music in terms of phrasing as old jazz was in terms of sonority.

In their extremes, jazz phrasing and jazz sonority seem mutually exclusive. Where jazz sonority is at its strongest—for example, in the "jungle" solos of Tricky Sam Nanton, Bubber Miley, or Cootie Williams with Duke Ellington's band—jazz phrasing stops. The "jungle" sound dictates the phrasing, and this sound exists for its own sake, beyond jazz phrasing. On the other hand, where jazz phrasing appears at its most highly cultivated stage—as in the tenor improvisations of Stan Getz, the flute solos of Hubert Laws, or the alto lines of the Lee Konitz of the fifties—jazz sonority seems largely suspended. The musical proceedings are so unilaterally dictated by the phrasing that it does not appear possible to produce sounds that have an expressive meaning outside the flow of the phrase.

A similar, if not quite so precise, relationship exists between swing and improvisation. Both are factors of spontaneity. Thus it may come about that when spontaneity is expressed in the extreme through the medium of swing, improvisation will recede. Even when a record by Count Basie's band does not contain a single improvised solo, no one questions its jazz character. But if improvisation is given too free a rein, swing recedes, as in many unaccompanied solos or in some free-jazz recordings. This suppression of swing by freedom is already illustrated by the very first totally "free" record in jazz history—Lennie Tristano's "Intuition."

Thus the relationships among the elements of jazz change constantly. In the thirties, when sonority in terms of New Orleans jazz had already receded and fluent phrasing in terms of modern jazz had not as yet been fully developed, swing celebrated such unquestioned victories that swing (the element) and Swing (the style) were not even differentiated in terminology. There have always been forms of jazz that seek to project the jazz essence into a single element of jazz. The ragtime pianists had swing, but hardly any improvisation and no sonority. The early New Orleans bands did have jazz sonority, but they had more march rhythm than swing and a form of collective improvisation that sooner or later led to ever-repeated head arrangements. In the realm of Swing style there is a kind of big-band music in which improvisation, sonority, and sometimes even phrasing largely take a back seat—and yet it swings marvelously. During the fifties Jimmy Giuffre often projected the whole jazz essence into a single Lester Young–inspired phrase. On the other hand—as is made clear by just these "exceptional examples"—at the real peaks of jazz, all three jazz elements are present simultaneously, if in varying relationship to one another: from Louis Armstrong through Coleman Hawkins and Lester Young to Charlie Parker, Miles Davis, and John Coltrane.

It is important to note, too, that swing, improvisation, and sonority (or phrasing) are elements of intensity. As much as they may differ from each other, just so much do they concur in creating intensity.

Swing creates intensity through friction and superimposition of the levels of time.

Improvisation creates intensity through the fact that the road from musician to sound is shorter and more direct than in any other type of musical production.

In sonority and phrasing, intensity is produced by the immediacy and directness with which a particular human personality is projected into sound.

It may thus be assumed that the main task and real meaning of the basic jazz elements rest in the creation of structured intensity. This understanding is also contained in free jazz with its ecstatic heat, as idiosyncratic as the interpretation of the three basic elements in this music may often appear.

In all these differentiations the question of quality—stature—is decisive. One might almost be tempted to adopt it as a fourth "element of jazz" within our definition. If, for example, Stan Kenton or Keith Jarrett has found a place in jazz—a place that was perhaps disputed at some points of their development but nevertheless basically is accepted—this is due to the quality and stature of their music, which are indisputable, even though much might be said against these two musicians in terms of jazz essentials. Moreover, this point similarly applies to the European, or to any other, musical culture. Even if it were possible to give a precise definition of what "classical" music is, a music that contained all the elements of this definition and yet lacked the stature—the quality—of the great classical works would still not be "classical."

It is important in this context to discuss some thoughts that were developed by the American writer and scholar Robert M. Pirsig. Pirsig (in his book *Zen and the Art of Motorcycle Maintenance*) has shown that definitions are "square," because quality is defined "entirely outside the analytic process." Thus the aspect of quality, necessarily, is excluded from any attempt at definition. Pirsig: "When you subtract quality you get squareness."

Jazz fans may feel that such considerations are too intellectual, and yet they explain why we who belong to the jazz world are left strangely dissatisfied with any attempt at definition. Jazz scholars may develop ever more extensive and refined definitions, but the real point eludes them; indeed, it *must* necessarily elude them, for reasons that Pirsig has shown (more extensively than can be summarized here). What remains excluded from the range of the definition musicians know better than all scholars. We have quoted Fats Waller before: "It's not *what* you play, but *how* you play it."

This state of affairs explains why thousands of cocktail, pop, and rock groups all over the world play a kind of music that might fulfill all—or almost all—requirements of all definitions to date, and that yet cannot be called jazz. In countless "commercial" groups, there *also* is improvisation, sometimes even jazz phrasing and jazz sounds; they often even swing, and yet their music is not jazz. On the other hand, as we have shown, with genuine jazz musicians the presence of only *one* element of "jazzness" is often sufficient to insure the jazz character of their music.

It is necessary to understand this: Jazz has to do with quality. Quality is felt rather than rationally comprehended. This has been realized subconsciously by musicians for as long as jazz has existed. For them music has to be first and foremost "good" to be perceived as jazz. All other criteria play a secondary role, however important they may be.

There is another fact that must be considered in this context. The constant use of the elements, styles, musicianship, techniques, and ideas of jazz in commercial music forces the jazz musician unceasingly to create something new. In this sense, André Hodeir remarked that today's innovation is tomorrow's cliché.

The flair for the cliché, however, is not only connected with the abuses of jazz in commercial music; it lies in the nature of jazz itself. Almost every blues strophe has been turned into a cliché. All the famous blues lines exist as ever-recurring "entities": "I've been drinkin' muddy water, sleepin' in a hollow log . . . ," "My baby treats me like a low-down dog . . . ," "Broke and hungry, ragged and dirty too . . . ," " 'cause the world is all wrong . . . ," "But the meanest blues I ever had . . . ," "I'm just as lonely, lonely as a man can be . . . ," "Can't eat, can't sleep . . . ," "I wanna hold you, baby, hold you in my arms again . . . ," "I'm gonna buy myself a shotgun . . . ," "Take me back, baby . . . ," "I love you, baby, but you sure don't treat me right . . . ,"and so forth. The great blues singers used them as they pleased, taking a line from here and another from there, adapting them to each other, and often not even that.

What holds true for the lyrics also applies to the music. When Jimmy Smith, Horace Silver or David Murray records a blues, both the arrangement and the improvised solos are saturated with structural elements from half a century of blues history. Everything played by exponents of classicism is saturated with elements from Charlie Parker records that, though not in themselves clichés, certainly lend themselves to cliché making. Or, to reach back into jazz tradition: in every third or fourth blues by Bessie Smith one hears phrases, or even entire lines, that might just as easily have been heard in other contexts from other blues singers. Every boogie consists of nothing but a constantly changing montage of "entities" made up of ostinatos and largely standardized melodic phrases. Almost every improvised break on old records by the Hot Five or Hot Seven, by Johnny Dodds or King Oliver, by Jimmie Noone or Kid Ory, is mutually interchangeable. So are the breaks that set off the four-bar blues phrases from each other—whether they be played by singers accompanying themselves on the guitar or by the most famous of jazz musicians. There are half a hundred, perhaps not even that many, "model breaks" from which all others are derived.

The further one goes back, the more apparent this model character becomes. What Marshall Stearns, Alan Lomax, and Alfons Dauer discovered of African elements in jazz consists almost without exception of such connective models and "entities"; they were not only taken over from African music as "entities" but often had this character within African music itself. Their model nature is so compact that they have survived through centuries almost without changing. Consider the tango: the rhythm was brought by the slaves from Africa, and today it exists in African folklore as much as in the great Argentinian tango tradition, in temperamental folk dances, lasciviously slow dance and bar music, in boogie-woogie basses, and in hundreds of intermittent stages. Everywhere there is the identical ostinato figure—the model with its tendency toward the cliché.

All jazz consists of such "models." They are fragments—such as the downward-descending lines of old blues or modern funk—that have something of the aura of the words with which fairy tales begin: "Once upon a time . . . ." This, too, is a model element. And as it is in the fairy tales, where elements-turned-symbols become content, so it is in jazz: The evil witch casts a spell on the noble prince, and hard-hearted king turns soft when he catches sight of the lovely shepherdess, and at last prince and shepherdess find each other and the shepherdess turns out to be a bewitched princess. Witch and prince, magic and hard-heartedness, king and shepherdess . . . all of these are elements of motives that can be joined together in inexhaustible combinations. It is thanks to postmodern jazz that the model character of such elements has been clearly revealed.

While Western concert music in the process of its ever-increasing tendency toward abstraction has lost almost all the old models and entities; while there is hardly a structural and formal element that has not been questioned—theme and variation, the sonata form, the triad—while we now long for the attainment of new and connective models and elements in concert music, and can only attain them by taking up once again the old models and elements that in the meantime have become questionable; and while in doing this we are historicizing—meanwhile, all these things are present in jazz in the most natural, self-evident, and living way.

Model, element, entity, cliché, may coincide—literally and note for note. But as model, as element, and as entity they have meaning; as cliché they are meaningless. But *since* they can coincide there is a constant tendency toward the cliché inherent in the models, elements, and entities. To a great extent, it is on the basis of this tendency that jazz constantly renews itself. The most fascinating thing about jazz is its aliveness. Jazz runs counter to all academicism—that very academicism that has made great European music the exclusive concern of the well-bred bourgeoisie.

The aliveness of jazz is such that standards are constantly overthrown—even where the old models and entities remain relevant. This complicates the position of jazz criticism. It has been reproached for being without standards.

In reality, it is remarkable that jazz criticism has so many standards. Often the evolution of jazz proceeds so rapidly that the kind of standards arrived at in European music, frequently formed one or two generations after the particular music has been alive, are meaningless. Jazz standards without flexibility tend to acquire violent and intolerant aspects.

We insist: The point is not to define standards and to test an art form against them; the point is to have the art and constantly reorient the standards in its image. Since this is inconvenient, one attempts to avoid it—within and outside of jazz. But it is above all jazz, as a music of revolt against all that is too convenient, which can demand of its listeners that they revise standards valid years ago and be prepared to discover new norms.

Nearly one hundred years after it began, jazz is still what it was then: a music of protest; that, too, contributes to its aliveness. It cries out against social and racial and spiritual discrimination, against the clichés of picayune bourgeois morality, against the functional organization of modern mass society, against the depersonalization inherent in this society, and against that categorization of standards that leads to the automatic passing of judgments wherever these standards are not met.

Many American musicians, particularly blacks, understand protest as a matter of race. No doubt it is that. But their music would not have been understood all over the world, and it would not have received almost immediate acceptance by musicians of all races, colors, and political systems, if the racial aspect were the crucial factor. Here as elsewhere the racial element of jazz has long transcended itself and become universal. It has become part of the worldwide protest against a domination-oriented society, which is perceived as a threat by millions of cultured people in all fields all over the world in every country and social system—in short, by those who are shaping the judgment to be passed on our epoch by future generations: a threat not only to themselves and their creative productivity but to essential human dignity and worth.

DISCOGRAPHY

Discography

The sheer number and diversity of musicians discussed in *The Jazz Book*—its unique strength—makes it impossible to include every artist mentioned in the text. I've listed albums by selected key figures, and I have often identified albums that contain important performances referred to by Joachim Berendt and Gunther Huesmann. Where appropriate (or where I couldn't resist), I've also added brief comments of my own. In every case, of course, responsibility for what is included or omitted is mine.

As you'll see, the discography includes an index of sorts in that it cross-references many musicians who appear as sidefolk—some chosen because they're major figures too, some because they've left interesting trails through the recording world. But here, as well, listings are limited by space considerations.

In a given entry, the year(s) of recording is listed first. Selected musicians on the album are then identified in the following order: brass, reeds, keyboards, vibes, strings (including guitar and bass), drums, percussion, and vocalists. Each of these categories is arranged from highest to lowest pitch. (In other words, for brass, trumpeters come before trombonists, who come before tuba players.) A word about alphabetization: Nicknamed figures such as Fats Waller are listed by last name as you'd expect, but King Pleasure and Sun Ra are found under K and S respectively, because their full names are adopted pseudonyms.

Since many readers use *The Jazz Book* as an introduction to the music, and since novice listeners often complain that jazz records aren't easy to find, I've habitually listed U.S. reissues of classic material instead of foreign compilations, despite reservations I may have about sound quality or other aspects of the American productions.

For those who are interested in foreign or hard-to-find jazz recordings, the best mail-order source by far in North America is North Country Distributors (Redwood, NY 13679-9612; 315-287-2852).

As they appear here, catalog numbers do not include the lettered prefixes or numerical suffixes that indicate format. For example, most but not all major labels designate CDs with the suffix -2 and cassettes with -4. Issues on foreign labels licensed to American distributors, such as Enja, often carry different catalog numbers in North America than they do overseas, and it's conceivable that an album listed here may be reissued under a different number in the future. (In a few instances, Canadian numbers may differ from those used in the United States.) Where multiple catalog numbers exist, listings here are for current U.S. issues.

All recordings are available on compact disc except as noted. While hundreds of classic jazz sessions have been reissued on CD, much essential material has not. Therefore some LPs and/or out-of-print albums are listed because there is a fair chance that the material will turn up on CD—either in the same or different form—or because the music is too important to ignore. For instance, the discography includes significant recordings from the Savoy catalog, a motherlode of great stuff that was sold and withdrawn from the market shortly before this book went to press.

Most serious fans get in the habit of prowling through used record stores, searching for the gems that record companies have neglected to reissue. One good retail and mail-order source for out-of-print albums is the Jazz Record Center (135 W. 29th St., 12th Floor, New York, NY 10001; 212-594-9880).

I hope that this discography captures the breadth and expansive spirit of *The Jazz Book*. Like the main text, it's designed for browsing as much as for reference.

—*Kevin Whitehead*

Abbreviations

a.o.	and others	**cl**	clarinet
arr	arranger/arranged/	**cnt**	cornet
	arrangement	**comp**	composer/
as	alto saxophone		composition
b	bass	**d**	drums
b cl	bass clarinet	**el**	electric
bars	baritone saxophone	**flgh**	flugelhorn
cel	cello	**flt**	flute

fr hn	french horn	**rds**	reeds
g	guitar	**ss**	soprano saxophone
g syn	guitar synthesizer	**syn**	synthesizer
kbds	keyboards	**tba**	tuba
ldr	big band leader	**tbn**	trombone
mba	marimba	**tpt**	trumpet
misc instr	miscellaneous	**ts**	tenor saxophone
	instruments	**vcl**	vocal
ob	oboe	**vib**	vibraphone
org	organ	**vln**	violin
p	piano	**xyl**	xylophone
perc	percussion		

JOHN ABERCROMBIE (el g, g syn), *Getting There* (1987, with Michael Brecker, Marc Johnson, Peter Erskine), ECM 833 494

RABIH ABOU-KHALIL (oud), *Nafas* (1988, with Glen Velez), ECM 835 781

MUHAL RICHARD ABRAMS (p, syn, ldr), *The Hearinga Suite* (1989, with Jack Walrath, John Purcell, Marty Ehrlich, Diedre Murray, Fred Hopkins, Warren Smith, Andrew Cyrille a.o.), Black Saint 120 103   *See also* Anthony Braxton, Hal Willner.

GEORGE ADAMS (ts, flt, vcl), *Paradise Space Shuttle* (1978, with Al Foster a.o.), Timeless 127   *See also* Gil Evans.

PEPPER ADAMS (bars), *The Master* (1980, with Tommy Flanagan, George Mraz, Leroy Williams), Muse 5213   *See also* Thad Jones, Toots Thielemans.

CANNONBALL ADDERLEY (as), *Them Dirty Blues* (1960, with Nat Adderley, Bobby Timmons, Barry Harris, Sam Jones, Louis Hayes), Landmark 1301   *See also* Miles Davis, Dinah Washington, Joe Williams.

AIR (trio), *Air Lore* (1979: Henry Threadgill, Fred Hopkins, Steve McCall; includes arrs. of Jelly Roll Morton and King Oliver comps.), RCA/Bluebird 6578

TOSHIKO AKIYOSHI (p, ldr)/Lew Tabackin (ts, flt), *Toshiko Akiyoshi/Lew Tabackin Big Band* (late 1970s, with Jimmy Knepper a.o.), RCA/Novus 3106

PHEEROAN AKLAFF (d), *see* Anthony Davis, Craig Harris, Oliver Lake, James Newton, Henry Threadgill, Yosuke Yamashita

AMIN ALI (el b), *see* Music Revelation Ensemble

GERI ALLEN (p), *see* Charlie Haden, Oliver Lake

HENRY "RED" ALLEN (tpt), *see* Sidney Bechet, Fletcher Henderson, Jelly Roll Morton

MOSE ALLISON (p, vcl), *Ever Since the World Ended* (1987, with Bennie Wallace, Arthur Blythe, Bob Malach, Kenny Burrell a.o.), Blue Note 48015   *See also* Al Cohn.

LAURINDO ALMEIDA (g)/Bud Shank (as), *Brazilliance, Vol. 1* (1953), World Pacific 96339

BARRY ALTSCHUL (d), *see* Anthony Braxton, Dave Holland

ALBERT AMMONS (p), *see* Collections: *Barrelhouse Boogie*

GENE AMMONS (ts), *Boss Tenor* (1960, with Tommy Flanagan, Doug Watkins, Art Taylor, Ray Baretto), Fantasy/OJC 297

GENE AMMONS/SONNY STITT (ts), *see* Collections: *Jazz Club: Tenor Sax*

RAY ANDERSON (tbn), *Blues Bred in the Bone* (1988, with John Scofield, Anthony Davis, Mark Dresser, Johnny Vidacovich), Gramavision 79445   *See also* Bass-Drum-Bone, Bennie Wallace.

ARCADO (string trio), *Arcado* (1989: Mark Feldman, Hank Roberts, Mark Dresser), JMT 834 429

LOUIS ARMSTRONG (cnt, tpt, vcl), *Louis Armstrong/King Oliver* (disc split with King Oliver sessions—see Oliver; 1924, with Buster Bailey, Sidney Bechet, Lil Hardin a.o.), Milestone 47017

——— *The Hot Fives* (1925–26, with Johnny Dodds, Kid Ory, Johnny St. Cyr a.o.), Columbia 44049

——— *The Hot Fives & Hot Sevens* (1927–28, with Dodds, St. Cyr, Lonnie Johnson, Earl Hines, Baby Dodds, Zutty Singleton a.o.), Columbia 44422

——— *Louis Armstrong and Earl Hines* (1927–28, with Don Redman, Singleton a.o.), Columbia 45142

——— *Laughin' Louie* (1932–33: orchestra with Charlie Green, Louis Jordan, Budd Johnson, Sid Catlett, Chick Webb a.o.), RCA/Bluebird 9759   *See also* King Oliver, Bessie Smith, Jack Teagarden, Collections: *Riverside History of Classic Jazz.*

ART ENSEMBLE OF CHICAGO (quintet), *Nice Guys* (1978: Lester Bowie, Roscoe Mitchell, Joseph Jarman, Malachi Favors, Don Moye), ECM 827 876

SVEND ASMUSSEN (vln), *see* Collections: *Jazz Club: Violin*

LOVIE AUSTIN (p), *see* Collections: *Riverside History of Classic Jazz*

ALBERT AYLER (ts), *Lörrach/Paris 1966* (quintet), Hat Art 6039

AZIMUTH (trio), *Azimuth '85* (Kenny Wheeler, John Taylor, Norma Winstone—not to be confused with the Brazilian trio Azymuth), ECM 827 520

BUSTER BAILEY (cl, ss), *see* Lionel Hampton, Billie Holiday, John Kirby, King Oliver, Bessie Smith

DEREK BAILEY (g, el g), *Company 5* (1977, with Leo Smith, Anthony Braxton, Steve Lacy, Evan Parker, Tristan Honsinger, Maarten Altena), Incus 28 [LP]

MILDRED BAILEY (vcl), *Her Greatest Performances* (1929–46, with Roy Eldridge, Charlie Shavers, Benny Goodman, Chu Berry, Coleman Hawkins, Red Norvo a.o.), Columbia Special Products JC3 22 [3-LP set]   *See also* Benny Goodman.

CHET BAKER (tpt, vcl), *see* Charlie Haden, Gerry Mulligan

BILLY BANG (vln), *see* String Trio of New York

GATO BARBIERI (ts), *see* Don Cherry, Charlie Haden, Jazz Composers Orchestra

GEORGE BARNES (g), *see* Ruby Braff

CHARLIE BARNET (as, ss, ldr), *Clap Hands, Here Comes Charlie* (1939–41, with Lena Horne a.o.), RCA/Bluebird 6273

KENNY BARRON (p), *see* Nick Brignola, Stan Getz

COUNT BASIE (p, ldr), *One O'Clock Jump* (1937, with Buck Clayton, Lester Young, Herschel Evans, Claude Williams, Walter Page, Jo Jones, Jimmy Rushing a.o.; including "Time Out"), MCA 42324

———— *The Essential Count Basie, Vol. 1* (1936, 1939, with Clayton, Benny Morton, Young, Buddy Tate, Freddie Green, Page, Jones, Rushing, Helen Humes a.o.; includes "Oh, Lady Be Good," 2 tracks with Basie, org.), Columbia 40608

———— *April in Paris* (1955–56, with Joe Newman, Thad Jones, Henry Coker, Benny Powell, Frank Foster, Frank Wess, Green, Joe Williams a.o.), Verve 825 575

———— *For the First Time!* (1974, with Ray Brown, Louie Bellson; includes 2 tracks with Basie, org), Pablo 2310 712   *See also* Benny Goodman, Mel Tormé.

BASS-DRUM-BONE (trio), *Wooferlo* (1987: Ray Anderson, Mark Helias, Gerry Hemingway), Soul Note 121 187

ALVIN BATISTE (cl), *see* Clarinet Summit

SIDNEY BECHET (ss, cl), *The Victor Sessions—Master Takes 1932–1943* (with Henry "Red" Allen, Tommy Ladnier, Charlie Shavers, Rex Stewart, Vic Dickenson, J. C. Higginbotham, Mezz Mezzrow, Albert Nicholas, Earl Hines, Jelly Roll Morton, Willie the Lion Smith, Wellman Braud, Sid Catlett, Kenny Clarke, Baby Dodds, Zutty Singleton a.o.; essential music), RCA/Bluebird 2402 [3-CD box]

———— *Sidney Bechet and Friends, Compact Jazz* (1949–56, with Clarke and with French and Dutch musicians), PolyGram/Verve 840 633   *See also* Earl Hines.

BIX BEIDERBECKE (cnt, p), *Singin' the Blues* (1927, with Frankie Trumbauer, Eddie Lang a.o.; including "In a Mist"), Columbia 45450   *See also* Collections: *Riverside History of Classic Jazz.*

RICHIE BEIRACH (p), *see* Jeremy Steig

LOUIE BELLSON (d, ldr), *East Side Suite* (1987, with Clark Terry a.o.), Musicmasters 60161   *See also* Count Basie.

HAN BENNINK (d, perc, misc instr), *see* Peter Brötzmann, ICP Orchestra, Misha Mengelberg

BENGT BERGER (perc, ldr), *Bitter Funeral Beer* (1981, with Don Cherry a.o.), ECM 839 308

BERLIN CONTEMPORARY JAZZ ORCHESTRA, *Berlin Contemporary Jazz Orchestra* (1989, with Benny Bailey, Kenny Wheeler, Gerd Dudek, Willem Breuker, Ernst Ludwig Petrowsky, Misha Mengelberg, Aki Takase, Ed Thigpen a.o.; comps. by Wheeler, Mengelberg), ECM 841 777

TIM BERNE (as), *Fractured Fairy Tales* (1989, with Herb Robertson, Mark Feldman, Hank Roberts, Mark Dresser, Joey Baron), JMT 834 431   *See also* Mark Helias, John Zorn.

CHU BERRY (ts), *Giants of the Tenor Sax* (disc split with Lucky Thompson session—*see* Thompson; 1938 and 1941, with Roy Eldridge, Hot Lips Page, Danny Barker, Sid Catlett a.o.), Commodore 7004   *See also* Mildred Bailey, Benny Carter, Lionel Hampton, Bessie Smith.

GREETJE BIJMA (vcl), *see* Five Voices

ED BLACKWELL (d), *see* Jane Ira Bloom, Don Cherry, Ornette Coleman, Mal Waldron

EUBIE BLAKE (p), *Memories of You* (from piano rolls, 1915–73), Biograph 112

RAN BLAKE (p), *see* Jeanne Lee

ART BLAKEY (d), *New Sounds* (disc split with James Moody sessions—*see* Moody; 1947, with Kenny Dorham, Walter Bishop a.o.), Blue Note 84436

————*A Night at Birdland, Vol. 1* (1954, with Clifford Brown, Lou Donaldson, Horace Silver, Curly Russell), Blue Note 46519 [cassette, 81521]

———— *1958–Paris Olympia* (with Lee Morgan, Benny Golson, Bobby Timmons, Jymie Merritt, includes live versions of the Blakey classics "Moanin'" and "Blues March"), PolyGram/Fontana 832 659

———— *Album of the Year* (1981, with Wynton Marsalis, Bobby Watson, Billy Pierce, James Williams, Charles Fambrough), MCA 33103 [Timeless 155]   *See also* Thelonious Monk, Herbie Nichols, Annie Ross, Jimmy Smith.

TERENCE BLANCHARD (tpt), *see* Donald Harrison

CARLA BLEY (p, org), with Paul Haines (lyrics), *Escalator Over the Hill* (1968–71, with Don Cherry, Michael Mantler, Enrico Rava, Sharon Freeman, Jimmy Knepper, Roswell Rudd, Howard Johnson, Perry Robinson, Jimmy Lyons, Gato Barbieri, Leroy Jenkins, John McLaughlin, Karl Berger, Don Preston, Jack Bruce, Charlie Haden, Paul Motian, Sheila Jordan, Jeanne Lee, Linda Ronstadt a.o.), ECM/JCOA 839 310

———— *Social Studies* (1980, with Mantler, Earl McIntyre, Joe Daley, Carlos Ward, Tony Dagradi, Steve Swallow a.o.), ECM 831 831   *See also* Charlie Haden, Hal Willner.

PAUL BLEY (p), *The Floater Syndrome* (1962–63, with Steve Swallow, Pete LaRoca; CD reissue of LPs *Floater* & *Syndrome*), Savoy 4427 [out of print]

JANE IRA BLOOM (ss), *Mighty Lights* (1982, with Fred Hersch, Charlie Haden, Ed Blackwell), Enja 79662

HAMIET BLUIETT (bars), *see* Kip Hanrahan, World Saxophone Quartet

ARTHUR BLYTHE (as), *In Concert* (1977, with Abdul Wadud, Bob Stewart a.o.; CD reissue of LPs *Metamorphosis* and *The Grip*), India Navigation 1029   *See also* Mose Allison, James Newton.

JEAN-PAUL BOURELLY (el g), *see* Miles Davis, Cassandra Wilson

JOSEPH BOWIE (tbn), *see* Ethnic Heritage Ensemble

LESTER BOWIE (tpt), *Works* (anthology, 1980–85, with Art Ensemble of Chicago, Brass Fantasy, includes Stanton Davis, Rasul Siddik, Vincent Chancey, Frank Lacy, Steve Turre, Bob Stewart, Phillip Wilson a.o.), ECM 837 274   *See also* Art Ensemble of Chicago, David Murray.

JOANNE BRACKEEN (p), *Special Identity* (1981, with Eddie Gomez, Jack DeJohnette), Antilles 422 848 813

RUBY BRAFF (cnt)/George Barnes (g), Quartet, *Salutes Rodgers and Hart,* (1974), Concord Jazz 6007

ANTHONY BRAXTON (rds, flt), *Live* (1975–76, with Kenny Wheeler, George Lewis, Dave Holland, Barry Altschul), RCA/Bluebird 6626

—————— *Creative Orchestra Music 1976* (with Jon Faddis, Leo Smith, Wheeler, Lewis, Roscoe Mitchell, Muhal Richard Abrams, Richard Teitelbaum, Holland, Altschul, Warren Smith, Phillip Wilson a.o.), RCA/Bluebird 6579

—————— *Composition 113* (1983, solo soprano sax), Sound Aspects 003

—————— *Prag 1984 (Quartet Performance)* (with Marilyn Crispell, John Lindberg, Gerry Hemingway), Sound Aspects 038   See also Derek Bailey, Globe Unity Orchestra, Dave Holland, Max Roach, Richard Teitelbaum.

MICHAEL BRECKER (ts), *see* John Abercrombie

WILLEM BREUKER (rds, ldr) Kollektief, *Parade* (1990–91, with Arjen Gorter, the Mondriaan Strings a.o.; includes arrs. of comps. by Erik Satie and Kurt Weill), BVHaast 9101   See also Berlin Contemporary Jazz Orchestra, Peter Brötzmann.

NICK BRIGNOLA (bars), *On a Different Level* (1989, with Kenny Barron, Dave Holland, Jack DeJohnette), Reservoir 112

BIG BILL BROONZY (g, vcl), *see* Collections: *Riverside History of Classic Jazz*

PETER BRÖTZMANN (ts, bars) Octet, *Machine Gun* (1968, with Willem Breuker, Evan Parker, Fred van Hove, Han Bennink, Peter Kowald a.o.; one of the most raw and extreme European free jazz recordings), FMP 24   See also Globe Unity Orchestra, Last Exit, Phil Minton.

CLIFFORD BROWN (tpt)/Max Roach (d), *Clifford Brown and Max Roach* (1954, quintet), PolyGram/EmArcy 814 645   See also Art Blakey, Dinah Washington.

MARION BROWN (as), *see* Archie Shepp

RAY BROWN (b), *see* Count Basie, Stephane Grappelli, Charlie Parker, Oscar Peterson, Sonny Rollins, Soprano Summit

DAVE BRUBECK (p), *Jazz at Oberlin* (1953, with Paul Desmond a.o.), Fantasy/OJC 046

—————— *Time Out* (1959, with Desmond, Eugene Wright, Joe Morello), Columbia 40585

JACK BRUCE (el b, vcl), *see* Carla Bley, Mark Nauseef

BILL BRUFORD (d, perc), *Feels Good to Me* (1977, with Kenny Wheeler, Allan Holdsworth, Jeff Berlin a.o.), E.G. 33/Caroline 1524

JANE BUNNETT (ss, flts)/Don Pullen (p), *New York Duets* (1989), Music & Arts 629

KENNY BURRELL (g), *see* Mose Allison, Donald Byrd, Billie Holiday

GARY BURTON (vib, mba), *see* Ralph Towner, Collections: *Jazz Club: Vibraphone*

DON BYAS (ts), *Don Byas On Blue Star* (1947–52, with Billy Taylor a.o.), PolyGram/EmArcy 833 405   *See also* Oscar Pettiford, Joe Turner, Collections: *Jazz Club: Tenor Sax.*

DONALD BYRD (tpt)/Kenny Burrell (g), *All Night Long* (1956, with Jerome Richardson, Hank Mobley, Mal Waldron, Doug Watkins, Art Taylor), Fantasy/OJC 427   *See also* Dexter Gordon.

BENNY CARTER (as, tpt, ldr), *Benny Carter/ 1933* (with Max Kaminsky, J. C. Higginbotham, Chu Berry, Wayman Carver, Teddy Wilson, Sid Catlett a.o.; includes "Symphony in Riffs," "Lonesome Nights"), Prestige 7643 [LP]

BENNY CARTER/AMERICAN JAZZ ORCHESTRA, *Central City Sketches* (1987, with Eddie Bert, Jimmy Knepper, John Purcell, Lew Tabackin, John Lewis, Ron Carter, Mel Lewis a.o.; includes "Symphony in Riffs," "Lonesome Nights"), Musicmasters 60126   *See also* Ella Fitzgerald, Lionel Hampton, Billie Holiday, McKinney's Cotton Pickers, Ben Webster, Collections: *Three Great Swing Saxophones.*

BETTY CARTER (vcl), *Look What I Got!* (c. 1986, with Don Braden, Benny Green, Winard Harper a.o.), Verve 835 661   *See also* King Pleasure.

JOHN CARTER (cl), *Fields* (1988, with Bobby Bradford, Benny Powell, Marty Ehrlich, Terry Jenoure, Don Preston, Fred Hopkins, Andrew Cyrille), Gramavision 79425   *See also* Clarinet Summit.

RON CARTER (b), *see* Benny Carter, Miles Davis, Gil Evans, Herbie Hancock, Kronos Quartet, Pharoah Sanders, Stanley Turrentine

WAYMAN CARVER (as, ts, flt), *see* Benny Carter, Ella Fitzgerald, Chick Webb

SID CATLETT (d), *see* Louis Armstrong, Sidney Bechet, Chu Berry, Benny Carter, Benny Goodman, Billie Holiday

SERGE CHALOFF (bars), *The Fable of Mabel* (1954, with Charlie Mariano, Dick Twardzik, Jimmy Woode a.o.), Black Lion 760923   *See also* Buddy DeFranco, Woody Herman.

PAUL CHAMBERS (b), *see* Miles Davis, Benny Golson, Dexter Gordon, J. J. Johnson, Wes Montgomery, Oliver Nelson

VINCENT CHANCEY (fr hn), *see* Lester Bowie

DON CHERRY (tpt), *Complete Communion* (1965, with Gato Barbieri, Henry Grimes, Ed Blackwell), Blue Note 84226 [LP, out of print]   *See also* Bengt Berger, Carla Bley, Codona, Ornette Coleman, Trilok Gurtu, Charlie Haden, Jazz Composers Orchestra, Sun Ra.

CHARLIE CHRISTIAN (el g), *The Genius of the Electric Guitar* (1939–41, with Cootie Williams, Benny Goodman, Lionel Hampton, Fletcher Henderson, Dave Tough, Jo Jones a.o.), Columbia 40846   *See also* Dizzy Gillespie.

CL-4 (clarinet quartet), *Seltsam ist Propheten Lied* (1987: Theo Jorgensmann, Dieter Kuhr, Gerald Doecke, Eckart Koltermann), Konnex 5399 [LP]

CLARINET SUMMIT (quartet), *In Concert at the Public Theatre* (1981: Alvin Batiste, John Carter, Jimmy Hamilton, David Murray), India Navigation 1062

SONNY CLARK (p), *see* Dexter Gordon, Jackie McLean, Howard Rumsey

KENNY CLARKE (d), *see* Sidney Bechet, Miles Davis, Dexter Gordon, Milt Jackson, King Pleasure, Fats Navarro, Charlie Parker, Oscar Pettiford, Collections: *The Bebop Revolution*

JAY CLAYTON (vcl), *see* Vocal Summit

CODONA (trio), *Codona* (1978: Don Cherry, Nana Vasconcelos, Collin Walcott), ECM 829 371

AL COHN (ts) featuring Zoot Sims (ts), *Al and Zoot* (1957, with Mose Allison a.o.), MCA 31372   *See also* Maynard Ferguson, Woody Herman, Buddy Rich, Collections: *Jazz Club: Tenor Sax.*

NAT KING COLE (p, vcl), *Hit That Jive, Jack: The Earliest Recordings 1940–41* (with Oscar Moore, Wesley Prince; in fact, not the trio's earliest recordings, but never mind), MCA/Decca 42350

ORNETTE COLEMAN (as), *The Shape of Jazz to Come* (1959, with Don Cherry, Charlie Haden, Billy Higgins), Atlantic 1317

———— *Free Jazz* (1960, with Cherry, Freddie Hubbard, Eric Dolphy, Haden, Scott LaFaro, Higgins, Ed Blackwell), Atlantic 1364

————— *At the "Golden Circle" Stockholm, Vol. 1* (1965, with David Izenzon, Charles Moffett), Blue Note 84224

————— *New York Is Now* (1968, with Dewey Redman, Jimmy Garrison, Elvin Jones; 1 track with Coleman, vln), Blue Note 84287

————— *Dancing in Your Head* (1973 and 1976, with Robert Palmer [cl], Charles Ellerbee, Bern Nix, Jamaaladeen Tacuma [listed as Rudy McDaniel], Ronald Shannon Jackson, the Master Musicians of Joujouka, Morocco), A&M 75021 0807 *See also* Pat Metheny.

STEVE COLEMAN (as), *see* Dave Holland, Strata Institute, Cassandra Wilson

BUDDY COLLETTE (as, flts), *see* Barney Kessel, Buddy Rich, Howard Rumsey

JOHN COLTRANE (ts, ss), *Olé Coltrane* (1961, with Freddie Hubbard, Eric Dolphy [listed as George Lane], McCoy Tyner, Art Davis, Reggie Workman, Elvin Jones), Atlantic 1373

————— *John Coltrane and Johnny Hartman* (1963, with Tyner, Jimmy Garrison, Jones), MCA 5661

————— *A Love Supreme* (1964, with Tyner, Garrison, Jones), MCA 5660

————— *Live at the Village Vanguard Again* (1966, with Pharoah Sanders, Alice Coltrane, Garrison, Rashied Ali; includes Garrison's "flamenco" bass solo), Impulse 9124 [LP, out of print] *See also* Miles Davis, Thelonious Monk, Collections: *Jazz Club: Tenor Sax.*

EDDIE CONDON (g), *Jammin' at Commodore* (disc split with Bud Freeman session—*see* Freeman; 1938, with Bobby Hackett, George Brunies, Jack Teagarden, Pee Wee Russell, Freeman, Joe Bushkin, Jess Stacy, Lionel Hampton [d], George Wettling a.o.), Commodore 7007.

————— *The Definitive Eddie Condon and His Jazz Concert All-Stars, Vol. 1* (1944, with Hackett, Hot Lips Page, Muggsy Spanier, Benny Morton, Edmond Hall, Russell, Stacy, Bob Haggart, Wettling, Lee Wiley a.o.), Stash 530 *See also* Bud Freeman, Fats Waller, Collections: *At the Jazz Band Ball, Riverside History of Classic Jazz.*

TOM CORA (cel), *Gumption in Limbo* (1990, solo), Sound Aspects 042 *See also* David Moss.

CHICK COREA (p, el p, syn), *Piano Improvisations, Vol. 2* (1971), ECM 829 190

————— *Return to Forever* (1973, with Joe Farrell, Stanley Clarke, Airto, Flora Purim), ECM 811 978

———— *Akoustic Band* (1989, with John Patitucci, Dave Weckl), GRP 9582   *See also* Miles Davis, Wayne Shorter.

LARRY CORYELL (g), *The Essential Larry Coryell* (1968–74, with Randy Brecker, John McLaughlin, Ralph Towner, Glen Moore, Chuck Rainey, Miroslav Vitous, Billy Cobham, Elvin Jones, Alphonse Mouzon, Collin Walcott a.o.), Vanguard 75/76   *See also* Jazz Composers Orchestra.

IDA COX (vcl), *see* Collections: *Riverside History of Classic Jazz*

MARILYN CRISPELL (p), *Circles* (1990, with Oliver Lake, Peter Buettner, Reggie Workman, Gerry Hemingway), Victo 012   *See also* Anthony Braxton.

ANDREW CYRILLE (d), *see* Muhal Richard Abrams, John Carter, Charlie Haden, Leroy Jenkins

TADD DAMERON (p, arr), *see* Fats Navarro

EDDIE DANIELS (cl), . . . *This Is Now* (1990, with Billy Childs a.o.), GRP 9635

KENNY DAVERN (ss, cl), *see* Soprano Summit

ANTHONY DAVIS (p), *Hemispheres* (1983, with Leo Smith, George Lewis [tbn], J. D. Parran, David Samuels, Rick Rozie, Pheeroan akLaff a.o.), Gramavision 79428   *See also* Ray Anderson, Leroy Jenkins, David Murray.

WILD BILL DAVIS (org), *see* Duke Ellington, Johnny Hodges

EDDIE "LOCKJAW" DAVIS (ts), *Griff & Lock* (1960, with Junior Mance a.o.), Fantasy/OJC 264 [LP]   *See also* Collections: *Jazz Club: Tenor Sax.*

MILES DAVIS (tpt), *Birth of the Cool* (1949–50, with Lee Konitz, J. J. Johnson, Kai Winding, Gerry Mulligan, John Lewis, Kenny Clarke, Max Roach a.o.; includes arrs. by Gil Evans, Lewis, Mulligan), Capitol 92862

———— *Kind of Blue* (1959, with Cannonball Adderley, John Coltrane, Bill Evans, Wynton Kelly, Paul Chambers, Jimmy Cobb), Columbia 40579

———— *Sketches of Spain* (1959–60, arr. by Gil Evans), Columbia 40578

———— *Nefertiti* (1967, with Wayne Shorter, Herbie Hancock, Ron Carter, Tony Williams), Columbia 46113

———— *Bitches Brew* (1969, with Shorter, Benny Maupin, Chick Corea, Larry Young [el p], Joe Zawinul, John McLaughlin, Dave Holland, Jack DeJohnette, Lenny White a.o.), Columbia 40577

——— *Aura* (1984, with Palle Mikkelborg, McLaughlin, Niels-Henning Ørsted Pedersen, Bo Stieff, Marilyn Mazur a.o.), Columbia 45332

——— *Amandla* (1989, with Kenny Garrett, George Duke, Jean-Paul Bourelly, Marcus Miller, Al Foster, Omar Hakim, Don Alias a.o.), Warner Brothers 25873   *See also* Charlie Parker, Sarah Vaughan.

BUDDY DEFRANCO (cl), *Crosscurrents* (disc split with Bill Harris and Lennie Tristano sessions—*see* Harris, Tristano; 1949, with Earl Swope, Al Cohn, Serge Chaloff, Teddy Charles, Jimmy Raney, Oscar Pettiford, Max Roach a.o.), Capitol 11060 [LP, out of print]   *See also* Terry Gibbs, Art Tatum, Mel Tormé.

JACK DEJOHNETTE (d, p, kbds), *Album Album* (1984, with David Murray, John Purcell, Howard Johnson, Rufus Reid), ECM 823 467   *See also* Joanne Brackeen, Nick Brignola, Miles Davis, Keith Jarrett, Pat Metheny, Wayne Shorter, Joe Zawinul.

PACO DE LUCIA (g), *see* John McLaughlin

PAUL DESMOND (as), *see* Dave Brubeck

AL DI MEOLA (g), *see* John McLaughlin

DIRTY DOZEN BRASS BAND (octet), *Voodoo* (1987, with Dizzy Gillespie, Branford Marsalis, Dr. John), Columbia 45042

BABY DODDS (d), *see* Louis Armstrong, Sidney Bechet, Johnny Dodds, Earl Hines, Jelly Roll Morton, King Oliver

JOHNNY DODDS (cl), *South Side Chicago Jazz* (1927–29, with Louis Armstrong, Barney Bigard, Lil Hardin, Earl Hines, Baby Dodds a.o.), MCA/Decca 42326   *See also* Louis Armstrong, Jelly Roll Morton, King Oliver.

ERIC DOLPHY (as, b cl, flt), *Out to Lunch* (1964, with Freddie Hubbard, Bobby Hutcherson, Richard Davis, Tony Williams), Blue Note 84163   *See also* Ornette Coleman, John Coltrane, Andrew Hill, Charles Mingus, Oliver Nelson, George Russell.

KENNY DORHAM (tpt), *see* Art Blakey, Benny Golson, Andrew Hill

PIERRE DØRGE (g, ldr), New Jungle Orchestra, *Even the Moon Is Dancing* (1985, with Harry Beckett, John Tchicai, Johnny Dyani, Marilyn Mazur a.o.), SteepleChase 1208

RAY DRAPER (tba), *see* Max Roach

MARK DRESSER (b), *see* Ray Anderson, Arcado, Tim Berne

PAQUITO D'RIVERA (as, cl), *see* Dizzy Gillespie, Daniel Ponce

RAY DRUMMOND (b), *see* Ricky Ford, Wayne Horvitz, The Jazztet

URSULA DUDZIAK (vcl), *see* Vocal Summit

BILLY ECKSTINE (vcl), *see* Dizzy Gillespie, Earl Hines, George Shearing

MARTY EHRLICH (rds, flt), *see* Muhal Richard Abrams, John Carter

ROY ELDRIDGE (tpt, vcl), *see* Mildred Bailey, Chu Berry, Fletcher Henderson, Billie Holiday, Gene Krupa, Artie Shaw

DUKE ELLINGTON (p, ldr), *The Brunswick Era, Vol. 1 (1926–1929)* (with Bubber Miley, Arthur Whetsol, Joe Nanton, Barney Bigard, Otto Hardwick, Johnny Hodges [as,ss], Harry Carney, Sonny Greer a.o.; includes "East St. Louis Toodle-Oo," "Jubilee Stomp," "Birmingham Breakdown," "Black and Tan Fantasy"), MCA/ Decca 42325

———— *The Great Ellington Units* (1940–41; dates led by Bigard, Hodges, Rex Stewart, with Ray Nance, Cootie Williams, Lawrence Brown, Juan Tizol, Ben Webster, Billy Strayhorn, Jimmy Blanton, Greer), RCA/Bluebird 6751

———— *The Blanton/Webster Band* (1940–42), with Williams, Stewart, Nanton, Brown, Tizol, Bigard, Hodges, Hardwick, Webster, Carney, Ellington, Ivie Anderson a.o.; includes "Concerto for Cootie," "Cotton Tail," "A Portrait of Bert Williams," "Sepia Panorama," "The Flaming Sword"), RCA/Bluebird 5659

———— Ellington/Strayhorn, *Piano Duets: Great Times!* (1950, with Oscar Pettiford [cel], Jo Jones a.o.), Fantasy/OJC 108

———— *At Newport* (1956, with Cat Anderson, Nance, Clark Terry, Jimmy Hamilton, Russell Procope, Hodges, Paul Gonsalves, Carney, Jimmy Woode, Sam Woodyard a.o.) Columbia 40587

———— *The New Orleans Suite* (1970, with Cat Anderson, Williams, Hodges [1 session only], Procope, Gonsalves, Carney, Wild Bill Davis [1 track] a.o.), Atlantic 1580

DON ELLIS (tpt, ldr), *Electric Bath* (c. 1968, includes odd-meter and quarter-tone music), Columbia 9585 [LP, out of print]   *See also* George Russell.

KAHIL EL'ZABAR (perc, vcl), *see* Ethnic Heritage Ensemble, Edward Wilkerson

JAMES EMERY (g), *see* String Trio of New York

BOOKER ERVIN (ts), *see* Charles Mingus, Collections: *Jazz Club: Tenor Sax*

ETHNIC HERITAGE ENSEMBLE (trio), *Ancestral Song* (1987: Edward Wilkerson, Joseph Bowie, Kahil El'Zabar), Silkheart 108

KEVIN EUBANKS (g, el g), *see* Oliver Lake, Dianne Reeves

ROBIN EUBANKS (tbn), *see* Dave Holland

BILL EVANS (p), *Sunday at the Village Vanguard* (1961, with Scott LaFaro, Paul Motian), Fantasy/OJC 140

——— *Since We Met* (1974, with Eddie Gomez, Marty Morell), Fantasy/OJC 622   *See also* Miles Davis, J. J. Johnson, Oliver Nelson.

GIL EVANS (p, el p, arr, ldr), *Out of the Cool* (1961, with Johnny Coles, Jimmy Knepper, Budd Johnson, Ron Carter, Elvin Jones, Charli Persip), MCA/Impulse 5653

——— *Live at Sweet Basil, Vol. 1* (1984, with Lew Soloff, Hannibal Marvin Peterson, Tom Malone, Chris Hunter, George Adams, Howard Johnson, Hiram Bullock, Pete Levin, Mark Egan, Adam Nussbaum a.o.), Gramavision 79442   *See also* Miles Davis, Helen Merrill, Claude Thornhill.

TAL FARLOW (el g), *see* Red Norvo

ART FARMER (flgh), *Something to Live For: The Music of Billy Strayhorn* (1987, with Clifford Jordan, James Williams, Rufus Reid, Marvin "Smitty" Smith), Contemporary 14029   *See also* The Jazztet.

JOE FARRELL (ts, ss, flt), *see* Chick Corea, Pat Martino, Collections: *Jazz Club: Tenor Sax*

MARK FELDMAN (vln), *see* Arcado, Tim Berne

MAYNARD FERGUSON (tpt, ldr), *The Birdland Dreamband* (1956, with Ernie Royal, Eddie Bert, Jimmy Cleveland, Herb Geller, Al Cohn, Budd Johnson, Ernie Wilkins, Hank Jones, Milt Hinton, Osie Johnson a.o.), RCA/Bluebird 6455   *See also* Ben Webster.

ELLA FITZGERALD (vcl), *1937–1938* (with Mario Bauza, Taft Jordan, Louis Jordan, Wayman Carver [ts], Chick Webb a.o.; includes "A-Tisket A-Tasket"), Classics 506

——— *The Harold Arlen Songbook, Vol. 1* (1960–61, with Benny Carter a.o.), Verve 817 527

——— *Clap Hands, Here Comes Charlie!* (1961, with Herb Ellis, Gus Johnson a.o.), Verve 835 646   *See also* Benny Goodman.

FIVE VOICES (a cappella quintet), *Direct Sound* (1989: Greetje Bijma, Shelley Hirsch, Anna Homler, David Moss, Carles Santos), Intakt 015

TOMMY FLANAGAN (p)/Hank Jones (p), *Our Delights* (1978, duo), Galaxy 5113   *See also* Pepper Adams, Gene Ammons, Lambert, Hendricks & Ross, Sonny Rollins.

RICKY FORD (ts), *Saxotic Stomp* (1987, with James Spaulding, Charles Davis, Kirk Lightsey, Ray Drummond, Jimmy Cobb), Muse 5349

AL FOSTER (d), *see* George Adams, Miles Davis, Adam Makowicz, Carmen McRae

POPS FOSTER (b), *see* Jelly Roll Morton

BUD FREEMAN (ts), *Jammin' at Commodore* (disc split with Eddie Condon sessions—see Condon; 1938, with Bobby Hackett, Pee Wee Russell, Jess Stacy, Condon, Dave Tough a.o.), Commodore 7007   *See also* Eddie Condon, Jack Teagarden, Collections: *At the Jazz Band Ball.*

CHICO FREEMAN (ts), *Spirit Sensitive* (1979, with John Hicks, Cecil McBee, Billy Hart, Don Moye), India Navigation 1045

SHARON FREEMAN (fr hn, p), *see* Carla Bley, Hal Willner

DAVID FRIEDMAN (vib, mba), *see* Bob Moses, Wayne Shorter

BILL FRISELL (el g, g syn, banjo), *Lookout for Hope* (1987, with Hank Robert a.o.), ECM 833 495   *See also* Marc Johnson, Bob Moses, Paul Motian, Power Tools, Hal Willner, John Zorn.

FRED FRITH (el g, misc instr)/Rene Lussier (el g, misc instr), *Nous Autres* (1986), Victo 01   *See also* David Moss, John Zorn.

WOLFGANG FUCHS (ss, b cl, contrab cl)/Hans Koch (ss, ts, b cl)/Evan Parker (ss, ts)/Louis Sclavis (cl, b cl, ss), *Duets, Dithyrambisch* (1989, excellent set of detailed, spirited, free-improvised duets), FMP 19/20

CURTIS FULLER (tbn), *see* The Jazztet

DIAMANDA GALAS (vcl), *see* John Zorn

THE GANELIN TRIO, *Non Troppo* (1982: Vyacheslav Ganelin, Vyacheslav Chekasin, Vladimir Tarasov), Hat Art 6059

JAN GARBAREK (ts, ss)/Bobo Stenson (p), *Witchi-Tai-To* (1973, with Palle Danielsson, Jon Christensen), ECM 833 330   *See also* Charlie Haden, Keith Jarrett.

ERROLL GARNER (p), *Concert by the Sea* (1955, with Denzil Best, Eddie Calhoun), Columbia 40589   *See also* Charlie Parker.

STAN GETZ (ts), *Jazz Samba* (1962, with Charlie Byrd a.o.), Verve 810 061

—— *Dynasty* (1971, with Eddy Louiss, René Thomas, Bernard Lubat), Verve 839 118

—— *Anniversary* (1987, with Kenny Barron, Rufus Reid, Victor Lewis), EmArcy 838 769   *See also* Woody Herman, Collections: *Jazz Club: Tenor Sax.*

TERRY GIBBS (vib)/Buddy DeFranco (cl), *Chicago Fire* (1987), Contemporary 14036   *See also* Collections: *Jazz Club: Vibraphone.*

DIZZY GILLESPIE (tpt, ldr), *The Development of an American Artist, 1940–1946* (with Cab Calloway, Billy Eckstine, Coleman Hawkins, Les Hite, Lucky Millinder, Boyd Raeburn & their orchs., Don Byas, Lucky Thompson, Milt Jackson, Charlie Christian, Ray Brown, Oscar Pettiford, Kenny Clarke, Sarah Vaughan a.o.), Smithsonian Collection of Recordings R004 [2 LP-set; mail-order only, P.O. Box 207, Colchester VT 05449–2071]

—— *Live at the Royal Festival Hall* (1989, with Claudio Roditi, Arturo Sandoval, Slide Hampton, Steve Turre, Paquito D'Rivera, James Moody, Ignacio Berroa, Airto Moreira, Flora Purim a.o.), Enja 79658   *See also* Dirty Dozen Brass Band, Lionel Hampton, Charlie Parker, Collections: *Afro-Cuban Jazz, The Bebop Revolution.*

EGBERTO GISMONTI (g, p), *see* Charlie Haden

JIMMY GIUFFRE (cl, ts, bars), *The Jimmy Giuffre 3* (1956, with Jim Hall, Ralph Peña), Atlantic 90981   *See also* Woody Herman, Shorty Rogers.

GLOBE UNITY ORCHESTRA (free-jazz big band), *Pearls* (1975 and 1977, with Enrico Rava, Manfred Schoof, Kenny Wheeler, Günter Christmann, Albert Mangelsdorff, Paul Rutherford, Anthony Braxton, Peter Brötzmann, Rüdiger Carl, Gerd Dudek, Evan Parker, Michel Pilz, Alexander von Schlippenbach, Peter Kowald, Buschi Niebergall, Paul Lovens), FMP 0380 [LP]

BENNY GOLSON (ts), *Modern Touch* (1957, with Kenny Dorham, J. J. Johnson, Wynton Kelly, Paul Chambers, Max Roach; includes "Out of the Past"), Riverside 6070 [LP, out of print]   *See also* Art Blakey, The Jazztet.

EDDIE GOMEZ (b), *see* Joanne Brackeen, Bill Evans

JERRY GONZALEZ (tpt, flgh, perc), *Rumba Para Monk* (1988–89, with Carter Jefferson, Larry Willis a.o.; includes Afro-Cuban arrs. of Thelonious Monk comps.), Sunnyside 1036

BENNY GOODMAN (cl, ldr), *Trio and Quartet Sessions, Vol. 1—After You've Gone* (1935–36, with Teddy Wilson, Lionel Hampton, Gene Krupa, Helen Ward), RCA/Bluebird 5631

—— *Sing, Sing, Sing* (1935–38, with Bunny Berrigan, Ziggy Elman, Harry James, Vido Musso, Jess Stacy, Krupa, Ella Fitzgerald, Ward a.o.; includes arrs. by Count Basie, Fletcher Henderson, Jimmy Mundy, Mary Lou Williams), RCA/Bluebird 5630

—— *Roll 'Em* (1937–39, with James, Elman, Musso, Henderson, Stacy, Krupa, Mildred Bailey a.o.; includes arrs. by Henderson, Mundy, Williams), Columbia 40588

—— *Clarinet a la King* (1939–41, with Billy Butterfield, Elman, Cootie Williams, Georgie Auld, Johnny Guarnieri, Henderson, Mel Powell, Wilson, Sid Catlett, Jo Jones, Peggy Lee a.o.; includes title track, "Superman" and arrs. by Henderson, Mundy, Powell, Eddie Sauter), Columbia 40834   *See also* Billie Holiday, Bessie Smith, Jack Teagarden.

DEXTER GORDON (ts)/Wardell Gray (ts), *The Chase* (1947), Spotlite 130 [LP]

—— *Ballads* (1962–65 and 1978, with Donald Byrd, Freddie Hubbard, Sonny Clark, Kenny Drew, Barry Harris, Horace Parlan, Bud Powell, Paul Chambers, Niels-Henning Ørsted Pedersen, Kenny Clarke, Billy Higgins, Philly Joe Jones, Art Taylor a.o.), Blue Note 96579

—— *Homecoming: Live at the Village Vanguard* (1976, with Woody Shaw, Ronnie Mathews, Stafford James, Louis Hayes), Columbia 46824   *See also* Lionel Hampton, Fats Navarro, Charlie Parker, Collections: *Jazz Club: Tenor Sax.*

STEPHANE GRAPPELLI (vln)/Stuff Smith (vln), *Violins No End* (1957, with Oscar Peterson, Herb Ellis, Ray Brown, Jo Jones), Pablo 2310 907   *See also* Django Reinhardt, Collections: *Jazz Club: Violin.*

WARDELL GRAY (ts), *see* Dexter Gordon, Charlie Parker, Collections: *Jazz Club: Tenor Sax.*

CHARLIE GREEN (tbn), *see* Louis Armstrong, Fletcher Henderson, Bessie Smith

FREDDIE GREEN (g), *see* Count Basie, Billie Holiday, Lambert, Hendricks & Ross, Diane Schuur, Sarah Vaughan, Lester Young

JOHNNY GRIFFIN (ts), *see* Eddie "Lockjaw" Davis, Wes Montgomery, Collections: *Jazz Club: Tenor Sax.*

TRILOK GURTU (perc, vcl), *Usfret* (1987–88, with Don Cherry, L. Shankar, Ralph Towner, Jonas Hellborg a.o.), CMP 33   *See also* Mark Nauseef, Oregon.

CHARLIE HADEN (b, ldr), *Liberation Music Orchestra* (1969, with Don Cherry, Roswell Rudd, Gato Barbieri, Dewey Redman, Howard Johnson, Carla Bley, Andrew Cyrille, Paul Motian a.o.), MCA/Impulse 39125

———— Haden/Jan Garbarek (ts, ss)/Egberto Gismonti (g, p), *Magico* (1979), ECM 823 474

———— Haden/Paul Motian (d), feat. Geri Allen (p), *Etudes* (1987), Soul Note 121 162

———— *Silence* (1987, with Chet Baker, Enrico Pieranunzi, Billy Higgins), Soul Note 121 172   *See also* Carla Bley, Jane Ira Bloom, Ornette Coleman, Adam Makovicz, John McLaughlin, Pat Metheny, Hal Willner.

JIM HALL (el g), *see* Jimmy Giuffre, Lee Konitz, Lambert, Hendricks & Ross, Sonny Stitt

JIMMY HAMILTON (cl, ts), *see* Clarinet Summit, Duke Ellington

SCOTT HAMILTON (ts), *Radio City* (1990, with Connie Kay a.o.), Concord Jazz 4428

LIONEL HAMPTON (vib, p, vcl, ldr), *Hot Mallets* (1937–39, small-group sessions, with Ziggy Elman, Dizzy Gillespie, Harry James, Rex Stewart, Cootie Williams, Lawrence Brown, Buster Bailey, Mezz Mezzrow, Vido Musso, Benny Carter, Johnny Hodges, Chu Berry, Herschel Evans, Coleman Hawkins, Budd Johnson, Ben Webster, Harry Carney, Clyde Hart, Billy Kyle, Jess Stacy, Danny Barker, Charlie Christian, Milt Hinton, John Kirby, Cozy Cole, Sonny Greer, Jo Jones a.o.), RCA/Bluebird 6458

———— *Flying Home 1942–1945* (with Ernie Royal, Earl Bostic, Arnett Cobb, Dexter Gordon, Illinois Jacquet, Al Sears, Charlie Fowlkes, Milt Buckner a.o.), MCA/Decca 42349   *See also* Louis Armstrong, Charlie Christian, Eddie Condon, Benny Goodman, Illinois Jacquet.

HERBIE HANCOCK (p, syn), *Maiden Voyage* (1965, with Freddie Hubbard, George Coleman, Ron Carter, Tony Williams), Blue Note 84195

———— *The Quintet: V.S.O.P. Live* (1976, with Hubbard, Wayne Shorter, Carter, Williams), Columbia 34976

———— *Future Shock* (1983, with Bill Laswell, Daniel Ponce a.o.; including "Rockit"), Columbia 38814   *See also* Miles Davis, Wynton Marsalis, Jaco Pastorius, Wayne Shorter, Joe Zawinul.

KIP HANRAHAN (producer), *Cab Calloway Stands in for the Moon* (1987–88, with Olu Dara, Eddie Harris, David Murray, Hamiet Bluiett, Don Pullen, Steve Swallow, Ishmael Reed a.o.), American Clave 1015

BILL HARRIS (tbn), *Crosscurrents* (disc split with Buddy DeFranco and Lennie Tristano sessions—*see* DeFranco, Tristano; 1949, 1 track with Shelly Manne a.o.), Capitol 11060 [LP, out of print]   *See also* Woody Herman.

CRAIG HARRIS (tbn, didgeridu) and Tailgaters Tales, *Shelter* (1986, with Don Byron, Anthony Cox, Pheeroan akLaff a.o.), JMT 870 008

DONALD HARRISON (as, ss, C-melody s)/Terence Blanchard (tpt), *Black Pearl* (1988, with Reginald Veal, Carl Allen a.o.), Columbia 44216

BILLY HART (d), *see* Chico Freeman, James Newton, Pharoah Sanders, Joe Zawinul

JON HASSELL (tpt), *Power Spot* (1983–84, with Brain Eno, J.A. Deane a.o.), ECM 828 466.

COLEMAN HAWKINS (ts), *Classic Tenors* (disc split with Lester Young session—*see* Young; 1943, with Ellis Larkins, Oscar Pettiford, Shelly Manne a.o.), Signature 38446   *See also* Mildred Bailey, Dizzy Gillespie, Lionel Hampton, Fletcher Henderson, McKinney's Cotton Pickers, Thelonious Monk, Max Roach, Pee Wee Russell, Bessie Smith, Collections: *The Bebop Revolution, Esquire's All-American Hot Jazz Sessions, Three Great Swing Saxophones, Jazz Club: Tenor Sax.*

MARK HELIAS (b), *The Current Set* (1987, with Herb Robertson, Robin Eubanks, Greg Osby, Tim Berne, Victor Lewis, Nana Vasconcelos), Enja [German] 5041   *See also* Bass-Drum-Bone.

JONAS HELLBORG (b), *see* Trilok Gurtu

GERRY HEMINGWAY (d, perc), *see* Bass-Drum-Bone, Anthony Braxton, Marilyn Crispell

JULIUS HEMPHILL (as, flt), *Dogon A.D.* (1972, with Baikida Carroll, Abdul Wadud, Phillip Wilson), Arista/Freedom 1028 [LP, out of print]   *See also* World Saxophone Quartet.

FLETCHER HENDERSON (p, ldr), *Hocus Pocus* (1927–36, with Henry "Red" Allen, Tommy Ladnier, Joe Smith, Rex Stewart, Charlie Green, Jimmy Harrison, J. C. Higginbotham, Benny Morton, Russell Procope, Coleman Hawkins, John Kirby a.o.; includes "Singin' the Blues," "Sugar Foot Stomp," "Variety Stomp," "St. Louis Shuffle"), RCA/Bluebird 9904   *See also* Charlie Christian, Benny Goodman, Bessie Smith.

JOE HENDERSON (ts), *Inner Urge* (1964, with McCoy Tyner, Bob Cranshaw, Elvin Jones), Blue Note 84189 *See also* Andrew Hill, Lee Konitz, Lee Morgan, Larry Young, Collections: *Jazz Club: Tenor Sax.*

JON HENDRICKS (vcl), *see* King Pleasure, Lambert, Hendricks & Ross

WOODY HERMAN (cl, as, vcl, ldr), *The Thundering Herds 1945–1947* (with Pete Candoli, Shorty Rogers, Bill Harris, John LaPorta, Herbie Steward, Stan Getz, Flip Phillips, Zoot Sims, Serge Chaloff, Jimmy Rowles, Red Norvo, Billy Bauer, Chubby Jackson, Don Lamond, Buddy Rich, Dave Tough a.o.; includes "Woodchopper's Ball" [remake], "Four Brothers," "Bijou"), Columbia 44108 *See also* Mel Tormé.

J. C. HIGGINBOTHAM (tbn), *see* Benny Carter, Fletcher Henderson, Jelly Roll Morton

BILLY HIGGINS (d), *see* Ornette Coleman, Dexter Gordon, Charlie Haden, Hank Jones, Lee Morgan, Art Pepper

ANDREW HILL (p), *Point of Departure* (1967, with Kenny Dorham, Eric Dolphy, Joe Henderson, Richard Davis, Tony Williams), Blue Note 84167

EARL HINES (p, ldr), *Piano Man* (1939–42, with Sidney Bechet, Baby Dodds, Billy Eckstine [1 track each], Omer Simeon, Budd Johnson a.o.; most sides with orchestra), RCA/Bluebird 6750

———— *Up to Date* (1964, with Ray Nance, Johnson a.o.: trio and quartet), RCA/Bluebird 6462

———— *Earl Hines Plays Duke Ellington* (1971–75, terrific, solo), New World 361/362 *See also* Louis Armstrong, Sidney Bechet, Johnny Dodds.

MILT HINTON (b), *see* Maynard Ferguson, Lionel Hampton, Pee Wee Russell, Ben Webster

JOHNNY HODGES (as)/Wild Bill Davis (org), *In a Mellotone* (1966, with Lawrence Brown, Bobby Durham a.o.), RCA/Bluebird 2305 *See also* Duke Ellington, Lionel Hampton, Billie Holiday.

ART HODES (p), *see* Collections: *Riverside History of Classic Jazz*

JAY HOGGARD (vib), *The Little Tiger* (1990, with Benny Green a.o.), Muse 5410 *See also* James Newton.

ALLAN HOLDSWORTH (el g), *I.O.U.* (1981), Enigma 73252 *See also* Bill Bruford.

BILLIE HOLIDAY (vcl), *The Quintessential Billie Holiday, Vol. 1, (1933–1935)* (with Roy Eldridge, Jack Teagarden, Benny Goodman, Johnny Hodges, Ben Webster, Joe

Sullivan, Teddy Wilson, John Kirby, Cozy Cole, Gene Krupa a.o.; includes "What a Little Moonlight Can Do"), Columbia 40646

———— *The Quintessential Billie Holiday, Vol. 4 (1937),* (with Buck Clayton, Cootie Williams, Buster Bailey, Edmond Hall, Hodges, Lester Young, Harry Carney, Wilson, Freddie Green, Kirby, Walter Page, Cole, Jo Jones a.o.; includes "Easy Living," "Me, Myself and I"), Columbia 44252

———— *The Quintessential Billie Holiday, Vol. 9 (1940–1942)* (with Eldridge, Jimmy Hamilton, Benny Carter, Wilson, Young a.o.; includes "Mandy Is Two"), Columbia 47031

———— *Lady Day* (1939 and 1944, with Frankie Newton, Vic Dickenson, Sid Catlett a.o.; includes "Strange Fruit"), Commodore 7001

———— *Lady Sings the Blues* (1954 and 1956, with Harry "Sweets" Edison, Charlie Shavers, Tony Scott, Paul Quinichette, Wynton Kelly, Kenny Burrell, Barney Kessel, Red Callendar, Chico Hamilton a.o.), Verve 833 770

DAVE HOLLAND (b), *Conference of the Birds* (1972, with Anthony Braxton, Sam Rivers, Barry Altschul), ECM 829 373

———— *The Razor's Edge* (1987, with Kenny Wheeler, Robin Eubanks, Steve Coleman, Marvin "Smitty" Smith), ECM 833 048   *See also* Anthony Braxton, Nick Brignola, Miles Davis, Hank Jones, Adam Makowicz.

JOHN LEE HOOKER (g, vcl), *John Lee Hooker Sings the Blues: That's My Story* (1960, with Sam Jones, Louis Hayes), Fantasy/OBC 538

FRED HOPKINS (b), *see* Muhal Richard Abrams, Air, John Carter, Oliver Lake, David Murray, Henry Threadgill

PAUL HORN (flt), *Inside* (1968, solo at the Taj Mahal), Epic 26466 [cassette only]

WAYNE HORVITZ (p)/John Zorn (as)/Ray Drummond (b)/Bobby Previte (d), a k a The Sonny Clark Memorial Quartet, *Voodoo* (1985), Soul Note 120 109

———— Horvitz (p, kbds)/Butch Morris (cnt)/Robert Previte (d, perc, syn, p), *Nine Below Zero* (1986), Sound Aspects 014   *See also* David Moss, John Zorn.

FREDDIE HUBBARD (tpt), *Breaking Point* (1964, with James Spaulding, Ronnie Mathews a.o.), Blue Note 84172   *See also* Ornette Coleman, John Coltrane, Dexter Gordon, Herbie Hancock, Oliver Nelson.

DANIEL HUMAIR (d), *see* Joachim Kühn

ALBERTA HUNTER (vcl), *Amtrak Blues* (1980, with Vic Dickenson, Frank Wess a.o.), Columbia 36430

BOBBY HUTCHERSON (vib), *see* Eric Dolphy, Dianne Reeves, Collections: *Jazz Club: Vibraphone*

MARJORIE HYAMS (vib), *see* George Shearing, Collections: *Jazz Club: Vibraphone*

ABDULLAH IBRAHIM [a k a Dollar Brand] (p, vcl, ss), *Children of Africa* (1976, with Cecil McBee, Roy Brooks), Enja 79618

ICP [INSTANT COMPOSERS POOL] ORCHESTRA, *Performs Herbie Nichols/Thelonious Monk* (1984 and 1986, with George Lewis [tbn], Wolter Wierbos, Steve Lacy, Misha Mengelberg, Larry Fishkind, Han Bennink a.o.; arr. Mengelberg), ICP 026

ED JACKSON (as), *see* 29th Street Saxophone Quartet, Tom Varner

MILT JACKSON (vib), *Opus de Jazz* (1955, with Frank Wess, Hank Jones, Eddie Jones, Kenny Clarke), Savoy 1116 [LP, out of print]   *See also* Modern Jazz Quartet, Collections: *Jazz Club: Vibraphone.*

RONALD SHANNON JACKSON (d) and the Decoding Society, *Mandance* (1982, with Vernon Reid, Melvin Gibbs a.o.), Antilles 422 846 397   *See also* Ornette Coleman, Last Exit, Power Tools.

ILLINOIS JACQUET (ts), *The Black Velvet Band* (1947, 1949, 1967, with Henry Coker, J. J. Johnson, Leo Parker, John Lewis, Lionel Hampton, Jo Jones, Shadow Wilson a.o.), RCA/Bluebird 6571   *See also* Lionel Hampton.

AHMAD JAMAL (p), *Poinciana* (1951–52 and 1955, trios), Epic/Portrait 44394

KEITH JARRETT (p), *Fort Yawuh* (1973, with Dewey Redman, Charlie Haden, Paul Motian—"the American quartet"), MCA/Impulse 33122

———— *Belonging* (1974, with Jan Garbarek, Palle Danielsson, Jon Christensen— "the European quartet"), ECM 829 115

———— *The Köln Concert* (1975, solo), ECM 810 067

———— *Standards, Vol. 1* (1983, with Gary Peacock, Jack DeJohnette), ECM 811 966

JAZZ COMPOSERS ORCHESTRA, *The Jazz Composers Orchestra* (1968, with Don Cherry, Roswell Rudd, Gato Barbieri, Pharoah Sanders, Cecil Taylor, Larry Coryell a.o.; comp. by Michael Mantler), ECM/JCOA 1001/2

THE JAZZTET (sextet), *Back to the City* (1986, with Art Farmer, Benny Golson, Curtis Fuller, Mickey Tucker, Ray Drummond, Marvin "Smitty" Smith), Contemporary 14020

BLIND LEMON JEFFERSON (g, vcl), *see* Collections: *Riverside History of Classic Jazz*

EDDIE JEFFERSON (vcl), *The Godfather of Vocalese* (1976, with Richie Cole, Mickey Tucker, Rick Laird a.o.), Muse 6013

J. F. JENNY-CLARK (b), *see* Joachim Kühn

LEROY JENKINS (vln), *Space Minds, New Worlds, Survival of America* (1978, with George Lewis, Anthony Davis, Andrew Cyrille), Tomato 2696512

TERRY JENOURE (vln, vcl), *see* John Carter

BUDD JOHNSON (rds), *see* Louis Armstrong, Gil Evans, Maynard Ferguson, Earl Hines, Sarah Vaughan

BUNK JOHNSON (cnt), *see* Collections: *Riverside History of Classic Jazz*

HOWARD JOHNSON (rds, tba), *see* Carla Bley, Jack DeJohnette, Gil Evans, Charlie Haden, Bob Moses

JAMES P. JOHNSON (p), *see* Collections: *Riverside History of Classic Jazz*

J. J. JOHNSON (tbn)/Kai Winding (tbn), *The Great Kai and J. J.* (1960, with Bill Evans, Paul Chambers, Tommy Williams, Roy Haynes, Art Taylor), MCA/Impulse 42012 [cassette 39109]   *See also* Miles Davis, Benny Golson, Illinois Jacquet, King Pleasure, Charlie Parker, Sonny Stitt, Collections: *Esquire's All–American Hot Jazz Sessions.*

LONNIE JOHNSON (g, vcl), *Steppin' on the Blues* (1925–32, with Eddie Lang, Clarence Williams, Victoria Spivey a.o.), Columbia 46221   *See also* Louis Armstrong.

MARC JOHNSON (b), *Bass Desires* (1985, with Bill Frisell, John Scofield, Peter Erskine), ECM 827 743   *See also* John Abercrombie.

PETE JOHNSON (p), *see* Joe Turner, Collections: *Riverside History of Classic Jazz*

ELVIN JONES (d), *see* Ornette Coleman, John Coltrane, Joe Henderson, Gil Evans, Rahsaan Roland Kirk, Lee Konitz, Steve Lacy

HANK JONES (p), *The Oracle* (1989, with Dave Holland, Billy Higgins), EmArcy 846 376   *See also* Maynard Ferguson, Tommy Flanagan, Milt Jackson, Charlie Parker, Lucky Thompson.

JO JONES (d), *see* Count Basie, Charlie Christian, Benny Goodman, Stephane Grappelli, Lionel Hampton, Billie Holiday, Illinois Jacquet, Pee Wee Russell, Ben Webster, Lester Young

THAD JONES (tpt, ldr)/Mel Lewis (d, ldr), *New Life* (1976, with Cecil Bridgewater, Janice Robinson, Earl McIntyre, Jerry Dodgion, Frank Foster, Pepper Adams, Walter Norris, George Mraz a.o.), A&M 75021 0810   *See also* Count Basie.

SCOTT JOPLIN (p), *see* Collections: *Riverside History of Classic Jazz*

SHEILA JORDAN (vcl), *see* Carla Bley, Bob Moses, George Russell

STANLEY JORDAN (el g), *Cornucopia* (1986–89, with Kenny Kirkland, Charnett Moffett, Jeff Watts a.o.), Blue Note 92356

HENRY KAISER (el g, syn)/Sergei Kuriokhin (syn), *Popular Science* (1988–89), Rykodisc 20118

STAN KENTON (p, ldr), *The Concert in Miniature Broadcasts, 1952–1953* (with Conte Candoli, Ernie Royal, Frank Rosolino, Lee Konitz, Richie Kamuca, Zoot Sims a.o.; includes arrs. by Bill Holman, Gerry Mulligan, Bill Russo), Artistry 001

FREDDIE KEPPARD (cnt), *see* Collections: *Riverside History of Classic Jazz*

BARNEY KESSEL (el g), *Easy Like* (1953 and 1956, with Buddy Collette, Bud Shank, Claude Williamson, Red Mitchell, Shelly Manne a.o.), Fantasy/OJC 153   *See also* Billie Holiday, Charlie Parker, Shorty Rogers, Artie Shaw.

STEVE KHAN (el g), *Blades* (1982, with Anthony Jackson, Steve Jordan, Manolo Badrena), Passport 88001 [LP, out of print]   *See also* Hal Willner.

KING PLEASURE [CLARENCE BEEKS] (vcl), *King Pleasure Sings/Annie Ross Sings* (split session with Annie Ross—*see* Ross; 1952–54, with J. J. Johnson, Kai Winding, Lucky Thompson, John Lewis, Percy Heath, Kenny Clarke, Betty Carter, John Hendricks, Dave Lambert a.o.), Fantasy/OJC 217

JOHN KIRBY (b), *The Biggest Little Band 1937–1941* (with Frankie Newton, Charlie Shavers, Buster Bailey, Pete Brown, Russell Procope, Billy Kyle, O'Neill Spencer a.o.), Smithsonian Collection of Recordings R013 [2-LP set; mail-order only, *see* note under Dizzy Gillespie]   *See also* Fletcher Henderson, Billie Holiday, Chick Webb, Ben Webster.

RAHSAAN ROLAND KIRK (rds, flt), *Rip, Rig and Panic/Now Please Don't You Cry, Beautiful Edith* (2 LPs on 1 CD; 1965, with Jaki Byard, Richard Davis, Elvin Jones; 1967, with Lonnie Liston Smith, Ronnie Boykins, Grady Tate), EmArcy 832 164

JIMMY KNEPPER (tbn), *see* Toshiko Akiyoshi, Carla Bley, Benny Carter, Gil Evans, Helen Merrill, Charles Mingus

HANS KOCH (ss, ts, b cl), *see* Wolfgang Fuchs

LEE KONITZ (as), *Subconscious–Lee* (1949–50, with Warne Marsh, Lennie Tristano, Billy Bauer, Denzil Best, Shelly Manne a.o.; including "Rebecca"), Fantasy/OJC 186

———— *The Lee Konitz Duets* (1967, with Marshall Brown, Joe Henderson, Richie Kamuca, Dick Katz, Karl Berger, Jim Hall, Ray Nance, Eddie Gomez, Elvin Jones), Fantasy/OJC 466   *See also* Miles Davis, Stan Kenton, Claude Thornhill, Lennie Tristano.

KRONOS QUARTET (strings), *Monk Suite* (1984, with Ron Carter, Chuck Israels, Eddie Marshall; includes Thelonious Monk compositions and improvs arranged for strings—it works), Landmark 1505

GENE KRUPA (d, ldr), "Roy Eldridge with the Gene Krupa Orchestra featuring Anita O'Day," *Uptown* (1941–42 and 1949; all sides under Krupa's leadership), Columbia 45448   *See also* Benny Goodman, Billie Holiday.

JOACHIM KÜHN (p)/Daniel Humair (d)/J.F. Jenny–Clark (b), *Live 1989,* CMP 43   *See also* Rolf Kühn.

ROLF KÜHN (cl, syn), *Rolf Kühn,* (1978 and 1980, with Charlie Mariano, Joachim Kühn, Philip Catherine, Niels-Henning Ørsted Pedersen, Alphonse Mouzon a.o.), Blue Flame 40162 [cassette 60162]   *See also* Oscar Pettiford.

SERGEI KURIOKHIN (p, syn), *see* Henry Kaiser, Anatoly Vapirov

STEVE LACY (ss), *Reflections: Steve Lacy Plays Thelonious Monk* (1958, with Mal Waldron, Buell Neidlinger, Elvin Jones), Fantasy/OJC 063

———— *Momentum* (1987, with Steve Potts, Bobby Few, Irene Aebi a.o.), RCA/Novus 3021   *See also* Derek Bailey, ICP Orchestra, Helen Merrill, Hal Willner.

OLIVER LAKE (as, ss, flt), *Expandable Language* (1984, with Geri Allen, Kevin Eubanks, Fred Hopkins, Pheeroan akLaff), Black Saint 120 074   *See also* Marilyn Crispell, World Saxophone Quartet.

JOSEPH LAMB (p), *see* Collections: *Riverside History of Classic Jazz*

LAMBERT, HENDRICKS & ROSS [Dave Lambert, Jon Hendricks, Annie Ross] (vcl trio), *The Swingers* (1959, with Zoot Sims, Tommy Flanagan, Russ Freeman, Freddie Green, Jim Hall a.o.), EMI/Pacific Jazz 46849

—————— Dave Lambert, *see* King Pleasure   *See also* Annie Ross.

EDDIE LANG (g), *see* Bix Beiderbecke, Lonnie Johnson, Joe Venuti

LAST EXIT (quartet), *Iron Path* (1988: Peter Brötzmann, Sonny Sharrock, Bill Laswell, Ronald Shannon Jackson), Virgin/Venture 91015

BILL LASWELL (el b), *see* Last Exit

YUSEF LATEEF (ts, flt, ob) *Eastern Sounds* (1961, with Barry Harris a.o.), Fantasy/OJC 612   *See also* Collections: *Jazz Club: Tenor Sax.*

HUBERT LAWS (flt), *see* Jaco Pastorius, Joe Zawinul

LEADBELLY [HUDDIE LEDBETTER] (g, vcl), *Alabama Bound* (1940, with The Golden Gate Jubilee Quartet; chilling, beautifully illustrates the links between blues and gospel music), RCA 9600

JEANNE LEE (vcl)/Ran Blake (p), *The Legendary Duets* (1961), RCA/Bluebird 6461   *See also* Carla Bley, Bob Moses, Vocal Summit.

GEORGE LEWIS (cl), *see* Collections: *Riverside History of Classic Jazz*

GEORGE LEWIS (tbn), *see* Anthony Braxton, ICP Orchestra, Leroy Jenkins, David Murray, Richard Teitelbaum

JOHN LEWIS (p), *see* Benny Carter, Miles Davis, Illinois Jacquet, Modern Jazz Quartet, Sonny Stitt

MEADE LUX LEWIS (p), *see* Collections: *Barrelhouse Boogie, Riverside History of Classic Jazz*

MEL LEWIS (d), *see* Benny Carter, Thad Jones, Helen Merrill, Gerald Wilson

DAVID LIEBMAN (ss), *The Loneliness of the Long Distance Runner* (1985, solo with overdubs), CMP 24   *See also* John McLaughlin.

ABBEY LINCOLN (vcl), *see* Max Roach

JOHN LINDBERG (b), *see* Anthony Braxton, String Trio of New York

ARTO LINDSAY (el g), *see* David Moss, John Zorn

DIDIER LOCKWOOD (el vln), *see* Collections: *Jazz Club: Violin*

LOOSE TUBES (big band), *Open Letter* (1987, with Iain Ballamy, Django Bates a.o.), E.G. 55/Caroline 1501

EDDIE LOUISS (org), *see* Stan Getz

JOE LOVANO (ts), *see* Paul Motian

JIMMIE LUNCEFORD (ldr), *Harlem Shout (1935–1936)* (with Sy Oliver, Eddie Durham, Willie Smith [as, cl] a.o.; includes "Hittin' the Bottle") MCA/Decca 1305 [LP, out of print]

RENE LUSSIER (el g, misc instr), *see* Fred Frith

MACHITO (perc, ldr), *see* Collections: *Afro-Cuban Jazz*

ADAM MAKOWICZ (p), *Naughty Baby* (1987, with Charlie Haden, Dave Holland, Al Foster; all-Gershwin program), RCA/Novus 3022

ALBERT MANGELSDORFF (tbn), *see* Globe Unity Orchestra, United Jazz & Rock Ensemble

SHELLY MANNE (d), *My Fair Lady* (1956, with André Previn, Leroy Vinnegar), Fantasy/OJC 336   *See also* Coleman Hawkins, Barney Kessel, Lee Konitz, Shorty Rogers, Sonny Rollins.

MICHAEL MANTLER (tpt, ldr), *see* Carla Bley, Jazz Composers Orchestra

CHARLIE MARIANO (ss, flt, as), & the Karnatka College of Percussion, *Jyothi* (1983, with T.A.S. Mani a.o.), ECM 811 548 [available in Europe only]   *See also* Serge Chaloff, Rolf Kühn, United Jazz & Rock Ensemble.

BRANFORD MARSALIS (ts, ss), *Random Abstract* (1987, with Kenny Kirkland, Delbert Felix, Lewis Nash, Jeff Watts), Columbia 44055   *See also* Dirty Dozen Brass Band, Wynton Marsalis.

WYNTON MARSALIS (tpt), *Wynton Marsalis* (1981, with Branford Marsalis, Herbie Hancock, Kenny Kirkland, Ron Carter, Charles Fambrough, Clarence Seay, Jeff Watts, Tony Williams), Columbia 37574

——— *The Wynton Marsalis Quartet Live at Blues Alley* (1986, with Marcus Roberts, Bob Hurst, Watts), Columbia 40675

——— *The Majesty of the Blues* (1988, with Todd Williams, Roberts, Reginald Veal, Herlin Riley a.o.), Columbia 45091   *See also* Art Blakey.

WARNE MARSH (ts), *Noteworthy* (1956, 1977, 1979, with Sam Jones, Roy Haynes a.o.), Discovery 945   *See also* Lee Konitz, Lennie Tristano.

PAT MARTINO (el g), *Strings!* (1967, with Joe Farrell, Cedar Walton a.o.), Fantasy/OJC 223

LYLE MAYS (p, syn, org), *see* Pat Metheny, Bob Moses

MARILYN MAZUR (perc), *see* Miles Davis, Pierre Dørge

M'BOOM (percussion ensemble), *Collage* (1984, with Max Roach, Warren Smith, Freddie Waits a.o.), Soul Note 121 059

BOBBY MCFERRIN (vcl), *The Voice* (1984, solo), Elektra/Musician 60366   *See also* Vocal Summit, Hal Willner.

MCKINNEY'S COTTON PICKERS (big band), *The Band Don Redman Built (1928–1930)* (with Rex Stewart, Benny Carter, Redman, Coleman Hawkins, Fats Waller, Kaiser Marshall a.o.), RCA/Bluebird 2275

JOHN MCLAUGHLIN (g, el g), *My Goals Beyond* (1971, with Dave Liebman, Jerry Goodman, Mahalakshmi, Charlie Haden, Billy Cobham, Airto Moreira, Badal Roy), Rykodisc 10051

—— The Mahavishnu Orchestra, *The Inner Mounting Flame* (1972, with Goodman, Jan Hammer, Rick Laird, Cobham), Columbia 31067

—— *Shakti* (1975, with L. Shankar, Zakir Hussain a.o.), Columbia 46868

—— John McLaughlin/Al Di Meola (g)/Paco De Lucia (g), *Passion, Grace & Fire,* Columbia 36845   *See also* Carla Bley, Larry Coryell, Miles Davis, Wayne Shorter, Tony Williams.

JACKIE MCLEAN (as), *Tippin' the Scales* (1962, with Sonny Clark, Butch Warren, Art Taylor), Blue Note 84427   *See also* Charles Mingus.

CARMEN MCRAE (vcl), *Carmen Sings Monk* (1988, with Clifford Jordan, Charlie Rouse, Eric Gunnison, Larry Willis, George Mraz, Al Foster), RCA/Novus 3086

JAY MCSHANN (p, ldr), *The Early Bird Charlie Parker* (1941–43, with Parker, Paul Quinichette, Gus Johnson a.o.), MCA 1338 [LP, out of print]   *See also* Ben Webster.

MISHA MENGELBERG (p)/Han Bennink (d, perc), *Ein Partietischtennis* (1974), SAJ 03 [German LP, dist. by FMP]   *See also* Berlin Contemporary Jazz Orchestra, ICP Orchestra.

HELEN MERRILL (vcl)/Gil Evans (arr), *Collaboration* (1987, with Jimmy Knepper, Steve Lacy, Joe Beck, Buster Williams, Mel Lewis a.o.), EmArcy 834 205

PAT METHENY (g, el g)/Lyle Mays (p, syn, org), *As Falls Wichita, So Falls Wichita Falls* (1980, with Nana Vasconcelos), ECM 821 416

————— Pat Metheny/Ornette Coleman (as), *Song-X* (1985, with Charlie Haden, Denardo Coleman, Jack DeJohnette), Geffen 24096

STEPHAN MICUS (misc instr), *Twilight Fields* (1987), ECM 835 085

MULGREW MILLER (p), *Wingspan* (1987, with Kenny Garrett, Steve Nelson, Charnett Moffett, Tony Reedus) Landmark 1515   *See also* Dianne Reeves, Woody Shaw.

CHARLES MINGUS (b, ldr), *Pithecanthropus Erectus* (1956, with Jackie McLean, Mal Waldron a.o.), Atlantic 8809

————— *New Tijuana Moods* (1957, with Jimmy Knepper, Dannie Richmond a.o.; includes "Ysabel's Table Dance"), RCA/Bluebird 5644 [cassette 5635]

————— *Mingus Ah Um* (1959, with Knepper, John Handy, Booker Ervin, Shafi Hadi, Horace Parlan, Richmond; includes "Better Git It in Your Soul," "Goodbye Pork Pie Hat," "Open Letter to Duke"), Columbia 40648

————— *Mingus at Antibes* (1960, with Ted Curson, Eric Dolphy, Ervin, Bud Powell, Richmond; includes "Better Git Hit in Your Soul" [sic], "What Love?"), Atlantic 90532

————— *Let My Children Hear Music* (1971, with orchestra), Columbia 31039 [LP, out of print; 1 track on CD *Shoes of the Fisherman's Wife,* Columbia 44050]   *See also* Red Norvo.

PHIL MINTON (vcl), *The Berlin Station* (1984 and 1986, with Peter Brötzmann, Tony Oxley a.o.), SAJ 57 [LP, dist. by FMP]

ROSCOE MITCHELL (rds, flt), *see* Art Ensemble of Chicago, Anthony Braxton

HANK MOBLEY (ts), *see* Donald Byrd, Collections: *Jazz Club: Tenor Sax*

MODERN JAZZ QUARTET, *Fontessa* (1956: John Lewis, Milt Jackson, Percy Heath, Connie Kay), Atlantic 1231

————— *Pyramid* (1959; includes "Django"), Atlantic 1325

MIFF MOLE (tbn), *see* Collections: *Riverside History of Classic Jazz*

THELONIOUS MONK (p), *Monk's Music* (1957, with Ray Copland, Gigi Gryce, John Coltrane, Coleman Hawkins, Wilbur Ware, Art Blakey), Fantasy/OJC 084

————— *Monk's Dream* (1962, with Charlie Rouse a.o.), Columbia 40786

WES MONTGOMERY (el g), *Full House* (1962, with Johnny Griffin, Wynton Kelly, Paul Chambers, Jimmy Cobb), Fantasy/OJC 106

TETE MONTOLIU (p), *Tete!* (1974, with Niels-Henning Ørsted Pedersen, Albert "Tootie" Heath), SteepleChase 1029

JAMES MOODY (ts), *New Sounds* (disc split with Art Blakey session—*see* Moody; 1948, with Cecil Payne, Art Blakey a.o.; includes "Cu-Ba"), Blue Note 84436 *See also* Dizzy Gillespie.

AIRTO MOREIRA (perc), *see* Chick Corea, Dizzy Gillespie, John McLaughlin, Wayne Shorter, Weather Report

FRANK MORGAN (as), *Lament* (1986, with Cedar Walton, Buster Williams, Billy Higgins), Contemporary 14021

LEE MORGAN (tpt), *The Sidewinder* (1963, with Joe Henderson, Barry Harris, Bob Cranshaw, Billy Higgins), Blue Note 84157

LAWRENCE "BUTCH" MORRIS (cnt), *see* Wayne Horvitz, David Murray

JELLY ROLL MORTON (p), *His Complete Victor Recordings* (1926–30 and 1939, with Henry "Red" Allen, Bubber Miley, J. C. Higginbotham, Barney Bigard, Johnny Dodds, Albert Nicholas, Omer Simeon, Sidney Bechet, Russell Procope, Johnny St. Cyr, Wellman Braud, Pops Foster, Cozy Cole, Baby Dodds, Zutty Singleton a.o.), RCA/Bluebird 2631 *See also* Sidney Bechet, Collections: *Riverside History of Classic Jazz.*

PINGUIN MOSCHNER (tba), *Tuba Love Story* (1984, solo), Sound Aspects 05 [LP]

BOB MOSES (d, ldr), *When Elephants Dream of Music* (1982, with Terumasa Hino, Howard Johnson, Jeremy Steig, Lyle Mays, David Friedman, Steve Swallow, Nana Vasconcelos, Sheila Jordan, Jeanne Lee a.o.), Gramavision 8203 [LP, out of print]

DAVID MOSS (d, perc, vcl), *Dense Band* (1985, with John Zorn, Wayne Horvitz, Fred Frith, Arto Lindsay, Tom Cora, Christian Marclay a.o.), Moers Music 02040 [LP] *See also* Five Voices.

PAUL MOTIAN (d), *It Should Have Happened a Long Time Ago* (1984, with Joe Lovano, Bill Frisell), ECM 823 641 *See also* Carla Bley, Bill Evans, Charlie Haden, Keith Jarrett.

ALPHONSE MOUZON (d), *see* Larry Coryell, Rolf Kühn, Wayne Shorter, McCoy Tyner, Weather Report

GERRY MULLIGAN (bars, ldr), *The Best of the Gerry Mulligan Quartet with Chet Baker* (1952–53, with Chico Hamilton a.o.; includes "Walkin' Shoes"), EMI/Pacific Jazz 95481 *See also* Miles Davis, Stan Kenton.

MARK MURPHY (vcl), *Sings Nat's Choice: The Complete Nat Cole Song Books, Vols. 1 & 2*, (1983), Muse 6001

DAVID MURRAY (ts), *Live at the Lower Manhattan Ocean Club, Vols. 1 & 2* (1977, with Lester Bowie, Fred Hopkins, Phillip Wilson), India Navigation 1032

――― *Ming* (1980, with Olu Dara, Butch Morris, George Lewis, Henry Threadgill, Anthony Davis, Wilbur Morris, Steve McCall), Black Saint 120 045

――― *Spirituals* (1988, with Dave Burrell, Fred Hopkins, Ralph Peterson), DIW 841   *See also* Clarinet Summit, Jack DeJohnette, Kip Hanrahan, Music Revelation Ensemble, World Saxophone Quartet.

DIEDRE MURRAY (cel), *see* Muhal Richard Abrams, Henry Threadgill

SUNNY MURRAY (d), *see* Alexander von Schlippenbach

MUSIC REVELATION ENSEMBLE (quartet), *Elec. Jazz* (1990: David Murray, James Blood Ulmer, Amin Ali, Cornell Rochester), DIW 839

RAY NANCE (tpt, vln), see Duke Ellington, Earl Hines, Lee Konitz, Collections: *Jazz Club: Violin*

MILTON NASCIMENTO (vcl), *see* Wayne Shorter

MARK NAUSEEF (perc), *Wun-Wun* (1984, with Walter Quintus, Jack Bruce, Trilok Gurtu), CMP 25

FATS NAVARRO (tpt), *The Fabulous Fats Navarro, Vol. 1* (1947 and 1949, all sides under leadership of Tadd Dameron, with Kai Winding, Sahib Shihab, Dexter Gordon, Charlie Rouse, Cecil Payne, Kenny Clarke, Shadow Wilson a.o.), Blue Note 81531

OLIVER NELSON (as, ts, arr), *Blues and the Abstract Truth* (1961, with Freddie Hubbard, Eric Dolphy, George Barrow, Bill Evans, Paul Chambers, Roy Haynes), MCA/Impulse 5659

NEW ORLEANS RHYTHM KINGS (octet: Paul Mares, George Brunies, Leon Rappolo, Elmer Schoebel, Ben Pollack a.o.), *see* Collections: *Riverside History of Classic Jazz*

JAMES NEWTON (flt), *Echo Canyon* (1984, solo), Celestial Harmonies 13012

――― *The African Flower: The Music of Duke Ellington and Billy Strayhorn* (1985, with Olu Dara, Arthur Blythe, Sir Roland Hanna, Jay Hoggard, Billy Hart, Pheeroan akLaff a.o.), Blue Note 46292

LAUREN NEWTON (vcl), *see* Vienna Art Orchestra, Vocal Summit

HERBIE NICHOLS (p), *The Complete Blue Note Recordings of Herbie Nichols* (1955–56, with Teddy Kotick, Al McKibbon, Art Blakey, Max Roach), Mosaic 118 [mail-order only, 35 Melrose Place, Stamford, CT 06902]

RED NORVO (vib), *The Red Norvo Trio* (1950–51, with Tal Farlow, Charles Mingus), Savoy 2212 [LP, out of print]   *See also* Mildred Bailey, Woody Herman, Frank Sinatra, Collections: *Jazz Club: Vibraphone.*

ANITA O'DAY (vcl), *see* Gene Krupa

CHICO O'FARRILL (arr), *see* Collections: *Afro-Cuban Jazz*

KING OLIVER (cnt), *Louis Armstrong/King Oliver* (disc split with Louis Armstrong sessions—*see* Armstrong; 1923–24, with Armstrong, Johnny Dodds, Lil Hardin, Johnny St. Cyr, Baby Dodds a.o.), Milestone 47017   *See also* Collections: *Riverside History of Classic Jazz.*

OREGON (quartet), *Distant Hills* (1973: Paul McCandless, Ralph Towner, Glen Moore, Collin Walcott), Vanguard 79341

—— *Ecotopia* (1987: McCandless, Towner, Moore, Trilok Gurtu), ECM 833 120

ORIGINAL DIXIELAND JAZZ BAND (quintet with Nick LaRocca, Tony Spargo a.o.; first jazz recordings, 1917–18, scheduled for 1992 reissue by RCA/Bluebird)

ORIGINAL MEMPHIS FIVE (with Miff Mole), *see* Collections: *Riverside History of Classic Jazz*

NIELS-HENNING ØRSTED PEDERSEN (b), *see* Miles Davis, Dexter Gordon, Rolf Kuhn, Tete Montoliu

KID ORY (tbn), *see* Collections: *Riverside History of Classic Jazz*

GREG OSBY (as, ss), *see* Mark Helias, Dianne Reeves, Michele Rosewoman, Strata Institute

HOT LIPS PAGE (tpt), *see* Chu Berry, Eddie Condon, Lucky Thompson, Joe Turner

CHARLIE PARKER (as), *The Savoy Recordings (Master Takes), Vol. 1* (1944–47, with Miles Davis, Dizzy Gillespie, Tiny Grimes, Bud Powell, Tommy Potter, Max Roach a.o.), Savoy 4402 [out of print]

—— *The Savoy Recordings (Master Takes), Vol. 2* (1947–48, with Davis, Duke Jordan, John Lewis, Potter, Roach a.o.), Savoy 4407 [out of print]

———— *The Legendary Dial Masters, Vol. 1* (1946–47, with Davis, Dizzy Gillespie, Howard McGhee, J. J. Johnson, Wardell Gray, Lucky Thompson, Erroll Garner, Jordan, Dodo Marmarosa, Barney Kessel, Ray Brown, Red Callendar, Potter a.o.), Stash 23

———— *Compact Jazz* (1947–53, with Miles Davis, Red Rodney, Hank Jones, John Lewis, Ray Brown, Kenny Clarke, Roy Haynes, Buddy Rich, Max Roach, big band, chorus a.o.), PolyGram/Verve 833 288   *See also* Jay McShann, Collections: *Afro-Cuban Jazz.*

EVAN PARKER (ss, ts), *see* Derek Bailey, Peter Brotzmann, Wolfgang Fuchs, Globe Unity Orchestra

JACO PASTORIUS (el b), *Jaco Pastorius* (1975, with Hubert Laws, Dave Sanborn, Wayne Shorter, Herbie Hancock, Lenny White, Don Alias a.o.), Epic 33949   *See also* Weather Report.

CECIL PAYNE (bars), *see* James Moody, Fats Navarro

GARY PEACOCK (b), *see* Keith Jarrett

ART PEPPER (as, cl), *Landscape* (1979, with George Cables, Tony Dumas, Billy Higgins), Fantasy/OJC 676   *See also* Shorty Rogers.

OSCAR PETERSON (p), *Trio + One, Clark Terry* (1964, with Ray Brown, Ed Thigpen; includes Terry vcl on "Mumbles," "Incoherent Blues"), PolyGram/Mercury 818 840   *See also* Stephane Grappelli.

MICHEL PETRUCCIANI (p), *Oracle's Destiny* (1982, solo), Owl 79229

OSCAR PETTIFORD (b, cel), *Sessions 1958–1960* (with Dusko Gojkovic, Rolf Kühn, Don Byas, Hans Koller, Lucky Thompson, Attila Zoller, Kenny Clarke a.o.), Delta 11 096   *See also* Buddy DeFranco, Duke Ellington, Dizzy Gillespie, Coleman Hawkins.

DAVE PIKE (vib), *see* Collections: *Jazz Club: Vibraphone*

COURTNEY PINE (ts, ss), *Destiny's Song + The Image of Pursuance* (1987, with Mark Mondesir a.o.), Antilles 422 842 772

DANIEL PONCE (perc), *Arawe* (1987, with Lew Soloff, Steve Turre, Paquito D'Rivera, Vernon Reid, Ignacio Berroa, Tito Puente a.o.), Antilles 422 842 659

BENNY POWELL (tbn), *see* Count Basie, John Carter

BUD POWELL (p), *The Amazing Bud Powell, Vol. 2* (1951 and 1953, with Max Roach, Art Taylor a.o.), Blue Note 81504   *See also* Dexter Gordon, Charles Mingus, Charlie Parker, Sonny Stitt.

POWER TOOLS (trio), *Strange Meeting* (1987: Bill Frisell, Melvin Gibbs, Ronald Shannon Jackson), Antilles 422 842 648

BOBBY PREVITE (d), *see* Wayne Horvitz, John Zorn

DUDU PUKWANA (as, p), *In the Townships* (1973) Virgin/Earthworks 90884

DON PULLEN (p), *Evidence of Things Unseen* (1983, solo), Black Saint 120 080   *See also* Jane Bunnett, Kip Hanrahan.

JOHN PURCELL (rds, flt), *see* Muhal Richard Abrams, Benny Carter, Jack DeJohnette

FLORA PURIM (vcl), *see* Chick Corea, Dizzy Gillespie

GENE QUILL (as), *see* Phil Woods

BOYD RAEBURN (rds, ldr), *Man with the Horns* (1945–46, with Harry Babasin a.o.), Savoy 12025 [LP, out of print]   *See also* Dizzy Gillespie.

MA RAINEY (vcl), *see* Collections: *Riverside History of Classic Jazz*

JIMMY RANEY (el g) *A* (1954–55), Fantasy/OJC 1706   *See also* Buddy DeFranco.

ENRICO RAVA (tpt)/Dino Saluzzi (bandoneon) Quintet, *Volver* (1986, with Harry Pepl a.o.), ECM 831 395   *See also* Carla Bley, Globe Unity Orchestra.

DEWEY REDMAN (ts, musette), *see* Ornette Coleman, Charlie Haden, Keith Jarrett

DON REDMAN (rds, arr), *see* Fletcher Henderson, McKinney's Cotton Pickers

DIANNE REEVES (vcl), *I Remember* (1988 and 1990, with Greg Osby, Mulgrew Miller, Bobby Hutcherson, Kevin Eubanks, Charnett Moffett, Terri Lyne Carrington, Marvin "Smitty" Smith a.o.), Blue Note 90264

VERNON REID (el g, banjo), *see* Ronald Shannon Jackson, Daniel Ponce, John Zorn

DJANGO REINHARDT (g)/Stephane Grappelli (vln) with the Quintet of the Hot Club of France, *Souvenirs* (1938–39 and 1946), PolyGram/London 820 591

———— *Djangology 49* (1949, with Grappelli a.o.), RCA/Bluebird 9988

BUDDY RICH (d, ldr), *Compact Jazz* (1955–61, big bands, with Harry "Sweets" Edison, Sonny Criss, Phil Woods, Al Cohn, Benny Golson, Buddy Collette, Abe Most, Dave

McKenna a.o.; includes arrs. by Gigi Gryce, Ernie Wilkins), PolyGram/Verve 833 295   *See also* Woody Herman, Charlie Parker.

JEROME RICHARDSON (flt, ts), *see* Donald Byrd

SAM RIVERS (ss, ts, flt), *see* Dave Holland

MAX ROACH (d), *Deeds, Not Words* (1958, with Booker Little, Ray Draper, George Coleman, Art Davis), Fantasy/OJC 304

———— *We Insist! Freedom now suite* (1960, with Little, Julian Priester, Coleman Hawkins, Michael Olatunji, Abbey Lincoln a.o.), Candid 79002

———— Max Roach/Anthony Braxton (rds, flt), *One in Two-Two in One* (1979, duo), Hat Art 6030   *See also* Clifford Brown, Miles Davis, Buddy DeFranco, Benny Golson, M'BOOM, Herbie Nichols, Charlie Parker, Bud Powell, Sonny Rollins, Howard Rumsey, Sonny Stitt, Dinah Washington.

HANK ROBERTS (cel), *see* Arcado, Tim Berne, Bill Frisell

MARCUS ROBERTS (p), *see* Wynton Marsalis

HERB ROBERTSON (cnt, tpt, vcl), *see* Tim Berne

CORNELL ROCHESTER (d), *see* Music Revelation Ensemble

SHORTY ROGERS (tpt, flgh, arr), *The Complete Atlantic and EMI Jazz Recordings of Shorty Rogers* (1951–56, with Conte Candoli, Pete Candoli, Harry "Sweets" Edison, Herb Geller, Art Pepper, Bud Shank, Jimmy Giuffre, Bill Holman, Hampton Hawes, Lou Levy, Jimmy Rowles, Barney Kessel, Harry Babasin, Curtis Counce, Ralph Peña, Leroy Vinnegar, Shelly Manne a.o.; a definitive collection of '50s West Coast jazz), Mosaic 125 [mail-order only, *see* note under Herbie Nichols]   *See also* Woody Herman, Mel Tormé.

SONNY ROLLINS (ts), *Saxophone Colossus* (1956, with Tommy Flanagan, Doug Watkins, Max Roach), Fantasy/OJC 291

———— *Way Out West* (1957, with Ray Brown, Shelly Manne; includes a couple of typically offbeat Rollins selections, "I'm an Old Cowhand," "Wagon Wheels"), Fantasy/OJC 337

———— *The Solo Album* (1985), Milestone 9137   *See also* Collections: *Jazz Club: Tenor Sax.*

MICHELE ROSEWOMAN (p, syn, vcl), *Contrast High* (1988, with Greg Osby, Gary Thomas, Lonnie Plaxico a.o.), Enja 79607

ANNIE ROSS (vcl), *King Pleasure Sings/Annie Ross Sings* (split session with King Pleasure—*see* King Pleasure; 1952, with George Wallington, Percy Heath, Art Blakey a.o.), Fantasy/OJC 217   *See also* Lambert, Hendricks & Ross.

RICH ROTHENBERG (ts), *see* 29th Street Saxophone Quartet, Tom Varner

CHARLIE ROUSE (ts), *see* Carmen McRae, Thelonious Monk, Fats Navarro, Mal Waldron, Hal Willner

ROVA (sax quartet), *This Time We Are Both* (1989: Bruce Ackley, Steve Adams, Larry Ochs, Jon Raskin), New Albion 041

ROSWELL RUDD (tbn), *see* Carla Bley, Charlie Haden, Jazz Composers Orchestra

HOWARD RUMSEY (b) and his Lighthouse All-Stars, *Oboe/Flute* (1954 and 1956, with Bob Cooper, Bud Shank, Buddy Collette, Sonny Clark, Claude Williamson, Stan Levey, Max Roach) Fantasy/OJC 154

GEORGE RUSSELL (p, arr, ldr), *Ezz-thetics,* (1960, with Don Ellis, Dave Baker, Eric Dolphy, Steve Swallow, Joe Hunt) Fantasy/OJC 070 [LP]

——— *The Outer View* (1962, with Ellis, Garnett Brown, Paul Plummer, Swallow, Pete LaRoca, Sheila Jordan; includes "You Are My Sunshine"), Fantasy/OJC 616

——— *The African Game* (1983), Blue Note 46335

PEE WEE RUSSELL (cl)/Coleman Hawkins (ts), *Jazz Reunion* (1961, with Emmett Berry, Bob Brookmeyer, Nat Pierce, Milt Hinton, Jo Jones), Candid 79020 *See also* Eddie Condon, Bud Freeman, Collections: *Riverside History of Classic Jazz.*

DINO SALUZZI (bandoneon), *see* Enrico Rava

PHAROAH SANDERS (ts), *Karma* (1969, with Julius Watkins, James Spaulding, Lonnie Liston Smith, Ron Carter, Richard Davis, Reggie Workman, Billy Hart, Freddie Waits, Nathaniel Bettis, Leon Thomas), MCA/Impulse 39122   *See also* John Coltrane, Jazz Composers Orchestra.

ALEXANDER VON SCHLIPPENBACH (p)/Sunny Murray (d), *Smoke* (1989, duo), FMP 23   *See also* Berlin Contemporary Jazz Orchestra, Globe Unity Orchestra.

DIANE SCHUUR (vcl), *Diane Schuur & the Count Basie Orchestra* (1987, with Sonny Cohn, Bill Hughes, Eric Dixon, Frank Foster, Freddie Green a.o.; recorded after Basie's death, under Foster's leadership), GRP 1039

LOUIS SCLAVIS (cl, b cl, ss), *see* Wolfgang Fuchs

JOHN SCOFIELD (el g), *Shinola* (1981, with Steve Swallow, Adam Nussbaum), Enja 79656   *See also* Ray Anderson, Marc Johnson, Bennie Wallace.

JAMES SCOTT (p), *see* Collections: *Riverside History of Classic Jazz*

SHIRLEY SCOTT (org), *see* Stanley Turrentine

TONY SCOTT (cl), *African Bird–Come Back! Mother Africa* (1981 and 1984, with Glenn Ferris, Chris Hunter a.o.), Soul Note 1083 [LP]   *See also* Billie Holiday, Sarah Vaughan.

ZBIGNIEW SEIFERT (vln), *see* Collections: *Jazz Club: Violin*

BUD SHANK (as, flt), *see* Laurindo Almeida, Barney Kessel, Shorty Rogers, Howard Rumsey, Gerald Wilson

L. SHANKAR (vln), *see* Trilok Gurtu, John McLaughlin

ELLIOTT SHARP (el g, el b, ss, misc instr)/Carbon, *Datacide* (1190, with Zeena Parkins a.o.), Enemy 03516–26   *See also* John Zorn.

SONNY SHARROCK (el g), *see* Last Exit, Wayne Shorter

CHARLIE SHAVERS (tpt), *see* Mildred Bailey, Sidney Bechet, Billie Holiday, John Kirby, Collections: *Esquire's All-American Hot Jazz Sessions*

ARTIE SHAW (cl), *The Complete Gramercy Five Sessions* (1940 and 1945, with Billy Butterfield, Roy Eldridge, Johnny Guarnieri [harpsichord], Dodo Marmarosa, Barney Kessel a.o.), RCA/Bluebird 7637

————— *Blues in the Night* (1941 and 1944–45, with Eldridge, Max Kaminsky, Hot Lips Page, Georgie Auld, Guarnieri [p], Marmarosa, Kessel, Dave Tough a.o.), RCA/Bluebird 2432

WOODY SHAW (tpt), *Lotus Flower* (1982, with Steve Turre, Mulgrew Miller, Stafford James, Tony Reedus), Enja 79637   *See also* Eric Dolphy, Dexter Gordon, Mal Waldron, Larry Young, Joe Zawinul.

GEORGE SHEARING (p), *Lullaby of Birdland* (1949–54, with Marjorie Hyams, Cal Tjader, Chuck Wayne, Denzil Best, Candido Camero, Armando Pereza, Billy Eckstine a.o.), PolyGram/Verve 827 977 [2-LP set]

ARCHIE SHEPP (ts), *Fire Music* (1965, with Ted Curson, Marion Brown, David Izenzon a.o.), MCA/Impulse 39121

ANDY SHEPPARD (ts, ss, flts), *see* Keith Tippett

WAYNE SHORTER (ts, ss) *Super Nova* (1969, with John McLaughlin, Sonny Sharrock, Miroslav Vitous, Chick Corea [d, vib], Jack DeJohnette, Airto Moreira a.o., includes "Dindi"), Blue Note 84332

————— *Odyssey of Iska* (1970, with David Friedman, Ron Carter, Cecil McBee, Billy Hart, Alphonse Mouzon a.o.), Blue Note 84363

————— featuring Milton Nascimento (vcl), *Native Dancer* (1974, with Herbie Hancock, Airto a.o.), Columbia 46159 *See also* Miles Davis, Herbie Hancock, Weather Report, Joe Zawinul, Collections: *Jazz Club: Tenor Sax.*

HORACE SILVER (p), *Finger Poppin'* (1959, with Louis Hayes a.o.), Blue Note 84008 *See also* Art Blakey.

ZOOT SIMS (ts), *see* Al Cohn, Woody Herman, Stan Kenton, Lambert, Hendricks & Ross, Collections: *Jazz Club: Tenor Sax*

FRANK SINATRA (vcl), *The Legendary Concert: Melbourne, Australia–1959* (with Jerry Dodgion, Red Norvo a.o.), Bravura 102

ZUTTY SINGLETON (d), *see* Louis Armstrong, Sidney Bechet, Jelly Roll Morton, Fats Waller

BESSIE SMITH (vcl), *The Collection* (1923–33, with Louis Armstrong, Joe Smith, Charlie Green, Jimmy Harrison, Jack Teagarden, Buster Bailey, Benny Goodman, Coleman Hawkins [cl], Chu Berry, Fletcher Henderson, Clarence Williams a.o.), Columbia 44441 *See also* Collections: *Riverside History of Classic Jazz.*

JIMMY SMITH (org), *Cool Blues* (1958, with Lou Donaldson, Art Blakey a.o.), Blue Note 84441

LEO SMITH (tpt), *see* Derek Bailey, Anthony Braxton, Anthony Davis

MARVIN "SMITTY" SMITH (d), *see* Art Farmer, Dave Holland, The Jazztet, Dianne Reeves, Strata Institute

STUFF SMITH (vln), *see* Stephane Grappelli, Collections: *Jazz Club: Violin*

WILLIE THE LION SMITH (p), *see* Sidney Bechet, Joe Turner

MARTIAL SOLAL (p), *Bluesine* (1983, solo), Soul Note 121 060

SOPRANO SUMMIT (quintet) *Soprano Summit In Concert* (1976, with Kenny Davern, Bob Wilber, Marty Grosz, Ray Brown, Jake Hanna), Concord Jazz 4029

S.O.S. [Alan Skidmore (ts, d, perc)/Mike Osborne (as, perc)/John Surman (bars, ss, b cl, syn)], *S.O.S* (1973; English reed choir that anticipated rise of sax quartets), Ogun 400 [LP]

MUGGSY SPANIER (tpt), *see* Eddie Condon, Collections: *At the Jazz Band Ball, Riverside History of Classic Jazz*

JAMES SPAULDING (as, flt), *see* Ricky Ford, Freddie Hubbard, Pharoah Sanders, Sun Ra

BOBO STENSON (p), *see* Jan Garbarek

BOB STEWART (tba), *see* Arthur Blythe, Lester Bowie

REX STEWART (cnt), *see* Sidney Bechet, Duke Ellington, Lionel Hampton, Fletcher Henderson, McKinney's Cotton Pickers

JEREMY STEIG (flts)/Richie Beirach (p), *Leaving* (1976, duo), Storyville 4149   *See also* Bob Moses.

SONNY STITT (as, ts), *Sonny Stitt/Bud Powell/J. J. Johnson* (1949–50, Stitt [ts] with John Lewis, Max Roach a.o.), Fantasy/OJC 009

———— *Stitt Plays Bird* (1966, Stitt [as] with Lewis, Jim Hall, Richard Davis, Connie Kay), Atlantic 1418   *See also* Collections: *Jazz Club: Tenor Sax.*

STRATA INSTITUTE (small group), *C-I-P-H-E-R S-Y-N-T-A-X* (1988, with Steve Coleman, Greg Osby, David Gilmore, Bob Hurst, Marvin "Smitty" Smith, Tani Tabbal), JMT 834 425

STRING TRIO OF NEW YORK, *Natural Balance* (1986: Billy Bang, James Emery, John Lindberg), Black Saint 120 098

SUN RA (p, syn, ldr), *Purple Night* (1989, with Don Cherry, Julian Priester, Marshall Allen, James Spaulding, John Gilmore a.o.), A & M 75021 5324

JOHN SURMAN (sop, bars, b cl, recorder, p, syn), *Withholding Pattern* (1984, solo, overdubbed), ECM 825 407   *See also* S.O.S..

LEW TABACKIN (ts, flt), *see* Toshiko Akiyoshi, Benny Carter

AKI TAKASE (p), *see* Berlin Contemporary Jazz Orchestra

ART TATUM (p), *Solos* (1940), MCA/Decca 42327

———— *The Tatum Group Masterpieces, Vol. 7* (1956, with Buddy DeFranco, Red Callendar, Bill Douglass), Pablo 2405 430   *See also* Joe Turner.

ART TAYLOR (d), *see* Gene Ammons, Dexter Gordon, Jackie McLean, Bud Powell, Toots Thielemans

CECIL TAYLOR (p), *Indent* (1973, solo) Freedom 41038

——— *The Eighth* (1981, with Jimmy Lyons, William Parker, Rashid Bakr), Hat Art 6036   *See also* Jazz Composers Orchestra.

JOHN TAYLOR (p, org), *see* Azimuth

JOHN TCHICAI (ts), *see* Pierre Dørge

JACK TEAGARDEN (tbn, vcl), *That's A Serious Thing* (1929, 1934–39, 1947, 1959, includes dates led by Louis Armstrong, Bud Freeman, Benny Goodman, Teagarden, Fats Waller, Paul Whiteman), RCA/Bluebird 9986   *See also* Eddie Condon, Billie Holiday, Bessie Smith.

RICHARD TEITELBAUM (p, syn, interactive electronics), *Concerto Grosso* (1985, with George Lewis [tbn], Anthony Braxton), Hat Art 6004   *See also* Anthony Braxton.

CLARK TERRY (tpt, flgh, vcl), *see* Louie Bellson, Oscar Peterson

TOOTS [JEAN] THIELEMANS (harmonica), *Man Bites Harmonica!* (1957–58, with Pepper Adams, Kenny Drew, Wilbur Ware, Art Taylor), Fantasy/OJC 1738   *See also* John Zorn.

GARY THOMAS (ts, flt), *see* Michele Rosewoman

LEON THOMAS (vcl), *see* Pharoah Sanders

RENÉ THOMAS (el g), *see* Stan Getz

LUCKY THOMPSON (ts, ss), *Giants of the Tenor Sax* (disc split with Chu Berry sessions—*see* Berry; 1944, Thompson [ts only] with Hot Lips Page, Sid Catlett a.o., recorded under Page's leadership), Commodore 7004

——— *Lucky Strikes* (1964, with Hank Jones, Richard Davis, Connie Kay), Fantasy/OJC 194   *See also* King Pleasure, Charlie Parker, Collections: *The Bebop Revolution.*

CLAUDE THORNHILL (p, arr, ldr), *Claude Thornhill: Best of the Big Bands* (1940s, with Lee Konitz a.o.; includes arrs. by Gil Evans), Columbia 46152

HENRY THREADGILL (as, ts, cl, flt), Sextet [actually septet], *Easily Slip into Another World* (1987, with Rasul Siddik, Frank Lacy, Diedre Murray, Fred Hopkins, Pheeroan akLaff, Reggie Nicholson), RCA/Novus 3025   *See also* Air, David Murray.

STEVE TIBBETTS (g, el g, perc), *Exploded View* (1985–86), ECM 831 109

KEITH TIPPETT (p, perc)/Andy Sheppard (ss, ts, flts), *66 Shades of Lipstick* (1990, duo), E.G. 64/Caroline 1590

CAL TJADER (vib), *Jazz at the Blackhawk* (1957, with Vince Guaraldi a.o.), Fantasy/OJC 436   *See also* Collections: *Jazz Club: Vibraphone.*

MEL TORMÉ (vcl, p, d), *'Round Midnight: A Retrospective 1956–1968* (with bands led by Count Basie, Woody Herman, Marty Paich, Shorty Rogers a.o.), Stash 4

DAVE TOUGH (d), *see* Charlie Christian, Bud Freeman, Woody Herman, Artie Shaw

RALPH TOWNER (g)/Gary Burton (vib, mba), *Slide Show* (1985, duo), ECM 827 257   *See also* Larry Coryell, Trilok Gurtu, Oregon.

LENNIE TRISTANO (p), *Crosscurrents* (disc split with Buddy DeFranco and Bill Harris sessions—*see* DeFranco, Harris; 1949, with Lee Konitz, Warne Marsh, Billy Bauer, Denzil Best a.o.; includes "Wow," "Intuition," "Digression"), Capitol 11060 [LP, out of print]

——— *Live in Toronto 1952* (with Konitz, Marsh a.o.), Jazz Records [CD] 5

GIANLUIGI TROVESI (b cl, rds), *Les Bôites à Musique* (1988, trio), Splasc(h) 152

JOE TURNER (vcl), *I've Been to Kansas City* (1940–41, with Hot Lips Page, Edmond Hall, Don Byas, Pete Johnson, Sammy Price, Willie the Lion Smith, Art Tatum, Oscar Moore a.o.), MCA/Decca 42351

STEVE TURRE (tbn, shells), Lester Bowie, Dizzy Gillespie, Daniel Ponce, Woody Shaw

STANLEY TURRENTINE (ts) feat. Shirley Scott (org), *Let It Go* (1964 and 1966 with Ron Carter a.o.), GRP/Impulse 104

29TH STREET SAXOPHONE QUARTET, *The Real Deal* (1987: Ed Jackson, Bobby Watson, Rich Rothenberg, Jim Hartog), New Note 1006 [to be reissued by Antilles]

MCCOY TYNER (p), *Sahara* (1972, with Sonny Fortune, Calvin Hill, Alphonse Mouzon), Fantasy/OJC 311

——— *Atlantis* (1974, with Guilherme Franco a.o.), Milestone 55002   *See also* John Coltrane, Joe Henderson.

JAMES BLOOD ULMER (el g, vcl), *see* Music Revelation Ensemble

UNITED JAZZ + ROCK ENSEMBLE (big band), *Live in Berlin* (1981, with Ian Carr, Kenny Wheeler, Albert Mangelsdorff, Charlie Mariano, Wolfgang Dauner, Eberhard Weber a.o.), Mood 33620

WARREN VACHÉ (cnt) & the Beaux-Arts String Quartet, *Warm Evenings* (1989), Concord Jazz 4392

FRED VAN HOVE (org, p), *Church Organ* (1975, solo) SAJ 25 [German LP, dist. FMP]   *See also* Peter Brötzmann.

ANATOLY VAPIROV (rds, p, perc), *DeProfundis* (1981 and 1985, with Sergei Kuriokhin a.o.), Leo [England] 159 [LP]

TOM VARNER (fr hn), *Long Night Big Day* (1990, with Ed Jackson, Rich Rothenberg, Lindsey Horner, Phil Haynes), New World 80410

NANA VASCONCELOS (perc, vcl), *see* Codona, Mark Helias, Pat Metheny, Bob Moses

SARAH VAUGHAN (vcl), *The Divine Sarah Vaughan: The Columbia Years 1949–1953* (with Miles Davis, Tony Scott, Budd Johnson, Freddie Green, J. C. Heard a.o.), Columbia 44165

——— *Sassy Swings the Tivoli* (1963, live with trio), PolyGram/EmArcy 832 788   *See also* Dizzy Gillespie.

GLEN VELEZ (frame d, perc, vcl), *Internal Combustion* (1985), CMP 23   *See also* Rabih Abou-Khalil.

CHARLIE VENTURA (ts), *A Charlie Ventura Concert* (1949, with Conte Candoli, Ed Shaughnessy, Jackie Cain, Roy Kral a.o.), MCA/Decca 42330

JOE VENUTI (vln), *Violin Jazz* (1927–34, with Benny Goodman, Frankie Trumbauer, Bud Freeman, Adrian Rollini, Joe Sullivan, Eddie Lang a.o.), Yazoo 1062   *See also* Collections: *Jazz Club: Violin.*

VIENNA ART ORCHESTRA (big band), *Concerto Piccolo* (1980, with Herbert Joos, Wolfgang Reisinger, Christian Radovan, Wolfgang Puschnig, Lauren Newton a.o., cond. Matthias Ruegg), Hat Art 6038

MIROSLAV VITOUS (b), *see* Larry Coryell, Wayne Shorter, Weather Report, Joe Zawinul

VOCAL SUMMIT (quartet) & Bobby McFerrin (vcl), *Sorrow Is Not Forever—Love Is* (1982: Jay Clayton, Ursula Dudziak, Jeanne Lee, Lauren Newton), Moers Music 02004

ABDUL WADUD (cel), *see* Arthur Blythe, Julius Hemphill

COLLIN WALCOTT (perc, misc instr), *see* Codona, Larry Coryell, Oregon

MAL WALDRON (p), *The Seagulls of Kristiansund: Live at the Village Vanguard* (1976, with Woody Shaw, Charlie Rouse, Reggie Workman, Ed Blackwell), Soul Note 121 148   *See also* Donald Byrd, Charles Mingus.

T-BONE WALKER (el g, vcl), *The Complete Recordings of T-Bone Walker 1940–54* (with Al Killian a.o.), Mosaic 130 [mail-order only, *see* note under Herbie Nichols]

BENNIE WALLACE (ts), *Sweeping Through the City* (1984, with Ray Anderson, John Scofield, Mike Richmond, gospel quartet a.o.), Enja 79664   *See also* Mose Allison.

FATS WALLER (p, org), *The Joint Is Jumpin'* (1929–43, solo [p] and with Benny Carter [tpt], Tommy Dorsey, Gene Sedric, Irving Ashby, Eddie Condon, Slam Stewart, Zutty Singleton, George Wettling a.o.), RCA/Bluebird 6288

———— *Fats Waller in London* (1938, with Adelaide Hall a.o., includes 10 tracks with Waller, el org), DRG/Disques Swing 8442   *See also* McKinney's Cotton Pickers, Jack Teagarden.

CEDAR WALTON (p), *see* Pat Martino, Frank Morgan

DINAH WASHINGTON (vcl), *Compact Jazz* (1954–61, with Clifford Brown, Clark Terry, Max Roach a.o.; includes arrs. by Quincy Jones, Ernie Wilkins), PolyGram/Mercury 830 700   *See also* Ben Webster.

BOBBY [ROBERT] WATSON (as), *see* Art Blakey, 29th Street Saxophone Quartet

WEATHER REPORT (small group) *Weather Report* (1971: Wayne Shorter, Joe Zawinul, Miroslav Vitous, Alphonse Mouzon, Airto Moreira), Columbia 30661 [cassette only]

———— *Heavy Weather* (1976: Shorter, Zawinul, Jaco Pastorius, Alejandro Acuna, Manolo Badrena; includes "Birdland"), Columbia 34418

CHICK WEBB (d, ldr), *1929–1934* (with Mario Bauza, Hilton Jefferson, Louis Jordan, Wayman Carver, John Kirby a.o.), Classics 502   *See also* Ella Fitzgerald.

EBERHARD WEBER (b), *The Colors of Chloe* (1973, with Ack van Rooyen, Rainer Bruninghaus a.o.), ECM 833 331   *See also* United Jazz & Rock Ensemble.

BEN WEBSTER (ts), *The Complete Ben Webster on EmArcy* (1951–53, with Maynard Ferguson, Eddie Bert, Benny Carter, Jay McShann, Pee Wee Crayton, Milt Hinton, John Kirby, Jimmy Cobb, Jo Jones, Johnny Otis, Dinah Washington, The Ravens a.o.)   *See also* Duke Ellington, Lionel Hampton.

FRANK WESS (ts, flt), *see* Count Basie, Alberta Hunter, Milt Jackson

MIKE WESTBROOK (p, tba), *Westbrook–Rossini* (1986; arrs. of Rossini opera music for septet), Hat Art 6002

RANDY WESTON (p), *Portraits of Duke Ellington* (1989; Africanized quartet arrs. of Ellington comps.), PolyGram/Verve 841 313   *See also* Hal Willner.

KENNY WHEELER (tpt, flgh), *see* Berlin Contemporary Jazz Orchestra, Anthony Braxton, Bill Bruford, Glove Unity Orchestra, Dave Holland, United Jazz + Rock Ensemble

BOB WILBER (ss, cl), *see* Soprano Summit

EDWARD WILKERSON (rds, ldr) & Shadow Vignettes (big band), *Birth of a Notion* (with Mwata Bowden, Kahil El'Zabar, Reggie Nicholson a.o.; Wilkerson "directs" but doesn't play), Sessoms 0001 [LP]/Open Minds 2410 [CD]   *See also* Ethnic Heritage Ensemble.

CLARENCE WILLIAMS (p), *see* Bessie Smith, Collections: *Riverside History of Classic Jazz*

COOTIE WILLIAMS (tpt), *see* Duke Ellington, Lionel Hampton, Billie Holiday

JOE WILLIAMS (vcl), *Joe Williams Live* (1973, with Nat Adderley, Cannonball Adderley, George Duke a.o.), Fantasy/OJC 438   *See also* Count Basie.

MARY LOU WILLIAMS (p, arr), *see* Benny Goodman, Andy Kirk

TONY WILLIAMS (d, vcl), Tony Williams Lifetime, *Emergency!* (1969, with Larry Young, John McLaughlin) Verve 849 068   *See also* Miles Davis, Eric Dolphy, Herbie Hancock, Andrew Hill, Tony Williams.

HAL WILLNER (producer), *Amarcord Nino Rota* (1981, Rota comps. played by various groups; ldrs. include Muhal Richard Abrams, David Amram, Carla Bley, Jaki Byard, Sharon Freeman, Bill Frisell, Steve Lacy), Hannibal 9301

———— *That's the Way I Feel Now: A Tribute to Thelonious Monk* (1984, same concept, Monk comps.; ldrs. include Bley, Freeman, Steve Khan, Lacy, Bobby McFerrin, Charlie Rouse, Randy Weston, John Zorn), A & M 75021 6600

———— *Lost in the Stars: The Music of Kurt Weill* (1985, same concept; ldrs. include Bley, Charlie Haden, Zorn), A & M 75021 5104

CASSANDRA WILSON (vcl), *Point of View* (1985, with Grachan Moncur III, Steve Coleman, Jean-Paul Bourelly, Lonnie Plaxico, Mark Johnson), JMT 834 404

GERALD WILSON (tpt, ldr), *Moment of Truth* (1962, with Bud Shank, Teddy Edwards, Joe Pass, Jack Nimitz, Mel Lewis a.o.), EMI/Pacific Jazz 92928

PHILLIP WILSON (d), *see* Lester Bowie, Anthony Braxton, Julius Hemphill, David Murray

TEDDY WILSON (p), *see* Benny Carter, Benny Goodman, Billie Holiday

LEM WINCHESTER (vib), *see* Collections: *Jazz Club: Vibraphone*

KAI WINDING (tbn), *see* Miles Davis, J. J. Johnson, King Pleasure, Fats Navarro

NORMA WINSTONE (vcl), *see* Azimuth

PHIL WOODS (as)/Gene Quill (as), *Phil and Quill with Prestige* (1957, quintet), Fantasy/OJC 215 [LP]

WORLD SAXOPHONE QUARTET, *Plays Duke Ellington* (1986: Julius Hemphill, Oliver Lake, David Murray, Hamiet Bluiett), Elektra/Nonesuch 79137

——— *Dances and Ballads* (1987, personnel as above), Elektra/Nonesuch 79164

YOSUKE YAMASHITA (p), *Sakura* (1990, with Cecil McBee, Pheeroan akLaff), Antilles 422 849 141

JIMMY YANCEY (p), *see* Collections: *Barrelhouse Boogie, Riverside History of Classic Jazz*

LARRY YOUNG (org), *Unity* (1965, with Woody Shaw, Joe Henderson, Elvin Jones), Blue Note 84221   *See also* Miles Davis, Tony Williams.

LESTER YOUNG (ts, cl), and Friends, *Giant of the Tenor Sax* (1938 and 1944, with Buck Clayton, Bill Coleman, Dicky Wells, Joe Bushkin, Eddie Durham, Freddie Green, Walter Page, John Simmons, Jo Jones), Commodore 7002

——— *Classic Tenors* (disc split with Coleman Hawkins sessions—see Hawkins; 1943, with Coleman, Wells, Ellis Larkins, Green, Al Hall, Jones), Signature 38446   *See also* Count Basie, Billie Holiday, Collections: *Jazz Club: Tenor Sax.*

FRANK ZAPPA (el g)/The Mothers, *Grand Wazoo* (1972, with Ernie Watts, George Duke, Don Preston a.o.), Rykodisc 10026

JOE ZAWINUL (kbds), *Zawinul,* (1971, with Jimmy Owens, Woody Shaw, Wayne Shorter, Hubert Laws, Herbie Hancock, Miroslav Vitous, Jack DeJohnette, Billy Hart a.o.), Atlantic 1579   *See also* Miles Davis, Weather Report.

JOHN ZORN (as), *John Zorn Plays the Music of Ennio Morricone: The Big Gundown* (1984–85, with Tim Berne, Ned Rothenberg, Wayne Horvitz, Guy Klucevsek, Bill Frisell, Fred Frith, Robert Quine, Vernon Reid, Melvin Gibbs, Christian Marclay, Toots Thielemans, Bobby Previte, Diamanda Galas a.o.), Elektra/Nonesuch 79139

———— *Cobra* (1985–86, with J. A. Deane, Horvitz, Klucevsek, Frisell, Lindsay, Elliott Sharp, Zeena Parkins, Marclay, Previte a.o.), Hat Art 6040   *See also* Wayne Horvitz, David Moss, Hal Willner.

Collections

Afro-Cuban Jazz (1949–54, orchs. led by Dizzy Gillespie, Machito, Chico O'Farrill, with Charlie Parker, Flip Phillips a.o.), PolyGram/Verve 833 561 [2-LP set]

At the Jazz Band Ball (1929 and 1939, Eddie Condon with Jack Teagarden, Mezz Mezzrow, Joe Sullivan a.o. [2 tracks]; Muggsy Spanier with George Brunies, Joe Bushkin a.o. [16]; Bud Freeman with Max Kaminsky, Pee Wee Russell, Condon a.o. [4]), RCA/Bluebird 6752

Barrelhouse Boogie (1936–41, Meade Lux Lewis [2 tracks]; Jimmy Yancey [10]; Pete Johnson & Albert Ammons [9]), RCA/Bluebird 8334

The Bebop Revolution (1946–40, mostly Dizzy Gillespie, septet and orch.; also dates led by Kenny Clarke, Coleman Hawkins, Lucky Thompson, with Allen Eager a.o.), RCA/Bluebird 2177

Esquire's All-American Hot Jazz Sessions (1946–47, with dozens of prominent artists; included "How High the Moon" discussed in the chapter "The Elements of Jazz: Improvisation"), RCA/Bluebird 6757

Jazz Club: Tenor Sax (1948–80, includes Coleman Hawkins, "Picasso" [first unaccompanied jazz sax solo on record], Gene Ammons & Sonny Stitt, Don Byas & Ben Webster, Wardell Grey & Stan Getz, Johnny Griffin & Eddie "Lockjaw" Davis, Joe Farrell, Booker Ervin & Yusef Lateef, John Coltrane, Dexter Gordon, Joe Henderson, Hank Mobley, Sonny Rollins, Lester Young), PolyGram/Verve 840 031

Jazz Club: Vibraphone (1944–70, with Gary Burton, Don Elliot, Vic Feldman, Terry Gibbs, Lionel Hampton, Bobby Hutcherson, Marjorie Hyams [with George Shearing], Milt Jackson, Red Norvo, Dave Pike, Cal Tjader, Lem Winchester), PolyGram/Verve 840 034

Jazz Club: Violin (1957–79, with Svend Asmussen, Stephane Grappelli, Sugarcane Harris, Didier Lockwood, Ray Nance, Jean-Luc Ponty, Zbigniew Seifert, Stuff Smith, Michal Urbaniak, Joe Venuti), PolyGram/Verve 840 039

The Jazz Trumpet (1923–80, selections by 39 trumpeters), Prestige 3PCD 2301

Riverside History of Classic Jazz (pre–1920–53; very good survey of early jazz and jazz roots; includes ragtime from piano rolls [Scott Joplin, Joseph Lamb, James Scott], Harlem stride piano from piano rolls [Cliff Jackson, James P. Johnson], boogie-woogie piano [Art Hodes, Pete Johnson, Meade Lux Lewis, Cripple Clarence Lofton, Jimmy Yancey a.o.], classic blues singers [Ida Cox, Ma Rainey, Bessie Smith], country blues [Big Bill Broonzy, Blind Lemon Jefferson], early jazz by black artists [Louis Armstrong, Lovie Austin, Duke Ellington, Freddie Keppard, Jelly Roll Morton, King Oliver, Clarence Williams a.o.] and white artists [Eddie Condon, New Orleans Rhythm Kings, Original Memphis Five with Miff Mole, Muggsy Spanier, Wolverines with Bix Beiderbecke a.o.], New Orleans revivalists [Bunk Johnson, Kid Ory, George Lewis (cl), Lu Watters a.o.]), Riverside 005 [5-LP box]

Three Great Swing Saxophones (1929–46, Coleman Hawkins with the Mound City Blue Blowers, Fletcher Henderson, Lionel Hampton a.o.; includes "One Hour," "Body and Soul" [8 tracks]; Ben Webster with Bennie Moten, Duke Ellington, Rex Stewart, Chocolate Dandies a.o. [7]; Benny Carter with McKinney's Cotton Pickers, Hampton a.o. [7]), RCA/Bluebird 9863

Index

509

About the Authors

JOACHIM ERNST BERENDT, an internationally-known authority on jazz, is the author of twenty-three books, the founder of the Berlin *Jazztage,* and the producer of the record series "Jazz Meets the World." In 1945, he cofounded the radio station Südwestfunk, where he was director of the jazz division until 1987. Berendt has received numerous honors, including the Bundesfilmpreis, awarded by the German Federal Republic, the German Television Critics Award, and the Polish Culture Award. A resident of Baden-Baden, Germany, he lectures throughout the world.

GÜNTHER HUESMANN is a musicologist and a jazz programmer for the German radio stations Südwestfunk and Westdeutscher Rundfunk. He is also a contributor to the *New Grove Dictionary of Jazz.*

TIM NEVILL has been a translator and writer for over twenty-five years. He is also the translator of Joachim Berendt's *The Third Ear: On Listening to the World* and the editor and translator of texts by composer Karlheinz Stockhausen, entitled *Towards a Cosmic Music.*

KEVIN WHITEHEAD is a jazz critic who writes regularly for *Down Beat, Coda,* and *Cadence.* He is also the jazz critic for National Public Radio's "Fresh Air."